Flex® 3 Bible

Flex® 3 Bible

David Gassner

WILEY

Wiley Publishing, Inc.

Flex® 3 Bible

Published by
Wiley Publishing, Inc.
10475 Crosspoint Boulevard
Indianapolis, IN 46256
www.wiley.com

About the Author

David Gassner is president of Bardo Technical Services, an Authorized Adobe Training Center in Seattle, Washington and an Adobe Systems Rapid Engagement Services partner for Adobe Flex. As an author for Lynda.com, he has recorded video training titles on Flex, AIR, ColdFusion, and Dreamweaver. He holds Adobe developer and instructor certifications in Flex, ColdFusion, Flash, and Dreamweaver, and has been a regular speaker at Allaire, Macromedia, and Adobe conferences. As a contributor to *ColdFusion Journal* and *XML Journal,* he has assisted many developers with the integration of ColdFusion with Java, XML, and other development technologies.

David earned a B.A. from Pitzer College in Claremont, California (his home town), and an M.F.A. from the Professional Theater Training Program at U.C. San Diego. In his copious free time (and putting his M.F.A. to good use), he is Artistic Director of Theater Schmeater (www.schmeater.org), one of Seattle's oldest fringe theater companies. He shares his home with his wonderful wife Jackie (Go Mets!) and a feline comedian named Sylvester, and he receives occasional visits from his thoroughly adult kids, Thad, Jason, and Jenny.

For Jackie, who always says "why not?"

Credits

Senior Acquisitions Editor
Stephanie McComb

Project Editor
Martin V. Minner

Technical Editor
Drew Falkman

Copy Editor
Gwenette Gaddis Goshert

Editorial Manager
Robyn Siesky

Business Manager
Amy Knies

Sr. Marketing Manager
Sandy Smith

Vice President and Executive Group Publisher
Richard Swadley

Vice President and Executive Publisher
Bob Ipsen

Vice President and Publisher
Barry Pruett

Senior Project Coordinator
Kristie Rees

Graphics and Production Specialists
Carrie Cesavice, Abby Westcott

Quality Control Technicians
John Greenough, Jessica Kramer

Proofreading
Christine Sabooni

Indexing
Infodex Indexing Services

Cover Design
Michael Trent

Cover Illustration
Joyce Haughey

Contents at a Glance

Contents

Contents

Contents

Contents

Contents

Contents

Contents

Contents

Preface

When Macromedia first released Flash MX in 2002, the product was branded as the new way to build Rich Internet Applications (known by the acronym RIA). The term was invented at Macromedia to describe a new class of applications that would offer the benefits of being connected to the Internet, including access to various types of Web-based services, but would solve many of the nagging issues that had been inherent in browser-based applications since the mid-1990s. By using Flash Player to host graphically rich applications delivered as Flash documents, issues such as the ongoing differences between Web browsers in implementation of Cascading Style Sheets (CSS) and JavaScript would be overcome. And because such applications would be able to leverage Flash Player's original strengths, including animation and delivery of rich media (audio and video) to the desktop, the applications could be both functional and visually compelling.

The first push into the new frontier of RIAs met with mixed success. Products built and delivered with Flash MX and ColdFusion MX (Macromedia's recommended middleware application server software at the time) could be very impressive. Perhaps the best known of this class was the iHotelier hotel reservations application, still used by many large hotels around the world to present a Flash-based interface that allows customers to find and reserve hotel rooms from a visually intuitive single-screen interface. Users could input information and get nearly instantaneous response without having to navigate the multi-page interface of classic HTML-based Web applications.

Meanwhile, developers who were creating these applications were madly pulling their hair out. Building data-centric applications in Flash meant that you were working with a binary source file, making it difficult to integrate with source control systems. At the time, ActionScript wasn't particularly object-oriented (although this part of the situation improved drastically with the release of ActionScript 2 in Flash MX 2004), and there was no enforcement of code placement standards. Its loose data typing and lack of strong compile-time error checking or debugging tools led to phenomena such as "silent failure" — the moment when something that's supposed to happen doesn't, and no information is offered as to the reason.

In large multi-developer environments, figuring out where to put the code in a Flash document was a significant part of the application planning, because the product wasn't really designed for application development. And the ActionScript editor built into Flash gave experienced developers fits. Particularly for Java developers who were used to sophisticated code editors, working in Flash slowed productivity and increased developer frustration.

Flex 1 was Macromedia's first response to these issues. Released initially as a server-based product, Flex was designed to let enterprise application developers use a workflow they were accustomed to. Flex Builder 1, built on top of the Dreamweaver code base, was a first stab at providing a better code editor, and was included for those organizations that purchased a server license. Issues remained, but developers who were accustomed to building applications in source code were able to use their usual workflows, and multiple developers could collaborate more easily, because Flex applications were built as source code files that could be shared.

Flex 2 went further with the delivery of ActionScript 3, a true object-oriented language. The Flex 2 SDK was free, and Flex Builder 2 was the first version of the IDE delivered as an Eclipse plug-in. The IDE's licensing changed to a per-developer model, identical to the model used by other successful developer tools. For enterprise application developers, the situation got better and better.

Now, with the release of Flex 3, Adobe offers developers the ability not only to build better Web-based applications, but also to leverage their skills to deliver desktop applications using the Adobe Integrated Runtime. Anything you can do in Flex on the Web, you can now do in Flex on the desktop. The Flex 3 SDK has expanded with new classes, such as the AdvancedDataGrid. And Flex Builder 3 is compatible with the latest release of the Eclipse workbench.

This book offers a comprehensive overview of Flex application development. Detailed explanations of building applications using the Flex framework (the class library containing the building blocks of Flex applications) are combined with explorations of how to integrate applications with the most popular Web service architectures and application servers. The book is not designed as a replacement for the Flex 3 documentation (which at last count included multiple publications and over 2,000 pages). Instead, it offers a combination of reference, tutorial, and tips for building and delivering Flex application to the Web and the desktop that take you through learning Flex in a natural sequence.

Many other books may be helpful as you learn Flex. The ActionScript programming language is worthy of an entire book and is described admirably in the *ActionScript 3 Bible* by Roger Braunstein, Mims H. Wright, and Joshua J. Noble. The *AIR Bible* by Peter Else, Benjamin Gorton, Ryan Taylor, and Jeff Yamada offers a deep dive into the unique capabilities of the Adobe Integrated Runtime. And for those who want to understand more about Flash Player, the venerable *Flash CS3 Professional Bible* by Robert Reinhardt and Snow Dowd is an invaluable reference.

Finally, for those like to listen as they learn, check out my own video training titles at Lynda.com (www.lynda.com), *Flex 3 Essential Training, Flex 3 Beyond the Basics, AIR Essential Training,* and *AIR for Flex Developers Beyond the Basics.*

Getting the most out of this book

Most chapters are accompanied by sample Flex applications and other source code that you can download from the Wiley.com Web site at www.wiley.com/go/flex3. Each chapter's sample files are independent from other chapters, so if you want to jump to a particular subject, you don't first have to go through the sample code for all the preceding chapters.

Many of the files from the Web site are delivered in Flex Project Archives. A Flex Project Archive is a new feature of Flex Builder 3, a file in .zip format that contains everything you need to import an existing project into Flex Builder. It's portable between operating systems, so you can import the file into any version of Flex Builder 3, whether on Windows, Mac OS X, or the new version for Linux that was in public beta at the time this was written.

If you're using the free Flex SDK (rather than Flex Builder), you can still use the Flex Project Archive files. Just extract them to a folder somewhere on your system. Following current best-practice recommendations, the project's application source code files are always in a subfolder of the archive root named src.

For chapters that deal with application servers such as BlazeDS, ColdFusion, ASP.NET, or PHP, you'll need to download and install that software to run the sample applications from the Web site. Each relevant chapter includes the URL from which the software can be downloaded and complete installation instructions. For these chapters, you typically are instructed to create a Flex project from scratch and then extract files from a .zip file from the Web site into the project (rather than importing a Flex Project Archive file).

Finally, you can let us know about issues you find in the book or offer suggestions for subjects you'd like to see covered in a future edition. Visit www.bardotech.com/flexbible to ask questions and offer feedback.

Using the book's icons

The following margin icons help you get the most out of this book:

NOTE Notes highlight useful information that you should take into consideration.

TIP Tips provide additional bits of advice that make particular features quicker or easier to use.

CAUTION Cautions warn you of potential problems before you make a mistake.

NEW FEATURE The New Feature icon highlights features that are new to Flex 3.

CROSS-REF Watch for the Cross-Ref icon to learn where in another chapter you can go to find more information on a particular topic.

ON the WEB This icon points you toward related files on the book's Web site, www.wiley.com/go/flex3.

WEB RESOURCE The Web Resource icon directs you to other material available online.

Acknowledgments

It's a truism, and it's also true, that no book of any length can be completed without the support and sufferance of family, friends, and colleagues.

First, I'd like to thank the great folks at Wiley Publishing who always took my calls. Stephanie McComb and Marty Minner were always willing to hear the newest idea and help me figure out what was next. Gwenette Gaddis Goshert pointed out grammatical *faux pas* that made this former English major blush. And Drew Falkman, fellow Flex instructor at Bardo Tech and aspiring screenwriter, ferreted out the technical issues without regard for my sensitive side.

The Adobe Certified Instructors who join me at Bardo Tech in teaching Adobe Flex to the world have taught me more about Flex than just about anyone. Thanks to Simeon Bateman, Drew Falkman (again), Alex Hearnz, Spike Milligan, and Jeanette Stallons.

Neil Salkind and Heather Brown at Studio B relieved me of having to worry about the business details.

Since early in this century, I've worked as a technical trainer and courseware developer with an extraordinary crew, the Adobe instructional development team members who have moved from Allaire to Macromedia to Adobe and never lost their stride: Matt Boles, Robert Crooks, Tina Goodine, Sue Hove, Deborah Prewitt, James Talbot, and Leo Schuman. They're always willing to discuss and argue the teaching points. And thanks also to other Adobe Flex instructors who are always willing to share their knowledge and insights: Emily Kim, David Hussein, Simon Slooten, and Jun Heider.

Members of the Adobe Flex product management team, including Matt Chotin and Phil Costa, pointed me in the right direction more times than they know. Jeff Vroom of the LiveCycle Data Services development team humbled himself to be my teaching assistant at a couple of Adobe conferences and is more the master of this material than I.

And finally, for my family who dealt with my being pretty much unavailable for anything at all for this long: my kids, Thad, Jason, and Jenny, and my extraordinary wife and best friend in the whole world, Jackie.

Part I

Flex Fundamentals

Chapter 1

About Flex 3

Flex 3 is the most recent version of a platform for developing and deploying software applications that run on top of the Adobe Flash Player. While such tools have existed for many years, the most recent toolkit from Adobe Systems allows programmers with object-oriented backgrounds to become productive very quickly using the skills they already have learned in other programming languages and platforms.

Since the release of Flex 2, the Flex development environment has encouraged a development workflow similar to that used in other desktop development environments such as Visual Studio, Delphi, and JBuilder. The developer writes source code and compiles an application locally and then uploads the finished application to a Web server for access by the user. That isn't how Flex started, however.

Flex was originally released by Macromedia as a server-based application deployment and hosting platform. In the early versions of the Flex product line, an MXML/ActionScript compiler was included in a Java-based Web application hosted on a Java 2 Enterprise Edition (J2EE) server. Application source code was stored on the server. When a user made a request to the server, the application was compiled "on request" and delivered to the user's browser, and hosted by the Flash Player.

This server-based compilation and application deployment model is still available in the most recent version of the server software now known as LiveCycle Data Services ES. But the version of the compiler that's delivered in LiveCycle Data Services isn't necessarily the same as the one that's available in both the Flex 3 Software Developers Kit (SDK) and Flex Builder 3. And most developers find it simpler to use the primary "local compilation" development model.

In this chapter, I describe the nature of Flex applications, the relationship between Flex applications and the Flash Player, and how Flex leverages the nearly ubiquitous distribution of Flash Player on multiple operating systems. I also describe how Flex applications can be packaged for deployment as desktop applications using the Adobe Integrated Runtime (AIR), formerly known as Apollo.

Learning the Fundamentals of Flex

The Flex product line allows developers to deploy applications that run on the Flash Player as Web applications and on the Adobe Integrated Runtime (AIR) as desktop applications. The compiled applications that you create with Flex are the same as those produced by the Adobe Flash authoring environment (such as Adobe Flash CS3), but the process of creating the applications is very different.

Getting to know Flex applications

A Flex application is software that you create using the various pieces of the Adobe Flex 3 product line, which includes the following:

- The Flex 3 Software Developers Kit (SDK)
- Flex Builder 3

One major difference between the SDK and Flex Builder is that the SDK is free, while Flex Builder is available only through a license that you purchase from Adobe Systems. But in addition to the Flex SDK that's at the core of Flex Builder, the complete development environment includes many tools that will make your application development more productive and less error-prone than working with the SDK and another editing environment.

Flex Builder 3 Professional (the more complete and expensive of the available Flex Builder licenses) also includes a set of components known as the Data Visualization Toolkit that aren't included in the SDK. The Data Visualization Toolkit includes the Flex Charting components for presenting data as interactive visual charts and a new component called the `AdvancedDataGrid` that presents relational data with groups, summaries, multi-column sorting, and other advanced features.

NEW FEATURE   The Flex Charting Controls were available as a separately licensed product in the Flex 2 product line. With Flex 3, the Charting Controls, the `AdvancedDataGrid` component, and other advanced controls are now available only as part of a Flex Builder 3 Professional license.

Flex programming languages

Flex 3 applications are written using two programming languages — ActionScript 3 and MXML:

- **ActionScript 3** is the most recent version of the ActionScript language to evolve in the Flash authoring environment over the lifetime of the product. A complete object-oriented language, ActionScript 3 is based on the ECMAScript edition 4 draft language specification. It includes most of the elements of object-oriented languages, including class definition syntax, class package structuring, strong data typing of variables, and class inheritance.

Flex as Open Source

In April 2007, Adobe Systems announced its intention to migrate the Flex SDK to an open-source project, to be licensed under the Mozilla Public License (MPL). This license allows developers to modify and extend source code, and to distribute components of the code (or the entire SDK). Any changes that developers make to the ActionScript files that make up the Flex SDK must in turn be made available to other developers. This does not affect the developer's own proprietary code. You still own the MXML and ActionScript code you write for your own applications.

Not all components in the Flex SDK are available in the open-source package. Some components, such as the Flex Charting Components and `AdvancedDataGrid`, are available only through commercial licenses. Also, Flex Builder is available only through a license that you purchase from Adobe.

The open-source Flex SDK is managed through the `http://opensource.adobe.com/wiki/display/flexsdk/` Web site. Additional information and ongoing discussion of the Flex open-source project is available at these Web sites:

- `http://groups.google.com/group/flex-open-source`
- `http://flex.org/`

To get a copy of the Mozilla Public License, visit `www.mozilla.org/MPL/`.

- **MXML** is a pure XML-based markup language that is used to define a Flex application and many of its components. Most of the elements in MXML correspond to an ActionScript 3 class that's delivered as part of the Flex class library.

When you compile a Flex application, your MXML code is rewritten in the background into pure ActionScript 3. MXML can be described as a "convenience language" for ActionScript 3 that makes it easier and faster to write your applications than if you had to code completely in ActionScript.

NOTE ActionScript 3 also is used in the Flash CS3 authoring environment for logical code, creating class definitions, and other programming tasks. Unlike Flex 3, which uses only version 3 of ActionScript, you can create Flash documents in Flash CS3 that use older versions of the language, such as ActionScript 2.

The diagram in Figure 1.1 describes the relationship between the Flex SDK's command-line compiler, Flex Builder, the MXML and ActionScript programming languages, and the Flash Player and Adobe Integrated Runtime.

MXML versus ActionScript 3

MXML and ActionScript can be used interchangeably in many situations. MXML is commonly used to declare visual layout of an application and many objects, but it's usually your choice as a developer as to when to use each language.

FIGURE 1.1

The Flex SDK and Flex Builder both compile source code in MXML and ActionScript, producing executable applications that are hosted by the Flash Player on the Web or the Adobe Integrated Runtime ("AIR") on the desktop.

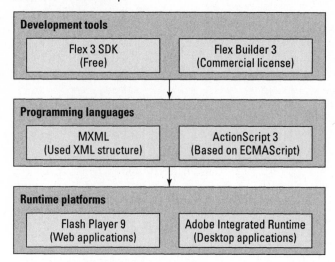

In these examples, I'm declaring an instance of an ActionScript class named Label. The Label class is part of the Flex class library that's included with both the Flex SDK and Flex Builder 3. Its purpose is to present a single line of text in a Flex application.

Declaring objects in MXML

The Label class is represented in MXML as a tag named <mx:Label/>. To create an instance of the Label class using MXML and set its text property to a value of Hello World, declare the tag and set the property as an XML attribute:

```
<mx:Label id="myLabel" text="Hello World"/>
```

This results in creating an instance of the Label class that is displayed in the application.

Declaring objects in ActionScript 3

The Label class also can be instantiated using ActionScript 3. When using the ActionScript 3 coding model, you first create the object using the class's constructor method and then add the object to the application's display list so it becomes visible. You can set the text property anytime after creating the object:

```
import mx.controls.Label;
var myLabel:Label = new Label();
myLabel.text = "Hello World";
this.addChild(myLabel);
```

This ActionScript code accomplishes exactly the same steps as the MXML code in the first example. Notice that it takes four lines of ActionScript instead of the single line of MXML code. The amount of code needed to accomplish any particular task is a common difference and one of the reasons MXML exists. MXML can significantly reduce the amount of code in your application without compromising its features or performance.

NOTE Assuming that the ActionScript code above is in a main application file, the prefix `this` in the method call `this.addChild()` would refer to the Application itself. If the same code were in an MXML component or ActionScript class, `this` would refer to the current instance of that component or class.

Flex versus Flash development

Developers tend to use Flex instead of Flash when they want to create software applications that have these characteristics:

- High level of interactivity with the user
- Use of dynamic data with application servers such as ColdFusion, ASP.NET, PHP, or J2EE
- Highly scaled applications in terms of the number of views, or screens, from which the user can select

In contrast, developers tend to use Flash when they are creating documents with these characteristics:

- Documents whose main purpose is to present visual animation
- Marketing presentations
- Hosting of Web-based video

Many applications that are built in Flash CS3 could be built in Flex, and vice versa. The selection of development environment, then, is frequently driven by a developer's background and existing skill set.

Developing in Flash

As described above, developers who use Flash are frequently focused on presenting animation, hosting video, and the like. Flash is generally considered superior for animation work because of its use of a timeline to control presentations over a designated period of time. Flash supports a variety of animation techniques that make use of the timeline, including these:

- Frame by frame animation
- Motion tweening
- Shape tweening

Flash also allows you to create animations using pure ActionScript code, but that approach also can be used in Flex. Developers who come from a graphic design background and are used to thinking visually appreciate the precision and visual feedback that the Flash development environment provides.

One drawback that application developers encounter with Flash is that the primary source document used in Flash, the .fla file format, is binary. As a result, it doesn't work well with the source control systems that application developers commonly use to manage their development projects, because you can't easily "diff," or discover differences between, different versions of a binary file.

Developing in Flex

Developers who use Flex to build their applications commonly have a background in some other programming language. Documents can be created and made useful in Flash without any programming, but a Flex application is almost entirely code-based. Animations are handled entirely through ActionScript, because Flex doesn't have a timeline as part of its development toolkit.

Flex also has superior tools for handling large-scale applications that have dozens or hundreds of views, or screens. Although Flash CS3 has a screen document feature, this feature hasn't received the development attention from Adobe that would make it a compelling architectural choice for these "enterprise" applications.

Finally, Flex applications are built in source code, which is stored in text files. These text files are easy to manage in source-code control applications such as CVS and Subversion. As a result, multi-developer teams who are dependent on these management tools find Flex development to be a natural fit to the way they already work.

The Flex Builder 3 design view feature has become more friendly and useful to graphic designers than in previous versions, but it isn't always intuitive to a designer who's used to "real" graphic design tools like Adobe's own Photoshop, Illustrator, and Fireworks.

Table 1.1 describes some of the core differences between Flex and Flash development.

TABLE 1.1

Differences between Flex and Flash Development

Task	Flex	Flash
Animation	Flex uses ActionScript classes called Effects to define and play animations. There is no timeline.	The Flash timeline allows animation frame-by-frame or tweening, and also supports programmatic animation with ActionScript.
Working with data	Flex has multiple tools for working with data and application servers, including the RPC components (HTTPService, WebService, and RemoteObject). It is also a natural fit for use with LiveCycle Data Services.	Flash can communicate with the same RPC sources as Flex, but its programming tools aren't as intuitive or robust.

Task	Flex	Flash
Design	Flex has a design view for WYSIWYG ("What You See Is What You Get") application layout, but has no visual tools for creating graphic objects from scratch.	Flash has very good graphic design tools, although not as complete a toolkit as Illustrator. However, it has excellent tools for importing and using graphics created in Photoshop and Illustrator.
Programming languages	Flex supports ActionScript 3 and MXML.	Flash supports all versions of ActionScript (but only one version per Flash document) and does not support MXML.
Code management	Flex applications are created as source code in text files, which are completely compatible with source-code management systems.	Flash documents are binary, which presents problems when building applications in multi-developer environments that require source-code management tools.

NOTE Applications built for development in the Adobe Integrated Runtime (AIR) can be created in either Flex or Flash. AIR applications can be created from any compiled Flash document or from HTML-based content.

Flex and Object-Oriented Programming

Flex application development is especially compelling for developers who are already acquainted with object-oriented programming (OOP) methodologies. Object-oriented programming is a set of software development techniques that involve the use of software "objects" to control the behavior of a software application.

Object-oriented programming brings many benefits to software development projects, including these:

- Consistent structure in application architectures
- Enforcement of contracts between different modules in an application
- Easier detection and correction of software defects
- Tools that support separation of functionality in an application's various modules

You'll find no magic bullets in software development: You can create an application that's difficult to maintain and at risk of collapsing under its own weight in an OOP language just as easily as you can create one that primarily uses procedural programming. But a good understanding of OOP principles can contribute enormously to a successful software development project.

And because ActionScript 3 is a completely object-oriented language, it serves Flex developers well to understand the basic concepts of OOP and how they're implemented in Flex development.

Object-oriented programming is commonly supported by use techniques known as modularity, encapsulation, inheritance, and polymorphism.

Modularity

Modularity means that an application should be built in small pieces, or modules. For example, an application that collects data from a user should be broken into modules, each of which has a particular purpose. The code that presents a data entry form, and the code that processes the data after it has been collected, should be stored in distinct and separate code modules. This results in highly maintainable and robust applications, where changes in one module don't automatically affect behavior in another module.

The opposite of modularity is *monolithic*. In monolithic applications such as the example in Listing 1.1, all the code and behavior of an application are defined in a single source-code file. These applications tend to be highly "brittle," meaning that changes in one section of the application run a high risk of breaking functionality in other areas. Such applications are sometimes referred to as *spaghetti code* because they tend to have code of very different purposes all wrapped around each other.

LISTING 1.1

A monolithic Flex application

```xml
<?xml version="1.0" encoding="utf-8"?>
<mx:Application xmlns:mx="http://www.adobe.com/2006/mxml">
  <mx:Model>
    ...data representation...
  </mx:Model>
  <mx:Script>
    ...ActionScript...
  </mx:Script>
  <mx:HBox>
    <mx:DataGrid>
     <mx:columns>
        <mx:DataGridColumn .../>
        <mx:DataGridColumn .../>
        <mx:DataGridColumn .../>
      </mx:columns>
    </mx:DataGrid>
    <mx:Form>
      <mx:FormItem label="First Name:">
        <TextInput id="fnameInput"/>
      </mx:FormItem>
      <mx:FormItem label="Last Name:">
        <TextInput id="lnameInput"/>
      </mx:FormItem>
      <mx:FormItem label="Address:">
        <TextInput id="addressInput"/>
      </mx:FormItem>
    </mx:Form>
  </mx:HBox>
</mx:Application>
```

In the above application, all the application's functionality is mixed together: data modeling, data collection, and logical scripting. Although the application might work, making changes without introducing bugs will be difficult, especially for a multi-developer team trying to work together on the application without constantly disrupting each other's work.

A modular application such as the version in Listing 1.2 breaks up functionality into modules that each handle one part of the application's requirements. This architecture is easier to maintain because the programmer knows immediately which module requires changes for any particular feature.

LISTING 1.2

A modular Flex application

```
<?xml version="1.0" encoding="utf-8"?>
<mx:Application xmlns:mx="http://www.adobe.com/2006/mxml">
  <mx:Script source="scriptFunctions.as"/>
  <valueObjects:AValueObject id="vo"/>
  <views:ADataGrid id="grid"/>
  <forms:AForm id="form"/>
</mx:Application>
```

Flex implements modularity through the use of MXML components and ActionScript classes that together implement the bulk of an application's functionality.

Encapsulation

Encapsulation means that a software object should hide as much of its internal implementation from the rest of the application as possible, and should expose its functionality only through publicly documented "members" of the object. A class definition that's properly encapsulated exposes and documents these object members to allow the application to set properties, call methods, handle events, and refer to constants. The documentation of the object members is known as the application programming interface (API) of the class.

In the Flex class library, class members include:

- **Properties:** Data stored within the object
- **Methods:** Functions you can call to execute certain actions of the object
- **Events:** Messages the object can send to the rest of the application to share information about the user's actions and/or data it wants to share
- **Constants:** Properties whose values never change

In Flex, encapsulation is fully implemented in ActionScript 3. Each member that you define in a class can be marked using an access modifier to indicate whether the particular method or property is `public`, `private`, `protected`, or `internal`. A `public` method, for example, allows the application to execute functionality that's encapsulated within the class, without the programmer who's calling the method having to know the details of how the action is actually executed.

For example, imagine a class that knows how to display a video in the Flash Player and allows the developer to start, stop, and pause the video, and control the video's audio volume. The code that executes these functions would have to know lots about how video is handled in Flash and the particular calls that would need to be made to make the audio louder or softer. The API of the class, however, could be extremely simple, including methods to execute each of these actions.

```
public class VideoPlayer()
{

  public function VideoPlayer(video:String):null
  { ... call video libraries to load a video ... }

  public function start()
  { ... call video libraries to play the video ... }

  public function stop()
  { ... call video libraries to stop the video ... }

  public function setVolume(volume:int):null
  { ... call video libraries to reset the volume ... }

}
```

The application that instantiates and uses the class wouldn't need to know any of the details; it just needs to know how to call the methods:

```
var myVideoPlayer:VideoPlayer = new VideoPlayer("myvideo.flv");
myVideoPlayer.start();
myVideoPlayer.setVolume(1);
```

We say, then, that the VideoPlayer class encapsulates complex behavior, hiding the details of the implementation from the rest of the application.

Inheritance

Inheritance refers to the ability of any class to extend any other class and thereby inherit that class's properties, methods, and so on. An inheritance model allows the developer to define classes with certain members (properties, methods, and so on) and then to share those members with the classes that extend them.

In an inheritance relationship, the class that already has the capabilities you want to inherit is called the *superclass,* or *base class,* or *parent class.* The class that extends that class is known as the *subclass,* or *derived class,* or *child class.* Unified Modeling Language (UML) is a standardized visual language for visually describing class relationships and structures. In this book, I frequently use UML diagrams such as the example in Figure 1.2 to describe how a class is built or its relationship to other classes.

FIGURE 1.2

This is an example of a UML diagram that describes a relationship between a base and a derived class.

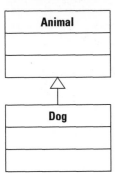

One class can extend a class that in turn extends another. UML diagrams can be extended to describe these relationships as well. The UML diagram in Figure 1.3 describes a three-tier inheritance relationship between a superclass named Animal and subclasses named Dog and Poodle.

FIGURE 1.3

This diagram describes a three-part inheritance relationship.

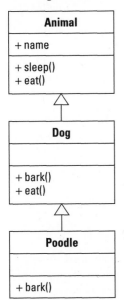

In Figure 1.2, methods of the superclass `Animal` are inherited by the subclass `Dog`. `Dog` has additional methods and properties that aren't shared with its superclass and that can override the superclass's existing methods with its own implementations. The same relationship exists between `Dog` and `Poodle`.

Because all versions of `Animal` sleep in the same way, calling `Dog.sleep()` or `Poodle.sleep()` actually calls the version of the method implemented in `Animal`. But because `Dog` has its own `run()` method, calling `Dog.run()` or `Poodle.run()` calls that version of the method. And finally, because all dogs bark in a different way, calling `Poodle.bark()` calls a unique version of the `bark()` method that's implemented in that particular class.

Inheritance allows you to grow an application over time, creating new subclasses as the need for differing functionality becomes apparent.

In Flex, the ActionScript inheritance model allows you to create extended versions of the components included in the Flex class library without modifying the original versions. Then, if an upgraded version of the original class is delivered by Adobe, a simple recompilation of the application that uses the extended class will automatically receive the upgraded features.

Polymorphism

Polymorphism means that you can write methods that accept arguments, or parameters, data typed as instances of a superclass, but then pass an instance of a subclass to the same method. Because all subclasses that extend a particular superclass share the same set of methods, properties, and other object members, the method that expects an instance of the superclass also can accept instances of the subclass and know that those methods can be called safely.

Polymorphism also can be used with a programming model known as an *interface*. An interface is essentially an abstract class that can't be directly instantiated. Its purpose is to define a set of methods and other object members and to describe how those methods should be written. But in an interface such as the one described in Figure 1.4, the method isn't actually implemented; it only describes the arguments and return data types that any particular method should have.

A class "implements" an interface by creating concrete versions of the interface's methods that actually do something. As with the relationship between super and subclasses, a method might be written that accepts an instance of the interface as an argument. At runtime, you actually pass an instance of the implementing class.

For example, you might decide that `Animal` should be abstract; that is, you would never create an instance of an Animal, only of a particular species. The following code describes the interface:

```
public interface Animal
{
  public function sleep()
  {}
}
```

FIGURE 1.4

This UML diagram describes the relationship between an interface and an implementing class.

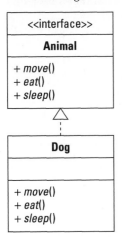

The interface doesn't actually implement these methods. Its purpose is to define the method names and structures. A class that implements the interface might look like this:

```
public class Dog implements Animal
{
  public function sleep()
  { ... actual code to make the dog sleep ... }
  public function bark()
  { ... actual code to make the dog bark ... }
}
```

Notice that a class that implements an interface can add other methods that the interface doesn't require. This approach is sometimes known as *contract-based programming*. The interface constitutes a contract between the method that expects a particular set of methods and the object that implements those methods.

Flex supports polymorphism both through the relationship between superclasses and subclasses and through creation and implementation of interfaces in ActionScript 3.

Understanding the Flash Player

Flex applications are executed at runtime by the Flash Player or the Adobe Integrated Runtime. In either case, they start as applications compiled to the .swf file format.

When you deploy a Flex application through the Web, it's downloaded from a Web server at runtime as a result of a request from a Web browser. The browser starts the Flash Player, which in turn runs the application.

The Adobe Integrated Runtime includes the Flash Player as one of its critical components. Other components include a Web browser kernel to execute HTML, CSS and JavaScript, and APIs for local file access and data storage. But the version of the Flash Player that's included with AIR is the same as the one that runs on users' systems as a Web browser plug-in or ActiveX control. As a result, any functionality that you include in a Flex application should work the same regardless of whether the application is deployed to the Web or the desktop.

The diagram in Figure 1.5 describes the architectural difference between the Flash Player's deployment in a Web browser versus the Adobe Integrated Runtime.

FIGURE 1.5

Flash Player installed with a Web browser versus the Adobe Integrated Runtime

Web deployment model

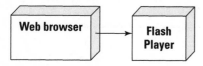

Flash Player called as ActiveX or plug-in

Desktop deployment model

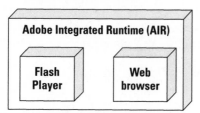

Flash Player and Web browser
integrated into runtime

Learning a little history about the Flash Player

FutureWave Software originally created a product called Future Splash Animator, which in turn evolved from a product called SmartSketch. The player for the animations was Java-based and was the ancestor of the current Adobe Flash Player. After its purchase by Macromedia, the product was renamed and released in 1996 as Macromedia Flash 1.0.

The product went through a steady evolution, starting with basic Web animation and eventually becoming a full-featured programming environment with rich media (video and audio) hosting capabilities.

During its time with Macromedia, Flash (the IDE) was packaged as part the Studio bundle and was integrated with other Studio products such as Dreamweaver and Fireworks. Macromedia positioned Flash MX and MX 2004 as development environments for what the company began to call *rich internet applications* (RIAs). Although the development environment that was Flash never fully satisfied the requirements of application developers (see the discussion in the section "Flex versus Flash development" of issues that are commonly encountered in Flash when developing true applications), the Flash Player continued to grow in its ability to host the finished applications, however they were built.

After Adobe Systems purchased Macromedia, Flash became a part of the Adobe Creative Suite 3 (CS3) product bundles. Along with this rebundling came increased integration with other CS3 products such as Illustrator and Photoshop. Other Adobe products such as AfterEffects and Premiere received new export features that allow their video-based output files to be integrated into Flash-based presentations.

Table 1.2 describes the major milestones in the history of the Flash Player.

TABLE 1.2

Flash Player History

Version	Year	New Features
Macromedia Flash Player 1	1996	Basic Web animation
Macromedia Flash Player 2	1997	Vector graphics, some bitmap support, some audio support; object library
Macromedia Flash Player 3	1998	The movieclip element; alpha transparency, MP3 compression; standalone player; JavaScript plug-in integration
Macromedia Flash Player 4	1999	Advanced ActionScript; internal variables; the input field object; streaming MP3
Macromedia Flash Player 5	2000	ActionScript 1.0; XML support; Smartclips (a component-based architecture); HTML 1.0 text formatting
Macromedia Flash Player 6	2002	Flash remoting for integration with application servers; screen reader support; Sorenson Sparc video codec
Macromedia Flash Player 7	2003	Streaming audio and video; ActionScript 2; first version associated with Flex
Macromedia Flash Player 8	2005	GIF and PNG graphic loading; ON VP6 video codec; faster performance; visual filters including blur and drop shadow; file upload and download; improved text rendering; new security features
Adobe Flash Player 9	2006	ActionScript 3; faster performance; E4X XML parsing; binary sockets; regular expressions
Adobe Flash Player 9 Update3	2007	H.264 video; hardware-accelerated full-screen video playback

Each new product bundling and relationship has increased the requirements for the Flash Player. As a result, the most recent version of the Player (version 9) has all the features I've described:

- Object-oriented programming with ActionScript 3
- Web-based animation
- Rich media hosting and delivery

NOTE In addition to the Flash Player that's delivered for conventional computers, Macromedia and Adobe have released versions of Flash Lite for hosting Flash content on devices such as cell phones and PDAs. None of the current versions of Flash Lite support ActionScript 3, so Flex applications currently can't be deployed on those platforms. Undoubtedly, this is a goal of future development by Adobe.

Flash Player penetration statistics

One of the attractions of the Flash Player is its nearly ubiquitous penetration rate in the Web. Each new version of the Player has achieved a faster rate of installation growth than each version before it; version 9 is no different. As of December 2007 (according to statistics published on Adobe's Web site), the penetration rate for Flash Player 7 was 99% or greater, Flash Player 8 was at 98% or greater, and Flash Player 9 already had a penetration rate of 93% or greater. Of course, these rates change regularly; for the most recent information on Flash Player penetration rates, visit:

```
http://www.adobe.com/products/player_census/flashplayer/
```

Penetration rates are very important to organizations that are deciding whether to build applications in Flex, because the availability of Flash Player 9 (required to run both Flex applications and Flash documents built with ActionScript 3) determines whether a Flex application will open cleanly or require the user to install or upgrade the Player prior to running the application. If a user needs to install the Flash Player, however, many ways exist to get the job done.

The Debug Flash Player

The Debug version of the Flash Player differs from the production version in a number of ways. As described in detail below, you can install the debug version of the Flash Player from installers that are provided with Flex Builder 3 and the Flex 3 SDK.

The Debug version of the Player includes these features:

- Integration with `fdb`, the command-line debugger that's included with the Flex 3 SDK
- Integration with Flex Builder debugging tools such as the `trace()` function and breakpoints
- Other debugging tools

To ensure that you're running the Debug player, navigate to this Web page in any browser that you think has the Player installed:

```
http://kb.adobe.com/selfservice/viewContent.do?externalId=tn_19245
```

As shown in Figure 1.6, you should see a Flash document that tells you which version of the Player is currently installed. When you load this document with the Debug Player, it displays a message indicating that you have the Content Debugger Player. This tool also tells you whether you're running the ActiveX or plug-in Player and what version.

FIGURE 1.6

Discovering your Flash Player version

Flash Player installation

As of this writing, Flash Player 9 is available for these operating systems:

- Windows
- Mac OS X
- Linux
- Solaris

For up-to-date information about current operating system support, including minimum browser and hardware requirements, visit this Web page:

```
http://www.adobe.com/products/flashplayer/productinfo/systemreqs/
```

The Flash Player can be installed on a user's computer system in a variety of ways:

- As an integrated Web browser plug-in
- As a standalone application
- As part of the Adobe Integrated Runtime

NOTE Regardless of how you install the Flash Player, users who install the Flash Player must have administrative access to their computer. On Microsoft Windows, this means that you must be logged in as an administrator. On Mac OS X, you must have an administrator password available during the installation.

Uninstalling the Flash Player

Before installing the Flash Player, make sure any existing installations have been removed. The process for uninstalling the Flash Player differs from one operating system to another, but in all cases you must close any browser windows before trying to uninstall the Player

On Windows XP, use the Control Panel's Add or Remove Programs feature, shown in Figure 1.7, and uninstall whatever versions of the Flash Player you find.

FIGURE 1.7

Windows XP's Add or Remove Programs feature, listing both the plug-in and ActiveX versions of the Flash Player

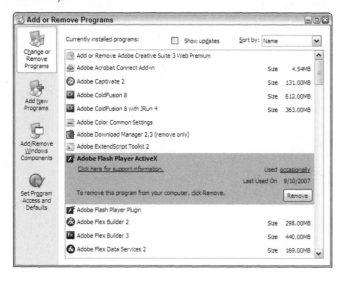

On Mac OS X, use the uninstaller application that's available for download from this Web page:

```
www.adobe.com/go/tn_14157
```

Installation with Flex Builder

As shown in Figure 1.8, when you install Flex Builder 3, you're prompted to install the debug version of the Flash Player as one of the last steps in configuring the installation. You should always accept this part of the installation, because it ensures that your system is equipped with the most recent version of the Player that you need for building, debugging, and testing your Flex applications.

FIGURE 1.8

The Flex Builder installer prompts you to install the Flash Player plug-in or ActiveX control on currently installed browsers.

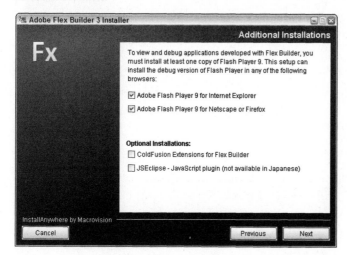

Before installing Flex Builder, make sure that you've closed any browser windows. If the installation detects open browser windows, it prompts you to close those windows before continuing the installation process.

Using Flex Builder installation files

If you need to reinstall the debug version of the Flash Player, you should use the version that's included with Flex Builder 3 or the Flex SDK. If you've installed Flex Builder, you can find the installation files in a subfolder within the Flex Builder installation folder. On Windows, this folder is named:

```
C:\Program Files\Adobe\Flex Builder 3\Player\Win
```

This folder has three files:

- **Install Flash Player 9 Plugin.exe:** The plug-in version for Firefox and Netscape
- **Install Flash Player 9 ActiveX.exe:** The ActiveX control for Internet Explorer
- **FlashPlayer.exe:** The standalone player (does not require installation — just run it!)

Before running any of the installers, be sure to close any open browser windows.

Installing the Flash Player from the Web

You also can get the Flash Player from the Adobe Web site. Select a download location depending on whether you want the production or debug version of the Player.

Downloading the production Flash Player

End users who want to run Flex applications and other Flash-based content can download the Flash Player installer from this Web page:

```
http://www.adobe.com/go/getflashplayer
```

When you see the page shown in Figure 1.9, you should see a link to download the Flash Player that's appropriate for your operating system and browser.

FIGURE 1.9

Downloading the Flash Player from Adobe.com

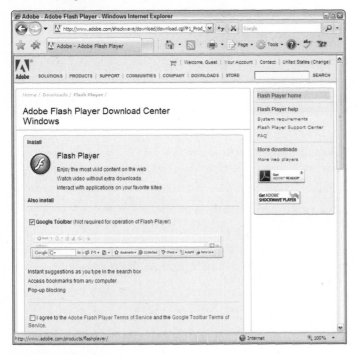

CAUTION The Flash Player that you download from this page is the production version, rather than the debug version. If you have the production version installed, you can test your applications, but you can't take advantage of debugging tools such as tracing, breakpoints, and expressions evaluation.

TIP The Flash Player Download Center may include a link to download the Google toolbar or other content. You do not have to download and install this unrelated content in order to get all the features of the Flash Player.

Downloading the debug Flash Player

To download the debug version of the Flash Player, visit this Web page:

http://www.adobe.com/support/flashplayer/downloads.html

As shown in Figure 1.10, you should see links for all versions of the Player, including both debug and production versions for a variety of operating systems and browsers.

FIGURE 1.10

This is the Adobe Flash Player Support Center.

> **TIP**   You might find an even more recent version of the Flash Player on the Adobe Labs Web page at http://labs.adobe.com. Adobe Labs hosts projects that are still in development, but that are far enough along that Adobe is sharing the current code with the community.

Flex 3 development tools

Flex developers have two sets of development tools: Flex Builder 3 and the Flex 3 SDK.

Flex Builder 3

Flex Builder 3 is an *integrated development environment* (IDE) for building Flex applications. This is the tool that most developers use to build Flex applications. I describe Flex Builder 3 in detail in Chapter 2.

The Flex Software Developers Kit (SDK)

The Flex class library and command-line tools you need to build Flex applications are completely free. As long as you don't need to use Flex Builder or certain components that require a license, you can download the Flex SDK from Adobe and build and deploy as many applications as you want. The obvious benefit is the cost. The drawback to this approach is that you'll have to select a text editor such Eclipse that doesn't have the specific support for Flex application development that you get with Flex Builder.

If you decide to use the Flex 3 SDK, download the most recent version from Adobe at www.adobe. com/go/flex. The SDK is delivered in a zipped archive file that can be extracted to any platform.

The SDK includes most of the class library you use to build Flex applications. The following components, however, require a license for deployment:

- Flex Charting components
- AdvancedDataGrid component
- Application profiling tools

As shown in Figure 1.11, if you decide to use these features without a license, any instances of the charting components or AdvancedDataGrid component are displayed in your application with a watermark indicating that you are using an evaluation version of the component.

In addition to the Flex class library, the Flex 3 SDK includes these command-line tools:

- mxmlc: A compiler for building Flex applications
- compc: A compiler for building component libraries, Runtime Shared Libraries (RSLs), and theme files
- fdb: A debugger to debug applications
- fcsh: The Flex Compiler Shell, which you can use to execute multiple compilation tasks without the overhead of having to launch a new Java Virtual Machine (JVM) for each task
- amxmlc: The AIR application compiler
- acompc: The AIR component compiler
- adl: The AIR debug application launcher
- optimizer: A tool for reducing ActionScript compiled file size and creating a "release version" of an application, component, or RSL

Detailed information about how to use each of these command-line tools is available in the Adobe publication *Building and Deploying Flex Applications*.

FIGURE 1.11

A watermarked charting component

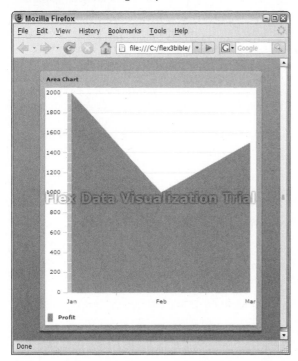

Using MXMLC, the command-line compiler

To compile a Flex application with mxmlc, the command-line compiler, it's a good idea to add the location of the Flex 3 SDK bin directory to your system's path. This allows you to run the compiler and other tools from any folder without having to include the entire path in each command. Figure 1.12 shows the command-line compiler.

TIP   When you install Flex Builder 3 on Microsoft Windows, the installer provides a menu choice that opens a command window and adds all directories containing Flex 3 components to the current path. To use this tool, select All Programs ⇨ Adobe ⇨ Adobe Flex 3 SDK Command Prompt from the Windows Start menu.

To compile an application from the command line, switch to the folder that contains your main application file. If you want to try this using the exercise files that are available for download with this book, switch to the chapter01 directory:

```
cd /flex3bible/chapter01
```

This directory contains a file called `HelloWorld.mxml`, a simple Flex application. To compile the application, run this command:

```
mxmlc HelloWorld.mxml
```

The command-line compiler at work

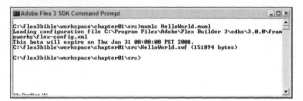

After the compilation is complete, your directory will contain a new file called `HelloWorld.swf`. This is the compiled application that you deploy to your Web server.

TIP The command-line compiler has many options for tuning your application. For complete details on how to use the compiler, see the Adobe publication *Building and Deploying Flex Applications.*

Getting Help

Documentation for Flex 3 is available from the Adobe Web site at:

```
www.adobe.com/support/documentation/en/flex/
```

The documentation is available in a variety of formats, including Acrobat PDF, HTML Help, and ASDocs HTML files.

The documentation includes these publications, among others:

- *Developing Flex Applications* contains extensive documentation on the functional tools that are available in the Flex framework.

- *Building and Deploying Flex Applications* focuses on application architecture, compiler tools, and deployment strategies.

- *ActionScript 3.0 Language and Components Reference* contains generated documentation of the Flex class library, including each class's properties, methods, and so on. This documentation also includes extensive code samples.

The documentation also is delivered in indexed, searchable format with Flex Builder 3. I describe how to explore and use this version of the documentation in Chapter 2.

Summary

In this chapter, I gave an introduction to the world of application development with Adobe Flex. You learned the following:

- Flex applications are built as source code and compiled into Flash documents.
- Flex applications can be run as Web applications with the Flash Player, delivered through a Web browser.
- Flex applications also can be run as desktop applications, hosted by the Adobe Integrated Runtime (AIR).
- The Flex Software Developers Kit (SDK) is completely free and available as an open-source project that's managed by Adobe Systems.
- Flex Builder 3 is a commercial integrated development environment for building Flex applications.
- Flex developers tend to have a background in object-oriented software development, but anyone who's willing to invest the time can become proficient in Flex application development.

Chapter 2

Using Flex Builder 3

Flex Builder 3 is Adobe's preferred development tool for building applications with the Flex Framework. Flex Builder is available for both the Windows and Mac OS X operating systems, and a Linux version of the product is planned for future release.

Although you can develop and deploy Flex applications to the Web or the desktop with the free Flex SDK, Flex Builder is a worthwhile investment that can increase developer productivity, reduce bugs, speed up coding, and generally make the process of developing a Flex application much more enjoyable.

Getting Flex Builder 3

You can get Flex Builder from Adobe as a free evaluation that lasts for 60 days, or you can purchase a license. Two licenses currently are available for Flex Builder 3:

- Flex Builder 3 Standard Edition includes everything you need to build basic Flex applications for the desktop and the Web, but it does not include the Flex Charting component library, the AdvancedDataGrid control, or certain other advanced development and testing tools.

- Flex Builder 3 Professional Edition includes the Flex Builder Standard Edition feature set and adds data visualization tools such as the Flex Charting components and AdvancedDataGrid control. The Professional license also includes the Flex Test Automation framework, which can be used along with Mercury QuickTest Professional to perform automated client testing on a Flex application.

Installing Flex Builder 3

Flex Builder 3 can be installed in two ways:

- As a standalone installation that includes everything you need
- As a plug-in on top of an existing installation of Eclipse

Regardless of which installation option you select, Flex Builder runs as a plug-in, or an integrated component, of another software product called Eclipse. So, before installing Flex Builder, it's first important to understand the nature of Eclipse.

NEW FEATURE Flex Builder 2 had a single installation application for each operating system. After you started the installation process, you selected whether to install Flex Builder with the standalone or the plug-in configuration. Flex Builder 3 has separate installation applications for the two configurations.

NOTE The plug-in installation requires Eclipse version 3.22 or later. When you select the standalone configuration, Flex Builder is installed with Eclipse 3. Eclipse 3 includes many new features that developers find valuable, including the ability to drag and drop code from one part of a source file to another.

Installing Flex Builder with the standalone configuration

The standalone installation of Flex Builder includes everything you need to get started building Flex applications. The installation includes these components in a single integrated package:

- The Java Runtime Environment (JRE) when installing on Windows
- The Flex Builder plug-in
- Optional installation of the ColdFusion Extensions for Eclipse
- Optional installation of the JSEclipse plug-in for editing JavaScript files

Running the standalone installer

Start the installer, and navigate through the first few screens. When prompted for the installation folder, select the location where you want to install the product.

On the next screen, shown in Figure 2.1, you're asked whether you want to install the debug version of Flash Player 9. Because this version of Flash Player is required for successful Flex application development, you should leave the options selected for all browsers.

This installation dialog box prompts you to decide which optional components you want to include in the Flex Builder installation.

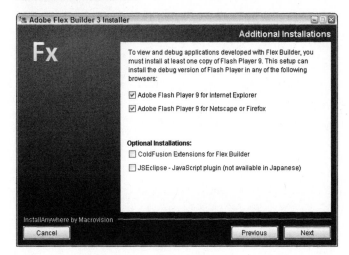

After accepting the summary screen (shown in Figure 2.2) and clicking Finish, the installation should be completed successfully.

The Pre-Installation Summary screen

Installing Flex Builder with the Eclipse workbench

Eclipse is an open-source software product that serves as a platform for building and deploying application development tools. Eclipse was originally developed by IBM as a Java integrated development environment. The software was then donated to the Eclipse Foundation, which describes itself as a "not-for-profit, member supported corporation." The purpose of the Eclipse Foundation is to organize and support ongoing development of Eclipse and related software. You can visit the Eclipse Foundation online at `http://www.eclipse.org`.

Eclipse is described as a *workbench*. It serves as a platform for many software products, each of which is typically devoted to development in a particular language or platform. These individual products are known as *plug-ins*. An Eclipse installation can host as many plug-ins as you like, for as many different programming languages as you work in. This allows you to do your development work in a single development environment and easily switch among Java, Flex, ColdFusion, XML, and any other languages for which you've installed the appropriate plug-ins.

Hundreds of plug-ins are available for the Eclipse workbench. Table 2.1 describes some Eclipse plug-ins that are commonly used by Flex application developers.

TABLE 2.1

Eclipse Plug-ins for Flex Developers

Plug-in	Description	Available From
Java Development Tools (JDT)	The most commonly used Eclipse-based Java development IDE; includes a Java editor with code editing, generation, debugging, and analysis tools	`http://www.eclipse.org/jdt/`
Web Tools Project	A set of tools for developing Web and Java EE applications	`http://www.eclipse.org/webtools/`
JSEclipse	A development environment for working with JavaScript	Included with Flex Builder
ColdFusion Extensions for Eclipse	A plug-in for ColdFusion developers that provides Remote Development Service (RDS) access to a ColdFusion server, along with tools to generate code for both ColdFusion and ActionScript	Included with Flex Builder
CFEclipse	An open-source, freely licensed plug-in for ColdFusion developers	`http://www.cfeclipse.org`

Getting Eclipse

When you install Flex Builder with the standalone installation option, you get a complete copy of Eclipse 3.3 as part of the installation. If you want to install Flex Builder using the plug-in installation option, you first need to download and install an Eclipse distribution.

Preparing to install Eclipse

Before installing an Eclipse distribution, you need to have the Java Runtime Environment (JRE) installed on your computer.

Mac OS X developers already have the JRE installed as part of the operating system's default configuration. Windows XP and Windows Vista developers should check for an existing JRE and install it if it isn't found.

As of this writing, the most recent version of the JRE (version 6) has not been fully tested with Eclipse 3.3, so I recommend that you install JRE 5 for use with Eclipse. If you're a Java developer, this doesn't affect your ability to develop with the latest version of the Java programming language, because you can always designate a different version of Java Standard Edition for any particular development project.

You can download and install JRE 5 from `http://java.sun.com/javase/downloads/index_jdk5.jsp`. Just follow the prompts to install the JRE, and you'll be ready to install Eclipse.

Selecting an Eclipse distribution

Many pre-packaged distributions of Eclipse are available. The basic product includes just the workbench and allows you to completely customize your installation. Other distributions include various combinations of plug-ins and configurations for common development scenarios.

Table 2.2 describes some of the common Eclipse distributions.

TABLE 2.2

Eclipse Distributions

Plug-in	Description	Available From
Eclipse IDE for Java Developers	Includes the JDT, a source code management client, XML editor, and other useful tools	`http://www.eclipse.org/downloads/`
Eclipse IDE for Java EE Developers	All of the above, plus Mylyn, for integration with Bugzilla, Trac, and JIRA (server environments for source code management)	`http://www.eclipse.org/downloads/`

continued

TABLE 2.2 *(continued)*		
Plug-in	**Description**	**Available From**
Eclipse Classic	Includes the JDT, plus tools for developers who want to create their own Eclipse plug-ins	`http://www.eclipse.org/downloads/`
Web Tools Platform All-in One	Includes text and graphics editors for a variety of languages and platforms; enables certain features of Flex Builder 3 for generation of Java server-side code	`http://www.eclipse.org/webtools/`

Installing Eclipse

Eclipse distributions are typically delivered as compressed archive files without formal setup applications.

Eclipse on Windows

On Windows, the Eclipse distribution is in the ZIP archive format. You install Eclipse on Windows simply by extracting the archive to any folder on your system.

For example, if you select the Eclipse IDE for J2EE Developers on Windows, version 3.3, the installation file will be named `eclipse-jee-europa-win32.zip`. Extract the .zip file to any folder on disk such as `C:\eclipse`.

To start Eclipse on Windows, run `eclipse.exe` from the Eclipse folder.

Eclipse on Mac OS X

On Mac OS X, the Eclipse distribution is in an archive format known as tarball. You install Eclipse on Mac OS X by extracting the archive to any folder on your system.

For example, if you select the Eclipse IDE for J2EE Developers on Mac OS X, version 3.3, the installation file will be named `eclipse-jee-europa-fall-macosx-carbon-tar.gz`. Extract the archive file to any folder on disk such as the Applications folder on your hard disk.

After installing Eclipse on Mac OS X, locate the Eclipse icon `Eclipse` in the Eclipse folder. Select the icon and press Cmd+O or double-click on the icon to start Eclipse.

Installing the Flex Builder plug-in

To install Flex Builder as a plug-in on top of your existing Eclipse installation, use the appropriate installation application for your operating system.

Eclipse Licensing

Eclipse is licensed under the Eclipse Public License Version 1.0 (EPL). This license allows you to freely download, install, and use Eclipse on as many computers as you like. The license is structured so that plug-ins that are created by software companies, non-profit organizations, or individuals can be distributed under open-source licenses (as with the Java Development Tools or CFEclipse) or sold as commercial products (as with Flex Builder).

Start the installer, and navigate through the first few screens. The plug-in installer asks for most of the same options as the standalone installer, but it also asks for two locations:

- The Choose Install Folder dialog box asks you to choose a location for the Flex SDK and other supporting files. Figure 2.3 shows the installation prompt for this information.

FIGURE 2.3

This dialog box asks for the location of the Install Folder.

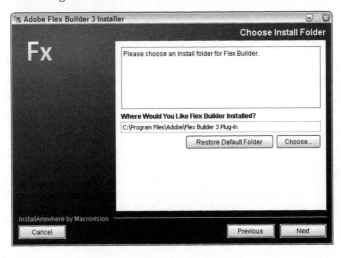

- The Choose Eclipse Folder to be Extended dialog box asks where you want Eclipse plug-ins to be installed. Figure 2.4 shows the installation screen for this information.

FIGURE 2.4

This dialog box asks you for the location of your Eclipse installation.

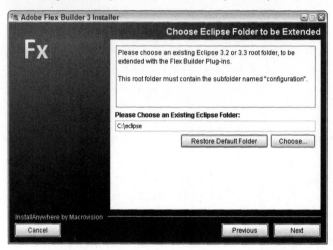

On the next screen, you're asked whether you want to install the debug version of Flash Player 9. Because this version of Flash Player is required for successful Flex application development, you should leave the options selected for all browsers.

CAUTION   **If you have a later version of the debug Flash Player already installed, the Flex Builder installation still replaces it with its own version. If you know you have a later version already installed, deselect the option to install the Flash Player to retain your current version.**

After accepting the summary screen and clicking Finish, the installation completes successfully.

Getting to Know the Eclipse Features

The Flex Builder 3 feature set combines the capabilities of the Eclipse workbench with customized tools that increase Flex application development productivity. Figure 2.5 shows the default Flex Builder layout the first time you open it after installation. In this section, I describe the basic tools of Eclipse: workspaces, projects, views, editors, and perspectives.

The Eclipse workspace

An Eclipse workspace consists of a collection of development projects, plus configuration settings for both the built-in Eclipse features and certain customized features that are part of Flex Builder.

When Eclipse first starts up, you're prompted to select a workspace. The default workspace folder will differ based on whether you're using Flex Builder's standalone configuration or the plug-in, but the location is your personal folder. Table 2.3 shows the specific locations you'll see for different operating systems.

FIGURE 2.5

Flex Builder in the default Flex Development perspective

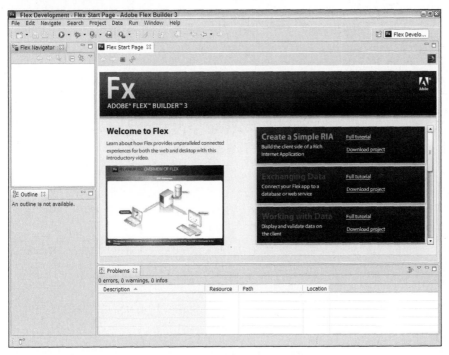

TABLE 2.3

Default Workspace Locations by Operating System

Operating System	Default Workspace Location
Windows XP	C:\Documents and Settings\[username]\My Documents\Flex Builder 3
Windows Vista	C:\Users\[username]\Documents\Flex Builder 3
Mac OS X	/Users/[username]/Documents/Flex Builder 3

The most visible and important purpose of an Eclipse workspace is to serve as a table of contents for a set of projects. The workspace, however, does more; it maintains all the information you need to manage your projects, including configuration settings for Eclipse, Flex Builder, and other plug-ins you might have installed.

Select File ➪ Switch Workspace from the Eclipse menu to switch workspaces. Workspaces you've used previously may be displayed on the menu; if the workspace you want is available, just select it.

To select a different workspace (whether new or one that already exists), select Other from the sub-menu. As shown in Figure 2.6, type the name of the workspace folder or use the folder browsing tool to select it. If you type the name of a folder that doesn't yet exist, it is created for you.

FIGURE 2.6

This dialog box asks for a new workspace location.

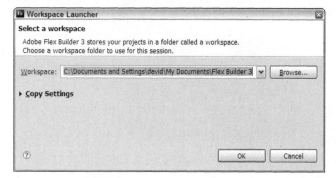

When you select a new workspace, Eclipse automatically restarts to allow any file or folder locks to be released.

Eclipse projects

An Eclipse project contains all the resources needed for a particular application or group of related applications. The basic Eclipse project contains only a reference to a particular root folder. Most projects you create will be for a particular programming language or platform and will be associated with a particular Eclipse plug-in such as Flex Builder, CFEclipse, the JDT, or others.

 A single project can be referenced in multiple workspaces.

Because the project creation process can vary widely for various plug-ins, I describe the details of Flex project creation in a later section.

Eclipse views

An Eclipse view is a user interface panel that serves a specific function. Some of the views you use in Flex Builder are part of the Eclipse workbench and are common to all Eclipse plug-ins. For example, the Problems view, which displays current compilation errors and warnings, is used in most plug-ins. Other views are unique to Flex Builder and are useful only in the context of Flex application development.

To open a view that currently isn't displayed on the screen, select Window ⇨ Show View ⇨ Other. As shown in Figure 2.7, all views from all installed plug-ins are available.

FIGURE 2.7

This dialog box allows you to select from all views from all installed plug-ins.

Managing a view's layout

Each view can be used in either docked or detached mode. Docking positions for views include the top, bottom, left, and right of the workspace window.

To move a docked view:

1. Click and drag the view's tab.

2. Move the view until the cursor displays a black line indicating where the view will be docked.

3. Release the mouse button to drop the view in its new location.

Figure 2.8 shows the process of docking a view.

As shown in Figure 2.9, to detach a view, right-click the view's tab (Ctrl-click on the Mac), and select Detached from the context menu. After a view has been detached, it can be moved anywhere on your screen, including moving to a second monitor you use in spanned mode.

FIGURE 2.8

Docking a view

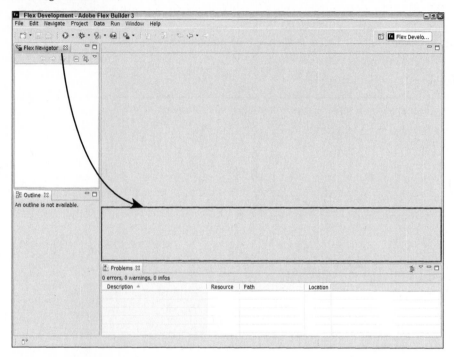

FIGURE 2.9

Detaching a view

TIP To maximize a view to full screen, double-click the view's tab. Double-clicking the tab again restores it to its original size.

Eclipse editors

An editor is special kind of view that's designed to support development for a particular programming language. The basic Eclipse installation includes a text editor that can be used to edit any text file. Each plug-in includes its own unique editors. For example, the Flex Builder plug-in includes editors for MXML and ActionScript files.

The editor is placed in the center of the workspace window and cannot be detached. To open multiple editors on a single file, right-click the editor tab and select New Editor. As shown in Figure 2.10, the same file is opened again in a separate editor view. When you have multiple editors open in this way, any changes you make in one of the editors is immediately reflected in the others. In Flex Builder, this allows you to have one editor open in Design view and the other open in Source view simultaneously.

FIGURE 2.10

Multiple editors open to a single source file.

Document editor 1 in Source view

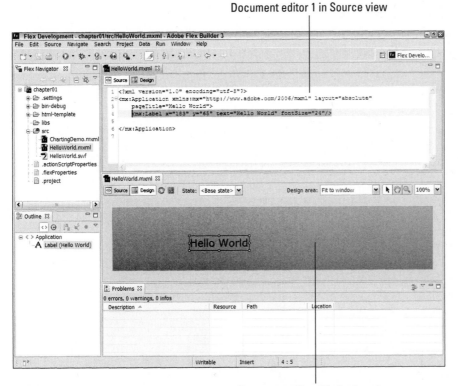

Document editor 2 in Design view

Eclipse perspectives

An Eclipse perspective is a particular arrangement of views. Each plug-in typically includes one or more predefined perspectives. For example, Flex Builder 3 includes these perspectives:

- Flex Development
- Flex Debugging
- Flex Profiling

If you install Flex Builder with the standalone configuration, the default perspective is Flex Development. You can select a different perspective in two ways:

- From the Eclipse menu, select Window ⇨ Perspective and select a perspective.
- As shown in Figure 2.11, use the Perspective selection tool in the upper-right corner of the workspace window.

FIGURE 2.11

Selecting a perspective from the perspective selection tool

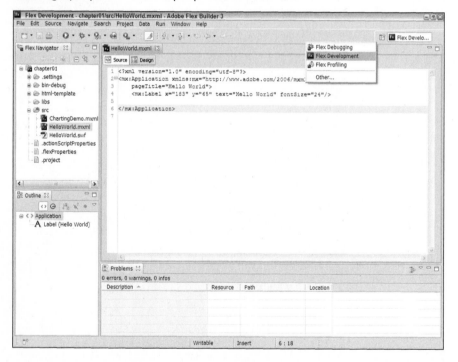

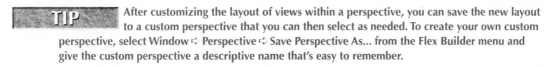 After customizing the layout of views within a perspective, you can save the new layout to a custom perspective that you can then select as needed. To create your own custom perspective, select Window ➪ Perspective ➪ Save Perspective As... from the Flex Builder menu and give the custom perspective a descriptive name that's easy to remember.

Configuring Eclipse

Most configuration options for Eclipse are available from the Preferences dialog box. Select Window ➪ Preferences from the Eclipse menu to open the dialog box shown in Figure 2.12.

FIGURE 2.12

The Eclipse Preferences dialog box

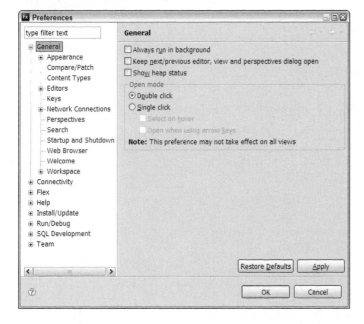

The General section of the Preferences dialog box allows you to change configurations that are common to all Eclipse plug-ins. Some preferences that you might want to customize are deeply buried in the tree of options. I describe some of the preferences that are frequently used, but I also encourage you to explore this area of the product.

Changing fonts

The standard font that's used to present text in the MXML, ActionScript, and text editors is configurable in the General section of the Preferences dialog box. To find this setting in the Preferences dialog box (shown in Figure 2.13):

1. Select General ⇨ Appearance ⇨ Colors and Fonts from the tree control on the left.

2. In the Colors and Fonts configuration tree on the right, select Basic ⇨ Text Font.

3. Click the Change button, and select the font from the font selection dialog box that appears.

4. After selecting a font, click OK to return to the Preferences dialog box, and click OK again to save your changes.

FIGURE 2.13

Selecting a text font

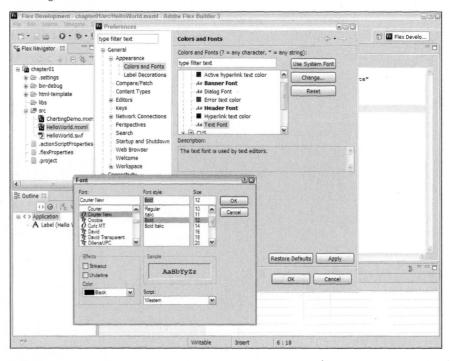

Selecting a Web browser

When you test a Flex Web application, you run the application in Flash Player, hosted by a Web browser of your choice. Flex Builder uses the Eclipse Web Browser configuration option. By default, this option uses your system browser (the same browser that's used when you navigate to a URL from an e-mail client or other link on your system).

Using the Eclipse Preferences dialog box, you can override this setting and select a specific Web browser. With the Preferences dialog box open, select General ➪ Web Browser from the tree of configuration options. As shown in Figure 2.14, you see a list of available browsers. The default selection tells Eclipse to use the system default browser. Select the browser you prefer, and click OK to save your changes. The next time you test a Flex application, it opens in the browser you selected.

FIGURE 2.14

Selecting a Web browser

Many other configuration options are available, but most are useful or relevant only when working with a particular kind of file or application. I describe these options at other points in the book.

Touring the Flex Builder Interface

Flex Builder has a common set of tools that you use to create and test Flex applications, whether it's installed with the standalone or plug-in configuration. In this section, I describe the most common tasks related to Flex application development: creating a Flex project and finding Help resources.

Creating Flex projects

An Eclipse project is a collection of application resources. When using Flex Builder, you should create your projects as a resource known as a *Flex project*. In addition to standard Eclipse project settings, a Flex project contains many configuration options that are designed specifically for Flex developers.

Select File ⇨ New ⇨ Flex Project from the Flex Builder menu to create a new Flex project.

In the New Flex Project wizard's first screen, shown in Figure 2.15, provide the following information:

FIGURE 2.15

This is the first screen in the New Flex Project wizard.

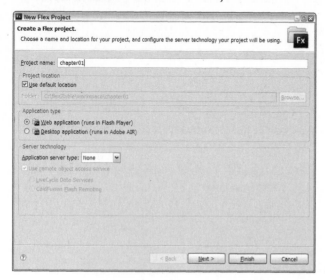

- The Project name can contain letters, numbers, the $ symbol, and the _ (underscore) symbol. You can't include spaces or any other special characters.

- The Project location can be anywhere on your disk. The default location is a folder named just like the project, placed under the workspace folder, but you don't have to put it there. This is where the project configuration and primary source code files, and possibly compiled applications, are stored.

- The Application type is set to either Web application or Desktop application.

  - Selecting Web application causes the application to be delivered through the browser and run in Flash Player.

  - Selecting Desktop application creates an application that installs for use with the Adobe Integrated Runtime ("AIR") and runs as a native application on the user's desktop.

NOTE   Flex Builder 3 does not allow you to create a single project whose applications can be deployed on either Flash Player or AIR. Each project must specify one and only one of these deployment options. Flex Builder can share resources between multiple projects so that each project is created as a shell for a particular deployment option, and the bulk of an application's resources are maintained in a third project known as a Flex Library Project.

The options in the Server Technology section allow you to select an application server. These application servers are directly supported by Flex Builder:

- ASP.NET
- ColdFusion
- J2EE (also known as Java EE)
- PHP

NEW FEATURE When you select ColdFusion, you also are prompted to select either LiveCycle Data Services or ColdFusion Flash Remoting as a communications option. This is because ColdFusion 8 now includes an option to integrate LiveCycle Data Services (formerly known as Flex Data Services) into its basic installation.

NOTE If you are using an application server with your Flex application, make sure the application server is installed and tested prior to creation of the Flex Project.

For the purposes of this section, I'll assume you've set the application server type to None. For options specific to particular application servers, see Chapter 24 through Chapter 29.

The next screen of the Flex Project wizard asks you to provide the Compiled Flex application location, also known as the Output folder. The default is a subfolder of the project root named *bin*. This folder contains a compiled version of the application, which you'll use for debugging and testing. The production version of the application is created in a separate step after the project has been created.

The last screen of the Flex Project wizard, shown in Figure 2.16, asks for this information:

- The Main source folder is where you place the .mxml and .as source code files that constitute your application source. Your application .mxml files are placed in this folder. You can also create subfolders of the Main source folder to contain component and class files. These subfolders are known as *packages*.
- The Output folder URL is the http address you'll use to test the application in a Web browser. This option appears only when you're creating a Web application. By leaving this option blank in a Web project that doesn't use an application server, you indicate that you want to run the application by loading the compiled application from the hard disk. Using this default configuration has the advantage of not requiring a Web server for testing (similar to loading an HTML Web page into the browser from the local disk).
- The Application ID is a unique identifier assigned to your application. This option appears only when you are creating a Desktop application for deployment on the Adobe Integrated Runtime.

NEW FEATURE In Flex Builder 2, the Main source folder defaulted to the project root folder. In Flex Builder 3, the Main source folder is now a subfolder named *src*.

FIGURE 2.16

This dialog box asks for the source folder, the main application filename, and the Output folder URL when creating a Web application.

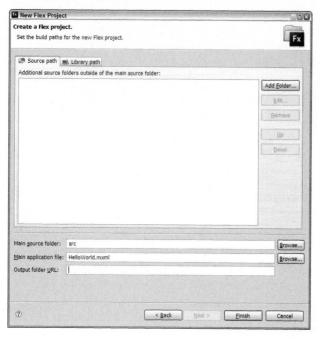

- The Main application file is the source code file that defines your application. Flex application files always have a file extension of .mxml. A single project can contain more than one application, but you can create only a single application during project creation. Other applications have to be created after the project is open.

NOTE The first part of the application filename (the part before the file extension of .mxml) becomes an ActionScript class name during the compilation process. This is why you must follow class naming conventions when you name your application file. An ActionScript class name can include letters, numbers, and the $ symbol, and the _ (underscore) symbol, but must begin with a letter, the $ symbol, or the _ (underscore) symbol; you can't start a class or application filename with a number.

To accept your project configurations, click the Finish button to create the Flex Project and the main application file.

The Flex Builder user interface

Flex Builder 3 adds unique tools to Eclipse to facilitate Flex application development. These tools include Editors and Views. In this section I describe these important tools.

The MXML editor

Flex Builder includes two editors for use in creating your Flex applications. The MXML editor is used to work with MXML files, whether they represent application files or custom components.

When you double-click a file with the .mxml file extension from the Eclipse Navigator view, the file is opened in the MXML editor. This editor has two views of its own: Source view and Design view. Whether the file opens initially in Design view or Source view depends on what view you've used most recently on other files.

As shown in Figure 2.17, you select whether you want to use Source view or Design view by clicking one of the buttons at the top of the MXML editor.

FIGURE 2.17

Source view and Design view selection buttons

TIP   You can toggle between Source view and Design view with the keyboard shortcut Ctrl+~.

The ActionScript editor

The ActionScript editor is designed for editing of files containing pure ActionScript code. This editor can be useful whether you're a Flex developer or a Flash developer, because both products now can use the latest version of the ActionScript programming language.

When you double-click a file with the .as file extension from the Eclipse Navigator view, the file is opened in the ActionScript editor, as shown in Figure 2.18.

FIGURE 2.18

The ActionScript editor

```
1  // ActionScript file
2  [Bindable]
3  private var currentResult:Number;
4
5  [Bindable]
6  private var currentInput:String;
7
8  private function initApp():void
9  {
10    input.addEventListener("click", clickHandler);
11    input.addEventListener("calculate", calculate);
12  }
13
14 private function calculate(event:Event):void
15  {
16    currentResult += Number(currentInput);
17  }
18
19 private function clickHandler(event:TextEvent):void
20  {
21    currentInput += event.text;
22  }
23
```

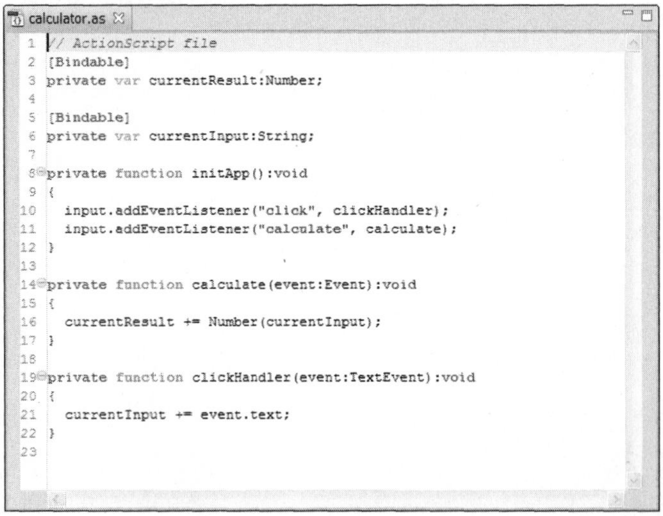

Both the MXML and ActionScript editors include these features to make coding faster and more productive:

- Language color-coding
- Auto-import of external ActionScript classes
- Auto-completion of MXML tags and attributes
- Auto-completion of variable symbol names
- Code hinting for function arguments and class members
- Intelligent language search for symbols and their declarations

Flex Builder views

Flex Builder 3 includes custom Eclipse views that serve particular purposes.

Flex Navigator view

The Flex Navigator view, shown in Figure 2.19, displays a tree of folders and files and allows you to locate and open any project resource. This view is displayed by default in both the Flex Development and the Flex Debugging perspectives. When using any of the Flex perspectives, you can open the view by selecting Window ⇨ Flex Navigator from the Eclipse menu.

FIGURE 2.19

The Flex Navigator view

You can create new project resources directly within the Flex Navigator view by right-clicking (Ctrl-clicking on the Mac) any project folder. From the context menu that appears, as shown in Figure 2.20, select the kind of resource you want to create.

Outline view

The Outline view, shown in Figure 2.21, displays a tree of the objects that have been declared in an MXML or ActionScript file. This view is displayed by default only in the Flex Development perspective. Select Window ⇨ Outline from the Eclipse menu to open this view in any other perspective.

The Outline view lets you easily locate code representing any declared variable or object, whether the object has been declared in MXML or ActionScript.

To locate code representing any variable or object using the Outline view, click the object in the view. The cursor in the current editor then jumps to that part of the code and selects the code that declares the object.

FIGURE 2.20

Creating a project resource from the Flex Navigator view

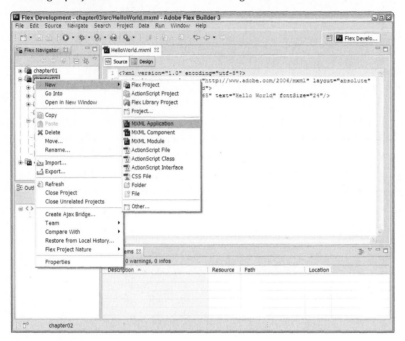

FIGURE 2.21

The Outline view

Problems view

The Problems view, shown in Figure 2.22, displays current compilation errors and warnings. When your code contains a bug, the Problems view shows you these details:

- The Description of the problem (an error message)
- The Resource containing the problem (a source code file)
- The Path of the resource (the folder containing the problem file)
- The Location of the problem (the line number)

Double-click a problem in the Problems view to jump to the problem code. If the file containing the problem isn't currently open, Flex Builder opens the file and places the cursor in the appropriate editor.

FIGURE 2.22

The Problems view

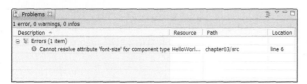

TIP   Keep only one project open at a time. If you have the Build Automatically feature turned on (the default setting), Flex Builder recompiles all open projects whenever any source file in any of the projects has been modified and saved.

If you have any remaining errors or warnings in projects you have open but aren't using, it slows Flex Builder's compilation process and keeps those errors and warnings in the Problems view until you fix them or close the project.

Design views

These views are used only when an editor is in Design view:

- The Flex Properties view allows you to set object properties through a simple user interface and generates the appropriate MXML code to represent your selections.
- The Components view allows you to drag and drop common user interface components, including both Containers and Controls, into your application.
- The States view allows you to manage alternate presentation States through Design view and generates code to represent the alternate states.

Debugging views

These views are primarily used when debugging a Flex application:

- The Console view displays tracing information and other detailed debugging messages.
- The Debug view contains controls for stepping through code, terminating a debugging session, and resuming a debugging session.
- The Variables view displays the values of all pre-declared variables that are currently in scope while application execution is stopped on a breakpoint.
- The Breakpoints view allows you to manage your breakpoints.
- The Expressions view allows you evaluate and inspect arbitrary ActionScript expressions while application execution is stopped on a breakpoint.

These views are described in greater detail in Chapter 6.

Getting Help

The documentation for the Flex development platform is delivered as part of the Flex Builder installation. You can access the documentation in a variety of ways:

- Explore the Help contents.
- Search for specific terms.
- Use context-sensitive Help.

Exploring the Help contents

In Flex Builder, you can get to the Help contents, shown in Figure 2.23, from the menu choice Help ➪ Help Contents. The Help Contents screen opens in a separate window.

The Help Contents screen contains entries for all the Flex documentation and also for any Eclipse plug-ins you may have installed. For example, if you installed JSEclipse, the Adobe plug-in for JavaScript development, during the installation process, you'll see an entry for that plug-in on the Help screen.

The main documentation for Flex is under Adobe Flex 3.0 Help. Under this heading, you'll find these links:

- Using Flex Builder 3
- Flex 3 Developer's Guide
- Building and Deploying Flex 3 Applications

- Creating and Extending Flex 3 Components

- Developing AIR applications with Flex

- Programming ActionScript 3.0

- Adobe Flex 3 Language Reference

Each of these links takes you to an extensive publication describing that aspect of Flex development.

FIGURE 2.23

The Help Contents screen

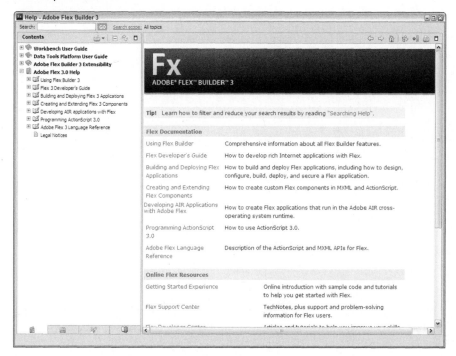

Searching for Help terms

The Flex Builder Help system allows you to search for any terms you need to find. You can search from within Flex Builder, or if you already have the Help Contents screen open, you can search without returning to the Flex Builder interface.

Searching in the Flex Builder interface

In the Flex Builder interface, select Help ➪ Search from the menu. A Help view, shown in Figure 2.24, appears on the right. Enter your search terms, and click Go to execute the search.

FIGURE 2.24

Using the Help view

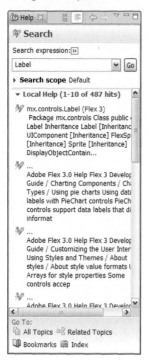

If your Help search is successful, a list of found links is displayed. Click any link to display that Help page in a Help editor. As shown in Figure 2.25, when the Help page is opened, your search terms are highlighted.

FIGURE 2.25

A Help page with highlighted search terms in the Eclipse interface

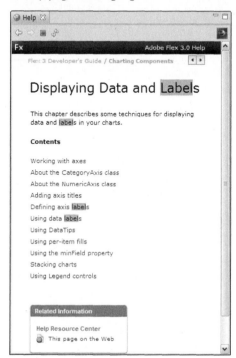

Searching in the Help Contents window

You also can search for terms in the Help Contents window:

1. Select Help ⇨ Help Contents from the Flex Builder menu.

2. Click in the Search input box, and type a term.

3. Click the GO button.

As with searching in the Flex Builder interface, a successful search displays links to pages that contain your terms, as shown in Figure 2.26. Click any link to display the Help page. The page is displayed in a separate pane of the Help window.

TIP   When a Help page is displayed in either the Eclipse interface or the external Help window, it's hosted by an internal Web server component that starts up in the background. You may find that the first Help page you open takes some time as the server starts up in the background. After it's started, though, it stays open for the duration of your Eclipse session.

FIGURE 2.26

Searching in the Help window

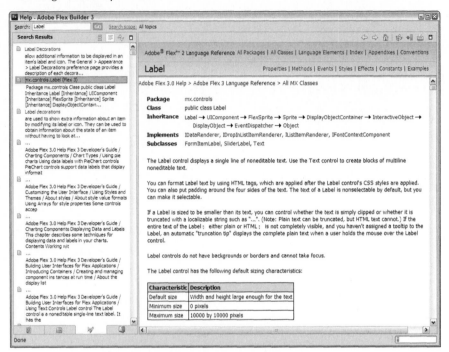

Using Dynamic Help

The Dynamic Help feature allows you to find Help topics related to the content you're currently editing. For example, suppose you're working with the `DataGrid` component and want to find out what properties, methods, or events are available. You can easily jump to a Help topic related to that component and display the information in an Eclipse editor or in a separate Help window.

Displaying Dynamic Help in an Eclipse editor

To display a Dynamic Help topic in an Eclipse editor:

1. Place the cursor anywhere in the class type declaration or MXML tag for which you want help.

2. Press F1 to display a list of related links in a Help view with the title Related Topics.

3. Click the appropriate link to display the Help topic in an editor.

As shown in Figure 2.27, Dynamic Help is displayed in a separate Help view.

FIGURE 2.27

Dynamic Help from an MXML editor

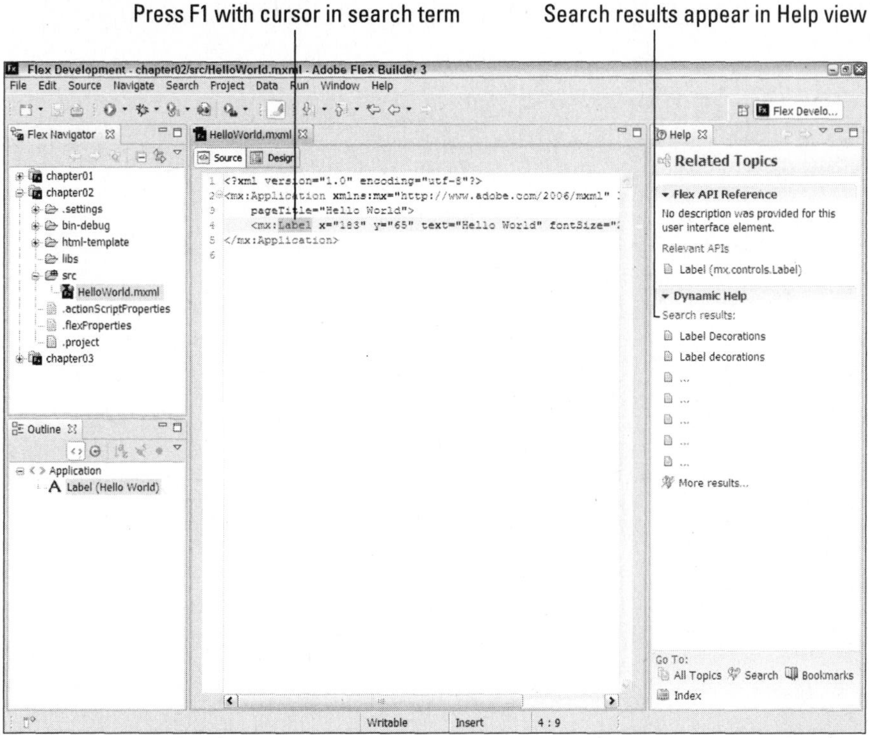

Press F1 with cursor in search term   Search results appear in Help view

When you place the cursor in an ActionScript class declaration or MXML tag for which
Flex Builder has API documentation, the first link under Related Topics is usually the
ActionScript documentation for that class, listed under a heading of Relevant APIs.

After using the Dynamic Help feature, be sure to close the Help view on the right
before continuing to work on your code. If you leave it open, it continues to execute
searches each time you move the cursor to a new location in the code, creating a very "jumpy" editing experience.

Displaying Dynamic Help in a separate window

To display dynamic help in a separate window:

1. Place the cursor anywhere in the class type declaration or MXML tag for which you want
   help.

2. Press Shift+F2.

The Help topic should be correctly selected and displayed in a separate Help window.

Searching for Code

Flex Builder and Eclipse have a number of tools that allow you to search for and locate code. Two of the tools are part of the Eclipse workbench, and a third is part of the Flex Builder plug-in.

Using Eclipse search tools

Eclipse has two tools that allow you to search for code: Find/Replace and Find in Files. The first is designed to locate code one file at a time; the second can search for code in multiple files.

Using Find/Replace

The Find/Replace dialog box, shown in Figure 2.28, lets you search for code in the currently opened file. This dialog box is available only in an MXML editor that's currently open in Source view. Select Edit ⇨ Find/Replace (keyboard shortcut Ctrl+F) from the Flex Builder menu to open this dialog box.

FIGURE 2.28

The Find/Replace dialog box

> **TIP**   After you execute a Find operation with the Find/Replace dialog box, you can repeat the operation with the menu choices Find Next and Find Previous on the Flex Builder Edit menu. The keyboard shortcuts for these operations in the standalone version of Flex Builder are Ctrl+K for Find Next and Ctrl+Shift+K for Find Previous.

Using Find in Files

The Find in Files dialog box, shown in Figure 2.29, also known as the File Search tool, allows you to search across multiple files in a project, directory, or workspace. It has many options that allow you to fine-tune your search. Select Edit ➪ Find in Files from the Flex Builder menu to open this dialog box.

The Find in Files (File Search) dialog box

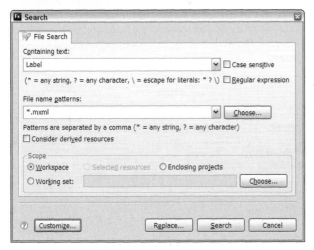

To use this tool, make these selections:

- Set the Containing text field to the string you want to find.
- Select case sensitivity and whether you're searching with a regular expression.
- Set the filename patterns field to indicate what kind of files you want to search. For example, if you want to limit your search to ActionScript files and classes, set this value to *.as.
- Set the Scope to the Workspace, Selected resources, or Enclosing projects.

Click the Search button to execute the operation. Results are displayed in a Search view that contains links to all found resources, as shown in Figure 2.30.

FIGURE 2.30

The Search view, presenting found resources

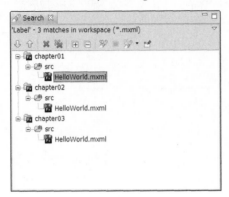

Using Flex Builder code model search tools

Flex Builder 3 adds new search tools that are based on the code model. With these tools you can:

- Search for object references
- Search for object declarations
- Refactor code

Searching for references

If you know where a variable or object's declaration is located, you can use the code model tools to locate all the object's references:

1. In an MXML editor, place the cursor anywhere in the variable declaration.

2. Select Search ⇨ References from the Flex Builder menu. Alternatively, you can right-click the variable declaration and select References from the context menu.

3. Select the scope of the search from these options:

   - Workspace
   - Project
   - File

The results of the search are displayed in the Search view.

Searching for a declaration

If you know where a variable or object is used, you can use the code model tools to locate the object's original declaration:

1. In an MXML editor, place the cursor anywhere in the variable reference.
2. Select Search ➪ Declarations from the Flex Builder menu. Alternatively, you can right-click the variable declaration and select Declarations from the context menu.
3. Select the scope of the search from these options:
   - Workspace
   - Project
   - File

The results of the search are displayed in the Search view.

Flex Builder adds a new option called Mark Occurrences. This feature causes any variable name or type reference to be highlighted wherever it occurs in the source code file you're editing. For example, if you place the cursor in an <mx:Label> declaration, all <mx:Label> declarations in the current file are highlighted. Similarly, if you place the cursor in a variable such as myVar, all references or declarations of that variable are highlighted.

As shown in Figure 2.31, you can toggle this feature on and off from the Flex Builder toolbar by clicking the icon with the image of a highlighter pen.

NEW FEATURE The Mark Occurrences option is a new feature in Flex Builder 3.

FIGURE 2.31

Toggle button for Mark Occurrences

Refactoring variable names

When you refactor code, you globally rename object references or types. This is very different from a global search-and-replace operation that's based on string values. In a global search and replace, you can make a mess if you accidentally find substrings that are part of something else. With code refactoring, the search is based on internal references that are known to the Flex compiler and Flex Builder's code modeling tools.

To globally rename a variable with the code refactoring tool:

1. Place the cursor in any of the variable's reference or declarations.
2. Select Source ➪ Refactor ➪ Rename from the Flex Builder menu. (Or you can right-click in the variable and select Refactor ➪ Rename from the context menu, or press the keyboard shortcut Ctrl+Alt+R.)

3. In the Rename Variable dialog box, shown in Figure 2.32, enter the new variable name.

The Rename Variable dialog box

4. You can preview refactoring changes by clicking the dialog box's Preview button. The preview dialog box, shown in Figure 2.33, displays the Original and Refactored source code.

Previewing refactoring changes

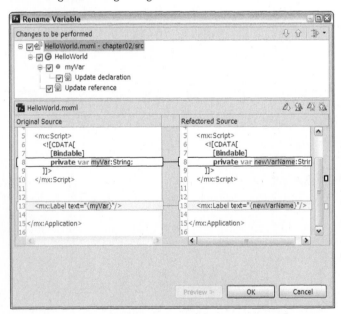

5. Click OK to accept the changes and globally rename the variable.

Refactoring source code files

Renaming ActionScript and MXML files also is considered a refactoring operation, because these files represent ActionScript types that must be maintained consistently throughout a project.

To refactor a file, just rename the file in the Flex Navigator view, as shown in Figure 2.34:

1. Select a file, and press F2 (or right-click, and select Rename from the context menu).
2. In the Rename Class dialog box, enter a new filename.
3. Optionally preview the changes.
4. Click OK to accept the changes.

Any references to the changed file are updated through the current project, including the class declaration and constructor name.

FIGURE 2.34

Renaming an ActionScript class file

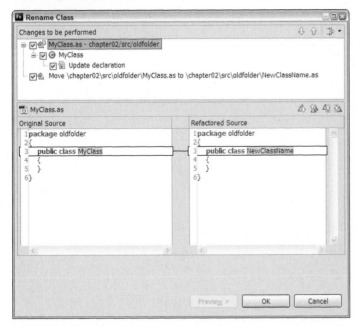

TIP If you rename an ActionScript class file from the Flex Navigator view within Flex Builder, the class declaration and constructor method (if it exists) within the file are updated to match the filename.

CAUTION If you move an ActionScript class from one folder to another by dragging it within the Flex Navigator view, the package declaration within the file is not updated by the code refactoring engine; it must be updated manually.

Summary

In this chapter, I described the nature and behavior of Flex Builder 3. You learned the following:

- Flex Builder 3 is a plug-in designed for the Eclipse workbench.

- Flex Builder 3 is available for the Windows and Mac OS X operating systems; a Linux version is planned for future release.

- Flex Builder's standalone configuration includes everything you need to build Flex applications, including Eclipse 3.3.

- Flex Builder's plug-in installation option allows you to install Flex Builder on top of an existing Eclipse installation.

- The Flex Builder plug-in installation requires Eclipse 3.22 or later.

- Flex Builder can be used by both Flex and Flash developers to edit their ActionScript files.

- Flex Builder adds many tools in the form of Views and Editors to make coding faster and more productive.

- Many tools that are a part of the Eclipse workbench are critical to effective use of Flex Builder.

Chapter 3

Building a Basic Flex Application

I n this chapter, I describe how to create and deploy a basic "Hello World" Flex application.

The code samples and screen shots in this chapter assume that you're using Flex Builder to build the application. If you're using the Flex SDK and your own text editor, the steps will be similar, but you won't have access to some of the code completion and other productivity tools I describe.

After the application is built, I describe the fundamental nature of a Flex application, including the relationship between the application .swf file and the supporting HTML files. I describe the contents of the HTML "wrapper" file that's generated for you in Flex Builder and its associated JavaScript library file.

Finally, I describe how to deploy the Flex application into a Web site in these ways:

- As a distinct application that opens in its own window
- As an applet that's displayed as part of an existing Web page
- As a desktop application deployed on the Adobe Integrated Runtime

By the end of this chapter, you should have a good sense of what a Flex application is and how it's delivered to the user.

Creating a "Hello World" Application

In all programming languages, your first task is to write a "Hello World" application. This most simple of applications typically contains no more than a single line of text output. This simple Flex application does a bit more: It uses XML-formatted data, presented in a DataGrid component, to say hello to the world.

Throughout these instructions, I assume that you're using the standalone version of Flex Builder. Where the steps are different in the plug-in version, I provide alternative steps in a Tip.

Switching workspaces

As described in Chapter 2, your first step is to create a Flex Project. The project hosts the application and its assets. Throughout the instructions, I assume that you have downloaded the book's sample files from the publisher's Web site. Follow these steps to switch to a new workspace:

1. Open Flex Builder 3.

2. From the menu, select File ➪ Switch Workspace.

3. Select a new workspace subfolder under the flex3bible folder that contains the downloaded book files. For example, if you are working on Microsoft Windows and the book files are in a folder named C:\flex3bible, the name of the workspace folder would be C:\flex3bible\workspace. When you have done this, click OK.

   After selecting the workspace, you should see that Flex Builder closes and reopens. The new workspace, shown in Figure 3.1, should display the Flex Welcome Screen and the default Flex Development perspective. The newly created workspace is empty and contains no projects.

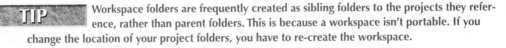 Workspace folders are frequently created as sibling folders to the projects they reference, rather than parent folders. This is because a workspace isn't portable. If you change the location of your project folders, you have to re-create the workspace.

Creating the project

Follow these steps to create a project:

1. From the menu, select File ➪ New ➪ Flex Project.

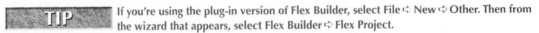 If you're using the plug-in version of Flex Builder, select File ➪ New ➪ Other. Then from the wizard that appears, select Flex Builder ➪ Flex Project.

2. In the first screen, shown in Figure 3.2, enter a Project name of **chapter03**.

3. Select the Default location option as checked. On Windows, the Project location defaults to C:\flex3bible\chapter03.

4. Set the Application type to Web application (runs in Flash Player).

5. Set the Application server type to None, and click Next.

FIGURE 3.1

The default Flex Development perspective in a new workspace

Navigator view

Perspective selector tool

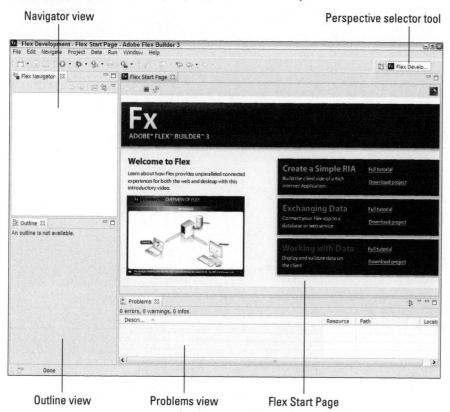

Outline view   Problems view   Flex Start Page

---

6. On the Configure Output screen, shown in Figure 3.3, accept the Output folder setting of `bin-debug`. This is the location of the compiled debug version of the application and its supporting files.

7. Click Next.

NEW FEATURE In Flex Builder 2, the default Output folder setting was `bin`, and the resulting folder contained both the debug and the release version of the compiled application. In Flex Builder 3, the Output folder defaults to `bin-debug` to distinguish it from the separate `bin-release` folder created when you export a release version.

8. On the Create a Flex project screen, shown in Figure 3.4, accept these default settings:

  - Main source folder: `src`

  - Main application file: `HelloWorld.mxml`

  - Output folder url: Accept the default setting, leaving it blank

FIGURE 3.2

The first screen of the New Flex Project wizard

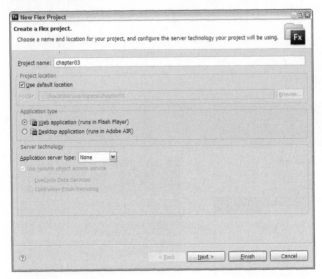

FIGURE 3.3

The second screen of the New Flex Project wizard

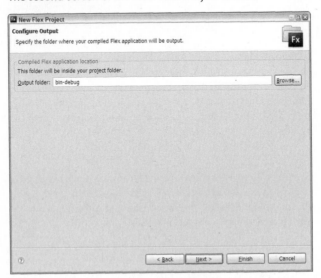

FIGURE 3.4

The third screen of the New Flex Project wizard

9. Click Finish to create the project and the main application file.

As shown in Figure 3.5, you should see the main application file appear in the Editor view. If you're working in a completely new workspace, the file should appear in Source view; that is, you should see the application's source code.

FIGURE 3.5

The new main application file in Source view

Saying hello

Follow these steps to display a simple message in your Flex application:

1. Notice that the `Application` tag's `layout` property is set to `absolute`. This means that objects placed on the application screen in Design view will maintain their absolute positions relative to the application's top-left corner.

2. Click Design to see what the application will look like as you build it.

   When you use Design view, you see the Components view in the lower-left corner, as shown in Figure 3.6.

FIGURE 3.6

The Components view

3. In the Components view's tree, open the Controls leaf and locate the `Label` control.

4. Drag a `Label` object into the application, and place it approximately in the center of the application.

5. With the Label control still selected, look at the Flex Properties view in the lower-right corner of Flex Builder.

6. In the Common section of the Flex Properties view, shown in Figure 3.7, set the `Label` control's `text` property to `Hello World`.

7. In the Text section of the Flex Properties view, set the `Label` control's `fontSize` to `24`.

8. Save your changes with this menu selection by choosing File ➪ Save.

9. Run the application in a browser by choosing Run ➪ Run HelloWorld.

   As shown in Figure 3.8, you see that the application opens in a browser window and looks just like it did in Flex Builder's Design view.

FIGURE 3.7

The Common section of the Flex Properties view with a Label control selected

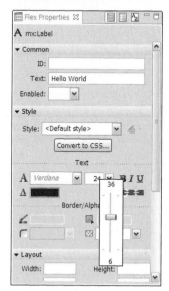

FIGURE 3.8

The finished application running in a Web browser

 **TIP** In the standalone version of Flex Builder, you also can use the keyboard shortcut Ctrl+F11 to run the current application.

Understanding the html-template Folder

Each Flex Project contains a folder called `html-template`. This folder contains models for the HTML and supporting files that run your application in the browser. Whenever you save changes to your source code, Flex Builder automatically rebuilds your application using the HTML model file to generate an HTML wrapper. At the same time, it copies the contents of the `html-template` folder to the output folder that contains the compiled application. Figure 3.9 shows the structure of the `html-template` folder.

 **TIP** The `html-template` folder and its contents do not need to be copied to the Web server to deploy the application. These files are used only during the compilation process.

FIGURE 3.9

The `html-template` folder structure

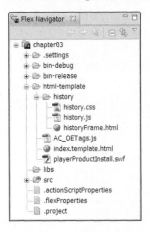

 **TIP** The Flex project has a `Build Automatically` property that causes your applications to be automatically compiled every time you save changes to any source code file. If you want your applications to be recompiled only when you choose, change the property in Flex Builder by selecting **Project ➪ Build Automatically**. Use the same menu choice to turn the property back on.

During the compilation process, most of the files in the `html-template` directory are simply copied to the output folder that contains the debug version of the project's applications. The HTML wrapper file that you use at runtime is generated based on a model file in `html-template` named `index.template.html`.

HTML template files

The `html-template` directory contains these files:

- `index.template.html` is a model file that is the basis for the generated HTML "wrapper" files that call the application at runtime.

- AC_OETags.js is a JavaScript library containing functions are used at runtime to load Flash Player. This file also contains "sniffer" code that can discover whether Flash Player is currently loaded on the user's desktop and, if so, which version.

- playerProductInstall.swf is a Flash application that's used to upgrade a user's system when Flash Player 6.65 or higher is installed.

- The history subfolder contains files to implement the history management feature (for non-IE browsers only):

  - historyFrame.html is a model for an HTML page that's loaded into an <iframe> in the main page at runtime.

  - history.js is a JavaScript library containing functions that are called by historyFrame.html.

  - history.css contains Cascading Style Sheet (CSS) rules to suppress the visibility of the history frame in the main page.

With the exception of index.template.html, all files in the html-template directory are copied to the output folder in their exact current states whenever you compile the application. And when you create a "release" version of the application, they're copied to the release output folder as well.

The HTML wrapper model file

The model HTML file contains a combination of these elements:

- HTML code
- Calls to JavaScript functions that are stored in AC_OETags.js
- The <iframe> that calls the history management files
- Placeholders for values that are passed to the generated version of the file

In this section, I describe each part of the file and its purpose.

The HTML <head> section

The <head> section of the model HTML file contains links to a set of CSS and JavaScript files. The first <link> tag incorporates the history.css file from the history folder:

```
<link rel="stylesheet" type="text/css" href="history/history.css"
    />
```

The <title> element contains a variable that's filled in from the Application's pageTitle property:

```
<title>${title}</title>
```

To fill in this value in the generated HTML wrapper page, set the `pageTitle` property in the `<mx:Application>` start tag:

```
<mx:Application xmlns:mx="http://www.adobe.com/2006/mxml"
    layout="absolute" pageTitle="Hello World">
```

The next section is a `<style>` element that contains basic page formatting instructions:

```
<style>
body { margin: 0px; overflow:hidden }
</style>
```

The `margin` style's value of `0px` means that Flash Player won't have any space between its borders and the edges of the Web page. The `overflow` style's setting of `hidden` means that if the size of Flash Player (or another element in the page) overflows the boundaries of the page, the remainder are hidden. If you want the page to show scrollbars instead, change the value of the `overflow` style to `scroll`.

The HTML <body> section

The `<body>` element of the Web page starts by declaring JavaScript variables that determine which version of Flash Player is required by the application:

```
<script language="JavaScript" type="text/javascript">
<!--
// Globals
// Major version of Flash required
var requiredMajorVersion = ${version_major};
// Minor version of Flash required
var requiredMinorVersion = ${version_minor};
// Minor version of Flash required
var requiredRevision = ${version_revision};
// -->
</script>
```

The `version_major`, `version_minor`, and `version_revision` parameters can be set through the project's properties:

1. Select Project ➪ Properties from the Flex Builder menu.
2. In the Properties dialog box, select the Flex Compiler section, as shown in Figure 3.10.
3. In the Required Flash Player version option, change the version numbers as needed.

TIP When you create a new Flex Project in Flex Builder 3, the required version in the project properties is set to 9,0,28 by default. The version of Flash Player that was delivered with the Flex Builder 3 in February 2008 was 9,0,115.

FIGURE 3.10

Setting the required Flash Player version number

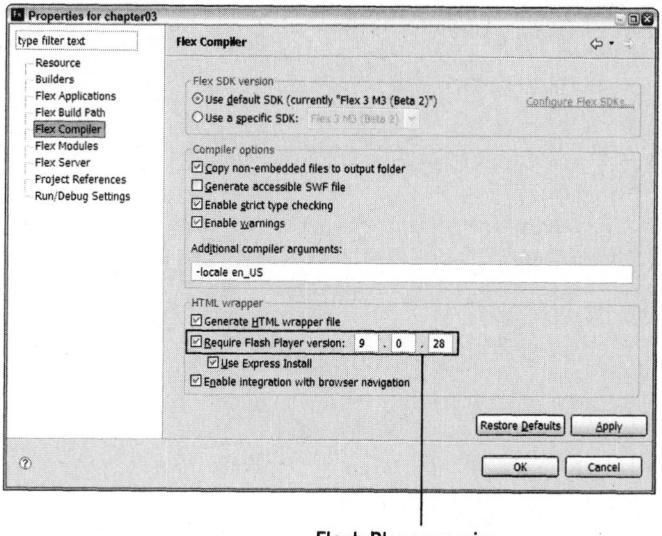

Flash Player version

The next section of the HTML wrapper calls a JavaScript function named DetectFlashVer()
and checks whether the user has at least version 6,0,65. This is the version that's required for use
of the Flash-based upgrade. It then calls the function again and checks whether the user has the
version required to run the application:

```
var hasProductInstall = DetectFlashVer(6, 0, 65);
var hasRequestedVersion = DetectFlashVer(
    requiredMajorVersion, requiredMinorVersion, requiredRevision);
```

If the user has at least version 6,0,65, but not the version required to run the application, the
HTML wrapper runs the Flash-based installer:

```
if ( hasProductInstall && !hasRequestedVersion ) {
  var MMPlayerType = (isIE == true) ? "ActiveX" : "PlugIn";
  var MMredirectURL = window.location;
    document.title = document.title.slice(0, 47) +
      " - Flash Player Installation";
    var MMdoctitle = document.title;

  AC_FL_RunContent(
    "src", "playerProductInstall",
    "FlashVars", "MMredirectURL="+MMredirectURL+'&MMplayerType='+
            MMPlayerType+'&MMdoctitle='+MMdoctitle+"",
    "width", "${width}",
    "height", "${height}",
```

```
        "align", "middle",
        "id", "${application}",
        "quality", "high",
        "bgcolor", "${bgcolor}",
        "name", "${application}",
        "allowScriptAccess","sameDomain",
        "type", "application/x-shockwave-flash",
        "pluginspage", "http://www.adobe.com/go/getflashplayer"
    );
}
```

The JavaScript function called above runs `playerProductInstall.swf`, the Flash-based upgrade installer, which tries to upgrade the user's browser to the latest version of Flash Player from the Adobe Web site. If any errors are encountered (if the user doesn't have administrative rights to his computer, for example), the Flash-based upgrade installer fails with a useful error message (rather than just hanging and letting the user wonder what happened).

The next section of code runs the Flex application if the user has the required version of the Flash Player:

```
} else if (hasRequestedVersion) {
    // if we've detected an acceptable version
    // embed the Flash Content SWF when all tests are passed
    AC_FL_RunContent(
        "src", "${swf}",
        "width", "${width}",
        "height", "${height}",
        "align", "middle",
        "id", "${application}",
        "quality", "high",
        "bgcolor", "${bgcolor}",
        "name", "${application}",
        "allowScriptAccess","sameDomain",
        "type", "application/x-shockwave-flash",
        "pluginspage",
"http://www.adobe.com/go/getflashplayer");
    }
```

The JavaScript function called above instantiates Flash Player and passes it certain parameters. Some parameters, such as `quality`, `types`, and `allowScriptAccess`, have fixed values. The following parameters' values are set dynamically, based on information such as properties and styles of the Flex application and the application name:

- `src`: The name of the application file (without the .swf extension)

- `width`: The width of the application as defined in the <mx:Application> tag (defaults to 100 percent)

- `height`: The height of the application as defined in the <mx:Application> tag (defaults to 100 percent)

- `id`: The name of the application file, without the .swf extension

- bgcolor: The application's backgroundColor style, as defined in the application's <mx:Application> tag or in a CSS declaration for the Application type selector

- name: The name of the application file, without the .swf extension

These are some other key parameters you can pass to AC_FL_RunContent() and to the embed/ object tags:

- wmode: How Flash handles layering/transparency (options include window, transparent, and opaque)

- menu: Whether to allow the zoom/print left-click options (options include true and false)

- allowFullScreen: To allow to go full screen (options include true and false)

- allowScriptAccess: Security for scripting. Options: never, always, and sameDomain

The last bit of JavaScript code handles the condition that exists when Flash Player hasn't been installed or the user's browser has a version older than 6,0,65:

```
} else {  // flash is too old or we can't detect the plugin
  var alternateContent =
    'Alternate HTML content should be placed here. '
    + 'This content requires the Adobe Flash Player. '
    + '<a href=http://www.adobe.com/go/getflash/>Get Flash</a>';
  document.write(alternateContent);  // insert non-flash content
  }
```

This code simply displays some HTML content to users who don't have the right version of Flash Player and can't run the Flash-based upgrade installer.

CAUTION You can customize this HTML as desired, but you should always do so in the HTML model page, rather than the version that's generated in the output folders. If you customize the generated files directly, they'll just be overwritten the next time you compile the application.

The HTML <noscript> section

This <noscript> element at the bottom of the page contains code to instantiate Flash Player in browsers that don't support JavaScript:

```
<noscript>
  <object classid="clsid:D27CDB6E-AE6D-11cf-96B8-444553540000"
  id="${application}" width="${width}" height="${height}"
  codebase="http://fpdownload.macromedia.com/get/
    flashplayer/current/swflash.cab">
  <param name="movie" value="${swf}.swf" />
  <param name="quality" value="high" />
  <param name="bgcolor" value="${bgcolor}" />
  <param name="allowScriptAccess" value="sameDomain" />
```

```
  <embed src="${swf}.swf" quality="high" bgcolor="${bgcolor}"
    width="${width}" height="${height}"
    name="${application}" align="middle"
    play="true" loop="false"
    quality="high" allowScriptAccess="sameDomain"
    type="application/x-shockwave-flash"
  pluginspage="http://www.adobe.com/go/getflashplayer">
  </embed>
  </object>
</noscript>
```

This section of code is executed only in browsers that don't support JavaScript at all or where the user has disabled JavaScript through her browser's security settings. This circumstance is rare, but not unheard of, in current browser installations.

The only real drawback to loading Flash Player in this manner is that if the user is working with Microsoft Internet Explorer, loading Flash Player without JavaScript code can result in an odd user experience: To interact with the application, first the user must click the Flash document (the Flex application) or press the spacebar. This is an irritant, but certainly not crippling.

 If you add or change parameters, they must applied to both the JavaScript and the `embed` and `object` tag versions in the HTML wrapper file.

The JavaScript library file

The HTML wrapper file makes calls to JavaScript functions that are stored in a JavaScript library file named `AC_OETags.js`. This file appears in the `html-template` folder and is copied to the output folder during the compilation process without any modifications.

The JavaScript library file defines these functions:

- `ControlVersion()`: Returns version of currently installed Flash Player ActiveX control when running in Internet Explorer
- `GetSwfVersion()`: Returns version of currently installed Flash Player plug-in when running in Firefox or another browser that supports the plug-in architecture
- `AC_FL_RunContent()`: Runs the Flash Player and calls a designated Flash document

The library also defines other supporting functions that serve purposes such as parsing arguments to be passed to Flash Player.

History management files

The `html-template` folder contains a subfolder called `history`. This folder in turn contains these three files:

- `historyFrame.html`
- `history.js`
- `history.css`

These files are called by the HTML wrapper file from an `<iframe>` element. Their purpose is to implement a feature known as history management when using a `ViewStack`, `TabNavigator`, or `Accordion` container. This feature allows the user to navigate forward and backward through an application's view state with the browser's Forward and Back buttons in Web browsers other than Microsoft Internet Explorer.

Deploying the Application

You've created the application, and it runs beautifully in your development and testing environment. Now you want to share the applications with your users. This section describes how to create a version of the application that's suitable for public release and make the application available to your audience.

Creating the release version

The version of the application that's created in your output folder, and that you normally run during the testing and debugging phase of development, is the "debug" version of the application. This compiled .swf file is significantly larger than the version you'll ultimately deploy for your users, because it contains additional internal information and symbols that are used during the debug process.

NEW FEATURE In Flex Builder 2, the debug and release versions of the application were placed in a single output folder. To deploy the application, you copied all files except the HTML and .swf files with the word debug in their filenames to the Web server. Flex Builder 3 now separates the debug and release versions into separate folders and requires a manual export process for the release version.

To create a release version of a Flex Web application, follow these steps:

1. From the Flex Builder menu, select Project ⇨ Export Release Version.

2. In the Export Release Version dialog box, shown in Figure 3.11, make these choices:

    a. Select the application you want to export.

    b. Indicate whether you want to enable the View Source feature.

    c. Select a folder to which you want to export the release version.

3. Click Finish to export the release version.

TIP A release version folder contains only a single application (and its supporting files) by default. In contrast, the `bin-debug` folder contains the debug versions of all applications in a project.

After exporting the release version, you should have a new folder containing the compiled application and its supporting files. This version of the application is optimized for delivery to the user. It doesn't contain debug information, and as a result it's significantly smaller than the debug version.

FIGURE 3.11

The Export Release Version dialog box for a Web application

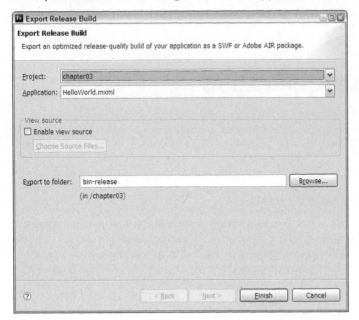

The size of a basic "Hello World" compiled application file with a single Label control will be either 235k for the debug version, or 144k for the release version. Clearly, you want your users to be downloading and using the release version!

Testing the release version

You can test the release version of a Flex Web application by opening its HTML wrapper file in a Web browser. Here's how:

1. From the Flex Navigator view, open the release version folder and locate the HTML wrapper file. This file has the same name as the application itself, but with a .html file extension.

2. Right-click the HTML file, and select Open With ⇨ Web Browser.

The application opens in a Web browser nested with an Eclipse editor view, as shown in Figure 3.12.

CAUTION When you run the release version as described above, the application always opens from the local file system, rather than from any Web server you might have configured. If you need to test the application with a Web server, you have to manually configure the server, or place your bin-release folder within your Web server's document root folder, then open the file from a Web browser using the appropriate URL.

FIGURE 3.12

Running the release version running in a Web Browser editor view

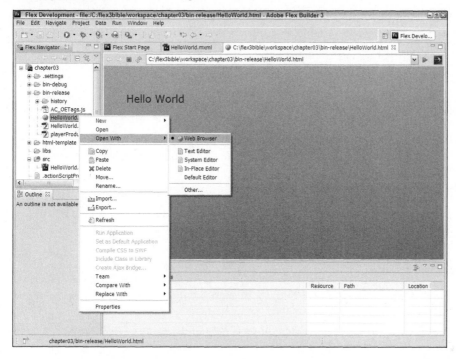

Deploying the release version

To deploy the release version of the application, just upload all files in the release version folder to your Web site using FTP or whatever method you typically use to deploy other files to your Web site. These files will include the following:

- The compiled application file in .swf format
- The HTML wrapper
- The JavaScript library
- `playerProductInstall.swf`
- The `history` folder

Then provide the URL of the HTML wrapper page to your users. For example, if the release version of the application named `registration` is uploaded to a subfolder of my Web site, `www.bardotech.com`, and the HTML wrapper file is named `registration.html`, then the deployment URL is this:

```
http://www.bardotech.com/registration/registration.html
```

Programmers commonly make users navigate to a Flex application in a new browser window. The new window then has a fresh "history," which means the browser's Back button is disabled and the user can't accidentally unload the application by trying to go back to a previous screen.

The following HTML code would open the application from the home page of my Web site:

```
<a href="registration/registration.html" target="_blank"/>
```

Integrating an application into an existing Web page

Some Flex applications are designed to be presented as "applets" or some application that represents only part of a Web page. This is easy to accomplish if you have some working knowledge of HTML. Here's how:

1. Create a region of a Web page where you want to host the application. Design it just as you would to host an image, an ActiveX control, or a Java applet. You can use HTML tables or more modern <div> tags with CSS to control the size and position of the hosting region.

2. In the Flex application code, set the Application tag's height and width to a specific number of pixels that will make the application size match the available space in the Web page. For example, if you have a <div> tag in the hosting page that's 300 pixels high and 200 pixels wide, use this code in the Flex application to size it appropriately:

    ```
    <mx:Application xmlns:mx="http://www.adobe.com/2006/mxml"
      height="300" width="200">
    ```

    When the application is compiled, the height and width settings are passed into the generated HTML file.

3. Copy all the JavaScript includes and initialization code from the <head> section of the generated HTML wrapper file to the <head> section of the hosting HTML page. Be sure to include these lines of code:

    ```
    <link rel="stylesheet" type="text/css"
      href="history/history.css" />
    <script src="AC_OETags.js" language="javascript"></script>
    <script src="history/history.js"
        language="javascript"></script>
    <script language="JavaScript" type="text/javascript">
      var requiredMajorVersion = 9;
      var requiredMinorVersion = 0;
      var requiredRevision = 28;
    </script>
    ```

NOTE The code above has been stripped of comments that appear in the generated version of the HTML wrapper file and are not required to run the application.

4. Copy the `<script>` and `<noscript>` sections from the `<body>` of the HTML wrapper into the target HTML page's application hosting region. The complete code is in the following code listing.

Listing 3.1 shows the finished code in the `<body>` section of a hosting HTML after being extracted and stripped of commenting.

LISTING 3.1

Code in the `<body>` section of a hosting HTML page

```
<!-- A div tag hosting a Flex application -->
<div id="flexApp">
<script language="JavaScript" type="text/javascript">
var hasRequestedVersion = DetectFlashVer(
  requiredMajorVersion, requiredMinorVersion, requiredRevision);

if ( hasProductInstall && !hasRequestedVersion ) {
  var MMPlayerType = (isIE == true) ? "ActiveX" : "PlugIn";
  var MMredirectURL = window.location;
  document.title = document.title.slice(0, 47) +
    " - Flash Player Installation";
  var MMdoctitle = document.title;

  AC_FL_RunContent("src", "playerProductInstall","FlashVars",
    "MMredirectURL="+MMredirectURL+'&MMplayerType='+MMPlayerType+
    '&MMdoctitle='+MMdoctitle+"",
    "width", "200", "height", "300",
    "align", "middle", "id", "HelloWorld",
    "quality", "high", "bgcolor", "#869ca7",
    "name", "HelloWorld", "allowScriptAccess","sameDomain",
    "type", "application/x-shockwave-flash",
    "pluginspage", "http://www.adobe.com/go/getflashplayer");
} else if (hasRequestedVersion) {
  AC_FL_RunContent(
    "src", "HelloWorld",
    "width", "200", "height", "300",
    "align", "middle", "id", "HelloWorld",
    "quality", "high", "bgcolor", "#869ca7",
    "name", "HelloWorld", "allowScriptAccess","sameDomain",
    "type", "application/x-shockwave-flash",
    "pluginspage", "http://www.adobe.com/go/getflashplayer"
  );
  } else {
    var alternateContent = 'Alternate HTML content should be placed
  here. '
    + 'This content requires the Adobe Flash Player. '
```

continued

85

LISTING 3.1   *(continued)*

```
        + '<a href=http://www.adobe.com/go/getflash/>Get Flash</a>';
      document.write(alternateContent);   // insert non-flash content
    }
// -->
</script>
<noscript>
  <object classid="clsid:D27CDB6E-AE6D-11cf-96B8-444553540000"
    id="HelloWorld" width="100%" height="100%"
    codebase="http://fpdownload.macromedia.com/get/flashplayer/
  current/swflash.cab">
    <param name="movie" value="HelloWorld.swf" />
    <param name="quality" value="high" />
    <param name="bgcolor" value="#869ca7" />
    <param name="allowScriptAccess" value="sameDomain" />
    <embed src="HelloWorld.swf" quality="high" bgcolor="#869ca7"
      width="100%" height="100%" name="HelloWorld" align="middle"
      play="true" loop="false" quality="high"
      allowScriptAccess="sameDomain" type="application/x-shockwave-
  flash"
      pluginspage="http://www.adobe.com/go/getflashplayer">
    </embed>
  </object>
</noscript>
</div>
```

TIP Because the application can be opened in a number of ways, borrowing the generated HTML wrapper code ensures that all application properties such as `height` and `width` are copied to all the places in the code where they're needed.

CAUTION When you deploy a hosted Flex applet to a Web server, be sure to include all the same files as before: the JavaScript library, history files, and upgraded .swf file (`player ProductInstall.swf`).

As shown in Figure 3.13, the application will look like a part of the HTML page, but will offer all the dynamic functionality that you've programmed.

Integrating Flex applications with Dreamweaver CS3

Dreamweaver CS3 is the common application of choice for Web site developers who are not necessarily developers. Because compiled Flex applications are simple Flash documents, though, it's possible to use Dreamweaver's Web page code generation capabilities to import a Flex application into an existing Web page.

FIGURE 3.13

A Flex application running in an HTML file as an applet

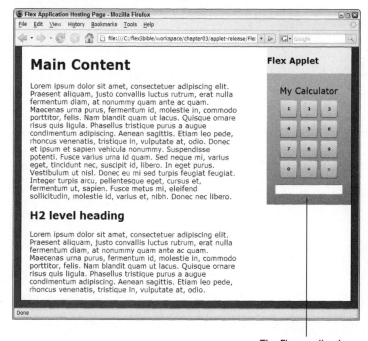

The Flex application

CAUTION   When you integrate Flex using Dreamweaver CS3, you won't have the integrated history management feature, because Dreamweaver treats the Flex application as though it's a simple Flash document.

To integrate a Flex application into a Web page with Dreamweaver CS3, follow these steps:

1. In the Flex application code, set the Application tag's `height` and `width` to a specific number of pixels that will make the application size match the available space in the Web page. For example, if you have a `<div>` tag in the hosting page that's 300 pixels high and 200 pixels wide, use this code in the Flex application to size it appropriately:

```
<mx:Application xmlns:mx="http://www.adobe.com/2006/mxml"
  height="300" width="200">
```

2. After generating the release version of the Flex application, copy the compiled .swf application file from the release version folder into your Dreamweaver site.

3. In Dreamweaver, place the cursor in the region where you want the Flex application to appear.

4. Select Insert ➪ Media ➪ Flash from the Dreamweaver menu.

   As shown in Figure 3.14, a browsing dialog box prompts you to select a Flash document.

TIP   You can also start the process of inserting a Flash document in Dreamweaver by dragging or selecting the Flash document from the Assets panel, or by pressing the keyboard
shortcut Ctrl+Alt+F.

5. Select the Flex application .swf file.

FIGURE 3.14

Selecting a Flex application as a Flash document in Dreamweaver

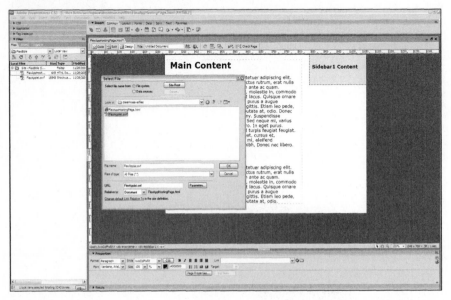

6. If prompted for Object Tag Accessibility Attributes, as shown in Figure 3.15, enter the
   Title you want to make available to Web site visitors who use screen reader software.

FIGURE 3.15

Setting accessibility attributes in Dreamweaver

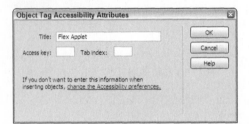

As shown in Figure 3.16, the application initially appears as a disabled region of the page.

FIGURE 3.16

The application appearing as a disabled region in Dreamweaver's Design view

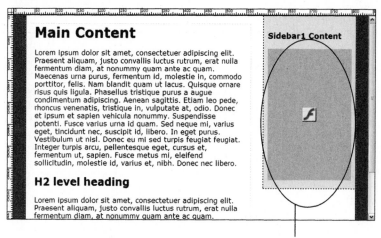

The disabled Flex application in Dreamweaver's Design view

7. With the disabled Flash document selected in Dreamweaver's Design view, click the Play button in the Properties panel to run the application, as shown in Figure 3.17.

FIGURE 3.17

Dreamweaver's Properties panel with the Play button

Click to play the Flex application

8. Save the hosting Web page.

As shown in Figure 3.18, when you save the page, Dreamweaver informs you that it adds to the site a file named `Scripts/AC_RunContent.js`. This file contains the same sort of dynamic JavaScript functionality as the version that's generated in Flex Builder and must be deployed to the Web site to ensure that the Flex application is displayed correctly.

FIGURE 3.18

Dreamweaver added the JavaScript library to the site.

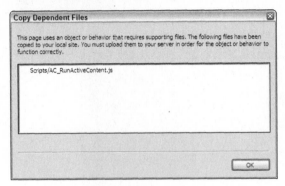

CAUTION The JavaScript code that's generated in Dreamweaver does not include the ability to detect the user's Flash Player version or automatically upgrade the user if he has an older Flash Player version. Also, this code does not allow the user to control all of the parameters passed in the embed and object versions of the code that runs the Flash Player.

Summary

In this chapter, I described how to use Flex Builder 3 to create and manage Flex projects and applications. You learned the following:

- When using Flex Builder, Flex applications are built in Flex projects.
- Flex applications are compiled into .swf files and require additional supporting files when they're deployed.
- The files in the html-template folder are used to model generated HTML wrapper files.
- Compiled files in the default bin-debug folder are meant for debugging and testing and are significantly larger than the version you deploy to your Web site.
- You should create a release version of your Flex application for deployment to a Web site.
- A release version folder normally contains the release version of a single application.
- You can integrate a Flex application into an existing Web page by sizing it correctly and copying code from the generated HTML file into the hosting page.
- You can use Dreamweaver CS3's Flash import tools to integrate a Flex application into a Web page.

Chapter 4

Understanding the Anatomy of a Flex Application

I n this chapter, I describe the basic architecture of a Flex application from the point of view of a developer.

In previous chapters, I described the role of Flash Player in hosting a Flex application at runtime, regardless of whether you use the version of the Player that's hosted by a Web browser (a Web application) or the version that's embedded in the Adobe Integrated Runtime (a desktop application).

In either case, Flash Player "plays" the application with a bit of software known as the ActionScript Virtual Machine (the *AVM*). Flash Player 9 (the version that runs Flex 3 applications) includes two versions of the AVM. The first is for older documents and applications built in Flash and Flex 1.x that use ActionScript 1 and 2. The other, newer AVM is for documents and applications that use ActionScript 3.

NOTE   Flash Player 9 can run either ActionScript 2 or ActionScript 3, but not both simultaneously. Prior to the introduction of Flash CS3, which supports the newer version of the language, a Flash component built with ActionScript 2 that was incorporated into a Flex 2 application would have its ActionScript code ignored by the Flash Player at runtime.

Flash Player is doing the work at runtime, interpreting your ActionScript code and executing the application's functionality. And while a Flex application is typically built in a combination of MXML and ActionScript code, Flash Player understands only compiled ActionScript.

Importing Flex Project Archive Files

Most of the sample files for this book from the Wiley Web site are delivered in Flex Project Archive files that you can import directly into a Flex Builder workspace. Follow these steps to import the archive file for each chapter that's delivered in this format:

1. Select File Í Import Í Flex Project from the Flex Builder menu.

2. Browse and select the archive file for the current chapter from the Web site files.

3. Click Finish to import the project.

A project archive includes source code, other application assets, and project property settings. After importing the archive file you can immediately compile and run any of its applications.

As I described previously, MXML is a façade, or a convenience language, for ActionScript. In this section of the book, I describe the relationship between the two programming languages and explain how a Flex application is architected.

ON the WEB   To use the sample code for this chapter, import the `chapter04.zip` Flex project archive file from the Web site files into your Flex Builder workspace.

MXML and ActionScript 3

Two versions of the MXML programming language have been developed. In the first version, which was used in Flex 1.0 and 1.5 applications, MXML was rewritten into ActionScript 2 during the compilation process. In Flex 2 and 3, you use a version of MXML that compiles into ActionScript 3.

During the process that generates the compiled Flex application, MXML code is first translated into ActionScript 3. This is all done behind the scenes so you don't have to worry about it. You can see how this process works by adding a compiler option to your project properties:

1. Right-click a Flex Project in the Flex Navigator view, and select Properties from the context menu.

2. In the Properties dialog box, select Flex Compiler.

3. As shown in Figure 4.1, modify the Additional compiler arguments field by adding this argument setting:

   `-keep-generated-actionscript=true`

4. Click OK to save the changes.

5. After the project has been rebuilt, look in the Flex Navigator view in the source root. A new generated subfolder is created that contains many ActionScript files, as shown in Figure 4.2.

FIGURE 4.1

Setting a compiler argument to keep generated ActionScript code

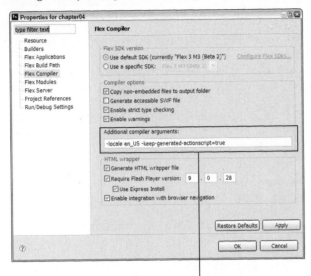

Compiler argument to keep generated ActionScript

FIGURE 4.2

The new generated code subfolder in the project source-code root folder

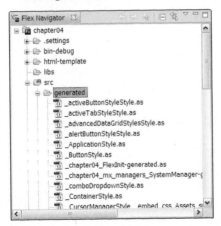

TIP

Keeping generated classes doesn't have any benefit for your application's functionality or performance. I show the feature only to illustrate how the compiler translates MXML code in the background.

Even a very simple "Hello World" application generates a large number of ActionScript files. Most are boilerplate interpretations of internal ActionScript classes that must be available to the compiler for every Flex application. But look for the file representing your specific application to see how your specific MXML code is interpreted.

If you have a main application file named `HelloWorld.mxml`, you'll find generated ActionScript files named `HelloWorld-generated.as` and `HelloWorld-interface.as` in the project source root's generated subfolder. `Helloworld_generated.as` is the primary generated application file. Review this generated code to understand how your MXML code is interpreted.

The code below is part of the generated application file in ActionScript and represents the instantiation of a Flex `Application` at runtime with a single child `Label` control:

```
public class HelloWorld  extends mx.core.Application
{
//   instance variables
//   type-import dummies
//   Container document descriptor
private var _documentDescriptor_ : mx.core.UIComponentDescriptor
   =
  new mx.core.UIComponentDescriptor({
  type: mx.core.Application
  ,
  propertiesFactory: function():Object { return {
    childDescriptors: [
      new mx.core.UIComponentDescriptor({
        type: mx.controls.Label
        ,
        propertiesFactory: function():Object { return {
          text: "Hello World"
        }}
      })
    ]
  }}
  })
}
```

Compare the generated ActionScript code with the MXML it replaces:

```
<?xml version="1.0" encoding="utf-8"?>
<mx:Application xmlns:mx="http://www.adobe.com/2006/mxml">
  <mx:Label text="Hello World"/>
</mx:Application>
```

That's the power of the MXML programming language!

Understanding MXML

MXML is a pure XML-based markup language that is a convenience language for ActionScript 3. In this and previous chapters, I've shown examples of how you can accomplish certain tasks in either language, and in most cases the MXML version requires significantly less code.

MXML is XML!

As pure XML, MXML follows all conventions and syntax rules that are common to all such languages, including the following:

- **XML is case sensitive.** All element and attribute names must be declared exactly as they're defined in the language documentation.

- **All tags must have end tags or use empty tag syntax.** For instance, the `<mx:Label>` element usually doesn't need an end tag, so it's declared as `<mx:Label/>`. The extra slash character indicates that no end tag is needed.

- **Element tags can't be overlapped.** In HTML, you might get away with overlapping element tag containership, such as `<b><i>My Text</b></i>`. In HTML, the browser typically just figures it out and does the right thing. In XML, this sort of markup breaks the hierarchical parent-child relationship between elements that's required for the XML processor to correctly parse the file.

- **Every XML document has a single root element.** In an MXML application file designed for Web deployment, the root element is always `<mx:Application>`. For AIR applications, the root element is `<mx:WindowedApplication>`. In MXML component files, the root element is whatever existing class you want to extend. But no matter what, you must have a single root element.

- **XML attribute values must be wrapped in quotation marks.** This is another supposed requirement of HTML that you can sometimes ignore in a browser environment. In XML, if you forget the quotation marks around an attribute value, the compiler just gives up and displays an error.

Other XML rules are important to understanding the coding requirements of MXML, including the use of CDATA blocks and XML comments, but the bottom line is that MXML is a real XML language. So if a rule is true for XML, it's true for MXML as well.

XML as a programming language

Although XML was originally designed to represent data for exchange over the Internet, it isn't the only XML-based language to gain popularity as an application development tool. These languages have been used effectively to build or add functionality to software applications:

- **XSLT** (Extensible Stylesheet Language Transformations): A language that's defined by the World Wide Web Consortium (W3C) and implemented in many products and platforms to transform XML from one "flavor" into another

- **XUL** (XML User Interface Language): A language for defining application interfaces that's incorporated into the Mozilla Web browser kernel

What Does MXML Stand For?

Adobe's documentation doesn't say whether MXML is an acronym or, if it is, what it abbreviates. Whereas most XML-based languages have clear meanings, this one is just, well, MXML. Some developers have guessed that it stands for "Macromedia Extensible Markup Language" because it was invented at Macromedia prior to the company's acquisition by Adobe. Other suggestions include "Multidimensional XML" and "Maximum eXperience Markup Language" (based on Macromedia's old mantra, "Experience Matters").

Adobe isn't saying. So that means you get to make up your own version here. MXML stands for (write in your vote): _____.

- **XAML** (Extensible Application Markup Language): A language developed by Microsoft that's very similar in purpose and design to MXML, and used to define applications that run in Microsoft's SilverStream player

To be productive with an XML-based programming language, it's important to understand some basic XML concepts and how they affect programming techniques. In this section, I describe the concepts of namespaces, reserved characters, and other XML concepts that you might find helpful.

XML namespaces

A namespace in XML gives a language designer a way of defining and binding together element and attribute names into a language that can then be recognized by an XML processor. The string that's used to identify a namespace in XML is known as a *URI Reference*.

 The technical description of XML namespaces is available at the W3C's Web site: `www.w3.org/TR/REC-xml-names/#sec-namespaces`

The URI, or Uniform Resource Identifier, that identifies an XML namespace is typically created as a combination of the following:

- The Web address of the organization that manages the XML language
- A subdirectory structure indicating the name of the language and, optionally, the year in which the language was defined

The namespace URI for Flex 2 and 3 applications looks like this:

```
http://www.adobe.com/2006/mxml
```

This means that this version of MXML was defined in 2006 by Adobe Systems.

NOTE An older version of the MXML language was used in Flex 1.x. The namespace URI for that version of the language was:

```
http://www.macromedia.com/2004/mxml
```

This version of the language is distinguished from the current version by both the domain name (from when Flex was owned by Macromedia) and the year of its definition.

As the first step in the Flex compilation process, the Flex compiler reads the XML markup in the application. If it sees a namespace other than the one it expects, it generates a compiler error.

CAUTION An XML namespace URI is case sensitive and must be spelled exactly as indicated in the previous example. Changing even a single character from lowercase to uppercase causes the compiler to fail.

TIP Even though a namespace URI looks like a Web address, it's really just a simple string. The Flex compiler does not use the URI to make any requests to the Adobe Web site, and you don't need access to the Internet to compile a Flex application.

XML namespace prefixes

A namespace prefix is an arbitrary string that's assigned to a namespace URI as an alias. You define a namespace prefix with the xmlns attribute, separated from the prefix by a colon (:). Herein lies the key benefit of namespaces: different types of XML can be used in the same document by matching the prefix with an identifier (the URI), and the XML parser can handle each type in its own unique way.

In a default Flex application, the <mx:Application> root element defines a namespace prefix of mx with this syntax:

```
<mx:Application xmlns:mx="http://www.adobe.com/2006/mxml">
</mx:Application>
```

The mx prefix is then used in every declaration of an MXML element, such as the Label:

```
<mx:Label text="Hello World"/>
```

This means that the Label element is a member of the XML language that's defined by the mx prefix's bound URI.

NOTE Every MXML file, including MXML component and module files, requires the standard MXML namespace URI to be declared in the XML file's root element.

TIP Namespace prefixes are arbitrary. That means you can use any prefix you like, as long as you're consistent. The mx prefix that's used in the Flex documentation and code samples is in reality a recommendation, and not a technical requirement. This code would work just as well:

```
<?xml version="1.0" encoding="utf-8"?>
<harry:Application
  xmlns:harry="http://www.adobe.com/2006/mxml">
  <harry:Label text="Hello World"/>
</harry:Application>
```

But it would be just plain silly. I strongly recommend that you use the mx prefix as described throughout the product documentation and code samples.

Namespace prefixes and XML child elements

You can declare any object property or event handler using XML child element syntax instead of an XML attribute. For instance, the two following code snippets are functionally identical.

Version 1 with an attribute:

```
<mx:Label text="Hello World"/>
```

Version 2 with a child element:

```
<mx:Label>
  <mx:text>Hello World</mx:text>
</mx:Label>
```

Notice that the text property of the Label control has the same value in both cases, but observe two significant differences in the syntax styles:

- The child element declaration of <mx:text> requires the mx namespace prefix to indicate that the element is a member of the MXML language, while the XML attribute version doesn't need (and can't use) the prefix.

- The attribute version requires quotation marks around the property value to satisfy the XML requirement that all attribute values must be quoted, while the child element doesn't need them.

In many cases, deciding which syntax to use is a coin flip; in others, the choice is pretty clear.

Using CDATA blocks

In XML, CDATA blocks are used to protect literal characters from XML processors that would otherwise interpret them as part of the XML markup, rather than the document's content. This is particularly important in Flex when you're trying to create ActionScript code that's nested within an MXML document.

In Flex Builder, when you create an <mx:Script> section to host some ActionScript, Flex Builder adds a CDATA block automatically if you follow the right sequence in adding the tag. Try this:

1. Place the cursor in an MXML application just underneath the <mx:Application> start tag. (The <mx:Script> section can go anywhere in the document as long as it's a direct child of the root element, but it's frequently placed in this location.)

2. Type this string:

   ```
   <s
   ```

   You should see a list of available MXML tags.

3. Press Enter (Return on the Mac) to select the <mx:Script> tag.

4. Type a closing > character to close the tag.

You should see that Flex Builder auto-completes the `<mx:Script>` tag set and creates a CDATA block between the tags:

```
<mx:Script>
  <![CDATA[
  ]]>
</mx:Script>
```

The cursor is placed inside the CDATA block; this is where the ActionScript code should be placed.

The purpose of the CDATA block is to ensure that characters that are considered *reserved* by the XML processor are interpreted as scripting characters, rather than XML markup. XML considers these characters to be reserved:

```
<  >  &  "  '
```

All five characters have clear meanings in both ActionScript and XML, so if you don't protect the code, the XML processor will think, for example, that the < character is part of the tag syntax, rather than meaning "less than" as it does for ActionScript, and you get a parser error when you try to compile.

CDATA blocks also are sometimes used to protect literal text in other MXML elements. For example, the `Label` and `Text` controls support an `htmlText` property that allows you to present simple HTML 1.0 content. In this example, the `<b>` tags are correctly interpreted because they're wrapped in a CDATA block:

```
<mx:Label>
  <mx: htmlText>
  <![CDATA[
    <b>This text is bold!</b>
  ]]>
  </mx:htmlText>
</mx:Label>
```

Without the CDATA block, the HTML tag characters would confuse the Flex compiler, because it would interpret the `<b>` element as part of the MXML code and not as HTML.

XML entities

On rare occasions, you'll encounter a situation where a reserved character just has to be placed in an XML structure, and the alternative is to write many lines of ActionScript code. To solve these cases, XML provides the concept of entities — strings that are aliases for the characters that XML considers to be reserved.

These are the entities for the five XML reserved characters (these may look familiar; they are the same in HTML):

```
&amp; = & (ampersand)
&lt; = < (less than)
```

> ; > = (greater than)

" ; = " (double quote)

' ; = ' (apostrophe/single quote)

Here's a scenario where this comes in handy. Imagine that you want to set an object's `enabled` property using a Boolean binding expression. The object should be enabled only when a certain value is less than 0. You might first try the binding like this:

```
<mx:Button label="Click Me" enabled="{someValue < 3}"/>
```

The above code will cause the compiler to fail because according to XML syntax rules, the < character isn't permitted within an attribute value. You can solve this issue in a number of ways, but the one with the least amount of code that also retains the same logic looks like this:

```
<mx:Button label="Click Me" enabled="{someValue &lt; 3}"/>
```

The XML processor that's at the core of the Flex compiler accepts this code and translates < , the XML entity, to the literal < character before the ActionScript parser does its part. The code may look odd, but it works.

MXML and containership

You can use MXML to declare both visual and non-visual objects. When using the markup language to declare visual objects, positioning of code determines both containership and the order of objects in the application's visual presentation.

The `Application` itself is a container that contains other visual objects such as containers and controls. In the following code, the `Application` contains a `VBox` container, and the `VBox` container contains 3 `Label` controls. The order of presentation is determined by the order of the code.

```
<?xml version="1.0" encoding="utf-8"?>
<mx:Application xmlns:mx="http://www.adobe.com/2006/mxml"
  backgroundColor="#999999" layout="absolute">
  <mx:Canvas backgroundColor="#cccccc" width="50%" height="50%"
    horizontalCenter="0" verticalCenter="0">
    <mx:VBox backgroundColor="#eeeeee"
      horizontalCenter="0" verticalCenter="0"
    paddingTop="20" paddingBottom="20"
    paddingRight="20" paddingLeft="20">
    <mx:Label text="This is Label 1"/>
    <mx:Label text="This is Label 2"/>
    <mx:Label text="This is Label 3"/>
    </mx:VBox>
  </mx:Canvas>
</mx:Application>
```

In this application, the Canvas container is inside the Application; the VBox container is inside the Canvas; the Label controls are inside the VBox; and the Label controls display in the order in which they're declared. The application's visual presentation is shown in Figure 4.3.

FIGURE 4.3

An application with multiple containers and controls

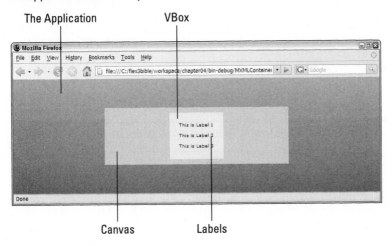

The Application   VBox

Canvas   Labels

If you want to move the Label controls up or down relative to each other, the easiest approach is to change the order of the code.

The visual objects that are nested within a container such as the Application are considered to be part of the container's display list. This is the list of visual objects that make up what the user sees at runtime.

TIP You can add visual objects to the container's display list at runtime with ActionScript code. Every container has methods named addChild() and addChildAt() that are designed for this purpose; another method named setChildIndex() lets you move objects around within the container's display list.

MXML and non-visual classes

You also can use MXML to declare non-visual ActionScript class instances. The following code declares an instance of the WebService class that's used to make calls to SOAP-based Web services.

```
<mx:WebService id="myService"
  wsdl="http://www.bardotech.com/services/Myservice?wsdl"/>
```

These sort of non-visual controls are known as *faceless* components, because they don't have visual representation in the application. Faceless components must be declared as direct child elements of the MXML file's root element such the `<mx:Application>` element in a main application file. This code, for example, would be incorrect and would generate the compiler error shown in Figure 4.4:

```xml
<?xml version="1.0" encoding="utf-8"?>
<mx:Application xmlns:mx="http://www.adobe.com/2006/mxml"
  <mx:VBox>
    <mx:WebService id="myService"
      wsdl="http://www.bardotech.com/services/Myservice?wsdl"/>
  </mx:VBox>
</mx:Application>
```

FIGURE 4.4

The Problems view displaying a compiler error for incorrectly placed faceless controls

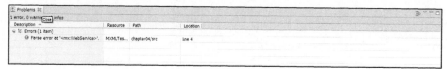

Since VBox is a visual container, it can contain only other visual objects. To fix this problem, move the `<mx:WebService>` declaration outside the `<mx:VBox>` container so that it becomes a direct child element of the `<mx:Application>` element.

Understanding ActionScript 3

ActionScript 3 is the most recent version of the programming language that drives both Flash and Flex. ActionScript 3 is an implementation of the ECMAScript 4th Edition recommendation. ECMAScript in turn was originally based on Netscape's JavaScript.

A complete description of ActionScript 3 is beyond the scope of this book, but it's worth an overview of the language's basic syntax.

 A formal description of the ECMAScript 4th Edition standard is available in PDF format at www.ecmascript.org/es4/spec/overview.pdf.

 In addition to ActionScript 3, subsets of the ECMAScript 4th edition interim recommendation also have been implemented in Microsoft's JScript.NET.

ActionScript syntax

ActionScript 3, and the language recommendation on which it's modeled, ECMAScript, share syntax with languages such as C, C++, C#, and Java. Like these languages, ActionScript has these syntactical features:

- All identifiers and keywords are case sensitive.
- Keywords are always lowercase.
- Statements end with a ; (semicolon) character, as in

  `x = 0;`

- Boolean expressions used in conditional clauses are wrapped in parentheses, as in

  `if (aBoolean)`

- `{}` (brace) characters are used to denote code blocks.

 The semicolon character at the end of lines is optional when you code one statement per line, but is used nearly universally to improve code readability.

Declaring variables

As in JavaScript, ActionScript 3 variables are declared with the `var` keyword. The variable name is usually followed by a data type declaration using what's known as *post-colon* data typing syntax. The following ActionScript declaration creates a `public` variable named `myValue`, typed as a `String`:

```
public var myValue:String;
```

The type declaration isn't required, but if you leave it out the compiler generates a warning. If you want to use a "loose" type declaration that allows the variable to hold values of any type, use the wild card * character after the colon:

```
public var myLooseValue:*;
```

Using access modifiers

An *access modifier* is a keyword that defines a class member's visibility and availability to the rest of the application. In code placed outside function declarations, the variable declaration is preceded by an access modifier keyword that determines the variable's visibility to the rest of the application.

CROSS-REF When you declare a variable outside a function, you're really declaring a property of a component or class. When the code is in the main MXML application file, the property is a member of the `Application` component. This aspect of declaring object members, including how to declare other component members such as functions and constants, is described in Chapter 5.

You can use any one of these access modifiers in a variable declaration placed outside a function:

- `public`: All code throughout an application can access the variable.
- `private`: Only code in the current component or class can access the variable.

- `protected`: Only code in the current component or class, or any its subclasses, can access the variable.

- `internal`: Only code in the current component or class, or any other component or class in the same package, can access the variable.

You use only one access modifier for any particular variable declaration.

CAUTION If you don't include an access modifier in a variable declaration placed outside a function, the compiler generates a warning and the access for that member is set to the default of `internal`. In ActionScript 2, the same code would have resulted in a default access of `public` and no compiler warning would have been generated.

TIP Unlike in JavaScript, where the presence or absence of the `var` keyword can determine variable lifetime and visibility, in ActionScript `var` is required whenever you declare a variable or an object property (described in Chapter 5).

Declaring variables within functions

Variables declared within functions don't require or accept access modifiers. By declaring the variable within the function, you restrict its visibility and lifetime to the duration of the function itself. This ActionScript code declares a variable within a function:

```
private function myFunction()
{
  var myVar:String;
}
```

Once the function has completed execution, any variables declared within its body expire.

Initializing variable values

You can set initial values in a variable declaration by adding the assignment operator (a single = character) and the value after the variable name. The following code creates a variable named `myValue` and assigns its initial value at the same time:

```
public var myValue:String = "Hello World!";
```

TIP Variable declarations, including those that set declare and set a variable's initial value, can be placed either inside or outside functions. Code that modifies an existing variable's value, however, must be placed inside a function.

Using ActionScript operators

ActionScript shares operators with languages such as C, C++, C#, and Java. Table 4.1 lists common mathematical and comparison operators that work in all of these languages.

TABLE 4.1

ActionScript 3 Operators

Operator	Purpose	Example

+	Mathematical addition and string concatenation	Addition:
		`var result:Number = 1 + 1;`
		Concatenation:
		`var result:String = "Hello " + "world";`

-	Mathematical subtraction	`var result:Number = 20 - 10;`
/	Mathematical division	`var result:Number = 20 / 2;`
*	Mathematical multiplication	`var result:Number = 20 * 2;`
%	Modulus (returns remainder from integer division)	`var result:int = 12 % 5;`
==	Equals	`var is:Boolean=` `(value1 == value2)`
!=	Assignment	`var value:Number=1;`
>	Greater than	`if (value > 3) {}`
<	Less than	`if (value < 3) {}`
&&	Logical AND	`if (value1 > 3 && value1 < 10) {}`
||	Logical OR	`if (value1 < 3 || value2 > 10) {}`

The language includes many more operators, categorized as Logical, Relational, Assignment, and Bitwise operators. Again, if you have a background in C, Java, or similar languages, you can let that experience be your guide.

Conditional statements

ActionScript uses two types of conditional statements. The more common formulation uses an `if` keyword with a Boolean expression to determine whether code will be executed. You can then optionally add `else` and `else if` clauses to the statement.

A simple `if` statement looks like this:

```
if (some Boolean expression)
{
  ... do something ...
}
```

For example, if you want to evaluate whether a user has selected a row in a `DataGrid` or `List` control, you might code it like this:

```
if (myDataGrid.selectedIndex != -1)
{
  var myData:Object = myDataGrid.selectedItem;
}
```

The Boolean expression works because `DataGrid` and `List` controls have a `selectedIndex` property that indicates the ordinal position of the currently selected data element. If nothing is selected, this property always returns _1.

You can optionally add `else` and `else if` clauses to an `if` statement like this:

```
if (some Boolean expression)
{
  ... do this!
}
else if (some other expression)
{
  ... do that!
}
else
{
  ... do something else!
}
```

When using these optional clauses, you can have as many `else if` clauses as you need and a single `else` clause that is always at the end of the whole code section.

```
private function onLoad():void
{
  if (str == "dfsd")
    Alert.show("dfsd")
  else if (str == "kks")
    Alert.show("kks")
  else if (str == "yes")
    Alert.show("yes")
}
```

You can also use `switch` statements to evaluate a single expression against multiple possible values:

```
switch (some expression)
{
  case value1:
    ... do something ...
    break
  case value2:
    ... do something else ...
```

```
      default:
         ... do another thing ...
   }
```

The expression you evaluate with a `switch` statement can be of any data type.

Looping

Looping constructs look basically the same as in Java, JavaScript, C, and other similar languages. A `for` loop allows you to loop a given number of times.

```
for (var i:int=0; i<10; i++)
{
   ... do this 10 times ...
}
```

The `for` statement establishes a *counter* variable (named `i` in the above example); in the second part of the expression, it causes the loop to continue as long as `i` is less than 10; and in the third part, it increments the variable's value by 1 each time through the loop.

You also can use a `while` statement to execute a loop:

```
var i:int = 0;
while (i<10)
{
  do this 10 times!
  i++;
}
```

In this example, the `while` statement is used to loop a specific number of times. It also can be used to evaluate any Boolean expression and determine whether to continue the looping process or break out of the loop and continue with the remainder of the code.

 TIP   In many cases, the choice of a `for` or a `while` loop is a style choice that's completely up to the programmer.

Combining MXML and ActionScript

Many tasks can be accomplished with either MXML or ActionScript code, and only a few are restricted to one language or the other. Most Flex applications use both. The main application file is always in MXML, and that file can then contain or refer to ActionScript code in a variety of ways.

The <mx:Script> tag

The `<mx:Script>` tag set can wrap ActionScript code that becomes a part of the Application or component that the current MXML file represents. The advantage of including the scripting in the MXML file is that all the code for a particular component is in one place. Disadvantages include:

- Some developers find that mixing declarative (MXML) and programmatic (ActionScript) syntax in a single file can look odd and be a bit confusing.

- Because Flex Builder 3 provides code management tools for ActionScript stored in external files that aren't available in MXML files, you might find that you want to take advantage of these tools.

In terms of functionality and application performance, either of these approaches works fine. So it's purely a question of style and preference.

If you decide to include ActionScript in an MXML file, create the `<mx:Script>` element as a pair of tags wrapped around a CDATA block. Then place all your scripting inside the CDATA block:

```
<mx:Script>
  <![CDATA[
    Scripting goes here
  ]]>
</mx:Script>
```

TIP To insert a CDATA block into a source code file, place the cursor where you want the CDATA to appear, and then select Source ⇨ Insert CDATA Block from the Flex Builder menu. Or use the keyboard shortcut Ctrl+Shift+D.

Using external ActionScript files

You can link an MXML file to an external ActionScript file with the source property of the `<mx:Script/>` element. The ActionScript file should have a file extension of .as and can contain as much ActionScript code as you need.

Any code in the external file is considered to be a part of the MXML file and the ActionScript class it represents. And because the external file isn't in XML format, you don't need the `<mx:Script>` element or the CDATA block to protect the code.

Follow these steps to create an external ActionScript file:

1. Select File ⇨ New ⇨ ActionScript File from the Flex Builder menu. (Don't select ActionScript Class — that's a different sort of file I'll describe in a later chapter.)

2. In the New ActionScript File dialog box, select the folder in which you want to create the file. External ActionScript files can go anywhere in the project, because you'll explicitly refer to the file's location when you link to it from an MXML file. I usually place the file in the same folder as the MXML file it's linked to.

3. Enter the name of the file. It should have a file extension of .as, but the rest of the filename is up to you. I usually match the name of the MXML file it's linked to, so for an application named HelloWorld.mxml, the name of the external ActionScript file would be helloWorld.as.

4. Click Finish to create the file.

> **TIP**
>
> Notice that in this usage, the external ActionScript filename starts with a lowercase character. This doesn't have any technical effect on the code, but it's a way of indicating that it's a simple file containing ActionScript code, as opposed to an ActionScript class (which, by object-oriented programming conventions, has an initial uppercase character).

After the file has been created, you link to it from the MXML file with the `<mx:Script>` element and add a `source` property pointing to the external file. The application in Listing 4.1 embeds its ActionScript code in an `<mx:Style>` tag set.

> **CAUTION**
>
> Any particular `<mx:Script>` element can contain nested ActionScript or use the `source` property to link to an external ActionScript file, but it cannot do both at the same time. You can, however, have as many `<mx:Script>` declarations in a single MXML file as you need.

LISTING 4.1

An MXML application CalculatorWithScript.mxml with nested ActionScript

```
<?xml version="1.0" encoding="utf-8"?>
<mx:Application xmlns:mx="http://www.adobe.com/2006/mxml"
layout="vertical" xmlns:components="components.*">

  <mx:Script>
    <![CDATA[

      [Bindable]
      private var currentResult:Number;
      [Bindable]
      private var currentInput:String;

      private function initApp():void
      {
        input.addEventListener("click", clickHandler);
        input.addEventListener("calculate", calculate);
      }

      private function calculate(event:Event):void
      {
        currentResult += Number(currentInput);
      }

      private function clickHandler(event:TextEvent):void
      {
        currentInput += event.text;
      }
    ]]>
```

continued

LISTING 4.1   *(continued)*

```
  </mx:Script>

  <components:ButtonTile id="input"/>
  <components:ResultOutput id="output"/>

</mx:Application>
```

ON the WEB   The code in Listing 4.1 is available in the Web site files in the `chapter04` project's `src` folder as `CalculatorWithScript.mxml`.

Listing 4.2 shows the same application after the ActionScript has been moved to an external file.

LISTING 4.2

MXML application Calculator.mxml with linked ActionScript file

```
<?xml version="1.0" encoding="utf-8"?>
<mx:Application xmlns:mx="http://www.adobe.com/2006/mxml"
  layout="vertical" xmlns:components="components.*">

  <mx:Script source="calculator.as"/>

  <components:ButtonTile id="input"/>
  <components:ResultOutput id="output"/>

</mx:Application>
```

ON the WEB   The code in Listing 4.2 is available in the Web site files in the `chapter04` project's `src` folder as `Calculator.mxml`.

You have just as much code to manage, but the XML markup is cleaner and easier to read. And, as shown in Listing 4.3, the ActionScript file now contains only the programmatic code:

LISTING 4.3

External ActionScript file calculator.as

```
// ActionScript file
[Bindable]
private var currentResult:Number;

[Bindable]
```

```
private var currentInput:String;

private function initApp():void
{
  input.addEventListener("click", clickHandler);
  input.addEventListener("calculate", calculate);
}

private function calculate(event:Event):void
{
  currentResult += Number(currentInput);
}

private function clickHandler(event:TextEvent):void
{
  currentInput += event.text;
}
```

ON the WEB The code in Listing 4.3 is available in the Web site files in the **chapter04** project's **src** folder as **calculator.as**.

Managing ActionScript code with Flex Builder

Whether you're working with MXML or ActionScript, Flex Builder's Outline view allows you to easily find function and variable declarations within the source code. The Outline view appears in the lower-right corner of Flex Builder in the default Flex Development perspective.

Using Outline view with ActionScript

When working with MXML, the default Outline view displays a tree of MXML elements. As shown in Figure 4.5, the <mx:Script> element shows up as a single selectable object.

FIGURE 4.5

Flex Builder's Outline view in MXML mode

To navigate to a specific function or variable declaration using the Outline view, click the Show class view icon at the top of the view. As shown in Figure 4.6, you're now able to click a declaration and jump to that bit of code.

FIGURE 4.6

Outline view and the Class view buttons

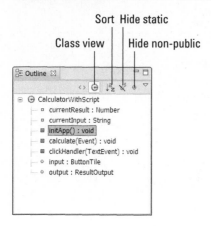

When using the Outline's Class view, you can change the display with these other options that are accessed from buttons at the top of the Outline view:

- **Sort** displays variables and functions in alphabetical order.
- **Hide Static Functions and Variables** hides variables and functions that are marked with the `static` modifier.
- **Hide Non-Public Members** hides variables and functions that aren't marked with the `public` access modifier.

 You need to click an item only once in the Outline view to jump to the matching code.

 From any object reference in the ActionScript file, hold down the Ctrl key and click the reference to jump to that object's declaration. This works whether the declaration is in the ActionScript file or an external MXML file and for both custom classes and Flex library classes whose source code has been provided by Adobe.

Managing ActionScript code in external files

When you store ActionScript code in an external file, Flex Builder gives you some additional code management tools.

Code folding

Code folding refers to the ability of the Flex Builder editor to fold, or collapse, certain sections of code. In an MXML editor, code folding is based on the source file's MXML elements. As shown in Figure 4.7, an MXML file displays code folding icons at the beginning of each MXML element. You'll see a folding icon for the `<mx:Script>` tag that allows you to collapse that section of code to a single line.

FIGURE 4.7

Code folding icons in an MXML file

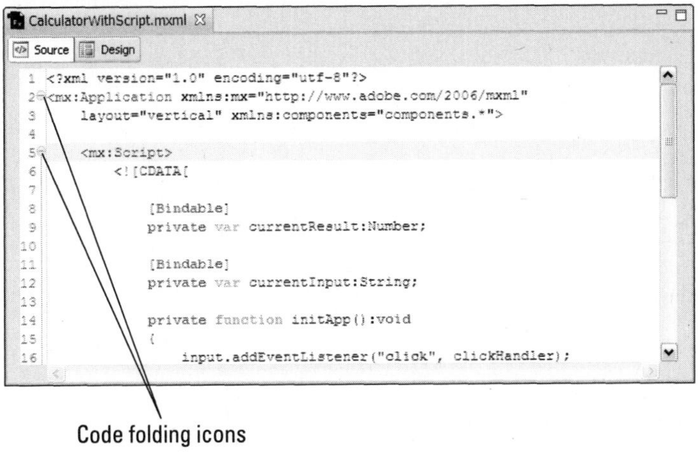

Code folding icons

Clicking the icon reduces the MXML element at that line to a single line of displayed code. Then, when you move the cursor over the folding icon, you see a pop-up window showing the first of code in the collapsed section, as shown in Figure 4.8. Clicking the icon again expands it to full display.

In an external ActionScript external file, because you are using Flex Builder's ActionScript editor, code folding lets you collapse function declarations instead of MXML elements. As shown in Figure 4.9, you can click any function's folding icon and reduce it to a single line of code.

You also can collapse all functions in a file to single-line display:

- Right-click in the column of line numbers.
- As shown in Figure 4.10, select Folding ➪ Collapse Functions to reduce all functions to single-line displays.

Now all functions are displayed as single lines of code, as shown in Figure 4.11.

And finally, moving the cursor over a folded icon that is in a collapsed state displays the contents of the folded function, as shown in Figure 4.12.

113

FIGURE 4.8

Displaying collapsed MXML code

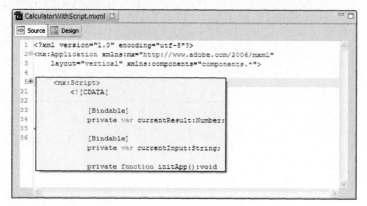

FIGURE 4.9

Code folding icons in an ActionScript file

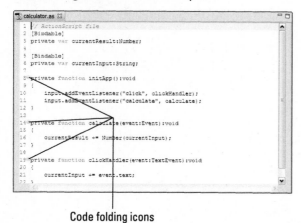

Code folding icons

Collapsing all functions

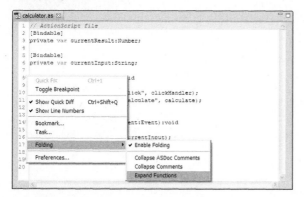

Functions displayed as single lines of code

```
 1  // ActionScript file
 2  [Bindable]
 3  private var currentResult:Number;
 4
 5  [Bindable]
 6  private var currentInput:String;
 7
 8  private function initApp():void
13
14  private function calculate(event:Event):void
18
19  private function clickHandler(event:TextEvent):void
20
```

Displaying the contents of a folded function

```
 1  // ActionScript file
 2  [Bindable]
 3  private var currentResult:Number;
 4
 5  [Bindable]
 6  private var currentInput:String;
 7
 8  private function initApp():void
13  {
14      input.addEventListener("click", clickHandler);
18      input.addEventListener("calculate", calculate);
19  }
20
```

Organizing import statements

An `import` statement informs the compiler about the location of ActionScript classes it needs to compile an application or component. Most ActionScript classes must be explicitly imported to be recognized by the compiler. This `import` statement makes a class named `ArrayCollection` available to the compiler:

```
import mx.collections.ArrayCollection;
```

In Flex Builder 2, the development environment helped you build an import list by creating `import` statements for classes you referred to as you typed. But later, if you removed a class reference from the body of the code, the `import` statement would be left in the file. This doesn't cause any harm to the application (`import` statements on their own don't add size or functionality to a compiled application), but it could be confusing later when you opened the file and saw `import` statements that had nothing to do with the code's functionality.

Flex Builder 3' ActionScript editor adds the ability to organize an ActionScript file's `import` statements with a simple menu selection or keyboard shortcut. When you organize imports, unused `import` statements are removed and the ones you need are left in alphabetical order, grouped by package.

Consider this list of `import` statements:

```
import mx.controls.Alert;
import flash.net.FileFilter;
import flash.net.URLRequest;
import mx.collections.ArrayCollection;
import mx.validators.Validator;
import flash.net.FileReference;
```

To organize this list, select Source ➪ Organize Imports from the Flex Builder menu. (Or press the keyboard shortcut Ctrl+Shift+O.) After organization, the list now looks like this:

```
import flash.net.FileFilter;
import flash.net.FileReference;
import flash.net.URLRequest;

import mx.controls.Alert;
import mx.validators.Validator;
```

The import statement for the unused class is removed, and the remaining statements are alphabetized and grouped.

 This ability to organize `import` statements currently is available only in ActionScript source code files and does not work in MXML files.

Using the Application Container

The `Application` container is always declared as the root element of an MXML application file. It represents the top level of the application's containership hierarchy.

`Application` is defined as an ActionScript class with the fully qualified name `mx.core.Application`. The Application class supports these important properties that are not part of other containers. Table 4.2 shows the application properties.

TABLE 4.2

Application Properties

Property	Purpose	Example
application	A static property that returns a reference to the current Application.	Application.application.height = 400;
controlBar	A read-only property that returns a reference to an `Application ControlBar` within the `Application`.	var myCB:ApplicationControlBar = this.controlBar;
frameRate	The number of frames per second at which changes are reflected in Flash Player. The default is 24 frames/second.	<mx:Application frameRate="60"/>
pageTitle	A value that's passed through to the HTML wrapper and displayed in place of the ${title} placeholder.	<mx:Application pageTitle="My Flex App"/>
parameters	An ActionScript Object containing name/value pairs that are passed into the Flash Player into a FlashVars string passed into the Flash Player.	Opening the application with a URL containing query string variables: "flashvars", "state=new" Reading the variable in the Flex application: var currentState:String = this.parameters.state;
url	The URL with which the Application .swf file was opened.	var currentURL:String = this.url;

> **TIP**
> You can make typing appear to be smoother in a Flex application by increasing the `frameRate`. For example, if the cursor is in a **TextArea** or **TextInput** control and you hold down a key at 24 frames/second, the effect can be a bit "jumpy." That is, the characters may not appear at an even rate. Setting the **frameRate** to 60 or 90 frames/second may noticeably improve this "animation." In theory, this could have a negative effect on CPU usage on the client system, but in testing on a modern computer, it's difficult to see a difference.

CAUTION   The `url` property refers to the URL through which the application `.swf` file was loaded, not the HTML wrapper file. For example, when running the `URLDemo.mxml` application from the local disk, the browser's `url` is displayed as:

```
file:///C:/flex3bible/workspace/chapter04/
   bin-debug/URLDemo.html
```

The `Application.url` property returns this value:

```
file:///C:/flex3bible/workspace/chapter04/
   bin-debug/URLDemo.swf
```

Passing application parameters

You pass parameters to the application from the browser using a special Flash Player variable named `flashVars`. If you're using simple `<object>` and `<embed>` tags to call Flash Player from an HTML wrapper file, the `flashVars` variable is passed from the HTML wrapper file in this form:

```
<object classid="clsid:D27CDB6E-AE6D-11cf-96B8-444553540000"
   id="${application}" width="${width}" height="${height}"
   codebase="http://fpdownload.macromedia.com/get/
         flashplayer/current/swflash.cab">
   <param name="movie" value="${swf}.swf" />
   <param name="quality" value="high" />
   <param name="bgcolor" value="${bgcolor}" />
   <param name="allowScriptAccess" value="sameDomain" />
   <param name="flashVars" value="state=New" />
   <embed src="${swf}.swf" quality="high" bgcolor="${bgcolor}"
     width="${width}" height="${height}" name="${application}"
     align="middle" play="true"
     loop="false" quality="high"
     allowScriptAccess="sameDomain"
     type="application/x-shockwave-flash"
     pluginspage="http://www.adobe.com/go/getflashplayer"
     flashVars="state=New">
   </embed>
</object>
```

Notice that the `flashVars` property is passed twice: once for the `<object>` tag (for Internet Explorer), and once for the `<embed>` tag (for plug-in based browsers such as Firefox).

If you're using the JavaScript code in the HTML wrapper file that's generated by Flex Builder, pass the `flashVars` variable like this:

```
AC_FL_RunContent(
   "src", "${swf}",
   "width", "${width}",
   "height", "${height}",
   "align", "middle",
   "id", "${application}",
```

```
"quality", "high",
"bgcolor", "${bgcolor}",
"name", "${application}",
"allowScriptAccess","sameDomain",
"type", "application/x-shockwave-flash",
"pluginspage", "http://www.adobe.com/go/getflashplayer",
"flashVars", "state=New");
```

The format of the `flashVars` variable is the same as the `queryString` portion of a URL. Variables and their values are separated by the = character, and multiple values are separated by the & character. You don't need additional quotation marks around parameter values, so a `flashVars` variable containing two parameters might look like this:

```
"flashVars", "firstName=Bob&lastName=Smith"
```

This code would result in two parameters named `firstName` and `lastName` with values of `Bob` and `Smith`.

To retrieve these values at runtime, use the `Application` object's `parameters` property. The `parameters` property is a dynamic object that allows you to address its named properties with dot notation, as in:

```
private var fullName:String =
    Application.application.parameters.firstName + " " +
    Application.application.parameters.lastName;
```

TIP The expression `Application.application` allows you to get a reference to the `application` object from most locations in the application's code. If the code you're writing is in the main application file, though, you can simplify it with:

```
private var fullName:String =
    this.parameters.firstName + " " +
    this.parameters.lastName;
```

Controlling application dimensions

The default values for the `Application` component's width and height are both 100 percent. These values are passed to Flash Player through the HTML wrapper file that's generated by Flex Builder. For example, this code:

```
<mx:Application height="300" width="200">
</mx:Application>
```

results in these values being passed to Flash Player in the generated HTML wrapper page:

```
AC_FL_RunContent(
    "src", "HelloWorld",
    "width", "200",
    "height", "300",
    ... other parameters ...);
```

These dimension properties also are passed into, and are part of, the `.swf` application file.

> **TIP** You can pass different explicit values into the HTML wrapper code that calls Flash Player by modifying the HTML template. This causes the Flex application to be stretched or compressed to match Flash Player's dimensions.

Setting the layout property

The `Application` component's `layout` property controls how its nested visual objects are laid out on the screen. The `layout` property has these possible values:

- `vertical` (the default)
- `horizontal`
- `absolute`

Vertical and horizontal layout

Settings of `vertical` and `horizontal` cause the application to lay out its nested visual objects automatically. As shown in Figure 4.13, a layout setting of `vertical` makes objects in the `Application`'s display list appear in a single column.

FIGURE 4.13

An application with `vertical` layout

> **TIP** The `Application`'s `horizontalAlign` style defaults to center, so objects laid out with either `horizontal` or `vertical` layout are placed in the horizontal center of the application. Other possible values include `left` and `right`.

Figure 4.14 shows what happens when you change the `Application` object's `layout` property to `horizontal`. Objects in the display list are laid out in a row from left to right.

FIGURE 4.14

An application with `horizontal` layout

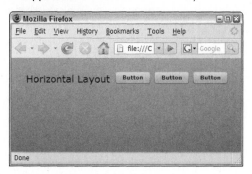

> **TIP** A layout setting of `horizontal` or `vertical` requires the application to calculate the quantity and size of the nested controls at runtime, and then in a second pass to place them on the screen. This calculation has to be re-executed each time the application is resized (for example, if the user resizes the browser). On slower computers, this process can seem a bit sluggish. One solution to improve client-side performance in this situation is to switch to `absolute` layout, because the application then doesn't have to do this calculation.

Absolute layout

An application with `absolute` layout allows each object to be placed in a specific position relative to the top-left corner of the application. As shown in Figure 4.15, `absolute` layout has the additional advantage of being able to overlap objects. When objects have `alpha` settings that allow transparency, as is the case with default settings of the `Button` component, you can make objects show through each other from back to front.

> **TIP** The z-index, or relative depth, of overlapping visual objects is controlled by their order in the container's display list. When declared in MXML, the last declared object has the highest z-index and overlaps any other objects with which it shares screen space.

FIGURE 4.15

An application with `absolute` layout and overlapping

Other containers in the Flex framework besides `Application` support the `layout` property, including these:

- `Panel`
- `TitleWindow`
- `WindowedApplication` (used only in desktop applications deployed with AIR)

I describe those in detail in Chapter 9.

Summary

In this chapter, I described the basic anatomy of a Flex application. You learned the following:

- MXML and ActionScript 3 are the two programming languages you use for Flex development.
- ActionScript 3 is based on the ECMAScript 4th Edition recommendation.
- ActionScript's syntax is similar to Java, JavaScript, C, C++, and C#.
- MXML is a "convenience" language that compiles into ActionScript.
- MXML is a pure XML-based language.
- You can combine MXML and ActionScript in a number of ways.
- The `Application` class is the root element in a Flex application designed for Web deployment.
- The `Application` class's layout property can be set to `horizontal`, `vertical`, or `absolute`.

Chapter 5

Using Bindings and Components

In Chapter 1, I described the object-oriented concept of *modularity* and described how dividing an application into small pieces can increase developer productivity and improve long-term maintenance of an application. I also described the concept of *encapsulation* that encourages developers to create application building blocks that hide the details of a feature's implementation from the rest of the application, and only expose tools in the module's public interface that are needed to set and get the module's information and execute its functions.

In this chapter, I describe some of the basic building blocks of a Flex application that can improve its modularity and make it easier to manage over time. I start with a look at binding expressions and describe how they help you easily move data around an application. A binding expression can move data from one object to another at runtime without explicit event handling or ActionScript statements. I describe a couple of binding syntax styles and show when to use each.

This chapter also includes a description of how to create and use custom MXML components in a Flex application. In the last section of this chapter, I describe how to package and manage multiple components and classes in a component library, using a Flex Builder Library Project.

ON the WEB To use the sample code for this chapter, import the `chap-ter05.zip` Flex project archive file from the Web site files into your Flex Builder workspace.

IN THIS CHAPTER

Using binding expressions

Creating MXML components

Instantiating MXML components

Creating component properties and methods

Using component libraries

Using Binding Expressions

As previously described, a binding expression lets you move data from one object to another at runtime without having to handle complex events or write lots of ActionScript code.

> **TIP** Binding expressions represent only one possible approach to managing data within a Flex application. Because they generate automatic event broadcasters and listeners, they can create significant application activity when overused. Sometimes it's best just to assign object properties using ActionScript code.

The purpose of a binding is to "listen" for changes to an expression and to "broadcast" the expression's value to an object's property. The expression that returns the value is known in a binding as the *source*. The expression to which you pass the value when it changes is known as the *destination*.

Let's look at this example of two Label controls.

```
<mx:Label id="sourceLabel" text="some value"/>
<mx:Label id="destinationLabel"/>
```

If you want the first control's text property value to be displayed in the second control, you would refer to the first as the source and the second as the destination.

Flex supports three binding syntax styles:

- A simple, shorthand MXML-based version that wraps a binding expression in an attribute of an MXML declaration
- A longhand MXML-based version that uses the <mx:Binding> tag
- A longhand ActionScript-based version that uses the mx.binding.utils.BindingUtils class

> **TIP** The longhand ActionScript-based version of creating a binding has some limitations compared to MXML. While the BindingUtils class allows you to create a binding at runtime, it does not support the use of simple ActionScript or E4X expressions, and it doesn't have as good a set of error and warning detection as bindings declared in MXML.

Shorthand MXML binding expressions

In the shorthand MXML version, you start by assigning an id, or unique identifier, to the source control. This becomes the instance name of your object for future reference:

```
<mx:Label id="sourceLabel" text="some value"/>
```

In the destination control's declaration, you use an ActionScript expression that refers to the source control's text property, wrapped in {} characters:

```
<mx:Label text="{sourceLabel.text}"/>
```

At runtime, if the source control's text property changes, the destination control is updated at the same time.

Using <mx:Binding>

The longhand MXML binding syntax uses an <mx:Binding/> tag with properties of source
and destination to define the two expressions:

```
<mx:Binding source="sourceLabel.text"
    destination="sourceLabel.text"/>
```

The <mx:Binding> tag can be used when the destination object is declared in ActionScript code,
rather than MXML. Because shorthand syntax works only in the context of an MXML declaration,
it just doesn't work for this case.

In the following code, a value entered into a TextInput control is passed to a pre-declared variable named myVar whenever the user makes a change. That variable's value is then passed to the
Label control using a shorthand binding expression.

```
<mx:Script>
  <![CDATA[
    [Bindable]
    private var myVar:String
  ]]>
</mx:Script>

<mx:Binding source="myInput.text" destination="myVar"/>
<mx:TextInput id="myInput"/>
<mx:Label text="{myVar}"/>
```

TIP You might not use the <mx:Binding> tag in the simplest Flex applications, but the
first time you need to pass a value to an object or expression that's declared in
ActionScript, you'll find it a valuable tool.

Making expressions bindable

Most object properties in the Flex framework's library are automatically bindable, meaning that if
the property's value changes at runtime, the new value is *broadcast* to the listening destination
object. When you declare your own variables in ActionScript, their values aren't automatically
bindable; you have to mark them with a [Bindable] metadata tag to indicate that they should
share new values with the rest of the application.

Consider this code:

```
<mx:Script>
  <![CDATA[
    private var myVar:String="Hello World";
  ]]>
</mx:Script>
<mx:Label id="destinationLabel" text="{myVar}"/>
```

The variable `myVar` will share its value with the `destinationLabel` control at application startup, but because the variable isn't marked as bindable, any changes at runtime won't be passed to the control. In fact, the compiler notices this problem and generates a compiler warning, as shown in Figure 5.1.

A compiler warning for a binding to a non-bindable expression

To fix this and get rid of the compiler warning, add the `[Bindable]` metadata tag above the variable declaration:

```
<mx:Script>
  <![CDATA[
    [Bindable]
    private var myVar:String="Hello World";
  ]]>
</mx:Script>
<mx:Label id="destinationLabel" text="{myVar}"/>
```

The compiler warning disappears, and if the source expression's value changes at runtime, the `Label` control correctly displays the new value.

Using MXML Components

As described previously, modularity means that you break up an application into pieces that are focused on particular application tasks. A modular application tends to be more stable and maintainable than one that mixes many types of functionality into a single source code file.

Flex supports the object-oriented concept of modularity through the use of custom MXML components and ActionScript classes. In this section, I describe how to create and incorporate MXML components in a Flex application.

Creating MXML components

Like the application itself, an MXML component is built in a source code file with an extension of `.mxml`. At compilation time, an MXML component is turned into an ActionScript class where the

The View in Model-View-Controller

Asingle Flex application can have dozens or hundreds of "views" — that is, screens or visual representations of data that execute particular functions, collect data, or present information to the user. If you try to implement all of these views in a single source code file, the result can be a mess.

Similarly, the application may need to call many different external functions to get data and implement many object structures in application memory in which to hold that data at runtime. In classic model-view-controller application architecture, these parts of the application are known as *models*.

You can create view components with either MXML or ActionScript, but for most purposes an MXML component is the simplest approach. And after you create the components, you need a way to share data with them and make them do things. In this chapter, I describe how to build the Flex application's views as MXML components and how to design the components to hold and receive data.

name of the class matches the first part of the component's filename. So for example, if you create a file named `MyComponent.mxml`, the resulting ActionScript class is named `MyComponent`.

TIP   I strongly recommend that you create components in subfolders of the project source root folder, rather than the source folder itself. This allows you to group components by purpose into *packages*. For example, you might have one folder for forms, another for DataGrid and List components (data-aware components), a third for navigational tools, and so on. The names of the folders are completely up to you.

TIP   Because an MXML component is really an ActionScript class, I recommend that you follow object-oriented naming conventions for class definitions. Specifically this means that component filenames usually start with an initial uppercase character and use mixed-case after that. This is a convention, not a technical requirement, but it's one that most developers follow.

Component inheritance

Each MXML component extends, or is derived from, an existing ActionScript class. You indicate which class the current component extends with the MXML file's root element. So a class named `MyComponent.mxml` that extends the `VBox` container looks like this:

```
<?xml version="1.0" encoding="utf-8"?>
<mx:VBox xmlns:mx="http://www.adobe.com/2006/mxml">
</mx:VBox>
```

CAUTION   Notice that the MXML component file's root element includes the standard MXML namespace and prefix declaration of
`xmlns:mx="http://www.adobe.com/2006/mxml"`. This is required in all MXML files.

The preceding MXML code results in the inheritance relationship described by the UML diagram in Figure 5.2.

FIGURE 5.2

The inheritance relationship between VBox, the superclass, and the custom component, the subclass

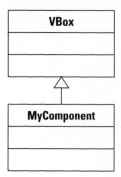

Using the New MXML Component wizard

To create a new MXML component with Flex Builder, first create a folder in the project's source root to contain the component. Then use the New MXML Component wizard to create the component source code file.

Creating a component folder

To create a component folder, follow these steps:

1. Right-click the project's src folder in the Flex Navigator view.
2. Select New ⇨ Folder.
3. Enter a new folder name of **components**, and click Finish.

 Folder names that represent packages, by convention, are usually all lowercase. For example, the folder containing form components should be named forms, not Forms or FORMS.

Creating the MXML component

To create the MXML component, follow these steps:

1. Right-click the new folder in the Flex Navigator view.
2. Select New ⇨ MXML Component.
3. As shown in Figure 5.3, enter a component filename of **MyComponent.as**.
4. Select VBox from the Based on: list.
5. Remove the default values in the Width and Height settings, leaving them blank. This creates a VBox component that automatically resizes based on the size and quantity of its nested controls.

6. Click Finish to create the new MXML component.

The component opens in Flex Builder in either Source or Design view, depending on what view you used most recently.

The New MXML Component wizard

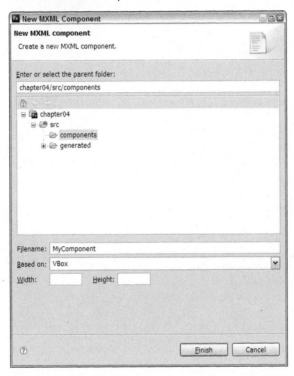

Adding content to the component

To add content to the component, follow these steps:

1. If the component opened in Source view, click the Design button.

2. Locate the Style section of the Flex Properties view.

3. Click the background color selector's paint bucket icon, shown in Figure 5.4, to choose a background color.

4. In the color selector dialog box, if you know the hexadecimal value of the color you want, enter it in the background color field (labeled with a # character). Otherwise, use the color pallet to select a color. Then click OK to complete the selection.

FIGURE 5.4

The background color selector

Background color selector

5. Drag 3 Label components from the Components view into the Design view.

6. Double-click each Label component to edit its text property and add this custom text:

   ■ **Label 1**: These Label components

   ■ **Label 2**: are inside my custom

   ■ **Label 3**: component.

7. Click Source to look at the generated source code. The source code for the component looks like this:

```
<?xml version="1.0" encoding="utf-8"?>
<mx:VBox xmlns:mx="http://www.adobe.com/2006/mxml"
  backgroundColor="#9DEDE8">
  <mx:Label text="These Label components"/>
  <mx:Label text="are inside my custom"/>
  <mx:Label text="component."/>
</mx:VBox>
```

Reverse Domain Package Names

Some developers prefer to create their components and ActionScript classes in a folder structure that includes their organization's domain information and an application identifier. Instead of a simple folder named `forms`, you might have a folder structure named `com/bardotech/myapplication/forms`. Because the folder structure represents a *package* in class management terms, this creates a globally unique identifying system for each group of components. A file named `MyForm.as` in the above folder is known by its fully qualified name as `com.bardo.tech.myapplication.forms.MyForm`.

Notice that the domain name `bardotech.com` becomes a package structure of `com.bardotech`. This convention of reversing the parts of a domain name in a package structure is described in the documentation for the Java programming language and has been adopted by some Flex developers.

In Java, this practice is very strongly encouraged. Because the Java Virtual Machine searches for classes in its classpath at runtime, as well as at the time of compilation, using globally unique class names ensures that if a library of classes with conflicting names just happens to be in your application's classpath, using globally unique package identifiers reduces the possibility of class naming conflicts.

In ActionScript, the source path is used only during the compilation process. By the time you run the application, it's already been compiled into the .swf byte code format. The ActionScript Virtual Machine uses only the classes that are compiled into the application, but it doesn't use the source path to go searching for classes as they're needed at runtime. As a result, this particular reason for the globally unique package name only applies to the world of ActionScript when you incorporate third-party code libraries in the form of .swc files (component libraries) and .rsl files (runtime shared libraries) where you don't control the names of the classes.

You may still want to use these sorts of package names in code libraries that are shared between multiple projects to ensure that compile-time conflicts don't emerge. But for code that's unique to a single application, these deeply nested package names don't have any technical benefit.

Instantiating MXML components

You use MXML components by creating instances of the components in your application. You can instantiate a component using either MXML or ActionScript code.

Instantiating a component with MXML

If the MXML component represents a visual object such as a container or control, it's most commonly instantiated using MXML code. Before an MXML component can be instantiated, you must declare a custom XML namespace prefix that's associated with the folder in which the component's source code file is stored.

The custom namespace prefix is best declared in the MXML file's root element start tag, the value of which contains the folder location of your components (in dot notation) and usually ends with an asterisk to indicate that all components in this folder are available in this namespace:

```
<mx:Application xmlns:mx="http://www.adobe.com/2006/mxml"
    xmlns:mycomps="components.*">
```

You then instantiate the component with standard XML syntax, using the namespace prefix and the component name as an XML element:

```
<mycomps:MyComponent id="comp1"/>
```

> **TIP**   A custom namespace that you declare for a particular folder also serves as an `import` declaration for all classes in that folder. If you need to refer to components or classes in that folder in other parts of the MXML file, a separate `import` statement is not required.

You also can declare the namespace prefix directly within the component instantiation like this:

```
<mycomps:MyComponent id="comp1" xmlns:mycomps="components.*"/>
```

This works, but the namespace prefix is available only for the single component instance. When you place the namespace prefix in the current MXML file's root element, you can then declare as many instances of any component in the `components` folder.

The namespace prefix is arbitrary; that is, you can name it anything. I recommend, however, that you assign a prefix that's the same as the folder name, as in:

```
xmlns:components="components.*"
```

This has two benefits:

- Because the namespace prefix matches the folder name, you'll recognize the component file's location when you look at the code.

- Flex Builder can create the second version of the namespace declaration for you if you follow a particular sequence in coding the object. I describe this sequence in the next section's tutorial.

Instantiating an MXML component

Here's how you create an application that instantiates the custom MXML component:

1. Create a new MXML application in the current project.

2. Place the cursor within the `<mx:Application>` root element tag set.

3. Type the **<** character, and then **my**, the first couple of characters in the component name. (This string is unique enough to display a small number of items in the list of available ActionScript classes.)

   As shown in Figure 5.5, the list of available classes appears and the custom component is displayed.

FIGURE 5.5

Selecting the custom component

> **TIP**   If the list of available classes disappears, press Ctrl+spacebar to bring it back. This works in Flex Builder wherever code hinting is available.

4. Press Enter (Return on the Mac) to select the custom component from the list of available ActionScript classes.

   Flex Builder completes the code with the namespace prefix and the tag name:

   ```
   <components:MyComponent
   ```

5. Type **/>** to complete the tag.

   The code should now look like this:

   ```
   <components:MyComponent/>
   ```

6. Look at the `<mx:Application>` start tag.

   You should see that the `<mx:Application>` tag has been populated with the required namespace prefix to support the selected component. The tag looks like this:

   ```
   <mx:Application xmlns:mx="http://www.adobe.com/2006/mxml"
      layout="vertical" xmlns:components="components.*">
   ```

7. Save and run the application.

Figure 5.6 shows the application with a single instance of the custom MXML component.

FIGURE 5.6

An application with a component

Inserting a custom component instance in Design view

You also can instantiate the custom component in Design view by simply dragging it from Flex Builder's Components view.

1. Click Design to switch to Design view.

2. In the Components view in the lower-left corner of Flex Builder, open the Custom section. You should see your new custom component.

3. As shown in Figure 5.7, drag the custom component from the Components view into the application.

The component instance should appear in the application's Design view.

CAUTION When you drag a component into Design view and the component's namespace prefix hasn't been previously defined, Flex Builder creates an automatically numbered namespace prefix such as **ns1** (for "namespace 1"). It also creates the MXML code that instantiates the component using paired tags, instead of the preferred empty tag syntax. The resulting generated code looks like this:

```
<?xml version="1.0" encoding="utf-8"?>
<mx:Application xmlns:mx="http://www.adobe.com/2006/mxml"
  xmlns:ns1="components.*">
  <ns1:MyComponent>
  </ns1:MyComponent>
</mx:Application>
```

This code works fine, but you may decide to manually change the namespace to something more meaningful, such as the name of the folder in which the component source code is stored.

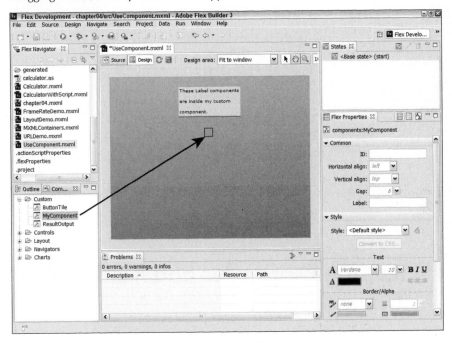

FIGURE 5.7

Dragging a custom component into an application

Instantiating a component with ActionScript

Since an MXML component is really an ActionScript class definition, you can instantiate the component with pure ActionScript code. As with any pre-built component in the Flex framework, you follow these steps:

- Create an `import` statement that refers to the component as a class.
- Declare a variable with its data type set to the component as a class.
- Instantiate the component using a no-arguments constructor method call.
- Add the component instance to the application's display list.

Listing 5.1 shows the code for an application that creates and displays a single instance of the custom component upon application startup.

ON the WEB The code in Listing 5.1 is available in the Web site files in the **chapter05** project's **src** folder as **UseComponentWithAS.mxml**.

LISTING 5.1

Instantiating a custom component with ActionScript

```
<?xml version="1.0" encoding="utf-8"?>
<mx:Application xmlns:mx="http://www.adobe.com/2006/mxml"
  layout="vertical" creationComplete="initApp()">
  <mx:Script>
    <![CDATA[
      import components.MyComponent;
      private function initApp():void
      {
        var comp:MyComponent = new MyComponent();
        this.addChild(comp);
      }
    ]]>
  </mx:Script>
</mx:Application>
```

Adding Properties and Methods to Components

Components and classes can have *member* objects. A member object is a pre-declared item that's instantiated along with the class. ActionScript classes support these member types:

- **Properties** to hold dynamic data values
- **Constants** to hold fixed data values
- **Methods** to execute actions
- **Events** to send messages to other parts of the application
- **Styles** to controls a visual object's presentation

In this section, I describe how to define properties, constants, and methods in an MXML component.

Component properties

A *property* is a variable that's owned by a class definition. In ActionScript 3, all variables are actually properties of some object. If you declare a variable in an application source file, that variable is actually a property of the application object.

Setting properties

The syntax to declare a property looks like this:

```
[access modifier] var [variable name]:[data type];
```

A `public` property named `currentValue` with a data type of `String` is declared with this code:

```
public var currentValue:String;
```

You can set the property's initial value upon object instantiation with this code:

```
public var currentValue:String = "Default value";
```

TIP In browser-based JavaScript, the `var` keyword is optional and can be used to control a variable's scope: A variable declared in a function with var is local to the function, while a variable declared without `var` is global to the current HTML page. In ActionScript, the `var` keyword is always used to mark any variable or property declaration.

TIP The use of post-colon syntax to statically type a variable is the subject of some controversy. This syntax is part of the ECMAScript recommendation and was implemented by Macromedia with the goal of standardization with the rest of the industry. Some Java developers find the syntax odd, because in Java static data typing is accomplished with the data type before the variable name:

```
public String currentValue;
```

The data typing result is the same, but the syntax is just turned around.

CROSS-REF The available access modifiers for variables and properties are described in Chapter 4.

CAUTION As with simple variable declarations, if you don't include an access modifier with a property or method declaration, the compiler generates a warning and the access for that member is set to the default of `internal`. In ActionScript 2, the same code would have resulted in a default access of `public` and no compiler warning would have been generated.

TIP If you want a property's data type to be dynamic, where you can assign any value at runtime, use this syntax:

```
public var myVar:*;
```

The * character means that the property's data type can be anything. This is possible because, unlike Java, ActionScript 3 is a loosely typed language that offers tools for strict typing when you need or want them.

Static properties

A *static property* is a value that's the same for all instances of the component; it also can be referred to by other parts of the application without having to instantiate the component at all. You make a property static by adding the `static` keyword after the access modifier:

```
public static var myStaticVar:String;
```

The variable declared above will have the same value for all instances of the component in which it's declared.

Making a property bindable

As described earlier in this chapter, properties are bindable only if you explicitly mark them with the [Bindable] metadata tag. A property that's marked as bindable always broadcasts changes in its value to objects within the component. A property that's also marked as public broadcasts changes to the application or other module that instantiates the component.

In Listing 5.2, a component has a bindable public variable named valueToDisplay. A Label control within the component displays the property's value.

LISTING 5.2

A component with a bindable public property

```
<?xml version="1.0" encoding="utf-8"?>
<mx:VBox xmlns:mx="http://www.adobe.com/2006/mxml">

  <mx:Script>
    <![CDATA[
      [Bindable]
      public var valueToDisplay:String;
    ]]>
  </mx:Script>

  <mx:Label text="{valueToDisplay}" fontSize="24"/>

</mx:VBox>
```

ON the WEB   The code in Listing 5.2 is available in the Web site files in the chapter05 project's src/components folder as CompWithBindableProp.mxml.

TIP   In an MXML component, each property that you want to be bindable needs its own [Bindable] tag. With ActionScript class definitions, you can mark all the class's properties as bindable with a single instance of the [Bindable] metadata tag placed before the class declaration.

TIP   You also can declare a property with MXML. For example, this code declares the same String property as in the previous example:

```
<mx:String id="valueToDisplay"/>
```

A property that's declared in this way is implicitly marked as public and bindable, so the public access modifier and the [Bindable] metadata tag aren't required.

Passing data to a component property

You can pass data to a component property with either dot syntax in ActionScript or MXML property declarations. To pass data using an MXML property declaration, declare the property as an XML attribute of the object declaration and set the value as either a literal or binding expression.

This is an example of passing a literal value:

```
<components:MyComponent valueToDisplay="Hello World"/>
```

This is an example of using a binding expression:

```
<components:MyComponent valueToDisplay="{aBindableValue}"/>
```

In either case, the value is passed to the public property. And because that property is marked as bindable within the component, its new value is then passed to any control or expression that's bound to it.

Using constants

A *constant* is a property whose value is set at the time of declaration and never changes. Common uses of constants in ActionScript include:

- Aliases for literal values within components that are referred to multiple times. For example, this private constant represents the literal string "All Products":

  ```
  private const ALLPRODUCTS:String="All Products";
  ```

- Aliases for properties of objects that are used externally. For example, custom event classes frequently have static public constants whose values are names of custom events for which the current event class is used:

  ```
  public static const SELECTED:String="selected";
  ```

> **TIP** By object-oriented convention, constant identifiers are spelled in all uppercase, as in `SELECTED`. This distinguishes them in your code from property identifiers, which are spelled with an initial lowercase character and optional mixed case thereafter.

> **TIP** Because a constant's value never changes, it doesn't make sense to make it bindable. In fact, if you mark a constant declaration with the `[Bindable]` metadata tag, a compiler error results.

Component methods

A *method* is a function that belongs to a class or component definition. The dictionary meaning of the word "method" is "a way of doing something, especially a systematic way." This makes sense in the context of class definitions; a method defines how a class accomplishes a particular task.

Depending on your background with various programming languages, you might think of a method as a *function* or a *subroutine*. In fact, methods are marked in ActionScript with the `function` keyword.

Defining methods

Use this syntax to define a method in a component:

```
[access modifier] function [methodName](
[argument declarations] ):[data type]
{
}
```

A sample method might look like this:

```
public function getValue():String
{
  return someValue;
}
```

As with properties, methods are marked with one of these four access modifiers:

- `public`: All code through an application can call the method.
- `private`: Only code in the current component or class can call the method.
- `protected`: Only code in the current component or class, or any its subclasses, can call the method.
- `internal`: Only code in the current component or class, or any other component or class in the same package, can call the method.

As with properties, if you don't include an access modifier with a method declaration, the access defaults to `internal`.

The code in Listing 5.3 creates a component with two `public` properties named `firstName` and `lastName` and one `public` method named `getFullName()` that returns a concatenated string. The component also contains two `Label` controls that display the current values of the two properties.

LISTING 5.3

A component with a public method

```
<?xml version="1.0" encoding="utf-8"?>
<mx:VBox xmlns:mx="http://www.adobe.com/2006/mxml">
  <mx:Script>
    <![CDATA[
      [Bindable]
      public var firstName:String;
      [Bindable]
      public var lastName:String
      public function getFullName():String
      {
        return firstName + " " + lastName;
      }
    ]]>
```

```
  </mx:Script>
  <mx:Label text="First Name: {firstName}"/>
  <mx:Label text="Last Name: {lastName}"/>
</mx:VBox>
```

ON the WEB The code in Listing 5.3 is available in the Web site files in the **chapter05** project's **src/components** folder as **UseComponentWithAS.mxml**.

Calling component methods

You call component methods with either ActionScript statements or binding expressions. Listing 5.4 shows an application that uses the component in Listing 5.3 and displays the concatenated value returned from the component's public method.

LISTING 5.4

An application calling a component method in a binding expression

```
<?xml version="1.0" encoding="utf-8"?>
<mx:Application xmlns:mx="http://www.adobe.com/2006/mxml"
  layout="vertical" xmlns:components="components.*">

  <components:CompWithMethods
    id="myComp"
    firstName="Peter"
    lastName="Programmer"/>

  <mx:Label text="{myComp.getFullName()}"/>

</mx:Application>
```

ON the WEB The code in Listing 5.4 is available in the Web site files in the **chapter05** project's **src** folder as **UseComponent.mxml**.

When you call a component method in a binding expression, it executes only upon initial object construction (for example, upon application startup). There's no way in this syntax to tell the Flex Framework that the method should be called again:

```
<mx:Label text="{myComp.getFullName()}"/>
```

However, it's a simple matter to call the function with an ActionScript statement. In Listing 5.5, the component's property values are passed in with expressions that bind to visual controls in the application, and the application calls the component's getFullName() method to retrieve and display the resulting concatenated value.

LISTING 5.5

Calling a component method with an ActionScript statement

```
<?xml version="1.0" encoding="utf-8"?>
<mx:Application xmlns:mx="http://www.adobe.com/2006/mxml"
  layout="vertical" xmlns:components="components.*">

  <components:CompWithMethods id="myComp"
    firstName="{firstNameInput.text}"
    lastName="{lastNameInput.text}"/>

  <mx:TextInput id="firstNameInput"/>
  <mx:TextInput id="lastNameInput"/>

  <mx:Label id="fullNameOutput"/>
  <mx:Button label="Get Full Name"
    click="fullNameOutput.text=myComp.getFullName()"/>

</mx:Application>
```

ON the WEB The code in Listing 5.4 is available in the Web site files in the **chapter05** project's **src** folder as **CallComponentMethodWithAS.mxml**.

Using Component Libraries

A component library is an archive file in zip format that has a file extension of .swc. Component libraries that are compatible with Flex 3 applications can be created in three tools:

- Flash CS3
- The Flex SDK's compc command-line component compiler
- A Flex Library Project created and managed in Flex Builder

In this section, I describe how to create and use a component library in Flex Builder 3 with a Flex Library Project.

Creating component libraries

A Flex Library Project is designed to create a component library: an archive file that contains compiled MXML components and ActionScript classes. Unlike a Flex Project, which contains complete applications, a Library Project contains only the building blocks of an application. Its purpose is to create component library files that contain pre-built ActionScript code and related assets that can be dropped into a Flex application for immediate use.

Creating a library project

Follow these steps to create a Library Project in Flex Builder 3:

1. Select File ⇨ New ⇨ Flex Library Project from the Flex Builder menu.

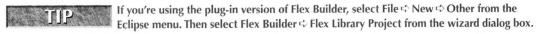

> **TIP** If you're using the plug-in version of Flex Builder, select File ⇨ New ⇨ Other from the Eclipse menu. Then select Flex Builder ⇨ Flex Library Project from the wizard dialog box.

2. In the New Flex Library Project wizard, shown in Figure 5.8, provide a Project name, select the Use default location checkbox and the Use default SDK radio button, and indicate whether AIR libraries should be included.

FIGURE 5.8

The first screen of the New Flex Library Project wizard

3. Click Next.

4. In the next screen, shown in Figure 5.9, browse to select locations for Main source folder and Output folder.

5. If any assets such as image or XML files should be included with the component library, click the Assets tab.

> **TIP** When you first create the Library Project, you may not have assets to add right away. You can easily add assets to the project later through the Project Properties.

6. Click Finish to create the project.

FIGURE 5.9

The second screen of the New Flex Library Project wizard

When a Flex Library Project is first created, a compiler error often indicates that nothing is currently in the library, as shown in Figure 5.10.

FIGURE 5.10

A compiler error in an empty Flex Library Project

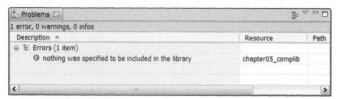

Creating a project's folder structure

As with components that are built in a Flex Project, you'll commonly create subfolders that represent the packages in which various components are stored. Unlike Flex Projects, which have a default `src` folder that acts as the source code root, a Flex Library Project sets the project root as the default source root. With this default setting, the package subfolders should be created under the project root.

Follow these steps to create a component in a Library Project:

1. If the project doesn't have a subfolder in which to create the component, right-click the project in the Flex Navigator view and select New ⇨ Folder.

2. In the New Folder wizard, shown in Figure 5.11, enter the new folder name and click Finish.

FIGURE 5.11

Creating a project subfolder

3. Right-click the folder in which you want to create the component, and select New ➪ MXML Component.

4. Create the component using the same options as in a Flex Project: Enter the Filename, select which component the custom component is based on, and enter or clear any width or height properties.

5. Click Finish to create the component.

After the component has been built, look in the project's output folder (the output folder's default name is bin-debug). You'll find a new file with a name consisting of the project name and a file extension of .swc. For example, a Library Project named MyCompLibrary generates a component library file named MyCompLibrary.swc.

Incorporating component libraries

You incorporate component libraries into Flex applications in two ways:

- Add a component library to a Flex Project's source path.
- Copy the component library into Flex Project's libs folder.

Adding a component library to a project's build path

Each Flex Project has a *build path* that consists of a list of folders and component libraries whose components and classes are available to the current project. The build path includes a source path of folders in which ActionScript and MXML source code is stored, and a library path of component libraries. The build path is set in the project properties dialog box.

Follow these steps to add a component library to a Flex Project's build path:

1. In the Flex Navigator view, select a Flex Project.

2. Select Project ➪ Properties from the Flex Builder menu.

> **TIP** You also can right-click the project in the Flex Navigator view and select Properties from the context menu.

3. Select Flex Build Path in the Project Properties dialog box.

4. As shown in Figure 5.12, click the Library path tab.

The Library path screen allows you to add the component libraries in these ways:

- For Library Projects that are managed in the current Flex Builder workspace, click Add Project. As shown in Figure 5.13, select the Library Project and click OK. All components and classes in the selected Library Project become available to the current Flex Project.

- For component libraries that you've built in another workspace or received from another developer, you can do either of the following:

  - Add a folder containing one or more .swc files.

  - Add an individual .swc file to the Flex Project build path.

FIGURE 5.12

Setting the Flex Build Path in the Project Properties dialog box

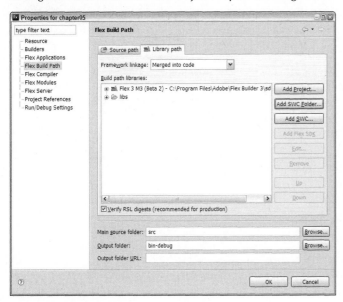

FIGURE 5.13

Adding a Library Project to a Flex Project's Library path

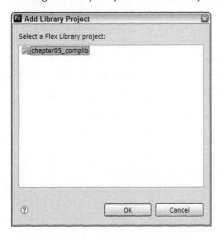

Using the libs folder

Every new Flex Project has a folder named `libs` that's already a part of the project's library path.

NEW FEATURE The `libs` folder has been added to the default Flex project structure in Flex Builder 3. Flex Builder 2 had tools that would allow you to create such an automatically included library folder, but didn't do the work for you.

To use the `libs` folder, copy a .swc file into the project's `libs` folder, as shown in Figure 5.14. The classes and component in the component library are now immediately available to the Flex Project.

FIGURE 5.14

A component library in a Flex Project's `libs` folder

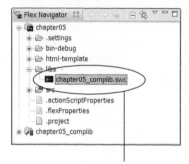

Component library

CAUTION When you copy a component library file that you created into the `libs` folder, you detach it from the Flex Library project that manages its source code. Each time you modify the library's code, you have to then re-copy the compiled library to the Flex project to make the modified code available. The `libs` folder is most effectively used when you add libraries that you have received from other developers, when you aren't managing the library's source code.

Regardless of how you create and use a component library, it's a valuable architecture that lets you package and manage one or more components for use and reuse in your Flex applications.

TIP You can't run an MXML application from directly within a Flex library project. During library project development, you should create a Flex project with at least one application that's used to test library project components and classes.

Summary

In this chapter, I described the use of binding expression and MXML components in developing Flex applications. You learned the following:

- Bindings are used to move data between objects and expressions.
- Bindings can be created with binding expressions or the `<mx:Binding/>` tag.
- A binding creates a broadcaster/listener relationship between two ActionScript expressions.
- An MXML component is a building block of a Flex application that encapsulates functionality.
- MXML components are frequently used to create the view modules in a model-view-controller application architecture.
- MXML components are really classes that support properties, methods, and other members of the ActionScript class architecture.
- Component libraries can be used to package and manage components and classes.
- Component libraries are useful for sharing code with multiple projects and applications.

Chapter 6

Debugging Flex Applications

Flex Builder 3 includes powerful tools that allow you to easily debug and fine-tune your applications. Of course, software without bugs is a myth—at least at the beginning of a software development project. In many cases, the question of whether you complete your application within the time you originally estimate depends on how quickly you can find and fix an application's defects, or bugs.

As with many good integrated development environments, Flex Builder includes a variety of tools to help you find and fix an application's issues and understand what's happening inside the application at runtime, including these tools:

- The trace() function sends runtime messages to the Flex Builder console and other logging targets.

- The <mx:TraceTarget/> tag defines runtime tracing for network communications.

- Breakpoints suspend application execution and allow inspection of internal application state at runtime.

- Variable and expression tools allow you to inspect the value of various ActionScript expressions.

- Profiling tools allow you to see what's happening at runtime in terms of performance and memory usage.

In this chapter, I describe the tools you can use to debug and test your Flex applications.

ON the WEB To use the sample code for this chapter, import the **chapter06.zip** Flex project archive file from the Web site files into your Flex Builder workspace.

Debugging Basics

Debugging simply means that when you run an application, you want special debugging information that helps you find and fix application issues. Debugging with Flex requires the right kind of file and the right kind of runtime environment. Before executing debugging tasks, you need to be sure of two things:

- You are using the debug version of the application.
- You are running the application in debug mode.

The debug version of the application

When you create a Flex Project in Flex Builder 3, the New Flex Project wizard creates an *output* folder in which the debug version of the application and its supporting files are created. As described in Chapter 3, the application's debug version file size is significantly larger than the release version that you deploy to your Web site or users' desktops because it includes special information and functionality that can be used in a debugging session both by Flex Builder's debugging tools and by the fdb command-line debugger.

The default name of the output folder is bin-debug. The name of the compiled debug version of the application is the same as the main application source file, but it has the .swf file extension.

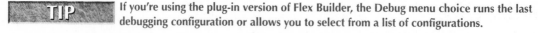 In Flex Projects that don't use an application server, this is normally a subfolder of the project's source root folder, such as src/bin-debug. In projects that do use an application server, the bin-debug folder is typically created under the document root of the testing Web server, and then made accessible in the Flex Navigator view through an Eclipse linked folder.

Running an application in debug mode

Follow these steps to run an application in debug mode:

1. Open the application you want to debug in Flex Builder.
2. Select Run ➪ Debug [application source file] from the Flex Builder menu.

TIP If you're using the plug-in version of Flex Builder, the Debug menu choice runs the last debugging configuration or allows you to select from a list of configurations.

You also can debug an application with the Debug button on the toolbar. This button is next to the Run button and can be used in two ways:

- When you click the Debug button, Flex Builder launches a debug session with the currently displayed application, or the default application if the current file is a component or class source file.
- When you click the arrow on the edge of Debug button, as shown in Figure 6.1, you see a list of the current project's applications and can select one to debug.

FIGURE 6.1

Launching a debug session

Selecting an application to debug

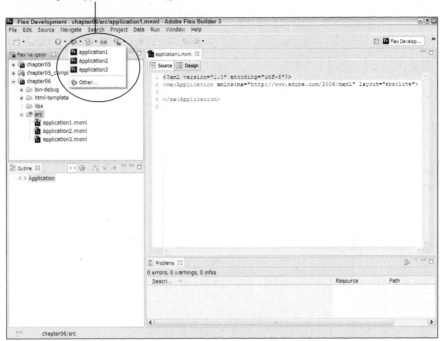

When you debug a Web application, it opens in the browser with the same URL as when you run in standard mode. You can tell that a debug session is running in Flex Builder though: As shown in Figure 6.2, Flex Builder's Console view appears whenever a debug session starts and displays a debugging message indicating which file is being debugged.

FIGURE 6.2

The Console view during a debug session

Managing the Console view

The Console view in its default state displays text messages without any word wrapping. You can change this behavior through the view's preferences:

1. Right-click anywhere in the Console view, and select Preferences.

2. As shown in Figure 6.3, select the Fixed width console option and set a line length between 80 characters (the default) and 1000 characters.

The Console view preferences dialog box

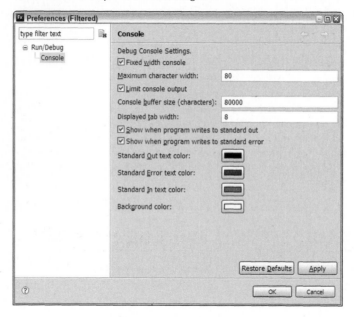

3. Change any other options, and click OK.

The Console view now word wraps long lines so you don't have to scroll horizontally to see entire messages.

Terminating a debugging session

You want to always explicitly terminate a debugging session before trying to run or debug an application again. You can terminate a debugging session in many ways:

■ Select Run ➪ Terminate from the Flex Builder menu.

■ As shown in Figure 6.4, click the square red Terminate button in the Console view.

- Click the square red Terminate button in the Debug view (visible in the Flex Debugging perspective).

- Close the browser in which the application is running (for a Web application).

- Close the application (for a desktop application).

FIGURE 6.4

The Console view's Terminate button

Terminate Debugging

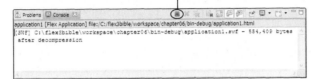

TIP When you terminate a Web application's debugging session from within Flex Builder, the browser sometimes closes automatically, depending on which Web browser and operating system you're using and whether any other tabs or browser windows are open. For example, provided that no other sites are open, Internet Explorer and Firefox on Windows always close automatically. Firefox on the Mac doesn't always close automatically. The fact that this behavior differs from one operating system to another is not a cause for concern.

Using trace() and the Logging API

Flex gives you the ability to generate and send logging messages to Flex Builder and other logging targets at runtime. Tracing is typically useful when you're trying to get runtime information about the following:

- Variable values

- Order of application execution

- Whether various bits of code are being executed as expected

In its simplest use, logging is accomplished through use of the `trace()` method. More advanced logging techniques are also available through an interface known as the Logging API.

Using the trace() function

The `trace()` function is *global* to Flash Player; that is, it's always available without your having to reference or import an ActionScript class. The purpose of the `trace()` method is to send a text message to a logging target. In its simplest form, `trace` is called with a `String` value:

```
trace('A tracing message');
```

You also can pass in variables and concatenated expressions that can result in a `String`:

```
trace("The value of myVariable is " + myVariable);
```

In fact, any object that can serialize to a `String` can be passed to `trace()`. In this example, an `Array` of `String` values is passed to `trace()`:

```
trace(['hello', 'world']);
```

The resulting trace message looks like this:

```
hello,world
```

Trace messages in Flex Builder's Console view

When you debug a Flex application, the value you pass into `trace()` is displayed in Flex Builder's Console view.

TIP Calls to `trace()` are ignored when you run, rather than debug, an application. These calls are also stripped from an application's release version, so you can leave any calls to `trace()` in an application without affecting runtime performance or file size.

Try these steps to see the `trace()` method at work:

1. Create a new Flex application with the following code:

```
<?xml version="1.0" encoding="utf-8"?>
<mx:Application xmlns:mx="http://www.adobe.com/2006/mxml"
  layout="vertical">

  <mx:Button label="Call Trace" click="trace('Button
  clicked')"/>

</mx:Application>
```

2. Click Debug or press F11 to debug the application.

3. Click Call Trace in the application to call `trace()`.

4. Switch back to Flex Builder, and look at the Console view.

   As shown in Figure 6.5, you should see the tracing message displayed in the Console view.

A tracing message in the Console view

Tracing message in the Console view

Sending tracing messages to flashlog.txt

Messages also can be saved to a text file named flashlog.txt. The flashlog.txt file is created by the debug Flash Player in a particular folder on your system.

Configuring Flash Player with mm.cfg

You configure the use of flashlog.txt with another file named mm.cfg. This file contains parameters that control what messages are sent to, and saved in, the file. The location of mm.cfg differs by operating system. Table 6.1 shows the location for each operating system that's supported by Flash Player.

Location of mm.cfg

Operating System	Location
Macintosh OS X	/Library/Application Support/Macromedia
Windows 95/98/ME	%HOMEDRIVE%\%HOMEPATH%
Windows 2000/XP	C:\Documents and Settings\username
Windows Vista	C:\Users\username
Linux	/home/username

To save both error reporting and tracing messages to the flashlog.txt file, add these parameters on their own separate lines in mm.cfg:

```
ErrorReportingEnable=1
TraceOutputFileEnable=1
```

After these settings have been created, the next time you debug a Flex application or Flash document, the flashlog.txt is created automatically. Each time you call trace(), the message is saved to the file, in addition to being sent to Flex Builder's Console view.

Location of flashlog.txt

The `flashlog.txt` file is placed in a particular location that differs by operating system. Table 6.2 shows the location of `flashlog.txt` for each operating system on which Flash Player is supported.

TABLE 6.2	
Location of flashlog.txt	
Operating System	**Location**
Macintosh OS X	/Users/username/Library/Preferences/Macromedia/Flash Player/Logs/
Windows 95/98/ME/2000/XP	C:\Documents and Settings\username\Application Data\Macromedia\Flash Player\Logs
Windows Vista	C:\Users\username\AppData\Roaming\Macromedia\Flash Player\Logs
Linux	/home/username/.macromedia/Flash_Player/Logs/

TIP   Both `mm.cfg` and `flashlog.txt` are simple text files and can be viewed and edited with any text editor.

Using the Logging API

The Logging API is an advanced architecture that lets you filter logging messages that are generated by the Flex Framework, and send messages to a logging target of your choice. The Logging API consists of an ActionScript interface named `ILogger`, a class that implements ILogger named `LogLogger`, a singleton class named `Log`, and a predefined tracing target class named `TraceTarget`. You can extend the API by creating your own versions of `ILogger` implementations and tracing targets, but you also can make very good use of the API with just these pre-built components.

TIP   ActionScript 3 allows developers to use interfaces to define the required elements of a class definition. An interface isn't the same thing as a class. For example, it doesn't implement any code in its method definitions, and you can't create an instance of an interface directly. Its purpose is to establish a contract that must be fulfilled by any classes that claim to implement its members.

In the Flex framework, interfaces are always named within an initial uppercase `I`, followed by a descriptive name. For example, the interface named `ILogger` can be described simply as "the Logger interface."

Using the Log class

You get started with the Logging API by creating a `Logger` object using the `Log` class's static `getLogger()` method. You can create custom logger objects that are sensitive to particular categories of events, and you can automatically include that category information in logging messages.

The syntax for `getLogger()` is:

```
private var myLogger:ILogger = Log.getLogger("myCategory");
```

The category you pass into `getLogger()` must be a non-blank string. If the category you provide is registered by an existing class that implements `ILogger`, you get an instance of that class. Otherwise, you get an instance of a class named `mx.logging.LogLogger` that implements basic logging functions.

The Logging API supports these levels, in ascending order of panic:

- ALL
- DEBUG
- INFO
- WARN
- ERROR
- FATAL

The Log class implements these methods that allow you to determine whether a logging target has been defined for various logging levels:

- isDebug():Boolean
- isInfo():Boolean
- isWarn():Boolean
- isError():Boolean
- isFatal():Boolean

Using Logger objects

A logger class implements the `ILogger` interface. The interface includes these methods to send messages to a logging target:

- debug(message:String, ... rest):void
- error(message:String, ... rest):void
- fatal(message:String, ... rest):void
- info(message:String, ... rest):void
- warn(message:String, ... rest):void
- log(level:int, message:String, ... rest):void

After you've created a logger object, you send a logging message with one of the above methods. Most methods create a message with a specific logging level. For example, to send a message with a level of DEBUG, you call the logger object's `debug()` method:

```
myLogger.debug("My debug message");
```

The debugging levels are defined as constants in a class named `mx.logging.LogEventLevel`. You also can send logging messages with the logger object's `log()` method and explicitly pass in the appropriate level:

```
myLogger.log(LogEventLevel.DEBUG, "My debug message");
```

> **TIP** The use of the `LogEventLevel` class' constants to select a logging level is considered a best practice. As with event names, any typos in the names of the constants result in compiler errors, as opposed to runtime errors or silent failures that you may encounter when using simple strings.

Logging levels are used to filter which messages are handled by various logging targets.

Self-logging components

The Logging API can be used to create a self-logging component. For example, the application in Listing 6.1 is a `Button` component that logs each click event to a logging target.

LISTING 6.1

A self-logging button component

```
<?xml version="1.0" encoding="utf-8"?>
<mx:Button xmlns:mx="http://www.adobe.com/2006/mxml"
  creationComplete="init()">
  <mx:Script>
    <![CDATA[
      import mx.logging.Log;
      import mx.logging.ILogger;
      private var myLogger:ILogger = Log.getLogger("Button Events");
      private function init():void {
        addEventListener(MouseEvent.CLICK, logEvent);
      }
      private function logEvent(event:MouseEvent):void {
        if (Log.isDebug()) {
          myLogger.debug("LoggingButton " +
          event.target.id + " was clicked");
        }
      }
    ]]>
  </mx:Script>
</mx:Button>
```

> **ON the WEB** The code in Listing 6.1 is available in the Web site files in the `chapter06` project's `src/debug` folder as `LoggingButton.mxml`.

 The code sample in Listing 6.1 uses the Flex event model to handle component events. The event model is described in Chapter 7.

Using tracing targets

A tracing target is a class that can receive and process tracing messages. The `TraceTarget` class is included in the Flex Framework and is ideally suited to use in Flex applications.

When you use the `TraceTarget` class, the output of the Logging API behaves just like output you create with the `trace()` method. The messages appear in Flex Builder's Console view and, if you've configured Flash Player as described above, are saved in `flashlog.txt`.

The `TraceTarget` class supports these properties:

- `fieldSeparator:String`: A string value to separate other values included in a logging message; defaults to a single space character
- `includeCategory:Boolean`: Indicates whether to include the logging message's category in the logging message
- `includeDate:Boolean`: Indicates whether to include the current date in the logging message
- `includeLevel:Boolean`: Indicates whether to include the logging level in the logging message
- `includeTime:Boolean`: Indicates whether to include the current time in the logging message
- `level:int`: A logging level that this target will handle; defaults to `LogEventLevel.ALL`

You can instantiate `TraceTarget` with either MXML or ActionScript. Use this syntax to instantiate the class in its simplest form:

```
<mx:TraceTarget/>
```

 The `TraceTarget` MXML declaration does not require an `id` property. Unless you need to call its methods or properties directly, the object can be declared anonymously.

In its default form, `TraceTarget` becomes a tracing target that handles all logging levels. However, the tracing messages you see include only the messages themselves and none of the other available logging data such as date, time, level, and category. To include all that information and separate the data elements from each other with a | (pipe) character, use this syntax:

```
<mx:TraceTarget id="myTarget"
  includeCategory="true"
  includeLevel="true"
  includeDate="true"
  includeTime="true"
  fieldSeparator="|"/>
```

Finally, to make a tracing target display messages only for a particular logging level, use this syntax:

```
<mx:TraceTarget id="myTarget"
  includeCategory="true"
  includeLevel="true"
  includeDate="true"
  includeTime="true"
  fieldSeparator="|"
  level="{LogEventLevel.DEBUG}"/>
```

 In the last example, the `LogEventLevel` class would have to be imported before being referenced in the `TraceTarget.level` binding expression:

```
import mx.logging.LogEventLevel;
```

The resulting trace output generated by the self-logging button component in Listing 6.1 would look like this:

```
12/4/2007|12:09:39.256|[DEBUG]|buttonEvents|LoggingButton myLoggingButton was
  clicked
```

The application in Listing 6.2 uses the self-logging button and a `TraceTarget` object. The `TraceTarget` object is configured only to handle messages with a logging level of DEBUG and to include all available information in each message.

LISTING 6.2

An application with a self-logging component

```
<?xml version="1.0" encoding="utf-8"?>
<mx:Application xmlns:mx="http://www.adobe.com/2006/mxml"
  layout="vertical" xmlns:debug="debug.*">
  <mx:Script>
    <![CDATA[
      import mx.logging.LogEventLevel;
    ]]>
  </mx:Script>

  <mx:TraceTarget id="myTarget"
    includeCategory="true"
    includeLevel="true"
    includeDate="true"
    includeTime="true"
    level="{LogEventLevel.DEBUG}"
    fieldSeparator="|"/>

  <debug:LoggingButton id="myLoggingButton" label="Log Click Event"/>

</mx:Application>
```

ON the WEB   The code in Listing 6.2 is available in the Web site files in the `chapter06` project's `src` folder as `UseLoggingButton.mxml`.

The Logging API can help you build applications that keep you informed about their actions during a debugging session without having to make constant calls to the `trace()` method. With some advanced ActionScript programming, you also can create your own custom logger and tracing target classes.

Using Breakpoints

A breakpoint allows you to suspend application execution at runtime and inspect the application's current state. Once in a breakpoint, you can look at variable values, evaluate arbitrary ActionScript expressions, and take other actions that help you figure out what's happening.

Setting and clearing breakpoints

Breakpoints can be set on any line that includes at least one ActionScript statement. For example, this code declares a button component but has no ActionScript code:

```
<mx:Button label="Debug"/>
```

If you set a breakpoint on the line containing that MXML declaration, the breakpoint is ignored by the debugger.

If, however, the same MXML declaration includes an event handler that executes some ActionScript code, it becomes a valid target for a breakpoint:

```
<mx:Button label="Debug" click="clickHandler()"/>
```

Because this version of the declaration executes an ActionScript statement, placing a breakpoint on that line successfully suspends the application when the user clicks the button.

Setting and removing breakpoints in an MXML or ActionScript editor

You can set or remove a breakpoint in an MXML or ActionScript editor. To do so, perform one of these actions:

- Place the cursor on the line where you want the breakpoint, and press Ctrl+Shift+B.
- Double-click the line number in the editor.
- As shown in Figure 6.6, right-click the line number in the editor, and select Toggle Breakpoint.

FIGURE 6.6

Right-click a line number to see this context menu, and select Toggle Breakpoint.

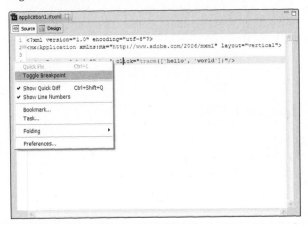

As shown in Figure 6.7, the breakpoint appears as a small dot to the left of the line number.

FIGURE 6.7

A Breakpoint represented by a small icon next to a line number

Breakpoint indicator

Using the Breakpoints view

Flex Builder's Breakpoints view shows you the application's current breakpoints and allows you to add, remove, enable, or disable breakpoints as needed.

The Breakpoints view is displayed in the Flex Debugging perspective. To use the Breakpoints view:

1. Select Window ➪ Perspective ➪ Flex Debugging from the Flex Builder menu.

2. As shown in Figure 6.8, click the Breakpoints tab in the upper-right corner of the Flex Builder interface.

FIGURE 6.8

The Breakpoints tab in the Flex Debugging perspective

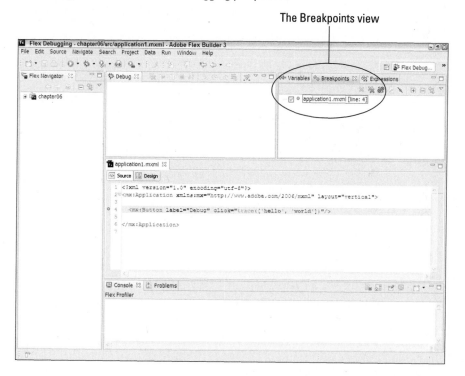

The Breakpoints view, shown in Figure 6.9, displays all breakpoints for the current project.

FIGURE 6.9

The Breakpoints view

Show Breakpoints Supported
by Selected Target

Remove All   Go to File

Remove   Skip All

The Breakpoints view includes these tools:

- **Remove:** Removes the currently selected breakpoint
- **Remove All:** Removes all breakpoints in the current project
- **Show Breakpoints:** Supported by Selected Target: shows breakpoints only for a selected debug target
- **Go to File for Breakpoint:** Opens file for current breakpoint and moves cursor to that position
- **Skip All Breakpoints:** Causes debugging session to ignore breakpoints

Click the appropriate button to use any of the above tools. The Remove All Breakpoints tool requires you to confirm the operation.

Exporting breakpoints to an external file

The Breakpoints view allows you to export and import breakpoint definitions to external files. A breakpoints file has a file extension of .bkpt. Follow these steps to export breakpoints:

1. Right-click anywhere in the Breakpoints view, and select Export Breakpoints from the context menu.

2. In the Export Breakpoints dialog box, shown in Figure 6.10, select the following:

   - Which breakpoints you want to export
   - The file to which you want to export breakpoints
   - The Overwrite existing file without warning checkbox (if you want to overwrite your existing file)

3. Click Finish to create the breakpoints file.

FIGURE 6.10

The Export Breakpoints dialog box

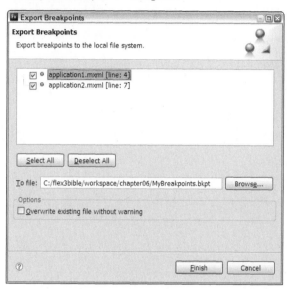

A breakpoints export file is in XML format. Listing 6.3 shows the contents of a typical breakpoints file.

LISTING 6.3

An exported breakpoints file

```xml
<?xml version="1.0" encoding="UTF-8"?>
<breakpoints>
 <breakpoint enabled="true" persistant="true" registered="true">
  <resource path="/chapter06/src/application1.mxml" type="1"/>
  <marker lineNumber="4"
    type="com.adobe.flexbuilder.debug.flash.lineBreakpoint.marker">
   <attrib name="org.eclipse.debug.core.enabled" value="true"/>
   <attrib name="org.eclipse.debug.core.id"
    value="com.adobe.flexbuilder.debug"/>
   <attrib name="message"
    value="Line breakpoint: application1.mxml [line: 4]"/>
   <attrib
    name="com.adobe.flexbuilder.debug.flash.instantiationInfoCount"
    value="1"/>
  </marker>
 </breakpoint>
```

continued

LISTING 6.3   *(continued)*

```
<breakpoint enabled="true" persistant="true" registered="true">
 <resource path="/chapter06/src/application2.mxml" type="1"/>
  <marker lineNumber="7"
   type="com.adobe.flexbuilder.debug.flash.lineBreakpoint.marker">
   <attrib name="org.eclipse.debug.core.enabled" value="true"/>
   <attrib name="org.eclipse.debug.core.id"
    value="com.adobe.flexbuilder.debug"/>
   <attrib name="message"
    value="Line breakpoint: application2.mxml [line: 7]"/>
   <attrib
    name="com.adobe.flexbuilder.debug.flash.instantiationInfoCount"
    value="0"/>
   <attrib
  name="com.adobe.flexbuilder.debug.flash.instantiationOkCount"
    value="0"/>
  </marker>
 </breakpoint>
</breakpoints>
```

Importing breakpoints from an external breakpoint file

Follow these steps to import an external breakpoints file:

1. Right-click anywhere in the Breakpoints view, and select Import Breakpoints from the context menu.

2. In the Import Breakpoints dialog box, shown in Figure 6.11, select these options, if appropriate:

   ▨ Whether you want to update existing breakpoints

   ▨ Whether you want to automatically create breakpoint working sets

3. Click Finish to import the breakpoints file.

The breakpoints in the external file are imported and are immediately available in the Breakpoints view.

FIGURE 6.11

Importing a breakpoints file

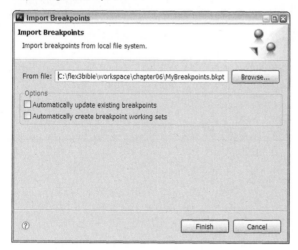

Using breakpoints in a debugging session

After you've set breakpoints, you can use them during a debugging session by executing the code on which the breakpoints are set.

When an application is running in debug mode and is suspended at a breakpoint, Flex Builder tries to take system focus. If you are not currently using the Flex Debugging perspective, a dialog box, shown in Figure 6.12, prompts you to switch to that perspective.

FIGURE 6.12

When a breakpoint has been activated, you're prompted to open the Flex Debugging perspective with the Confirm Perspective Switch dialog box.

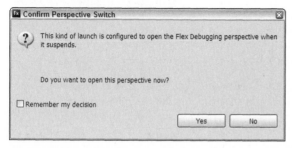

TIP The Confirm Perspective Switch dialog box has an option that allows you to remember the decision to switch to the Flex Debugging perspective when you encounter a breakpoint. If you select this option, Flex Builder always switches to this perspective automatically in future uses of breakpoints. This can be turned on and off by checking an option in the Run/Debug section of Flex Builder's Preferences dialog box.

After a breakpoint has been activated, Flex Builder shows you the current code execution position with the Debug Current Instruction Pointer, shown in Figure 6.13. If you move the cursor over the pointer icon, you see a pop-up window displaying information about the current line.

FIGURE 6.13

The Debug Current Instruction Pointer and current line information

Inspecting variables and expressions

When a breakpoint is active during a debugging session, Flex Builder allows you to inspect values of variables and objects that are in the application's scope. You can use two views for this purpose:

- The Variables view
- The Expressions view

Using the Variables view

The Variables view displays a tree of declared variables and object properties that are in scope at the point of the current instruction. Information in the Variables view is available only during a breakpoint; when you resume application execution, the Variables view no longer displays data.

The Variables view always has a tree item labeled this. The item refers to the application when the breakpoint is on a line of code in the Application scope, or to the current component or class when the breakpoint is in that scope.

As shown in Figure 6.14, when you click the expansion icon with the + character next to this, you see a list of all properties of the application or current object. A tree item representing an object has an inherited branch that displays properties declared in the current object's inheritance hierarchy.

NEW FEATURE Flex Builder 3 added the `inherited` branch to separate properties that are declared within the current class from those declared in its superclasses.

FIGURE 6.14

The Variables view

TIP The Variables tree is *recursive*; that is, you can click down to any object within the application, and then click the `inherited` ⇨ `$parent` item under the button and return to the `Application` object.

When you place a breakpoint inside a function, the Variables view displays tree items for any variables that are declared within the function. For example, the following code declares a variable named myVar data typed as a `Number`:

```
private function myFunction():void
{
  var myVar:Number=1;
} //place breakpoint here
```

When you stop code execution with a breakpoint on the function's final line, the resulting Variables view displays the value of myVar as 1, as shown in Figure 6.15.

FIGURE 6.15

Displaying a local variable in the Variables view

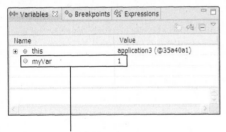

A local variable

Using the Expressions view

In many cases, evaluating an arbitrary ActionScript expression is useful. Here are some cases that come to mind:

- An expression that's deeply nested in the Variable view and hard to locate
- A compound expression that executes calculations that aren't pre-declared in the application code

The Expressions view is available in the Flex Debugging perspective and lets you evaluate these expressions easily. As with the Variables view, information in the Expressions view is available only during a breakpoint; when you resume application execution, the Expressions view no longer displays data.

To use the Expressions view, first click the Expressions tab in the Flex Debugging perspective's upper-right area, shown in Figure 6.16.

FIGURE 6.16

The Expressions tab

Expressions tab

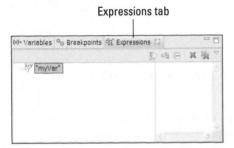

Adding an expression

You can add an expression either in the Expressions view or in the MXML or ActionScript editor that refers to an expression.

To add an expression in the Expressions view, right-click anywhere in the view and select Add Watch Expression from the context menu. Type the expression into the Add Watch Expression dialog box, shown in Figure 6.17.

FIGURE 6.17

Adding a watch expression

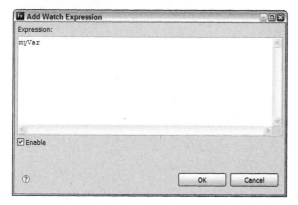

To add an expression from within an MXML ActionScript editor, right-click the expression in the code and select Watch "<variable name>" from the context menu. You should see the expression added to the Expressions view.

TIP You also can evaluate a pre-coded expression during a breakpoint in an MXML or ActionScript editor by moving the mouse over the expression. A tool tip is displayed showing the expression's name and current value.

Controlling application execution with the Debug view

When a breakpoint is active in a debugging session, Flex Builder's Debug view lets you step through, resume, or terminate application execution. The Debug view, shown in Figure 6.18, has these tools:

- **Resume:** This resumes code execution. If a breakpoint is encountered prior to allowing you to interact with the application, you return to Flex Builder. Otherwise, you can switch back to the application and continue interactions.

- **Suspend:** When an application is running, selecting this tool suspends the application without a predefined breakpoint and allows you to inspect variables and expressions.

- **Terminate:** This terminates the debugging session. The Terminate button in the Console view is identical in appearance and function.

- **Disconnect:** This disconnects the debugger when debugging remotely.

- **Step Into:** When called with the cursor on a function call, this steps into the function call.

- **Step Over:** When called with the cursor on a function call, this executes the function and moves to the next line of code.

- **Step Return:** This completes the current function and stops at the next line of code after the function has been called.

TIP When you step through code in Flex Builder, code execution pauses on each ActionScript statement, expression evaluation, and variable declaration. At times you'll find that you even step into the source code of Flex internal library classes, where available.

FIGURE 6.18

The Debug view

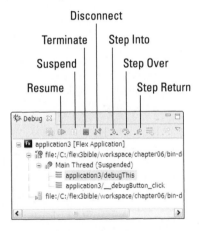

The Debug view tools described above also are available as menu selections and, in most cases, keyboard shortcuts. For example, to terminate a debugging session, select Run ➪ Terminate from the Flex Builder menu or press Ctrl+F2 on Windows or Cmd+F2 on Mac OS X. Figure 6.19 shows the Run menu as it appears during a debugging session. Notice that each feature's keyboard shortcut is noted on the menu.

FIGURE 6.19

Flex Builder's Run menu during a debugging session

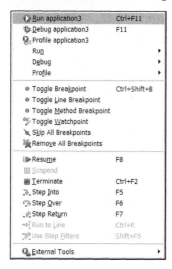

Profiling Flex Applications

Flex Builder includes tools for profiling Flex applications at runtime, providing valuable information about the frequency and duration of method calls, the size and number of object instances in memory, and overall memory usage.

NEW FEATURE   The Flex profiling tools are a new feature of Flex Builder 3. They are included only with a Flex Builder 3 Professional license.

The profiling tools are packaged in a new Flex Builder perspective named the Flex Profiling perspective. You can profile an application from the Flex Builder tool bar or menu.

Follow these steps to run an application in profiling mode:

1. Close any open browser windows. (If you have a browser window already open, profiling may not start correctly.)

2. Select Run ➪ Profile from the Flex Builder menu and select the application you want to profile. You also can click the Profile button on the toolbar.

3. When a profiling connection has been established, you're prompted for profiling options, as shown in Figure 6.20. Select options and click Resume.

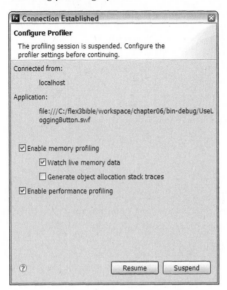

FIGURE 6.20

Selecting profiling options

4. Once the application has resumed execution in the browser, execute application functions and switch back to Flex Builder to see how the application is performing internally.

As shown in Figure 6.21, the Memory Usage view displays a graph showing overall memory usage.

FIGURE 6.21

The Memory Usage view in the Flex Profiling perspective

As shown in Figure 6.22, the Live Objects view displays statistical data about objects in Flash Player memory.

The Live Objects view in the Flex Profiling perspective

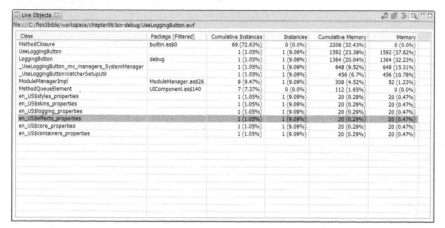

Live Objects ⊠

file:///C:/flex3bible/workspace/chapter06/bin-debug/UseLoggingButton.swf

Class	Package (Filtered)	Cumulative Instances	Instances	Cumulative Memory	Memory
MethodClosure	builtin.as$0	69 (72.63%)	0 (0.0%)	2208 (32.43%)	0 (0.0%)
UseLoggingButton		1 (1.05%)	1 (9.09%)	1592 (23.38%)	1592 (37.62%)
LoggingButton	debug	1 (1.05%)	1 (9.09%)	1364 (20.04%)	1364 (32.23%)
_UseLoggingButton_mx_managers_SystemManager		1 (1.05%)	1 (9.09%)	648 (9.52%)	648 (15.31%)
_UseLoggingButtonWatcherSetupUtil		1 (1.05%)	1 (9.09%)	456 (6.7%)	456 (10.78%)
ModuleManagerImpl	ModuleManager.as$26	9 (9.47%)	1 (9.09%)	308 (4.52%)	52 (1.23%)
MethodQueueElement	UIComponent.as$140	7 (7.37%)	0 (0.0%)	112 (1.65%)	0 (0.0%)
en_US$styles_properties		1 (1.05%)	1 (9.09%)	20 (0.29%)	20 (0.47%)
en_US$skins_properties		1 (1.05%)	1 (9.09%)	20 (0.29%)	20 (0.47%)
en_US$logging_properties		1 (1.05%)	1 (9.09%)	20 (0.29%)	20 (0.47%)
en_US$effects_properties		1 (1.05%)	1 (9.09%)	20 (0.29%)	20 (0.47%)
en_US$core_properties		1 (1.05%)	1 (9.09%)	20 (0.29%)	20 (0.47%)
en_US$containers_properties		1 (1.05%)	1 (9.09%)	20 (0.29%)	20 (0.47%)

Summary

In this chapter, I described tools that help you debug a Flex application. You learned the following:

- The trace() method lets you send debugging messages to Flex Builder's Console view at runtime.

- The flashlog.txt file also receives tracing and error messages when configured with the mm.cfg file.

- The locations of flashlog.txt and mm.cfg differ between operating systems.

- The Logging API lets you create self-logging components and filter logging messages based on logging level and category.

- Breakpoints let you suspend application execution so you can inspect variables and object properties at runtime.

- The Variables view displays pre-declared variables and object property values when the application is suspended.

- The Expressions view lets you evaluate arbitrary ActionScript expressions at runtime.

- The Debug view lets you step through code and otherwise control application execution during a debugging session.

Chapter 7

Working with Events

F lex applications are *event-driven*, which means that with the exception of the first phases of application startup, every action is the result of some trigger that causes the action to take place.

Many events are produced by internal functions within the Flex framework that don't necessarily have anything to do with a user's interactions with the application. These are sometimes known as *system* events. Other events, known as *user* events, are designed to inform you of actions taken by the user. These actions, known as user *gestures*, consist of key presses or mouse actions such as moving the mouse or pressing one of its buttons.

Regardless of how an event is generated, you can capture and handle the event in a number of ways. During event handling, you have access to information about the event from a variable known as an *event object*.

And when you need to share information between an application's components, you can create and dispatch your own custom events to move information and data around the application as needed.

This chapter describes the Flex event architecture: how to find out what events occur and when, what data you can get from them, and how to build your own event architecture.

ON the WEB To use the sample code for this chapter, import the chapter07.zip Flex project archive file from the Web site files into your Flex Builder workspace.

IN THIS CHAPTER

The Flex event architecture

Handling events with MXML

Handling events with addEventListener()

Declaring and dispatching custom events

Creating and using custom event classes

The Flex Event Architecture

The ActionScript objects you use to build Flex applications communicate with each other and share data by dispatching events. For example, consider a `Button` control that's declared with MXML:

```
<mx:Button label="Click Me"/>
```

As an instance of the `mx.controls.Button` class, this object supports many properties and methods that we know as the members of the Button class. The Button is capable of generating many events. Each of these events also is considered a member of the class.

To find out which events are supported by a particular class, look at the API documentation for that class. To get to the API documentation quickly in Flex Builder, place the cursor anywhere in the MXML or ActionScript component or class declaration and press F1 on Windows or Cmd + ? on Mac OS X. Then click the links for the appropriate class documentation that appear in the Help view.

The class's member types are listed at the top of the API documentation. Any class that is capable of generating events displays an `Events` link, as shown in Figure 7.1.

FIGURE 7.1

The Events link in the API documentation for the Button class

When you click the `Events` link, the Help view navigates to the Events section of the documentation. As shown in Figure 7.2, you may initially see only a short list of events that are supported by the class. These are the events that are defined locally in the current class. For example, the Button class has three events that are defined locally: `buttonDown`, `change`, and `dataChange`. You also see a Show Inherited Events link that, when clicked, expands the list to include events that are inherited from the current class's inheritance hierarchy.

FIGURE 7.2

A list of events that are defined locally in the Button class

Click to show inherited events

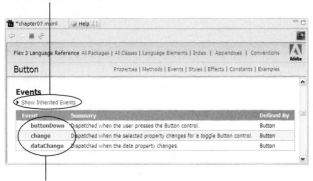

Locally defined events

When you click Show Inherited Events, you see all events that are available to the current class. For example, the Button class's most commonly used event is named click. This event is defined in another class named InteractiveObject, one of the Button class's superclasses. This information is available in the documentation, as shown in Figure 7.3.

FIGURE 7.3

The Button's click event is defined in a superclass named InteractiveObject.

The click event

The event is defined in this class

Handling Events in MXML

You can handle events in two different ways in Flex applications:

- With XML attribute-based event handlers in MXML object declarations
- With the addEventListener() method

The first event handling strategy is designed for ActionScript objects that are declared in MXML; the other works for any object, whether declared in MXML or ActionScript.

Creating event handlers in MXML

An MXML event handler uses an XML attribute where the attribute's name matches the name of the event being handled. For example, the Button class's click event uses an XML attribute that's also named click. The value of the XML attribute is an ActionScript statement that causes some action to take place.

Executing a single ActionScript statement in an event handler

If you need to execute a single ActionScript statement for any particular event, you can place the ActionScript code directly in the MXML-based event handler. In the following code, when the user clicks the Button component, the click event is handled and the ActionScript statement in the click XML attribute is executed:

```
<mx:Button label="Click Me"
  click="messageLabel.text='You clicked the button'"/>
<mx:Label id="messageLabel"/>
```

> **TIP** Notice in the above code that the literal string You clicked the button is wrapped in single quotes. This is because the click XML attribute's value (the ActionScript statement) is wrapped in double quotes. In ActionScript, single and double quotes are interchangeable as long as you match them up correctly.

> **NOTE** In browser-based JavaScript, the Dynamic HTML (DHTML) equivalent of this event architecture uses event names starting with the word "on" and finishing with the actual event. For example, in JavaScript, you'd use this code to handle an onClick event:

```
<input type="button" onClick="doSomething()"/>
```

The result is the same as in MXML: The event handler consists of a markup-based attribute that calls scripting code to be executed upon the event being dispatched. Only the event naming pattern is different.

A simple event handling application

Follow these steps to create a simple application that uses an MXML-based event handler:

1. Create a new application with the layout property set to vertical.
2. Add a Label component to the application with an id property set to myLabel.

3. Add a `Button` component to the application with a `label` property set to `Click Me` and a `click` event handler with ActionScript code that changes the `Label` control's `text` property to a value of `You Clicked!`.

   The completed application's code is shown in Listing 7.1.

4. Run the application, and click the button to see the `Label` control's `text` property change.

LISTING 7.1

An application with a simple MXML-based event handler

```
<?xml version="1.0" encoding="utf-8"?>
<mx:Application xmlns:mx="http://www.adobe.com/2006/mxml"
   layout="vertical">
  <mx:Label id="myLabel"/>
  <mx:Button label="Click Me" click="myLabel.text='You clicked!'"/>
</mx:Application>
```

ON the WEB The code in Listing 7.1 is available in the Web site files in the `chapter07` project's `src` folder as `SimpleEvent.mxml`.

Handling events with ActionScript functions

When you need to execute more than a single ActionScript statement in response to an event, you should create a custom function. The function allows you to add as much code as you need. The event handler function can be very simple:

```
private function clickHandler():void
{
   ... add ActionScript code here ...
}
```

Now all the code you want to call is wrapped inside `clickHandler()`, so to execute the code, call the function from the object's event handler:

```
<mx:Button label="Click Me" click="clickHandler()"/>
```

TIP You can name your event handler functions anything you like. The convention of naming the function with word "handler" at the end isn't a technical requirement, but it helps you identify the function's purpose.

If you have more than a single object whose events you need to handle, name the event handler functions to identify the event that's being handled and the object that's dispatching the event. For example, if you have two buttons with functions to save or cancel an operation, you might name the event handler functions **saveClickHandler()** and **cancelClickHandler()**. To call the functions you'd then use this code:

```
<mx:Button label="Save" click="saveClickHandler()"/>
<mx:Button label="Cancel" click="cancelClickHandler()"/>
```

Using an event handler function

Follow these steps to create an application that uses an event handler function:

1. Create a new application with the `layout` property set to `vertical`.

2. Add a `Label` component to the application with an `id` property set to `myLabel`.

3. Add an `<mx:Script>` tag set at the top of the application.

4. Within the `<mx:Script>` block, add a private function named `clickHandler()` that changes the `Label` control's `text` property to a value of `You Clicked!`.

5. Add a `Button` component to the application with a `label` property set to `Click Me`.

6. In the `Button` component's `click` event handler, call the `clickHandler()` function.

   The completed application's code is shown in Listing 7.2.

7. Run the application, and click the button to see the `Label` control's `text` property change.

LISTING 7.2

Using an event handler function

```
<?xml version="1.0" encoding="utf-8"?>
<mx:Application xmlns:mx="http://www.adobe.com/2006/mxml"
   layout="vertical">
  <mx:Script>
    <![CDATA[
      private function clickHandler():void
      {
        myLabel.text="You clicked the button";
      }
    ]]>
  </mx:Script>
  <mx:Label id="myLabel"/>
  <mx:Button label="Click Me" click="clickHandler()"/>
</mx:Application>
```

ON the WEB The code in Listing 7.2 is available in the Web site files in the `chapter07` project's `src` folder as `EventWithFunction.mxml`.

TIP Event handler functions typically return `void`, meaning that their purpose is to take some action but not return any value. When using an MXML-based event handler, this architecture is optional. As described below, when setting up an event handler with the `addEventListener()` function, the return data type of `void` is required.

Working with event objects

Every event that's dispatched in the Flex framework creates a variable known as an *event object*. The purpose of an event object is to share information about the nature of the event, including the event's name, the object that dispatched the event, the context of the event, and detailed information that might be useful in understanding what happened.

The event object's variable name

To handle an event and get information from the event object, you typically create an event handler function that's designed to receive the event object as an argument. When the event occurs, you then call the event handler function and pass the event object as its argument. For the duration of an MXML-based event handler, the name of the event object is always the same: event (always spelled in lowercase). So, assuming you've created a clickHandler() function that's designed to receive an event argument, the syntax of the MXML object declaration becomes this:

```
<mx:Button label="Click Me" click="clickHandler(event)"/>
```

Using event object arguments

The event object is always an instance of an ActionScript class named flash.events.Event or a subclass of this Event class. When you create an event handler function to receive an event object, you can always data type the argument as the Event class:

```
private function clickHandler(event:Event):void
{
  myLabel.text="You clicked the button";
}
```

Tip

All event objects can be handled as the Event class as they're passed into an event handler function, even if their true type is a subclass of the Event class. This convenient shortcut is made possible by ActionScript's support for polymorphism, where objects can be cast as and handled as their superclass types. As long as you don't need to refer to event object properties that are only implemented in the subclass, such as MouseEvent, typing the event object as Event doesn't have any negative effect on the application's performance or functionality.

Using event object properties

As shown in the UML diagram in Figure 7.4, the Event class supports properties and methods that let you get information about the event and in some cases control its behavior. (The diagram shows only certain key properties and methods of the Event class. See the class's API documentation for a complete list.)

FIGURE 7.4

UML diagram of the Event class

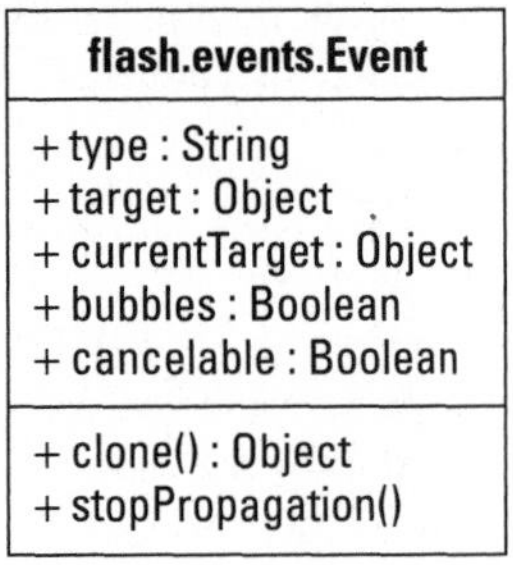

flash.events.Event
+ type : String + target : Object + currentTarget : Object + bubbles : Boolean + cancelable : Boolean
+ clone() : Object + stopPropagation()

These are the key properties of the Event class:

- type:String: The name of the event that was dispatched as a String. For example, when the click event is handled, the value of the event object's type property is "click."

- target:Object: A reference to the object that dispatched the event. Because the target property points to the object, any of that object's properties are then available with extended dot syntax. For example, a Button component's id property would be available as event.target.id, and its label as event.target.label.

NOTE Other key properties of the Event class are described below in the section on event bubbling.

When you pass an event object to an event handler function as an argument, you have access to all the event object's properties for the duration of the function. To capture information about the event, use the properties that are of interest:

```
private function clickHandler(event:Event):void
{
  myLabel.text="You clicked the button labeled " +
    event.target.label;
}
```

TIP When writing code that refers to event.target, you might notice that properties like label that aren't available on all ActionScript classes aren't suggested by Flex Builder code completion tools. This is because the expression event.target is known to the Flex compiler and to Flex Builder as an instance of the ActionScript Object class, and only properties that are implemented in that class will be suggested for auto-completion.

If you know that event.target refers to a Button in the context of a particular event handler function, you can safely refer to the Button class's properties (such as label). The code will compile and execute correctly, even if Flex Builder's code completion isn't able to help you write it.

Using event object properties in an application

Follow these steps to create an application that uses event object properties:

1. Create a new application with the layout property set to vertical.

2. Add a Label component to the application with an id property set to myLabel.

3. Add an <mx:Script> tag set at the top of the application.

4. Within the <mx:Script> block, add a private function named clickHandler() that receives an argument named event, data typed as the Event class.

5. Add this code to clickHandler() to display the event type and the id of the event target:

   ```
   myLabel.text="The " + event.type +
       " event was dispatched by " + event.target.id;
   ```

6. Add a Button component to the application with a label property set to Click Me.

7. In the Button component's click event handler, call the clickHandler() function and pass the event object as a function argument.

   The completed application's code is shown in Listing 7.3.

8. Run the application, and click the button to see the Label control's text property change.

LISTING 7.3

Using event object properties

```xml
<?xml version="1.0" encoding="utf-8"?>
<mx:Application xmlns:mx="http://www.adobe.com/2006/mxml"
   layout="vertical">

  <mx:Script>
    <![CDATA[
      private function clickHandler(event:Event):void
      {
        myLabel.text="The " + event.type +
          " event was dispatched by " + event.target.id;
      }
    ]]>
  </mx:Script>

  <mx:Label id="myLabel"/>
  <mx:Button label="Click Me" click="clickHandler(event)"/>

</mx:Application>
```

ON the WEB   The code in Listing 7.3 is available in the Web site files in the chapter07 project's src folder as EventObjectProperties.mxml.

Event class inheritance

Event objects are created as specific class types depending on the nature of the event that's dispatched. For example, events having to do with mouse actions are typically instances of a class name flash.events.MouseEvent. As shown in the UML diagram in Figure 7.5, MouseEvent, ResultEvent, TextEvent, and dozens of other classes in the Flash and Flex class libraries are directly extended from the standard Event class.

FIGURE 7.5

All event classes are directly extended from the Event superclass

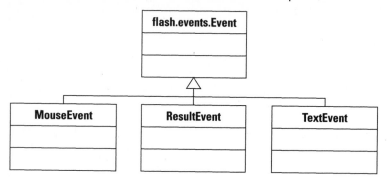

When an event class such as MouseEvent extends Event, it inherits that superclass's basic properties such as type and target. The subclass typically defines additional properties that are useful for that particular event. The MouseEvent class adds properties to track button state, mouse cursor position, and other useful information. Some of these properties include:

- altKey:Boolean: Set to true if the Alt key is held down when the event is dispatched; otherwise false.

- ctrlKey:Boolean: Set to true if the Ctrl key is held down when the event is dispatched; otherwise false.

- shiftKey:Boolean: Set to true if the Shift key is held down when the event is dispatched; otherwise false.

- commandKey:Boolean: Set to true if the command key on the Mac is held down when the event is dispatched; otherwise false. Always set to false on Windows.

- localX:int: The number of pixels from the left border where the user clicked an object dispatching the event.

- localY:int: The number of pixels from the top border where the user clicked an object dispatching the event.

- stageX:int: The number of pixels from the left border where the user clicked the *stage* (Flash Player region).

- stageY:int: The number of pixels from the top border where the user clicked the stage (Flash Player region).

■ `buttonDown:Boolean`: Set to `true` if the primary mouse button is pressed when the event is dispatched; otherwise `false`.

Which event class will I get?

To find out what specific class will be dispatched for a particular event, you can use one of these strategies:

■ Debug the application, and inspect the event object in the Variables view.

■ Read the API documentation for the object whose event you're handling.

■ Place the mouse cursor over the `event` object where it's passed into the event handler function in Flex Builder 3 and get a tool tip describing the class name.

Debugging the event object

Follow these steps to debug the application and inspect the event object:

1. Place a breakpoint in the event handler function on a line of ActionScript code or, if the function is empty, on the line with the function's closing brace:

```
private function clickHandler(event:MouseEvent):void
{
} //place breakpoint here
```

2. Debug the application.

3. Trigger the event that calls the event handler function (for example, by clicking a button).

4. When the breakpoint suspends the application, inspect the function's `event` argument in the Flex Debugging perspective's Variables view.

As shown in Figure 7.6, the Variables view displays the event object's type and all its current property values.

Reading the documentation

Documentation for every event in the Flex Framework includes the type of the event object that will be dispatched when the event occurs. For example, the documentation for the `Button` class's `click` event shows that the event object is an instance of `flash.events.MouseEvent`. To find this information:

1. Place the cursor in the object declaration in Source view.

2. Press F1 to display a list of Help subjects.

3. Click the link for the class or component you're using.

4. In the API documentation, click the `Events` link.

5. Locate the event you're interested in, and click its link.

As shown in Figure 7.7, you should see the specific type of the class that will be dispatched for that event.

FIGURE 7.6

The event object's type displayed in the Variables view

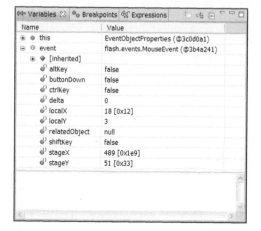

FIGURE 7.7

Documentation for the `click` event

The type of the click event's event object

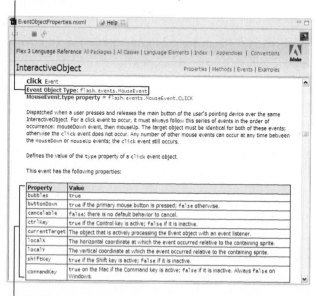

The event object's properties

Handling specific event objects

To capture information that's available only in one of the extended event classes, set an event handler function's event argument to that class. For example, this event handler function expects an instance of MouseEvent:

```
private function clickHandler(event:MouseEvent):void
{
  myLabel.text="You clicked; was the alt key pressed? " +
    event.altKey;
}
```

The altKey property is available only because the event argument is declared as the subclass that supports that property. If the event argument instead is declared as the Event superclass, the altKey property isn't recognized by the compiler and a compiler error results.

The complete application shown in Listing 7.4 is an application that captures a MouseEvent and displays the status of the keys on the keyboard at the moment the event is dispatched.

LISTING 7.4

An application that handles a MouseEvent object

```
<?xml version="1.0" encoding="utf-8"?>
<mx:Application xmlns:mx="http://www.adobe.com/2006/mxml"
  layout="vertical">

  <mx:Script>
    <![CDATA[
      private function clickHandler(event:MouseEvent):void
      {
        myLabel.text="The " + event.type +
          " event was dispatched by " + event.target.id;
        altLabel.text="Alt key pressed: " + event.altKey;
        ctrlLabel.text="Ctrl key pressed: " + event.ctrlKey;
        shiftLabel.text="Shift key pressed: " + event.shiftKey;
      }
    ]]>
  </mx:Script>

  <mx:Label id="myLabel"/>
  <mx:Label id="altLabel"/>
  <mx:Label id="ctrlLabel"/>
  <mx:Label id="shiftLabel"/>

  <mx:Button label="Click Me" click="clickHandler(event)"/>

</mx:Application>
```

Event Class Inheritance and Polymorphism

The fact that you can define an event handler function to expect either the specific event class such as MouseEvent, or its superclass such as Event, is a reflection of the support for polymorphism in ActionScript's implementation of object-oriented programming. The concept of polymorphism is described in detail in Chapter 1. Merriam-Webster defines polymorphism as "the quality or state of existing in or assuming different forms." In this case, the different forms the event object takes are its native type (MouseEvent) or its superclass type (Event).

One reason some developers set an event object to the superclass is because they don't know the event's native class type and don't want to take time to look it up. It sounds like just being lazy, but in many cases the specific properties of the native type just aren't needed in that situation, and using the Event superclass makes for faster programming.

Developers also can use the superclass type to make a function reusable by events that dispatch different native types, again where they don't need the specific properties that are supported by the native types. This is the true purpose of implementing polymorphism in object-oriented languages: to support code that's reusable in many different circumstances.

ON the WEB   The code in Listing 7.4 is available in the Web site files in the chapter07 project's src folder as MouseEventObjectProperties.mxml.

Handling Events with addEventListener()

You also can set up event handlers with a method named addEventListener(). This method is defined in an ActionScript class named EventDispatcher, which appears in the inheritance hierarchy of every ActionScript class that's able to dispatch events. Stated more briefly, you can call addEventListener() from any object that knows how to dispatch an event.

Setting up an event listener

The following MXML code declares a Button component with a click event handler:

```
<mx:Button id="myButton" label="Click Me"
  click="clickHandler(event)"/>
```

The following code calls addEventListener() instead of the MXML-based event handler:

```
myButton.addEventListener("click", clickHandler);
```

The first argument you pass to addEventListener() is the name of the event you're listening for. The second argument is the name of the function you want to call when the event is dispatched.

CAUTION Notice that you pass the name of the function as the second argument, not the complete code required to call the function. You're designating which function to call, rather than calling the function immediately.

The object from which you call `addEventListener()` always calls the listener function with the same signature, passing a single argument data typed as the appropriate event class for that event. Event listener functions designed to be used with `addEventListener()` always have the same signature:

```
[access modifier] function [functionName](
  event:[event class data type]):void
{}
```

So a function designed to receive an instance of `MouseEvent` always looks like this:

```
private function clickHandler(event:MouseEvent):void
{
  ... execute event handling code ...
}
```

You typically call `addEventListener()` during application startup, where it can replace an MXML-based event handler definition. For example, you might set up your event listeners in a function named `initApp()` that's called upon the Application component's `creationComplete` event. The application in Listing 7.5 uses this strategy. Notice the following:

- The `initApp()` function returns `void`.
- The `initApp()` function is called during application startup upon the Application's `creationComplete` event.
- The MXML-based declaration of the `Button` component doesn't have a `click` event handler; this would be redundant and in fact would result in the event handler function being called twice.

LISTING 7.5

An application that uses addEventListener()

```
<?xml version="1.0" encoding="utf-8"?>
<mx:Application xmlns:mx="http://www.adobe.com/2006/mxml"
   layout="vertical"
  creationComplete="initApp()">
  <mx:Script>
    <![CDATA[
      private function initApp():void
      {
        myButton.addEventListener("click", clickHandler);
      }
      private function clickHandler(event:MouseEvent):void
```

continued

LISTING 7.5 *(continued)*

```
      {
        myLabel.text="The " + event.type +
          " event was dispatched by " + event.target.id;
      }
    ]]>
  </mx:Script>
  <mx:Button id="myButton" label="Click Me"/>
</mx:Application>
```

ON the WEB The code in Listing 7.5 is available in the Web site files in the `chapter07` project's `src` folder as `UsingAddEventListener.mxml`.

Using event name constants

Each event class in the Flex framework implements constants that have values equal to the names of events for which the event class is used. For example, the `MouseEvent` class has many constants that reflect the names of events for which this event class is dispatched (shown with their equivalent values):

- `CLICK` = "click"
- `MOUSE_DOWN` = "mouseDown"
- `MOUSE_UP` = "mouseUp"
- `MOUSE_MOVE` = "mouseMove"
- `RIGHT_CLICK` = "rightClick"
- `MOUSE_WHEEL` = "mouseWheel"

There are more, but you get the picture. You use these constants in calls to `addEventListener()` instead of phrasing the event name as a literal string. For example, instead of this code:

```
myButton.addEventListener("click", clickHandler);
```

you can use this:

```
myButton.addEventListener(MouseEvent.CLICK, clickHandler);
```

When you use event name constants, you reduce the risk of typing errors in your code. When you use literal strings to indicate which event you want to listen for, it's easy to misspell the name. For example, this code would result in an event listener that will never be triggered, because no event name is `clik`:

```
myButton.addEventListener("clik", clickHandler);
```

Because the event name is phrased as a literal string, the compiler has no way of knowing that it's misspelled. Of course, you can make the same mistake with an event name constant:

```
myButton.addEventListener(MouseEvent.CLIK, clickHandler);
```

But in this case, the compiler would complain, as shown in Figure 7.8, telling you that there is no such property or constant as CLIK in the MouseEvent class, and you'd be able to find and fix the error at a much earlier stage of development.

FIGURE 7.8

A compiler error resulting from a misspelled event name constant

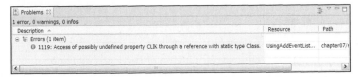

Another advantage of using event name constants comes from Flex Builder's code completion tool. As shown in Figure 7.9, when you type the name of the MouseEvent class and add a period, you see a list of available constants that are members of the class. You can then select the appropriate event name and ensure that it's typed correctly from the beginning.

FIGURE 7.9

Flex Builder's code completion tool with event name constants

Flex Builder's code completion with event name constants

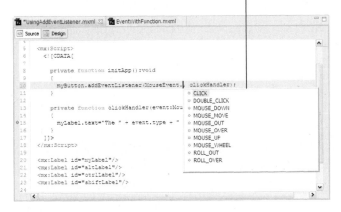

Removing an event listener

You can remove an event listener that was set up with `addEventListener()` with the `removeEventListener()` method. This method also is defined in the `EventDispatcher` class and can be called from any object that dispatches events.

The basic syntax for `removeEventListener()` is the same as `addEventListener()`:

```
myButton.removeEventListener(MouseEvent.CLICK, clickHandler);
```

The `addEventListener()` and `removeEventListener()` methods allow you to add and remove event listeners as needed whenever an application's requirements change logically at runtime.

Using Event Bubbling

Event bubbling refers to the process of dispatching events through multiple levels of inheritance. Consider this application code, which defines a `Button` control inside a `VBox` container:

```
<?xml version="1.0" encoding="utf-8"?>
<mx:Application xmlns:mx="http://www.adobe.com/2006/mxml"
    layout="vertical">
  <mx:VBox id="myContainer">
    <mx:Button label="Click me" id="myButton"/>
  </mx:VBox>
</mx:Application>
```

When the `Button` component is clicked, it dispatches a `click` event. All event objects have a Boolean property named `bubbles`. When this property's value is set to `true`, as it is by default with the `MouseEvent` class, the event first is dispatched by the object that was clicked, then by its container, and so on up the display tree until it's dispatched by the application itself.

Each time the event bubbles up another containership level, the event object is cloned and the new version contains all the original properties and the stored values of the original. But one property is changed: Each new copy of the event object has a `currentTarget` property that refers to the object that's currently dispatching the event. In the meantime, each event object's `target` property continues to reference the object that originally dispatched the event.

The application in Listing 7.6 uses a two-level containership hierarchy: a `Button` inside a `VBox` inside an Application. All objects handle the `click` event and dispatch the event object to a `clickHandler()` function, where the target and `currentTarget` are logged.

LISTING 7.6

An application that tracks simple event bubbling

```xml
<?xml version="1.0" encoding="utf-8"?>
<mx:Application xmlns:mx="http://www.adobe.com/2006/mxml"
   layout="vertical"
  verticalAlign="middle" click="clickHandler(event)">

  <mx:Script>
    <![CDATA[
      private function clickHandler(event:Event):void
      {
        eventLog.text += "target=" + event.target.id +
          ", currentTarget=" + event.currentTarget.id + "\n\n";
      }
    ]]>
  </mx:Script>

  <mx:Label text="Application"/>
  <mx:VBox id="myContainer" height="50%" width="50%"
    horizontalAlign="center" verticalAlign="middle"
    backgroundColor="#eeeeee"
    click="clickHandler(event)">
    <mx:Label text="myContainer"/>
    <mx:Button label="myButton" id="myButton"
      click="clickHandler(event)"/>
  </mx:VBox>
  <mx:TextArea id="eventLog" height="110" width="50%"/>
</mx:Application>
```

ON the WEB The code in Listing 7.6 is available in the Web site files in the **chapter07** project's **src** folder as **EventBubblingSimple.mxml**.

As shown in Figure 7.10, each time the event is handled, the target property always points to the Button component, while the currentTarget changes with each new call to the event handler function.

TIP Event bubbling works only if the parent container declares the event you want to handle. For example, if you try to handle a change event from a ComboBox in a parent VBox in MXML, an error occurs because the compiler says there is no change event to listen for. To overcome this limitation, create your own custom component based on the container you want to use, and explicitly declare the selected event as a member of the new version of the container.

FIGURE 7.10

A simple event bubbling demonstration

Using Custom Events

You use custom events to communicate information and data between application components. As described previously, Flex applications are built with a modular architecture, with functionality divided between multiple components. When a component needs to share information with the rest of the application, it does so by dispatching an event.

The following MXML component displays three choices of Small, Medium, and Large in a group of RadioButton components:

```
<?xml version="1.0" encoding="utf-8"?>
<mx:VBox xmlns:mx="http://www.adobe.com/2006/mxml">
  <mx:RadioButtonGroup id="sizeGroup"/>
  <mx:RadioButton value="Small" label="Small"
    groupName="sizeGroup"/>
  <mx:RadioButton value="Medium" label="Medium"
    groupName="sizeGroup"/>
  <mx:RadioButton value="Large" label="Large"
    groupName="sizeGroup"/>
</mx:VBox>
```

ON the WEB The above code is available from the Web site files' `chapter07` project as `components/SizeSelectorStart.mxml`.

When the user clicks a radio button to make a selection, the component can share the following information with the rest of the application:

- The user selected something.
- The user selected a particular bit of data.

In order to share the information, you'll need to follow these steps within the component:

1. Define a custom event that the MXML component is capable of dispatching.

2. Create an event object at runtime.

3. Populate the event object with data.

4. Dispatch the event object.

In the application that instantiates the custom component, you'll follow these steps:

1. Create an event handler using either an MXML-based event attribute or the `addEventListener()` method.

2. Create a custom event handler function that extracts the data from the dispatched event object.

Declaring custom events

You declare custom events in a component with the `<mx:Metadata>` tag and a metadata tag named `[Event]`. Start by adding the `<mx:Metadata>` tag set as a child of the component root:

```
<mx:VBox xmlns:mx="http://www.adobe.com/2006/mxml">
  <mx:Metadata>
  </mx:Metadata>
  ... remainder of component code ...
</mx:VBox>
```

Within the `<mx:Metadata>` tag set, add one `[Event]` metadata tag for each custom event you want to declare. The syntax of the `[Event]` metadata tag is:

```
[Event(name="[custom event name]", type="[event object type]")]
```

The `[Event]` metadata tag has these two attributes:

- name: A string that identifies your custom event, and can be of any value. Just as the Flex framework uses event names like `click`, `change`, and `mouseMove`, you can select any meaningful string as long as it doesn't contain any spaces or special characters. This value is required.

- type: The name of an event class that will be instantiated and dispatched to an event listener. The default is the standard `flash.events.Event` class.

If you only need to dispatch an event that informs the event listener that the event occurred, and don't need to share specific data, you can use a shorthand form of the `[Event]` tag that omits the type attribute:

```
[Event(name="sizeSelected")]
```

If you need to share specific data with the event listener and use a special event class that is designed to contain that data, include the type property and refer to the fully qualified event class name:

```
[Event(name="sizeSelected", type="flash.events.TextEvent")]
```

> **TIP**   The TextEvent class is already part of the Flash class library and has a text property you can use to package and share a simple String value when you dispatch a custom event. If you only need to share a String, it doesn't make sense to create a custom event class — you'd just be reinventing a wheel.

Adding an event declaration to a custom component and testing it

Follow these steps to add an event declaration to a custom MXML component:

1. Open components/SizeSelector.mxml from the chapter07 project from the Web site.

2. Place the cursor after the starting <mx:VBox> tag.

3. Add an <mx:Metadata> tag set.

4. Within the <mx:Metadata> tag set, declare a custom event named sizeSelected that dispatches an event object typed as flash.events.TextEvent. The code to declare the event looks like this:

```
<mx:Metadata>
  [Event(name="sizeSelected", type="flash.events.Event")]
</mx:Metadata>
```

5. Save the file.

6. Create a new MXML application named CustomEventApp.mxml in the chapter07 project.

7. Declare an instance of the SizeSelectorStart component with MXML:

```
<components:SizeSelectorStart/>
```

8. Place the cursor after the SizeSelector tag name and before the ending /> characters.

9. Press the spacebar to see a list of available class members.

10. Type **size** to filter the list.

    As shown in Figure 7.11, you should see that the list displays the new sizeSelected event as a member of the component.

11. Remove the partial event attribute size (you learn how to use this attribute in the next section) so you have only the tag declaration with no event listener.

12. Save and run the application.

A custom event shown in Flex Builder's code completion tool

As shown in Figure 7.12, the application displays the component but isn't yet handling the custom event.

The application with the custom component

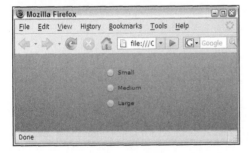

Dispatching custom events

To dispatch a custom event, follow these steps:

1. Create an instance of the event class you declared as the event type.
2. When you instantiate the event object, set its `type` property as the name of the custom event. All event classes in the Flex framework have a constructor method that allows you to set the event name as you instantiate the object:

```
var myEvent:Event = new Event("[my event name]");
```

3. Populate the event object with data, if applicable.

4. Call the component's `dispatchEvent()` method, and pass the event object as the only argument:

   ```
   dispatchEvent(myEvent);
   ```

The complete code to dispatch a `TextEvent` class for an event named `sizeChanged` looks like this:

```
var e:TextEvent = new TextEvent("sizeChanged");
e.text = "some value I want to share";
dispatchEvent(e);
```

Follow these steps to dispatch an event from the custom component:

1. Re-open components/SizeSelector.mxml from the chapter07 project.

2. Add an `<mx:Script>` tag set after the `<mx:Metadata>` tag set.

3. Within the script section, create a private function name `clickHandler()` that receives an event argument typed as `Event` and returns `void`.

4. Add this code to the event handler function:

   ```
   var e:TextEvent = new TextEvent("sizeSelected");
   e.text = sizeGroup.selection.value as String;
   dispatchEvent(e);
   ```

5. Add an event handler named `itemClick` to the `RadioButtonGroup` component, and call the new function, passing the event object:

   ```
   <mx:RadioButtonGroup id="sizeGroup"
      itemClick="clickHandler(event)"/>
   ```

6. Save the file.

The completed component code is shown in Listing 7.7.

LISTING 7.7

A completed component that dispatches a custom event with data

```
<?xml version="1.0" encoding="utf-8"?>
<mx:VBox xmlns:mx="http://www.adobe.com/2006/mxml">
  <mx:Metadata>
    [Event(name="sizeSelected", type="flash.events.Event")]
  </mx:Metadata>
  <mx:Script>
    <![CDATA[
      private function clickHandler(event:Event):void
      {
        var e:TextEvent = new TextEvent("sizeSelected");
        e.text = sizeGroup.selection.value as String;
        dispatchEvent(e);
      }
```

```
    ]]>
  </mx:Script>
  <mx:RadioButtonGroup id="sizeGroup" itemClick="clickHandler(event)"/>
  <mx:RadioButton value="Small" label="Small" groupName="sizeGroup"/>
  <mx:RadioButton value="Medium" label="Medium" groupName="sizeGroup"/>
  <mx:RadioButton value="Large" label="Large" groupName="sizeGroup"/>
</mx:VBox>
```

ON the WEB The code in Listing 7.7 is available in the `chapter07` project from the Web site as `components/SizeSelectorComplete.mxml`.

TIP The `RadioButtonGroup` component's `selection.value` property must be explicitly cast as a `String`, because the API declares it as an `Object` and the `String` type is expected by the `TextEvent` class's `text` property.

Handling custom events

Event handling with custom events looks just like handling events that are predefined by classes in the Flex framework. You can handle a custom event in these two ways:

- With an MXML-based event attribute that executes explicit ActionScript code
- With the `addEventListener()` method

Handling a custom event with MXML

To handle an event with an MXML declaration, add an XML attribute named for the event to the MXML declaration of the object that will dispatch the event. When the event is dispatched, call a custom event handler function and pass the event object as an argument:

```
<components:SizeSelectorComplete
  sizeSelected="sizeSelectedHandler(event)"/>
```

Create a custom event handler function that expects the appropriate event class as its event argument:

```
private function sizeSelectedHandler(event:TextEvent):void
{
   ... process event data here ...
}
```

When the event occurs, the event handler function is executed and the data can then be appropriately handled.

Follow these steps to handle a custom event with an MXML event handler:

1. Open `CustomEventApp.mxml` from the `chapter07` project.
2. Add a `Label` component at the end of the application with an `id` of `sizeMessage`.
3. Add an `<mx:Script>` tag set to the application.

4. Create a private function named `sizeSelectedHandler()` that receives an event argument typed as `TextEvent` and returns `void`.

5. Within the event handler function, set the `text` property of the `sizeMessage` object to the text property of the event object. The function should now look like this:

```
private function sizeSelectedHandler(event:TextEvent):void
{
   sizeMessage.text = "You selected " + event.text;
}
```

6. Save and run the application, and click a radio button.

As shown in Figure 7.13, you should see that the selected radio button's value is displayed in the application.

FIGURE 7.13

The completed application handling a custom event

> **ON the WEB** The completed application is available in the Web site files as `CustomEventAppComplete.mxml` in the `chapter07` project.

Using Custom Event Classes

Custom event classes can be used when you need to share complex data with the application or other components. For example, a data entry form component might need to share more than a single string value when the user clicks the form's button to indicate that data entry is complete.

An ActionScript class that's designed to be used as an event object has these requirements:

- The custom event class must be extended from `flash.events.Event`.

- The custom event class's constructor method should call the `Event` class's constructor method and pass the name of the event using a virtual method named `super()`.

- Data elements that are wrapped inside the event class are declared as public properties.

- If the event class is designed to bubble upward through the container hierarchy, two additional requirements must be met:
  - The custom event class's `bubbles` property must be set to `true`.
  - The custom event class must declare a `clone()` method that overrides the version declared in the superclass `Event`.

Creating the ActionScript class

Custom event classes are designed as ActionScript classes that extend the Event class. You can place the custom event class in any folder within a project source root; typically they're created in a folder simply named `events`.

Using the New ActionScript Class wizard

Follow these steps to create a custom event class that holds data for a Login form:

1. In the `chapter07` project's source root, right-click the `events` subfolder and select New ➪ ActionScript class.

2. In the New ActionScript Class wizard, shown in Figure 7.14, enter **LoginEvent** as the Name of the new class.

FIGURE 7.14

The New ActionScript Class wizard

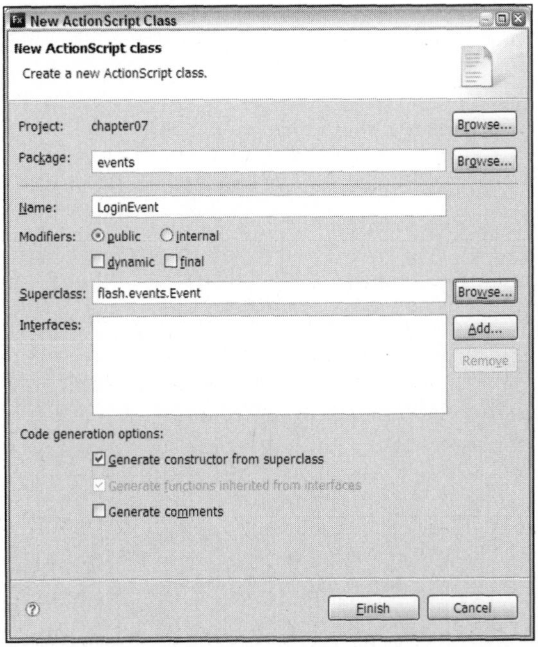

3. Click Browse next to the Superclass text box.

4. In the Open Type dialog box, shown in Figure 7.15, type **Event** to browse to the `flash.events.Event` class.

The Open Type dialog box

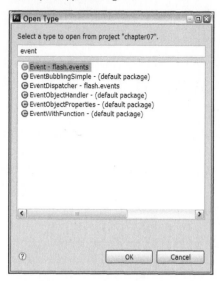

5. Click OK to select the Event class.

6. Select the Generate constructor from superclass option.

7. Click Finish to create the `LoginEvent` class.

The generated class code should now look like this:

```
package events
{
  import flash.events.Event;
  public class LoginEvent extends Event
  {
    public function LoginEvent(type:String,
      bubbles:Boolean=false, cancelable:Boolean=false)
    {
      super(type, bubbles, cancelable);
    }
  }
}
```

> **TIP**   Notice that the call to the `super()` method passes the type (the name of the event) and the `bubbles` and `cancelable` properties. The last two properties are marked as optional, by setting default values of `false`. This means that when you create an instance of the `LoginEvent` class, you only need to pass the name of the event if you don't need the `bubbles` or `cancelable` properties set to `true`:

```
var myEvent:LoginEvent = new LoginEvent("myEventName");
```

Declaring public properties

Each data value you want to wrap into the custom event class should be declared as a public property. For example, a data value for the user's password in a login data entry form would be declared as:

```
public var password:String;
```

Follow these steps to add user and password data elements to the custom event class:

1. In the generated `LoginEvent.as` file, place the cursor inside the class declaration.

2. Declare two public properties named `username` and `password`, both data typed as `String`:

```
public var username:String;
public var password:String;
```

Declaring event name constants

If you know the name of certain custom events for which the custom event class is designed, you can declare static event name constants that serve the same purpose of such constants as `MouseEvent.CLICK`; they help you accurately code the rest of the application.

For example, if the `LoginEvent` class will be used for a custom event named `login`, you would declare the event name constant with:

```
public static const LOGIN:String="login";
```

When you listen for the event using `addEventListener()`, you can use the constant with this code:

```
myComponent.addEventListener(LoginEvent.LOGIN, loginHandler);
```

The ActionScript class in Listing 7.8 declares custom properties and event name constants.

LISTING 7.8

The custom event class with properties and event name constants

```
package events
{
  import flash.events.Event;
  public class LoginEvent extends Event
  {
    public var username:String;
    public var password:String;
    public static const LOGIN:String="login";
    public function LoginEvent(type:String,
      bubbles:Boolean=false, cancelable:Boolean=false)
    {
      super(type, bubbles, cancelable);
    }
  }
}
```

ON the WEB The code in Listing 7.8 is available in the Web site files as `events/LoginEvent.as` in the `chapter07` project.

Overriding the clone() method

The Event class has a method named `clone()` that's used during the bubbling process to create new copies of the event object for each level of bubbling. As described previously, the event object's `currentTarget` property changes its value each time the event is dispatched to point to the container or control that's currently dispatching the event. By creating a new copy on each dispatch, the `currentTarget` for previous versions of the event object doesn't change.

CAUTION When you override a method in ActionScript, you must include the override keyword in the method declaration:

```
override public function superMethod():void
{}
```

If you don't include the override keyword and the method name matches one that's already declared in the current class's inheritance hierarchy, the compiler generates an error.

Keep in mind these rules for overriding the `clone()` method:

- The method must be marked with `override` and `public`.
- The method's return data type should be `Event`.

- Within the method:
  - Instantiate the current custom event class.
  - Populate the new copy with data from the current copy.
  - Return the new copy.

The `clone()` method for the `LoginEvent` class would look like this:

```
override public function clone():Event
{
  var newEvent:LoginEvent = new LoginEvent(type);
  newEvent.username = username;
  newEvent.password = password;
  return newEvent;
}
```

Notice that the current object's `type` property (the name of the current event) is passed to the new copy of the event object in the constructor method call.

> **TIP** If you don't make an event bubble, it doesn't need a `clone()` method. By default, custom event classes have their `bubbles` property set to `false`. To turn bubbling on whenever you use the custom event class, pass a value of `true` to the superclass's constructor method's second argument, as in:
>
> ```
> super(type, true, cancelable);
> ```

Dispatching a custom event class

When you dispatch a custom event class, follow these steps, which are the same as for pre-built event classes in the Flex framework:

1. Define a custom event that sets the type as the new custom ActionScript class.
2. Create an event object typed as the custom event class at runtime.
3. Populate the event object with data.
4. Dispatch the event object.

To declare a custom event named `login` that dispatches an instance of the `LoginEvent` class described above, the code within the custom Form component would look like this:

```
<mx:Metadata>
  [Event(name="login", type="events.LoginEvent")]
</mx:Metadata>
```

At runtime, you would create an instance of the event class, passing the event name into the constructor method:

```
var e:LoginEvent = new LoginEvent("login");
```

The next step is to populate the event object with data. Assuming you have TextInput controls with their id properties of userNameInput and passwordInput, the code would be:

```
e.username = userNameInput.text;
e.password = passwordInput.text;
```

Finally, dispatch the event just as you would with one of the pre-built event classes:

```
dispatchEvent(e);
```

Listing 7.9 shows a Form component that declares and dispatches the custom event using the custom event class.

LISTING 7.9

A Form component that dispatches a custom event object

```xml
<?xml version="1.0" encoding="utf-8"?>
<mx:Form xmlns:mx="http://www.adobe.com/2006/mxml">
  <mx:Metadata>
    [Event(name="login", type="events.LoginEvent")]
  </mx:Metadata>
  <mx:Script>
    <![CDATA[
      import events.LoginEvent;
      private function doLogin():void
      {
        var e:LoginEvent = new LoginEvent("login");
        e.username = userNameInput.text;
        e.password = passwordInput.text;
        dispatchEvent(e);
      }
    ]]>
  </mx:Script>
  <mx:FormItem label="User Name:">
    <mx:TextInput id="userNameInput"/>
  </mx:FormItem>
  <mx:FormItem label="Password:">
    <mx:TextInput id="passwordInput"/>
  </mx:FormItem>
  <mx:FormItem>
    <mx:Button label="Log In" click="doLogin()"/>
  </mx:FormItem>
</mx:Form>
```

ON the WEB   The code in Listing 7.9 is available in the Web site files as components/LoginForm.mxml in the chapter07 project.

Handling a custom event class

You handle an event that uses a custom event class in two ways — the same as with the Flex framework's pre-built event classes:

- With an MXML-based event handler
- With addEventListener()

In either case, you create a custom event handler function that expects an event argument typed as your custom event class:

```
private function loginHandler(event:LoginEvent):void
{}
```

 Unlike the event classes in the **flash.events** package, your custom event classes must be imported prior to use:

```
import events.LoginEvent;
```

Flex Builder can create **import** statements for you as you type. For example, as you type the string **LoginEvent** in the event handler function signature, Flex Builder presents a list of classes that match what you've typed. When you select your class, the **import** statement for that class is added at the top of the ActionScript code.

 If you don't see the list of available classes, press Ctrl+spacebar to trigger Flex Builder's code completion tool.

Within the event handler function, extract data as needed. The complete event handler function might look like this:

```
private function loginHandler(event:LoginEvent):void
{
  messageLabel.text = "You logged as " + event.username +
    " with a password of " + event.password;
}
```

Then, to call the event handler function, use an MXML-based event handler, as in:

```
<components:LoginForm login="loginHandler(event)"/>
```

Or, if you prefer to use addEventListener(), call this code as the application starts up:

```
myForm.addEventListener(LoginEvent.LOGIN, loginHandler);
```

Either way, the loginHandler() function is called and the data is delivered to the application.

Summary

In this chapter, I described the Flex event architecture and how you can create your own events to share data between application components. You learned the following:

- Flex applications are event-driven.
- Every component that dispatches events includes `EventDispatcher` in its inheritance hierarchy.
- You handle events with either MXML-based event handlers or the `addEventListener()` method.
- Event handler functions receive a single `event` argument and return `void`.
- You can declare and dispatch custom events from your custom components.
- You can create custom event classes to store and send data from custom components to the rest of the application.
- To make a custom event class `bubble`, set its `bubble` property to `true` and override the `Event` class's `clone()` method.
- You handle custom events and event classes with the same architecture as pre-built classes in the Flex framework.

Part II

The Flex Class Library

Chapter 8

Using Flex Controls

Through previous chapters, I've described various aspects of Flex application development and declared instances of *controls* such as Label and Button.

Flex uses two types of visual components:

- **Containers** are visual components that can contain other objects.
- **Controls** are visual components that display information or provide the application with user interaction capabilities.

A Flex control can serve two purposes:

- All controls help you create the visual presentation of the application.
- Interactive controls allow the user to provide you with information through data entry and mouse gestures (such as moving the mouse or clicking its buttons).

In this chapter, I describe the nature of Flex controls and show the interface and usage of commonly used controls in data entry forms and other visual presentations.

ON the WEB   To use the sample code for this chapter, import the
chapter08.zip Flex project archive file from the Web site
files into your Flex Builder workspace. In addition to the specific applications
in the Listings in this chapter, the Web site files include sample applications for
most of the controls described here.

IN THIS CHAPTER

Understanding Flex controls

Using text controls

Using layout controls

Using button controls

Using interactive controls

Presenting images

Instantiating and Customizing Controls

As described previously, a Flex control is really an ActionScript class that can be instantiated either with an MXML tag-based declaration or an ActionScript statement.

In order to determine the behavior and use of a control, you need to know a control's public interface, or its *API*. Because a control is written as an ActionScript class, to get information from the control and to be able set its appearance, you need to know the control's members, their requirements, and their behavior:

- Properties
- Methods
- Events
- Styles
- Effects
- Constants

This information is available in the Flex API documentation for each of the framework's included controls.

Instantiating controls with MXML and ActionScript

When you instantiate a control with MXML, it's known as *declarative* instantiation:

```
<mx:Button id="myButton"/>
```

The same code in ActionScript is known as *programmatic* instantiation:

```
var myButton:Button = new Button();
this.addChild(myButton);
```

Either way, the result is a visual object that's created in Flash Player memory and displayed in the parent class. The behavior of the object is determined by its API and internal implementation.

Setting control properties and styles

A control's properties and styles can be set in two ways:

- Upon instantiation with MXML attributes
- With ActionScript code

Properties and styles that are set with MXML attributes are done pretty much the same way. This `Label` control has a `text` property and a `color` style:

```
<mx:Label id="myLabel" text="my text value" color="#ff0000"/>
```

But when you use ActionScript code to reset the object's properties and styles at runtime, the syntax is different. Properties are set with simple dot syntax:

```
myLabel.width = 100;
```

Styles are set with a method named `setStyle()` that takes two arguments: the style name and its new value:

```
myLabel.setStyle("fontWeight", "bold");
```

Styles are described in more detail in Chapter 10, but you need to understand this fundamental difference between properties and styles as you acquaint yourself with the controls that are described in this chapter.

Understanding the UIComponent class

As with any other ActionScript class, a control's members are a combination of those that are declared locally in the class and those that are declared in the class's inheritance hierarchy.

Each control, such as `Label`, is extended from a superclass named `UIComponent`. The UML diagram in Figure 8.1 describes the inheritance relationship between `UIComponent` and classes that extend the container and control classes.

FIGURE 8.1

This UML diagram describes the relationship between the `UIComponent` and the container and control classes.

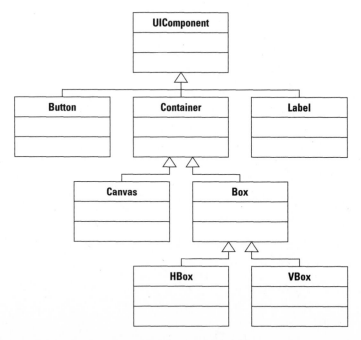

Visual components can be directly extended from UIComponent, as with Label and Button, or they can have UIComponent as one of the classes in their inheritance hierarchy, as with VBox, HBox, and Canvas. In this section, I describe the class's properties and styles that are inherited by all visual components.

UIComponent properties

Table 8.1 describes key properties that are declared in the UIComponent class and inherited by all visual components.

TABLE 8.1

Key UIComponent Properties

Property	Data Type	Description
currentState	String	Determines which named "view state" is currently displayed.
enabled	Boolean	Determines whether a component can receive user interactions, and in some cases, whether a "disabled" style will be used in its display.
height	Number	The height of the component in pixels. In MXML, you can also set height to a percentage setting such as "100%," but in ActionScript, the percentage would be set through the percentHeight property.
id	String	This becomes the component's instance (variable) name. Each component id within the scope of the application or the current custom component must be unique. The value of the id property cannot be reset at runtime. Components that are instantiated in MXML without an id property are anonymous and cannot be directly addressed in ActionScript or binding expressions.
maxHeight	Number	The maximum height of the component in pixels.
maxWidth	Number	The maximum width of the component in pixels.
minHeight	Number	The minimum height of the component in pixels.
minWidth	Number	The minimum width of the component in pixels.
percentHeight	Number	Percent height relative to the component's parent. This returns a meaningful value only if explicitly set.
percentWidth	Number	Percent width relative to the component's parent. This returns a meaningful value only if explicitly set.
states	Array	An array containing one or more view state definitions. (See Chapter 15 for more information on view states.)
styleName	String	A previously declared CSS style name (sometimes known as a CSS class) whose properties the component inherits.

Property	Data Type	Description
toolTip	String	A string that appears in a tool tip when the mouse hovers over the component.
transitions	Array	An array containing one or more view state transition definitions.
visible	Boolean	Whether the control is visible.
width	Number	The width of the control in pixels. In MXML, you also can set width to a percentage setting such as "100%," but in ActionScript, the percentage would be set through the percentWidth property.
x	Number	The number of pixels from the left edge of the control's parent to the left edge of the control. This is meaningful only in a container with absolute layout.
y	Number	The number of pixels from the top edge of the control's parent to the top of the control. This is meaningful only in a container with absolute layout.

Many more UIComponent properties are available that are used less frequently than those listed in Table 8.1. See the API documentation for a complete list.

Using Text Controls

The Flex framework includes five controls that are designed to display or accept text:

- Label: A single-line display control
- Text: A variable-height display control
- TextInput: A single-line data entry control
- TextArea: A variable-height data entry control
- RichTextEditor: A compound data entry control that accepts text and property settings and converts its content to HTML 1.0 code

Common properties of text controls

All five text controls support a common set of properties and styles, and each supports certain properties and styles that are unique to that control's functions and requirements.

Properties that are implemented by all text controls are described in Table 8.2.

TABLE 8.2

Common Properties of Text Controls

Property	Data Type	Description
condenseWhite	Boolean	Indicates whether extra white space (space characters, tabs, and line feeds) is removed from text with HTML 1.0 markup. This is not supported in RichTextEdit.
htmlText	String	Text that contains HTML 1.0 markup.
Text	String	Simple text that contains no HTML markup.

The text property

The text property is used to set or get simple string values with all text controls. As with all properties, its value can be accessed in either MXML or ActionScript.

To set the text property in MXML, you can use either an XML text attribute or a nested child <mx:text> tag set. This Label control has its text property set through an attribute:

```
<mx:Label id="myLabel" text="Hello World"/>
```

This Label control has its text property set through a nested child element:

```
<mx:Label id="myLabel">
  <mx:text>Hello World</mx:Text>
</mx:Label>
```

The two preceding Label declarations are functionally identical.

 **Notice that child elements that set properties require the mx namespace prefix. Property, style, and event listener attributes do not require the mx namespace prefix.**

To set or get the text property in ActionScript, use simple dot syntax:

```
myLabel.text = "A new string";
```

The htmlText property

The htmlText property accepts HTML 1.0 markup that modifies the display and behavior of the control. Although all five text controls support htmlText, both TextInput and TextArea typically support only displaying HTML (rather than accepting markup text as data entry).

Flash Player has limited HTML parsing and display capabilities. These HTML tags are supported in Flash Player 9:

- <a> (anchor)
- <b> (bold)

- `<br>` (break)
- `<font>` (font)
- `<img>` (image)
- `<i>` (italics)
- `<li>` (list item)
- `<p>` (paragraph)
- `<textformat>` (text format)
- `<u>` (underline)

Important limitations in Flash Player HTML support include the following:

- HTML tables are not supported.
- CSS within HTML markup is not supported.
- Flash Player 9 does not support ordered (numbered) lists.
- Only a single unordered (bulleted) list style is supported.
- Wrapping text in an `<a>` tag set creates a hyperlink, but does not affect color or underlining of text.
- Tags must be declared in lowercase.

Because HTML markup includes tag characters that can be misinterpreted by the Flex compiler, you usually can't use a simple MXML attribute to set the `htmlText` property's value. This `Label` control tries to use `htmlText` to set bold text:

```
<mx:Label htmlText="This text <b>is bold</b>"/>
```

The code looks like it should work, but it results in this compiler error:

```
The value of attribute "htmlText" must not contain the '<'
    character.
```

Since < is a reserved character in XML, using HTML markup in this manner isn't acceptable. You can get around this issue in three ways and successfully display HTML text: with an initialization function, with XML entities, and with a CDATA section.

Using an initialization function

An initialization function is executed during the initialization phase of an object's life cycle. A function that sets `htmlText` might look like this:

```
private function initText():void
{
  htmlLabel.htmlText = "This text <b>is bold</b>";
}
```

Because the HTML markup is wrapped inside ActionScript code, the rules for XML reserved characters no longer apply and you can add as many HTML tags as you need.

You call the initialization function upon the component's `initialize` event:

```
<mx:Label id="htmlLabel" initialize="initText()"/>
```

As shown in Figure 8.2, the application displays the text as defined in the `htmlText` property.

FIGURE 8.2

A `Label` displaying HTML text

Using XML entities

As described in Chapter 4, all XML reserved characters have *entities* that can be used as aliases for those characters. You can use these entities instead of their literal equivalents in the `htmlText` property:

```
<mx:Label htmlText="This text &lt;b&gt;is bold&lt;/b&gt;"/>
```

This example results in the same display as the first, but it's obviously very difficult to read and generally not recommended.

Using CDATA

Instead of using XML entities to replace the reserved characters in HTML markup, you're better off wrapping literal HTML markup inside a CDATA section. As described in Chapter 4, the CDATA block protects literal text from XML interpretation. To use the CDATA section, first declare the `htmlText` property as a child element instead of an attribute. Then wrap the HTML text inside the CDATA section:

```
<mx:Label>
  <mx:htmlText>
    <![CDATA[ This text <b>is bold</b> ]]>
  </mx:htmlText>
</mx:Label>
```

Because the reserved characters are wrapped inside the CDATA section, you can add as much literal markup text as you like without encountering XML parsing problems.

 **TIP** You can wrap existing text inside a CDATA section by first selecting the text and then selecting Source ⇨ Add CDATA Block from the Flex Builder menu.

Using the condenseWhite property

The condenseWhite property applies only to text set through the htmlText property. If applied to a control with text set through the text property, the value of condenseWhite is ignored. A Boolean value that defaults to false, when set to true it "normalizes" extra white space within the text.

In this code, a Text control displays a long text value set through the htmlText property:

```
<mx:Text width="200" condenseWhite="true">
  <mx:htmlText>
    <![CDATA[
    The quick <font color="#ff0000">red</font>
      fox jumped over the lazy brown dog.
    The quick <font color="#ff0000">red</font>
      fox jumped over the lazy brown dog.
    The quick <font color="#ff0000">red</font>
      fox jumped over the lazy brown dog.
    ]]>
  </mx:htmlText>
</mx:Text>
```

Figure 8.3 shows how the Text control is displayed with condenseWhite set to its default value of false. Notice that the extra line feeds and spaces in the code are displayed in the application.

FIGURE 8.3

HTML text with condenseWhite set to false

Figure 8.4 shows how the Text control is displayed with condenseWhite set to true. The extra line feeds and spaces in the code have been removed.

FIGURE 8.4

HTML text with `condenseWhite` set to `true`

> **TIP**   All text controls except the `RichTextEdit` control support the `condenseWhite` property. Use this property when displaying text (rather than accepting data entry), so when used with the `TextInput` or `TextArea` controls, it should be paired with an `editable` property set to `false`.

Text display controls

Two controls are designed exclusively for display of text: `Label` and `Text`. They're primarily distinguished from each other by how they handle text values that are too long to fit on a single line: The `Label` control truncates long text, whereas the `Text` control wraps the words and grows vertically as needed.

The Label control

The `Label` control displays a single line of text. By default, this control shrinks or grows horizontally to accommodate the width of its `text` property.

The truncateToFit property

The `Label` control's `truncateToFit` property is a `Boolean` value that determines whether text will be truncated. When set to the default value of `true`, text that is longer than can fit (given the control's current width) is truncated, and the control displays the surviving text followed by an ellipsis (...). In addition, when the user moves the mouse over the control, a tool tip pops up displaying the control's full text.

This `Label` control's `truncateToFit` property is set to the default of `true`:

```
<mx:Label width="200"
    text="The quick red fox jumped over the lazy brown dog."/>
```

Figure 8.5 shows that the `Label` control truncates the text and adds the ellipsis at the end. When the mouse hovers over the control, the tool tip shows the complete text.

FIGURE 8.5

A Label with truncateToFit set to true

This Label has the same width limitation, but truncateToFit is set to false:

```
<mx:Label width="200" truncateToFit="false"
   text="The quick red fox jumped over the lazy brown dog."/>
```

The result will be that the text is still truncated, but the ellipsis characters aren't added and the tool tip isn't available when the mouse hovers over the control.

The selectable property

The Label and Text controls share a Boolean property named selectable. When set to true, the user can select some or all of the control's text, right-click to see a context menu, and copy the selected text to the clipboard, as shown in Figure 8.6.

FIGURE 8.6

Right-click a selectable control to see the context menu

The Text control

The Text control also is used exclusively to display text, but unlike the Label, it can wrap text and expand vertically to show as much text as necessary.

If you don't set the `Text` control's `width` property, it expands to whatever width is needed to display its value on a single line. To cause word wrapping and vertical expansion, set the `width` to an absolute dimension in pixels or a percent value such as `100%` of the control's container.

This `Text` control has a long string value and a `width` set to 200 pixels:

```
<mx:Text width="200"
    text="The quick red fox jumped over the lazy brown dog."/>
```

As shown in Figure 8.7, the `Text` control wraps the text and expands vertically to display the entire text value.

FIGURE 8.7

A `Text` control with long text that wraps and expands vertically

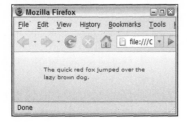

Limitations of the Label and Text controls

Both the `Label` and the `Text` control have these limitations:

- No support for background colors or images
- No support for borders
- No support for scrollbars

If you want backgrounds, borders, or scrollbars with displayed text, use the `TextInput` or `TextArea` controls with their `editable` property set to `false`.

Text entry controls

The Flex framework includes three text entry controls: `TextInput`, `TextArea`, and `RichTextEdit`.

The TextInput control

The `TextInput` control accepts a single line of data entry. This instance of the `TextInput` control is displayed with all default properties and styles:

```
<mx:TextInput id="myInput"/>
```

The TextInput control doesn't have its own label property, so it's commonly combined with a Label control and wrapped in an HBox, or wrapped in a FormItem container, which has its own label. When combined with an HBox and a Label, it looks like this:

```
<mx:HBox>
  <mx:Label text="Enter some text:"/>
  <mx:TextInput id="myInput"/>
</mx:HBox>
```

As shown in Figure 8.8, the TextInput control is displayed as a rectangular region with a default background color of white.

A simple TextInput control

In addition to having the same properties described previously that manage text display such as text, htmlText, and condenseWhite, the TextInput control defines certain properties that are of particular use in controlling data entry. Table 8.3 lists these properties.

TABLE 8.3

TextInput Properties

Property	Data Type	Description
displayAsPassword	Boolean	When set to true, causes entered characters to be displayed as "*" characters. Defaults to false.
editable	Boolean	When set to false, prevents control from receiving focus or data entry. Defaults to true.
horizontalScroll Position	Number	When the control's content is scrolled, indicates pixel position of left-most displayed content.
length	Number	A read-only property indicating the number of characters in the text property that's currently displayed.

continued

TABLE 8.3	(continued)	
Property	**Data Type**	**Description**
maxChars	int	The maximum number of characters the control accepts. If you exceed the maxChars value, you don't see a visible error message, but the control stops accepting entry.
restrict	String	Determines which characters the user can enter.
selectionBeginIndex	int	The index position of the first selected character.
selectionEndIndex	int	The index position of the last selected character.

Using the restrict property

The restrict property allows you to restrict which characters can be typed into a TextInput control. The property's value defaults to null, meaning the user can enter any character. Any other value means the user can enter only those characters, or ranges of characters, that are listed.

The restrict property accepts either literal individual characters or ranges of characters, with no delimiter between each selection. For example, a restrict value of abc means you can enter any of the three characters a, b, or c.

To enter a range of characters, separate the beginning and ending characters of the range with a hyphen. A restrict value of a-z0-9 allows any alphabetical or numeric character.

The restrict property is case-sensitive, so if its value is set to A-Z, the user can enter only lowercase characters. Any characters that are entered in lowercase are converted to uppercase automatically. To allow alphabetical characters to be entered in either uppercase or lowercase, enter the range twice, as in A-Za-z. If you want to include the dash (-) or backslash (\) as permitted characters, you must first use the escape character, the backslash (\).

 When a value is typed into a text control that isn't allowed by the control's restrict property, the user doesn't see an error — the typed value is just ignored.

Using selection properties

The properties selectionBeginIndex and selectionEndIndex allow you to programmatically select sections of text or find out what range of text is currently selected. This function selects all of a TextInput control's text and calls the control's setFocus() method to ensure that it has focus after the function has been executed:

```
private function selectText():void
{
  myInput.selectionBeginIndex = 0;
  myInput.selectionEndIndex = myInput.text.length;
  myInput.setFocus();
}
```

This function determines which text is currently selected and uses the String class's subString() method to get the selected text:

```
private function showSelectedText():void
{
   var beginIndex:int = myInput.selectionBeginIndex;
   var endIndex:int = myInput.selectionEndIndex;
   var selectedText:String =
      myInput.text.substring(beginIndex, endIndex);
   myInput.setFocus();
   myInput.selectionBeginIndex = beginIndex;
   myInput.selectionEndIndex = endIndex;
   Alert.show(selectedText, "Selected Text");
}
```

NOTE When the TextInput control loses focus, its selections are lost. The code in the preceding example resets the control's focus and selection index values to ensure that its original state is restored after the function has been executed.

TIP When using the selection index properties, remember that all indexing in ActionScript is zero-based. If selectionBeginIndex is set to a value of 1, the second character is the first one that's selected.

The TextArea control

The TextArea control implements most properties and methods of the TextInput control, but it works better when long values are to be entered. Unlike TextInput, it allows line feeds and wraps text that is too long to fit on a single line.

The TextArea control automatically creates a vertical scrollbar if its text or htmlText value is too long to be displayed given the control's current size. This TextArea control has a specified height and width of 150 pixels each and a text value that's long enough to trigger a vertical scrollbar:

```
<mx:TextArea id="myTextArea" width="150" height="150">
  <mx:text>
  <![CDATA[Lorem ipsum dolor sit amet, consectetuer adipiscing
   elit. Praesent aliquam, justo convallis luctus rutrum, erat
   nulla fermentum diam, at nonummy quam ante ac quam. Maecenas
   urna purus, fermentum id, molestie in, commodo porttitor,
   felis. Nam blandit quam ut lacus. Quisque ornare risus quis
   ligula.
   ]]>
  </mx:text>
</mx:TextArea>
```

As shown in Figure 8.9, the TextArea displays a vertical scrollbar to accommodate the long text.

FIGURE 8.9

A `TextArea` control with a vertical scrollbar

TIP   In the preceding code sample, the `text` value is a single unbroken string. Any spaces or line feeds are respected and displayed the `TextArea` component (unless text is set through the `htmlText` property with `condenseWhite` set to `true`).

The RichTextEditor control

The `RichTextEditor` control is a compound control that allows entry of text and these formatting features:

- Font family
- Font size in pixels
- Bold, italics, and underlining
- Font color
- Text alignment
- Bulleted lists
- Hyperlinks

As the user selects formatting options, they're interpreted into HTML 1.0 markup that can be understood by Flash Player. The value of the HTML markup is available through the control's `htmlText` property, which is a bindable value.

This `RichTextEditor` control's `title` property results in a `String` value displayed in the control's upper-left area. The `Text` control displays the editor's current `htmlText` property through a binding expression:

```
<mx:RichTextEditor id="myEditor" title="My Rich Text Editor"/>
<mx:Text text="{myEditor.htmlText}" width="400"/>
```

As shown in Figure 8.10, the control's `htmlText` property is displayed in the `Text` control as the user makes changes.

FIGURE 8.10

The `RichTextEdit` control

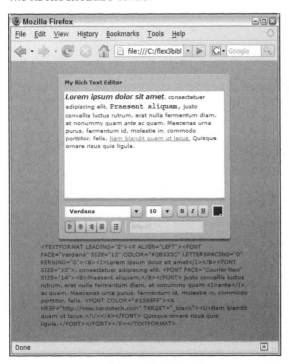

Using Layout Controls

A layout control creates visual output, but it isn't designed to be interactive in same way as a `Button`, `TextInput`, or other such control. These three controls affect layout but don't create any interaction with the user:

- `HRule`: A horizontal rule
- `VRule`: A vertical rule
- `Spacer`: An invisible control that can change other components' positions in horizontal or vertical layout

HRule and VRule

The HRule and VRule controls display a single line in the application. HRule creates a horizontal line, while VRule creates a vertical line. Each displays a primary line called the stroke and a secondary line called the shadow. You control the stroke and shadow colors and widths separately through distinct style settings.

Both HRule and VRule support the properties described in Table 8.4 to determine the control's appearance.

TABLE 8.4

HRule and VRule Properties

Property	Data Type	Description	Default
Width	Number	The width of the control	HRule: 100 VRule: 2
Height	Number	The height of the control	HRule: 2 VRule: 100
strokeColor	uint	The control's stroke line color	0xC4CCCC
strokeWidth	Number	The width of the primary line in pixels	2
shadowColor	uint	The control's shadow line color	0xEEEEEE

HRule and VRule objects are typically used to visually separate other visual components. This application displays two controls in vertical layout separated with an HRule control:

```
<?xml version="1.0" encoding="utf-8"?>
<mx:Application xmlns:mx="http://www.adobe.com/2006/mxml"
    verticalGap="25">
  <mx:RichTextEditor id="myEditor" title="My Rich Text Editor"/>
  <mx:HRule strokeColor="#000000" width="{myEditor.width}"/>
  <mx:Text text="{myEditor.htmlText}" width="{myEditor.width}"/>
</mx:Application>
```

As shown in Figure 8.11, the HRule appears between the other two controls.

FIGURE 8.11

A `RichTextEditor`, an `HRule`, and a `Text` control

The Spacer control

The `Spacer` control is invisible and "pushes" other objects in an application or other container that uses vertical or horizontal layout. Its `width` and `height` properties, set to `Number` values, dictate how much additional space they add to the layout.

 The `Spacer` control isn't useful in absolute layout containers, because the controls dictate their absolute positions through x and y properties or through constraint-based layout.

This application uses a `Spacer` with a `height` of 100 pixels to add vertical separation between two controls:

```
<?xml version="1.0" encoding="utf-8"?>
<mx:Application xmlns:mx="http://www.adobe.com/2006/mxml">
  <mx:RichTextEditor id="myEditor" title="My Rich Text Editor"/>
  <mx:Spacer height="100"/>
  <mx:Text text="{myEditor.htmlText}" width="400"/>
</mx:Application>
```

As shown in Figure 8.12, the space between the controls includes both the size of the `Spacer` and the `verticalGap` of the application.

FIGURE 8.12

Two controls separated with a `Spacer`

The Invisible Spacer creates this space

Using Button Controls

The Flex framework includes these button controls that allow interaction with the user:

- `Button`
- `LinkButton`
- `CheckBox`
- `RadioButton`
- `PopupButton`

As shown in the UML diagram in Figure 8.13, the `Button` control is implemented as the super-class for all other button controls. As a result, any event or property implemented in a `Button` is available in all the other controls described in this section.

FIGURE 8.13

Button controls inheritance hierarchy

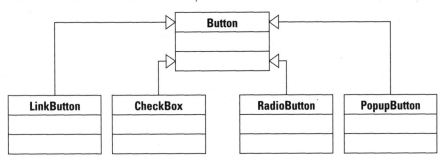

The Button control

The Button control is displayed as a rectangular object that can display a label and a graphical icon. One of the most commonly used interactive controls, you typically use event listeners with the Button and call ActionScript in reaction to its click event.

This simple Button control has a label of "Click Me" and a click event listener that displays an Alert dialog box:

```
<mx:Button label="Click Me" click="Alert.show('You clicked')"/>
```

Using a toggle Button

The Button control behaves by default as a *command* button to indicate that some action should be executed. To use the Button as a control that switches between two states, set its toggle property to true. The Button control has a Boolean property named selected that defaults to false. When toggle is set to true, each click event causes the selected property to switch back and forth between true and false.

This Button control's toggle property is set to true. Each time it's clicked, the selected property switches between true and false. The Label displays the selected property's current value through a binding expression:

```
<mx:Button id="toggleButton" label="Toggle Button"
    toggle="true"/>
<mx:Label text="Button selected: {toggleButton.selected}"/>
```

As shown in Figure 8.14, the control's appearance changes depending on the value of its selected property. If selected is false, it appears as a concave button; if true, its appearance flattens to indicate that it's selected.

FIGURE 8.14

Toggle buttons with the `selected` property set to `true` and `false`

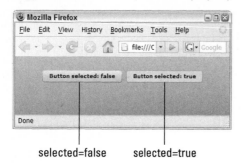

selected=false   selected=true

Using button icons

A button icon is a graphic that appears on the face of a `Button` control. You typically use an embedded graphic (rather than one that is downloaded from the server at runtime) for an icon, because embedding guarantees the best possible performance.

Button icons can be built in any supported graphic format: PNG, JPEG, GIF, and SWF. To embed a graphic for use as an icon, first declare it in the application as a bindable `Class` variable using the `[Embed]` metadata tag:

```
[Bindable]
[Embed(source="graphics/deleteIcon.png")]
public var myDeleteIcon:Class;
```

In the `Button` declaration, set the `icon` property to the embedded graphic variable using a binding expression:

```
<mx:Button id="deleteButton"
    label="Delete" icon="{myDeleteIcon}"/>
```

As shown in Figure 8.15, the `Button` control appears with the `icon` on the left and the `label` on the right.

FIGURE 8.15

A `Button` with an icon

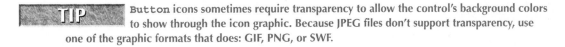

> **TIP** Button icons sometimes require transparency to allow the control's background colors to show through the icon graphic. Because JPEG files don't support transparency, use one of the graphic formats that does: GIF, PNG, or SWF.

Controlling the label position

The Button control's labelPlacement property determines the position of the label relative to the position of the icon and the Button control's dimensions. By default, the label is positioned in the center of a button with no icon, and to the right of an icon if it does exist. The possible values of labelPlacement include top, bottom, left, and right.

Figure 8.16 shows the effect of setting labelPlacement with a Button that uses a graphic icon.

FIGURE 8.16

A Button with an icon and labelPlacement set to different values

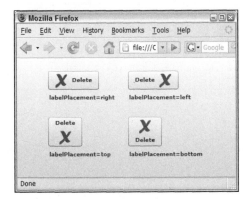

> **TIP** If you declare a Button object with an icon property but no label, the Button object's height and width are set dynamically to accommodate the size of the icon image.

The LinkButton control

The LinkButton control performs all the actions of the Button, but it has an appearance and behavior more like a traditional HTML hyperlink.

In its initial state, the LinkButton is transparent and shows only its label and icon (if any). As shown in Figure 8.17, when the cursor hovers over a LinkButton, its background color changes and a mouse cursor shaped as a pointing hand appears.

> **TIP** Because the LinkButton control extends Button, it supports all its superclass's properties and methods. Some, however, aren't very useful with the LinkButton. For example, while the toggle property is available with LinkButton, setting it to true doesn't cause any difference in appearance when the user clicks it to set selected to true or false.

FIGURE 8.17

The LinkButton with the mouse hovering over it

The CheckBox control

The CheckBox control allows the user to toggle its state to true or false. As shown in Figure 8.18, its selected property causes an icon shaped as a check mark inside a box to be displayed. When selected is false, the icon appears as an empty box.

FIGURE 8.18

A Checkbox object with its selected property set to true

Just as with the Button control that it extends, CheckBox supports the label property. The label appears by default to the right of the icon and is a clickable object; that is, clicking the icon and the label both have the same effect of toggling selected to true or false.

This CheckBox control displays a label of "Option selected":

```
<mx:CheckBox id="myCheckBox" label="Option selected"/>
```

At runtime, you determine or set whether the control is checked through its selected property:

```
private function checkSelected():void
{
  if (myCheckBox.selected)
  {
    Alert.show("You selected the CheckBox");
  }
```

```
    else
    {
      Alert.show("You didn't select the CheckBox");
    }
}
```

Using RadioButton controls

RadioButton controls are designed to be used in groups of controls representing mutually exclusive options. For example, this control represents the value "Small" and has its label set to the same value:

```
<mx:RadioButton value="Small" label="Small"/>
```

To group multiple radio buttons, use a control named RadioButtonGroup. This control is a non-visual object and provides a way to group RadioButton controls together so that only one of them can be selected at any given time. The RadioButtonGroup control is assigned an id property. Then each RadioButton joins the group by naming the RadioButtonGroup in its groupName property.

This is a group of mutually exclusive RadioButton controls, because they all share the same groupName property:

```
<mx:RadioButtonGroup id="buttonGroup"/>
<mx:RadioButton value="Small" label="Small"
  groupName="buttonGroup"/>
<mx:RadioButton value="Medium" label="Medium"
  groupName="buttonGroup"/>
<mx:RadioButton value="Large" label="Large"
  groupName="buttonGroup"/>
```

> **TIP** RadioButtonGroup is implemented as an invisible control rather than a visual container. This gives you the freedom to arrange RadioButton controls anywhere on screen, rather than visually grouped together.

The application in Listing 8.1 displays a group of RadioButton controls grouped with a RadioButtonGroup. When the user clicks Check Status, an Alert dialog displays the selected value.

LISTING 8.1

A group of radio buttons

```
<?xml version="1.0" encoding="utf-8"?>
<mx:Application xmlns:mx="http://www.adobe.com/2006/mxml"
   layout="vertical"
  backgroundColor="#eeeeee">
```

continued

LISTING 8.1 (continued)

```
<mx:Script>
  <![CDATA[
    import mx.controls.Alert;
    private function checkSelected():void
    {
      Alert.show("You selected " + buttonGroup.selectedValue);
    }
  ]]>
</mx:Script>
<mx:RadioButtonGroup id="buttonGroup"/>
<mx:VBox>
  <mx:RadioButton value="Small" label="Small"
 groupName="buttonGroup"/>
  <mx:RadioButton value="Medium" label="Medium"
 groupName="buttonGroup"/>
  <mx:RadioButton value="Large" label="Large"
 groupName="buttonGroup"/>
</mx:VBox>
<mx:Button label="Check status" click="checkSelected()"/>
</mx:Application>
```

ON the WEB The code in Listing 8.1 is available in the Web site files in the **chapter08** project's **src** folder as **RadioButtonGroup.mxml**.

Figure 8.19 shows the application displaying the resulting RadioButton controls.

FIGURE 8.19

An application with RadioButton controls

TIP The RadioButtonGroup control dispatches an **itemClick** event whenever any of its member RadioButton controls are selected. This allows you to handle **click** events for the entire group with a single event handler.

Other Data Entry Controls

The Flex framework includes these other controls that can be used to collect data from the application's user:

- NumericStepper
- DateField
- DateChooser
- ColorPicker

Each of these controls is designed to support data entry for a particular type of data.

The NumericStepper control

The NumericStepper is a compound control that's designed for numeric data entry. It includes a TextInput control for direct entry and a set of buttons that increment and decrement the control's current value.

The NumericStepper doesn't have its own label property, so it's typically paired with a Label or wrapped in a FormItem container, which has its own label property. This code declares a simple NumericStepper wrapped in an HBox with a Label:

```
<mx:HBox>
  <mx:Label text="Enter value:"/>
  <mx:NumericStepper id="myStepper"/>
</mx:HBox>
```

As shown in Figure 8.20, the control displays its value property and allows the user to change it.

FIGURE 8.20

A NumericStepper control

The NumericStepper supports these properties that determine its behavior:

- minimum: The minimum permitted value; defaults to 0
- maximum: The maximum permitted value; defaults to 10

241

- `stepSize`: The amount to increment or decrement when the control's buttons are clicked; defaults to 1
- `maxChars`: The maximum length of the value that can be directly typed into the control

This `NumericStepper` has a `minimum` value of 5, a `maximum` value of 25, and a `stepSize` of 5:

```
<mx:NumericStepper id="myStepper"
  minimum="5" maximum="25" stepSize="5"/>
```

The `NumericStepper` control's `value` property is bindable and can be used in a binding expression or ActionScript statement to get the value the user has entered:

```
<mx:Label text="You entered: {myStepper.value}"/>
```

Date controls

Two data entry controls are designed to show or select a date value:

- `DateChooser` displays a calendar from which the user selects a date.
- `DateField` displays a `TextInput` and a small calendar icon. When either is clicked, a calendar is displayed for date selection.

The DateChooser control

The `DateChooser` control presents an interactive calendar that displays a month and year and allows the user to do the following:

- Navigate forward and back one month at a time
- Select a single date, multiple dates, or a range of dates with mouse operations

The following code declares a simple `DateChooser` control:

```
<mx:DateChooser id="myDateChooser"/>
```

The `DateChooser` control supports `Boolean` properties named `allowMultipleSelection` and `allowDisjointSelection` that respectively allow multiple and non-contiguous dates to be selected. Changing either property causes changes in the control's visual presentation.

As shown in Figure 8.21, the `DateChooser` is presented as a visual calendar from which the user makes selections.

FIGURE 8.21

A DateChooser control

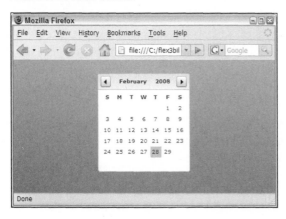

The DateField control

The DateField control presents the user with an input control and a small calendar icon. By default, when the user clicks either the icon or the input, a calendar control pops up that looks the same as the DateChooser and allows the user to make his selection. Unlike the DateChooser component, DateField allows only a single date value to be selected.

The following code declares a simple DateField control:

```
<mx:DateField id="myDateField"/>
```

As shown in Figure 8.22, the DateField is presented as an input control and icon which, when clicked, present a calendar control.

FIGURE 8.22

A DateField control

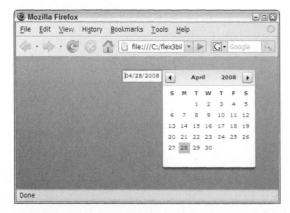

The DateField control has a Boolean property named editable that's set to false by default. When set to true, the user can click into the input area and type a date value.

Date entry properties and methods

The DateChooser and DateField controls share a common set of properties that allow you to control their behavior and collect their data. Table 8.5 describes these properties and their capabilities.

TABLE 8.5

Date Entry Control Properties

Property	Data Type	Description	Default
selectedDate	Date	The currently selected date value.	Null
showToday	Boolean	Determines whether the current date is highlighted.	true
dayNames	Array	An array of String values used as labels for the day names.	["S", "M", "T", "W", "T", "F", "S"]
minYear	int	The minimum allowed year.	1900
maxYear	int	The maximum allowed year.	2100
disabledDays	Array	An array of integer values indicating by zero-based index days that aren't selectable.	[] Setting of [0,6] would disable Sunday and Saturday
disabledRanges	Array of Object	A set of disabled ranges. Each range has named properties of rangeStart and rangeEnd typed as Date values.	[]
selectableRange	Object	A selectable range. Requires named properties of rangeStart and rangeEnd typed as Date values.	null

Other useful properties are described in the API documentation for DateField and DateChooser.

Using Interactive Controls

Beyond the data entry controls described previously, certain controls are designed for user interaction that can be used in a variety of applications. In this section, I describe the ScrollBar and Slider controls.

The ScrollBar controls

There are two versions of the ScrollBar control:

- HScrollBar is for a horizontal scrollbar.
- VScrollBar is for a vertical scrollbar.

A ScrollBar control has four graphic elements: a track, a button, and two arrows. The user changes the control's current value by clicking and dragging the button, clicking above or below the button, or clicking one of the arrows. The ScrollBar returns its current value through its scrollPosition property. The scrollPosition property isn't bindable, so typically it handles ScrollBar interactions by listening for the scroll event, which is dispatched each time the position of the button changes.

ScrollBar properties

The VScrollBar and HScrollBar are extended from the ScrollBar superclass, which implements the properties described in Table 8.6:

TABLE 8.6

ScrollBar Properties

Property	Data Type	Description	Default
scrollPosition	Number	The position of the scroll button relative to the top of a VScrollBar or the left of an HScrollBar. This property is bindable.	null
minScrollPosition	Number	The minimum value of scrollPosition.	0
maxScrollPosition	Number	The maximum value of scrollPosition.	0
pageSize	Number	Determines delta of change in pixels when user clicks before or after the scroll button.	0

The scroll event

The scroll event is dispatched each time the user interacts with the ScrollBar control. Its event object is typed as an event class named mx.events.ScrollEvent, which has a position property containing the new scrollPosition. In the application in Listing 8.2, the HScrollBar control's new scrollPosition is displayed in a Label control whose text property is changed each time the scroll event is handled:

LISTING 8.2

An application with a horizontal scrollbar

```
<?xml version="1.0" encoding="utf-8"?>
<mx:Application xmlns:mx="http://www.adobe.com/2006/mxml"
  layout="vertical">

  <mx:Script>
    <![CDATA[
      import mx.events.ScrollEvent;
      [Bindable]
      private var scrollPos:Number;

      private function scrollHandler(event:ScrollEvent):void
      {
        scrollPos = event.position;
      }
    ]]>
  </mx:Script>

  <mx:Label id="scrollLabel" fontSize="18" fontWeight="bold"
    text="Current scroll position: {scrollPos}"/>
  <mx:HScrollBar id="myScrollBar" width="300"
    minScrollPosition="0" maxScrollPosition="300" pageSize="100"
    scroll="scrollHandler(event)"/>

</mx:Application>
```

ON the WEB The code in Listing 8.2 is available in the Web site files in the `chapter08` project's `src` folder as `ScrollBarDemo.mxml`.

Figure 8.23 shows the `HScrollBar` and `Label` component in the application.

FIGURE 8.23

An `HScrollBar` and a `Label` displaying its current position

The Slider controls

There are two versions of the Slider control:

- HSlider is for a horizontal slider.
- VSlider is for a vertical slider.

A Slider control displays a track and a "thumb" graphic that allows the user to select a value by clicking and dragging the thumb. You allow the slider to select any value within a range or restrict it to selecting values at particular intervals. The control also can display two thumb icons to represent starting and ending values.

The user interacts with the Slider control by clicking and dragging the thumb icon or by clicking before or after the thumb. If the user clicks before or after the thumb, it slides to the selected position. If the Slider has implemented snapping through the snapInterval property, the thumb slides to the snapping position that's closest to where the mouse click occurred.

The Slider controls return their current value through the value property. The value property is bindable, so you can handle Slider interactions through either binding expressions or events. Each time the Slider control's value changes, it dispatches the change event.

Slider properties

The VSlider and HSlider are extended from the Slider superclass, which implements the properties described in Table 8.7.

TABLE 8.7

Slider Properties

Property	Data Type	Description	Default
value	Number	The currently selected value of the Slider based on thumb position. Relevant only when thumbCount is 1.	0
values	Array	An array of values. Relevant only when thumbCount is greater than 1.	[]
thumbCount	int	The number of thumbs that are displayed. Possible values are 1 and 2.	1
minimum	Number	Minimum value of the Slider.	0
maximum	Number	Maximum value of the Slider.	10
snapInterval	Number	When set, enforces snapping to particular intervals between minimum and maximum. If set to 0, sliding is continuous.	0

continued

TABLE 8.7		(continued)		
Property	**Data Type**	**Description**		**Default**
tickInterval	Number	A numeric value used to calculate interval of tick marks. Forexample, if minimum is 0, and maximum is 10, a tickInterval of 2 creates 4 tick marks. The default value of 0 displays no tick marks.		9
tickValues	Array	Determines display of tick marks on the Slider. All values should be between minimum and maximum. Use as alternative to tickInterval.		undefined
labels	Array	An array of strings used as labels. Typically contains same number of items as tickValues.		undefined

The following code declares a Slider with tick marks and labels. Its value is displayed in a Label control through a binding expression.

```xml
<?xml version="1.0" encoding="utf-8"?>
<mx:Application xmlns:mx="http://www.adobe.com/2006/mxml">
  <mx:Label id="sliderLabel" fontSize="18" fontWeight="bold"
    text="Current slider position: {mySlider.value}"/>
  <mx:HSlider id="mySlider" width="300"
    minimum="0" maximum="300"
    tickInterval="50" snapInterval="50"
    labels="{['0','50','100','150','200','250','300']}"/>
</mx:Application>
```

Figure 8.24 shows the resulting application running in Flash Player.

FIGURE 8.24

A horizontal slider with snapping and tick marks

Slider events

The Slider controls also support a set of events that let you detect and handle changes to the Slider control's value with ActionScript event handlers. Slider events include the following:

- change: Dispatched when the control's value property changes as a result of a user gesture
- thumbDrag: Dispatched when the user drags the thumb icon
- thumbPress: Dispatched when the user presses on the thumb icon with the left mouse button
- thumbRelease: Dispatched when the user releases the thumb icon

All these events dispatch an event object typed as mx.events.SliderEvent.

Working with Images

The Flex framework presents images with the Image control. This control can be used to present images that are downloaded from a server at runtime, loaded from the local hard disk at runtime (for AIR applications only, since Flex-based Web applications don't have access to the local file system), or embedded in the Flex application.

Using the Image control

As with all visual controls, the Image control can be declared in either MXML or ActionScript. You control which image is presented with the source property.

When used to load images at runtime, the source property is set to a full URL path (subject to Flash Player security restrictions) or a location that's relative to the application location.

> **TIP** For Web applications, the location is the Web server and folder from which the application's SWF file was downloaded. For desktop applications, the location is the disk folder in which the binary application is installed.

Flash Player can load these types of images at runtime:

- JPEG
- GIF
- PNG
- SWF

> **TIP** When you load an .swf file with the Image control, it's loaded as a static image. If the .swf file was built in Flash, only the Flash document's first frame is displayed. If you want to load an .swf file built in Flex or Flash and retain its animations and other functionality, use the SWFLoader control instead of Image.

This code declares an Image control that loads a graphic file named flower1.jpg at runtime from a graphics subfolder of the application's location folder:

```
<mx:Image source="graphics/flower1.jpg"/>
```

Figure 8.25 shows the application displaying the graphic.

FIGURE 8.25

An application displaying an image with the Image control

Resizing images

The Image control sizes itself by default based on the native dimensions of the original graphic image file. For example, if the image is 200 pixels wide by 300 pixels high and you don't declare a specific size, the control sizes itself to those dimensions.

You can resize images at runtime with the Image control's height and width properties. Both properties reflect the image size in pixels. If you set only one of these dimension properties, the Image control automatically calculates and resets the other dimension to maintain the image's original aspect ratio (the ratio of width to height).

If you set both the height and width and don't exactly match the original aspect ratio, also set the control's maintainAspectRatio property to false to allow it to skew the image.

```
<mx:Image source="graphics/flower1.jpg"
  height="200" width="400"
  maintainAspectRatio="false"/>
```

Figure 8.26 shows the image with explicit height and width properties and maintainAspectRatio set to false.

An image with specific width and height and maintainAspectRatio set to false

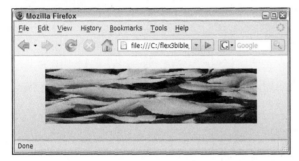

Embedding images

When you embed an image in a Flex application, you expand the size of the application by the size of the graphic file. At runtime an embedded image is displayed instantly, rather than having to be loaded from the Web or disk; the result is an improvement in perceived application performance.

You can embed images in a Flex application in two ways. If you want to embed an image once and always display it in the same location, use this syntax:

```
<mx:Image source="@Embed('graphics/flower1.jpg')"/>
```

Because you're embedding the image in a particular instance of the Image control, you can't easily reuse the embedded image elsewhere in the application. If you want an embedded image that can easily be bound to various controls, use the [Embed] metadata tag and a Class variable declaration inside a Script section:

```
[Embed(source="graphics/flower1.jpg")]
[Bindable]
public var flowerImage:Class;
```

Then set the Image control's source property to the variable name using a binding expression:

```
<mx:Image source="{flowerImage}"/>
```

> **TIP** When you embed images with the [Embed] metadata tag, you have the freedom to display the embedded image anywhere in the application. This is the same technique described earlier when using embedded images as Button control icons.

Changing images at runtime

You can change the source of an Image control at runtime in a few different ways. The control's source property can be reset to a String indicating the relative location of an image to be loaded at runtime or to a variable that references an embedded image. This code embeds two images and switches the source of the Image control to one of the variable references when the button is clicked:

```
<mx:Script>
  <![CDATA[
    [Embed(source="graphics/flower1.jpg")]
    [Bindable]
    public var flowerImage1:Class;
    [Embed(source="graphics/flower2.jpg")]
    [Bindable]
    public var flowerImage2:Class;
  ]]>
</mx:Script>

<mx:Image id="myImage" source="{flowerImage1}"/>
<mx:Button label="Change Image"
   click="myImage.source=flowerImage2"/>
```

You also can set the source property using a binding expression. This code uses a group of RadioButton controls to allow the user to switch between the two embedded images:

```
<mx:Image source="{flowerGroup.selectedValue}"/>
<mx:RadioButton value="{flowerImage1}" label="Image 1"
   groupName="flowerGroup" selected="true"/>
<mx:RadioButton value="{flowerImage2}" label="Image 2"
   groupName="flowerGroup"/>
<mx:RadioButtonGroup id="flowerGroup"/>
```

You also can change images at runtime with the Image control's load() method. The load() method accepts a single argument that can be either a String for a runtime loaded image or a variable referencing an embedded image. This code shows a Button with a click event handler that causes a new image to be loaded at runtime:

```
<mx:Image id="myImage" source="graphics/flower1.jpg"/>
<mx:Button label="Change Picture"
   click="myImage.load('graphics/flower2.jpg')"/>
```

> **TIP** It doesn't matter whether you use the load() method or simply change the value of the source property. Both actions have the same effect on the Image control.

Summary

In this chapter, I described the nature of Flex controls and the details of some of the most useful controls in the Flex framework. You learned the following:

- Flex visual components consist of containers and controls.
- A container is a visual component that contains other objects.
- A control executes some feature of a Flex application.
- Controls can be used for application layout, to display data, and to collect data from the user.
- Text controls include Label, Text, TextInput, TextArea, and RichTextEditor.
- Layout controls include HRule, VRule, and Spacer.
- Button controls include Button, CheckBox, RadioButton, and PopupButton.
- Other data entry controls include NumericStepper, DateField, DateChooser, and ColorPicker.
- Interactive controls include HScrollBar, VScrollBar, HSlider, and VSlider.
- The Image control displays images that are loaded at runtime or embedded in the Flex application.

Chapter 9

Using Layout Containers

A s described in Chapter 8, there are two types of visual components in Flex:

- *Containers* are visual components that can contain other objects.
- *Controls* are visual components that display information or provide the application with user interaction capabilities.

The layout of a Flex application is determined through a combination of the application's containership hierarchy and the use of absolute layout tools. Applications are typically designed with a combination of vertical or horizontal flow-style containers that lay out their nested child components automatically, and absolute layout components whose nested child components either set their positions with x and y or constraint properties.

The Flex framework includes two types of containers:

- *Layout containers* are rectangular regions that contain other visual components (containers or controls). Examples of layout containers include:
  - VBox
  - HBox
  - Canvas
  - Panel

IN THIS CHAPTER

Understanding containers

Using box containers

Using vertical and horizontal layout containers

Using the panel container

Using constraint-based layout

Sizing containers and controls

- *Navigator containers* wrap around other containers in a stack that contains the layers of the application's navigation system. The Flex framework includes three navigator containers:

    - ViewStack
    - TabNavigator
    - Accordion

In this chapter, I describe the pre-built layout containers in the Flex framework and how you use them to determine the application's visual appearance.

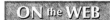 To use the sample code for this chapter, import the `chapter09.zip` Flex project archive file from the Web site files into your Flex Builder workspace.

Using Simple Box Containers

The three simple Box containers in the Flex framework implement different layout styles:

- VBox: A rectangular area that lays out its nested child objects in a single column from top to bottom
- HBox: A rectangular area that lays out its nested child objects in a single row from left to right
- Canvas: A rectangular area that places its nested child objects in specific positions relative to either top/left anchors or constraint-based anchors

These three containers support the height and width properties to determine their dimensions. If you don't declare these properties, the containers size themselves automatically to accommodate their child objects.

Using vertical and horizontal layout containers

As shown in the UML diagram in Figure 9.1, the VBox and HBox components are extended from a superclass named Box.

TIP While you're allowed to use the superclass Box component and set its `direction` property to either `vertical` or `horizontal`, which is the only difference between the subclasses, most often you already know which layout you want and can use the specific subclass.

The Box, VBox, and HBox components place their nested child visual components using two logical passes through the containership. In the first pass, the quantity and size of the nested child objects are collected. In the second pass, the nested objects are placed on the screen. Each time the Box component is resized, it re-executes this sizing and placement task.

FIGURE 9.1

The inheritance hierarchy for Box, VBox, and HBox

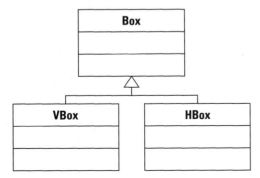

The VBox container

The VBox container behaves like the Application component when its layout is set to vertical: It lays out nested visual components in a single column from top to bottom. The application in Listing 9.1 uses a VBox to lay out three TextInput controls.

LISTING 9.1

Using the VBox container

```xml
<?xml version="1.0" encoding="utf-8"?>
<mx:Application xmlns:mx="http://www.adobe.com/2006/mxml"
   layout="vertical">
  <mx:Style>
    TextInput { font-size:24 }
  </mx:Style>
  <mx:VBox
    borderStyle="solid" borderColor="#000000" borderThickness="4"
    horizontalAlign="center"
    paddingBottom="10" paddingLeft="10" paddingRight="10"
   paddingTop="10">
    <mx:TextInput text="TextInput 1"/>
    <mx:TextInput text="TextInput 2"/>
    <mx:TextInput text="TextInput 3"/>
  </mx:VBox>
</mx:Application>
```

ON the WEB The code in Listing 9.1 is available in the Web site files as VBoxDemo.mxml in the chapter09 project.

Figure 9.2 shows the resulting application running in the Web browser.

FIGURE 9.2

An application using the VBox container

The HBox container

The HBox container behaves like the Application component when its layout is set to horizontal: It lays out nested visual components in a single column from top to bottom. The application in Listing 9.2 uses an HBox to lay out three TextInput controls.

LISTING 9.2

Using the HBox container

```
<?xml version="1.0" encoding="utf-8"?>
<mx:Application xmlns:mx="http://www.adobe.com/2006/mxml"
  layout="vertical">
 <mx:Style>
   TextInput { font-size:24 }
 </mx:Style>
 <mx:HBox
   borderStyle="solid" borderColor="#000000" borderThickness="4"
   horizontalAlign="center"
   paddingBottom="10" paddingLeft="10" paddingRight="10"
  paddingTop="10">
   <mx:TextInput text="TextInput 1"/>
   <mx:TextInput text="TextInput 2"/>
   <mx:TextInput text="TextInput 3"/>
 </mx:HBox>
</mx:Application>
```

Figure 9.3 shows the resulting application running in the Web browser.

FIGURE 9.3

An application using the HBox container

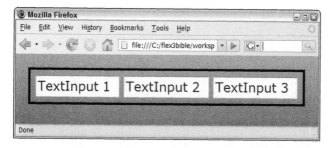

Using the Canvas container

The Canvas container behaves like the Application component when its layout is set to absolute. As shown in Figure 9.4, the Canvas container extends the Container class directly.

Objects that are nested within a Canvas determine their positions in one of these ways:

■ Traditional absolute-layout properties of x and y (the number of pixels from the left and top of the Canvas container)

■ Constraint-based positioning using anchors of left, right, top, bottom, horizontalCenter, and verticalCenter

■ Advanced constraints using row-based and column-based anchors

Visual components that are nested in a Canvas can use the following properties to set their positions relative to the Canvas container's top-left corner:

■ x: The number of horizontal pixels from the Canvas container's left border

■ y: The number of vertical pixels from the Canvas container's top border

The following code declares a Label component nested in a Canvas. The Label control's top-left corner is 10 pixels from the top and left of the Canvas:

```
<mx:Canvas>
  <mx:Label x="10" y="10" text="Hello World!"/>
</mx:Canvas>
```

The inheritance hierarchy of the Canvas container

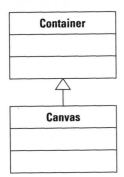

One benefit of the Canvas, Application, and other containers that support absolute positioning is the ability to layer objects on top of each other. Paired with alpha styles that control transparency, you can create visual effects where one object appears "behind" another, but shows through the "top" object.

The code in Listing 9.3 declares a Canvas container wrapped around three TextInput controls and three VBox containers. The VBox containers are arranged so that they overlap each other, and the backgroundAlpha setting of .5 creates a 50 percent transparency effect.

A Canvas container with overlapping objects

```
<?xml version="1.0" encoding="utf-8"?>
<mx:Application xmlns:mx="http://www.adobe.com/2006/mxml"
   layout="vertical">
  <mx:Style>
    TextInput { font-size:24 }
  </mx:Style>
  <mx:Canvas borderStyle="solid" borderColor="#000000"
  borderThickness="4"
    width="400" height="313">
    <mx:TextInput text="TextInput 1"/>
    <mx:TextInput text="TextInput 2" x="71" y="47"/>
    <mx:TextInput text="TextInput 3" x="141" y="97"/>

    <mx:VBox width="100" height="100" backgroundColor="#FFFFFF"
      backgroundAlpha=".5" x="224" y="144"/>
```

```
    <mx:VBox width="100" height="100" backgroundColor="#666666"
      backgroundAlpha=".5" x="249" y="169"/>
    <mx:VBox width="100" height="100" backgroundColor="#000000"
      backgroundAlpha=".5" x="274" y="194"/>
  </mx:Canvas>

</mx:Application>
```

ON the WEB   The code in Listing 9.3 is available in the Web site files as `CanvasDemo.mxml` in the `chapter09` project.

Figure 9.5 shows the resulting application displayed in a browser. Notice the overlapping objects and the borders that show through.

FIGURE 9.5

A `Canvas` container with overlapping objects

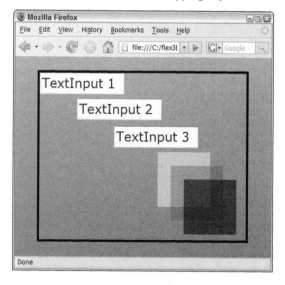

Using container styles

The `VBox` and `HBox` containers support styles that help to determine placement of nested objects. These styles, described in Table 9.1, control the alignment and the area around and between objects nested within the container.

TABLE 9.1

Box Container Styles

Style	Description	Possible Values/ Data Type	Default Value
verticalAlign	Collective vertical alignment of objects within the container	top middle bottom	top
horizontalAlign	Collective horizontal alignment of objects within the container	left center right	left
verticalGap	Number of vertical pixels between objects; applies to VBox only	Number	6
horizontalGap	Number of vertical pixels between objects; applies to HBox only	Number	6
paddingLeft	Number of pixels from left edge of container to first nested object	Number	0
paddingRight	Number of pixels from right edge of container to first nested object	Number	0
paddingTop	Number of pixels from top edge of container to first nested object	Number	0
paddingBottom	Number of pixels from bottom edge of container to first nested object	Number	0

The application in Listing 9.4 places nested visual components within a VBox container that sets gap, border, and padding styles using CSS syntax and MXML style attributes.

LISTING 9.4

An application with box styles

```
<?xml version="1.0" encoding="utf-8"?>
<mx:Application xmlns:mx="http://www.adobe.com/2006/mxml"
   layout="vertical"
  backgroundColor="#eeeeee">
  <mx:Style>
    TextInput {
      font-size:24;
      border-style:solid;
      border-color:black;
      border-thickness:4;
```

```
      }
   </mx:Style>
   <mx:Spacer height="20"/>
   <mx:VBox
      borderStyle="solid" borderColor="#000000" borderThickness="4"
      horizontalAlign="center"
      paddingBottom="20" paddingLeft="20" paddingRight="20"
    paddingTop="20"
      verticalGap="20" backgroundColor="white">
      <mx:TextInput text="TextInput 1"/>
      <mx:TextInput text="TextInput 2"/>
      <mx:TextInput text="TextInput 3"/>
   </mx:VBox>
</mx:Application>
```

ON the WEB   The code in Listing 9.4 is available in the Web site files as
VBoxGapAndPadding.mxml in the **chapter09** project.

The diagram in Figure 9.6 shows the placement of gap and padding styles in a VBox container.

FIGURE 9.6

Using gap and padding styles

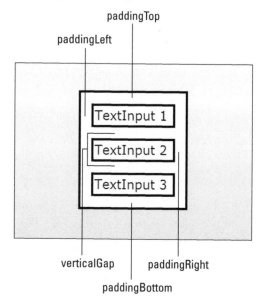

TIP The alignment, gap, and padding styles have no effect on objects nested inside a `Canvas` container, because the objects' positions are determined solely by their absolute positioning properties.

TIP Developers who are familiar with Cascading Style Sheets as implemented in Web browsers might be curious about the lack of margin styles. In HTML-based CSS, the "box model" includes padding on the inside of an object's borders, the borders themselves, and margins outside the borders that create space outside an object. Flex-based CSS omits the margin settings and implements only padding and border styles. The details of applying these and other styles are described in Chapter 10.

Using the Panel Container

The `Panel` container creates a rectangular region that looks like a dialog box. Unlike the `VBox`, `HBox`, and `Canvas`, which don't have any default visual appearance, a `Panel` is used when you want to wrap content inside a visual presentation that sets it off from the rest of the application.

A simple `Panel` is declared in MXML with a pair of `<mx:Panel>` tags. The `Panel` container's nested components are declared between the paired tags:

```
<mx:Panel>
   ... place contents here ...
</Panel>
```

Panel properties

The `Panel` shares many properties with the `Application` and `Box` containers.

Using the layout property

Like the `Application` component, it supports the `layout` property and allows the `Panel` container's nest components to be laid out with `vertical`, `horizontal`, or `absolute` positioning. As with `Application`, the default value is `vertical`.

Using title and status

The `Panel` container has two properties that place labels in the container's header region:

- The `title` property places a label in a bold font in the left side of the `Panel` header.
- The `status` property places a label in normal font in the right side of the `Panel` header.

The code in Listing 9.5 declares a `Panel` with a `title` and a `status` property, and contains a set of `Label` controls.

LISTING 9.5

A Panel containing three Label controls

```xml
<?xml version="1.0" encoding="utf-8"?>
<mx:Application xmlns:mx="http://www.adobe.com/2006/mxml"
    layout="vertical"
  backgroundColor="#cccccc">
  <mx:Panel title="My Panel" status="A test panel" width="200">
    <mx:Label text="Label 1"/>
    <mx:Label text="Label 2"/>
    <mx:Label text="Label 3"/>
  </mx:Panel>
</mx:Application>
```

ON the WEB The code in Listing 9.5 is available in the Web site files as `PanelDemo.mxml` in the `chapter09` project.

Figure 9.7 shows a `Panel` containing the three `Label` controls and displaying the `title` and `status` values in the `Panel` header.

FIGURE 9.7

A `Panel` with `title` and `status` properties

TIP While a `Panel` looks like a dialog box, it's typically presented "in line" with the rest of the application layout, rather than as a pop-up window. When you present pop-up windows, you typically use the `TitleWindow` container or the Alert class, both of which extend the `Panel` container and share its capabilities but are specifically designed for that use.

Panel styles

The Panel container supports all the Box styles described previously and adds other styles that are specific to its functions and abilities.

The Panel container and transparency

The Panel container has a borderAlpha style that controls the level of transparency in the container's title bar, control bar, and sides. Alpha values in Flex are set to a range of 0 to 1, where 0 is fully transparent and 1 is fully opaque. The default borderAlpha for a new Panel is .4, meaning that it has an opaqueness of 40 percent and the background color or image can show through the panel's outside area.

 The Panel container displays a drop shadow by default. To remove the shadow, set the Panel object's dropShadowEnabled property to false.

The code in Listing 9.6 displays three Panel containers with borderAlpha settings of 0, .4 (the default), and 1.

LISTING 9.6

Panel containers with different borderAlpha values

```
<?xml version="1.0" encoding="utf-8"?>
<mx:Application xmlns:mx="http://www.adobe.com/2006/mxml"
  backgroundColor="#333333" layout="horizontal">
    <mx:Panel title="borderAlpha=0" width="200" borderAlpha="0"
      color="#ffffff">
    ... nested labels ...
  </mx:Panel>
    <mx:Panel title="borderAlpha=.4" width="200" borderAlpha=".4">
    ... nested labels ...
  </mx:Panel>
    <mx:Panel title="borderAlpha=1" width="200" borderAlpha="1">
    ... nested labels ...
  </mx:Panel>
</mx:Application>
```

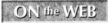 The code in Listing 9.6 is available in the Web site files as PanelTransparency.mxml in the chapter09 project.

Figure 9.8 shows the three Panel containers with the differing levels of transparency against a dark Application background.

Panel containers with differing borderAlpha settings

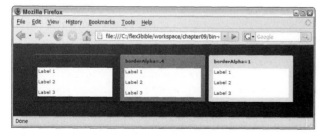

Controlling Panel corners

By default, a Panel presents rounded corners in the header and square corners in the footer. To instead present round corners for both the header and footer, set roundedBottomCorners to true, like this:

```
<mx:Panel title="My Panel" roundedBottomCorners="true">
   ...nested content...
</mx:Panel>
```

The Panel container also supports the cornerRadius style, which determines the amount of curve in the container's corners. The default cornerRadius is 4 pixels. Setting this value to 0 results in square corners at the top and bottom of the container; increasing the value creates a softer curve.

The code in Listing 9.7 creates a Panel container with rounded corners at both top and bottom and a cornerRadius of 15.

A Panel container with modified corner styles

```
<?xml version="1.0" encoding="utf-8"?>
<mx:Application xmlns:mx="http://www.adobe.com/2006/mxml">
  <mx:Panel title="A panel with rounded corners" width="200"
    roundedBottomCorners="true" cornerRadius="15">
    <mx:Label text="Label 1"/>
    <mx:Label text="Label 2"/>
    <mx:Label text="Label 3"/>
  </mx:Panel>
</mx:Application>
```

ON the WEB The code in Listing 9.7 is available in the Web site files as **PanelCorners.mxml** in the **chapter09** project.

Figure 9.9 shows the application with a `Panel` with rounded top and bottom corners and a `cornerRadius` of 15.

A `Panel` with rounded top and bottom corners

The ControlBar container

The `ControlBar` container is designed to be nested as the last component within a `Panel` or a `TitleWindow`. This container mimics the behavior of the `HBox` container, laying out its nested components horizontally, and creates a footer region below the other `Panel` container's nested objects with a style that matches the title bar. In addition to providing a container for objects in the `Panel` container's footer, it rounds the `Panel` container's bottom corners in the same manner as the `roundedBottomCorners` style. The code in Listing 9.8 creates a `Panel` with a `ControlBar`.

A Panel with a ControlBar

```
<?xml version="1.0" encoding="utf-8"?>
<mx:Application xmlns:mx="http://www.adobe.com/2006/mxml"
   layout="vertical"
  backgroundColor="#cccccc">
  <mx:Panel title="A Panel with a ControlBar">
    <mx:Label text="Label 1"/>
    <mx:Label text="Label 2"/>
    <mx:Label text="Label 3"/>
    <mx:ControlBar>
      <mx:Button label="Button 1"/>
      <mx:Button label="Button 2"/>
      <mx:Button label="Button 3"/>
    </mx:ControlBar>
  </mx:Panel>
</mx:Application>
```

ON the WEB The code in Listing 9.8 is available in the Web site files as `ControlBarDemo.mxml` in the `chapter09` project.

Figure 9.10 shows the resulting application. Notice that the `Button` controls in the `ControlBar` lay out horizontally.

FIGURE 9.10

A `Panel` with a `ControlBar`

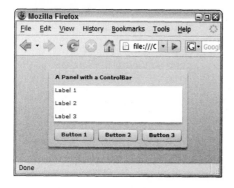

TIP The `ControlBar` container always lays out its nested components horizontally. If you want to stack objects in a `ControlBar` vertically or place them with absolute positions, declare a `VBox` or `Canvas` container inside the `ControlBar`.

To separate controls within a `ControlBar` so that they "glue" themselves to the far left and right edges, add a `Spacer` control between the controls with a width of 100:

```
<mx:ControlBar>
  <mx:Button label="Button 1"/>
  <mx:Spacer width="100%"/>
  <mx:Button label="Button "/>
</mx:ControlBar>
```

Figure 9.11 shows that the component after the `Spacer` is pushed to the far right edge of the `ControlBar`.

FIGURE 9.11

A ControlBar with a Spacer

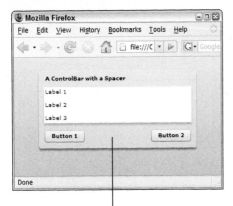

The invisible Spacer

Using Constraint-Based Layout

Constraint-based layout allows you to place objects on the screen using anchors other than a container's top-left corner. You can implement constraint-based layout easily using Flex Builder's Design and Flex Properties views or with a code-based approach. And, using the new ConstraintRow and ConstraintColumn classes, you can anchor objects to regions other than the borders of the container.

NOTE   Constraint-based layout works only in containers that support absolute layout. When used in the Application, Panel, or TitleWindow containers, the container's layout property must be set to absolute for constraint properties to have an effect. Because the Canvas container always uses absolute layout, constraint properties work within that container without any other changes to its property values. Constraint-based layout does not work in VBox, HBox, ControlBar, or other containers that don't support absolute layout.

Positioning components in Design view

Flex Builder's Design view has tools that can create constraint properties through a combination of selecting options in the Flex Properties view and dragging an object with anchors in the Design view editor. Figure 9.12 shows the Constraints interface in the Flex Properties view. This interface appears whenever a component in a container with absolute layout is selected in Design view.

FIGURE 9.12

The Constraints interface in the Flex Properties view

The Constraints user interface

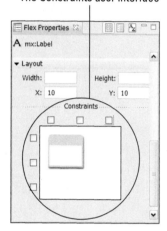

Follow these steps to create an application a text logo that's anchored to the application's bottom-right corner:

1. Open any Flex Builder project.

2. Select File ⇨ New ⇨ MXML Application from the Flex Builder menu.

3. As shown in Figure 9.13, enter **UsingConstraints.mxml** as the application filename and set the `layout` property to `absolute`.

4. If the application opens in Source view, click the Design button.

5. Drag a `Label` control from the Components view into the application. Place it anywhere on the screen.

6. Set the new `Label` control's `text` property to **My Logo**.

7. With the `Label` control still selected, click the Bold button in the Flex properties view.

FIGURE 9.13

Creating an application with absolute layout

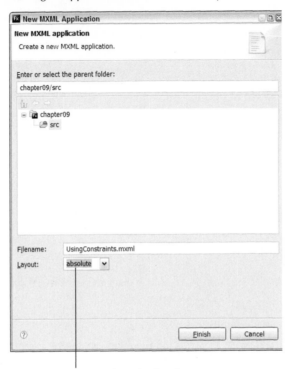

Use of constraints requires absolute layout

8. Set the Label control's font size to 18 pixels.

9. In the Constraints interface at the bottom of the Flex Properties view, place check marks in the right anchor and the bottom anchor, as shown in Figure 9.14.

10. Drag the Label component toward the bottom-right corner of the Application until it snaps to the padding alignment guides.

   You should see in the Constraints interface that the number of pixels from each anchor changes as you drag the Label control in Design view.

 The completed version of the preceding exercise is available in the Web site files as UsingConstraintsComplete.mxml in the chapter09 project.

FIGURE 9.14

The Constraints interface

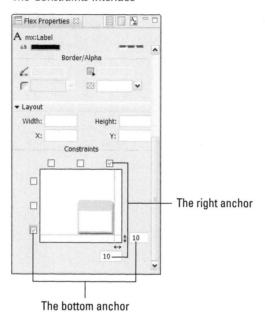

The right anchor

The bottom anchor

Using constraint properties

Each visual component supports six constraint properties. Each of the properties is data typed as a Number and indicates the number of pixels from the named anchor:

- left: This property sets the number of pixels from the left edge of the container to the left edge of the nested component.

- right: This property sets the number of pixels from the right edge of the container to the right edge of the nested component.

- top: This property sets the number of pixels from the top edge of the container to the top edge of the nested component.

- bottom: This property sets the number of pixels from the bottom edge of the container to the bottom edge of the nested component.

- horizontalCenter: This property sets the number of pixels from the horizontal center of the container to the horizontal center of the nested component. A positive number offsets the component to the right of the container's horizontal center; a negative number offsets to the left.

■ verticalCenter: This property sets the number of pixels from the vertical center of the container to the vertical center of the nested component. A positive number offsets the component below the container's vertical center; a negative number offsets the component above the vertical center.

The following code is generated by Design view as the user sets properties in the Constraints interface and drags the component around the screen:

```
<mx:Label text="My Logo" right="10" bottom="10"
    fontWeight="bold" fontSize="18"/>
```

The right and bottom properties are set to values of 10 pixels each. As shown in Figure 9.15, each time the user resizes the application, the Label control changes its position relative to the application's bottom-right corner.

FIGURE 9.15

A Label's position controlled by constraint-based properties

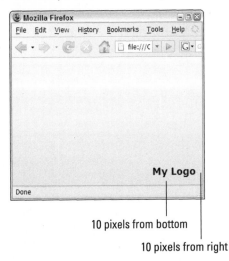

10 pixels from bottom

10 pixels from right

Sizing Containers and Controls

Four strategies are available to determine the dimensions of a container or control at runtime:

■ **Content:** Component dimensions are determined dynamically based on the cumulative size of the component's child objects.

■ **Absolute:** Component dimensions are determined by its width and height properties set to numeric values, interpreted as pixels.

- **Percentage:** Component dimensions are determined by percentage of available space.
- **Constraints:** Component dimensions are determined by constraint-based anchor properties.

Content-based sizing

Content-based sizing means that a container or control expands to accommodate its contents. In the absence of any other sizing properties, this happens automatically. With containers, this means that the container sizes itself to accommodate and display its nested contents. With controls, this means that the control sizes itself to display its internal objects. For example, if you don't set a Button control's height or width properties, it sizes itself to display its full label and icon.

Default dimensions

Each container has a default height and width. For example, if you create a Panel with this code, it has no nested components and no title property that would affect its height or width:

```
<mx:Panel>
</mx:Panel>
```

Then Panel container's default dimensions are driven by the size of its default border, gap, and padding styles. On my test system, the Panel container's default height is 40 pixels and its default width is 52 pixels.

Other containers have different default dimensions. In the absence of nested content, the VBox, HBox, and Canvas set their height and width to 0.

Minimum and maximum dimensions

You can set properties to constrain content-based sizing. These properties set minimum and maximum dimensions to place limits on a container's ability to dynamically grow and shrink:

- minHeight: The container's minimum height in pixels
- minWidth: The container's minimum width in pixels
- maxHeight: The container's maximum height in pixels
- maxWidth: The container's maximum width in pixels

This VBox container has a minimum width and height of 200 pixels each:

```
<mx:Panel minWidth="200" minHeight="200">
... nested components ...
</mx:Panel>
```

The container can still expand if its contents require more space, but it can't contract to less than 200 pixels in either dimension.

Absolute sizing

Absolute sizing means that you set a component's `width` and `height` properties in absolute pixel values. This `Panel` container is always displayed as 200 pixels high by 200 pixels wide, regardless of its nested contents:

```
<mx:Panel width="200" height="200">
</mx:Panel>
```

When you use absolute sizing and a container is too small to display its nested contents, by default it displays scrollbars that allow the user to scroll to see the contents. Figure 9.16 shows a Panel container with nested `Label` components. Because nested components can't be displayed in the container's available space, it displays both vertical and horizontal scrollbars.

FIGURE 9.16

A `Panel` with scrollbars

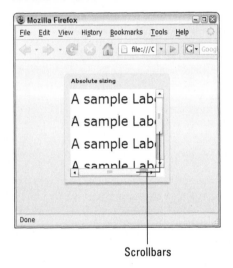

Scrollbars

Percentage sizing

Percentage sizing means that you set a dimension as a percentage of available space. When you set a component's size in MXML, you can declare percentage sizing with either the `height` and `width` properties or with `percentHeight` and `percentWidth`.

Percentage sizing with height and width

When you set percentage sizing with the `height` and `width` properties, you declare the values with a percentage expression, such as 50%. This `Label` control's width is 50 percent of the available space within its container:

```
<mx:Label text="A sample Label" width="50%"/>
```

Percentage sizing with percentHeight and percentWidth

When you set percentage sizing with the `percentHeight` and `percentWidth` properties, you use numeric expressions such as 50. This `Label` control's width is also 50 percent of the available space within its container:

```
<mx:Label text="A sample Label" percentWidth="50"/>
```

> **TIP** The `height` and `width` properties cannot be set to new percentage values at runtime with ActionScript statements. Instead, always use `percentHeight` and `percentWidth` in ActionScript.

> **TIP** The `percentHeight` and `percentWidth` properties return meaningful values only if they've been previously set through MXML declarations or ActionScript commands. Their values are not recalculated at runtime.

Using percentage ratios

When you declare multiple components within a container and set sizes by percentage, you can declare a total percentage of greater than 100 percent. This VBox contains three TextInput controls, each with a width property of 100 percent:

```
<mx:HBox width="450" borderStyle="solid" borderColor="#000000"
  paddingBottom="10" paddingLeft="10"
  paddingRight="10" paddingTop="10">
  <mx:TextInput width="100%"/>
  <mx:TextInput width="100%"/>
  <mx:TextInput width="100%"/>
</mx:HBox>
```

It might seem that this means the total width of the nested component is 300 percent and would exceed the available space. Instead, the Flex framework adds up the total percentage values and uses the ratio of the control's declared percentage value divided by the total to assign an actual percentage based on available space:

```
100% + 100% + 100% = 300% (the total)
For each component: 100% / 300% = 33.33%
```

> **TIP** If there is a combination of percentage-based and strict value sizing, space is allotted first to the strict values. Then if the remaining space is not enough to fulfill the percentage-based items, the same ratio division is calculated and applied.

Figure 9.17 shows the resulting display. Each TextInput control's width is set dynamically to 33.33% of the available horizontal space.

Using percentage ratios

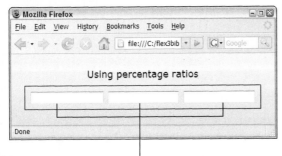

Calculated percentage ratio of 33.33% each

Constraint-based sizing

Constraint properties also can be used to control a component's size. When a component is nested in a container with absolute layout and two constraint properties in the vertical or horizontal dimension are set, the component "stretches" at runtime to keep its edges the correct distance from the two anchors. Listing 9.9 creates a Text control with right and left properties that keep its edges 50 pixels from each of the Application container's horizontal edges.

Using constraint-based sizing

```
<?xml version="1.0" encoding="utf-8"?>
<mx:Application xmlns:mx="http://www.adobe.com/2006/mxml"
  backgroundColor="#eeeeee" layout="absolute">

  <mx:Text id="myTextArea"
    left="50" right="50" top="20" textAlign="center"
    height="100%">
  <mx:text>
  <![CDATA[...text...]]>
  </mx:text>
  </mx:Text>

</mx:Application>
```

ON the WEB The code in Listing 9.9 is available in the Web site files as `ConstraintSizing.mxml` in the `chapter09` project.

Figure 9.18 shows the resulting display. When the user resizes the application, the Text control expands and contracts to keep its edges the correct distance from the constraint anchors.

FIGURE 9.18

A control with constraint-based sizing

The left constraint   The right constraint

Using Advanced Constraints

The Flex 3 framework added the ability to use constraints based on rows and columns that you define in a container using these properties:

- `constraintRows`: An array of `ConstraintRow` instances that divide a container vertically

- `constraintColumns`: An array of `ConstraintColumn` instances that divide a container horizontally

TIP As with all constraint-based features, constraint rows and columns work only in a container that supports absolute layout.

Declaring constraint rows and columns

You create rows and columns using MXML declarations. To divide a container vertically, first declare an `<mx:constraintRows>` tag set, then nest multiple `ConstraintRow` instances. Be sure to assign an `id` property to each `ConstraintRow`.

TIP   Constraint rows and columns are not visible to the user; they're used only at runtime to calculate component positions and sizes. And, unlike simple constraints, you cannot edit advanced constraints in Design view.

NOTE   Flex Builder 3's second public beta featured a new user interface that allowed you to create `ConstraintRow` and `ConstraintColumn` instances in Design view. This interface was removed prior to the product's final release, so advanced constraints must now be directly coded.

The first `ConstraintRow` always starts at the top of the container, and subsequent `ConstraintRow` instances are placed below the first. Each `ConstraintRow` instance's height property can be set to either an absolute numeric value indicating its height in pixels or a percentage value indicating its value in terms of percentage of available vertical space.

This code declares two `ConstraintRow` instances, each using 50 percent of the Application component's available vertical space:

```
<mx:constraintRows>
  <mx:ConstraintRow id="row1" height="50%"/>
  <mx:ConstraintRow id="row2" height="50%"/>
</mx:constraintRows>
```

Similarly, if you want to divide a container horizontally, you use `ConstraintColumn` instances wrapped in the `constraintColumns` property. Each column starts at the left edge of the container, and each subsequent column is added to its right. The following code sets up three columns, each filling 100 pixels of width:

```
<mx:constraintColumns>
  <mx:ConstraintColumn id="column1" width="100"/>
  <mx:ConstraintColumn id="column2" width="100"/>
  <mx:ConstraintColumn id="column3" width="100"/>
</mx:constraintColumns>
```

TIP   A container that supports absolute layout can declare both `constraintColumns` and `constraintRows` at the same time, allowing you to divide the container into grid-like regions.

Placing and sizing components with advanced constraints

You place or size components with constraint rows and columns using the same constraint properties described previously: `top`, `bottom`, `left`, `right`, `verticalCenter`, and `horizontalCenter`. Instead of assigning the property values with a simple numeric expression (as you would with simple constraints), you use a compound expression consisting of a constraint row or column `id` and a numeric value, separated with a colon. This declaration of the `bottom` constraint property means that a component should be placed 10 pixels from the bottom of a ConstraintRow with an id of row1:

```
bottom="row1:10"
```

Just as with simple constraints, you can use multiple constraint properties to control a component's size and make it stretch as a row or column expands. Listing 9.10 declares two constraint rows, each taking 50 percent of the application's available vertical space. Each of the VBox components sizes itself vertically, using the top and bottom constraint properties and anchoring itself to one of the constraint rows.

LISTING 9.10

An application with advanced constraints

```
<?xml version="1.0" encoding="utf-8"?>
<mx:Application xmlns:mx="http://www.adobe.com/2006/mxml"
  backgroundColor="#eeeeee" layout="absolute">

<mx:Application xmlns:mx="http://www.adobe.com/2006/mxml"
  backgroundColor="#eeeeee" layout="absolute">

  <mx:constraintRows>
    <mx:ConstraintRow id="row1" height="50%"/>
    <mx:ConstraintRow id="row2" height="50%"/>
  </mx:constraintRows>

  <mx:VBox top="row1:20" bottom="row1:20" horizontalCenter="0"
   width="50%"
    borderStyle="solid" backgroundColor="#666666"/>
  <mx:VBox top="row2:20" bottom="row2:20" horizontalCenter="0"
   width="50%"
    borderStyle="solid" backgroundColor="#999999"/>
</mx:Application>
```

ON the WEB The code in Listing 9.10 is available in the Web site files as `ConstraintSizing.mxml` in the `chapter09` project.

Figure 9.19 shows the resulting display. Each of the VBox containers uses width for horizontal sizing and horizontalCenter for horizontal placement, and sizes and places itself vertically with top and bottom properties that reference advanced constraint rows.

An application using advanced constraints

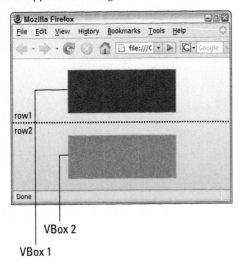

VBox 2

VBox 1

Summary

In this chapter, I described the use of layout containers, how to size components, and how to use constraint-based layout. You learned the following:

- The Flex framework uses two types of containers: layout containers to control the application design and navigation containers to control application navigation.

- The simple Box containers include VBox, HBox, and Canvas.

- The HBox and VBox containers place their nested components on the screen dynamically by calculating their cumulative size.

- The Canvas container always uses absolute layout to place objects based on x and y properties or with constraints.

- The Panel container creates a dialog-box presentation and supports the absolute property values of vertical, horizontal, and absolute.

- Constraint properties allow you to place and size objects with anchors to any of a container's borders or center positions.

- Components can be sized based on content, absolute dimensions, percentage dimensions, or constraints.

- Flex 3 adds advanced constraints that allow you to divide a container into multiple rows and columns.

Chapter 10

Using Cascading Style Sheets

Flex applications have a default visual appearance that's determined by a combination of graphics that are embedded in the Flex framework, known as *skins,* and various visual settings that are set through Cascading Style Sheet declarations.

About Cascading Style Sheets

Web site developers may already be familiar with the concept of Cascading Style Sheets (CSS), because this technology has been increasingly used to control the visual appearance of Web pages since its introduction in 1996.

The Cascading Style Sheet recommendation is created and published by the World Wide Web Consortium (W3C), the same organization that publishes the recommendations for HTML, XML, and other critical Internet technologies.

WEB RESOURCE Information about the World Wide Web Consortium's CSS recommendation and other CSS resources is available at `http://www.w3.org/Style/CSS/`.

It's up to the vendors who actually create the Web browsers and other products to implement CSS for their own platforms. Web browsers, for example, implement various subsets of the W3C recommendation; it's only in recent years that the major browsers such as Internet Explorer and Firefox have approached compatibility in their CSS implementations.

The use of CSS to control visual appearance isn't limited to Web-based technologies. Flex applications that are installed on the desktop with the Adobe Integrated Runtime (AIR) use CSS in exactly the same manner as Flex Web applications.

The Flex framework implements significant parts of the W3C's CSS recommendation and adds features that make the technology particularly effective for implementing Flex application graphic designs.

In this chapter, I describe using CSS in Flex to control an application's visual appearance. I start by describing how to declare and control style sheets in a number of ways. At the end of the chapter, I describe a particular aspect of Flex styles called *skinning* that allows you to replace the default graphics that control a Flex application's appearance.

ON the WEB To use the sample code for this chapter, import the `chapter10.zip` Flex project archive from the Web site files into your Flex Builder workspace.

What Is a Style Sheet?

A style sheet consists of rules that constitute a set of visual settings. Any particular style sheet can consist of three parts:

- **The selector** determines the scope of a set of rules that are declared in the style sheet. A single selector can declare multiple styles, each requiring a name and a value.
- **The style name** determines which style is being set.
- **The style value** determines the new style setting.

MXML-based declarations of styles and non-style properties look the same. This `VBox` container declares a `width` property and a `backgroundColor` style:

To know that one is a property and the other a style, you'd have to look it up in the product documentation. You encounter differences between styles and properties when you set their values in ActionScript or actual style sheet declarations, or when you read about their use in the product documentation. Table 10.1 describes some of the differences between styles and properties.

TABLE 10.1

Differences between Styles and Properties

Styles	Properties
Documentation is found in the Styles section for each component.	Documentation is found in the Properties section for each component.
Styles can be applied to multiple objects through embedded or external style sheets.	Properties can apply only to a single object.

Styles	Properties
When set at runtime with ActionScript, styles always use the `setStyle()` method.	Properties can be set at runtime in ActionScript with simple dot notation.
Multiple style rules can be compiled into `.swf` files and loaded at runtime.	Properties cannot be compiled into separate `.swf` files.

You can use these ways, among others, to declare styles in Flex:

- **Inline styles:** Declared as attributes in an object's MXML declaration
- **Embedded style sheets:** Declared within an MXML file in an `<mx:Style>` tag set
- **External style sheets:** Created as text files with a file extension of `.css`
- **Compiled style sheets:** Created as `.swf` files and can be loaded at application runtime

Regardless of how you declare a style, the name of the style and its value are always the same. For example, a style of `fontSize` is always set as a numeric value indicating the font height in terms of pixels. This style can be set in inline, embedded, external, or compiled style sheets, and its effect is always the same.

NOTE Unlike the HTML implementation of CSS, Flex applications do not support any unit of measurement other than pixels. If you try to use unit-of-measurement abbreviations like `pt`, `em`, or `px`, they are either ignored or result in a compiler error, depending on the context.

Using Inline Style Declarations

When you declare an object in MXML, you can declare any of its styles using XML attributes. The attribute's name matches the style's name, and the style's value is declared in various ways depending on its data type.

NOTE Unlike the Web browser implementation of CSS, Flex does not support a CSS `id` selector that would allow you to apply a style in an embedded or external style sheet to a single object by its `id` property. If you need to apply a style to a single object, use an inline style declaration.

This `Label` control declares its `color` style to a value of red using an inline style declaration and a hexadecimal color code:

```
<mx:Label text="Hello World" color="#ff0000"/>
```

CAUTION Many styles have two versions of their names. For example, the `fontSize` style has a name whose syntax is sometimes described as *camel case*, due to the use of uppercase characters in the middle of the style name. This style also can be declared in an embedded or external style sheet with the hyphenated name of `font-size`. However, when setting styles in an inline declaration, you must use the camel case version of the name, because the hyphenated version isn't recognized by the MXML parser.

TIP One of XML's fundamental syntax rules is that the order of attribute declaration isn't meaningful. In the MXML language, this means that you can declare property, style, and event listener attributes in any order because the order doesn't have any effect on the function or performance of the object you're declaring.

Using Style Selectors

You can declare complete style sheets either embedded within an MXML source code file or in a separate, external .css file. Either way, the style sheet contains one or more *selectors,* each of which determines the scope of a set of style declarations.

The Flex implementation of CSS has three kinds of selectors:

- **Type selectors** declare a set of styles that are applied to all instances of that ActionScript type.

- **Style name selectors** (traditionally known as *class* selectors) declare a set of styles within an arbitrarily named collection that is then applied to multiple components through the styleName property.

- **The global selector** declares a set of styles that are applied to all components within the application.

Regardless of which selector you use, the syntax is similar: the selector, followed by a block of style declarations wrapped in braces. Each style declaration consists of a name and a value, separated by a colon (:). The style declaration should be ended with a semicolon (;) to separate it from other style declarations.

Using type selectors

A type selector consists of the name of an ActionScript class that represents a visual component, followed by a code block containing one or more style declarations. This type selector declares a set of styles that are applied to all Label controls:

```
Label {
  color:#ff0000;
  font-size:14;
}
```

Because ActionScript class names are case-sensitive, type selectors must be spelled exactly the same as the names of the ActionScript visual components to which the styles are being applied.

CAUTION Type selectors can be declared only in the Application, not in a custom component. If you try to use a type selector in a component, a compiler warning is generated and the style(s) won't be applied.

TIP Property names in embedded or external style sheets can use either camel case or hyphenated syntax. Flex Builder 3's code completion tool always suggests camel case names in inline style declarations (which are required) and hyphenated syntax in embedded or external styles. Because you get help with hyphenated names in the latter context, all code samples in this chapter follow that standard.

Multiple type selectors

You can apply a set of styles to multiple types using a selector consisting of a comma-delimited list. This declaration applies to all instances of the Label, Text, TextInput, and TextArea controls:

```
Label, Text, TextInput, TextArea {
  color:#ff0000;
  font-size:14;
}
```

Type selectors and custom components

Type selectors also can be used to apply styles to instances of your own custom components. For example, if you create a custom component in an MXML file named MyComponent.mxml, its type is MyComponent. This style sheet applies styles to all instances of the custom component:

```
MyComponent {
  color:#ff0000;
  font-size:14;
}
```

Type selectors and class inheritance

When you declare a type selector in a style sheet, the selector's inheritable styles apply to all instances of that type and to all instances of any of the type's subclasses. For example, because the VBox and HBox containers are both extended from the Box superclass, the Box selector applies its style declarations for all instances of either container:

```
Box {
  background-color:silver;
  border-style:solid;
  border-color:black;
  border-thickness:2;
  padding-top:5;
  padding-bottom:5;
  padding-left:5;
  padding-right:5;
}
```

Figure 10.1 shows the resulting application with an HBox and VBox that use the same styles.

FIGURE 10.1

VBox and HBox using the Box selector styles

> **TIP** Type selectors that designate a superclass are inherited by subclasses even when the styles used in the selector are marked in the documentation as not implementing CSS inheritance. The documentation is describing which styles are inherited based on containership.

For example, if you apply font-based styles, which are inheritable, to a VBox selector, all text controls nested in VBox containers use those styles. Non-inheritable styles such as the border styles shown in the previous example are only applied to the VBox itself, and not to its nested child objects.

Class inheritance also is taken into account with custom components. If a custom component named MyComponent is extended from the VBox or HBox containers, it also would apply the inheritable styles declared in the Box selector.

Because the Canvas container isn't extended from Box, to apply the same styles to this container as well, you could use a multiple type selector:

```
Box, Canvas {
   ... style declarations ...
}
```

Using style name selectors

A style name selector, also sometimes known as a *class* selector, consists of any valid string, prepended with a period (.). Style names are typically created with an initial lowercase character and any mixture of uppercase and lowercase characters after that. This style name selector contains a single style declaration:

```
.redFont {
   color:#ff0000;
}
```

> **TIP** Style name selectors are identical in purpose and declaration syntax to the HTML concept of class selectors. As with the style class in HTML, a style name defines a set of rules that can be applied to any object arbitrarily.

A style name selector doesn't apply its styles to any object on its own. Instead, each object "opts in" to apply the selector's styles with the `styleName` property. This `Label` control uses the style rules in the `redFont` selector:

```
<mx:Label text="Hello World" styleName="redFont"/>
```

Style name selectors can be declared in the `Application` or within any custom component. If the same style name selector is declared at two levels of the application's containership and sets conflicting values for any particular style, the declaration in the custom component takes precedence.

> **TIP** You use the period as a prefix to the style name only in the selector definition, not in the `styleName` property. If you include the period in the `styleName` property, the settings are ignored.

Using the global selector

The global selector has a reserved name of `global` (always typed in all lowercase). Styles declared within the `global` selector are applied to all visual components in the entire application.

> **CAUTION** There aren't many styles that you'd want to apply to the entire application. This feature's use is typically restricted to setting default font styles such as `fontFamily` and `color`. It wouldn't make sense, for example, to apply border or padding styles to every object in the application.

This global declaration sets the default font family and color for the entire application:

```
global {
   font-family:Times New Roman, Times, serif;
   color:purple;
}
```

Using embedded style sheets

You can embed a style sheet in an MXML application or component with the `<mx:Style>` compiler tag set. As previously described, a style sheet embedded in a custom component can include only style name selectors. Style sheets embedded in the `Application` can contain a mixture of type, style name, and global selectors.

> **CAUTION** The `<mx:Style>` tag must be declared as a direct child element of the MXML file's root element. An `<mx:Style>` tag placed within any other child element in the MXML containership results in a compiler error.

The code in Listing 10.1 shows an application with an embedded style sheet. The embedded style sheet's selectors and rules are applied to the entire application.

LISTING 10.1

An embedded style sheet

```
<?xml version="1.0" encoding="utf-8"?>
<mx:Application xmlns:mx="http://www.adobe.com/2006/mxml"
   horizontalAlign="center"
  layout="horizontal">

  <mx:Style>

    global {
      font-family:Times New Roman, Times, serif;
      color:purple;
    }

    Box {
      background-color:silver;
      border-style:solid;
      border-color:black;
      border-thickness:2;
      padding-top:5;
      padding-bottom:5;
      padding-left:5;
      padding-right:5;
    }

    .redFont {
      color:#ff0000;
    }

  </mx:Style>

  <mx:VBox>
    <mx:Label text="Hello World" styleName="redFont"/>
    <mx:Button label="Click me"/>
  </mx:VBox>

  <mx:HBox>
    <mx:Label text="Hello World"/>
    <mx:Button label="Click me"/>
  </mx:HBox>

</mx:Application>
```

ON the WEB The code in Listing 10.1 is available in the Web site files as `EmbeddedStyles.mxml` in the `chapter10` project.

Using external style sheets

You can store style sheets in text files with a file extension of .css. As with embedded style sheets, an external style sheet contains a collection of style selectors, each declaring one or more style and value.

Flex Builder can create a new style sheet for you in a couple of ways:

- As a new blank style sheet file
- By exporting existing styles from Design view to a new external style sheet

Creating a blank style sheet

To create a new blank style sheet, select File ➪ New ➪ CSS File from the Flex Builder menu, or right-click in the Flex Navigator view and select New ➪ CSS File. As shown in Figure 10.2, set the filename and location of the CSS file.

FIGURE 10.2

Creating a new external style sheet

> **NOTE**   You can save external style sheets anywhere in your project. The `<mx:Style>` tag styles are added to the application at compile time and are not loaded at runtime, so the style sheet file technically doesn't have to be in the source folder; however, I recommend that you place it in the source folder or somewhere in its subfolder structure.

After you've created the external style sheet file, you can manually add selectors and properties. As shown in Figure 10.3, Flex Builder provides code completion support in external style sheets that helps you correctly type the property names and values. To get code completion help at any time, press Ctrl+spacebar to see available properties and values.

FIGURE 10.3

Code completion in an external style sheet

Press Crtl+Space for code completion

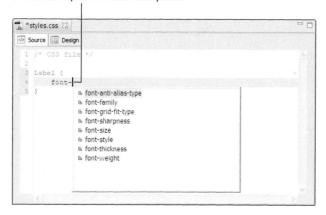

Listing 10.2 shows the contents of an external style sheet file. Notice that there is no `<mx:Style>` tag set, because this is no longer an MXML file.

LISTING 10.2

An external style sheet file

```
global {
    font-family:Times New Roman, Times, serif;
    color:purple;
}
Box {
    background-color:silver;
    border-style:solid;
    border-color:black;
    border-thickness:2;
    padding-top:5;
    padding-bottom:5;
    padding-left:5;
    padding-right:5;
```

```
}
.redFont {
  color:#ff0000;
}
```

ON the WEB The code in Listing 10.2 is available in the Web site files as `styles.css` in the chapter10 project.

To incorporate an external style sheet into an application, declare the `<mx:Style>` tag set with a source property referring to the style sheet file by its name and relative location:

```
<mx:Style source="styles.css"/>
```

CAUTION When you declare `<mx:Style>` with a `source` property, you cannot also include nested CSS declarations. You can, however, declare more than one `<mx:Style>` tag set in an application or component.

Listing 10.3 shows the application now referring to an external style sheet.

LISTING 10.3

An application referring to an external style sheet

```
<?xml version="1.0" encoding="utf-8"?>
<mx:Application xmlns:mx="http://www.adobe.com/2006/mxml"
  horizontalAlign="center" layout="horizontal">
  <mx:Style source="styles.css"/>
  <mx:VBox>
    <mx:Label text="Hello World" styleName="redFont"/>
    <mx:Button label="Click me"/>
  </mx:VBox>
  <mx:HBox>
    <mx:Label text="Hello World"/>
    <mx:Button label="Click me"/>
  </mx:HBox>
</mx:Application>
```

ON the WEB The code in Listing 10.3 is available in the Web site files as `ExternalStyles.mxml` in the chapter10 project.

Exporting existing styles

Flex Builder 3 adds a new feature that allows you to export inline styles of any component instance to an external style sheet and then link the current application to that external file.

When you export styles from a component instance, you can define what kind of selector the styles should be applied to the following:

- All components (the `global` selector)
- All components with style name
- The current specific component's name
- The current specific component's name plus a style name

Follow these steps to learn how this feature works:

1. Create a new MXML application named `ExportStyles.mxml` with its `layout` property set to `vertical`.

2. If the application opens in Source view, switch to Design view.

3. Drag a `Label` from the Components view into the application.

4. In the Flex Properties view, set the `Label` component's properties as follows:

   - text: **Hello World**
   - color: **#ff0000**
   - fontSize: **14**

5. Switch to Source view.

   Your application code should look like this:

   ```
   <?xml version="1.0" encoding="utf-8"?>
   <mx:Application xmlns:mx="http://www.adobe.com/2006/mxml"
     layout="vertical">

     <mx:Label text="Hello World" color="#ff0000" fontSize="14"/>

   </mx:Application>
   ```

6. Switch back to Design view, and select the `Label` control.

7. In the Flex Properties view, click Convert to CSS, as shown in Figure 10.4.

8. If prompted to save changes to the application, click Yes.

9. In the New Style Rule dialog box, shown in Figure 10.5, select New to create a new CSS style sheet.

10. In the New CSS File dialog box, name the new style sheet `newStyleSheet.css` in the project's `src` folder and click Finish.

11. In the New Style Rule dialog box, select Specific component and click OK.

    Flex Builder should now display the new CSS file in Design view.

12. Return to the application and switch to Source view.

FIGURE 10.4

Exporting styles from the Flex Properties view

Click to export styles

FIGURE 10.5

The New Style Rule dialog box

Style Data Types

When you set a style, you use syntax that's specific to the style's data type. Some styles require String values, others numeric values, and still others Array values containing specific numbers of items.

For example, the fontSize style requires a numeric value. When you set this value in an MXML inline attribute, you declare it as a String and it's converted to a Number by the Flex compiler:

```
<mx:Label text="Hello World" fontSize="14"/>
```

Other styles require specific String values. For example, the fontWeight style requires a String, but only accepts values of bold and normal:

```
<mx:Label text="Hello World" fontWeight="bold"/>
```

Styles that require color values accept a number of formats. The most common color code format is hexadecimal and consists of a six-character string defining the amount of red, green, and blue in the color. The string can be prefixed by either a hash or pound character (#) or by a zero and small x (0x). If you want to store this value in a variable, you can set the hex value without quotes to an int (integer) or uint (unsigned integer) data type. This Label sets its font color to blue with a hexadecimal code:

```
<mx:Label text="Hello World" color="0x0000FF"/>
```

Colors can also be declared using RGB percentage values. This syntax consists of the key word rgb, followed by a comma-delimited set of percentage values representing the amount of red, green, and blue. This syntax only works in embedded or external style sheets, not in inline declarations. This style declaration means that Label controls have a font color of red:

```
Label {
  color:rgb(100%, 0%, 0%);
}
```

You also can set color values with named colors. Color names that are recognized by the Flex compiler include Aqua, Black, Blue, Fuchsia, Gray, Green, Lime, Maroon, Navy, Olive, Purple, Red, Silver, Teal, White, and Yellow. This Label sets its font color to teal with a named color:

```
<mx:Label text="Hello World" color="teal"/>
```

Style values that are typed as Array are declared in MXML as comma-delimited lists wrapped in brackets. The Button control's fillColors style requires an array of two colors that are then used to create a background gradient. As with simple color values, you can use hexadecimal or named colors:

```
<mx:Button label="Click Me" fillColors="[blue, white]"/>
```

When you declare the Array values in an embedded or external style sheet, you still use the comma-delimited list, but don't include the brackets. This style sheet declaration sets the fillColors style for all Button controls in the application with a vertical gradient of blue and white:

```
Button {
  fill-colors:#0000ff,#000000;
}
```

The application's source now contains an `<mx:Style>` declaration pointing to the external style sheet, and the `Label` control's inline styles have been removed:

```
<?xml version="1.0" encoding="utf-8"?>
<mx:Application xmlns:mx="http://www.adobe.com/2006/mxml"
  layout="vertical">
  <mx:Label text="Hello World"/>
  <mx:Style source="newStyleSheet.css"/>
</mx:Application>
```

The external style sheet now contains the styles that were part of the `Label` declaration, now applied in a type selector:

```
/* CSS file */
Label
{
  color: #ff0000;
  fontSize: 14;
}
```

ON the WEB The complete code from the preceding exercise is available in the Web site files as `ExportStylesComplete.mxml` and `newStyleSheetComplete.css` in the `chapter10` project.

Using Compiled Style Sheets

Style sheets can be compiled into external .swf files and then loaded at runtime.

NOTE Neither Flash Player nor the Flex framework includes a CSS parser that would allow a Flex application to parse a "raw" CSS file at runtime. The ability to load a pre-compiled CSS file was added to Flex in version 2.0.1.

Compiling style sheets

Flex Builder 3 can create a compiled style sheet with a simple menu selection. These steps describe how to compile a style sheet:

1. Create a new external style sheet named `compiledstyles.css` in the current project's `src` folder.

2. Add a `Label` selector that sets the `color` to `blue`, the `font-size` to `18`, and the `font-weight` to `bold`:

    ```
    Label {
      color:blue;
      font-size:18;
      font-weight:bold;
    }
    ```

3. Save the external style sheet file.

4. As shown in Figure 10.6, right-click the style sheet file in the Flex Navigator view and select Compile CSS to SWF.

Using the Compile CSS to SWF option

The compiled SWF file is created in the same folder as the external style sheet, and is also copied to the project's output folder.

TIP   Once the Compile CSS to SWF option has been selected for any particular external style sheet, the compilation option remains selected for that file until you deselect it. Whenever Flex Builder rebuilds the project, the CSS file is recompiled as well.

You should see the new `compiledstyles.swf` file in the project source folder.

Loading compiled style sheets

The compiled style sheet file becomes an asset that can be dynamically loaded at runtime. Its styles can then immediately be applied to existing component instances in the application.

To load the precompiled application at runtime, use an ActionScript class named `StyleManager`. The class has a method named `loadStyleDeclarations()` that loads compiled style sheets and optionally updates the application's style declarations immediately.

Follow these steps to use the `StyleManager` class:

1. Create a new MXML application named `RuntimeStyles.css`.

2. Add a `Label` control with a `text` property of `Hello World`.

3. Add a `Button` control with a label of `Load Styles`. Set its click event listener to execute this code:

```
StyleManager.loadStyleDeclarations('compiledstyles.swf');
```

Listing 10.4 shows the completed application.

LISTING 10.4

An application loading a compiled style sheet at runtime

```
<?xml version="1.0" encoding="utf-8"?>
<mx:Application xmlns:mx="http://www.adobe.com/2006/mxml"
  layout="vertical">

  <mx:Label text="Hello World"/>

  <mx:Button label="Load Styles"
    click="StyleManager.loadStyleDeclarations(
      'compiledstyles.swf');"/>

</mx:Application>
```

ON the WEB The code in Listing 10.4 is available in the Web site files as `RuntimeStylesComplete.mxml` in the `chapter10` project.

4. Run the application.

5. Click Load Styles.

   When the application first loads, the `Label` control is displayed with its default font color, weight, and size. When you click Load Styles, the application loads the compiled style sheet and updates the `Label` control's presentation.

Using the `StyleManager` class, you also can unload styles, delay style updates, and react to various events in the process of working with dynamic styles.

WEB RESOURCE For more information on runtime loading of styles, visit `http://livedocs.adobe.com/labs/flex3/html/help.html?content=styles_10.html`.

Controlling Styles with ActionScript

You can control styles at runtime in many ways. These tasks are available:

- Loading of compiled style sheets (described in the preceding section)
- Setting and getting styles for individual component instances
- Modifying selectors and their properties
- Changing a component instance's style name

Setting and getting style information

Every visual component in the Flex framework supports methods named setStyle() and getStyle() that allow you to set or get any particular style's values. As described previously, you cannot use simple dot syntax to access style information (as you might with a component property). This code, for example, would produce a compiler error:

```
myLabel.fontSize=18;
```

The use of dot syntax to separate a component instance id and its members works with properties, but not with styles.

Instead, use the setStyle() method to reset a style's value at runtime:

```
myLabel.setStyle("fontSize", 18);
```

And use the getStyle() method to get a style's value:

```
var currentSize:Number = myLabel.getStyle("fontSize");
```

The code in Listing 10.5 shows an application with Label control and two Button controls. Clicking Change Font Size results in modifying the Label control's font size at runtime. Clicking Get Font Size displays the Label control's current font size.

LISTING 10.5

Setting and getting style values

```
<?xml version="1.0" encoding="utf-8"?>
<mx:Application xmlns:mx="http://www.adobe.com/2006/mxml"
  layout="vertical">

  <mx:Label id="myLabel" text="Hello World" fontSize="10"/>

  <mx:Button label="Change Font Size"
    click="myLabel.setStyle('fontSize', 18)"/>
```

```
<mx:Button label="Get Font Size"
  click="myLabel.text='Current font size: ' +
  myLabel.getStyle('fontSize')"/>

</mx:Application>
```

 The code in Listing 10.5 is available in the Web site files as
SettingAndGettingStyles.mxml in the **chapter10** project.

As shown in Figure 10.7, the Label displays its own current font size when the second button is clicked.

FIGURE 10.7

The font size changes when the ActionScript code is executed.

 Styles are never bindable at runtime. This code, which tries to bind to a style's current value at runtime, succeeds upon application startup, but fails to execute when the target component's style changes at runtime:

```
<mx:Label text="{'Current font size: ' +
  myLabel.getStyle('fontSize')}"/>
```

Modifying style selectors at runtime

You can modify style selectors at runtime with the CSSStyleDeclaration and StyleManager classes. You can use one of these approaches:

- Create an instance of CSSStyleDeclaration bound to a style name or type selector.
- Create an instance of CSSStyleDeclaration without a selector, and then use the StyleManager class's setStyleDeclaration() method to bind the styles to the selector.

Using bound CSS declarations

To bind a `CSSStyleDeclaration` to a style selector, pass the selector as an argument to the class's constructor method:

```
var style:CSSStyleDeclaration = new CSSStyleDeclaration("Label");
```

Then, to change the styles in the selector, use the object's `setStyle()` method using the same syntax as with individual component instances:

```
style.setStyle("fontSize", 18);
```

When the `setStyle()` method is executed, the selector and any component instances it effects are updated immediately.

Binding CSS declarations with the StyleManager class

You can delay updates of styles by using unbound instances of `CSSStyleDeclaration`. To create an unbound style declaration, use the class's constructor method without any arguments:

```
var style:CSSStyleDeclaration = new CSSStyleDeclaration();
```

Set the style declaration's rules with the `setStyle()` method as described previously. Then, to bind the declaration to a style selector, call `StyleManager.setStyleDeclaration()` with three arguments:

- The style selector name
- The `CSSStyleDeclaration` instance
- A Boolean value indicating whether you want to update the styles immediately

The code in Listing 10.6 declares an unbound instance of `CSSStyleDeclaration`, sets two styles, and then binds and updates the styles.

LISTING 10.6

Binding CSS declarations with StyleManager

```
<?xml version="1.0" encoding="utf-8"?>
<mx:Application xmlns:mx="http://www.adobe.com/2006/mxml"
   layout="vertical">
  <mx:Script>
    <![CDATA[
      private function setLabelStyles(size:Number, weight:String):void
      {
        var style:CSSStyleDeclaration = new CSSStyleDeclaration();
        style.setStyle("fontSize", size);
        style.setStyle("fontWeight", weight);
        StyleManager.setStyleDeclaration("Label", style, true);
```

```
    }
  ]]>
</mx:Script>
<mx:Style>
  Label {
    font-size:12;
  }
</mx:Style>
<mx:Label text="Hello World"/>
<mx:Button label="Change Label Styles"
  click="setLabelStyles(18, 'bold')"/>
</mx:Application>
```

 The code in Listing 10.6 is available in the Web site files as `ChangingSelectors.mxml` in the `chapter10` project.

CAUTION The `setStyle()` method is particularly resource-intensive, as it has to look up the entire inheritance tree to be correctly applied.

Graphical Skinning of Visual Components

Skinning refers to the process of applying a set of graphics that replace a visual component's default appearance. You can create skins either graphically or programmatically. In this section, I describe the process of creating and applying programmatic skins.

Creating graphical skins

A graphical skin is an image that is designed to replace the default appearance of a Flex visual component. You can create graphical skins in these formats:

- GIF
- PNG
- JPG
- SWF

Using bitmap graphics as skins

When a skin graphic will always be displayed with the same dimensions, you can use bitmap graphics built in any of these formats and have the freedom to use any graphical editing application you like. Many applications successfully create `.png`, `.gif`, and `.jpg` format graphic files, including Adobe Fireworks, Photoshop, and Illustrator.

When you create a bitmap graphic to use as a skin, the original graphic should be sized exactly as you want it to appear in Flex. For example, all the graphical skins that will be used to visually represent the CheckBox controls typically share the same dimension of width and height (to create a square appearance).

Graphical skins are assigned to visual components through the styles API. The Styles documentation for any particular visual component will include both simple styles that require values typed as String, Number, and Array values and skinning styles that require embedded graphics. For example, the CheckBox component supports these graphical skins to represent the box and tick mark area of the control:

- upIcon
- downIcon
- overIcon
- upSelectedIcon
- downSelectedIcon
- overSelectedIcon
- disabledIcon
- disabledSelectedIcon

In order to properly skin the CheckBox component, each icon style should have a graphic assigned to it. To assign a skin, add the appropriate style name, followed by an Embed() declaration that references the graphic file. This declaration means the downIcon.png graphic is displayed when the mouse button is down over a CheckBox with a selected property of true:

```
downSelectedIcon: Embed(source="skins/downSelectedIcon.png");
```

Assuming you've created a bitmap graphic for each button state, the CheckBox selector might look like this:

```
CheckBox
{
  upIcon: Embed(source="skins/upIcon.png");
  downIcon: Embed(source="skins/downIcon.png");
  overIcon: Embed(source="skins/overIcon.png");
  disabledIcon: Embed(source="skins/disabledIcon.png");
  selectedUpIcon: Embed(source="skins/selectedUpIcon.png");
  selectedOverIcon: Embed(source="skins/selectedOverIcon.png");
  selectedDownIcon: Embed(source="skins/selectedDownIcon.png");
  selectedDisabledIcon:
    Embed(source="skins/selectedDisabled.png");
}
```

As shown in Figure 10.8, the CheckBox component is now displayed with the graphics you assigned.

FIGURE 10.8

FIGURE 10.8

A skinned `CheckBox` component

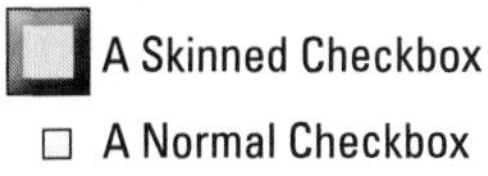

☐ A Skinned Checkbox

☐ A Normal Checkbox

Bitmap versus vector graphics

The first three types of graphics listed here are bitmap graphics, meaning that they store information about individual pixels in the graphic file. These types of graphics don't always scale well when stretched to accommodate a visual component that's been resized. A graphic created as a `.png` file may look fine when presented in its original size, but when its size is expanded at runtime, it shows the raw pixels in a phenomenon known as *pixelating* or *stair steps*.

Figure 10.9 shows a bitmap graphic in its original size of 30 pixels height and width and the same graphic displayed at three times its original size.

FIGURE 10.9

The effect of scaling on a bitmap graphic

Normal Size   3x normal size

With a bitmap image, the graphic is distorted and pixelated when it's expanded to a scale greater than 100 percent of its original size.

ON the WEB A Flex application file that displays the bitmap graphic is available in the Web site files as `BitMapScaling.mxml` in the `chapter10` project.

Vector graphics store their information mathematically instead of one pixel at a time. As a result, when these graphics are scaled to a larger size, they don't distort in the same way. You can create vector graphics with either Adobe Flash or Illustrator CS3.

Figure 10.10 shows a vector graphic created in Flash with its original size of 30 pixels height and width and the same graphic displayed at three times its original size.

FIGURE 10.10

The effect of scaling on a vector graphic

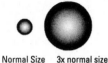

Normal Size   3x normal size

With the vector graphic, the edges of the graphic are recalculated as its scale is increased. The resulting smooth lines and gradients are clearly a better result than with the bitmap approach.

ON the WEB   A Flex application file that displays the vector graphic is available in the Web site files as `VectorScaling.mxml` in the `chapter10` project.

Creating vector-based skins in Flash CS3

The Flex framework uses a skinning library built in Flash CS3 to determine a Flex application's default visual appearance. The Flash source file that's used to build the graphical skinning library is named `AeonGraphical.fla` and is stored in this folder under the Flex Builder installation folder:

```
sdks/3.0.0/frameworks/themes/AeonGraphical/src
```

If you have Flash CS3, you can open this file and see how it's built. Follow these steps to build it yourself:

1. Open Flash CS3.
2. Open `AeonGraphical.fla` from `sdks/3.0.0/frameworks/themes/AeonGraphical/src` under the Flex Builder installation folder. Figure 10.11 shows the Flash file's *stage*, which contains one instance of each skinning graphic.

FIGURE 10.11

The Flash skinning source file, `AeonGraphical.fla`

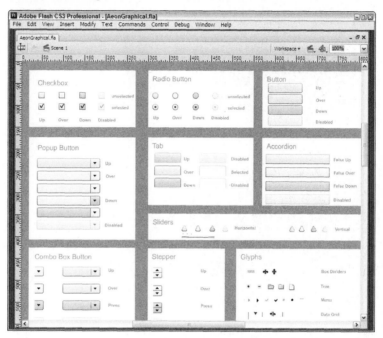

3. Select Window ⇨ Library from the Flash menu to open the Library panel. As shown in Figure 10.12, each skinning graphic is stored as a symbol in the Flash document library.

FIGURE 10.12

The Flash skinning source file's Library panel

Follow these steps to create a new skinning graphic in Flash CS3:

1. Create a new graphic object in Flash.

2. Convert the graphic to a MovieClip symbol.

3. Add *linkage* to export the graphic for use in ActionScript.

4. Publish the Flash document to .swf format.

After the Flash document has been created, you're ready to use the skinning graphic in a Flex application.

If you're working with Flash and have downloaded the exercise files from the Web site, follow these steps to view a document showing simple skinning graphics for the CheckBox component:

1. Open Flash CS3.

2. Open CheckBoxSkins.fla from the chapter10 project's src/skins subfolder. As shown in Figure 10.13, the Flash source file displays eight symbol instances.

FIGURE 10.13

The Flash stage with symbol instances

Symbol Instances

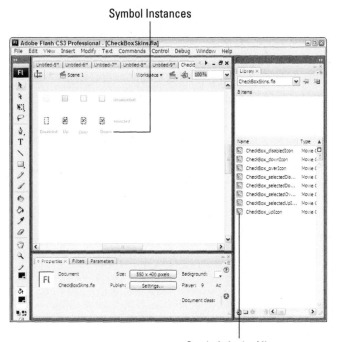

Symbols in the Library

3. Select Window ➪ Library to open the Library panel.

4. Double-click any symbol to open it in edit mode.

   Notice that each skin consists of simple graphic and optional text elements.

 To zoom in on the symbol and display it in a larger size, press Ctrl+=.

5. Click Scene 1 to return to the document stage.

6. Right-click any symbol in the library, and select Linkage.

As shown in Figure 10.14, the Linkage properties for each symbol have a class consisting of the component name and the skinning style name, separated by an underscore (_) character.

FIGURE 10.14

Setting symbol Linkage properties

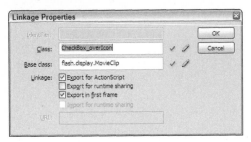

Flash symbols that will be used as graphical skins have these requirements:

- At least one instance of each symbol must be placed on the stage. If no instances of a symbol are on the stage, Flash doesn't include the symbol in the compiled .swf file.

- Each symbol must have an external class set through its Linkage properties.

- If any ActionScript code is included in the symbol, the document must be published as a Flash 9 document using ActionScript 3, because Flash Player 9 cannot execute both ActionScript 2 and ActionScript 3 in the same document.

After publishing a document as an .swf file, you're ready to use the Flash symbols as graphical skins.

Declaring Flash-based skins

As described previously, graphical skins are assigned to visual components through the styles interface. When you assign a Flash symbol as a graphical skin, the syntax is similar to that for a bitmap graphic, but you also need to tell the Flex compiler which symbol to use.

This declaration assigns the CheckBox component's downSelectedIcon skin to the appropriate symbol from a compiled Flash document:

```
downSelectedIcon: Embed(source="skins/CheckBoxSkins.swf",
    symbol="CheckBox_downSelectedIcon");
```

Importing skin artwork

Flex Builder 3 adds a new feature that allows you to import bitmap or vector-based graphical skins and create the required style sheet declarations. The resulting output is stored in an external style sheet that can then be linked into the application with an <mx:Style> tag set.

You can import vector-based skins that are created in Flash CS3 or Illustrator CS3. In this section, I describe how to prepare skins for import in Flash and then how to import them into your project.

Preparing symbols in Flash for import

Before you can import graphical skins with the Flex Builder skin artwork import tool, the skins must be exported to a Flash component library. A component library is an archived file in .zip format with a file extension of .swc.

Follow these steps to export multiple MovieClip symbols from Flash CS3:

1. In the Flash document that contains the symbols, ensure that each symbol you want to export has Linkage properties with a valid class name.

> **TIP** For the best import results, set the symbol's Linkage class name as the name of the Flex component for which the graphical icon will be used and the skin name as described in the Flex documentation, separated by the underscore (_) character. When you import this symbol, the import tool suggests binding the graphic to the component and skin style name with this information. For example, the symbol for the `CheckBox` component's `upIcon` style would have a Linkage class name of `CheckBox_upIcon`.

2. Add one instance of each symbol to the stage.
3. Select all symbols you want to export, and select Modify ⇨ Convert to Symbol from the Flash menu.
4. In the Convert to Symbol dialog box, enter any descriptive string as the Name, and enter **Movie Clip** as the Type.
5. Right-click the new symbol in the Library, and select Linkage from the context menu.
6. In the Linkage Properties dialog box, select Export for ActionScript.
7. As shown in Figure 10.14, set the Class to a valid ActionScript class name (no spaces or other special characters are allowed), and click OK to save the Linkage properties.
8. Right-click the new symbol in the Library panel, and select Export SWC File.
9. Save the file into the Flex project folder.

You're now ready to import the graphical skin symbols.

Importing skin artwork

Flex Builder's skin artwork import tool can import graphical skins from these kinds of files:

- Flash component libraries in .swc format
- Flash .swf files created in Illustrator CS3
- Bitmap graphics in .png, .gif, and .jpg format

Follow these steps to import graphics from a Flash component library created using the steps in the preceding section:

1. Select File ⇨ Import ⇨ Skin Artwork from the Flex Builder menu.
2. As shown in Figure 10.15, select the radio button for SWC or SWF file and then choose the .swc file you created in Flash.

3. Select a new or existing .css file in which the skin style rules should be created.

4. Select an application you want to use the graphical skins.

5. Click Next.

6. In the Import Skin Artwork dialog box, shown in Figure 10.15, select each Symbol Class you want to import and assign it a Style Selector and a Skin Part.

FIGURE 10.15

The Import Skin Artwork dialog box

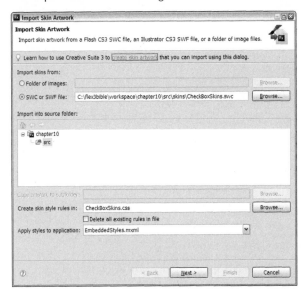

> **TIP**   The settings shown in Figure 10.15 are assigned automatically by the import tool, because the skin symbol class names match the component and skin style names as described previously.

7. Click Finish to import the skin symbols.

The .css file you select now contains skin style declarations wrapped in the selectors you selected. Listing 10.7 shows the resulting style sheet declaration code.

LISTING 10.7

Imported style sheet declarations

```
CheckBox
{
    disabledIcon: Embed(skinClass="CheckBox_disabledIcon");
    downIcon: Embed(skinClass="CheckBox_downIcon");
```

```
overIcon: Embed(skinClass="CheckBox_overIcon");
selectedDisabledIcon:
  Embed(skinClass="CheckBox_selectedDisabledIcon");
selectedDownIcon: Embed(skinClass="CheckBox_selectedDownIcon");
selectedOverIcon: Embed(skinClass="CheckBox_selectedOverIcon");
selectedUpIcon: Embed(skinClass="CheckBox_selectedUpIcon");
upIcon: Embed(skinClass="CheckBox_upIcon");
}
```

ON the WEB The code in Listing 10.7 is available in the Web site files as `CheckBoxSkins.css` in the `chapter10` project.

Because the skin symbols are now stored as ActionScript classes in a component library, this syntax assigns each of them to the appropriate style name:

```
overIcon: Embed(skinClass="CheckBox_overIcon");
```

The import tool also explicitly adds the component library to the Flex project's build path, as shown in Figure 10.16. Each Flash symbol is exported as an ActionScript class in the component library, the library is in the project's build path, and the style declarations bind the Flash symbol classes to the Flex visual components.

FIGURE 10.16

The Flex project build path after importing Flash-based skinning symbols

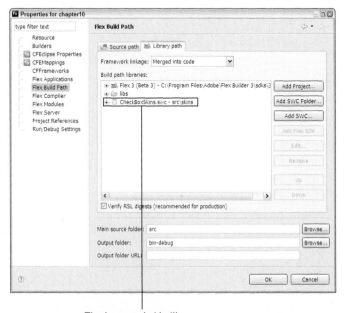

The imported skin library

A complete Flash-based skin library will contain many graphic symbols wrapped in a component library and an associated .css file that binds the symbols to the visual components during the compilation process.

Summary

In this chapter, I described the use of Cascading Style Sheets to effect the visual presentation of Flex applications. You learned the following:

- Cascading Style Sheets (CSS) are implemented in the Flex framework as the primary mechanism for controlling a Flex application's visual appearance.
- You can declare styles with inline style declarations, and with embedded or external style sheets.
- Styles can be controlled at runtime with ActionScript code.
- Skins are one type of style that can be used to dramatically change an application's appearance.
- You can create skinning graphics in bitmap or vector formats.
- Vector graphics designed for use as skins can be created in Illustrator CS3 or Flash CS3.
- You can import skin artwork with Flex Builder's import tool.

Chapter 11

Working with Text

When you present text in a Flex application, many choices and tools can determine how text is presented and processed. Text values can be "hard-coded" in an application, retrieved from a data source (such as database on a server), and stored in memory as constants or variables.

When text is presented to the user in visual control, you select many font settings, including the font typeface and its size, weight, and style. In this chapter, I describe the various tools available for text processing and presentation in Flex. I describe these strategies and techniques:

- Selecting device fonts for text display that are already installed on the client computer.

- Embedding fonts to tightly control text display regardless of the state of the client computer.

- Formatting of text values with the `formatter` family of classes

CROSS-REF Any discussion of text presentation in Flex must include the use of Cascading Style Sheets (CSS) to select font typefaces and styles, and the use of visual controls that are specifically designed for text presentation, such the `Label` and `Text` controls. Previous chapters included detailed descriptions of both subjects. In this chapter, I describe uses of styles that are specifically oriented around text presentation, and I expand on the use of the `Label` and `Text` controls in presenting text to the user.

ON the WEB To use the sample code for this chapter, import the `chapter11.zip` Flex project archive from the Web site files into your Flex Builder workspace.

Controlling Fonts with Cascading Style Sheets

As described in Chapter 10, CSS is one of the most important tools you have for modifying the appearance of text on the screen. In this section, I describe specific styles and their values that you can use to change how `Label`, `Text`, `TextInput`, or `TextArea` controls present data.

Some font styles can be used with both device and embedded fonts, while others are used only with embedded fonts.

These styles apply to all fonts:

- `fontFamily` to determine the typeface
- `color` to determine the typeface color
- `fontSize` to determine the font size
- `fontWeight` to select a bold font
- `fontStyle` to select an italicized font
- `textDecoration` to select an underlined font
- `letterSpacing` to determine the horizontal space between characters

These styles have an effect only on embedded fonts:

- `kerning` to enable adjustments to the horizontal gap between characters
- `fontAntiAliasType` to enable the use of these advanced anti-aliasing styles
    - `fontGridType` to determine whether to measure fonts based on pixels or subpixels
    - `fontThickness` to determine the thickness of font glyph edges
    - `fontSharpness` to determine the sharpness of font glyphs

Selecting Fonts

You select which typeface you want to use with the `fontFamily` (or `font-family`) style. This `Label` control presents its text with the `Arial` typeface with an inline style declaration:

```
<mx:Label fontFamily="Arial" text="Hello World"/>
```

When you declare the `fontFamily` style in an embedded or external style sheet, you can use either the camel case version of the style name, `fontFamily`, or the hyphenated version, `font-family`. This type selector sets an application's default font for the `Label` and `Text` controls to `Times New Roman`:

```
<mx:Style>
  Label, Text {
    font-family:"Times New Roman";
  }
</mx:Style>
```

TIP   When you designate a typeface that has spaces in its name, always wrap the font name in quotation marks. If you don't use quotes, the CSS parser squeezes the spaces out of the font name, resulting in a font name that might not be recognized by Flash Player.

For example, a font declared with a name of `Bookman Old Style Bold` without surrounding quotes is transformed internally to `BookmanOldStyleBold` and no longer matches up correctly with its actual font on the client system.

CAUTION   If you misname a typeface in a `fontFamly` declaration, Flash Player renders the unrecognized font as the client system's default `serif` typeface, which is typically Times Roman.

Two types of fonts can be used in Flex applications:

- **Device fonts** are typefaces that are already installed on the client system.
- **Embedded fonts** are typefaces that are embedded in a compiled Flex application and delivered to the client system as part of the application .swf file.

The pros and cons of using device versus embedded fonts are listed in Table 11.1.

TABLE 11.1

Pros and Cons of Device and Embedded Fonts

	Pros	Cons
Device fonts	Allow you to minimize the size of the compiled Flex application and speed the download of the application during startup (for Web applications) or installation (for desktop applications).	Limited to those fonts that are installed universally, so your graphic design capabilities are limited. Do not support advanced anti-aliasing and font rotation.
Embedded fonts	Allow you to use any font to which you have access during development. Support advanced ani-aliasing and font rotation.	Result in a larger compiled application .swf file. If not managed carefully, embedded fonts can result in a "bloated" application file and significantly slow download and installation.

Using device fonts

When you declare a device font, you should declare a list of fonts you'd like to use in order of preference. The last item in the list should be a generic device font name that selects a font based on what's available on the client system.

This CSS declaration sets the fontFamily style as a list with a first preference of Helvetica and a last preference of the generic font family _sans:

```
<mx:Style>
  Label, Text {
    font-family:Helvetica, Arial, "_sans";
  }
</mx:Style>
```

The first choice, Helvetica, is typically available on Mac OS X, but not on Windows. If that font isn't found by Flash Player on the client system, it then looks for the second choice, Arial, which is installed by default on both Windows and Mac OS X. The final choice, _sans, refers to the general family of sans serif fonts. If Flash Player doesn't find either of the first two choices, it uses the client system's default font of that family.

Three generic device font names are recognized by Flash Player:

- _sans refers to smoother typefaces that are generally selected for their easy readability on computer screens. This family includes such fonts as Arial, Helvetica, and Verdana.

- _serif refers to typefaces that have non-structural visual details added to the ends of font lines. This font family includes such fonts as Times Roman (and its variants such as Times New Roman) and Baskerville.

- _typewriter refers to fixed pitch typefaces that look like they were created on typewriters. This font family includes such fonts as Courier (and its variants such as Courier New) and Prestige Elite.

CAUTION   If you designate only a single typeface in a fontFamily declaration and that font doesn't exist on the client system, Flash Player replaces the font as needed. In this case, the application might not appear to the user as it was originally designed.

Using embedded fonts

When you embed a font in a Flex application, you guarantee that the font will be available to the client system.

Embedded fonts offer great advantages to graphic designers:

- You can strongly "brand" an application's appearance with fonts that are unique to a particular company's design standards.

- Embedded fonts can be rotated, whereas device fonts always are rendered in their default horizontal layout.

- Embedded fonts support advanced anti-aliasing, which allows you to control the sharpness of the font to a fine degree.

- Embedded fonts support transparency, whereas device fonts are always opaque.

Embedded fonts have these limitations:

- Only TrueType or OpenFace fonts can be embedded directly within Flex applications with simple style declarations or ActionScript metadata tags.

- Embedded fonts aren't always legible at sizes less than 10 pixels.

TIP You can embed other font styles such as PostScript Type 1 or bitmap fonts, but these fonts must first be embedded in a Flash document to *vectorize* them, and only then can they be embedded in a Flex application.

CAUTION Fonts that you've downloaded or purchased from a font vendor aren't always licensed for use in a Flash document or Flex application. Check your license for any restrictions on a font's use.

Declaring embedded fonts with CSS

You can embed a font with the @font-face style selector in an embedded or external style sheet. This selector supports all font styles listed previously, plus these additional style names:

- src:local to select a device font to embed by its system font name

- src:url to select a device font by its file location

- fontFamily to designate a font name that can be used for the rest of Flex application

Each embedded font declaration must include the fontFamily to create an alias by which the embedded font will be referenced in the rest of the application and either src:local or src:url to designate the font to embed.

Embedding by font file location

You can embed a font that you haven't installed in your operating system by referring to the font by its file location. Font files can be referred to from anywhere in your file system, but for convenience you should copy the font file somewhere in your project and then refer to it with a relative file location.

This @font-face declaration embeds a font by its filename and assigns a fontFamily of Goudy:

```
@font-face {
  src:url("../fonts/GOUDOS.TTF");
  font-family:"Goudy";
}
```

After the font has been embedded, you can use the fontFamily style to use the font in a particular text control with an inline style declaration or in a set of controls with a style selector. This Label control uses the embedded font:

```
<mx:Label fontFamily="Goudy" text="An embedded font"/>
```

This type selector assigns the embedded font to `Label` and `Text` controls:

```
<mx:Style>
  Label, Text {
    font-family: Goudy;
  }
</mx:Style>
```

Embedding font variations with font files

Fonts that support variations in presentation such as bold and italics are delivered as individual font files. When embedding a font by its filename, you must declare each variation with a separate `@font-face` selector. If you set all of a font's selectors with the same `fontFamily`, you can then refer to the individual fonts from an inline style declaration or a style selector by simply including the appropriate font style.

These `@font-face` declarations embed all three of a font's available variations and assign the same `fontFamily` to each. The `font-weight` and `font-style` settings in each `@font-face` selector determine when each font file will be used.

The application in Listing 11.1 uses the Goudy font with all its variations and a set of `Label` controls that use the font in multiple sizes and variations of appearance.

LISTING 11.1

```
<?xml version="1.0" encoding="utf-8"?>
<mx:Application xmlns:mx="http://www.adobe.com/2006/mxml"
  backgroundColor="white" verticalGap="0">
  <mx:Style>
    @font-face {
      src:url("../fonts/GOUDOS.ttf");
      font-family:"Garamond";
    }
    @font-face {
      src:url("../fonts/GOUDOSB.ttf");
      font-family:"Goudy Old Style";
      font-weight:bold;
    }
    @font-face {
      src:url("../fonts/GOUDOSI.ttf");
      font-family:"Goudy Old Style";
      font-style:italic;
    }
  </mx:Style>
  <mx:Label text="Goudy Old Style 18"
    fontFamily="Goudy Old Style" fontSize="18"/>
  <mx:Label text="Goudy Old Style 30"
    fontFamily="Goudy Old Style" fontSize="30"/>
```

```
<mx:Label text="Goudy Old Style 72"
    fontFamily="Goudy Old Style" fontSize="72"/>
<mx:Label text="Goudy Old Style italic"
    fontFamily="Goudy Old Style" fontSize="72" fontStyle="italic"/>
<mx:Label text="Goudy Old Style bold"
    fontFamily="Goudy Old Style" fontSize="72" fontWeight="bold"/>
</mx:Application></mx:Application>
```

ON the WEB The code in Listing 11.1 is available in the Web site files as `EmbedFontByFileName.mxml` in the `chapter11` project.

WEB RESOURCE In these examples, I'm using a font named Goudy Old Style, which is included by default on both Windows and Mac OS X. You can download more specialized fonts from various Web sites, including `www.1001freefonts.com`.

Embedding by system font name

To embed a font that's been installed in the operating system, use the `src:local` style and refer to the font by its system name. The font's system name is usually the same as the font filename (without the file extension), but to be sure of the system name, you can open the font file and view the system name information. Figure 11.1 shows a font file displayed in Windows XP and the font's system name.

FIGURE 11.1

A font file displayed in Windows XP with the font's system name

The system font name

TIP

On Mac OS X, fonts are stored in the system hard disk's `/System/Library/Fonts` folder. As with Windows, you can preview a font by locating and double-clicking the font file. The font is displayed in the Font Book application, which is included with the operating system.

This declaration embeds a font using the font's system name after the font has been installed in the operating system:

```
@font-face {
  src:local("Goudy Old Style");
  font-family:"Goudy";
}
```

CAUTION

If you type the name of a system font incorrectly, the compiler generates an error.

As with a declaration by font filename, the `font-family` style determines the name by which the font is known in the rest of the application. This `Label` control uses the embedded font:

```
<mx:Label text="Goudy Font" fontFamily="Goudy"/>
```

Embedding font variations with system font names

When you embed by system font name, you still have to declare each font variation individually, but you can use the same system font name and `font-family` for each declaration, and you distinguish each by the use of the `font-weight` or `font-style` declarations. The application in Listing 11.2 declares the Goudy font with the system font name and then uses the font in a set of text controls.

LISTING 11.2

Embedding fonts by system font name

```
<?xml version="1.0" encoding="utf-8"?>
<mx:Application xmlns:mx="http://www.adobe.com/2006/mxml"
  backgroundColor="white">
  <mx:Style>
    @font-face {
      src:local("Goudy Old Style");
      font-family:"Goudy";
    }
    @font-face {
      src:local("Goudy Old Style");
      font-family:"Goudy";
      font-weight:bold;
    }
    @font-face {
      src:local("Goudy Old Style");
      font-family:"Goudy";
```

```
        font-style:italic;
    }
</mx:Style>
<mx:Text text="Goudy 10" fontFamily="Goudy" fontSize="10"/>
<mx:Text text="Goudy 18" fontFamily="Goudy" fontSize="18"/>
<mx:Text text="Goudy 30" fontFamily="Goudy" fontSize="30"/>
<mx:Text text="Goudy italic" fontFamily="Goudy" fontSize="72"
    fontStyle="italic"/>
<mx:Text text="Goudy bold" fontFamily="Goudy" fontSize="72"
    fontWeight="bold"/>
</mx:Application>
```

ON the WEB The code in Listing 11.2 is available in the Web site files as
EmbedFontBySystemName.mxml in the **chapter11** project.

Figure 11.2 shows the application using the embedded font. The application's appearance is the
same regardless of whether the fonts are embedded with file or system names.

FIGURE 11.2

A Flex application using an embedded font

Embedding fonts with Flex Builder's Design view

Flex Builder 3's enhanced Design view can generate a certain amount of CSS code to declare an
embedded font. These generated declarations are always created in an external style sheet and represent only the base font style (and not any variations such as font weight or style).

NEW FEATURE The CSS Editor's Design view is a new feature of Flex Builder 3. In addition to supporting preview of embedded fonts, it allows you to preview most styles when applied to the Flex framework's visual controls.

Follow these steps to create an external style sheet with an embedded font declaration:

1. Select File ➪ New CSS File from the Flex Builder project to create a new external style sheet file.

2. In the New CSS File dialog box, name the new file `fontStyles.css` and click Finish.

3. In Source view of the CSS editor, manually add a `Label` selector to the file without any style declarations. Be sure to declare a code block after the `Label` selector with the { } characters. The `Label` selector should look like this:

```
Label {
}
```

4. Click Design to switch to Design view.

   As shown in Figure 11.3, Design view previews the `Label` control without any custom styles applied.

FIGURE 11.3

The CSS Design view editor previewing the `Label` control

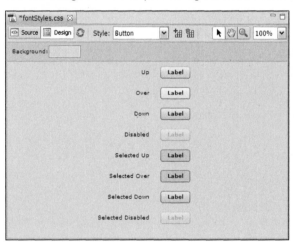

5. Look at the Flex Properties view's Text section, and locate the pull-down list of fonts, as shown in Figure 11.4.

   Notice that the pull-down list displays the standard five device fonts, and in a section at the bottom of the list, it shows all fonts currently installed on the system listed by their system font name.

Available system fonts

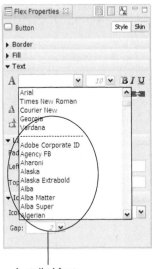

Installed fonts

6. Select a font you'd like to embed. If you're working with the Windows operating system, try a font that may not appear on Mac OS X, such as Comic Sans MS.

7. After selecting the font, Design view refreshes itself and the preview buttons display the select typeface. If the refresh operation doesn't occur, click Design view's Refresh button.

8. Switch to Source view to view the generated style declarations.

The generated code looks like this:

```
/* CSS file */

Label {
   fontFamily: "Comic Sans MS";
}
@font-face
{
   fontFamily: "Comic Sans MS";
   fontWeight: normal;
   fontStyle: normal;
   src: local("Comic Sans MS");
}
```

When you generate font style declarations in this manner, you get only a declaration for the base font, not for such variations as bold and italics.

9. To add the bold variation for the embedded font, select the entire `@font-face` selector with its nested styles and copy it to the clipboard.

10. Paste the `@font-face` selector at the bottom of the style sheet file.

11. Change the new selector's `font-weight` style to **bold**.

12. Save the changes to the style sheet file.

Listing 11.4 shows the contents of the completed style sheet.

LISTING 11.4

The external style sheet after manual changes to generated code

```
Label {
  fontFamily: "Comic Sans MS";
}
@font-face
{
  fontFamily: "Comic Sans MS";
  fontWeight: normal;
  fontStyle: normal;
  src: local("Comic Sans MS");
}
@font-face
{
  fontFamily: "Comic Sans MS";
  fontWeight: bold;
  fontStyle: normal;
  src: local("Comic Sans MS");
}
```

ON the WEB The code in Listing 11.4 is available in the Web site files as `fontStylesFinishd.css` in the **chapter11** project.

CAUTION The completed CSS file on the Web site was generated on a Windows-based development system. If you open it on a Mac or other system that doesn't include the Comic Sans MS font, Flex Builder's Design view may not preview the styles correctly.

Follow these steps to use the generated styles in a Flex application:

1. Create a new MXML application named `ImportingFonts.mxml`.

2. In Source view, add two `Label` controls as follows:

   ```
   <mx:Label text="Embedded font normal"/>
   <mx:Label text="Embedded font bold" fontWeight="bold"/>
   ```

3. Add an <mx:Style/> tag with a source property set to the new external style sheet file:

```
<mx:Style source="fontStyles.css"/>
```

4. Save and run the application shown in Listing 11.5.

LISTING 11.5

An application using embedded fonts in an external style sheet

```
<?xml version="1.0" encoding="utf-8"?>
<mx:Application xmlns:mx="http://www.adobe.com/2006/mxml"
   layout="vertical"
  backgroundColor="#eeeeee">
  <mx:Style source="fontStyles.css"/>
  <mx:Label text="Embedded font normal"/>
  <mx:Label text="Embedded font bold" fontWeight="bold"/>
</mx:Application>
```

ON the WEB The code in Listing 11.5 is available in the Web site files as `ImportingStylesFinished.mxml` in the **chapter11** project.

CAUTION As mentioned previously, the completed sample applications on the Web site were created on a Windows-based development system. If you open them in Flex Builder on Mac OS X or another system that doesn't include the application's expected fonts, compiler errors will be generated.

As shown in Figure 11.5, you should see that the two Label controls use the normal and bold variations of the selected typeface.

FIGURE 11.5

An application showing two variations of an embedded font

Embedding ranges of characters in CSS

When you embed a typeface, you significantly increase the size of the compiled Flex application. For example, in the previous example where two font files were embedded in the application, the compiled debug version of the application increased in size from 152,533 bytes to 308,776 bytes, or roughly twice the original size. This is because font definition files contain font outlines for every possible character, frequently including outlines for non-Latin characters that you might never use in your application.

You can restrict which characters of a typeface are embedded in your application by declaring the unicodeRange style. This style takes an array of range designators, each starting and ending with a Unicode character in hexadecimal code.

TIP Unicode is a standard for encoding characters on computer systems that uses unique numbers, known as *code points*, for each character. Flex uses the most common encoding style, where each character description starts with the string U+ and ends with a 4-character hexadecimal representation of the code point. For example, the Unicode expression U+0021 represents the exclamation point, U+005A represents an uppercase Z character, and so on.

WEB RESOURCE A PDF document containing a chart of the Basic Latin alphabet in Unicode is available at http://unicode.org/charts/PDF/U0000.pdf. Charts of other character sets are available in PDF format at www.unicode.org/charts. Complete information about the Unicode standard is available at www.unicode.org.

The following declaration embeds a broad range of basic Latin Unicode characters that would normally be used in an English language Flex application. The Unicode range of U+0021, representing the exclamation point (!),through U+007E, representing the the tilde (~) includes all uppercase and lowercase alpha characters, numeric characters, and most common punctuation:

```
@font-face
{
  fontFamily: "Comic Sans MS";
  src: local("Comic Sans MS");
  unicodeRange:U+0021-U+007E;
}
```

After adding this unicodeRange setting to both embedded fonts in the preceding example, the compiled application in the release build is 174,954 bytes — a bit larger than the application without any embedded fonts (152,533 bytes), but significantly smaller than the version with both fonts embedded with all their character outlines (308,776 bytes). The result is an application that downloads and installs more quickly, but still has all the text display functionality you need.

For European languages such as French, where an extended Latin alphabet is required, you can add additional ranges of characters that include versions of the Latin alphabet characters with accents and other required annotations. This style declaration embeds both the set of characters known in Unicode as Basic Latin and another set of characters known as Latin Extended A:

```
@font-face
{
  fontFamily: "Comic Sans MS";
```

```
src: local("Comic Sans MS");
unicodeRange:
  U+0021-U+007E, //Basic Latin
  U+0100-U+017F; //Latin Extended A
}
```

> **TIP** The Flex Builder installation contains a file named **flash-unicode-table.xml** in the **sdks/3.0.0/framesworks** folder. This file contains definitions of common Unicode character ranges. The file is not processed with the command-line compiler or Flex Builder, but it can serve as a handy reference to common Unicode ranges.

Declaring embedded fonts with ActionScript

You also can embed fonts with the ActionScript [Embed] metadata tag by either font location or system name. The [Embed] tag must be placed inside an <mx:Script> tag set and include either a source attribute for fonts embedded by filename or a systemFont attribute for fonts embedded by system name.

An [Embed] declaration also requires these attributes:

- fontName to select an alias by which the font will be known to the rest of the application
- mimeType always set to application/x-font

The [Embed] tag is always followed by a variable declaration typed as Class. This variable is never accessed directly in ActionScript code, so its name can be anything you like. This [Embed] tag embeds a font by filename and assigns a fontName of myEmbeddedFont:

```
[Embed(source='../fonts/MyCustomFont.ttf',
  fontName='myEmbeddedFont',
  mimeType='application/x-font')]
private var font1:Class;
```

> **TIP** The name of variable declared after the [Embed] metatdata tag is arbitrary and is only used internally to store the font. It isn't referred to in other ActionScript code, so you can name the variable anything you like.

> **TIP** The [Embed] metadata tag also supports a unicodeRange attribute that can be used to limit which font characters are embedded.

A font that's been installed in the operating system can be embedded using the system font name instead of the filename:

```
[Embed(systemName='MyCustomFont',
  fontName='myEmbeddedFont',
  mimeType='application/x-font')]
private var font1:Class;
```

In either case, you then use the font in a text control by assigning the `fontFamily` style to the new font name:

```
<mx:Label fontFamily="myEmbeddedFont" text="An embedded font"/>
```

Declaring embedded fonts in ActionScript gives you the same benefits as CSS declarations and has the same requirements:

- Each individual font file must be declared separately.

- Each font variation, such as bold or italics, must be declared separately even if the variation isn't stored in a separate file.

> **NOTE** Flex Builder's Design view CSS editor creates a small advantage in using CSS declarations over ActionScript, but you still have to customize the code that the CSS editor generates. So the choice of embedding fonts using CSS or ActionScript is purely a coding preference and is not driven by any strong benefits or drawbacks that might be inherent in either approach.

Manipulating Embedded Fonts

One advantage of embedded fonts over device fonts is the ability to change their visual appearance using these tools:

- **Font rotation** to change the orientation of a text control
- **Advanced anti-aliasing** to render text in clear, high-quality resolution

Rotating fonts

You can rotate a text control that uses an embedded font with the control's rotation property. The value of the rotation property defaults to 0 (indicating standard control layout). A positive value from 1 to 180 indicates that the control is rotated clockwise, while a negative value from -1 to -180 causes the control to rotate counter-clockwise. Values outside these ranges are added to or subtracted from 360 to get a valid value.

The code in Listing 11.6 embeds a system font and then uses the font in a control that's rotated 90 degrees counter-clockwise to turn the control on its side.

LISTING 11.6

A rotated control with an embedded font

```
<?xml version="1.0" encoding="utf-8"?>
<mx:Application xmlns:mx="http://www.adobe.com/2006/mxml"
   layout="absolute"
  backgroundColor="white">
```

```
    <mx:Style>
      @font-face {
        src:local("Comic Sans MS");
        font-family:"Comic";
        unicodeRange:U+0041-U+007E;
      }
    </mx:Style>
    <mx:Label id="rotatedControl" text="Rotated Text" fontFamily="Comic"
      rotation="-90" top="{rotatedControl.width + 10}" left="10"
      fontSize="36"/>
</mx:Application>
```

ON the WEB The code in Listing 11.6 is available in the Web site files as `RotatingFonts.mxml` in the **chapter11** project.

Figure 11.6 shows the resulting application, with the control placed in the application's upper-left corner.

FIGURE 11.6

A rotated control using an embedded font

The object's calculated position at runtime

When you rotate a visual control, its calculated upper-left corner is still based on the control's virtual position when it isn't rotated. A Flash developer would refer to this as the object's "registration point" — the point in the object from which its x and y properties are calculated. The position of the x/y coordinate doesn't change for Flex visual controls, even when the object's font is rotated at runtime.

To properly place such a control, you need to take into account the x and y properties and their true meaning. The top property's calculation used in Listing 11.6 binds to the control's width and uses this value to offset itself vertically. If you place the rotated control in an application with absolute layout, as shown in Listing 11.6, in Design view it appears to run off the screen, as shown in Figure 11.7. At runtime, the top property is calculated correctly and the object is positioned 10 pixels from the top of the application.

FIGURE 11.7

A control's virtual and runtime display positions, shown in Flex Builder's Design view

The control's display position

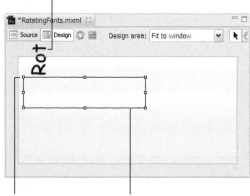

x=0, y=0 at this point   The control's virtual position

The rotation property can be set at runtime through bindings or through ActionScript statements. The code in Listing 11.7 binds a Label control's rotation property to a Slider control's value. As the user manipulates the Slider, the Label rotates.

LISTING 11.7

A Label control with an embedded font, rotating based on a Slider control's value

```
<?xml version="1.0" encoding="utf-8"?>
<mx:Application xmlns:mx="http://www.adobe.com/2006/mxml"
    layout="absolute"
  backgroundColor="white">
  <mx:Style>
    @font-face {
```

```
        src:local("Comic Sans MS");
        font-family:"Comic";
        unicodeRange:U+0041-U+007E;
      }
   </mx:Style>

   <mx:VSlider id="mySlider"
     top="10" left="10" height="150"
     minimum="-180" maximum="180" value="0"
     tickInterval="45" snapInterval="45"/>

   <mx:Label id="rotatedControl" text="Rotated Text" fontFamily="Comic"
     rotation="{mySlider.value}" top="{this.height / 2}"
     left="{this.width / 2}" fontSize="18" liveDragging="true"/>

</mx:Application>
```

ON the WEB   The code in Listing 11.7 is available in the Web site files as
`RotatingFontsWithSlider.mxml` in the `chapter11` project.

Figure 11.8 shows the resulting application, with the control rotated based on the `Slider` control's current `value`.

FIGURE 11.8

As the user manipulates the `Slider` control, the `Label` control's `rotation` property updates based on the binding expression.

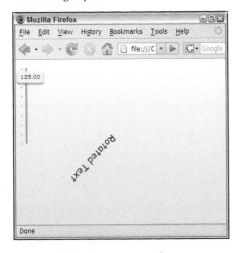

Using advanced anti-aliasing

Advanced anti-aliasing refers to the ability of Flash Player to make embedded fonts more readable by smoothing the font's edges during the rendering process. When you embed a font, its `fontAntiAliasType` style is set to `advanced` by default. If you don't want to use this feature on a particular font, set the style's value to `normal` in the embedding declaration:

```
@font-face {
  src:source("Garamond");
  font-family:"GaramondWithoutAntialiasing";
  font-anti-alias-type:normal;
}
```

When advanced anti-aliasing is enabled, you can set these styles to effect the font's presentation:

- `fontGridFitType` determines how a text control fits to the pixel grid on the monitor. Values of `none`, `pixel`, and `subpixel` are available. The `pixel` setting works only for left-aligned text. The `subpixel` setting works only on LCD monitors and works for right- and center-aligned text.

- `fontSharpness` determines the sharpness of the font glyph. Values from -400 to 400 are available.

- `fontThickness` determines the width the font glyph. Values from -200 to 200 are available.

The code in Listing 11.8 creates an application with two embedded versions of the `Garamond` font. The first embedded font supports advanced anti-aliasing, while the second has the style set to `normal`. The two `Label` controls use the different embedded fonts. The control with advanced anti-aliasing enabled uses the `fontSharpness` and `fontThickness` styles.

LISTING 11.8

An application with advanced anti-aliasing styles

```
<?xml version="1.0" encoding="utf-8"?>
<mx:Application xmlns:mx="http://www.adobe.com/2006/mxml"
  backgroundColor="white" verticalGap="0">
  <mx:Style>
    @font-face {
      src:source("Garamond");
      font-family:"GaramondWithAntialiasing";
      font-anti-alias-type:advanced;
    }
    @font-face {
      src:source("Garamond");
      font-family:"GaramondWithoutAntialiasing";
      font-anti-alias-type:normal;
```

```
    }
  </mx:Style>
  <mx:Label text="Garamond with Advanced Antialiasing"
    fontFamily="GaramondWithAntialiasing" fontSize="24"
    fontSharpness="-400" fontThickness="0"/>
  <mx:Label text="Garamond without Advanced Antialiasing"
    fontFamily="GaramondWithoutAntialiasing" fontSize="24"/>
</mx:Application>
```

ON the WEB   The code in Listing 11.8 is available in the Web site files as **EmbedFontWithAntialiasing.mxml** in the **chapter11** project.

Figure 11.9 shows the resulting application. The first Label control has smoother, fuzzier edges created by the advanced antialiasing, while the second shows the control's default appearance with a sharper appearance.

FIGURE 11.9

Label controls with and without advanced anti-aliasing

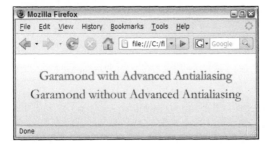

Formatting Text Values

The Flex framework includes a set of formatter classes that can be used to return particular types of data values as formatted strings. There are six classes in this group. The formatter class is the superclass from which all other classes are extended, and the other five classes are designed to format particular types of values.

The Formatter classes include the following:

- CurrencyFormatter to format numeric values as currencies
- DateFormatter to format date values
- NumberFormatter for format numeric values

- `PhoneFormatter` to format phone numbers
- `ZipCodeFormatter` to format zip codes

Each of the `formatter` classes has a set of properties that determine the format of the returned string, and a `format()` method that's used to process a value into a formatted string.

Creating formatter objects

You can create a `formatter` with either MXML or ActionScript. When declaring the class in ActionScript, you use the class name in an MXML declaration:

```
<mx:DateFormatter id="myDateFormatter"/>
```

CAUTION   The `formatter` classes are non-visual components, meaning that they don't implement the `IUIComponent` interface. As with all non-visual components, their MXML declarations must be placed as direct child elements of the **Application** or component root element. If you declare a **formatter** inside a visual container, a compiler error is generated and the application does not successfully compile.

To instantiate a `formatter` class in ActionScript, declare and instantiate a variable typed as the appropriate `formatter` class. Flex Builder should create an import statement for the class; if not, create it manually:

```
import mx.formatters.DateFormatter;
var myDateFormatter:DateFormatter = new DateFormatter();
```

Setting formatter properties

Each `formatter` class has its own set of properties that determine how it formats strings. The `DateFormatter`, for example, has a single `formatString` property that can be used to create a custom date format. The `formatString` property takes as its value a string consisting of masking tokens, combined with literal strings. Table 11.2 describes the tokens that can be used in a `DateFormatter` object's `formatString` property.

TABLE 11.1

DateFormatter formatString Tokens

Pattern token	Description
YY	Year as a two-digit number.
YYYY	Year as a four-digit number.
M	Month as a one- or two-digit number without padded zeroes.
MM	Month as a two-digit number with padded zero where necessary.
MMM	Month as a short name. Values include "Jan", "Feb", and so on.

Pattern token	Description
MMMM	Month as a long name. Values include "January", "February", and so on.
D	Day in month as a one- or two-digit number without padded zeroes.
DD	Day in month as a two-digit number with padded zero where necessary.
E	Day in week as a one- or two-digit number without padded zeroes. Sunday is interpreted as 0, Monday as 1, and so on.
EE	Day in week as a two-digit number with padded zero where necessary.
EEE	Day in week as a short name. Values include "Sun", "Mon", and so on.
EEEE	Day in week as a long name. Values include "Sunday", "Monday", and so on.
A	Returns "AM" for morning, "PM" for afternoon/evening.
J	Hour in day in 24-hour format.
H	Hour in day in 12-hour format.
N	Minutes in hour as a one- or two-digit number without padded zero.
NN	Minutes in hour as a two-digit number with padded zero where necessary.
S	Seconds in current minute.
SS	Seconds in current minute with padded zero

All text used in a `dateFormat` property other than the supported tokens is considered to be literal text. For example, a `formatString` of "EEEE, MMMM D, YYYY" on the first day of 2008 returns "Tuesday, January 1, 2008". The comma and space characters in the formatting string are returned along with the token replacements.

In contrast, the `CurrencyFormatter` and `NumberFormatter` classes have properties that affect thousand separators and decimal characters, the number of characters after a decimal, selection and placement of a currency symbol, and numeric rounding. The `ZipCodeFormatter` and `PhoneFormatter` classes have properties that affect the formatting of those values.

Using formatters in binding expressions

You can use a `formatter` class in a binding expression to change how a value is displayed in a text control. Follow these steps:

1. Create the `formatter` control, and set its formatting properties.

2. Add a text control that displays a value.

3. Set the text control's text property with a binding expression that wraps the value in the `formatter` control's `format()` method.

The application in Listing 11.9 uses a `DateFormatter` to format the `selectedDate` property of a `DateChooser` control.

LISTING 11.9

An application using a DateFormatter

```xml
<?xml version="1.0" encoding="utf-8"?>
<mx:Application xmlns:mx="http://www.adobe.com/2006/mxml"
  backgroundColor="white">
  <mx:DateFormatter id="myDateFormatter" formatString="EEEE, MMMM D,
  YYYY"/>
  <mx:DateChooser id="myDateChooser"/>
  <mx:Label fontSize="18"
    text="Selected date: {myDateFormatter.format(
      myDateChooser.selectedDate)}" />
</mx:Application>
```

ON the WEB   The code in Listing 11.9 is available in the Web site files as
`DateFormatterDemo.mxml` in the `chapter11` project.

Figure 11.10 shows the resulting application with the `Label` control displaying the date value's formatted string.

FIGURE 11.10

A formatted date value displayed in a `Label` control

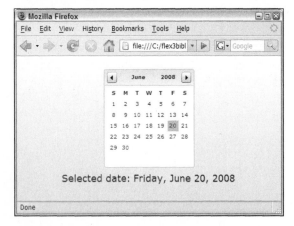

Using formatters in static methods

You may want to use a single formatting rule throughout an application. When you create a `formatter` class for each view component in an application, it can become cumbersome to update all the `formatter` object's formatting values when they have to be changed.

You can solve this by wrapping a `formatter` object in a static method that can be called from anywhere in an application. The nature of a static method is that it behaves the same in all circumstances, and it can be called from its class without having to first instantiate the class.

The code in Listing 11.10 shows a class with a static `formatDate()` method. The method accepts a value argument typed as an ActionScript `Object` so that the method can accept either a true date or a string that can be parsed as a date. It then instantiates the `DateFormatter` class local to the function, sets its `formatString` property to control the output, and returns a formatted value.

LISTING 11.10

A utility class with a static method to universally format date values

```
package utilities
{
  import mx.formatters.DateFormatter;
  public class FormatUtilities
  {
    public static function dateFormat(value:Object):String
    {
      var df:DateFormatter = new DateFormatter();
      df.formatString = "EEEE, MMMM D, YYYY";
      return df.format(value)
    }
  }
}
```

ON the WEB   The code in Listing 11.10 is available in the Web site files as `FormatUtilities.as` in the `src/utilities` folder of `chapter11` project.

To use this static method in an application or component, follow these steps:

1. Declare an `import` statement for the ActionScript class containing the static method.
2. Wrap the value you want to format in a call to the static method.

The code in Listing 11.11 uses the static method to format the date value.

LISTING 11.11

An application using a static formatting method

```
<?xml version="1.0" encoding="utf-8"?>
<mx:Application xmlns:mx="http://www.adobe.com/2006/mxml"
  backgroundColor="white">
  <mx:Script>
    <![CDATA[
      import utilities.FormatUtilities;
    ]]>
  </mx:Script>
  <mx:DateChooser id="myDateChooser"/>
  <mx:Label text="Selected date: {FormatUtilities.dateFormat(
    myDateChooser.selectedDate)}"
    fontSize="18"/>
</mx:Application>
```

ON the WEB The code in Listing 11.11 is available in the Web site files as `FormatWithStaticMethod.mxml` in the `chapter11` project.

When you use a static method to wrap formatting functionality, it becomes possible to change formatting rules for the entire application from a single source code file. The result is an application that's easier to maintain.

Summary

In this chapter, I described how to use device and embedded fonts to determine which typeface is used when displaying text. I also described the use of formatter classes to display values with specific formats. You learned the following:

- You can use device or embedded fonts to display text in various Flex controls.

- Device fonts make the compiled application as small as possible, resulting in faster download and installation.

- Embedded fonts expand graphic design possibilities and provide control of formatting choices such as control rotation and advanced anti-aliasing.

- You can select only certain ranges of characters in an embedded font to minimize the font's impact on the compiled application's size.

- Formatter classes allow you to present various types of values with formatted strings.

- You can declare a formatter object with MXML or ActionScript.

- You can use a formatter in a binding expression or by wrapping it in an ActionScript static method.

Chapter 12

Managing Application Navigation

I n any application that supports more than a single task on a single screen, you need to provide the user with a way of navigating from one area of the application to another. These areas of the application that can be presented only one screen at a time are commonly known as *views*.

In Flex applications, you handle navigation by switching between the application's views, or by modifying the current state of a view. Unlike classic Web applications, which define views as complete HTML pages that are requested and loaded by the browser one at a time, a Flex application's views are predefined and downloaded as part of the entire application. Unless you're using an advanced architecture such as runtime modules, switching from one view to another doesn't require new requests to a Web server, as it would in a Web site.

In this chapter, I describe how to manage navigation in a Flex application by managing stacks of views.

NOTE The term *view* will be used throughout this chapter to describe a rectangular visual presentation that presents and/or collects information from the user. The term is taken from the application development architecture known as model-view-controller, a way of breaking up an application into small parts with specific functions.

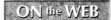 **WEB RESOURCE** These sites have extensive technical information about the role of views in model-view-controller style development:

```
http://ootips.org/mvc-pattern.html
http://c2.com/cgi/wiki?
    ModelViewControllerAsAnAggregateDesignPattern
http://st-www.cs.uiuc.edu/users/smarch/st-docs/mvc.html
```

ON the WEB To use the sample code for this chapter, import the `chapter12.zip` Flex project archive from the Web site files into your Flex Builder workspace.

Classic Web Navigation

Navigation in a Web site or an application built completely as a set of HTML pages is based on the capabilities of the Web browser. When a user clicks hyperlinks or submits information through HTML data entry forms, the Web browser handles navigation by sending HTTP requests to a Web server for each new page.

Classic Web applications, which dynamically generate their screens one page at a time, deliver each application view as a separate page upon request. The application's views don't exist in the browser until they're requested and delivered. And when the browser navigates to any new page, the current page is completely unloaded from memory.

NOTE This discussion of classic Web application architecture does not take into account AJAX-style development, which allows you to load more than one screen into browser memory at a time. Some, but not all, of the advantages of Flex development also can be realized with AJAX.

Classic Web application architecture has certain advantages, such as infinite scalability (measured by the number of views that are possible in an application without negatively affecting performance). But its limitations include the following:

- Classic Web applications can't store data persistently in client-side memory. As each page is unloaded from the browser, the data in its memory is lost.

  - Some Web architectures solve data persistence by passing data from page to page as the user navigates through the application. ASP.NET, for example, has an architecture known as the `ViewState` that passes data as part of each form post. This works with small amounts of data, but larger data packets can cause client-side performance issues because passing so much data to and from the server can create an impression of sluggishness.

  - Other Web architectures solve the state issue by storing session data on the server and synchronizing client access to the data with cookies (variables generated by the server and returned by the client on each new page request). While server-side session management relieves the client of the need to manage data persistently, server-side session management can create user scalability issues. Each time a new user visits the application, additional server memory is required.

- The browser has to rebuild the view each time it's visited. Because browsers have no inherent client-side state management, the graphical presentation of a page must be recalculated and rendered anew on each visit to the page. The browser offers caching of image and other assets to speed up this process, but graphical presentation in a Web page is necessarily limited.

- HTML and JavaScript aren't interpreted identically by every Web browser. In fact, one of the most costly and time-consuming aspects of classic Web application development is testing, because you must test on each combination of operating system, browser, and version that you want to support. Some Web application vendors handle this issue by limiting the platforms on which an application is supported. For example, Intuit's QuickBooks Online, while a powerful and reliable Web application, is supported only on Microsoft Internet Explorer on Windows — no Mac or Firefox users allowed!

Understanding Flex Navigation

Navigation in Flex applications is handled at two levels, with navigator containers and view states. The difference between these concepts can be described as one of the scale of visual change during a move from one presentation to another:

- **Navigator containers** should be used when you want to replace a rectangular region of a Flex application (a view) with a completely different visual presentation.

- **View states** should be used when you want to modify an existing view, by adding or removing visual components or by changing components' properties, styles, or event listeners.

In some cases, either a navigator container or a view state can get the job done, but for the most part, the choice is clear: Use a navigator container to move from one view to another, and use a view state to change an existing view.

 Detailed information about view states is available in Chapter 15.

Using Navigator Containers

You create a stack of views using one of the navigator containers provided in the Flex framework. The `ViewStack` class is the simplest of these navigator containers. You declare the `ViewStack` container as a parent container that nests a collection of view components, and displays only one of its nested views at any given time.

The `ViewStack` container doesn't have any user interface controls that allow the user to select a current view, so it's typically controlled either with ActionScript code or with navigator bar components that use the `ViewStack` as a data provider and dynamically generate interactive components to control navigation.

Declaring a ViewStack in MXML

To create a ViewStack in MXML, declare an <mx:ViewStack> tag set. Then declare each nested container within the <mx:ViewStack> tag set. You can nest either pre-built containers from the Flex framework or your own custom components. The containers you nest within the ViewStack can be either layout or navigator containers.

CAUTION Only containers can be nested directly within the ViewStack, TabNavigator, or Accordion navigator containers. This rule is enforced via the nested object's inheritance hierarchy: Each of the components nested directly within a ViewStack must include mx.core.Container as one of its superclasses. If you nest a control in a ViewStack that doesn't extend Container, a *type coercion* error is generated at runtime when the framework tries to cast the object as Container.

Each container nested within a navigator container, whether implemented as a ViewStack, TabNavigator, or Accordion, should have a label property. The label is an arbitrary String that's used in many circumstances to describe the container's purpose to the user. You don't always need the label property, but if you bind the stack to a navigator container that generates interactive components such as Buttons, or if you use the TabNavigator or Accordion containers, the value of each nested container's label is displayed on the interactive component that navigates to that child container.

This code creates a ViewStack with five views or layers:

```
<mx:ViewStack id="views">
  <mx:HBox/>
  <mx:VBox/>
  <mx:Canvas/>
  <mx:Panel/>
  <views:MyCustomComponent/>
</mx:ViewStack>
```

The first four views are instances of containers from the Flex framework, and the last is an instance of a custom component that's extended from a container component.

Using custom components in a navigator container

The views nested within a navigator container can be defined as custom components in MXML. As described previously, if you're going to nest a custom component in a navigator container, it must extend a component that includes mx.core.Container in its inheritance hierarchy. These components include HBox, VBox, Canvas, Panel, Form, and others.

The custom component in Listing 12.1 displays a Label and a DataGrid wrapped in a VBox container.

LISTING 12.1

A custom component suitable for use in a navigator container

```
<?xml version="1.0" encoding="utf-8"?>
<mx:VBox xmlns:mx="http://www.adobe.com/2006/mxml" width="400"
   height="300"
  backgroundColor="#FFFFFF">
  <mx:Label text="Author List" styleName="logo"/>
  <mx:DataGrid id="authorsGrid" width="100%" height="100%">
    <mx:columns>
      <mx:DataGridColumn dataField="title" headerText="First Name"/>
      <mx:DataGridColumn dataField="price" headerText="Last Name"/>
    </mx:columns>
  </mx:DataGrid>
</mx:VBox>
```

ON the WEB The code in Listing 12.1 is available in the Web site files as `views/Authors.mxml` in the `chapter12` project. View components named `Books.mxml` and `ShoppingCart.mxml` are used in these examples also.

Creating a ViewStack in Design view

You can use Flex Builder's Design view to visually create a `ViewStack` and its nested views. As described previously, each of the nested views must be a container, as an instance of either a Flex framework container class or a custom component that includes the `Container` class in its inheritance hierarchy.

NOTE Flex Builder's Design view refers to the layers of a `ViewStack` as *panes,* and the documentation sometimes refers to them as *panels.* These terms refer to the nested view containers within the `ViewStack`.

ON the WEB The steps in this section assume that you've downloaded the files from the Web site and imported the `chapter12` project.

Follow these steps to create a `ViewStack` in Design view:

1. Open `BookStore.mxml` from the `chapter12` project. Notice that the application already has an instance of a custom `Header` component and a few visual settings:

```
<?xml version="1.0" encoding="utf-8"?>
<mx:Application xmlns:mx="http://www.adobe.com/2006/mxml"
  xmlns:views="views.*"
  layout="vertical" horizontalAlign="left"
  backgroundGradientAlphas="[1.0, 1.0]"
  backgroundGradientColors="[#908D8D, #FFFFFF]">
  <mx:Style source="assets/styles.css"/>
  <views:Header/>
</mx:Application>
```

2. Run the application.

   As shown in Figure 12.1, you should see that the Header component displays an image, some text, and a background image.

FIGURE 12.1

The starting application with a custom Header component

3. Return to Flex Builder, and switch to Design view.

4. Look in the Components view's Navigators section, and drag a ViewStack into the application.

   As shown in Figure 12.2, the ViewStack is represented visually by a rectangular outlined area and a toolbar with + and – buttons to add and remove views, and < and > buttons to navigate from one view to the next.

5. Click the + button to add a new view to the ViewStack.

   As shown in Figure 12.3, the Insert Pane dialog box prompts you to select a component to instantiate as a layer of the ViewStack. The list of available components includes all containers from the Flex framework and all the application's custom components that are eligible for use in the context of a navigator container.

6. Set the Label of the new pane as **Catalog**.

7. Select Books from the list of available containers.

8. Click OK to add the new pane to the ViewStack.

FIGURE 12.2

A starting `ViewStack`

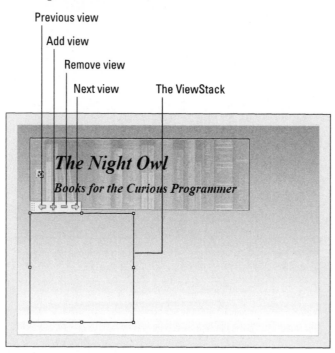

Previous view

Add view

Remove view

Next view   The ViewStack

The Night Owl

Books for the Curious Programmer

FIGURE 12.3

The Insert Pane dialog box

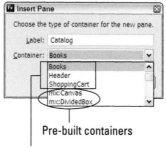

Custom components

Pre-built containers

9. Repeat Steps 5 through 8, and add an instance of the `Authors` container with a label of **Authors**.

10. Repeat Steps 5 through 8 again, and add an instance of the `ShoppingCart` container with a label of **Shopping Cart**.

11. Run the application.

    When the application appears, it should display the `Books` container, because it was the first layer declared within the `ViewStack`.

 The application displays only one layer at this point, because you haven't added any interactive components to control navigation.

12. Return to Flex Builder, and switch to Source view.

The generated `ViewStack` code looks like this:

```
<mx:ViewStack id="viewstack1" width="200" height="200">
  <views:Books label="Catalog" width="100%" height="100%">
  </views:Books>
  <views:Authors label="Authors" width="100%" height="100%">
  </views:Authors>
  <views:ShoppingCart label="Shopping Cart" width="100%"
    height="100%">
  </views:ShoppingCart>
</mx:ViewStack>
```

The Design view tool for generating `ViewStack` code makes a great start, but has these issues:

■ The `ViewStack` is always generated with an initial `height` and `width` of 200 pixels each. You can change the `ViewStack` dimensions in Design view by dragging the `ViewStack` handles, or in the Flex Properties view. And of course, you can always change or remove the dimensions completely in Source view.

■ Design view has no mechanism for visually reordering a `ViewStack` container's layers. If you want to change the order of the views, you must do so in Source view.

■ All containers' MXML declarations are generated with tag sets, such as:

```
<views:Books label="Catalog" width="100%" height="100%">
</views:Books>
```

Particularly when using custom components, the MXML code would be more efficient with empty tag syntax:

```
<views:Books label="Catalog" width="100%" height="100%"/>
```

This is purely a matter of code aesthetics though, and it doesn't have any negative effect on application functionality or performance.

After generating a `ViewStack` with Design view, be sure to revise the generated code as needed in Source view.

Working with navigator containers in ActionScript

When a navigator container is initially constructed and displayed, it displays the currently active view (by default, the first view declared in the stack). You can change the active view at runtime with ActionScript commands that reference one of these `ViewStack` properties:

- `selectedIndex:int` is the numeric index position of the active container within the stack.
- `selectedChild:Container` is the object reference of the active container within the stack.

Using selectedIndex

The `selectedIndex` property returns the index position of the currently active container, as determined by the order of the `ViewStack` container's display list. When declaring a `ViewStack` in MXML, the display list order and the order of MXML declaration are the same.

As with all index operations in ActionScript, indexing starts at 0. So the first container with the view stack is at position 0, the second at position 1, and so on.

To change the currently selected view by index, set the stack's `selectedIndex` property to the numeric index of the container you want to activate. This code makes the `viewstack1` container's second layer visible and active:

```
<mx:Button label="Authors" click="viewstack1.selectedIndex=1"/>
```

Because indexing always begins at 0, this `Button` would allow the user to navigate to the first layer of a stack:

```
<mx:Button label="First Layer"
    click="viewstack1.selectedIndex=0"/>
```

Using numChildren

The `numChildren` property returns the total number of layers in the stack as an `int` value. Taking into account the 0-based indexing offset, this `Button` would allow the user to navigate to the last layer of a stack:

```
<mx:Button label="Last Layer"
    click="viewstack1.selectedIndex=viewstack1.numChildren-1"/>
```

Navigating forward and backward through view stack layers

You can navigate forward and backward through layers of a view stack by incrementing or decrementing the stack's `selectedIndex` property. This `Button` would allow the user to move to the previous layer of a stack:

```
<mx:Button label="Authors" click="viewstack1.selectedIndex--"/>
```

TIP   The `selectedIndex` property of a `ViewStack` can't be set to less than 0. If the
`Button` control in the preceding code is clicked when the `ViewStack` container's
`selectedIndex` is already set to 0, the command is ignored and there is no runtime error.

You also can navigate forward through a stack, but if you set the `selectedIndex` to a value
greater than the stack's highest available index, an "array out of bounds" error results. You can prevent this by wrapping the code to navigate forward in a conditional clause that checks to be sure
that the last container in the stack isn't already active:

```
private function navForward():void
{
  if (viewstack1.selectedIndex != viewstack1.numChildren-1)
  {
    viewstack1.selectedIndex++;
  }
}
```

Alternatively, you can set the `Button` control's `enabled` property to `false` when
`selectedIndex` indicates that a forward or backward navigation either wouldn't work or would
result in a runtime error. Binding expressions that evaluate `selectedIndex` and return a
`Boolean` value to the `enabled` property can handle this task dynamically.

This `Button` control that navigates forward is enabled only when the `ViewStack` container's
`selectedIndex` isn't already set to the highest index:

```
<mx:Button label="Next &gt;&gt;"
  click="viewstack1.selectedIndex++"
  enabled="{viewstack1.selectedIndex != viewstack1.numChildren-
  1}"/>
```

Managing binding issues

In the preceding code example, the binding expression used in the `enabled` property might be
executed upon application startup before the `ViewStack` container's `numChidren` property can
be correctly evaluated. If this happens, you might see that the `Button` controls are incorrectly
enabled and disabled upon application startup.

To fix this sort of timing issue, call the `ViewStack` container's `executeBindings()` method
with a recursive argument of `true` to re-evaluate all of its dependent binding expressions. If you
call this method upon the `ViewStack` container's `creationComplete` event, it evaluates any
bound property values such as `numChildren` again and the `Button` control's `enabled` states
will be correctly calculated:

```
<mx:ViewStack id="viewstack1" width="400" height="200"
    creationComplete="executeBindings(true)">
  <views:Books label="Catalog" width="100%" height="100%"/>
```

```
      <views:Authors label="Authors" width="100%" height="100%"/>
      <views:ShoppingCart label="Shopping Cart" width="100%"
         height="100%"/>
   </mx:ViewStack>
```

The application in Listing 12.2 implements forward and backward navigation with a ViewStack and Button controls. Each Button control has its enabled property set through a binding expression, and the ViewStack re-executes its bindings upon its creationComplete event.

LISTING 12.2

An application using forward and backward navigation

```xml
<?xml version="1.0" encoding="utf-8"?>
<mx:Application xmlns:mx="http://www.adobe.com/2006/mxml"
  xmlns:views="views.*" layout="vertical" horizontalAlign="left"
  backgroundGradientAlphas="[1.0, 1.0]"
  backgroundGradientColors="[#908D8D, #FFFFFF]">
  <mx:Style source="assets/styles.css"/>
  <views:Header/>
  <mx:HBox>
    <mx:Button label="&lt;&lt; Previous"
      click="viewstack1.selectedIndex--"
      enabled="{viewstack1.selectedIndex != 0}"/>
    <mx:Button label="Next &gt;&gt;"
      click="viewstack1.selectedIndex++"
      enabled="{viewstack1.selectedIndex != viewstack1.numChildren-1}"/>
  </mx:HBox>
  <mx:ViewStack id="viewstack1" width="400" height="200"
      creationComplete="executeBindings(true)">
    <views:Books label="Catalog" width="100%" height="100%"/>
    <views:Authors label="Authors" width="100%" height="100%"/>
    <views:ShoppingCart label="Shopping Cart" width="100%"
    height="100%"/>
  </mx:ViewStack>
</mx:Application>
```

ON the WEB The code in Listing 12.2 is available in the Web site files as **BookStoreIndexNavigation.mxml** in the **chapter12** project.

Figure 12.4 shows the resulting application, with Previous and Next buttons to handle backward and forward navigation.

FIGURE 12.4

An application with forward and backward navigation

Using selectedChild

The ViewStack container's selectedChild property accesses the stack's currently visible view by its object reference. To use this property, each of the stack's nested containers should be assigned a unique id:

```
<mx:ViewStack id="viewstack1">
  <views:Books id="booksView"/>
  <views:Authors id="authorsView"/>
  <views:ShoppingCart id="cartView"/>
</mx:ViewStack>
```

To select an active view by the container's unique id, set the ViewStack container's selectedChild:

```
<mx:Button label="Shoppping Cart"
  click="viewstack1.selectedChild=cartView"/>
```

Notice that there are no quotes around the cartView container's id when it's assigned in this way. You're accessing the id as a variable or component instance id, not a String value.

TIP   When navigating with selectedChild set to a container's unique id, because your navigation will be hard-coded, you typically don't need to assign a label property to each container. The label property becomes useful when dynamically generating user interface controls for navigation.

The application in Listing 12.3 implements navigation using Button controls for each of the nested containers in a ViewStack. Each Button control explicitly navigates to its container by the container's unique id.

LISTING 12.3

An application using explicit navigation by unique id

```
<?xml version="1.0" encoding="utf-8"?>
<mx:Application xmlns:mx="http://www.adobe.com/2006/mxml"
  xmlns:views="views.*" layout="vertical" horizontalAlign="left"
  backgroundGradientAlphas="[1.0, 1.0]"
  backgroundGradientColors="[#908D8D, #FFFFFF]">
  <mx:Style source="assets/styles.css"/>
  <views:Header/>
  <mx:HBox>
    <mx:Button label="Catalog"
      click="viewstack1.selectedChild=booksView"/>
    <mx:Button label="Authors"
      click="viewstack1.selectedChild=authorsView"/>
    <mx:Button label="Shoppping Cart"
      click="viewstack1.selectedChild=cartView"/>
  </mx:HBox>
  <mx:ViewStack id="viewstack1" width="400" height="200">
    <views:Books id="booksView" width="100%" height="100%"/>
    <views:Authors id="authorsView" width="100%" height="100%"/>
    <views:ShoppingCart id="cartView" width="100%" height="100%"/>
  </mx:ViewStack>
</mx:Application>
```

ON the WEB   The code in Listing 12.3 is available in the Web site files as BookStoreReferenceNavigation.mxml in the chapter12 project.

Figure 12.5 shows the resulting application, with explicit Button controls to handle navigation to each nested container.

FIGURE 12.5

An application with explicit navigation by unique `id`

Managing creation policy

The `ViewStack`, `TabNavigator`, and `Accordion` containers support a property named `creationPolicy` that manages the manner in which their nested view containers are instantiated at runtime. These are possible values of `creationPolicy`:

- `auto` (the default)
- `all`
- `none`
- `queued`

When `creationPolicy` is set to the default of `auto`, only the initially active view is completely instantiated at first. The other view containers also are instantiated, but their child controls are left `null`. Any attempt to address these objects in ActionScript code while they're not yet instantiated results in a null error.

This behavior is known as *deferred instantiation* and is a strategy for optimizing client-side performance in Flash Player. In a navigator container that contains dozens of views or more, if the application has to instantiate all the content before the user can interact with anything, significant delays can occur. To prevent this issue, the default behavior makes content visible as early as possible.

You see the effect of deferred instantiation when you try to initialize some property of a nested component before the user decides to visit that content at runtime and get a runtime error. You can solve this by setting the navigator container's `creationPolicy` property to `all`, meaning that all the views are instantiated during the navigator container's instantiation. This strategy can work fine in a small- to medium-size application that doesn't have a large number of nested views.

Alternatively, you can set `creationPolicy` to `none`, meaning that you don't want the nested components ever to be instantiated automatically, and then take complete control over the process by explicitly calling the nested container's `createComponentsFromDescriptors()` method when you see fit.

> **TIP** The `Container` class implements such methods as `addChild()`, `addChildAt()`, and `removeChild()` that allow you to explicitly control the contents and order of a container's nested child objects at runtime. You can use these methods to control not just which objects have been instantiated, but which are currently nested children of a navigator container.

> **TIP** The `creationPolicy` property is also implemented in layout containers. Layout containers instantiate their child objects all at the same time by default. If you prefer to take control over the instantiation process, set the layout container's `creationPolicy` property to `none`, and then instantiate the child objects as necessary using with the container's `createComponentsFromDescriptors()` method.

Finally, the effect of setting `creationPolicy` to `queued` means that you want to instantiate all objects automatically, but instead of creating all objects simultaneously (as with the setting of `all`), each nested view component's content is instantiated only after the prior component's instantiation has been completed.

Managing navigator container dimensions

By default, navigator containers size to the first visible child container. Any subsequent navigation results in bumping the child container up to the top left if it is smaller than the instantiated size, or the implementation of scrollbars if the container is larger.

You can set the height and width of a navigator container using absolute pixel dimensions, percentage dimensions, or dynamic sizing. You can use two common strategies for handling navigator container sizing:

- Set the navigator container's dimensions to specific pixel or percentage dimensions, and then set the nested container sizes to 100 percent height and width. Each of the nested view containers then resizes to fill the available space in the navigator container.

- Set the nested containers to specific pixel dimensions, and set the navigator container's `resizeToContent` property to `true`. The navigator container then resizes to accommodate each newly active view as the user navigates through the application.

CAUTION   Setting `resizeToContent` to `true` forces the navigator container to re-measure and re-draw itself as the user navigates through the application. This can cause interesting and unintended visual effects, particularly when the navigator container has a visible border or background.

Using Navigator Bar Containers

If you want a user to be able to navigate to any container within a `ViewStack`, you can use one of the navigator bar containers that are included with the Flex framework. The framework uses four navigator bar containers:

- `ButtonBar`: Generates one `Button` control for each nested container

- `ToggleButtonBar`: Generates one `Button` control for each nested container and shows the current selection through the `Button` control's `toggle` behavior

- `LinkBar`: Generates one `LinkButton` control for each nested container

- `TabBar`: Generates one `Tab` for each nested container

TIP   You won't find a Tab component or ActionScript class in the Flex 3 documentation, but it's used internally as a style selector to manage a TabBar's visual presentation. Because each Tab is an instance of this internal class, you can change certain styles such as the amount of padding within each Tab:

```
<mx:Style>
  Tab {
    padding-left:10;
    padding-bottom:0;
    padding-top:0;
    padding-right:10;
  }
</mx:Style>
```

Using an Array as a dataProvider

Each of the navigator bar containers has a `dataProvider` property that you bind to a `ViewStack`. The navigator bar then generates one interactive component for each of the stack's nested containers.

Navigator bars generate nested controls based on information provided through their `dataProvider` property. The `dataProvider` can be either an `Array` of values (either simple strings or complex objects) or can be bound to a `ViewStack`.

This code generates a `LinkBar` using a `dataProvider` set as an `Array` of complex objects:

```
<mx:LinkBar itemClick="clickHandler(event)">
  <mx:dataProvider>
    <mx:Object>
      <mx:label>Adobe</mx:label>
      <mx:url>http://www.adobe.com</mx:url>
    </mx:Object>
    <mx:Object>
      <mx:label>Google</mx:label>
      <mx:url>http://www.google.com</mx:url>
    </mx:Object>
    <mx:Object>
      <mx:label>Microsoft</mx:label>
      <mx:url>http://www.microsoft.com</mx:url>
    </mx:Object>
  </mx:dataProvider>
</mx:LinkBar>
```

> **TIP**   In the preceding MXML declaration, the `<mx:Object>` tags are not explicitly wrapped in an `<mx:Array>` tag set. This is a bit of shorthand; the MXML compiler understands that the `dataProvider` requires an `Array` and correctly interprets the declaration of multiple `<mx:Object>` tag sets as an `Array` of `Object` instances.

> **TIP**   The `label` and `url` property names are arbitrary and not predefined in the `Object` class, but the `mx` prefix is required because they're declared within the `<mx:Object>` tag set. The value of the `label` property is used in the labels of the navigator bar container's generated controls because the container's `labelField` property defaults to `label`. You can use any other named object property for this purpose by setting the `labelField` to the property you want to use.

Handling navigator bar events

When a navigator bar's `dataProvider` is set as an `Array` of data, it doesn't automatically do anything when the user clicks one of its controls. Instead, you listen for the navigator bar's `itemClick` event and react to it by executing some ActionScript code.

The `itemClick` event generates an event object typed as `mx.events.ItemClickEvent`. This object has an item property that references underlying data of the interactive component that was clicked. Within an event handler function, the expression `event.item` returns the underlying data, and from that point you can reference the selected object's data properties.

With the preceding `Array` of `Object` instances as a navigator bar's `dataProvider`, the expression `event.item.label` returns the `label` property of the selected data item when an interactive control is clicked, and `event.item.url` returns its `url` property.

The application in Listing 12.4 handles the `itemClick` event of a `LinkBar` control and responds by navigating to the selected URL.

LISTING 12.4

An application using a navigator bar container with an Array as the dataProvider

```
<?xml version="1.0" encoding="utf-8"?>
<mx:Application xmlns:mx="http://www.adobe.com/2006/mxml"
   layout="vertical">
  <mx:Script>
    <![CDATA[
      import mx.controls.Alert;
      import mx.events.ItemClickEvent;
      private function clickHandler(event:ItemClickEvent):void
      {
        var request:URLRequest=new URLRequest(event.item.url);
        navigateToURL(request);
      }
    ]]>
  </mx:Script>
  <mx:LinkBar itemClick="clickHandler(event)">
    <mx:dataProvider>
      <mx:Object>
        <mx:label>Adobe</mx:label>
        <mx:url>http://www.adobe.com</mx:url>
      </mx:Object>
      <mx:Object>
        <mx:label>Google</mx:label>
        <mx:url>http://www.google.com</mx:url>
      </mx:Object>
      <mx:Object>
        <mx:label>Microsoft</mx:label>
        <mx:url>http://www.microsoft.com</mx:url>
      </mx:Object>
    </mx:dataProvider>
  </mx:LinkBar>
</mx:Application>
```

ON the WEB   The code in Listing 12.4 is available in the Web site files as
NavBarWithArrayData.mxml in the chapter12 project.

Using a ViewStack as a dataProvider

When you pass a ViewStack to a navigator bar as its dataProvider, the navigator bar generates one interactive control for each of the ViewStack container's nested views. Each nested container's label property is passed to each generated Button, LinkButton, or Tab for display.

You set a ViewStack as a dataProvider with a binding expression:

```
<mx:ToggleButtonBar dataProvider="{viewstack1}"/>
```

The application in Listing 12.5 uses a ToggleButtonBar that generates one toggle button for each nested container of a ViewStack.

LISTING 12.5

An application using a navigator bar container

```
<?xml version="1.0" encoding="utf-8"?>
<mx:Application xmlns:mx="http://www.adobe.com/2006/mxml"
  xmlns:views="views.*" layout="vertical" horizontalAlign="left"
  backgroundGradientAlphas="[1.0, 1.0]"
  backgroundGradientColors="[#908D8D, #FFFFFF]">
  <mx:Style source="assets/styles.css"/>
  <views:Header/>
  <mx:ToggleButtonBar dataProvider="{viewstack1}"/>
  <mx:ViewStack id="viewstack1" width="400" height="200">
    <views:Books label="Catalog" width="100%" height="100%"/>
    <views:Authors label="Authors" width="100%" height="100%"/>
    <views:ShoppingCart label="Shopping Cart" width="100%"
  height="100%"/>
  </mx:ViewStack>
</mx:Application>
```

ON the WEB   The code in Listing 12.5 is available in the Web site files as BookStoreNavBar.mxml in the chapter12 project.

Figure 12.6 shows the resulting application, with generated toggle button controls to handle navigation to each nested container.

FIGURE 12.6

An application using a navigator bar container

Managing navigator bar presentation

Each of the navigator bar containers has a `direction` property that can be used to lay out the container vertically. For example, this `LinkBar` stacks its generated `LinkButton` controls vertically:

```
<mx:LinkBar dataProvider="{viewstack1}" direction="vertical"/>
```

The application in Listing 12.6 uses a vertical `LinkBar` wrapped in an `HBox` container. Binding expressions are used to match the component's width and height properties as needed.

LISTING 12.6

An application using a vertical navigator bar container

```
<?xml version="1.0" encoding="utf-8"?>
<mx:Application xmlns:mx="http://www.adobe.com/2006/mxml"
  xmlns:views="views.*" layout="vertical" horizontalAlign="left"
  backgroundGradientAlphas="[1.0, 1.0]"
  backgroundGradientColors="[#908D8D, #FFFFFF]">
<mx:Style source="assets/styles.css"/>
<views:Header id="header"/>
```

```
    <mx:HBox width="{header.width}">
      <mx:LinkBar dataProvider="{viewstack1}"
        direction="vertical"
        backgroundColor="white" backgroundAlpha=".8"
        height="{viewstack1.height}"/>
      <mx:ViewStack id="viewstack1" width="100%" height="200">
        <views:Books label="Catalog" width="100%" height="100%"/>
        <views:Authors label="Authors" width="100%" height="100%"/>
        <views:ShoppingCart label="Shopping Cart" width="100%"
    height="100%"/>
      </mx:ViewStack>
    </mx:HBox>
  </mx:Application>
```

ON the WEB The code in Listing 12.6 is available in the Web site files as **BookStoreVerticalNav.mxml** in the **chapter12** project.

Figure 12.7 shows the resulting application, with a LinkBar displaying stacked LinkButton controls.

FIGURE 12.7

An application using a vertical navigator bar container

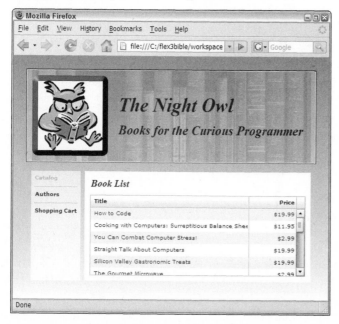

Using Menu Controls

Flex provides three menu controls that can be used to create styles of navigation interfaces. They include the Menu, the MenuBar, and the PopupMenuButton. Of these three controls, the Menu and MenuBar define their menus with a hierarchical data structure, represented as XML, and notify you of user selections with both an itemClick and change event.

The PopupMenuButton control differs from the other menu controls, in that it displays only a single-level menu and notifies you of a user selection with its change event. This section describes the details of using the Menu and MenuBar controls. PopupMenuButton is described in Chapter 13.

You can use the Menu and MenuBar controls, combined with event listeners and ActionScript event handler functions, to create a customized navigation interface.

Menu data providers

The data that determines the structure of a Menu or MenuBar is typically represented hierarchically and can be one of these types:

- A String containing valid XML text
- An XMLNode
- An XMLList
- Any object that implements ICollectionView
- An Array

Any other object passed as a menu data provider is automatically wrapped in an Array with the object as its first and only item.

The most common sort of data used to determine menu structure is an XMLList. You can declare an XMLList in the application with MXML code and nested XML markup:

```
<mx:XMLList id="menuData">
  <menuitem label="Lists">
    <menuitem label="Catalog" view="catalogView"/>
    <menuitem label="Authors" view="authorsView"/>
  </menuitem>
  <menuitem label="Shopping">
    <menuitem label="Shopping Cart" view="cartView"/>
  </menuitem>
</mx:XMLList>
```

You can select any element and attribute names you like in the XML structure, but you should follow these recommendations when using a menu control with a ViewStack:

- Each menu item should have a consistently named attribute to serve as the visible label for each menu node. In the preceding example, this attribute is named label. Notice that all menu items at all levels of the hierarchy have this attribute.

■ Menu items that cause navigation should have an attribute whose value matches the unique id of a nested container in a ViewStack. This can help you simplify the ActionScript code you write to handle the menu control's events.

To use the data in a menu control, pass the XMLList structure to the control as its dataProvider property in a binding expression. Also set the menu control's labelField to an E4X expression that references the label attribute in each menu node:

```
<mx:MenuBar id="myMenuBar" dataProvider="{menuData}"
    labelField="@label"/>
```

CROSS-REF Detailed information about retrieving XML and parsing it with E4X is available in Chapters 21 and 22.

CAUTION If you forget to set the menu control's labelField to a consistently named attribute or property of the underlying data, the labels of the menu items sometimes present raw XML because the control doesn't have any instructions for parsing the data.

Handling menu events

When the user selects an item from either the Menu or MenuBar control, it dispatches an itemClick event that generates an event object typed as mx.events.MenuEvent. This event object has an item property that references the underlying data that drove the creation of the selected menu item. Within an event handler function, the expression event.item references the data, and the E4X expression can be used to access the selected XML node's attributes. For example, the expression event.item.@view references the XML node's view attribute.

You can listen for the itemClick event with MXML or ActionScript. This MenuBar has an attribute-based itemClick event listener that passes the event object to a custom event handler function named menuClickHandler():

```
<mx:MenuBar id="myMenuBar" dataProvider="{menuData}"
    labelField="@label" itemClick="menuClickHandler(event)"/>
```

To listen for the same event with an ActionScript statement, use the addEventListener() method to listen for the event named by the constant MenuEvent.ITEM_CLICK:

```
navMenu.addEventListener(MenuEvent.ITEM_CLICK, menuClickHandler);
```

The custom event handler can then access the selected XML node's attributes and use them to execute navigation. This event handler function retrieves the node's view attribute with an array-style expression to change the active view container of the ViewStack:

```
import mx.events.MenuEvent;
private function menuClickHandler(event:MenuEvent):void
{
  viewstack1.selectedChild = this[event.item.@view];
}
```

Using the Menu control

The Menu control presents a set of cascading menus in response to a user event. Because this control is always presented in response to an event, and not as a static part of the application's visual interface, it can be instantiated only with ActionScript, not with MXML.

To create a Menu, instantiate it with the Menu class's static createMenu() method and pass two arguments:

- The Menu object's parent container
- The Menu object's data provider

Then present the Menu with its show() method, passing optional xShow and yShow coordinates as arguments. This event handler function responds to a mouse event by creating a Menu with a data provider named menuData and the Application as the parent window, and then displays it at the mouse event's stageX and stageY coordinates.

The application in Listing 12.7 uses a Menu populated with an XMLList as its dataProvider.

LISTING 12.7

Using the Menu control

```
<?xml version="1.0" encoding="utf-8"?>
<mx:Application xmlns:mx="http://www.adobe.com/2006/mxml"
   layout="vertical">
 <mx:Script>
   <![CDATA[
     import mx.events.MenuEvent;
     import mx.controls.Alert;
     import mx.controls.Menu;
     private function showMenu(event:MouseEvent):void
     {
        var navMenu:Menu = Menu.createMenu(this, menuData);
        navMenu.labelField="@label";
        navMenu.addEventListener(MenuEvent.ITEM_CLICK,
   menuClickHandler);
        navMenu.show(event.stageX,event.stageY);
     }

     private function menuClickHandler(event:MenuEvent):void
     {
        Alert.show("You selected " + event.item.@label, "Menu
   Selection");
     }
   ]]>
 </mx:Script>
```

```
<mx:XMLList id="menuData">
  <menuitem label="Lists">
      <menuitem label="Catalog" view="catalogView"/>
      <menuitem label="Authors" view="authorsView"/>
  </menuitem>
  <menuitem label="Shopping">
    <menuitem label="Shopping Cart" view="cartView"/>
  </menuitem>
</mx:XMLList>
<mx:Label text="Click for Menu" mouseUp="showMenu(event)"/>
</mx:Application>
```

ON the WEB The code in Listing 12.7 is available in the Web site files as `MenuDemo.mxml` in the `chapter12` project.

Figure 12.8 shows the resulting application. The Menu pops up when the mouse button is released while over the Label control.

FIGURE 12.8

Using the Menu control

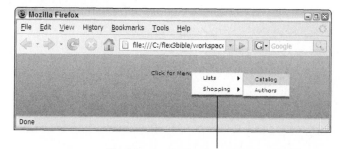

The Menu control responding to a mouse event

Using the MenuBar control

The MenuBar control presents a horizontal list of menu items with cascading pull-down sub-menus. It uses the same sort of data and generates the same events as the Menu control. Unlike the Menu, it's designed to be placed in a static position in the application and serve as a navigation or functional menu, so it's typically declared in MXML:

```
<mx:MenuBar id="myMenuBar" dataProvider="{menuData}"
    labelField="@label" itemClick="menuClickHandler(event)"/>
```

The application in Listing 12.8 uses a MenuBar for navigation in the sample bookstore application. Notice that the MenuBar is wrapped in an ApplicationControlBar that "glues" the navigation control to the top of the screen.

LISTING 12.8

Using the MenuBar control

```
<?xml version="1.0" encoding="utf-8"?>
<mx:Application xmlns:mx="http://www.adobe.com/2006/mxml"
  xmlns:views="views.*" layout="vertical" horizontalAlign="left"
  backgroundGradientAlphas="[1.0, 1.0]"
  backgroundGradientColors="[#908D8D, #FFFFFF]">
  <mx:Script>
    <![CDATA[
      import mx.events.MenuEvent;
      private function menuClickHandler(event:MenuEvent):void
      {
        viewstack1.selectedChild = this[event.item.@view];
      }
    ]]>
  </mx:Script>
  <mx:Style source="assets/styles.css"/>
  <mx:XMLList id="menuData">
    <menuitem label="Lists">
        <menuitem label="Catalog" view="catalogView"/>
        <menuitem label="Authors" view="authorsView"/>
    </menuitem>
    <menuitem label="Shopping">
      <menuitem label="Shopping Cart" view="cartView"/>
    </menuitem>
  </mx:XMLList>
  <mx:ApplicationControlBar dock="true">
    <mx:MenuBar id="myMenuBar"
      dataProvider="{menuData}"
      labelField="@label" itemClick="menuClickHandler(event)"/>
  </mx:ApplicationControlBar>
  <views:Header/>
  <mx:ViewStack id="viewstack1" width="400" height="200">
    <views:Books id="catalogView" label="Catalog"
      width="100%" height="100%"/>
    <views:Authors id="authorsView" label="Authors"
      width="100%" height="100%"/>
    <views:ShoppingCart id="cartView" label="Shopping Cart"
      width="100%" height="100%"/>
  </mx:ViewStack>
</mx:Application>
```

 The code in Listing 12.8 is available in the Web site files as `BookStoreMenuBar.mxml` in the `chapter12` project.

Figure 12.9 shows the resulting application, with the `MenuBar` nested within the `ApplicationControlBar`.

FIGURE 12.9

Using the `MenuBar` control

The MenuBar control

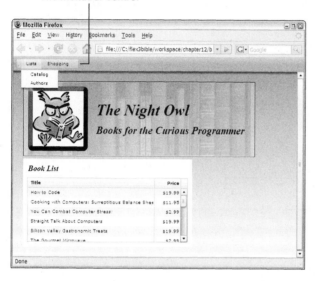

Using Other Navigator Containers

The `TabNavigator` and `Accordion` navigator containers provide the same form of navigation functionality as the `ViewStack` in that they nest a stack of containers and display only one of the containers at a time. Unlike the `ViewStack`, though, the `TabNavigator` and `Accordion` have their own user interface to allow the user to navigate between views.

The TabNavigator container

The `TabNavigator` container provides a set of tabs, similar in appearance to a `TabBar`, but more visually integrated with the rest of the container. Unlike the `ViewStack`, which is invisible by default, the `TabNavigator` has a default border.

The MXML syntax of the TabNavigator is identical to that of the ViewStack: You wrap its nested containers within the appropriate MXML tag set. As with the ViewStack, you can wrap only those components within a TabNavigator that include the Container class in their inheritance hierarchy:

```
<mx:TabNavigator id="views">
  <mx:HBox/>
  <mx:VBox/>
  <mx:Canvas/>
  <mx:Panel/>
  <views:MyCustomComponent/>
</mx:TabNavigator >
```

For example, in the bookstore application that's been used previously in this chapter, to use a TabNavigator instead of a ViewStack, you'd follow these steps:

1. Change the MXML tag set wrapping the custom components from <mx:ViewStack> to <mx:TabNavigator>.

2. Delete any navigator bar control or custom navigator controls that you might have been using to provide a navigation interface.

Listing 12.9 shows the application using a TabNavigator instead of a ViewStack.

LISTING 12.9

An application using a TabNavigator

```
<?xml version="1.0" encoding="utf-8"?>
<mx:Application xmlns:mx="http://www.adobe.com/2006/mxml"
  xmlns:views="views.*" layout="vertical" horizontalAlign="left"
  backgroundGradientAlphas="[1.0, 1.0]"
  backgroundGradientColors="[#908D8D, #FFFFFF]">
  <mx:Style source="assets/styles.css"/>
  <views:Header/>
  <mx:TabNavigator id="viewstack1" width="400" height="300">
    <views:Books label="Catalog" width="100%" height="100%"/>
    <views:Authors label="Authors" width="100%" height="100%"/>
    <views:ShoppingCart label="Shopping Cart" width="100%"
  height="100%"/>
  </mx:TabNavigator>
</mx:Application>
```

ON the WEB   The code in Listing 12.9 is available in the Web site files as **BookStoreTabNav.mxml** in the **chapter12** project.

Figure 12.10 shows the resulting application, with a TabNavigator providing the navigation interface. Notice that the tabs are visually integrated with the container that wraps the application content.

An application using a TabNavigator

The TabNavigator's dynamic tabs

The Accordion container

The Accordion navigator container provides navigation through a set of *headers* that slide vertically to expose or hide nested views as needed.

WEB RESOURCE The Accordion container slides only vertically, not horizontally. Doug McCune has created and shared a horizontal Accordion that you can download from http:// dougmccune.com/blog/2007/01/27/horizontal-accordion-component-for-flex.

The MXML syntax of the Accordion is identical to that of the ViewStack: You wrap its nested containers within the appropriate MXML tag set. As with the ViewStack and TabNavigator, you can wrap only those components within an Accordion that include the Container class in their inheritance hierarchy:

```
<mx:Accordion id="views">
  <mx:HBox/>
  <mx:VBox/>
  <mx:Canvas/>
  <mx:Panel/>
  <views:MyCustomComponent/>
</mx:Accordion >
```

For example, in the bookstore application that's been used previously as an example in this chapter, to use an Accordion instead of a ViewStack, you'd follow these steps:

1. Change the MXML tag set wrapping the custom components from <mx:ViewStack> to <mx:Accordion>.

2. Delete any navigator bar control or custom navigator controls that you might have been using to provide a navigation interface.

Listing 12.10 shows the application using an Accordion instead of a ViewStack.

LISTING 12.10

An application using an Accordion

```
<?xml version="1.0" encoding="utf-8"?>
<mx:Application xmlns:mx="http://www.adobe.com/2006/mxml"
  xmlns:views="views.*" layout="vertical" horizontalAlign="left"
  backgroundGradientAlphas="[1.0, 1.0]"
  backgroundGradientColors="[#908D8D, #FFFFFF]">
  <mx:Style source="assets/styles.css"/>
  <views:Header/>
  <mx:Accordion id="viewstack1" width="400" height="300">
    <views:Books label="Catalog" width="100%" height="100%"/>
    <views:Authors label="Authors" width="100%" height="100%"/>
    <views:ShoppingCart label="Shopping Cart" width="100%"
  height="100%"/>
  </mx:Accordion>
</mx:Application>
```

ON the WEB   The code in Listing 12.10 is available in the Web site files as BookStoreAccordion.mxml in the chapter12 project.

Figure 12.11 shows the resulting application, with an Accordion providing the navigation interface. Notice that the tabs are visually integrated with the container that wraps the application content.

FIGURE 12.11

An application using an `Accordion`

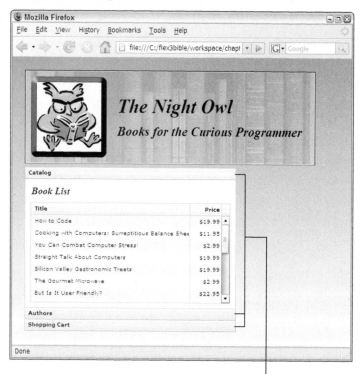

The Accordion container's headers

TabNavigator and Accordion keyboard shortcuts

The `TabNavigator` and `Accordion` containers support this set of keyboard shortcuts that allow the user to navigate with key presses instead of mouse gestures:

- **Page Down:** Navigates to next view, wrapping from last to first.
- **Down Arrow** and **Right Arrow:** Selects next tab or header, wrapping from last to first, but doesn't change the active view. Pressing Enter or the spacebar then triggers navigation.
- **Page Up:** Navigates to previous view, wrapping from first to last.
- **Up Arrow** and **Left Arrow:** Selects previous tab or header, wrapping from first to last, but doesn't change the active view. Pressing Enter or the spacebar then triggers navigation.
- **Home:** Navigates to first view.
- **End:** Navigates to last view.

Summary

In this chapter, I described techniques for creating navigation interfaces in Flex applications. You learned the following:

- Class Web applications handle navigation by requesting and loading individual Web pages into the browser one at a time.

- Flex applications contain all their views in the compiled application.

- The ViewStack container nests multiple view containers and displays only one at a time.

- You can manage navigation with ActionScript commands or with a navigator bar container.

- The navigator bar containers automate navigation when bound to a ViewStack.

- The menu controls can be used with event listeners and ActionScript to create a navigation interface.

- The TabNavigator and Accordion containers combine ViewStack functionality with their own navigation interfaces.

Chapter 13

Working with Pop-up Windows

I n applications that are built for windows-style operating systems, such as Microsoft Windows, Mac OS X, and the various windowing interfaces on Linux and other operating systems, pop-up windows are commonly used to get the user's attention, provide information, and collect data. Not all Flex applications have or require pop-up windows, but they're a common interface that users of these operating systems easily recognize and know how to use.

Flex applications are able to present pop-up windows in a variety of forms. Whether you want to display a simple information message or create a more customized user experience, you have these options:

- **The** `Alert` **class** creates a simple pop-up dialog box displaying simple `String` values. The `Alert` class also can be used to allow the user to confirm or cancel an operation before it's executed, and it can include a custom graphical icon.

- **The** `PopUpMenuButton` **control** displays a two-part `Button` control that displays a single-level pop-up menu when clicked.

- **The** `PopUpButton` **control** combines a `Button` with any other visual component that you want to display when clicked.

- **Custom pop-up windows** can be created with the `TitleWindow` container, and presented and managed with the `PopUpManager` class.

In this chapter, I describe each of these options and provide examples of how these classes and controls can be used.

ON the WEB To use the sample code for this chapter, import the `chapter13.zip` Flex project archive from the Web site files into your Flex Builder workspace.

Using the Alert Class

The mx.controls.Alert class can present dialog boxes as pop-up windows that either present simple informational messages or allow the user to accept or decline an operation. In addition, the pop-up windows generated by the Alert class can include a custom icon graphic in their presentation.

The Alert class displays a pop-up dialog box in response to a call to the class's static show() method. The syntax of the method is:

```
show(text:String = "", title:String = "",
   flags:uint = 0x4, parent:Sprite = null,
   closeHandler:Function = null,
   iconClass:Class = null, defaultButtonFlag:uint = 0x4):Alert
```

> **TIP**   All of the show() method's arguments are optional, but you almost always pass in the first text argument (the string you want to display in the body of the pop-up window).

> **TIP**   Before calling the Alert class's methods, it must be imported. You can import the Alert class with this explicit import statement:

```
import mx.controls.Alert;
```

You also can import the class with a wildcard statement that includes all classes in the mx.controls package:

```
import mx.controls.*;
```

Presenting pop-up windows with Alert.show()

The most common use of the Alert class is to present a simple dialog box with up to two text messages. To present this sort of dialog box, call the class's show() method and pass in two String arguments:

```
Alert.show("This is a simple informational message", "Alert
   Title");
```

The first String argument passed into Alert.show() appears in the body of the dialog box, and the second String appears as the dialog box title.

Figure 13.1 shows a simple Alert pop-up dialog box with the two text messages.

FIGURE 13.1

A simple `Alert` pop-up dialog box

Controlling Alert window modality

A pop-up window that's *modal* blocks the user from interacting with the rest of the application as long as the dialog box appears on the screen. In Flex, some pop-up windows are modal and others aren't.

When you present a pop-up dialog box with the `Alert` class, it's modal by default, so the user has to click a button or otherwise close the window before continuing his work with the rest of the application.

Modal pop-up windows in Flex have a special feature that lets the user know the application isn't currently available as long as the pop-up window is visible. When the pop-up window appears on the screen, the rest of the application is blurred so that its appearance clearly indicates to the user that he can't use it until he takes some action. The visual result, where the dialog box is presented in clear resolution and the remainder of the application is blurry, is a visual indicator that the user must take some action to continue.

The `Alert` pop-up window is modal by default. You can make the `Alert` class present a non-modal window by passing the `Alert.NONMODAL` constant into the `show()` method as a *flag*. The `Alert` class has constants designed for use as flags. The others are used to present specific buttons in the pop-up dialog box.

Flags are passed into the `show()` method as the third argument. This code creates a non-modal pop-up window:

```
Alert.show("This is a non-modal Alert window",
    "Non-modal Alert", Alert.NONMODAL);
```

Figure 13.2 shows the resulting non-modal pop-up window. Notice that the application in the background isn't blurry and can accept user focus.

A non-modal Alert dialog box

 TIP   You also can present a non-modal pop-up window with a custom container based on TitleWindow and managed with PopUpManager.

Managing Alert window buttons

You can present a pop-up window created by the Alert class with buttons labeled Yes, No, OK, and Cancel. You determine which buttons will be presented with the show() method's flags argument. To include more than one flag, separate them with the bitwise OR operator (|) and wrap the entire expression in parentheses.

This call to Alert.show() presents a dialog box with Yes and No buttons, shown in Figure 13.3:

```
Alert.show("This is an Alert dialog box with custom buttons",
  "Alert with Buttons",
  (Alert.YES | Alert.NO));
```

An Alert pop-up dialog box with custom buttons

Non-modal dialog boxes with multiple buttons

If you want to present an `Alert` dialog box with multiple buttons and make it non-modal, include the `Alert.NONMODAL` constant in the `flags` argument:

```
Alert.show("This is a non-modal Alert dialog box with custom
    buttons",
  "Non-modal Alert with Buttons",
  (Alert.YES | Alert.NO | Alert.NONMODAL));
```

Setting button labels

The labels of the various buttons are determined by these static properties of the `Alert` class:

- `yesLabel`: The label on the Yes button
- `noLabel`: The label on the No button
- `okLabel`: The label on the OK button
- `cancelLabel`: The label on the Cancel button

These properties should be set prior to calling the `Alert.show()` method. In addition, because buttons in the `Alert` dialog box don't automatically resize themselves based on their labels, you may need to explicitly set the `Alert.buttonWidth` property to specific width in terms of pixels:

```
private function alertWithButtonLabels():void
{
  Alert.yesLabel = "Fer sure!!!";
  Alert.noLabel = "NO WAY!!";
  Alert.buttonWidth = 100;
  Alert.show("This is an Alert dialog box with custom button
    labels",
      "Alert with Button Labels", (Alert.YES | Alert.NO));
}
```

Figure 13.4 shows an Alert dialog box with custom button labels.

CAUTION Changes to `Alert` button properties such as `buttonWidth`, `okLabel`, and `cancelLabel` survive only for a single call to `Alert.show()`. After the method has been called, the button labels return to their default values.

FIGURE 13.4

An Alert dialog box with custom button labels

Setting a default button

When an `Alert` pop-up window has multiple buttons, the first button is the default. If the user presses Enter or Return without any other window interactions, it's the equivalent of clicking that button. To change the default button, pass the selected button's flag constant in the `show()` method's seventh argument. Because you have to pass in all other arguments, just pass `null` in the arguments you aren't using:

```
Alert.show("This Alert dialog box's default button is Cancel",
   "Alert with default Button",
   (Alert.OK | Alert.CANCEL),
   null, null, null,
   Alert.CANCEL);
```

The user can click other buttons or press the Tab key to move focus from one button to another, but if he presses Enter or Return immediately upon the pop-up dialog box's appearance, the close event handler indicates that the default button was clicked.

Handling Alert window events

When you add multiple buttons to an `Alert` dialog box, you usually want to react in some way to whichever button the user clicks. When the user clicks any button to close the dialog box, an event object typed as `mx.events.CloseEvent` is generated. To find out which button was clicked, create a custom event handler function that accepts this event object as its only argument and returns `void`. Within the event handler function, the event object's `detail` property references the flag constant representing that button.

```
private function alertCloseHandler(event:CloseEvent):void
{
   if (event.detail == Alert.OK)
```

```
  {
    Alert.show("You clicked " + Alert.okLabel,
      "Close Event Handler");
  }
  else
  {
    Alert.show("You clicked " + Alert.cancelLabel,
      "Close Event Handler");
  }
}
```

TIP You may want to use the `close` event handler function even if your pop-up window only has a single button. For example, you can use it to store a reminder that the user has been warned about a particular condition so you don't have to show the pop-up window again.

You designate the event handler function by passing the function name as the `show()` method's fifth argument:

```
Alert.show("An Alert dialog box with close event handler",
  "Alert Event Handler", (Alert.OK | Alert.CANCEL),
  null, alertCloseHandler);
```

When the user clicks any of the pop-up dialog box's buttons, the `close` event is handled by the custom event handler and you have an opportunity to execute ActionScript code.

In the resulting application, shown in Figure 13.5, the user is informed as to which button was clicked.

FIGURE 13.5

The response to handling the `Alert` class `close` event

Using a custom graphical icon

You can display a graphical icon in the body of the `Alert` pop-up window with the `iconClass` argument. Graphical icons must be embedded in the application, so you first declare the graphic with the `[Embed]` metadata tag and assign it a `Class` variable name:

```
[Embed(source="assets/questionicon.png")]
private var questionIcon:Class;
```

In the call to `Alert.show()`, pass the `Class` variable representing the graphic as the sixth argument:

```
Alert.show("An Alert dialog box with custom icon",
    "Alert Event Handler", 0, null, null,
    questionIcon);
```

Figure 13.6 shows the `Alert` dialog box with the custom icon.

FIGURE 13.6

An Alert dialog box with a custom icon graphic

> **TIP**   Graphics designed for use as icons in the `Alert` pop-up window should be small and their backgrounds either should be transparent (a reason to use .gif, .png, or .swf files) or should match the `backgroundColor` style of the window. The `Alert` class's `backgroundColor` style is set to `#90A4AE` by default.

> **NOTE**   The graphic used in this example was created in Adobe Fireworks CS3, but you can use any graphics application you're familiar with to create the required assets.

The application in Listing 13.1 contains demo code for all of the preceding uses of the `Alert.show()` method.

LISTING 13.1

Using the Alert.show() method

```xml
<?xml version="1.0" encoding="utf-8"?>
<mx:Application xmlns:mx="http://www.adobe.com/2006/mxml"
   layout="vertical"
  backgroundColor="#eeeeee">
  <mx:Script>
   <![CDATA[
     import mx.events.CloseEvent;
     import mx.controls.Alert;
     [Embed(source="assets/questionicon.png")]
     private var questionIcon:Class;
     private function simpleAlert():void
     {
       Alert.show("This is a simple informational message", "Alert
   Title");
     }
     private function nonModalAlert():void
     {
       Alert.show("This is a non-modal Alert window", "Non-modal
   Alert",
         Alert.NONMODAL);
     }
     private function alertWithButtons():void
     {
       Alert.show("This is an Alert dialog box with multiple buttons",
         "Alert with Buttons", (Alert.YES | Alert.NO));
     }
     private function alertWithButtonLabels():void
     {
       Alert.yesLabel = "Fer sure!!!";
       Alert.noLabel = "NO WAY!!";
       Alert.buttonWidth = 100;
       Alert.show("This is an Alert dialog box with custom button
   labels",
         "Alert with Button Labels", (Alert.YES | Alert.NO));
     }
     private function alertWithDefaultButton():void
     {
       Alert.show("This Alert dialog box's default button is Cancel",
         "Alert with default Button", (Alert.OK | Alert.CANCEL),
         null, null, null, Alert.CANCEL);
     }
     private function alertWithCloseHandler():void
     {
```

continued

381

LISTING 13.1   *(continued)*

```
        Alert.show("An Alert dialog box with close event handler",
          "Alert Event Handler", (Alert.OK | Alert.CANCEL),
          null, alertCloseHandler);
      }
      private function alertCloseHandler(event:CloseEvent):void
      {
        if (event.detail == Alert.OK)
        {
          Alert.show("You clicked " + Alert.okLabel, "Close Event
    Handler");
        }
        else
        {
          Alert.show("You clicked " + Alert.cancelLabel,
            "Close Event Handler");
        }
      }
      private function alertWithCustomIcon():void
      {
        Alert.show("An Alert dialog box with custom icon",
          "Alert Event Handler", 0,null, null,
          questionIcon);
      }
    ]]>
  </mx:Script>
  <mx:Button label="Show Alert Message" click="simpleAlert()"
    width="{widestButton.width}"/>
  <mx:Button label="Show Non-modal Alert Message"
   click="nonModalAlert()"
    id="widestButton"/>
  <mx:Button label="Alert with Buttons" click="alertWithButtons()"
    width="{widestButton.width}"/>
  <mx:Button label="Alert with event handler"
    click="alertWithCloseHandler()" width="{widestButton.width}"/>
  <mx:Button label="Alert with Button Labels"
    click="alertWithButtonLabels()" width="{widestButton.width}"/>
  <mx:Button label="Alert with Default Button"
    click="alertWithDefaultButton()" width="{widestButton.width}"/>
  <mx:Button label="Alert with custom icon"
   click="alertWithCustomIcon()"
    width="{widestButton.width}"/>
</mx:Application>
```

ON the WEB The code in Listing 13.1 is available in the Web site files as `AlertDemos.mxml` in the `chapter13` project. The graphic file used in the custom icon example is available as `questionicon.png` in the project's `src/assets` folder.

Using CSS selectors with the Alert class

You can change the `Alert` pop-up window's appearance with these CSS selectors:

- **The `Alert` type selector** affects the body of the pop-up window. Most styles that you might use with the Panel container also work on the Alert dialog box.
- **The `.windowStyles` style name selector** affects the title area of the pop-up window. You can change the name of this class selector with the `Alert` class's `titleStyleName` style, but it should always be set on a global basis for the entire application. Setting this value with `setStyle()` for only one call to `Alert.show()` can result in incorrect sizing.

These styles can be set in the `Alert` type selector to change the overall appearance of the window:

- **Font styles** such as `color`, `fontSize`, `fontFamily`, and so on affect the text within the body of the window.
- **Background styles** such as `backgroundColor`, `backgroundImage`, and `backgroundAlpha` change the background of the window's center area.
- **Window styles**, including `cornerRadius` and `roundedBottomCorners`, affect the outer edges of the window.
- **Border styles** such as `borderStyle` and `borderColor` affect the outer border of the window.

Font styles also can be set in the `.windowStyles` selector to change the appearance of text in the window's header region.

CAUTION The `windowStyles` selector is also used by the Panel and TitleWindow containers. Any changes to the selector are applied to all instances of these containers as well as pop-up windows created by the `Alert` class.

The application in Listing 13.2 contains an embedded style sheet that changes styles for both the pop-up window's body and title area. The window has extreme round corners at the top and square corners at the bottom, a typewriter font in the body, and a sans serif font in the title.

LISTING 13.2

Changing the Alert window's appearance with styles

```
<?xml version="1.0" encoding="utf-8"?>
<mx:Application xmlns:mx="http://www.adobe.com/2006/mxml"
  backgroundColor="#eeeeee">
  <mx:Style>
```

continued

LISTING 13.2 *(continued)*

```
    Alert {
      color:#000000;
      background-color:#FFFFFF;
      font-family:Courier, "_typewriter";
      rounded-bottom-corners:false;
      corner-radius:15;
      border-color:#000000;
    }
    .windowStyles
    {
      font-family:Arial, "_sans";
      font-size:14;
      font-style:italic;
      color:#FFFFFF;
    }
  </mx:Style>
  <mx:Script>
    <![CDATA[
      import mx.controls.Alert;

      private function simpleAlert():void
      {
        Alert.show("This is an Alert dialog box with styles applied",
          "Alert Title");
      }
    ]]>
  </mx:Script>
  <mx:Button label="Alert with Style" click="simpleAlert()"/>
</mx:Application>
```

ON the WEB The code in Listing 13.2 is available in the Web site files as `AlertWithStyles.mxml` in the `chapter13` project.

As shown in Figure 13.7, the `Alert` dialog box uses the `Alert` and `.windowStyles` selectors to determine its visual presentation.

FIGURE 13.7

An `Alert` pop-up window, customized with Cascading Style Sheets

Using the PopUpMenuButton Control

The `PopUpMenuButton` control combines the functionality of a `Button` with a menu. It's presented as a two-part visual component including a simple `Button` and an icon representing a down arrow. When the user clicks the control, it presents a menu populated with items from its data provider.

CAUTION Unlike the `Menu` and `MenuBar` controls, the `PopUpMenuButton` doesn't support cascading menus. It's similar in some ways to the `ComboBox` control, in that it presents a single list of available items. But whereas the `ComboBox` presents only a single control and behavior, the Button control in the `PopUpMenuButton` supports all standard Button events.

Creating a data provider

The data provider for a `PopUpMenuButton` can be an `XMLList`, `XMLListCollection`, `Array`, or `ArrayCollection`. If you use an `XMLList`, ensure that each of its XML nodes contains only simple values in the form of attributes or child nodes with text. Because cascading menus aren't possible, you can't use a deeply nested XML structure.

This `XMLList` is designed as a compatible data source for the `PopUpMenuButton` control:

```
<mx:XMLList id="xSizes">
  <node label="Small" value="S"/>
  <node label="Medium" value="M"/>
  <node label="Large" value="L"/>
</mx:XMLList>
```

The data provider also could be expressed as this `ArrayCollection`:

```
<mx:ArrayCollection id="acSizes">
  <mx:Object>
    <mx:label>Small</mx:label>
    <mx:value>Small</mx:value>
  </mx:Object>
  <mx:Object>
    <mx:label>Medium</mx:label>
    <mx:value>M</mx:value>
  </mx:Object>
  <mx:Object>
    <mx:label>Large</mx:label>
    <mx:value>L</mx:value>
  </mx:Object>
</mx:ArrayCollection>
```

Whether you use an XML- or Array-based data set, the `PopUpMenuButton` displays a single-level menu when the user clicks the control's arrow icon, as shown in Figure 13.8.

FIGURE 13.8

A PopUpMenuButton control

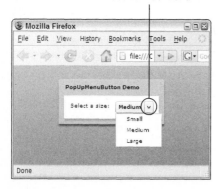

Handling events

As with the `Menu` and `MenuBar` controls, the `PopUpMenuButton` dispatches an `itemClick` event when the user selects an item from the pop-up menu. The same event is dispatched when the user clicks the Button portion of the control (the part of the control that displays its label). The `itemClick` event generates an event object typed as `mx.events.MenuEvent`, which has an item property that refers to the selected data item.

In the context of an event handler method, the expression event.item refers to the data item, and you can use E4X notation to refer to data node attributes or simple dot notation to refer to named properties of selected objects in an ArrayCollection.

The application in Listing 13.3 uses a PopUpMenuButton control with data populated from an XMLList. When the user clicks the Button portion of the control or selects an item from its menu, the itemClick event is dispatched and the message displayed indicates which item has been selected.

LISTING 13.3

Using the PopUpMenuButton control

```
<?xml version="1.0" encoding="utf-8"?>
<mx:Application xmlns:mx="http://www.adobe.com/2006/mxml">
  <mx:Script>
  <![CDATA[
    import mx.controls.Alert;
    import mx.events.MenuEvent;
    public function itemClickHandler(event:MenuEvent):void {
      Alert.show("Menu label: " + event.item.@label,
      "Menu value: " + event.item.@value);
    }
  ]]>
  </mx:Script>
  <!-- A data provider in E4X format. -->
  <mx:XMLList id="xSizes">
    <node label="Small" value="S"/>
    <node label="Medium" value="M"/>
    <node label="Large" value="L"/>
  </mx:XMLList>
  <mx:Panel title="PopUpMenuButton Demo" layout="horizontal"
    paddingTop="10" paddingLeft="10" paddingRight="10"
   paddingBottom="10">
    <mx:Label text="Select a size:"/>
    <mx:PopUpMenuButton id="p2" dataProvider="{xSizes}"
      labelField="@label" itemClick="itemClickHandler(event);"/>
  </mx:Panel>
</mx:Application>
```

ON the WEB   The code in Listing 13.3 is available in the Web site files as
PopUpMenuButtonDemo.mxml in the chapter13 project.

As shown in Figure 13.9, when the user clicks the Button portion of the control or selects an item from the pop-up menu, the itemClick event is handled.

FIGURE 13.9

Handling the `PopUpMenuButton` control's `itemClick` event

Using the PopUpButton control

The `PopUpButton` control allows you to create a `Button` made up of two sub-buttons, a main display button, and a pop-up button that, when clicked, presents any other visual control as a pop-up window. The only requirement for the component you use as the pop-up window is that it must include the `UIComponent` class in its inheritance hierarchy. You can use any pre-built container or control or any custom component as a pop-up window.

The `PopUpButton` control is commonly declared in MXML code somewhere in an Application or custom component:

```
<mx:PopUpButton id="myPopup" label="My Popup Button"/>
```

You then define the control's pop-up window and the window's events and data with ActionScript code.

Declaring the pop-up window

The pop-up window displayed by a `PopUpButton` is created at runtime and is typically instantiated in ActionScript code. You first create an instance of the component you want to use, but don't add it to the current `Application` or component's display list. The component is then bound to the `PopUpButton` with the `popUp` property.

This code declares an instance of a `DateChooser` control outside any functions. Then, in a function that's called upon application startup, the component is bound to the `PopUpButton` control's `popUp` property:

```
[Bindable]
private var myDateChooser:DateChooser = new DateChooser();

private function initPopUpButton():void {
  myDateChooser.selectedDate = new Date();
  myPopUpButton.popUp = myDateChooser;
}
```

Handling events and managing pop-up behavior

The rules for handling a `PopUpButton` control's events depend on which component you use as the pop-up window. For example, if you use a pre-built control such as the `DateChooser`, you depend on that control's data and events to manage behavior at runtime.

In the current example, when the user selects a date from the `DateChooser` control, it dispatches a `change` event with an event object typed as `mx.events.CalendarLayoutChangeEvent`. Because the `DateChooser` control has been instantiated with ActionScript code, any event listeners must be created with the `addEventListener()` method:

```
myDateChooser.addEventListener(CalendarLayoutChangeEvent.CHANGE,
  dateChangeHandler);
```

You can then call the `PopUpButton` control's `close()` method to close the pop-up window:

```
private function dateChangeHandler(
  event:CalendarLayoutChangeEvent):void {
    myPopup.close();
}
```

> **TIP** Even when objects aren't currently displayed on the screen, they still exist in application memory, allowing you access to any of their properties. In this example, you can use the `selectedDate` property of the `DateChooser` even after it's no longer displayed.

The application in Listing 13.4 uses a `PopUpButton` to display a DateChooser control as a pop-up window.

LISTING 13.4

Using a PopUpButton control

```
<?xml version="1.0"?>
<mx:Application xmlns:mx="http://www.adobe.com/2006/mxml"
  creationComplete="initPopUpButton()">
  <mx:Script>
    <![CDATA[
      import mx.events.CalendarLayoutChangeEvent;
      import mx.controls.DateChooser;
      [Bindable]
      private var myDateChooser:DateChooser = new DateChooser();
      private function initPopUpButton():void {
        myDateChooser.selectedDate = new Date();
        myDateChooser.addEventListener(
          CalendarLayoutChangeEvent.CHANGE, dateChangeHandler);
        myPopUpButton.popUp = myDateChooser;
        myPopUpButton.executeBindings(true);
      }
      private function dateChangeHandler(
        event:CalendarLayoutChangeEvent):void {
          myPopUpButton.close();
      }
    ]]>
  </mx:Script>
  <mx:DateFormatter id="df" formatString="M/D/YYYY"/>
  <mx:Panel title="Using the PopUpButton Control"
      paddingTop="10" paddingBottom="10" paddingRight="10"
  paddingLeft="10"
      layout="horizontal">
      <mx:Label text="Select a date:"/>
      <mx:PopUpButton id="myPopUpButton" width="135"
          label="{df.format(myDateChooser.selectedDate)}"/>
  </mx:Panel>
</mx:Application>
```

> **ON the WEB** The code in Listing 13.4 is available in the Web site files as `PopUpButtonDemo.mxml` in the `chapter13` project.

> **TIP** The `PopUpButton` component implements a Boolean `openAlways` property that can be used to display component's pop-up object when the user clicks the main button. The pop-up object is always displayed when you click the pop-up button or press the spacebar, regardless of the setting of the `openAlways` property.

Figure 13.10 shows the resulting application displaying the `DateChooser` control in response to a user clicking the `PopUpButton`.

FIGURE 13.10

Using the PopUpButton control

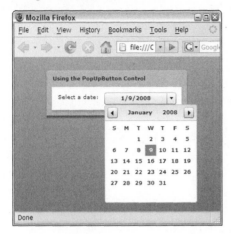

Working with Custom Pop-up Windows

You can create custom pop-up windows in a Flex application for many purposes:

- Presenting detailed information to the user that's too complex to easily fit into an `Alert` dialog box
- Collecting configuration and preference information before executing an operation
- Providing a pop-up window that can be reused as a custom component
- Collecting data through a data entry form wrapped in a pop-up window

A custom pop-up window component must be extended from a class that implements the `IFlexDisplayObject` interface. This interface is implemented by the `UIComponent` class, which in turn is in the inheritance hierarchy of all Flex containers and controls. This essentially means that any visual component can be used as a custom pop-up window.

Defining a custom pop-up window

Custom pop-up windows can be defined as custom MXML components. If you want to create a window that looks like a dialog box, you can use either the `Panel` or `TitleWindow` container.

CROSS-REF The `TitleWindow` is a subclass of the `Panel` that has the ability to display a close icon in its upper-right corner and dispatch a `close` event when the icon is clicked. Its details are described later in this chapter.

Creating the component

The steps for creating an MXML component that will be used as a pop-up window are the same as for any other MXML component:

1. Create a new MXML component.

2. Select the MXML component's base class.

3. Save the new component in your project as a file with the `.mxml` file extension.

The following code defines an MXML component designed to collect login information, and it might be saved as a file named `LoginWindow.mxml`:

```
<mx:Panel xmlns:mx="http://www.adobe.com/2006/mxml"
  title="Please Log In">
  <mx:Form>
    <mx:FormItem label="User Name:">
      <mx:TextInput id="userInput"/>
    </mx:FormItem>
    <mx:FormItem label="Password:">
      <mx:TextInput displayAsPassword="true" id="passwordInput"/>
    </mx:FormItem>
    <mx:FormItem direction="horizontal">
      <mx:Button label="Log In"/>
      <mx:Button label="Cancel"/>
    </mx:FormItem>
  </mx:Form>
</mx:Panel>
```

Sharing data with events

The custom component that will be used as a pop-up window should share information with the rest of the application using custom events. The `LoginWindow` component described in the preceding code sample would share events for logging in and for canceling the operation. In order to share the login information, you need to create a custom event class to contain the login data.

Listing 13.5 is a custom event class with public properties for the username and password values that will be collected by the custom component.

LISTING 13.5

A custom event class designed for use with a custom Login component

```
package events
{
  import flash.events.Event;
  public class LoginEvent extends Event
```

```
{
  public var username:String;
  public var password:String;

  public function LoginEvent(type:String, bubbles:Boolean=false,
    cancelable:Boolean=false)
  {
    super(type, bubbles, cancelable);
  }

  override public function clone():Event
  {
    var ev:LoginEvent = new LoginEvent(this.type);
    ev.username = this.username;
    ev.password = this.password;
    return ev;
  }

  }
}
```

ON the WEB   The code in Listing 13.5 is available in the Web site files as `LoginEvent.as` in the
chapter13 project's `src/events` folder.

When the user clicks the custom component's Log In button, the component shares data with the application by constructing and dispatching a custom event object:

```
var event:LoginEvent = new LoginEvent("login");
event.username = userInput.text;
event.password = passwordInput.text;
dispatchEvent(event);
```

And if the user clicks Cancel, the custom component dispatches a cancel event, with the event object typed as the standard Event class:

```
dispatchEvent(new Event("cancel"));
```

Listing 13.6 shows a completed custom component designed for use as a pop-up window that can share data with the application using custom events. Nothing in the preceding code indicates that this component will be used as a pop-up window; it could just as easily be declared with an MXML tag set in the application to appear inline in the application.

LISTING 13.6

A custom component ready for use as a pop-up window

```
<?xml version="1.0" encoding="utf-8"?>
<mx:Panel xmlns:mx="http://www.adobe.com/2006/mxml" title="Please Log
   In">
  <mx:Metadata>
    [Event(name="login", type="events.LoginEvent")]
    [Event(name="cancel", type="flash.events.Event")]
  </mx:Metadata>
  <mx:Script>
    <![CDATA[
      import events.LoginEvent;
      private function login():void
      {
        var event:LoginEvent = new LoginEvent("login");
        event.username = userInput.text;
        event.password = passwordInput.text;
        dispatchEvent(event);
      }
      public function setInitialFocus():void
      {
        userInput.setFocus();
      }
    ]]>
  </mx:Script>
  <mx:Form>
    <mx:FormItem label="User Name:">
      <mx:TextInput id="userInput"/>
    </mx:FormItem>
    <mx:FormItem label="Password:">
      <mx:TextInput displayAsPassword="true" id="passwordInput"/>
    </mx:FormItem>
    <mx:FormItem direction="horizontal">
      <mx:Button label="Log In" click="login()"/>
      <mx:Button label="Cancel"
        click=" dispatchEvent(new Event('cancel'));"/>
    </mx:FormItem>
  </mx:Form>
</mx:Panel>
```

ON the WEB The code in Listing 13.6 is available in the Web site files as `LoginWindow.mxml` in the `chapter13` project's `src/popups` folder.

Figure 13.11 shows the completed data entry form as it would appear if instantiated with this MXML code:

```
<popups:LoginWindow id="myLoginWindow"/>
```

FIGURE 13.11

The login window as a conventional `Panel` component

Using the PopUpManager class

The `PopUpManager` is a singleton class with static methods that you use to manage custom pop-up windows at runtime. It has two methods that can be used to present a pop-up window:

- `addPopUp()` adds a new top-level window using a component that's already been instantiated and is ready to use.
- `createPopUp()` creates a new instance of a component, presents the component as a pop-up window, and returns a reference.

Of these two methods, the `addPopUp()` method is more useful, because it allows you to construct and pre-configure a visual object prior to presenting it as a pop-up window.

The `PopUpManager` also has these methods that you use to manipulate the position and order of pop-up windows:

- `bringToFront()` gives top-level presentation and focus to a particular window.
- `centerPopUp()` positions a pop-up window in the horizontal and vertical center of its parent window.

Finally, `PopUpManager` has a `removePopUp()` method to remove top-level windows from the display when they're no longer needed, though they will still exist in application memory.

Adding a pop-up window

To add a new pop-up window to the application interface at runtime using the `addPopUp()` method, first declare an instance of the custom component you want to present. This declaration should be outside of any functions so the pop-up window reference persists between function calls:

```
private var popup:LoginWindow;
```

Within a function that you call to display the pop-up window, instantiate the component and create any required event listeners with accompanying event handler functions. The `LoginWindow` component in this example dispatches events named `login` and `cancel`, so it requires two `addEventListener()` calls:

```
popup = new LoginWindow();
popup.addEventListener("login", loginHandler);
popup.addEventListener("cancel", cancelHandler);
```

To present the window onscreen, call `PopUpManager.addPopUp()` with these arguments:

- `window:IFlexDisplayObject` is the component reference you just instantiated.
- `parent:DisplayObject` is the parent window over which the pop-up window is displayed.
- `modal:Boolean` determines whether the custom pop-up window is modal. If not passed in, it defaults to `false`.
- `childList:String` is the display child list in which you're adding the pop-up window. Possible values include `PopUpManagerChildList.APPLICATION`, `PopUpManagerChildList.POPUP`, and `PopUpManagerChildList.PARENT` (the default).

After adding the pop-up window to the application interface, you can center the window over its parent window with a call to `PopUpManager.centerPopUp()`. If necessary, you can ensure that the new window has top-level focus with a call to `PopUpManager.bringToFront()`.

This makes a call to `PopUpManager.addPopup()` to present the `LoginWindow` custom component as a modal pop-up window and then centers it on the parent component:

```
PopUpManager.addPopUp(popup, this, true);   .
PopUpManager.centerPopUp(popup);
```

 If you don't explicitly center the pop-up window with `PopUpManager.centerPopUp()`, the window appears in the top-left corner of the parent window.

Figure 13.12 shows the resulting pop-up window. Notice the application's blurry appearance in the background, indicating that the user must dismiss the window before interacting with the rest of the application.

FIGURE 13.12

The LoginWindow component as a pop-up window

Removing a pop-up window

To remove a pop-up window, use the PopUpManager class's static removePopUp() method. The method takes a single argument that references the pop-up window instance:

```
PopUpManager.removePopUp(popup);
```

You also can call the method from within the component to cause it to remove itself from the interface:

```
PopUpManager.removePopUp(this);
```

The application in Listing 13.7 uses the LoginWindow component as a pop-up window. In each of its custom event handler functions, it explicitly closes the pop-up window with a call to PopUpManager.removePopUp().

LISTING 13.7

An application using a custom pop-up window

```
<?xml version="1.0" encoding="utf-8"?>
<mx:Application xmlns:mx="http://www.adobe.com/2006/mxml">
  <mx:Script>
    <![CDATA[
      import events.LoginEvent;
      import mx.controls.Alert;
      import mx.managers.PopUpManager;
      import popups.LoginWindow;
      private var popup:LoginWindow;
      private function showLoginWindow():void
```

continued

LISTING 13.7   *(continued)*

```
    {
      popup = new LoginWindow();
      popup.addEventListener("login", loginHandler);
      popup.addEventListener("cancel", cancelHandler);
      PopUpManager.addPopUp(popup, this, true)
      PopUpManager.centerPopUp(popup);
      popup.setInitialFocus();
    }
    private function loginHandler(event:LoginEvent):void
    {
      Alert.show("You logged in as " + event.username +
        " with a password of " + event.password, "Login Successful");
      PopUpManager.removePopUp(popup);
    }
    private function cancelHandler(event:Event):void
    {
      Alert.show("You cancelled the login operation", "Login
  Cancelled");
      PopUpManager.removePopUp(popup);
    }
  ]]>
  </mx:Script>
  <mx:Button label="Log In" click="showLoginWindow()"/>
</mx:Application>
```

ON the WEB   The code in Listing 13.7 is available in the Web site files as
UseCustomPopUp.mxml.as in the chapter13 project.

Using the TitleWindow container

The TitleWindow container is a subclass of Panel, so it shares all of that container's features:
It contains a title bar, a caption, a border, and a content area, and like the Panel, it can host a
ControlBar container t wizard-like buttons at the bottom.

The TitleWindow adds the ability to display a close button in its upper-right corner, creating a
common visual interface for pop-up windows. To use the TitleWindow container as a custom
pop-up window with its own close icon, create the MXML component with a root element of
<mx:TitleWindow> instead of <mx:Panel>. Then set the component's showCloseButton
property to true:

```
    <?xml version="1.0" encoding="utf-8"?>
    <mx:TitleWindow xmlns:mx="http://www.adobe.com/2006/mxml"
      title="Please Log In"  showCloseButton="true">
        ... remainder of component is the same as for a panel ...
    </mx:TitleWindow>
```

When the `TitleWindow` component is displayed as a pop-up window, it now displays the close button, as shown in Figure 13.13.

FIGURE 13.13

A custom component extending `TitleWindow` and showing the close button

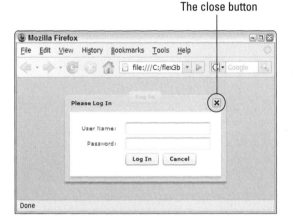

The close button

The `TitleWindow` container's close button doesn't actually close the pop-up window. Instead, it dispatches a `close` event with an event object typed as `mx.events.CloseEvent`. Upon instantiating the custom component (and prior to adding it as a pop-up window), create a listener for the `close` event:

```
popup.addEventListener(CloseEvent.CLOSE, closeHandler);
```

Then, in the event handler function, call `PopUpManager.removePopUp()` to remove the pop-up window from the application interface:

```
private function closeHandler(event:CloseEvent):void
{
  Alert.show("You canceled the login operation", "Login
   Canceled");
  PopUpManager.removePopUp(popup);
}
```

ON the WEB Versions of the pop-up window component and application that use the `TitleWindow` container instead of the `Panel` are available in the Web site files as `LoginTitle Window.mxml` and `UseTitleWindow.mxml.as` in the `chapter13` project.

Summary

In this chapter, I described how to create pop-up windows as part of a Flex application interface. You learned the following:

- Pop-up windows are typically used to present and collect information in a windowing style application.

- The `Alert` class is used to present simple informational messages and to allow a user to confirm or decline an operation.

- The `PopUpMenuButton` control combines a `Button` and single-level `Menu` that's similar in presentation to a `ComboBox`.

- The `PopUpButton` control can be used to present any visual container or control as a pop-up window.

- Custom pop-up windows are defined in the same way as any custom component.

- The `Panel` and `TitleWindow` containers present a dialog box-style interface.

- The `PopUpManager` singleton class is used to add and remove custom pop-up windows at runtime.

Chapter 14

Controlling Animation

IN THIS CHAPTER

Using effects

Using behaviors and triggers

Playing effects with ActionScript

Using tweening and masking effects

Using composite effects

Implementing drag-and-drop interfaces

Flash Player was originally created as a platform for presenting animation over the Web. Future Splash Animator, the original ancestor of the Flash authoring environment and Flash Player, was a Java-based software product that was integrated into the browser in much the same manner as Flash Player is today.

Millions of Flash developers worldwide create compelling content designed for presentation in a Web application. Animation and related visual wizardry is the most common goal, and the most common result, of documents developed in the Flash authoring environment and distributed through Flash Player.

Animation in Flash depends largely on use of the timeline: a visual interface that allows the developer to create animations frame by frame or through a process known as *tweening*. Flex application developers don't have the timeline available to them. In fact, one of Macromedia's most important motivations in creating Flex was to free developers with a coding background from having to work with the timeline at all. But a Flex application is still distributed and viewed through Flash Player. So when it's time to move objects around the screen, a Flex developer needs code-based approaches to make it happen.

In this chapter, I describe the use of effects and triggers to define and execute animation in a Flex application. I also describe how to implement drag-and-drop interfaces to create an intuitive way to move data around an application.

ON the WEB   To use the sample code for this chapter, import the chapter14.zip Flex project archive from the Web site files into your Flex Builder workspace.

Using Effects

An *effect* is an ActionScript class that defines changes in a visual component's position, visibility, scaling, and other properties over a period of time. The Flex framework includes many pre-built effect classes that can be applied to visual components and played with explicit ActionScript statements or upon certain built-in effect triggers.

Most pre-built effect classes in the Flex framework define changes to visual properties of control. The following effects cause changes to one or more of a visual component's properties over a period of time:

- AnimateProperty: Changes any numeric property of a visual component over a period of time. Properties with numeric values include width, height, scaleX, scaleY, x, y, and others.

- Blur: Applies a blur filter to a component. The same visual result can be accomplished programmatically with the BlurFilter class, but declaring it as an effect in a behavior takes less code and it can be applied gradually over time.

- Dissolve: Changes the alpha property of a component to affect transparency. An overlay rectangle of an arbitrary color is used to slowly hide or reveal the target component.

- Fade: Changes the alpha property of a component to affect transparency. It is similar to the Dissolve effect, but does not apply a colored overlay.

- Glow: Applies a glow filter to a component over a period of time. The same visual result can be achieved programmatically with the GlowFilter class, but declaring it as an effect in a behavior takes less code and it can be applied gradually over time.

- Iris: Uses a rectangular mask to reveal or hide an object over a period of time. Unlike the Zoom effect, this does not change the component's dimensions.

- Move: Changes the component's x and y properties over time. To use this effectively, the container in which the target component is nested should be a Canvas or an Application, Panel, or TitleWindow container with layout set to absolute.

- Resize: Changes the component's width and height over a period of time.

- Rotate: Rotates a component around a specific point. You can control the coordinates of the rotation point and the angle of rotation.

- WipeLeft, WipeRight, WipeUp, and WipeDown: Reveals or hides a component by applying or removing a masking rectangle over a period of time.

- Zoom: Changes the scale of a component over time, zooming into and out of a component's center point.

The following effects are non-visual in nature, but are played with the same strategy as the visual effect classes:

- Pause: Creates a time lag between multiple effects controlled in a Sequence (explained later in this chapter).

- SoundEffect: Plays an MP3 file. The MP3 file can be embedded or can be loaded at runtime.

Using effect classes

Effects can be executed automatically at runtime by assigning effect instances to special members of visual components called *triggers*. When a trigger occurs, the assigned effect is played.

Each effect class in the Flex framework has its own unique set of properties that control its behavior at runtime. When you pass an effect to a trigger using the effect's class name, you're accepting the effect class's default property values:

```
<mx:Image source="assets/flower1.jpg"
    showEffect="Fade" hideEffect="Fade"/>
```

TIP   When you pass the name of a class in an MXML attribute, you don't wrap the class name in a binding expression. Instead, you just pass the class name as a `String` and, in some circumstances, include its package. In this case, the `mx.effects` package doesn't have to be included when it's included in an MXML trigger declaration.

The Flex framework creates an instance of the event class at runtime and then plays it. When the effect has been completed, the instance created by the framework is destroyed. Using effect class names in this manner is convenient and easy for these reasons:

- You don't have to declare an `import` statement for effect classes when the effect class is used in an MXML trigger declaration.

- You don't have to remember the effect class's properties; when using the class in this manner, you cannot change its default behavior.

However, this method precludes the ability for controlling your effects, and because you frequently need to change an effect's default behavior, you should know how to set the property values of an effect's instance class.

Modifying effect class properties

You can override the default property values of any pre-built effect class with MXML or ActionScript code. To change the behavior of the Fade class, you can create an instance of the Fade class in MXML. Assign the MXML declaration a unique `id` so you can refer to the custom effect in your ActionScript code and binding expressions, and also set any of the class's properties to your custom values. This customized Fade effect has a customized `duration` of 2000 milliseconds:

```
<mx:Fade id="myFade" duration="2000"/>
```

Because an effect's `duration` is measured in milliseconds, a `duration` of 2000 means that the effect takes two seconds to play. The `duration` property's default value is 500 milliseconds, so the custom Fade effect plays much more slowly than the default.

To apply the custom effect to a component, reference the custom effect's `id` in a binding expression, applied to the target component's appropriate trigger. This declaration uses the custom myFade effect for both the showEffect and the hideEffect triggers:

```
<mx:Image id="myImage" source="assets/flower1.jpg" x="150"
    y="100"
    showEffect="{myFade}" hideEffect="{myFade}"/>
```

CAUTION Each effect class in the Flex framework has an equivalent *instance* class. For example, the `Fade` class is matched by a `FadeInstance` class. The instance class is used internally by the framework to create new instances of the effect each time it's played. You should never declare the effect instance classes directly though.

TIP Whenever an MXML property's value is assigned to a class instance or variable value, it should be expressed as a binding, wrapped in brace (`{}`) characters. This is true for data providers, transition targets, effect objects, and many other types of data. In some cases, the Flex compiler allows you to omit the braces from the expression, but it's a best practice to use them universally.

Using behaviors and triggers

A Flex *behavior* is a combination of a *trigger* and an *effect* that results in a visual animation or some other dynamic response to a change in application state.

Triggers play effects in response to a user gesture or change in application state. Triggers are similar to events, in that they occur when a user gesture or change in state is detected and reported by the Flex framework. But whereas an event such as `mouseDown` is handled with an event listener that executes arbitrary ActionScript code of your design, a trigger such as `mouseDownEffect` "plays" an effect class.

The Flex framework has many predefined triggers. Most triggers are defined in the `UIComponent` class and are supported by all visual components. These triggers are described in Table 14.1.

TABLE 14.1

Commonly Used Triggers

Name	Triggering Event	Description
addedEffect	added	Played when a component is added to a container's display list
creationComplete Effect	creation Complete	Played when a component has been completely created in Flash Player memory
focusInEffect	focusIn	Played when a component gains keyboard focus
focusOutEffect	focusOut	Played when a component loses keyboard focus
hideEffect	Hide	Played when a component's `visible` property is set to `false` or becomes invisible due to a navigator container changing its active container

Name	Triggering Event	Description
mouseDownEffect	mouseDown	Played when the user presses the mouse button while the mouse pointer is over the component
mouseUpEffect	mouseUp	Played when the user releases the mouse button while the mouse pointer is over the component
moveEffect	move	Played when the component is moved
removedEffect	removed	Played when the component is removed from a container's display list
resizeEffect	resize	Played when a component's dimensions change
rollOutEffect	rollout	Played when the mouse pointer moves so that it's no longer over a component
rollOverEffect	rollover	Played when the mouse pointer moves so that it becomes positioned over a component
showEffect	show	Played when a component's visible property is set to true or becomes visible due to a navigator container changing its active container

In addition to the triggers defined in the UIComponent class, certain triggers are defined for specific classes and their unique events. For example, the SWFLoader component's completeEffect trigger plays when a Flash .swf document has been completely loaded from the server.

TIP   Triggers are described in the Flex API documentation under each visual component's Effects section. Each trigger has an equivalent *triggering event*. For example, the triggering event for the mouseDownEffect trigger is mouseDown. You could accomplish the same result as a traditional behavior by listening for the triggering event and explicitly playing an effect class, but it would take significantly more code than a simple behavior declaration.

Declaring triggers in MXML

Triggers play effects when you apply them to a visual control. When an object is declared in MXML, you can apply the trigger with an MXML attribute declaration. In the following code, an Image control fades in and out of view when its visible property changes from true to false or back again:

```
<mx:Image source="assets/flower1.jpg"
    showEffect="Fade" hideEffect="Fade"/>
```

By default, the Image control appears and disappears abruptly. When the control's showEffect and hideEffect triggers are set to play the Fade effect, the control appears and disappears gradually.

Listing 14.1 shows a complete application that uses the showEffect and hideEffect triggers to play the Fade effect.

LISTING 14.1

Using a simple trigger

```xml
<?xml version="1.0" encoding="utf-8"?>
<mx:Application xmlns:mx="http://www.adobe.com/2006/mxml"
  layout="absolute" backgroundColor="#eeeeee">
  <mx:Image id="myImage" source="assets/flower1.jpg" x="150" y="100"
    showEffect="Fade" hideEffect="Fade"/>
  <mx:Button x="150" y="375" label="Show Image"
    click="myImage.visible=true"/>
  <mx:Button x="374" y="375" label="Hide Image"
    click="myImage.visible=false"/>
</mx:Application>
```

ON the WEB The code in Listing 14.1 is available in the Web site files as **SimpleTrigger.mxml** in the **chapter14** project.

Figure 14.1 shows the resulting application in the process of fading from visible to invisible. The screenshot on the left shows the Image control with full visibility, while the screenshot on the right shows the Image approximately 50 percent through the playing of the Fade effect.

Declaring triggers programmatically

Triggers are implemented internally as styles, so you can set a visual component's trigger in ActionScript with a call to the component's setStyle() method. The first argument in the call to setStyle() is the name of the trigger as a String. The second argument is an instance of the appropriate effect class.

The application in Listing 14.2 sets triggers on an Image control with the same result as in the MXML example, but it uses ActionScript to create the control, add it to the application, and set its behaviors.

FIGURE 14.1

A Fade effect in progress

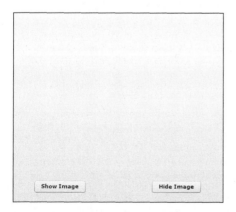

LISTING 14.2

Setting component triggers in ActionScript

```
<?xml version="1.0" encoding="utf-8"?>
<mx:Application xmlns:mx="http://www.adobe.com/2006/mxml"
  layout="absolute" backgroundColor="#eeeeee"
  creationComplete="initApp()">
  <mx:Script>
    <![CDATA[
      import mx.controls.Image;
      import mx.effects.Fade;
      private var myImage:Image = new Image();
      private function initApp():void
      {
        this.addChild(myImage);
        myImage.source = "assets/flower1.jpg";
        myImage.x=150;
        myImage.y=100;
        myImage.setStyle("showEffect", new Fade());
        myImage.setStyle("hideEffect", new Fade());
      }
    ]]>
  </mx:Script>
  <mx:Button x="150" y="375" label="Show Image"
    click="myImage.visible=true"/>
  <mx:Button x="374" y="375" label="Hide Image"
    click="myImage.visible=false"/>
</mx:Application>
```

 The code in Listing 14.2 is available in the Web site files as `SettingTriggers WithAS.mxml` in the `chapter14` project.

TIP When you refer to an effect class in ActionScript code, the class must be imported before it's referenced:

```
import mx.effects.Fade;
```

Playing effects in ActionScript

You can explicitly construct and play an effect with ActionScript code with these steps:

1. Declare an instance of an effect class as a variable.

2. Set the effect variable's `target` property to refer to the component you want to animate.

3. Set other properties to modify the effect's behavior.

4. Call the effect class's `play()` method.

The application in Listing 14.3 creates and plays customized Fade effects to handle the hiding and showing of a visual component.

LISTING 14.3

Defining and playing an effect with ActionScript

```
<?xml version="1.0" encoding="utf-8"?>
<mx:Application xmlns:mx="http://www.adobe.com/2006/mxml"
   layout="absolute"
  backgroundColor="#eeeeee">
  <mx:Script>
    <![CDATA[
      import mx.effects.Fade;
      private function showImage():void
      {
        var myFade:Fade = new Fade();
        myFade.target = myImage;
        myFade.alphaFrom = 0;
        myFade.alphaTo = 1;
        myFade.play();
      }
      private function hideImage():void
      {
        var myFade:Fade = new Fade();
        myFade.target = myImage;
        myFade.alphaFrom = 1;
        myFade.alphaTo = 0;
        myFade.play();
      }
    ]]>
  </mx:Script>
  <mx:Image id="myImage" source="assets/flower1.jpg" x="150" y="100"/>
  <mx:Button x="150" y="375" label="Show Image" click="showImage()"/>
  <mx:Button x="374" y="375" label="Hide Image" click="hideImage()"/>
</mx:Application>
```

ON the WEB   The code in Listing 14.3 is available in the Web site files as **PlayEffectWithAS.mxml** in the **chapter14** project.

TIP   Effect classes also have a **targets** property that takes an **Array** of visual components. When you call the effect class's **play()** method, the framework constructs one internal instance of the effect class for each target object and then plays them all simultaneously.

Using tweening and masking effects

Many of the pre-built effects in the Flex framework are specifically designed to show or hide a component with an animation instead of an abrupt appearance or disappearance.

Some of the effect classes accomplish this through a process known as *tweening*. A tweening effect changes an object's dimensions, transparency, or position over time, but doesn't directly affect how much of the object's surface is visible until the effect is complete. The Flex framework includes tween effects such as Move, Blur, Dissolve, Resize, and Rotate.

Other effect classes control a component's visibility through *masking*. A masking effect doesn't change the object's dimensions, transparency, or position; instead, it dynamically creates a visual object at runtime and uses that object to obscure or reveal the target component. The Flex framework includes such masking effects as Iris, WipeDown, WipeUp, WipeRight, and WipeLeft.

Both tweening and masking effects can be used to animate the process of showing or hiding a visual component. The application in Listing 14.4 demonstrates this, allowing you to apply selected effects to a control as its visible property is changed from true to false and back again.

LISTING 14.4

Showing and hiding a component with effects

```
<?xml version="1.0" encoding="utf-8"?>
<mx:Application xmlns:mx="http://www.adobe.com/2006/mxml"
   layout="absolute" backgroundColor="#eeeeee"
   creationComplete="changeEffect(event)">
  <mx:Script>
    <![CDATA[
      import mx.effects.*;
      private var myEffect:Effect;
      private function changeEffect(event:Event):void
      {
        switch (effectList.selectedItem)
        {
          case "Fade"      : myEffect = new Fade(); break;
          case "Dissolve"  : myEffect = myDissolve;  break;
          case "Iris"      : myEffect = new Iris(); break;
          case "Zoom"      : myEffect = new Zoom();break;
          case "WipeRight" : myEffect = new WipeRight(); break;
          case "WipeLeft"  : myEffect = new WipeLeft(); break;
          case "WipeUp"    : myEffect = new WipeUp(); break;
          case "WipeDown"  : myEffect = new WipeDown();
        }
        myImage.setStyle("showEffect", myEffect);
        myImage.setStyle("hideEffect", myEffect);
```

```
        }
    ]]>
  </mx:Script>
  <mx:Dissolve id="myDissolve" color="red"/>
  <mx:Label text="Showing and Hiding with Effects"
    fontSize="18" x="24" y="10"/>
  <mx:Image id="myImage" source="assets/flower1.jpg" x="158" y="72"/>
  <mx:Button x="158" y="321" label="Show Image"
    click="myImage.visible=true"/>
  <mx:Button x="382" y="321" label="Hide Image"
    click="myImage.visible=false"/>
  <mx:Label x="24" y="46" text="Select an Effect" fontWeight="bold"/>
  <mx:List id="effectList" change="changeEffect(event)"
    x="24" y="72" width="100" height="241"
    selectedIndex="0">
    <mx:dataProvider>
      <mx:String>Fade</mx:String>
      <mx:String>Dissolve</mx:String>
      <mx:String>Iris</mx:String>
      <mx:String>Zoom</mx:String>
      <mx:String>WipeRight</mx:String>
      <mx:String>WipeLeft</mx:String>
      <mx:String>WipeUp</mx:String>
      <mx:String>WipeDown</mx:String>
    </mx:dataProvider>
  </mx:List>
</mx:Application>
```

ON the WEB   The code in Listing 14.4 is available in the Web site files as **ShowAndHide.mxml** in the **chapter14** project.

Figure 14.2 shows the resulting application. To see the different effects:

- Select an effect from the list on the left.
- Click the buttons to show and hide the control.

Fade and Dissolve

The Fade and Dissolve effects are similar to each other in that they both affect the component's visibility and transparency over time. Both effect classes support properties of alphaFrom and alphaTo that can be used to control the direction and level of change in the component's visibility. The default values for these properties are 0 and 1, applied as appropriate to show or hide the target component completely.

FIGURE 14.2

Showing and hiding a component with effects

The Fade class implements a tweening effect that modifies the component's transparency level over a period of time. By default, the Fade effect changes the target component's alpha property from 0 to 1 when revealing it, and from 1 to 0 when hiding it. Whatever color or image is "behind" the target component shows through as its transparency level is changed.

The Dissolve class also implements a tweening effect, but it affects visibility by creating a rectangle object laid over the component and then changes the rectangle's opacity to show and hide the underlying component. At the end of the effect, the rectangle is destroyed. The advantage of the Dissolve effect over the Fade effect is that you can control the color of the overlaid rectangle and more effectively blend the effect into the application's background.

When declaring a custom Dissolve effect in MXML, set its color to match the application's background or any other color you like. This Dissolve effect uses a red rectangle that appears at the end of the effect when hiding the component and at the beginning of the effect when showing it:

```
<mx:Dissolve id="myDissolve" color="red"/>
```

Iris and Zoom

The Iris and Zoom effects both resize a component over time, increasing its size to show it and decreasing its size to hide it. The two effects' resizing strategies, however, are very different.

The Iris class implements a masking effect that reveals a component from the center out and hides it from the outer borders inward. The component's scale doesn't change when using the

Iris; only the amount of the component's surface that's visible to the user is modified. The Iris class supports properties of scaleXFrom, scaleXTo, scaleYFrom, and scaleYTo. Each of these properties' values can be set from 0, meaning the object is completely masked, to 1, meaning the object is completely visible.

The Zoom class implements a tweening effect that changes the scale of the component. The Zoom effect supports properties of zoomWidthFrom, zoomWidthTo, zoomHeightFrom, and zoomHeightTo. When hiding the component, its zoom properties go from 1 to 0.01, and when showing the component, its scale changes from 0.01 to 1.

The application in Listing 14.5 plays an Iris and a Zoom effect simultaneously on two controls.

LISTING 14.5

Using the Iris and Zoom effects

```
<?xml version="1.0" encoding="utf-8"?>
<mx:Application xmlns:mx="http://www.adobe.com/2006/mxml"
   layout="absolute"
  backgroundColor="#eeeeee">

  <mx:Zoom id="myZoom" duration="2000"/>
  <mx:Iris id="myIris" duration="2000"/>
  <mx:Image id="irisImage" source="assets/flower1.jpg" x="22" y="55"
    showEffect="{myIris}" hideEffect="{myIris}"/>
  <mx:Image id="zoomImage" source="assets/flower1.jpg" x="362" y="55"
    showEffect="{myZoom}" hideEffect="{myZoom}"/>
  <mx:Button x="241" y="330" label="Show Images"
    click="zoomImage.visible=true;irisImage.visible=true;"/>
  <mx:Button x="362" y="330" label="Hide Images"
    click="zoomImage.visible=false;irisImage.visible=false"/>
  <mx:Label x="22" y="24" text="Iris Image" fontSize="14"
    fontWeight="bold"/>
  <mx:Label x="362" y="24" text="Zoom Image" fontSize="14"
    fontWeight="bold"/>
</mx:Application>
```

ON the WEB The code in Listing 14.5 is available in the Web site files as **IrisAndZoom.mxml** in the **chapter14** project.

Figure 14.3 shows the difference between the Iris and Zoom effects. The screenshot reflects the appearance of two Image controls midway through playing the respective effects. The Iris effect masks the control, displaying only part of its surface, while the Zoom effect changes the object's size, showing it in its entirety but in a smaller scale.

FIGURE 14.3

The Iris and Zoom effects at work

The Iris effect masking the image

The Zoom effect scaling the image

Blur and Glow

The Blur and Glow classes implement tweening effects that use Flash Player's BlurFilter and GlowFilter classes to change a component's appearance over time. Unlike Iris, Zoom, and other effects that can be used effectively to show and hide a component, these filtering effects typically are used just to change an object's appearance but leave it visible.

The Blur effect supports properties of blurXFrom, blurXTo, blurYFrom, and blurYTo. The blurX properties determine the amount of horizontal blur, and the blurY properties determine the amount of horizontal blur.

The application in Listing 14.6 applies the Blur effect to an Image control. The effect is played explicitly upon a button's click event.

LISTING 14.6

Using the Blur effect

```
<?xml version="1.0" encoding="utf-8"?>
<mx:Application xmlns:mx="http://www.adobe.com/2006/mxml"
   layout="absolute"
  backgroundColor="#eeeeee">
  <mx:Blur id="myBlur" target="{myBlurredImage}" blurXTo="20"
  blurYTo="20"/>
```

```
<mx:Label x="22" y="24" text="Blurring an image" fontSize="14"
  fontWeight="bold"/>
<mx:Image source="assets/flower1.jpg" x="22" y="55"/>
<mx:Image id="myBlurredImage" source="assets/flower1.jpg" x="366"
  y="55"/>
<mx:Button x="22" y="315" label="Show Images" click="myBlur.play()"/>
</mx:Application>
```

ON the WEB The code in Listing 14.6 is available in the Web site files as `BlurDemo.mxml` in the `chapter14` project.

As shown in Figure 14.4, the application shows an image twice, with the Blur effect applied only to the second.

FIGURE 14.4

The Blur effect at work

The Glow effect applies a colored glow around a component's border. As with the Blur effect, the blurX and blurY properties determine the amount of blurriness to the effect, but instead of changing the whole component, only the glow area is affected.

In addition, the Glow effect supports these properties:

- color: A named color or hexadecimal color value that determines the color of the glow area
- inner: A Boolean value which, when set to true, causes the glow to be applied inward from the component's border area instead of the default outward glow

- knockout: A Boolean value which, when set to true, causes the surface area of the target component to be replaced with the color or component in the background

- alphaFrom and alphaTo: The amount of transparency to be applied

This Glow effect adds a red glow area around the outer edge of a target component. The alphaTo value of .5 means that after the effect has played, the glow area remains in place with 50 percent transparency.

```
<mx:Glow id="myGlowOn"
    blurXFrom="0" blurYFrom="0" blurXTo="20" blurYTo="20"
    color="#FF0000" alphaFrom="1.0" alphaTo="0.5"/>
```

CAUTION When applying a Glow filter, if you don't set alphaTo to a value less than 1, the visual result disappears after the effect has finished playing.

The application in Listing 14.7 plays a Glow effect upon the target component's rollOverEffect trigger and then plays a reverse effect to remove the glow upon the rollOutEffect trigger.

LISTING 14.7

Using the Glow effect

```
<?xml version="1.0" encoding="utf-8"?>
<mx:Application xmlns:mx="http://www.adobe.com/2006/mxml"
   layout="absolute"
  backgroundColor="#eeeeee">
  <mx:Glow id="myGlowOn"
    blurXFrom="0" blurYFrom="0" blurXTo="20" blurYTo="20"
    color="#ff0000" alphaFrom="1.0" alphaTo="0.5" knockout="true"/>
  <mx:Glow id="myGlowOff"
    blurXFrom="20" blurYFrom="20" blurXTo="0" blurYTo="0"
    color="#ff0000" alphaFrom=".5" alphaTo="1"/>
  <mx:Label x="22" y="24" text="Applying a Glow filter"
    fontSize="14" fontWeight="bold"/>
  <mx:Image source="assets/flower1.jpg" x="22" y="55"/>
  <mx:Image source="assets/flower1.jpg" x="366" y="55"
    rollOverEffect="{myGlowOn}" rollOutEffect="{myGlowOff}"/>
</mx:Application>
```

ON the WEB The code in Listing 14.7 is available in the Web site files as GlowDemo.mxml in the chapter14 project.

Figure 14.5 shows two Image controls. The Glow effect has been played on the second through the use of triggers.

FIGURE 14.5

Using the Glow effect

The Move effect

The Move class implements a tweening effect that does what it says: It moves the component on the screen to and from specific pixel positions over a period of time. The effect supports properties of xFrom, xTo, yFrom, and yTo that define the component's position at the beginning and end of the effect. The object's intermediate positions are then recalculated over the period of time defined by the effect's duration property.

When using the Move effect to control showing and hiding controls, you typically create two instances of the effect: one to show and one to hide. Each defines specific starting and ending coordinates and is applied to the target component's appropriate triggers.

CAUTION A Move effect's target component should always be nested in a Canvas or other container with absolute layout turned on. If the target component is nested in a container with vertical or horizontal layout and the container's dimensions change at runtime, the component's position is recalculated based on the container's layout rules.

The application in Listing 14.8 defines two Move effects that show and hide a target component by moving it on and off the application stage. Notice that the component's positions at the start and end of the effect are either defined as specific coordinates or calculated based on the target component's dimensions.

LISTING 14.8

Using the Move effect

```
<?xml version="1.0" encoding="utf-8"?>
<mx:Application xmlns:mx="http://www.adobe.com/2006/mxml"
  layout="absolute"
  backgroundColor="#eeeeee">
  <mx:Move id="moveOn"
    xFrom="{0-myImage.width}" xTo="150"
    yFrom="{0-myImage.height}" yTo="100"/>
  <mx:Move id="moveOff"
    xTo="{0-myImage.width}" xFrom="150"
    yTo="{0-myImage.height}" yFrom="100"/>
  <mx:Image id="myImage" source="assets/flower1.jpg" x="150" y="100"
    showEffect="{moveOn}" hideEffect="{moveOff}"/>
  <mx:Button x="150" y="375" label="Show Image"
    click="myImage.visible=true"/>
  <mx:Button x="374" y="375" label="Hide Image"
    click="myImage.visible=false"/>
</mx:Application>
```

> **ON the WEB** The code in Listing 14.8 is available in the Web site files as **MoveDemo.mxml** in the **chapter14** project.

Figure 14.6 shows the resulting application with the component in different positions as the effect is played.

The Rotate effect

The Rotate effect causes the target component to rotate in one direction or the other. You control the angle of rotation with the angleFrom and angleTo properties and values from 0 to 360. The rotation axis of the target component is controlled with the originX and originY properties, which default to the vertical and horizontal center point of the component.

This code defines a Rotate effect where the axis of rotation is dynamically calculated as the vertical and horizontal center of the object:

```
<mx:Rotate originX="{myImage.width/2}"
  originY="{myImage.height/2}"/>
```

> **CROSS-REF** An example of using the Rotate effect is included in the section on composite effects, later in this chapter.

FIGURE 14.6

Playing the Move effect

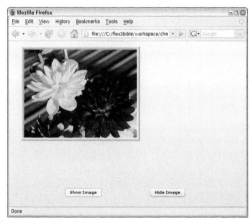

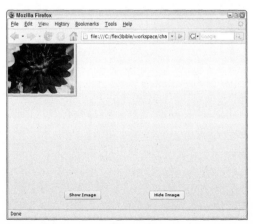

The wiping effects

Four wiping effects can mask a component using its top, bottom, left, and right borders as positions for the animation. The WipeRight, WipeLeft, WipeUp, and WipeDown effects are probably the simplest effects to use and understand. As with all effects, they support a duration property that controls the length of the effect.

In addition, the wiping effects support xFrom, xTo, yFrom, and yTo properties that control the beginning and ending position of the mask.

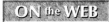 Examples of the wiping effects are available in the Web site files **ShowAndHide.mxml** in the **chapter14** project.

Using composite effects

A composite effect plays two or more effects either simultaneously or consecutively. The Flex framework has two composite effects:

- **The** Parallel **effect** plays two or more effects at the same time.
- **The** Sequence **effect** plays two or more effects consecutively, with each effect starting after the previous effect has finished.

Both Parallel and Sequence effects can be declared in either MXML or ActionScript and can nest as many child effects, simple or composite, as you need to get the desired visual result.

Using Parallel effects

To create a Parallel effect in MXML, declare an <mx:Parallel> tag set and assign a unique id. Then, within the tag set, nest two or more effects that you want to play simultaneously:

```
<mx:Parallel id="myParallelEffect">
...effect 1...
...effect 2...
...etc........
</mx:Parallel>
```

The effects defined with the <mx:Parallel> tag set don't need unique id properties, because the entire effect is played either through association with a target component trigger or by an explicit call to the Parallel class's play() method.

The application in Listing 14.9 defines Parallel effects that include a Move and a Rotate nested effects. The visual result is an object that appears to roll on and off the application stage. Notice that the Rotate effect in the second Parallel has its angleFrom set to 360 and angleTo set to 0. The result is a counterclockwise rotation.

LISTING 14.9

Using a Parallel effect

```
<?xml version="1.0" encoding="utf-8"?>
<mx:Application xmlns:mx="http://www.adobe.com/2006/mxml"
   layout="absolute"
  backgroundColor="#eeeeee">
  <mx:Parallel id="moveOn">
    <mx:Move
      xFrom="{0-myImage.width}" xTo="150"
      yFrom="100" yTo="100"/>
    <mx:Rotate originX="{myImage.width/2}"
  originY="{myImage.height/2}"/>
  </mx:Parallel>
  <mx:Parallel id="moveOff">
    <mx:Move
      xTo="{0-myImage.width}" xFrom="150"
      yFrom="100" yTo="100"/>
    <mx:Rotate originX="{myImage.width/2}" originY="{myImage.height/2}"
      angleFrom="360" angleTo="0"/>
  </mx:Parallel>
  <mx:Image id="myImage" source="assets/flower1.jpg" x="150" y="100"
    showEffect="{moveOn}" hideEffect="{moveOff}"/>
  <mx:Button x="150" y="375" label="Show Image"
    click="myImage.visible=true"/>
  <mx:Button x="374" y="375" label="Hide Image"
    click="myImage.visible=false"/>
</mx:Application>
```

ON the WEB The code in Listing 14.9 is available in the Web site files as **ParallelDemo.mxml** in the **chapter14** project.

Using Sequence effects

The Sequence effect plays two or more nested effects consecutively. In this code, a Sequence wraps two Move effects. The first nested effect moves the target object horizontally, and the second moves it vertically:

```
<mx:Sequence id="moveOn" target="{myImage}">
  <mx:Move
    xFrom="{0-myImage.width}" xTo="150"
    yFrom="0" yTo="0"/>
  <mx:Move yTo="100"/>
</mx:Sequence>
```

Sometimes when using a Sequence, you want to create a delay between effects. The Pause effect is designed explicitly for this purpose: You add a Pause between other nested effects with a duration indicating how long the delay should be in milliseconds. This version of the Sequence plays the same set of Move effects, but it adds a one-second delay between them:

```
<mx:Sequence id="moveOn" target="{myImage}">
  <mx:Move
    xFrom="{0-myImage.width}" xTo="150"
    yFrom="0" yTo="0"/>
  <mx:Pause duration="1000"/>
  <mx:Move yTo="100"/>
</mx:Sequence>
```

A Sequence effect can nest any number of child effects, allowing you to choreograph objects on the screen in sometimes elaborate ways. The application in Listing 14.10 causes an image to "bounce" across the screen with multiple Move effects nested within a Sequence. Notice these features of the application:

- The Application has its horizontalScrollPolicy and verticalScroll Policy set to off to prevent scrollbars from appearing as the visual control moves off the visible area of the stage.

- The Sequence effect handles its effectEnd event by placing the image back in its original starting position.

LISTING 14.10

```
<?xml version="1.0" encoding="utf-8"?>
<mx:Application xmlns:mx="http://www.adobe.com/2006/mxml"
   layout="absolute"
  horizontalScrollPolicy="off" verticalScrollPolicy="off">
  <mx:Script>
    <![CDATA[
      [Bindable]
      private var stageWidth:Number;
      [Bindable]
      private var stageHeight:Number;
      private function bounce():void
      {
        stageHeight = stage.height;
        stageWidth = stage.width;
        bouncingBall.play();
      }
      private function replaceBall():void
      {
        myImage.x = 0-myImage.width;
        myImage.y = 0-myImage.height;
      }
    ]]>
```

```
    </mx:Script>
    <mx:Sequence id="bouncingBall" target="{myImage}"
      effectEnd="replaceBall()">
      <mx:Move xTo="{stageWidth/5}"   yTo="{stageHeight-myImage.height}"/>
      <mx:Move xTo="{stageWidth/5*2}" yTo="{stageHeight-
    myImage.height*4}"/>
      <mx:Move xTo="{stageWidth/5*3}" yTo="{stageHeight-myImage.height}"/>
      <mx:Move xTo="{stageWidth/5*4}" yTo="{stageHeight-
    myImage.height*3}"/>
      <mx:Move xTo="{stageWidth}"     yTo="{stageHeight-myImage.height}"/>
    </mx:Sequence>
    <mx:Image id="myImage" source="@Embed('assets/ball.png')"
      x="{0-myImage.width}" y="{0-myImage.height}"/>
    <mx:Button label="Bounce Ball" click="bounce()" right="10"
      bottom="10"/>
</mx:Application>
```

ON the WEB The code in Listing 14.10 is available in the Web site files as `BouncingBall.mxml` in the `chapter14` project.

Figure 14.7 shows the resulting application and the various positions of the image as it moves across the screen.

FIGURE 14.7

A Sequence effect at work

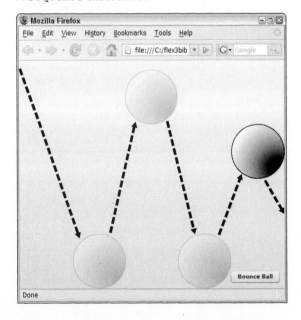

Using easing functions

An easing function allows you to modify the behavior of an event that transforms a component on the screen. By default, an effect transforms an object with a linear timeline. For example, a Move effect changes an object's position on the screen with constant speed and motion. An easing function allows you to redefine the object's movement mathematically and modify its rate of change so that, for example, it appears to speed up as it moves.

 **TIP** Easing functions are most commonly demonstrated with object movement, but they work with any visual effect, because all such effects transform objects over a period of time.

NOTE The easing functions included in the Flex framework are based on work by Robert Penner. More information on easing equations, including a valuable application for visualizing easing behavior, is available at his Web site at `http://robertpenner.com/easing/`.

The Flex framework includes a set of easing classes in the `mx.effects.easing` package, each of which modifies the rate of object transformation in a different way. The `Bounce` class, for example, can be used with a Move effect to cause the object to bounce against its final destination.

You use easing functions by assigning them to the effect's `easingFunction` property. You can either use the pre-built easing functions in the Flex framework, or you can define and use your own custom functions.

To use a pre-built easing function, follow these steps:

1. In a Script section, import the class that includes the easing function you want to use.

2. Set the effect's `easingFunction` property to the name of the class and function, using dot syntax. Don't include parentheses or pass any properties; include only the class and function name:

   ```
   easingFunction="Bounce.easeOut"
   ```

The application in Listing 14.11 uses the `Bounce.easeOut()` function to cause the `Image` control to bounce on a platform (created as a `Canvas` container) after dropping from the top of the application.

LISTING 14.11

Using an easing function

```
<?xml version="1.0" encoding="utf-8"?>
<mx:Application xmlns:mx="http://www.adobe.com/2006/mxml"
   layout="absolute"
  backgroundColor="#eeeeee">
  <mx:Script>
    <![CDATA[

      import mx.effects.easing.Bounce;
```

```
      private function dropBall():void
      {
        myImage.y=0-myImage.height;
        bouncingBall.play();
      }
    ]]>
  </mx:Script>
  <mx:Move id="bouncingBall" target="{myImage}"
    yTo="{platform.y-myImage.height}"
    easingFunction="Bounce.easeOut" duration="2000"
    suspendBackgroundProcessing="true"/>
  <mx:Image id="myImage" source="@Embed('assets/ball.png')"
    horizontalCenter="0" y="{0-myImage.height}"/>
  <mx:Button label="Bounce Ball" click="dropBall()" right="10"
   bottom="10"/>
  <mx:Canvas id="platform" width="200" height="75"
    backgroundColor="#666666" horizontalCenter="0" bottom="0"/>
</mx:Application>
```

ON the WEB   The code in Listing 14.11 is available in the Web site files as **EasingDemo.mxml** in the **chapter14** project.

As shown in Figure 14.8, the image drops from the top of the application and appears to bounce on the Canvas container.

FIGURE 14.8

Using an easing function

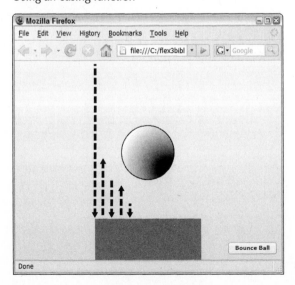

> **TIP**   The `suspendBackgroundProcessing` property causes all visual processing of the application to be suspended while an effect is being played. This can greatly improve effect performance, especially on a slower client computer. The only reason not to set this property to `true` is if the user has to be able to interact with the application while an effect is playing, or if you're trying to play more than one effect at the same time.

Using Drag-and-Drop Operations

Drag-and-drop interfaces allow users to give instructions to an application with simple mouse gestures. Pointing to an object that a person wants to manipulate is the most human of gestures, and grabbing and moving an object to change its current state is how we interact with the physical world in nearly every waking minute. The mouse turns that intuitive action into a computer instruction that graphical applications can interpret as needed.

Drag-and-drop operations can be created to represent various software operations:

- Selecting data
- Moving data from one location to another
- Deleting data
- Managing data relationships
- Modifying structures of information

As the designer and developer of a Flex application, you must select or create the drag-and-drop architecture that makes your interface the easiest to use.

Flex applications can implement drag-and-drop operations with two different approaches:

- `List`-based controls such as the `List` and `DataGrid` have built-in drag-and-drop capability.
- All visual controls can participate in drag-and-drop operations through a set of classes and events specifically designed for this purpose.

Implementing drag-and-drop with List controls

All `List`-based controls in the Flex framework have built-in support for drag-and-drop operations. These controls include:

- `List`
- `ComboBox`
- `DataGrid`
- `TitleList`

- HorizontalList

- Tree

Each of these controls supports a set of properties that turn on and control drag-and-drop operations:

- dragEnabled is a Boolean property that, when set to true, allows a user to select one or more items from a List control and drag them (and their underlying data) to another visual control in the application.

- dropEnabled is a Boolean property that, when set to true, allows a List control to accept a drop operation. When the user completes the operation, the target object adds the operation's underlying data to its data provider. If the initiating object's dragMoveEnabled property is set to true, the items that were dropped in the target object are removed from the initiating object's data source; otherwise, the initiating object's data provider is left in its current state.

- dragMoveEnabled is a Boolean property that, when set to true along with dragEnabled, causes items dragged from a List control be removed from the initiating control's data provider. This property also allows users to reorder data in a control's dataProvider if the control's dropEnabled property is set to true.

> **CAUTION** Setting **dragMoveEnabled** to true without also setting **dragEnabled** to true has no affect on the application. You must set **dragEnabled** to true to initiate a **List**-based drag-and-drop operation.

The following code creates a List control and a DataGrid control. The List control can initiate a drag-and-drop operation, and the DataGrid can accept the dropped data:

```
<mx:List dataProvider="{myData}" dragEnabled="true"/>
<mx:DataGrid dropEnabled="true">
```

Because the DataGrid control's dragMoveEnabled property isn't set to true, any objects dragged to the DataGrid are still displayed in the List after the operation is completed.

The application in Listing 14.12 uses List and DataGrid controls. Notice these features of the sample application:

- As the List row is dragged, an image of the row is generated and displayed as a visual indicator that the drag-and-drop operation is active. This image is known as the *drag proxy*.

- The drag proxy initially includes a white X in a red circle, indicating that the operation can't be completed yet. When the cursor moves over the target control with dropEnabled set to true, the white X and red circle disappear, indicating to the user that the operation can be completed.

- The DataGrid control's dragMoveEnabled property is set to true, so the data is added to the DataGrid and removed from the initiating List when the operation is completed.

LISTING 14.12

Using a List-based drag-and-drop operation

```xml
<?xml version="1.0" encoding="utf-8"?>
<mx:Application xmlns:mx="http://www.adobe.com/2006/mxml"
   layout="vertical"
   backgroundGradientAlphas="[1.0, 1.0]" xmlns:views="views.*"
   horizontalAlign="left" backgroundGradientColors="[#908D8D, #FFFFFF]">
  <mx:Script>
    <![CDATA[
      import utilities.FormatUtilities;
    ]]>
  </mx:Script>
  <mx:Model id="bookModel" source="model/books.xml"/>
  <mx:ArrayCollection id="acBooks" source="{bookModel.book}"/>
  <mx:Style source="assets/styles.css"/>
  <views:Header/>
  <mx:HBox>
    <mx:Panel id="catalogPanel" title="Catalog">
      <mx:List dataProvider="{acBooks}" labelField="title"
        height="300" width="200"
        dragEnabled="true" dragMoveEnabled="true"/>
    </mx:Panel>
    <mx:Panel title="Shopping Cart" height="{catalogPanel.height}"
      width="100%">
      <mx:DataGrid id="cart" width="100%" height="100%"
  dropEnabled="true">
        <mx:columns>
          <mx:DataGridColumn dataField="title" headerText="Title"
            width="300"/>
          <mx:DataGridColumn dataField="price" headerText="Price"
            labelFunction="FormatUtilities.currencyFormat"
            textAlign="right"/>
        </mx:columns>
      </mx:DataGrid>
    </mx:Panel>
  </mx:HBox>
</mx:Application>
```

ON the WEB The code in Listing 14.12 is available in the Web site files as
`ListDragAndDrop.mxml` in the `chapter14` project.

Figure 14.9 shows the drag-and-drop operation in action.

FIGURE 14.9

When a user drags an object into a `List` control that has `dropEnabled` set to `true`, the placement of the data in the target control's data provider is indicated by a horizontal line that appears near the mouse cursor's location.

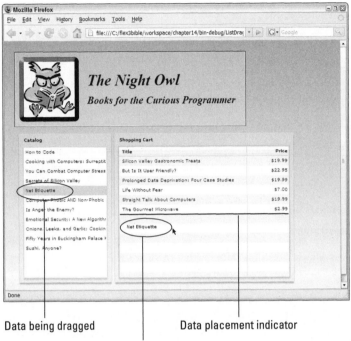

Data being dragged

The dynamic drag proxy

Data placement indicator

Implementing custom drag-and-drop operations

You also can implement drag-and-drop operations manually using a set of classes and events specifically designed for the purpose. The most critical tools for this job are these ActionScript classes:

- `DragSource` contains data and formatting information, and serves a messaging envelope containing the data you want to move.

- `DragManager` initiates and manages drag-and-drop operations containing whatever data you want the user to move in the application.

Initiating a drag-and-drop operation

The `DragSource` and `DragManager` classes are members respectively of the `mx.core` and `mx.managers` packages and must be imported before use:

```
import mx.core.DragSource;
import mx.managers.DragManager;
```

TIP Custom drag-and-drop operations can be initiated upon any mouse event; they typically start upon a `mouseDown`, which indicates the user has pressed the mouse button but hasn't yet released it.

To initiate a custom drag-and-drop operation, follow these steps:

1. Create an instance of the `DragSource` class with its no-arguments constructor method.

2. Populate the `DragSource` class with data by calling its `addData()` method.

3. Call the static method `DragManager.doDrag()` to start the drag-and-drop operation.

In the following code, a `mouseDown` event on an `Image` control that's generated in a `Repeater` is handled with a call to a custom method that will initiate the drag-and-drop operation:

```
<mx:Image source="{bookImage}" mouseDown="initiateDrag(event)"/>
```

The custom `initiateDrag()` method starts by creating a `DragSource` object and filling it with data with a call to the `addData()` method. `DragSource.addData()` has two required arguments:

- A reference to the data that's being moved
- A string that identifies the format of the data

TIP When you initiate a drag-and-drop operation with a `List` control with `dragEnabled` set to true, the name of the `format` is always `items`.

In the following method, the expression `event.target.getRepeaterItem()` returns a reference to the initiating object's underlying data. The `bookItem` format is an arbitrary string that identifies the type of data being moved. The `doDrag()` method receives three required arguments: a reference to the visual component that initiated the operation, the `DragSource` object containing the data, and a reference to the `MouseEvent` object that was passed into the current method:

```
private function initiateDrag(event:MouseEvent):void
{
  var source:DragSource = new DragSource();
  source.addData(event.target.getRepeaterItem(),"bookItem");
  DragManager.doDrag(event.target as UIComponent, source, event);
}
```

TIP You can call the `DragSource` class's `addData()` method multiple times to pass data in as many formats as you need. This is analogous to a clipboard operation, where data might be shared between applications in multiple formats through a copy-and-paste operation, but only formats that are common to the source and the target applications are used at any given time.

Creating a proxy image

A proxy image is displayed during a drag-and-drop operation as a visual indicator of the type or content of the data being moved. When you initiate drag-and-drop with List controls, the drag proxy image is created dynamically from the current screen display. For custom drag-and-drop operations, you're responsible for providing the drag proxy image.

> **TIP** If you don't provide a drag proxy image for a custom drag operation, a blank, partially transparent rectangle is created by the framework of the same shape and dimension as the object that initiates the operation. While this can work okay, the visual result is bland and uninformative.

Drag proxy images should be embedded in the application for the best possible performance. Follow these two steps for this part of the process:

1. Embed a graphic using the [Embed] metadata tag, and assign it a Class variable name.
2. Instantiate a BitMapClass object wrapped around a new instance of the embedded image Class.

> **TIP** A class used as a proxy image must implement the IFlexDisplayObject interface. Classes that can be used for this purpose include BitmapAsset, ButtonAsset, MovieClipAsset, MovieClipLoaderAsset, ProgrammaticSkin, SpriteAsset, SystemManager, TextFieldAsset, and UIComponent.

The following code embeds an image and wraps it in a BitMapAsset object that's suitable for use as a proxy image:

```
[Embed(source="assets/book.png")]
private var bookImage:Class;
private var bookProxy:BitmapAsset = BitmapAsset(new bookImage());
```

You cast the instance of the proxy image class as BitMapAsset to fulfill the requirement that the proxy image object implements IFlexDisplayObject interface.

To use the proxy image in a drag-and-drop operation, pass the proxy object as the fourth argument in the call to DragManager.doDrag():

```
DragManager.doDrag(event.target as UIComponent, source,
   event, bookProxy);
```

You also can control the position of the drag proxy image relative to the cursor position and the image's level of transparency. The doDrag() method's fifth and sixth arguments, xOffset and yOffset, determine the image's horizontal and vertical relative position, and the seventh argument, imageAlpha, determines the amount of transparency. This code uses the same proxy image but ensures that it's fully opaque and positioned to the top and left of the cursor:

```
DragManager.doDrag(event.target as UIComponent, source, event,
   bookProxy, 20, 20, 1);
```

> **TIP** Positive offset values for the proxy image place the image above and to the left of the cursor, while negative values place it below and to the right.

Handling the dragEnter event

A target control, located where the data will be dropped, detects a drag-and-drop operation by listening for the dragEnter event. When the mouse cursor moves over the target object, this event generates a DragEvent object. The DragEvent class has a dragSource property that references the DragSource object that contains the operation's underlying data.

The first step in handling the dragEnter event is to determine whether the operation contains data in a format you can deal with in the current context. You do this by calling the DragSource class's hasFormat() method and passing in a format string you can handle. If the selected format exists in the drag source, you then accept the operation by calling DragManager.acceptDragDrop() and passing in a reference to the object that accepts the operation.

This code detects a particular drag format and accepts the operation:

```
private function dragEnterHandler(event:DragEvent):void
{
  if (event.dragSource.hasFormat("bookItem"))
  {
    DragManager.acceptDragDrop(event.target as UIComponent);
  }
}
```

When you call acceptDragDrop(), the red icon with the white X on the proxy image disappears, indicating to the user that the data is ready to be dropped.

Handling the dragDrop event

When the user drops the data over an object that has already accepted the operation (as described in the preceding section), the object dispatches a dragDrop event. This event also generates a DragEvent object. In addition to the dragSource property described previously, this object also has a dragInitiator property that references the object that initiated the operation.

The DragSource class has a method named dataForFormat(). To retrieve data that should be acted upon, call the method and pass in the format of the data you want:

```
var dragData:Object = event.dragSource.dataForFormat("bookItem");
```

After you have a reference to the dropped data, you can manipulate it in a database, move it to other data buckets in the application, or simply remove it. The following code handles the drag-and-drop operation by first getting references to data through the initiating object's repeater and then removing the underlying data from the repeater's data provider:

```
private function dragDropHandler(event:DragEvent):void
{
  var dragData:Object =
   event.dragSource.dataForFormat("bookItem");
  var initiator:UIComponent = event.dragInitiator as UIComponent;
```

```
      var bookTitle:String = initiator.getRepeaterItem().title;
      acBooks.removeItemAt(initiator.repeaterIndex);
      Alert.show("Book deleted: " + bookTitle, "Deleted!");
   }
```

The application in Listing 14.13 uses a custom drag-and-drop operation to allow a user to delete data using a trash can icon.

LISTING 14.13

A custom drag-and-drop operation

```
<?xml version="1.0" encoding="utf-8"?>
<mx:Application xmlns:mx="http://www.adobe.com/2006/mxml"
   layout="vertical"
  backgroundGradientAlphas="[1.0, 1.0]" xmlns:views="views.*"
  horizontalAlign="left" backgroundGradientColors="[#908D8D, #FFFFFF]">
  <mx:Script>
   <![CDATA[
     import mx.controls.Alert;
     import mx.core.BitmapAsset;
     import mx.core.UIComponent;
     import mx.core.DragSource;
     import mx.managers.DragManager;
     import mx.events.DragEvent;
     import utilities.FormatUtilities;
     [Embed(source="assets/book.png")]
     [Bindable]
     private var bookImage:Class;
     private var bookProxy:BitmapAsset = BitmapAsset(new bookImage());
     private function initiateDrag(event:MouseEvent):void
     {
       var source:DragSource = new DragSource();
       var itemData:Object = event.currentTarget.getRepeaterItem();
       source.addData(event.target.getRepeaterItem(),"bookItem");
       DragManager.doDrag(event.target as UIComponent, source, event,
         bookProxy, 20, 20, 1);
     }
     private function dragEnterHandler(event:DragEvent):void
     {
       if (event.dragSource.hasFormat("bookItem"))
       {
         DragManager.acceptDragDrop(event.target as UIComponent);
       }
     }
     private function dragDropHandler(event:DragEvent):void
     {
```

continued

LISTING 14.13   (continued)

```
                var dragData:Object =
    event.dragSource.dataForFormat("bookItem");
                var initiator:UIComponent = event.dragInitiator as UIComponent;
                var bookTitle:String = initiator.getRepeaterItem().title;
                acBooks.removeItemAt(initiator.repeaterIndex);
                Alert.show("Book deleted: " + bookTitle, "Deleted!");
            }
        ]]>
    </mx:Script>
    <mx:Model id="bookModel" source="model/books.xml"/>
    <mx:ArrayCollection id="acBooks" source="{bookModel.book}"/>
    <mx:Style source="assets/styles.css"/>
    <views:Header id="header"/>
    <mx:HBox verticalAlign="top">

        <mx:Tile width="{header.width}">
            <mx:Repeater id="bookRepeater" dataProvider="{acBooks}"
                recycleChildren="true">
                <mx:HBox width="250">
                    <mx:Image source="{bookImage}"
    mouseDown="initiateDrag(event)"/>
                    <mx:Text text="{bookRepeater.currentItem.title}"
                        fontSize="10" fontWeight="bold" width="100%"
                        selectable="false"/>
                </mx:HBox>
            </mx:Repeater>
        </mx:Tile>
        <mx:Image source="@Embed('assets/garbagecan.png')"
            dragEnter="dragEnterHandler(event)"
            dragDrop="dragDropHandler(event)"/>
    </mx:HBox>
</mx:Application>
```

ON the WEB The code in Listing 14.13 is available in the Web site files as `CustomDragAndDrop.mxml` in the `chapter14` project.

Figure 14.10 shows the resulting application, with an embedded book graphic used both as a data icon and as a drag proxy image. When the user drags a book to the trash can, the data is deleted from the application.

FIGURE 14.10

A custom drag-and-drop operation

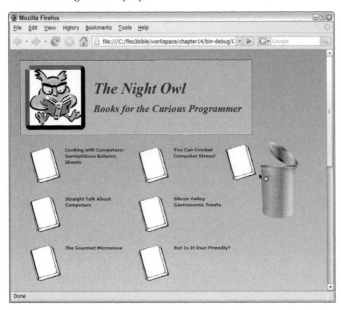

Custom drag-and-drop operations give you the freedom to react to user gestures in many ways. These are some other strategies you can use in your applications:

- You can explicitly handle `dragDrop` events on list-based controls instead of relying on the automatic list control behaviors. For example, you may react to the `dragDrop` event by calling a Web service and manipulating server-side data.

- In the case where an item can be dragged from multiple sources, you can detect the originator of a drag–and-drop operation like this:

```
if (Object(event.dragInitiator).id == "bookList")
{
   ... doWhatever() ...
}
```

- You can find out where the item is being dropped in a list-based control with `this.bookList.calculateDropIndex(event)` and passing the `DragEvent` object.

Summary

In this chapter, I described how to implement animation and drag-and-drop interfaces in Flex applications. You learned the following:

- An effect is an ActionScript class that defines changes in a visual component's position, visibility, scaling, and other properties over a period of time.
- The framework has many pre-built effect classes that control animation.
- Each effect class has a set of properties you can set to control animation.
- A behavior is a combination of a trigger and an effect.
- You can play an effect with explicit ActionScript statements or by associating it with a trigger.
- A trigger has an associated event, but it plays an effect instead of executing arbitrary ActionScript.
- You can define triggers in both MXML and ActionScript.
- Drag-and-drop operations can be used to create an intuitive interface for managing data in a Flex application.
- List-based controls implement drag-and-drop with the `dragEnabled` and `dropEnabled` properties.
- You can create highly customized drag-and-drop interfaces with the `DragManager` and `DragSource` classes.

Chapter 15

Managing View States

Flex applications define view states as particular presentations of a visual component. In each moment of the user's interactions with the application, each visual component presents itself in a particular form known as its current view state. Flex allows you to define as many different view states as you like for the `Application` and for each of its custom MXML components using declarative code, and then it lets you switch easily between states by setting the `Application` or custom component's `currentState` property.

View state management in Flex is designed primarily for application scenarios where the `Application` or component uses a significant portion of its33presentation in multiple situations and makes incremental changes to its presentation for each new situation. This sort of incremental change is different from application navigation, where the user moves between multiple different layers, or views, that don't share content with each other.

You can declare view states in MXML or ActionScript, although the MXML approach is used much more often. The ActionScript code to declare view states is long and verbose. I'll describe it later in this chapter so you have the syntax available, but I strongly recommend using MXML for view state management unless you have a very strong reason to work programmatically.

When you switch view states at runtime, you can make the change abruptly, or through the use of *transitions,* you can choreograph the change with Flex-based effects. (As described in Chapter 14, effects implement Flash-based animation to make objects appear, disappear, move, or change size using pre-defined animations.) A transition is a class that allows you to easily associate effects with view state changes.

In this chapter, I describe how to create and use view states in Flex applications and how to use transitions and effects to animate the changes.

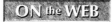 To use the sample code for this chapter, import the `chapter15.zip` Flex project archive from the Web site files into your Flex Builder workspace.

Understanding View States

View states are used to define incremental changes to an existing view. For example, a login form that initially requests a user name and password can, with the addition of a few more controls, also be used as a registration form. The initial presentation of the form is referred to as the component's *base state*. A set of incremental changes to the component is referred to as a *named state*.

View states are usually declared with MXML code. You can either code a view state manually or, using Flex Builder's Design view, generate the required code based on changes you make to a component at design time.

View states are identified by creating new `State` objects and setting their `name` property, which is a `String` value that you assign in MXML or ActionScript code. Each visual component that's displayed on the screen in a Flex application has a *base* view state. The base state is defined by all the object's current property and style settings, event handlers, and in the case of containers, nested child components in its display list, and it's represented by the main MXML in the document. The name of the base state is initially a blank String; all custom states must have a non-blank string as their `name`.

Examples of things you can change in a view state include:

- Adding and removing nested child objects in a container
- Setting values of properties and styles
- Changing handlers for events of the component or, in the case of a container, its nested child components

Each of these actions is known as an *override:* That is, you're overriding the state on which the new state is based.

NOTE When creating states in MXML, you can only define view states for an `Application` or a separate MXML component. You can't define view states for nested child components within an Application or component source code file. So to get started with view states, you first decide whether the view state will be defined at the application level or within a custom component. However, after you have made that choice, the process of declaring and controlling the view state is the same.

Defining View States in Design View

Flex Builder has a States view that shows up by default only when the Flex Development perspective is active and the current application or component is being edited in Design view. As shown in Figure 15.1, the States view has a toolbar that includes these buttons:

- New State
- Edit State Properties
- Delete State

Flex Builder's States view

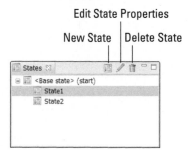

Creating a new state

You can create a new view state by clicking the New State button on the toolbar, or by right-clicking in the States view and selecting New State from the context menu. The New State dialog box, shown in Figure 15.2, asks for these properties:

- **Name:** A non-blank `String` value is required.
- **Based on:** This asks which state the new view state is based on. The default is a blank string, meaning the `Application` or component's base state.
- **Set as start state:** This check box allows you to assign the new state as the Application or component's starting state upon instantiation.

In the following example, an application contains a data entry form that asks the user for flight departure and return dates. In the form's default state, all information is requested. In an alternative state, controls are removed from the form for a one-way itinerary.

FIGURE 15.2

The New State dialog box in Design view

Try these steps to add a new state to an existing application and then add an incremental view state:

1. Open `ViewStatesDemo.mxml` from the `chapter15` project's `src` folder.

2. Run the application in a browser.

    As shown in Figure 15.3, the application displays a flight information data entry form, similar to those seen on popular travel booking Web sites. In the application's base state, it displays form controls for arrival and departure dates, but it doesn't make any changes if the user clicks the One Way radio button.

3. Return to Flex Builder. If the application currently is displayed in Source view, switch to Design view.

4. Locate the States view in the upper-right corner of Flex Builder.

    Notice that the States view displays a single state labeled `<Base state> (start)`.

FIGURE 15.3

The application's base state

5. As shown in Figure 15.4, right-click anywhere in the States view and select New State.

FIGURE 15.4

Creating a new view state from the States view's context menu

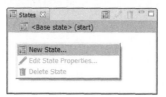

6. In the New State dialog box, set the new state's name to oneway and click OK.

 As with ActionScript identifiers, view state names are case-sensitive. Whatever you name the state in this step is how you'll refer to it in your ActionScript code.

As shown in Figure 15.5, the States view now displays the new view state and indicates with a selection bar which view state is currently active.

FIGURE 15.5

The States view with the new state set as currently active

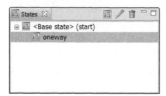

Defining a view state's overrides

To define a view state's override actions in Design view, first select the appropriate view state from the States view or the State selector. Then make changes to the Application or component with these design time actions:

- Add components to the state by dragging from the Components view.
- Remove components by selecting and deleting them.
- Change components' properties and styles through the Flex Properties view.
- Change event handlers through the Flex Properties view.

You can select the current view state either from the States view or, as shown in Figure 15.6, from the view state selection menu in the Design view editor toolbar.

FIGURE 15.6

The State selector in the Design view editor

> **TIP**
>
> If the Design view editor's width isn't sufficient to display all its toolbar icons, Flex Builder hides the States selector to adjust. If you don't see the States selector, try double-clicking the editor tab to display it in full-screen mode; the States selector should then appear.

> **TIP**
>
> When working with an application or component whose width or height exceeds the available dimensions of the Design view editor, you may not see scrollbars appear. Remember that you can use the Zoom and Pan tools to move around the design surface. Or, to generate design-time scrollbars, use the Design Area selector (in the Design view editor toolbar) to change from the default setting of Fit to Window to a specific size such as 1024 x 768.

Follow these steps to make incremental changes to the application:

1. Reopen ViewStatesDemo.mxml in Flex Builder's Design view.

2. Using either the States view or the State selector, set the current view state to oneway.

3. Select the Label control with the text value of Return, and press Delete to remove the control from the view state.

4. Select the DateField control in the same area of the application, and delete it as well.

5. To test the view states in Design view, set the Base state as currently active.

   You should see that the two controls you deleted are displayed in their original locations.

6. Switch back again to the oneway state.

   You should see that the two controls are removed from the current display.

Figure 15.7 shows the application's two view states in Design view, with the State selector controlling which state is currently active.

The application in its two states

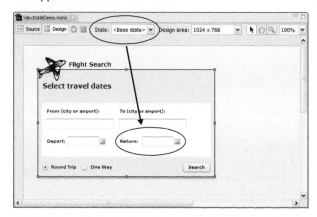

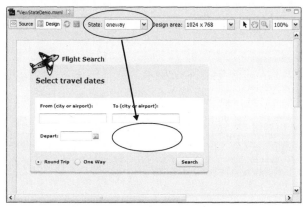

Listing 15.1 shows the application in its final state.

The view states application

```
<?xml version="1.0" encoding="utf-8"?>
<mx:Application xmlns:mx="http://www.adobe.com/2006/mxml"
  backgroundColor="#eeeeee" layout="absolute">
  <mx:states>
    <mx:State name="oneway">
      <mx:RemoveChild target="{label1}"/>
      <mx:RemoveChild target="{departDate}"/>
```

continued

LISTING 15.1   (continued)

```
      </mx:State>
  </mx:states>
  <mx:Style>
    Label, RadioButton { font-weight:bold }
    .windowStyles { font-size:16; }
  </mx:Style>
  <mx:Label text="Flight Search" fontSize="14"
    fontWeight="bold" x="106" y="33"/>
  <mx:Panel title="Select travel dates"
    layout="absolute" width="421" height="246" id="panel1" x="34" y="55"
    headerHeight="75" borderAlpha="1" >
    <mx:Label x="10" y="10" text="From (city or airport):"/>
    <mx:Label x="183" y="10" text="To (city or airport):"/>
    <mx:DateField x="61" y="77" id="returnDate"/>
    <mx:TextInput x="10" y="36" id="departInput"/>
    <mx:Label x="10" y="79" text="Depart:"/>
    <mx:TextInput x="183" y="36" id="returnInput"/>
    <mx:Label x="183" y="79" text="Return:" id="label1"/>
    <mx:DateField x="239" y="77" id="departDate"/>
    <mx:ControlBar>
      <mx:RadioButtonGroup id="typeGroup"/>
      <mx:RadioButton label="Round Trip" selected="true"
        click="currentState=''"/>
      <mx:RadioButton label="One Way" click="currentState='oneway'"/>
      <mx:Spacer width="100%"/>
      <mx:Button label="Search"/>
    </mx:ControlBar>
  </mx:Panel>
  <mx:Image x="31" y="24" source="assets/airplane.png"/>
</mx:Application>
```

ON the WEB   The code in Listing 15.1 is available in the Web site files as `ViewStatesComplete.mxml` in the `chapter15` project.

Switching View States at Runtime

All visual components support the `currentState` property to allow switching from one view state to another at runtime. The base state is always represented by an empty String or null value. The value of `currentState` is a simple `String`, so this code switches the current `Application` or component's state to oneway:

```
this.currentState = "oneway";
```

To return to the base state, set `currentState` to a blank string or `null`:

```
this.currentState = null;
```

Try the following steps with the airfare search application described in the preceding section:

1. Reopen `ViewStatesDemo.mxml` in Flex Builder, and switch to Source view.

2. Locate these `RadioButton` control declarations:

```
<mx:RadioButton label="Round Trip" selected="true"/>
<mx:RadioButton label="One Way"/>
```

3. Add a click event handler to the `RadioButton` control labeled `One Way` that changes the `currentState` to oneway:

```
<mx:RadioButton label="One Way" click="currentState='oneway'"/>
```

4. Add a click event handler to the `RadioButton` control labeled `Round Trip` that changes the `currentState` to a blank string (presenting the Base state):

```
<mx:RadioButton label="Round Trip" selected="true"
  click="currentState=null"/>
```

5. Run the application, and click the `RadioButton` controls to switch between view states.

You should see that the two controls appear and disappear as you click the `RadioButton` controls to switch view states.

You can also control view states with bindings. Instead of explicit ActionScript statements, set the Application or component's `currentState` property using a binding expression that gets its current value from a visual control or other data source.

In the following code, two `RadioButton` controls are grouped together with a `RadioButtonGroup`. Each `RadioButton` has its `value` set to an explicit state name or a blank string (the Base state):

```
<mx:RadioButtonGroup id="typeGroup"/>
<mx:RadioButton groupName="typeGroup"
  label="Round Trip" value="" selected="true"/>
<mx:RadioButton groupName="typeGroup"
  label="One Way" value="oneway"/>
```

In the `<mx:Application>` start tag, the `currentState` is set with a binding expression that executes each time the user clicks one of the `RadioButton` controls:

```
<mx:Application xmlns:mx="http://www.adobe.com/2006/mxml"
  currentState="{typeGroup.selectedValue}">
```

The application is functionally identical to the version using explicit ActionScript statements, but updates its current state based on the binding expression's evaluated result.

Declaring View States in MXML

A view state is represented by the <mx:State> tag set and is always assigned a name:

```
<mx:State name="myNewState">
... state declaration ...
</mx:State>
```

To declare one or more view states in an Application or custom component, wrap the <mx:State> declaration tags within <mx:states> tags:

```
<mx:Application xmlns:mx="http://www.adobe.com/2006/mxml">
<mx:states>
    <mx:State name="myFirstState">
    ... state declaration ...
    </mx:State>
    <mx:State name="mySecondState">
    ... state declaration ...
    </mx:State>
    ... additional states declared here ...
  </mx:states>
</mx:Application>
```

The <mx:states> element must always be declared as a child element of the Application or component root; you cannot nest state declarations within other child MXML tag sets unless they are in an <mx:Component> tag set (used with custom item renderers and editors, which are described in Chapters 17 and 18).

> **TIP**   Technically speaking, it doesn't matter whether the <mx:states> tag set is at the top, bottom, or middle of the MXML code, as long as it's a direct child of the MXML file's root element; however, the best practice is typically to declare child elements that represent component properties at the top of the code.

Within each <mx:State> declaration, you can include any number of state operations. In the following sections, I describe the use of each MXML tag that can be included in an <mx:State> tag set:

- <mx:AddChild/>
- <mx:RemoveChild/>
- <mx:SetEventHandler/>
- <mx:SetProperty/>
- <mx:SetStyle/>

Adding components

The <mx:AddChild> element adds a single visual component to a view state. The visual component can be a container that in turn contains other visual components, but only a single element can be directly nested within the <mx:AddChild> tag set.

The <mx:AddChild> tag has these attributes:

- relativeTo: This attribute is a reference to a container or control that's used as an anchor to determine placement of a component in the current application or custom component's display list.

- position: This attribute is a rule used in placing the added component. Possible values include before, after, firstChild, and lastChild. All four rules can be used relative to any component; firstChild and lastChild can be used only relative to a container. The default value is lastChild.

- target: This attribute is a reference to an existing object in memory. You can use this attribute instead of nesting a declaration of a new object, allowing you to refer to the object's methods and properties but wait to add it to the current display until the state changes.

This declaration adds a new LinkButton as the last child of a ControlBar with an id of myControlBar:

```
<mx:AddChild relativeTo="{controlbar1}" position="lastChild">
    <mx:LinkButton label="Log In" click="currentState=''"/>
</mx:AddChild>
```

Although you can directly nest only a single object within an <mx:AddChild> element, that object can contain other objects. This declaration adds a FormItem container that in turn nests a TextInput control:

```
<mx:AddChild relativeTo="{form1}" position="lastChild">
    <mx:FormItem label="Enter password again:">
      <mx:TextInput id="passwordInput2"/>
    </mx:FormItem>
</mx:AddChild>
```

You can include as many <mx:AddChild> elements in an <mx:State> tag set as you need to completely define the new view state.

Controlling the creation policy

When you declare an object within the <mx:AddChild> element, the object isn't instantiated immediately upon application startup. Instead, instantiation is deferred until the first time the view state is made active. This process is identical to how a navigator container uses deferred instantiation to improve client performance with multiple visual layers, and the logic is the same as well. If a user never visits a particular view state, the state's added components won't ever be needed, so the framework saves on memory and resources by waiting to see whether the component should be instantiated.

As with a navigator container, the AddChild class supports the creationPolicy property with a default value of auto. You can force instantiation of an object upon creation of the component that "owns" the view states by setting the <mx:AddChild> element's creationPolicy to all. In this example, the FormItem and its contents are instantiated immediately; this ensures that the TextInput control isn't left in a null state, which might cause data collection problems:

```
<mx:AddChild relativeTo="{form1}" position="lastChild"
  creationPolicy="all">
  <mx:FormItem label="Enter password again:">
    <mx:TextInput id="passwordInput2"/>
  </mx:FormItem>
</mx:AddChild>
```

CROSS-REF   For a more complete discussion of deferred instantiation and the `creationPolicy` property, see the section on the `ViewStack` container in Chapter 12.

State management

The state of a control when it appears and disappears during a state change isn't affected. For example, the `TextInput` control above is visible in an incremental state and isn't visible in the Base state. But although invisible, its current state (such as the value the user has typed) isn't disturbed. This is because the state management framework controls visibility by adding and removing the object from its container's display list, and not by creating or destroying it in memory. Once a control has been instantiated as part of a change to a named state, it stays in memory unless you explicitly remove it by setting it to `null` or you reset it by calling its constructor.

Removing components

The `<mx:RemoveChild>` element removes a component instance from an incremental view state. This tag is much simpler than the `<mx:AddChild>` and has fewer options.

To apply a `RemoveChild` command, assign the target object a unique `id`. Then declare the `<mx:RemoveChild>` element within the `<mx:State>` tag set, and assign the `target` property to the object you want to remove with a binding expression:

```
<mx:RemoveChild target="{objectToRemove}"/>
```

This tag has no other options and is applied only to a single object. If the object you remove is a container with nested objects, all those objects are removed as well.

As described previously, when you remove an object in a view state, the object stays in memory, but it is removed from its container's display list.

Overriding properties and styles

You override properties and styles in a view state with the `<mx:SetProperty>` and `<mx:SetStyle>` elements. Each of these elements supports these properties:

- `target`: A reference to the object whose property is being changed
- `name`: The name of the property or style to override as a String
- `value`: The new value of the property or style being changed

This declaration changes the text property of a `Label` control to a new value:

```
<mx:SetProperty target="{myLabel}" name="text"
  value="New Text Value"/>
```

The same sort of syntax is used to change styles:

```
<mx:SetStyle target="{myLabel}" name="fontWeight"
  value="bold"/>
```

> **CAUTION** You must use the correct tag to change properties or styles. If you try to use `<mx:SetStyle>` on a property, the code is ignored. If you try to use `<mx:SetProperty>` on a style, you get a runtime error when the view state management framework tries to set a property that doesn't exist. This is different from Flex 2, where properties and styles were both affected by the `<mx:SetProperty>` tag.

Overriding event handlers

You override event handlers with the `<mx:SetEventHandler>` tag. This tag has these properties:

- `target`: A reference to the object whose event handler is being changed
- `name`: The name of the event you want to change
- `handler`: ActionScript code you want to execute when the event is dispatched by the target object

For example, in an application where the view state management is being handled in reaction to clicks to a button, the button's initial code might be:

```
<mx:LinkButton id="stateButton"  label="Register as new user"
  click="currentState='register'"/>
```

This `<mx:SetEventHandler>` declaration causes the `stateButton` control's `click` event handler to switch back to the application's base state:

```
<mx:SetEventHandler target="{stateButton}"
  name="click" handler="currentState=''"/>
```

The application in Listing 15.2 presents a login data entry form wrapped in a `Panel` container.

LISTING 15.2

An application prior to adding view states

```
<?xml version="1.0" encoding="utf-8"?>
<mx:Application xmlns:mx="http://www.adobe.com/2006/mxml"
  layout="vertical" backgroundColor="#eeeeee">
  <mx:Panel title="Log In Form" id="panel1">
```

continued

LISTING 15.2   (continued)

```
        <mx:Form id="form1">
          <mx:FormItem label="User Name:">
            <mx:TextInput id="userNameInput"/>
          </mx:FormItem>
          <mx:FormItem label="Password:">
            <mx:TextInput id="passwordInput"/>
          </mx:FormItem>
        </mx:Form>
        <mx:ControlBar id="controlbar1">
          <mx:Button label="Log In"/>
          <mx:Spacer width="100%"/>
          <mx:LinkButton label="Register as new user" id="stateButton"/>
        </mx:ControlBar>
      </mx:Panel>
    </mx:Application>
```

As shown in Figure 15.8, the application's Form contains two TextInput controls wrapped in FormItem containers.

FIGURE 15.8

A data entry form before adding view states

The following code adds view state declarations to the application using <mx:AddChild>, <mx:SetProperty>, and <mx:SetEventHandler> override elements:

```
    <mx:states>
      <mx:State name="register">
        <mx:AddChild relativeTo="{form1}" position="lastChild">
```

```
        <mx:FormItem label="Enter password again:">
          <mx:TextInput id="passwordInput2"/>
        </mx:FormItem>
      </mx:AddChild>
      <mx:SetProperty target="{stateButton}" name="label"
        value="Return to login"/>
      <mx:SetEventHandler target="{stateButton}" name="click"
        handler="currentState=''"/>
      <mx:SetProperty target="{panel1}" name="title"
        value="Registration Form"/>
      <mx:SetProperty target="{button1}" name="label"
        value="Register"/>   </mx:State>
    </mx:states>
```

Figure 15.9 shows the application running in the new register state.

FIGURE 15.9

The application with the new view state active

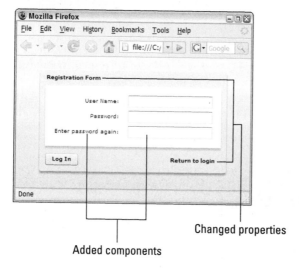

Changed properties

Added components

Listing 15.3 shows the completed application with all view state declarations and changes to the currentState property.

LISTING 15.3

Another application with complete view state declarations

```xml
<?xml version="1.0" encoding="utf-8"?>
<mx:Application xmlns:mx="http://www.adobe.com/2006/mxml"
  layout="vertical"
  backgroundColor="#eeeeee">
  <mx:states>
    <mx:State name="register">
      <mx:AddChild relativeTo="{form1}" position="lastChild">
        <mx:FormItem label="Enter password again:">
          <mx:TextInput id="passwordInput2"/>
        </mx:FormItem>
      </mx:AddChild>
      <mx:SetProperty target="{stateButton}" name="label"
        value="Return to login"/>
      <mx:SetEventHandler target="{stateButton}" name="click"
        handler="currentState=''"/>
      <mx:SetProperty target="{panel1}" name="title"
        value="Registration Form"/>
      <mx:SetProperty target="{button1}" name="label" value="Register"/>
    </mx:State>
  </mx:states>
  <mx:Panel title="Log In Form" id="panel1">
    <mx:Form id="form1">
      <mx:FormItem label="User Name:">
        <mx:TextInput id="userNameInput"/>
      </mx:FormItem>
      <mx:FormItem label="Password:">
        <mx:TextInput id="passwordInput"/>
      </mx:FormItem>
    </mx:Form>
    <mx:ControlBar id="controlbar1">
      <mx:Button label="Log In" id="button1"/>
      <mx:Spacer width="100%"/>
      <mx:LinkButton label="Register as new user" id="stateButton"
        click="currentState='register'" />
    </mx:ControlBar>
  </mx:Panel>
</mx:Application>
```

ON the WEB The code in Listing 15.3 is available in the Web site files as `UsingOverrides.mxml` in the `chapter15` project.

Declaring View States with ActionScript

You can manage view states in ActionScript as well as MXML using the same built-in classes. This approach isn't used as commonly as the MXML-based declarations, but it's good to know how to do it if your application needs to build view states dynamically.

> **TIP**
>
> If you're inclined to use ActionScript instead of MXML to declare view states, consider instead managing the current display list directly with methods such as `addChild()` and `removeChild()`.

Follow these steps to build a view state in ActionScript:

1. Import all classes in the `mx.states` package using a wildcard import statement:

   ```
   import mx.states.*;
   ```

2. For each override in the new state, create an instance of the appropriate override ActionScript class. Override classes include `AddChild`, `RemoveChild`, `SetProperty`, `SetStyle`, and `SetEventHandler`.

3. For each override object, set its required attributes exactly as in MXML. You can set override objects upon instantiation using the class constructor method; for example, this code creates a `SetProperty` object and passes all required properties:

   ```
   var setLabelProp:SetProperty =
     new SetProperty(myLabel, "label", "New Value");
   ```

   The first argument in the constructor method call is a reference to the object being modified, the second is the name of the property being overridden, and the last is its new value.

4. Create an instance of the `State` class with its no-arguments constructor, and set its name property:

   ```
   var newState:State = new State();
   newState.name="register";
   ```

5. Add each override object to the new `State` object's `overrides` array:

   ```
   newState.overrides.push(setLabelProp);
   ```

6. Add the new `State` object to the current application or component's `states` array:

   ```
   this.states.push(newState);
   ```

Setting override properties

When you create a new override object, you can set its properties either in the constructor method call (as shown in the preceding example) or after object construction using dot syntax. This code creates the same `SetProperty` object as in the preceding example, but it sets each of the properties explicitly after object construction:

```
var setLabelProp:SetProperty = new SetProperty();
setLabelProp.target = myLabel;
setLabelProp.name = myLabel;
setLabelProp.value = "New Value";
newState.overrides.push(setLabelProp);
```

Overriding event handlers

You can't assign arbitrary event handler code in ActionScript. Just as when setting event listeners with the addEventListener() method, you first create a custom event handler function that expects an event object argument of the appropriate type:

```
private function newClickHandler(event:Event):void
{
    this.currentState="";
}
```

Then to use the custom event handler, create an instance of the SetEventHandler class. Assign its target to the object that will dispatch the event and its name to the name of the event you're listening for. Then set the object's eventHandler property to the custom event handler function by its name, and add it to the new State object's overrides array:

```
var newEvHandler:SetEventHandler = new SetEventHandler();
newEvHandler.target = registerButton;
newEvHandler.name = "click";
newEvHandler.handlerFunction = newClickHandler;
newState.overrides.push(newEvHandler);
```

At runtime, the new event handler is used instead of the object's original event handler.

CAUTION The SetEventHandler class's handler property is designed only for use in MXML code. You cannot use it in ActionScript to create an event handler containing arbitrary code.

TIP In some instances, as with more complex states, it might be worthwhile to create custom components as subclasses of the State class and then add them as needed into the states array.

The application in Listing 15.4 declares a view state with ActionScript code upon application startup and then exercises the new view state as a response to clicks on the form's LinkButton controls.

LISTING 15.4

An application with a programmatically declared view state

```
<?xml version="1.0" encoding="utf-8"?>
<mx:Application xmlns:mx="http://www.adobe.com/2006/mxml"
    layout="vertical"
  backgroundColor="#eeeeee" creationComplete="initApp()">
  <mx:Script>
    <![CDATA[
      import mx.states.*;
      private function initApp():void
      {
        var newState:State = new State();
        newState.name="register";
```

```
            newState.overrides.push(
              new SetProperty(panel1, "title", "Registration Form"));
            newState.overrides.push(
              new SetProperty(button1, "label", "Register"));
            newState.overrides.push(
              new SetProperty(registerButton, "label", "Return to Log In"));

            //Add FormItem container with TextItem control
            var myFormItem:FormItem = new FormItem();
            myFormItem.label = "Enter password again:";
            var passwordInput2:TextInput = new TextInput();
            myFormItem.addChild(passwordInput2);
            var addFormItem:AddChild =
              new AddChild(form1, myFormItem, "lastChild");
            newState.overrides.push(addFormItem);

            //Override the LinkButton's event handler
            var newEvHandler:SetEventHandler = new SetEventHandler();
            newEvHandler.target = registerButton;
            newEvHandler.name = "click";
            newEvHandler.handlerFunction = newClickHandler;
            newState.overrides.push(newEvHandler);

            //Add the new state
            this.states.push(newState);
          }
          private function newClickHandler(event:Event):void
          {
            this.currentState="";
          }
      ]]>
    </mx:Script>
    <mx:Panel title="Log In Form" id="panel1">
      <mx:Form id="form1">
        <mx:FormItem label="User Name:">
          <mx:TextInput id="userNameInput"/>
        </mx:FormItem>
        <mx:FormItem label="Password:">
          <mx:TextInput id="passwordInput"/>
        </mx:FormItem>
      </mx:Form>
      <mx:ControlBar id="controlbar1">
        <mx:Button label="Log In" id="button1"/>
        <mx:Spacer width="100%"/>
        <mx:LinkButton id="registerButton"
          label="Register as new user"
          click="currentState='register'"/>
      </mx:ControlBar>
    </mx:Panel>
  </mx:Application>
```

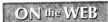 The code in Listing 15.4 is available in the Web site files as `OverridesWith`
`ActionScript.mxml` in the `chapter15` project.

Managing View States in Components

You can declare a view state inside a custom component using either MXML or ActionScript. When using MXML, the rules are the same as for an Application: You can only apply the view state to the entire component, not to its nested child objects.

You can then control that component's `currentState` either internally or from the component instance parent object. Remember that code within a custom component uses `this` to refer to the current instance of the component. The following code switches the `currentState` of the component instance to a new state:

```
this.currentState = 'myNewState';
```

Listing 15.5 defines a custom `Label` component that has a view state named `rollOverState`. When the component's `rollOver` event is dispatched, it changes to the new state; when the `rollOut` event occurs, it returns to its base state. The view state contains `<mx:SetStyle>` tags that override the component's `color` and `textDecoration` styles.

LISTING 15.5

A custom component with a view state

```
<?xml version="1.0" encoding="utf-8"?>
<mx:Label xmlns:mx="http://www.adobe.com/2006/mxml"
  rollOver="event.target.currentState='rollover'"
  rollOut="event.target.currentState=''"
  text="Rollover Label">
    <mx:states>
      <mx:State name="rollover">
        <mx:SetStyle name="color" value="#0000FF"/>
        <mx:SetStyle name="textDecoration" value="underline"/>
      </mx:State>
    </mx:states>
</mx:Label>
```

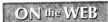 The code in Listing 15.5 is available in the Web site files as `components/RollOver`
`Label.mxml` in the `chapter15` project.

Using the custom component is a simple matter of declaring an instance and setting any standard Label properties or styles. The application in Listing 15.6 uses MXML to declare an instance of the component.

LISTING 15.6

Using a custom component with view states

```
<?xml version="1.0" encoding="utf-8"?>
<mx:Application xmlns:mx="http://www.adobe.com/2006/mxml"
   layout="vertical"
  backgroundColor="#eeeeee" xmlns:components="components.*">
  <components:RollOverLabel text="Test Rollover Label" fontSize="12"/>
</mx:Application>
```

ON the WEB The code in Listing 15.6 is available in the Web site files as `TestRollover.mxml` in the `chapter15` project.

Using Transitions

Transitions are a way of associating animations, implemented as Flex effects, with runtime changes from one view state to another. By default, when you switch to a view state that changes the visibility, size, or position of objects on the screen, the change is visually abrupt. A transition allows you to slow down and choreograph the change so that it's easier and more fun to watch.

As with view states, transitions are typically declared using MXML code. Each visual component has a `transitions` property. The `transitions` property is an `Array` containing multiple instances of the Transition class. To declare transitions in MXML, you create an `<mx:transitions>` tag set as a direct child of the application's or component's root element, often right after the `<mx:states>` declaration. Then nest as many `<mx:Transition>` tag sets with `<mx:transitions>` as you need:

```
<mx:Application>
  <mx:states>
    ...declare <mx:State> elements here...
  </mx:states>
  <mx:transitions>
    ...declare <mx:Transition> elements here...
  </mx:transitions>
  ... declare base state here ...
</mx:Application>
```

Declaring a transition

Each transition is declared as an `<mx:Transition>` tag with these properties:

- `fromState`: The name of the starting state
- `toState`: The name of the ending state

Each of these properties can be set to either an explicit state name or a wildcard (*), the default for both properties, to indicate that the transition applies to all state changes.

You then specify which animation you want to play by nesting the appropriate effect class within the `<mx:Transition>` tag set. The effect should have its target or targets property set to indicate which objects should be animated.

This transition is applied by moving from a state named `state1` to a state named `state2`. It has the effect of applying a `Fade` effect to an object that's being added in the state:

```
<mx:transitions>
  <mx:Transition fromState="state1" toState="state2">
    <mx:Fade target="{addedObject}"/>
  </mx:Transition>
</mx:transitions>
```

Using Parallel and Sequence effects in transitions

You also can use `Parallel` or `Sequence` effects to introduce more complex animation. This transition causes a `Move` and a `Zoom` to play simultaneously, creating the visual effect of an object "exploding" from the top-left corner of the application into its final position:

```
<mx:Transition fromState="*" toState="detail">
  <mx:Parallel target="{detailImage}">
    <mx:Move xFrom="0" yFrom="0" xTo="300" yTo="50"/>
    <mx:Zoom zoomHeightFrom="0" zoomWidthFrom="0"
      zoomHeightTo="1" zoomWidthTo="1"/>
  </mx:Parallel>
</mx:Transition>
```

The application in Listing 15.7 uses a `Transition` to animate presentation of a detail image. The function that changes to the detail state first sets up certain conditions:

- It saves the current image filename to a bindable variable that's then used as the source for the detail image object.
- It sets the custom `Move` effect's `xFrom` and `yFrom` properties based on the location of the `click` event's `MouseEvent.stageX` and `MouseEvent.stageY` properties. As a result, the detail image explodes onto the stage from the coordinates of the `mouseDown` event.

> **TIP** Transitions sometimes don't work if the result defined in the transition effect doesn't exactly match the result defined in the ending view state. For example, if you apply a `Move` effect to move an object to a coordinate of 0, and the ending view state defines a different coordinate, the move may happen abruptly and the effect may be ignored.

LISTING 15.7

An application with a transition

```xml
<?xml version="1.0" encoding="utf-8"?>
<mx:Application xmlns:mx="http://www.adobe.com/2006/mxml"
   layout="absolute"
  backgroundColor="#eeeeee" mouseUp="currentState=''">
  <mx:states>
    <mx:State name="detail">
      <mx:AddChild position="lastChild">
        <mx:Image id="detailImage" x="300" y="50"
          source="assets/{currentImage}"/>
      </mx:AddChild>
    </mx:State>
  </mx:states>
  <mx:transitions>
    <mx:Transition fromState="*" toState="detail">
      <mx:Parallel target="{detailImage}">
        <mx:Move id="customMove" xFrom="0" yFrom="0" xTo="300"
 yTo="50"/>
        <mx:Zoom zoomHeightFrom="0" zoomWidthFrom="0"
          zoomHeightTo="1" zoomWidthTo="1"/>
      </mx:Parallel>
    </mx:Transition>
  </mx:transitions>

  <mx:Script>
    <![CDATA[
      [Bindable]
      private var currentImage:String;
      private function showDetail(event:MouseEvent):void
      {
        customMove.xFrom = event.stageX;
        customMove.yFrom = event.stageY;
        currentImage = event.currentTarget.getRepeaterItem();
        currentState = "detail";
      }
    ]]>
  </mx:Script>
  <mx:ArrayCollection id="acFlowers">
    <mx:String>flower1.jpg</mx:String>
    <mx:String>flower2.jpg</mx:String>
```

continued

LISTING 15.7 *(continued)*

```
      <mx:String>flower3.jpg</mx:String>
      <mx:String>flower4.jpg</mx:String>
   </mx:ArrayCollection>
   <mx:Tile x="50" y="50">
      <mx:Repeater id="flowerRepeater" dataProvider="{acFlowers}">
         <mx:Image width="100" height="75"
            source="assets/{flowerRepeater.currentItem}"
            mouseDown="showDetail(event)"/>
      </mx:Repeater>
   </mx:Tile>
</mx:Application>
```

ON the WEB The code in Listing 15.7 is available in the Web site files as `TransitionDemo.mxml` in the `chapter15` project.

Summary

In this chapter, I described how to use view states to manage different looks in a Flex application. You learned the following:

- A view state is defined as a particular presentation of a visual component.

- You can declare view states in MXML or ActionScript code.

- Flex Builder's Design view can help you generate view state code that uses MXML declarations.

- You control which state is active at runtime by changing the value of the application or component's `currentState` property.

- You can declare view states within a custom component.

- Transitions allow you to associate effects (programmatic animations) with changes from one view state to another.

- You declare transitions with MXML code.

- Each transition can be associated with a `toState` and a `fromState`.

- You can associate `Parallel` or `Sequence` effects with a transition for more complex visual effects.

Part III

Working with Data

Chapter 16

Modeling and Managing Data

lex applications are *stateful;* that is, they have the ability to remember data persistently for the duration of the user's session in a way that classic Web applications usually don't. One of the most common tasks you must accomplish as an application developer is to create a framework for storing data that the application can use at runtime.

The content of an application's data can come from many sources: XML files, databases or other server-side resources, or remote functions wrapped by and exposed as SOAP-style or REST-style Web services. Regardless of how the data comes to an application, though, a Flex application stores the data in exactly the same way: as a data model.

In this chapter, I describe common techniques for modeling data in Flex applications. I start with creating single-object data models: ActionScript classes designed to hold one instance of a data entity at a time. (A data instance might represent a row in a database table or a single element in an XML file.) You can represent such data instances with the <mx:Model> tag, a generic data object, or more commonly you create your own custom ActionScript classes, known by the various design pattern names Value Object and Transfer Object.

In the second part of the chapter, I describe the use of data collections: ordered collections of data instances managed by the ArrayCollection class. I describe how and where to declare the ArrayCollection and then describe how to use this powerful class to filter, sort, bookmark, and traverse data in client application memory.

ON the WEB To use the sample code for this chapter, import the chapter16.zip Flex project archive from the Web site files into your Flex Builder workspace.

Creating a Data Model

A data model is a way of representing data (information) in a client application. It's a truism of database applications that you can't do much without knowing your data structure. Take an application that represents the personal information of your contact list. Whether you store this data in an e-mail client or a complex server-side database application such as SQL Server or mySQL, the software that manages the data has to know its structure.

In classic relational databases, data is stored in tables. Each table has columns that represent the bits of data that are created for each row in the table. A database table representing contact information might have any number of columns. Each column has a name and a data type. For example, a contacts table might have the data structure shown in Table 16.1.

TABLE 16.1

A Simple Database Table Structure

Column Name	Primary Key	Data Type	Length	Null OK
contactId	X	Integer		
firstName		String	50	
lastName		String	50	
dob		Date		X
address		String	50	x
city		String	20	x
zipCode		String	10	x
telephone		String	15	x

When data is returned to a Flex application in this structure, you need a way to store it. The goal is to create an object that can serve as a container for this data and can share this data structure to the best of the Flex framework's ability.

Figure 16.1 shows a UML diagram describing the structure of an object that would be able to hold this data.

You can create a data model to store the data in two ways: by using the `<mx:Model>` tag to declare a generic untyped data object and by creating a custom ActionScript class. Of these approaches, the custom ActionScript version is significantly more powerful and flexible. The `<mx:Model>` approach is fast and easy to code, and it might be used during early prototyping of an application, but an application that's built for durability and easy long-term maintenance generally requires custom ActionScript classes to represent data in Flex application memory.

FIGURE 16.1

A UML diagram describing a class with data structure

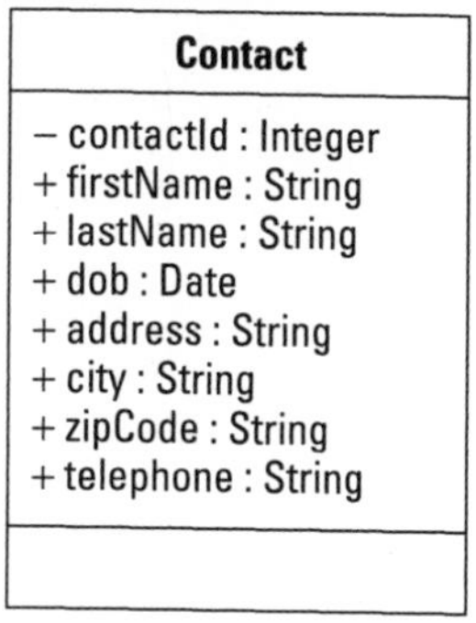

Contact
− contactId : Integer
+ firstName : String
+ lastName : String
+ dob : Date
+ address : String
+ city : String
+ zipCode : String
+ telephone : String

Using the <mx:Model> tag

The <mx:Model> tag compiles XML into a generic ActionScript Object. The data structure described in the UML diagram in Figure 16.1 could be implemented as a data object with this code:

```
<mx:Model id="myContact">
 <data>
  <contactId>1</contactId>
  <firstName>Joe</firstName>
  <lastName>Adams</lastName>
  <address>123 Main Street</address>
  <city>Anywhere</city>
  <state>WA</state>
  <zipCode>12345</zipCode>
  <dob>11/28/1959</dob>
  <telephone>555-123-4567</telephone>
 </data>
</mx:Model>
```

You also can fill Model properties dynamically from user interface components using binding expressions:

```
<mx:Model id="myContact">
 <data>
  <contactId>0</contactId>
  <firstName>{firstNameInput.text}</firstName>
  <lastName>{lastNameInput.text}</lastName>
  <dob>{myDataField.selectedDate}</dob>
  ... additional elements and bindings...
 </data>
</mx:Model>
```

At runtime, as the user interacts with form controls, the controls' values are passed to the Model object through the binding expressions.

> **CAUTION** The use of binding expressions to dynamically fill `Model` properties has an obvious benefit of creating and filling a data object declaratively, but this technique also has a drawback that might not be immediately apparent. When you fill a `Model` property from a binding expression, its initial value is `null`. If you don't explicitly set initial values with ActionScript statements, you can end up sending the data object to remote server functions such as Web services where `null` values can cause runtime errors. If you encounter this problem, an easy solution is to initialize the object's properties upon application startup in an initialization function:

```
myModel.firstName="";
myModel.last Name="";
```

On the other hand, setting default values is a built-in benefit of custom ActionScript classes used as value objects, described later in this chapter.

The application in Listing 16.1 declares a single data object using the `<mx:Model>` tag and then displays its values in `Label` controls with binding expressions.

LISTING 16.1

Declaring a data object with <mx:Model>

```xml
<?xml version="1.0" encoding="utf-8"?>
<mx:Application xmlns:mx="http://www.adobe.com/2006/mxml"
  backgroundColor="#eeeeee">

  <mx:Model id="myContact">
    <data>
      <contactId>1</contactId>
      <firstName>Joe</firstName>
      <lastName>Adams</lastName>
      <address>123 Main Street</address>
      <city>Anywhere</city>
      <state>WA</state>
      <zipCode>12345</zipCode>
      <dob>11/28/1959</dob>
      <telephone>555-123-4567</telephone>
    </data>
  </mx:Model>

  <mx:Label text="{myContact.firstName} {myContact.lastName}"/>
  <mx:Label text="{myContact.address}"/>
  <mx:Label text="{myContact.city}, {myContact.state}
  {myContact.zipCode}"/>
  <mx:Label text="{myContact.dob}"/>
  <mx:Label text="{myContact.telephone}"/>

</mx:Application>
```

ON the WEB The code in Listing 16.1 is available in the Web site files as `ModelDemo.mxml` in the `chapter16` project.

Benefits of <mx:Model>

The advantage of the `<mx:Model>` tag is its simplicity. It's very easy to declare a bit of hard-coded data with these benefits:

■ The object and all its properties are automatically bindable. You don't have to include the `[Bindable]` metadata tag, and you can refer to any of the object's properties with binding expressions, as in:

```
<mx:Label text="{myContact.firstName} {myContact.lastName}"/>
```

■ The `<mx:Model>` tag uses simple XML syntax to declare its property names.

After a data object has been declared with the `<mx:Model>` tag, you refer to its data using dot syntax. The object's `id`, assigned in the `<mx:Model>` start tag, actually refers to the model's root element if there is a sole root element. In the preceding example, this element is named `<data>`, but its name isn't important; you refer to the root by the model object's `id` and then to its named properties as child objects of the model:

```
myContact.firstName
```

Drawbacks of <mx:Model>

These drawbacks of the `<mx:Model>` tag prevent its being truly useful to model objects in production applications:

■ The properties are always `String` values; the `<mx:Model>` architecture doesn't give you any way to set specific data types.

■ You can declare only a single instance of an object. Unlike strongly typed ActionScript classes, which are designed to be instantiated as many times as necessary, if you want another data object you have to declare it explicitly.

■ Because `<mx:Model>` is a compiler tag that doesn't represent an ActionScript class, it has no methods or properties.

Importing data with <mx:Model>

The `<mx:Model>` tag does have one very useful capability: It can be used to embed data into an application at compile-time. This technique is useful only when two circumstances are true:

■ It should be a relatively small amount of data. Large amounts of embedded data result in an increase in the size of the compiled application. For applications that are deployed over the Web, embedding data results in a slower download and longer delay before the application starts for the first time. On the positive side, the data is instantly available to the application without having to be downloaded at runtime.

■ The data should be completely static. If any of the data under consideration might change during the lifetime of the application, you should load the data at runtime using the `HTTPService` component or another runtime loading mechanism.

To embed data with the `<mx:Model>` tag, first save it as an XML file. The names of the XML file's data elements can be anything you like; the only requirements are that the XML file be well-formed and have a single root element. The following XML structure is suitable for use with the `<mx:Model>` tag:

```
<?xml version="1.0" encoding="UTF-8"?>
<data>
  <book>
    <title_id>BU1032</title_id>
    <title>How to Program Good</title>
    <pub_id>1528</pub_id>
    <au_id>409-56-7008</au_id>
    <price>19.99</price>
    <notes>A guide to creating great software.</notes>
    <pubdate>2005-01-15</pubdate>
  </book>
  ... additional <book> elements ...
</data>
```

Assuming the preceding XML markup is saved in a text file named `books.xml` in the project source root's `data` subfolder, the code to import and embed the data looks like this:

```
<mx:Model id="bookData" source="data/books.xml"/>
```

As with hard-coded data, the `Model` element's `id` points to the XML structure's root element. From there, the data typing of each element depends on the number of elements with a particular name. If the preceding structure contains two or more `<book>` elements, the expression `bookData.book` returns an `Array`. If the XML structure's root element contains only a single child `<book>` element, the expression `bookData.book` instead returns an ActionScript Object.

> **TIP** To ensure that you always have an **Array** to work with, you can use the **ArrayUtil** `.toArray()` method wrapped around an expression that might return an Object due to the number of elements in the XML data structure. At application startup, declare a separate **Array** variable and fill it as shown here:

```
import mx.utils.ArrayUtil;
[Bindable]
private var bookArray:Array;
private function initApp():void
{
  bookArray = ArrayUtil.toArray(bookData.book);
}
```

Using Value Objects

A *value object*, also known variously as a *transfer object*, a *data transfer object*, and a *bean*, is a class designed to hold data for a single instance of a data entity. The design pattern is named Transfer Object in the world of Java Enterprise Edition (JEE) application server development, where it's implemented as a Java class.

WEB RESOURCE The Transfer Object design pattern is described in the J2EE design pattern catalog at `http://java.sun.com/blueprints/corej2eepatterns/Patterns/TransferObject.html`. In the most recent version on the Sun Web site, the graphics still refer to the design pattern as Value Object, its old name. Don't be confused; it's all the same pattern!

Value object classes have these advantages over the use of the `<mx:Model>` tag:

- Class properties can be strongly data typed. Each property is declared with standard variable declaration syntax and typically has a data type declared after the colon:

  ```
  public var myDateProperty:Date;
  ```

- Class properties can have default values. As when declaring a variable inside or outside a function, you can declare default values by appending the value after an = assignment operator. This code declares a `Date` property with the default set to the current date:

  ```
  public var myDateProperty:Date = new Date();
  ```

- When you integrate a Flex client application with an application server that supports Flash Remoting or the Data Management Service, client-side value object classes defined in ActionScript can be mapped to equivalent classes on the server (written in the server's native language, such as Java, ColdFusion, PHP, or C#). This allows you to pass data between the application tiers with minimal code in both tiers.

Using the New ActionScript Class wizard

You can use Flex Builder's ActionScript class wizard to create a simple ActionScript class. Follow these steps to create a new value object class to represent Book data:

1. Make sure you have the `chapter16` project open. Notice that the project's source root folder (src) contains a `valueObjects` subfolder.

2. Right-click the `valueObjects` folder, and select New ⇨ ActionScript Class.

3. As shown in Figure 16.2, set the class name as **Contact**.

4. Under Code generation options, leave the Generate constructor from superclass option selected.

5. Click Finish to create the new ActionScript class.

FIGURE 16.2

The New ActionScript Class wizard

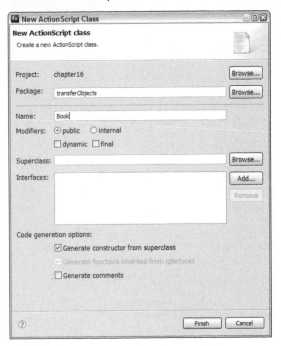

The completed ActionScript class is created in the file Contact.as in the valueObjects folder and should appear in the Source view editor as follows:

```
package valueObjects
{
  public class Contact
  {
    public function Contact()
    {
    }
  }
}
```

The class is ready to fill in with properties and other functionality.

Value object class syntax

Value objects are implemented in Flex as simple ActionScript classes, and their syntax is determined by basic ActionScript syntax requirements. In this section, I describe each part of a value object class, its purpose, and some best practice recommendations.

Declaring a package

A *package* is a collection of related classes. As in many other languages, including both Java and ColdFusion, packages are tied to the folder structure of an application's source code.

In ActionScript 3.0, each public ActionScript class must be wrapped inside a package declaration that's implemented as a code block. The package declaration tells the compiler where the class is stored, based on its subfolder within the project's source root folder or other locations in the project's build path.

As shown in Figure 16.3, the Contact value object class is stored in the `valueObjects` subfolder of the project's source root.

FIGURE 16.3
_____

The project structure, including the `valueObjects` subfolder

The package declaration looks like this:

```
package valueObjects
{
...public class declaration here...
}
```

> **CAUTION** When you generate a new class file with the New ActionScript Class wizard, the package declaration is created for you. However, if you move the class source code later, you're responsible for manually updating the package declaration in the class source code.

Declaring the public class

The class declaration for a public class is placed inside the package code block. Value object classes are always declared as public, so they can be used by the rest of the application. Also, value object classes typically don't explicitly extend any other class, as they usually don't have to inherit existing functionality.

The name of an ActionScript public class must match the name of the source code file in which it's defined. The name is case-sensitive, and by convention always has an initial upper-case character.

The public class declaration looks like this:

```
package valueObjects
{
  public class Contact
  {
    ...class members declared here...
  }
}
```

As noted in the preceding example, members of the class, including properties, functions, and constants, are declared inside the class declaration's code block.

> **TIP**   You can declare private classes in an ActionScript class source code file. These classes are available for use only by the public class in whose source code file the private class is declared. The private class doesn't actually have a `private` access modifier declaration, and it's declared outside the package declaration:

```
package valueObjects
{
  public class Book
  {
    public var page1:Page = new Page();
    public function Book()
    {
    }
  }
}
class Page
{
  public var pageNumber:int;
  public var text:String;
}
```

Declaring ActionScript class properties

ActionScript class properties are declared as variables, using this syntax:

```
[access modifier] var [property name]:[data type];
```

The access modifiers at the beginning of a property declaration should be one of these keywords:

- `public`: Properties that can be set and read by the rest of the application
- `private`: Properties that can only be set and read by instances of the class in which they're declared
- `protected`: Properties that can be set and read by the current class and by any of its subclasses
- `internal`: Properties that can be set and read by the current class and by any classes in the same package

The default access modifier is `internal`; if you leave the access modifier off a property declaration, the property is available only to the current class and any other classes in the same package. You'll also see a compiler warning indicating that you should include an explicit access modifier.

The name of a property is subject to naming rules for all ActionScript identifiers: It can include alpha, numeric, and underscore characters, and it must start with an alpha character or an underscore. The following naming conventions are considered to be best practices by most developers:

- The initial character in a property name should always be lowercase.
- Private properties have an initial underscore (_) character.

Neither of these conventions is a technical requirement, but by following them you create code that makes sense to other developers.

To add public properties representing the data structure in Table 16.1, follow these steps:

1. Open the `Contact.as` file you created in the previous exercise.
2. Place the cursor inside the class declaration's code block, but before the constructor method.
3. Declare each of the required properties with appropriate data types, as follows:

```
public var contactId:int=0;
public var firstName:String;
public var lastName:String;
public var dob:Date;
public var address:String;
public var city:String;
public var zipCode:String;
public var telephone:String;
```

4. Save the file to disk.

Making properties bindable

Value objects benefit from having their properties marked as bindable, so that as the property values change at runtime, they can broadcast those changes to any objects with binding expressions.

You can make individual properties bindable by adding the `[Bindable]` metadata tag before each property declaration. This code makes the `firstName` and `lastName` properties bindable, but doesn't do the same for the `contactId` property:

```
public var contactId:int=0;
[Bindable]
public var firstName:String;
[Bindable]
public var lastName:String;
```

Alternatively, you can add a single [Bindable] tag above the class declaration to make all its properties bindable:

```
package valueObjects
{
  [Bindable]
  public class Contact
  {
    public var contactId:int=0;
    ... remaining property declarations ...


  }
}
```

Follow these steps to make all the value object class's properties bindable:

1. Open `Contact.as`.

2. Place the cursor above the line with the class declaration, and add a [Bindable] metadata tag.

3. Save the changes to disk.

Listing 16.2 shows the completed value object Contact class.

LISTING 16.2

A completed value object class

```
package valueObjects
{
  [Bindable]
  public class Contact
  {
    public var contactId:int=0;
    public var firstName:String;
    public var lastName:String;
    public var dob:Date;
    public var address:String;
    public var city:String;
    public var zipCode:String;
    public var telephone:String;
    public function Contact()
    {
    }
  }
}
```

 Completed similar to Listing 16.2 is available in the Web site files as `ContactComplete.as` in the `chapter16` project.

Using private properties and accessor methods

If you prefer, you can use private properties and set and get accessor methods. This is a preferred syntax for some developers, because it follows the object-oriented practice of encapsulation and hiding data members from public usage.

To declare a private property in an ActionScript class, replace the public access modifier with the keyword `private`. If you like, you also can follow the practice of using an underscore (_) prefix as the property name's initial character:

```
private var _firstName:String;
```

To make the property accessible to the rest of the application, you then create set and get accessor methods. In ActionScript 3, these methods use explicit set and get keywords to indicate that the functions should be accessed by the class consumer as though they were properties.

A set accessor method receives a single argument and returns void. The body of the method sets the corresponding private variable's value from the argument:

```
public function set contactId(newValue:int):void
{
   this._contactId=newValue;
}
```

A get accessor method receives no arguments and returns the value of its corresponding private property:

```
public function get contactId():int
{
   return this._contactId;
}
```

> **TIP** Unlike in Java, where set and get accessor methods are enforced by the application frameworks that explicitly call value object methods such as `getFirstName()`, in ActionScript the set and get accessor methods are recognized as named properties by the compiler. As a result, you can't name a private property with the same identifier as a set or get accessor method. This is one reason the convention of prefixing private property names with the underscore character is commonly followed: It guarantees that the identifier for the private property and for its corresponding accessor methods are different from each other.

Listing 16.3 shows part of the ActionScript class using private properties and accessor methods, instead of public properties.

LISTING 16.3

Using private properties and set/get accessor methods

```
package valueObjects
{
  [Bindable]
  public class ContactPrivateVars
  {
    private var _contactId:int=0;
    private var _firstName:String;
    private var _lastName:String;
    ...more property declarations ...
    public function ContactPrivateVars()
    {
    }
    public function set contactId(newValue:int):void
    {
      this._contactId=newValue;
    }
    public function get contactId():int
    {
      return this.contactId;
    }
    public function set firstName(newValue:String):void
    {
      this.firstName = newValue;
    }
    public function get lastName():String
    {
      return this._lastName;
    }
    ... more set and get accessor methods ...
  }
}
```

ON the WEB   The code in Listing 16.3 is available in the Web site files as
`ContactPrivateVars.as` in the **chapter16** project.

 **TIP**   If a value object class might be extended by a subclass and you want to share the super-
class's properties, set the properties' access modifier to `protected` instead of `private`.

 **TIP**   Just as with public properties, you can make individual accessor method properties
bindable by adding the `[Bindable]` metadata tag before the method declaration:

```
[Bindable]
public function set firstName(newValue:String):void
```

```
{
  this._firstName = newValue;
}
 public function get firstName():String
{
  return this._firstName;
}
```

 **TIP** If you create a get accessor method for a private property, but not a set method, the property is considered "read-only" to the rest of the application.

TIP Accessor methods provide an opportunity to perform other tasks in addition to just getting and setting the properties. For example, if you want to use local shared objects, a set accessor method would provide an opportunity to save the new value to disk. Or, if a property is only available to users with a particular level of security, you can check permission before changing or returning the property.

Instantiating value object classes

You can create instances of value object classes using either MXML or ActionScript.

Instantiating with MXML

To create an instance of a value object class in MXML, follow these steps:

1. Declare a custom namespace prefix associated with the package containing the ActionScript class. The custom namespace prefix should be placed in the MXML file's root element (for example, in the <mx:Application> start tag):

```
<mx:Application xmlns:mx="http://www.adobe.com/2006/mxml"
  xmlns:valueObjects="valueObjects.*">
</mx:Application>
```

2. Declare an MXML tag using the custom namespace prefix, followed by the component name (without the .mxml extension). As with instances of pre-built components in the Flex framework, assign an id attribute to serve the object's unique identifier:

```
<valueObjects:ContactComplete id="myContact"/>
```

Setting object properties in MXML

A value object's properties can be set as either attributes or child elements. When assigning properties as XML attributes, you can include binding expressions to set values from visual components or other data sources. For example, this instance of the Contact object gets its property values from TextInput and other data entry controls:

```
<valueObjects:ContactComplete id="myContact"
  firstName="{firstNameInput.text}"
  lastName="{lastNameInput.text}"
  dob="{dobSelector.selectedDate}"/>
```

Alternatively, you can declare value object properties using child element syntax:

```
<valueObjects:ContactComplete id="myContact">
  <valueObjects:firstName>
    {firstNameInput.text}
  </valueObjects:firstName>
  <valueObjects:lastName>
    {lastNameInput.text}
  </valueObjects:lastName>
  <valueObjects:dob>
    {firstNameInput.text}
  </valueObjects:dob>
</valueObjects:ContactComplete>
```

> **TIP**
> The choice of using attributes or child elements in this case is purely one of coding style; both approaches result in passing values from visual controls to a value object's properties as the user interacts with the controls. Notice, however, that when using child element syntax, you must include the value object class's namespace prefix on each tag, while with attribute-style syntax the prefix isn't required (and in fact can't be used). As a result, attribute-style syntax is much more concise and, unsurprisingly, more popular.

The application in Listing 16.4 declares an instance of the Contact value object class and populates its public properties with binding expressions that refer to the properties of interactive controls.

LISTING 16.4

Using a value object in MXML

```
<?xml version="1.0" encoding="utf-8"?>
<mx:Application xmlns:mx="http://www.adobe.com/2006/mxml"
   layout="vertical"
  xmlns:valueObjects="valueObjects.*" backgroundColor="#ffffff">

  <valueObjects:ContactComplete id="myContact"
    firstName="{firstNameInput.text}"
    lastName="{lastNameInput.text}"
    dob="{dobSelector.selectedDate}"/>

  <mx:TextInput id="firstNameInput"/>
  <mx:TextInput id="lastNameInput"/>
  <mx:DateField id="dobSelector"/>

  <mx:Label text="{myContact.firstName}"/>
  <mx:Label text="{myContact.lastName}"/>
  <mx:Label text="{myContact.dob}"/>

</mx:Application>
```

 The code in Listing 16.4 is available in the Web site files as `UseTransferObject.mxml` in the `chapter16` project.

Instantiating value objects with ActionScript

Because a value object is an ActionScript class, you can create an instance of the class with this simple variable declaration. If you want to be able to use binding expressions to get data out of the class at runtime, be sure to include the `[Bindable]` metadata tag before the variable declaration:

```
private var myContact:Contact = new Contact();
```

You then set object properties with dot syntax:

```
myContact.firstName = firstNameInput.text
myContact.lastName = lastNameInput.text
myContact.dob = dobSelector.selectedDate;
```

Using customized constructor methods

After the value object is populated with data, you can send it to a server through a `RemoteObject` or `WebService` request, or store it persistently in client application memory for later use.

If you're planning to instantiate a value object class with ActionScript code, you might want to customize the class's constructor method to allow values to be set upon object construction. As with all ActionScript classes, the constructor method for a value object class follows these rules:

- The name of the constructor method is the same as the class name and is case-sensitive.

- You can have only a single constructor method. ActionScript 3.0 doesn't support method overloading (the ability to create two or more methods that share a name but differ by the number or data types of their arguments).

- A constructor method never returns a value and doesn't require a return data type declaration.

In this example, the constructor method has been customized to accept arguments containing initialization data:

```
public function ContactCustomConstructor(
   contactId:int, firstName:String, lastName:String, dob:Date,
   address:String, city:String, zipCode:String,
telephone:String)
 {
   this.contactId = contactId;
   this.firstName = firstName;
   this.lastName = lastName;
   this.dob = dob;
   this.address = address;
   this.zipCode = zipCode;
   this.telephone = telephone;
 }
```

In the preceding code, the names of arguments and the names of their corresponding public properties are identical. In the body of the constructor method, the prefix `this` is used to resolve ambiguity between the public property (referred to explicitly) and the argument of the same name. Without the prefix, the argument name takes precedence.

Using default argument values

In ActionScript 3.0, if you declare an argument in the constructor without a default value, the argument must be passed during object instantiation. This can cause a problem with objects that you also want to instantiate with MXML code, because this sort of instantiation always executes the class's constructor method but isn't capable of passing arguments:

```
<valueObjects:ContactCustomConstructor id="myContact"/>
```

Using the preceding constructor method signature, this MXML declaration would cause a compiler error and prevent you from successfully building or running the application.

You can solve this problem by adding default values to each of the constructor method's arguments, as in the following example:

```
public function ContactCustomConstructor(
   contactId:int=0, firstName:String=null, lastName:String=null,
   dob:Date=null, address:String=null, city:String=null,
   zipCode:String=null, telephone:String=null)
{
   if (contactId != 0)
     this.contactId = contactId;
   if (firstName != null)
     this.firstName = firstName;
   ... remaining property settings ...
}
```

If the class with this version of the constructor method is declared in MXML, the arguments are passed with their default values. Conditional code in the constructor method can then determine whether to pass the values to their corresponding public properties.

Using Data Collections

A data collection is an ordered list of data objects stored in client application memory. Flex provides an ActionScript class named `ArrayCollection` that's designed for this purpose. More than a simple `Array`, the `ArrayCollection` class has these advantages:

- Unlike an `Array`, an `ArrayCollection` reliably executes binding expressions that refer to its stored data.

- The `ArrayCollection` class implements a set of interfaces that provide client-side data filtering, sorting, bookmarking, and traversal.

- An `ArrayCollection` can be serialized for transport over the Web in requests to Web services, remoting services, and messaging services.

CROSS-REF In addition to the `ArrayCollection` class, the Flex framework also includes a class named `XMLListCollection` that serves many of the same purposes but is designed to manage hierarchical data represented in XML format. The `XMLListCollection` class is described in detail in Chapter 22.

Declaring an ArrayCollection

As with most ActionScript classes, `ArrayCollection` variables can be declared with either MXML or ActionScript. To declare an `ArrayCollection` in MXML, use the `<mx:ArrayCollection>` tag and assign an id property:

```
<mx:ArrayCollection id="myData"/>
```

When you declare an `ArrayCollection` with MXML, the variable is immediately instantiated and made bindable.

Alternatively, you can use this ActionScript code to declare and instantiate the `ArrayCollection` variable:

```
import mx.collections.ArrayCollection;
private var myData:ArrayCollection;
```

TIP The `ArrayCollection` class must be imported and explicitly instantiated when used in ActionScript code. When you use the `<mx:ArrayCollection>`, you don't need to import the class, and it's automatically instantiated.

Setting an ArrayCollection object's source property

The `ArrayCollection` class has a source property that refers to a raw `Array` containing its data. You can set an `ArrayCollection` object's source in a number of ways:

- By passing the `Array` into the `ArrayCollection` object's constructor method:
  ```
  myData = new ArrayCollection(myArray);
  ```
- With an ActionScript statement after the `ArrayCollection` has been instantiated:
  ```
  myData.source = ["red", "green", "blue"];
  ```
- In an MXML declaration, nested in `<mx:source>` tags:
  ```
  <mx:ArrayCollection id="acColors">
    <mx:source>
      <mx:String>Red</mx:String>
      <mx:String>Green</mx:String>
      <mx:String>Blue</mx:String>
    </mx:source>
  </mx:ArrayCollection>
  ```

TIP In the preceding MXML declaration, the `ArrayCollection` object's `source` property is already known by the compiler to be an `Array`. This is why you can then immediately declare individual data elements in a list. A long-hand version of this code might look like this:

```
<mx:ArrayCollection id="acColors">
  <mx:source>
    <mx:Array>
      <mx:String>Red</mx:String>
      <mx:String>Green</mx:String>
      <mx:String>Blue</mx:String>
    </mx:Array>
  </mx:source>
</mx:ArrayCollection>
```

If you're working with data that's been embedded into the application with the `<mx:Model>` tag, the model's repeating elements are exposed to the ActionScript environment as an `Array`. Because you always want to wrap the `Array` in an `ArrayCollection`, this code would accomplish the purpose:

```
<mx:Model id="bookData" source="data/books.xml"/>
<mx:ArrayCollection id="acBooks" source="{bookData.book}">
```

Accessing data at runtime

After an `ArrayCollection` object has been created, you can dynamically get, add, and remove data at runtime with the `ArrayCollection` class interface. The following `ArrayCollection` methods and properties are designed for this purpose:

- `addItem(item:Object)` appends a data item to the end of the collection.

- `addItemAt(item:Object, index:int)` adds a data item in the collection at the declared index position. Existing data items are shifted downward to make room for the new data item.

- `getItemAt(index:int, prefetch:int=0)` returns a data item at the declared index position. The optional prefetch argument is used when an `ArrayCollection` contains *managed* data to indicate how many rows of data should be fetched from the server.

- `removeItemAt(index:int)` removes a data item from the `ArrayCollection` object.

- `removeAll()` clears all items from the collection.

- `setItemAt(item:Object, index:int)` replaces a data item in the declared index position.

- `length:int` returns the number of items in the `ArrayCollection`.

CROSS-REF The term *managed data* refers to data that's managed by and accessed through Adobe LiveCycle Data Services' Data Management Service.

The application in Listing 16.5 shows the use of an `ArrayCollection` to manage data that's embedded from an XML file. When the user clicks the application's Remove Item button, the `ArrayCollection` object's `removeItemAt()` method is called to remove the selected data item.

LISTING 16.5

Using an ArrayCollection

```
<?xml version="1.0" encoding="utf-8"?>
<mx:Application xmlns:mx="http://www.adobe.com/2006/mxml"
   layout="vertical">

  <mx:Script>
    <![CDATA[
      private function removeDataItem():void
      {
        if (booksGrid.selectedIndex != -1)
        {
          acBooks.removeItemAt(booksGrid.selectedIndex);
        }
      }
    ]]>
  </mx:Script>

  <mx:Model id="bookData" source="data/books.xml"/>
  <mx:ArrayCollection id="acBooks" source="{bookData.book}"/>

  <mx:DataGrid id="booksGrid" dataProvider="{acBooks}"/>
  <mx:Button label="Remove Data" click="removeDataItem()"/>

</mx:Application>
```

ON the WEB   The code in Listing 16.5 is available in the Web site files as `DisplayBookCollection.mxml` in the `chapter16` project.

Managing data at runtime

The `ArrayCollection` class implements a number of interfaces to allow you to dynamically manage data in client application memory at runtime. These interfaces include:

- `ICollectionView`, with methods for filtering and sorting data at runtime
- `IList`, with the methods described previously for adding, removing, and accessing data at runtime

In addition, the `ArrayCollection` class's `createCursor()` method returns an `IViewCursor` object that allows you to bookmark and traverse data in memory, much like you might do with a server-side database that supports cursor operations. In this section, I describe the use of the `ICollectionView` and `IViewCursor` interfaces that support dynamic data management in the client application.

You can filter data that's managed by the `ArrayCollection` class without having to make additional calls to remote servers. This is a major benefit of Flex applications, compared to the model typically used in a classic Web application. In these applications, each time the user requests a filtered view of data, the application makes a call to a dynamic server page (whether built in ColdFusion, ASP.NET, PHP, or some other server technology). The dynamic server page executes a database query to get a filtered data set, and the application server returns a response formatted in HTML.

Flex applications are *stateful;* they have their own data management tools that can execute most data management operations without having to communicate with the server. As a result, these applications can support many more concurrent users, as each user contributes the processing power of their own local computer system to the task at hand.

Filtering data

The `ArrayCollection` class executes filtering through its `filterFunction` property. This property is designed to reference an ActionScript function that you create and customize. A function designed for filtering always has this signature:

```
private function functionName(item:Object):Boolean
```

The item argument can be either a generic ActionScript `Object` variable or a strongly typed value object. When you execute a filter, the `ArrayCollection` class loops through its source data and executes the filter function once for each data item. If the filtering function returns `true`, the current data item is included in the resulting filtered view; if it returns `false`, the data item is hidden and won't be visible to the user unless and until the filter is removed.

The following filtering function examines a property of a data item and compares it to a value provided by the user through a visual component. If the data item property and the user-provided value match, the function returns `true`, indicating that the data item should be included in the filtered view:

```
private function filterOnAuthor(item:Object):Boolean
{
  if (item.au_id == authorList.selectedItem.au_id)
  {
    return true;
  }
  else
  {
    return false;
  }
}
```

The preceding code also could be written more concisely, using the comparison of the two values as a Boolean expression:

```
private function filterOnAuthor(item:Object):Boolean
{
   return (item.au_id == authorList.selectedItem.au_id);
}
```

Because this function will be called by the ArrayCollection once for each of its data items, you should keep the filtering function brief.

To use the filter function, first assign the function to the ArrayCollection class's filter Function property by its name. Then call the ArrayCollection object's refresh() method to cause the filtering to happen:

```
acBooks.filterFunction=filterOnAuthor;
acBooks.refresh();
```

If the application's current state is such that you want to remove the filter, set filterFunction to a value of null and then again call the refresh() method. In the following code, a conditional statement evaluates whether the user has selected the first item in a ComboBox control. This item represents a value of "all records," so the filterFunction is set to null if the condition is true. Otherwise, the filterFunction is set to the custom ActionScript function designed to execute the filter. The call to refresh() is then executed at the end of the conditional block:

```
private function executeFilter():void
{
   if (authorList.selectedIndex == 0)
   {
      acBooks.filterFunction = null;
   }
   else
   {
      acBooks.filterFunction=filterOnAuthor;
   }
   acBooks.refresh();
}
```

The application in Listing 16.6 implements a filter using two data sets. The first data set, representing authors, is displayed in a ComboBox control. As the application starts up, an additional data item is added at the beginning of this data set representing a choice of All Authors.

At runtime, each time the user selects an author (or All Authors), the executeFilter() method is called. As a result, the filterFunction is set and the call to refresh() causes the filter to be applied.

LISTING 16.6

Implementing a filtering function

```
<?xml version="1.0" encoding="utf-8"?>
<mx:Application xmlns:mx="http://www.adobe.com/2006/mxml"
  layout="vertical"
  creationComplete="initApp()">
  <mx:Script>
    <![CDATA[
      private function initApp():void
      {
        acAuthors.addItemAt("All Authors", 0);
        authorList.selectedIndex = 0;
      }
      private function getAuthorName(item:Object):String
      {
        if (item is String)
        {
          return item as String;
        }
        else
        {
          return item.au_fname + " " + item.au_lname;
        }
      }
      private function filterOnAuthor(item:Object):Boolean
      {
        return (item.au_id == authorList.selectedItem.au_id);
      }
      private function executeFilter():void
      {
        if (authorList.selectedIndex == 0)
        {
          acBooks.filterFunction = null;
        }
        else
        {
          acBooks.filterFunction=filterOnAuthor;
        }
        acBooks.refresh();
      }
    ]]>
  </mx:Script>
  <mx:Model id="authorModel" source="data/authors.xml"/>
  <mx:Model id="bookModel" source="data/books.xml"/>
  <mx:ArrayCollection id="acAuthors" source="{authorModel.author}"/>
  <mx:ArrayCollection id="acBooks" source="{bookModel.book}"/>
  <mx:ComboBox id="authorList" dataProvider="{acAuthors}"
    labelFunction="getAuthorName" change="executeFilter()"/>
```

```
<mx:DataGrid id="bookGrid" dataProvider="{acBooks}" width="350">
  <mx:columns>
    <mx:DataGridColumn dataField="title" headerText="Title"/>
    <mx:DataGridColumn dataField="price" headerText="Price"/>
  </mx:columns>
</mx:DataGrid>
</mx:Application>
```

 The code in Listing 16.6 is available in the Web site files as `FilterDemo.mxml` in the chapter16 project.

CROSS-REF The application in Listing 16.6 includes the use of the `ComboBox` and `DataGrid` controls. These features of the Flex framework are described in Chapter 18.

Sorting data

The `ArrayCollection` sorts data through use of its `sort` property. The sort property references an instance of the `mx.collections.Sort` class. This class in turn has a `fields` property that references an `Array` containing instances of `mx.collections.SortField`.

The `SortField` class supports these `Boolean` properties that determine which named property of an `ArrayCollection` object's data items to sort on and how to execute the sort operation:

- `caseInsensitive` defaults to `false`, meaning that sort operations are case-sensitive by default.
- `descending` defaults to `false`, meaning that sort operations are ascending by default.
- `numeric` defaults to `false`, meaning that sort operations are text-based by default.

You can instantiate a `SortField` object and set all of its `Boolean` properties in the constructor method call, using this syntax:

```
var mySortField:SortField = new SortField(
    'propName', caseInsensitive, descending, numeric);
```

All the constructor method arguments are optional, so the following code creates a `SortField` object that sorts on a `lastName` field and uses the default settings of case-sensitive, ascending, and text:

```
var mySortField:SortField = new SortField('lastName');
```

To sort on multiple named properties, add the `SortField` objects to the array in the order of sort precedence — the first `SortField` object is the primary sort, and so on:

```
var mySort:Sort = new Sort();
mySort.fields = new Array();
mySort.fields.push(new SortField('price', false, false, true));
mySort.fields.push(new SortField('title'));
```

After creating the Sort object and populating its fields property with the Array of SortField objects, the last step is to assign the ArrayCollection object's sort property and call its refresh() method:

```
acBooks.sort = mySort;
acBooks.refresh();
```

TIP The implementation of sorting functionality as a collection of objects allows you to save a customized Sort object and reuse it elsewhere in your application.

The application in Listing 16.7 executes a sort operation using the ArrayCollection's sort property and two SortField objects.

LISTING 16.7

Executing a sort operation

```
<?xml version="1.0" encoding="utf-8"?>
<mx:Application xmlns:mx="http://www.adobe.com/2006/mxml">
  <mx:Script>
    <![CDATA[
      import mx.collections.SortField;
      import mx.collections.Sort;
      private function executeSort():void
      {
        var mySort:Sort = new Sort();
        mySort.fields = new Array();
        mySort.fields.push(new SortField('price', false, false, true));
        mySort.fields.push(new SortField('title'));
        acBooks.sort = mySort;
        acBooks.refresh();
      }
    ]]>
  </mx:Script>
  <mx:Model id="bookModel" source="data/books.xml"/>
  <mx:ArrayCollection id="acBooks" source="{bookModel.book}"/>
  <mx:DataGrid id="bookGrid" dataProvider="{acBooks}" width="350">
    <mx:columns>
      <mx:DataGridColumn dataField="title" headerText="Title"/>
      <mx:DataGridColumn dataField="price" headerText="Price"/>
    </mx:columns>
  </mx:DataGrid>
    <mx:Button label="Sort Data" click="executeSort()"/>
</mx:Application>
```

ON the WEB The code in Listing 16.7 is available in the Web site files as SortDemo.mxml in the chapter16 project.

The `Sort` class has a property named `compareFunction` that can be assigned to a custom ActionScript function. This is useful if you need to execute a sort operation that's based on comparisons of other than simple numeric or text values. The signature of the function you assign is as follows:

```
function [name](item1:Object, item2:Object,
  fields:Array = null):int
```

The function should return one of these values: _1 if the first item should appear above the second in the sorted view, 1 if the second item should appear first, and 0 if the two items are equivalent for purposes of sorting.

Using data cursors

The `ArrayCollection` class has a function named `createCursor()` that returns an object implementing the `IViewCursor` interface. The `IViewCursor` object has properties and methods supporting these client-side data management tasks:

- Traversing the data forward and backward
- Searching the data for particular values
- Accessing a particular object in the collection at the cursor's location
- Bookmarking data so you can easily return to bookmarked items

In order to use an `ArrayCollection` cursor object, declare a variable typed as the `IViewCursor` interface. It's typically best to declare this variable as a persistent property outside of any functions, so you can then refer to the object from anywhere else in the code:

```
import mx.collections.IViewCursor;
private var cursor:IViewCursor;

private function initApp():void
{
  cursor = acBooks.createCursor();
}
```

After the cursor has been created, you can then use its features to manage code in the client application.

Traversing data

The `IViewCursor` interface supports these properties and methods that allow you to move through data one item at a time and determine the current cursor position:

- `afterLast:Boolean` returns `true` if the current cursor position is after the last data item.
- `beforeFirst:Boolean` returns `true` if the current cursor position is before the first data item.

- `current:Object` returns a reference to the data item at the current cursor position.

- `moveNext():Boolean` moves the cursor to the next data item in the collection. This method returns `false` if the cursor can't move forward (because it's already at the end of the collection).

- `movePrevious():Boolean` moves the cursor to the previous data item in the collection. This method returns `false` if the cursor can't move backward (because it's already at the start of the collection).

 When you first create a cursor from a collection, the cursor's initial position is the collection's first item (unless the collection is empty).

The application in Listing 16.8 uses a cursor to loop through a collection and collect values from each of its data items.

LISTING 16.8

Using a cursor to traverse and collect data from a collection

```
<?xml version="1.0" encoding="utf-8"?>
<mx:Application xmlns:mx="http://www.adobe.com/2006/mxml"
  layout="vertical">

  <mx:Script>
    <![CDATA[
      import mx.controls.Alert;
      import mx.collections.IViewCursor;
      private var cursor:IViewCursor;
      private function collectData():void
      {
        cursor = acBooks.createCursor();
        var total:Number = 0;
        while (!cursor.afterLast)
        {
          total += Number(cursor.current.price);
          cursor.moveNext();
        }
        Alert.show("The average price of a book is " +
          formatter.format(total / acBooks.length));
      }
    ]]>
  </mx:Script>
  <mx:Model id="bookModel" source="data/books.xml"/>
  <mx:ArrayCollection id="acBooks" source="{bookModel.book}"/>
  <mx:CurrencyFormatter id="formatter" precision="2"/>
  <mx:DataGrid id="bookGrid" dataProvider="{acBooks}" width="350">
```

```
    <mx:columns>
      <mx:DataGridColumn dataField="title" headerText="Title"/>
      <mx:DataGridColumn dataField="price" headerText="Price"/>
    </mx:columns>
  </mx:DataGrid>

  <mx:Button label="Get Average Price" click="collectData()"/>
</mx:Application>
```

 The code in Listing 16.8 is available in the Web site files as **TraversingData.mxml** in the **chapter16** project.

Finding data with a cursor

The IViewCursor interface supports these methods to search an ArrayCollection for a data item:

- findAny(item:Object):Boolean locates an item with specific values anywhere in the ArrayCollection.

- findFirst(item:Object):Boolean locates the first item with specific values.

- findLast(item:Object):Boolean locates the last item with specific values.

Before executing any of these methods to locate data, the ArrayCollection must first be sorted with at least one of the properties on which you're searching included in the sort operation. Then, to locate a data item, create an object with matching named properties to the data that you want to search. For example, if you want to search on a title property of the objects in your collection, create a new Object with that named property set to the value you want to locate:

```
var searchObject:Object = {title:bookGrid.selectedItem.title};
var found:Boolean = cursor.findAny(searchObject);
```

If the search operation is successful, the function returns true. You can then get a reference to the data item that was located by referring to the cursor object's current property:

```
var foundObject:Object = cursor.current;
```

In the application in Listing 16.9, the application uses two ArrayCollection objects. The first is a catalog of data. When the user selects an item and clicks to add the object to the second ArrayCollection, a shopping cart — an IViewCursor — object is used to determine whether the object is already in the cart. If the object isn't found, it's added to the cart collection; if it is found, the object's quantity property is incremented by 1.

LISTING 16.9

Locating data with a cursor

```
<?xml version="1.0" encoding="utf-8"?>
<mx:Application xmlns:mx="http://www.adobe.com/2006/mxml"
   layout="vertical"
  creationComplete="initApp()">
  <mx:Script>
    <![CDATA[
      import mx.collections.SortField;
      import mx.collections.Sort;
      import mx.collections.IViewCursor;
      private var cursor:IViewCursor;
      private function initApp():void
      {
        var mySort:Sort = new Sort();
        mySort.fields = [new SortField('title')];
        acCart.sort = mySort;
        acCart.refresh();
      }
      private function addToCart():void
      {
        cursor = acCart.createCursor();
        var searchObject:Object = {title:bookGrid.selectedItem.title};
        if (cursor.findAny(searchObject))
        {
          cursor.current.quantity ++;
        }
        else
        {
          bookGrid.selectedItem.quantity=1;
          acCart.addItem(bookGrid.selectedItem);
        }
      }
      private function removeFromCart():void
      {
        acCart.removeItemAt(cartGrid.selectedIndex);
      }
    ]]>
  </mx:Script>
  <mx:Model id="bookModel" source="data/books.xml"/>
  <mx:ArrayCollection id="acBooks" source="{bookModel.book}"/>
  <mx:ArrayCollection id="acCart"/>
  <mx:CurrencyFormatter id="formatter" precision="2"/>
  <mx:HBox>
    <mx:Panel title="Catalog" >
      <mx:DataGrid id="bookGrid" dataProvider="{acBooks}" width="350">
        <mx:columns>
          <mx:DataGridColumn dataField="title" headerText="Title"/>
```

```
            <mx:DataGridColumn dataField="price" headerText="Price"/>
          </mx:columns>
        </mx:DataGrid>
        <mx:ControlBar>
          <mx:Button label="Add to Cart" click="addToCart()"
            enabled="{bookGrid.selectedIndex!=-1}"/>
        </mx:ControlBar>
      </mx:Panel>
      <mx:Panel title="Shopping Cart">
        <mx:DataGrid id="cartGrid" dataProvider="{acCart}" width="350"
          sortableColumns="false">
          <mx:columns>
            <mx:DataGridColumn dataField="title" headerText="Title"/>
            <mx:DataGridColumn dataField="quantity"
  headerText="Quantity"/>
          </mx:columns>
        </mx:DataGrid>
        <mx:ControlBar>
          <mx:Button label="Remove from Cart" click="removeFromCart()"
            enabled="{cartGrid.selectedIndex!=-1}"/>
        </mx:ControlBar>
      </mx:Panel>
    </mx:HBox>
  </mx:Application>
```

ON the WEB The code in Listing 16.9 is available in the Web site files as `SearchingData.mxml` in the `chapter16` project.

Bookmarking data

The `IViewCursor` interface defines these properties and methods that let you bookmark data items and then easily find them again:

- `bookmark:CursorBookmark` is a property that refers to the cursor's current bookmark.

- `seek(bookmark:CursorBookmark, offset:int = 0, prefetch:int = 0):void` is a method that can be used to locate a bookmark and reposition the cursor to that location, or to an offset relative to the bookmark location.

To create a bookmark, first position a cursor object on the data item you want to mark. Then create a variable typed as the `CursorBookmark` class that references the cursor's `bookmark` property:

```
import mx.collections.CursorBookmark;
private var myBookmark:CursorBookmark;
private function bookMarkIt():void
{
  myBookMark = cursor.bookmark;
}
```

To return the cursor to the bookmarked position, call the cursor's seek() method and pass the CursorBookmark object:

```
cursor.seek(myBookmark);
```

The application in Listing 16.10 uses a CursorBookmark object to "remember" which data item was most recently added to the shopping cart. When the user clicks the application's Add Another button, the cursor's seek() method is called to return to that data item and increment its quantity property.

LISTING 16.10

Using a cursor bookmark

```
<?xml version="1.0" encoding="utf-8"?>
<mx:Application xmlns:mx="http://www.adobe.com/2006/mxml"
   layout="vertical"
  creationComplete="initApp()">
  <mx:Script>
    <![CDATA[
      import mx.collections.CursorBookmark;
      import mx.collections.SortField;
      import mx.collections.Sort;
      import mx.collections.IViewCursor;
      private var cursor:IViewCursor;
      [Bindable]
      private var myBookmark:CursorBookmark;
      private function initApp():void
      {
        var mySort:Sort = new Sort();
        mySort.fields = [new SortField('title')];
        acCart.sort = mySort;
        acCart.refresh();
      }
      private function addToCart():void
      {
        cursor = acCart.createCursor();
        var searchObject:Object = {title:bookGrid.selectedItem.title};
        if (cursor.findAny(searchObject))
        {
          cursor.current.quantity ++;
        }
        else
        {
          bookGrid.selectedItem.quantity=1;
          acCart.addItem(bookGrid.selectedItem);
          cursor.findAny(searchObject);
        }
        myBookmark = cursor.bookmark;
```

```
      }
      private function addAnother():void
      {
        cursor.seek(myBookmark);
        cursor.current.quantity++;
        cartGrid.selectedItem=cursor.current;
      }
      private function removeFromCart():void
      {
        acCart.removeItemAt(cartGrid.selectedIndex);
      }
   ]]>
 </mx:Script>

 <mx:Model id="bookModel" source="data/books.xml"/>
 <mx:ArrayCollection id="acBooks" source="{bookModel.book}"/>
 <mx:ArrayCollection id="acCart"/>
 <mx:CurrencyFormatter id="formatter" precision="2"/>
 <mx:HBox>
   <mx:Panel title="Catalog" >
     <mx:DataGrid id="bookGrid" dataProvider="{acBooks}" width="350">
       <mx:columns>
         <mx:DataGridColumn dataField="title" headerText="Title"/>
         <mx:DataGridColumn dataField="price" headerText="Price"/>
       </mx:columns>
     </mx:DataGrid>
     <mx:ControlBar>
       <mx:Button label="Add to Cart" click="addToCart()"
         enabled="{bookGrid.selectedIndex!=-1}"/>
     </mx:ControlBar>
   </mx:Panel>
   <mx:Panel title="Shopping Cart">
     <mx:DataGrid id="cartGrid" dataProvider="{acCart}" width="350"
       sortableColumns="false">
       <mx:columns>
         <mx:DataGridColumn dataField="title" headerText="Title"/>
         <mx:DataGridColumn dataField="quantity"
 headerText="Quantity"/>
       </mx:columns>
     </mx:DataGrid>
     <mx:ControlBar>
       <mx:Button label="Remove from Cart" click="removeFromCart()"
         enabled="{cartGrid.selectedIndex!=-1}"/>
       <mx:Button label="Add Another" click="addAnother()"
         enabled="{myBookmark != null}"/>
     </mx:ControlBar>
   </mx:Panel>
 </mx:HBox>
</mx:Application>
```

495

ON the WEB The code in Listing 16.10 is available in the Web site files as `BookmarkingData.mxml` in the `chapter16` project.

Summary

In this chapter, I described how to model and manage data in a Flex application using value object classes, the `ArrayCollection` class, and the `IViewCursor` interface. You learned the following:

- You can model individual data items with the `<mx:Model>` tag or with custom ActionScript classes that implement the Value Object design pattern.

- Objects modeled with `<mx:Model>` can't declare default values or apply specific data types to their properties.

- Custom ActionScript classes that implement the Value Object design pattern can best model the structure of a server-side database table.

- The `<mx:Model>` tag can be used to embed data in an application.

- You should only embed data that's small in scope and won't change.

- The `ArrayCollection` class is an ActionScript class designed to manage data in a Flex client application.

- The `ArrayCollection` is a wrapper class around an `Array`, and does a better job than the `Array` of reliably executing bindings when its data changes.

- You can use the `ArrayCollection` class to sort and filter data in a client application without having to make additional requests to an application server.

- The `IViewCursor` interface provides the ability to traverse, search, and bookmark data stored in an `ArrayCollection`.

Chapter 17

Using List Controls

Most Flex applications are designed for the purpose of presenting and managing data in some form. As a result, one of the most popular families of visual controls in the Flex framework includes those known as *list controls*.

A list control is defined as a component that has a `dataProvider` property that allows you to populate the control with dynamic data. The data provided to a list control can be in the form of either hierarchical or relational data, and the type of data you want to present frequently determines which control you use. In addition to being able to display relational or hierarchical data, list controls have a common set of properties, methods, and events that allow the user to select one or more items with mouse and keyboard gestures.

The `mx.controls.List` component is the most fundamental of these controls. This component behaves like an HTML `<select>` control and displays a list of data items to the user as a list box. After you learn how to use the `List` control, you have most of the information you need to use other such controls. You can populate controls with data, listen for events indicating that the user has selected or started to drag data, set common styles, and so on.

CROSS-REF This chapter describes use of the single column list controls: `List` and `ComboBox`. It includes information on how to populate these controls with data, how to control data presentation with custom generation of item labels and renderers, and how to handle events indicating that the user wants to select and manipulate data. The unique capabilities of other list controls, including the `DataGrid`, `TileList`, and `HorizontalList`, are described in Chapter 18.

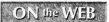 To use the sample code for this chapter, import the `chapter17.zip` project from the Web site files into any folder on your disk.

Table 17.1 shows a list of the components that have the ability to display dynamic data and support user interaction using the list control model.

TABLE 17.1

The List Controls

Control	Description
AdvancedDataGrid	A new feature of the Flex 3 class library, this component implements all the features of the List and DataGrid components, but adds the ability to group and aggregate data and can sort on multiple columns. This component is part of the Flex Data Visualization components and is available only with a Flex Builder Professional license.
ComboBox	This component presents a drop-down list of data items. The presentation of this component is similar to an HTML <select> control that has its size property set to 1. This component's editable property, when set to true, allows the user to enter an arbitrary string instead of selecting an item from the list.
DataGrid	This component presents a grid with multiple rows and columns. It is used to present data received from a server-side database or other data source that uses the spreadsheet-like rows-and-columns structure of relational database tables.
HorizontalList	This component presents a horizontal list of data items, typically rendered with a custom item renderer.
List	This component presents a list box of data items. The presentation of this component is similar to an HTML <select> control that has its size property set to a value greater than 1.
OlapDataGrid	Another new feature of the Flex 3 class library, this component expands on the AdvancedDataGrid and supports presentation of results from an OLAP query.
TileList	This component presents a grid of data items, typically rendered with a custom item renderer.
Tree	This component presents hierarchical data, commonly supplied by the contents of an XML file.

This chapter describes the details of working with all list controls, focusing on the simpler components: List, ComboBox, TileList, and HorizontalList. The following chapter describes the details of working with the DataGrid and related components.

TIP In addition to the components listed in Table 17.1, the Flex 3 class library adds a set of list controls designed for use in AIR applications. These controls provide the user with the ability to inspect and manipulate files and directories in the local file system and cannot be used in Flex applications that are deployed over the Web. They include the `FileSystemList`, `FileSystemComboBox`, `FileSystemDataGrid`, and `FileSystemTree` components.

Most of the information in this chapter and in Chapter 18 about list and `DataGrid` controls applies equally to these AIR-based controls, but these controls add functionality that allows them to populate their data from the directory and file contents of the local file system. They also implement additional properties and methods that are designed to support their unique purpose.

> **TIP**
>
> There are two unique components that extend a class named `ComboBase` and therefore must be considered members of the family of list controls as well. The `ColorPicker` control is designed to allow selection of a color value from a grid of "Web-safe" colors, and the `DateField` control presents a pop-up calendar control. The components aren't often thought of as list controls, but they support the same set of properties, methods, and events as their cousins.

Each of the list controls has its own unique visual presentation and behavior. As the developer, you select the control most suited to your application's requirements.

Figure 17.1 shows examples of the `List`, `ComboBox`, `DataGrid`, and `Tree` controls, each using the same set of data as its data provider.

FIGURE 17.1

Commonly used list controls

> **ON the WEB**
>
> The application displayed in Figure 17.1 is available in the Web site files as `ListControls.mxml` in the `chapter17` project.

Using Data Providers

The data you provide to a list control must be in the form of an ActionScript object, but for most purposes you typically provide data that's been wrapped in one of the data collection classes: either the `ArrayCollection` class for data that's in rows and columns or the `XMLListCollection` class for hierarchical data.

The `List` and `ComboBox` controls are distinguished from the `DataGrid` and its related controls in that they present only a single column of data. They can present data from a collection of complex objects, but by default they present only one value in each list item. In contrast, the `DataGrid` control is designed to present data in multiple columns.

Using hard-coded data providers

You can embed data in a Flex application for use by either a specific instance of a list control or as a separate data object that's then linked to a control through a binding expression. Hard-coding means that you declare actual data in the code, rather than retrieving it from an external data source at runtime.

CAUTION   As described in Chapter 16, when you embed data in a Flex application, the compiled application file expands accordingly. You should embed data only when it's a small amount of content and won't change during the lifetime of the application.

Nesting hard-coded data in a data provider

You can nest hard-coded data in the declaration of a list control's `dataProvider` by declaring the property with child-element syntax rather than attribute syntax. The following code presents a `List` control populated with a hard-coded data provider containing simple `String` values:

```
<mx:List id="sizeList">
  <mx:dataProvider>
    <mx:String>Small</mx:String>
    <mx:String>Medium</mx:String>
    <mx:String>Large</mx:String>
  </mx:dataProvider>
</mx:List>
```

You also can declare the `dataProvider` with hard-coded collections of complex objects by nesting multiple `<mx:Object>` declarations within the `<mx:dataProvider>` tag set:

```
<mx:List id="stateList">
  <mx:dataProvider>
    <mx:Object>
      <label>California</stateName>
      <capitol>Sacramento</capitol>
    </mx:Object>
    <mx:Object>
      <label>Oregon</stateName>
```

```
        <capitol>Salem</capitol>
      </mx:Object>
      <mx:Object>
        <label>Washington</stateName>
        <capitol>Olympia</capitol>
      </mx:Object>
    </mx:dataProvider>
  </mx:List>
```

Modifying data with the ArrayCollection API

At runtime, data that's hard-coded within a `dataProvider` is automatically wrapped inside an `ArrayCollection` object, so the `ArrayCollection` API can be used to access and manipulate the data. Even though the original data is hard-coded, this ActionScript statement code would add a new item to the `List` object's `dataProvider` when it contains simple String values:

```
sizeList.dataProvider.addItem('Extra Large');
```

And this code would add a new item when it contains complex objects:

```
stateList.dataProvider.addItem({state:'New York','Albany'});
```

The application in Listing 17.1 uses a `List` object with a hard-coded data provider and then allows the user to add data to the object with the `ArrayCollection.addItem()` method.

LISTING 17.1

A List control with hard-coded data

```
<?xml version="1.0" encoding="utf-8"?>
<mx:Application xmlns:mx="http://www.adobe.com/2006/mxml"
  layout="vertical">

  <mx:List id="sizeList" width="300">
    <mx:dataProvider>
      <mx:String>Small</mx:String>
      <mx:String>Medium</mx:String>
      <mx:String>Large</mx:String>
    </mx:dataProvider>
  </mx:List>

  <mx:HBox>
    <mx:Label text="New Item:"/>
    <mx:TextInput id="itemInput"/>
    <mx:Button label="Add Item"
      click="sizeList.dataProvider.addItem(itemInput.text)"/>
  </mx:HBox>

</mx:Application>
```

ON the WEB   The code in Listing 17.1 is available in the Web site files as `ListWithHardCoded` `Data.mxml` in the `chapter17` project.

Declaring separate data objects with MXML tags

You also can provide hard-coded data to a list control using the `<mx:Model>`, `<mx:Array>`, and `<mx:ArrayCollection>` tags. Regardless of which of these tags you select, the `dataProvider` of the `List` object is transformed to an `ArrayCollection` at runtime, so you should select whichever tag makes most sense to you, keeping in mind that only an `ArrayCollection` will broadcast updates to properties of complex objects at runtime.

The application in Listing 17.2 declares an `Array` with the `<mx:Array>` tag and then provides the data to the `List` object through a binding expression. Notice that even though the data is declared as an `Array`, you can still manipulate it at runtime by referencing the `List` object's `dataProvider` as an `ArrayCollection`.

LISTING 17.2

A List control with data provided through a binding expression

```
<?xml version="1.0" encoding="utf-8"?>
<mx:Application xmlns:mx="http://www.adobe.com/2006/mxml"
    layout="vertical">
  <mx:Array id="myData">
    <mx:String>Small</mx:String>
    <mx:String>Medium</mx:String>
    <mx:String>Large</mx:String>
  </mx:Array>
  <mx:List id="sizeList" width="300" dataProvider="{myData}"/>
  <mx:HBox>
    <mx:Label text="New Item:"/>
    <mx:TextInput id="itemInput"/>
    <mx:Button label="Add Item"
      click="sizeList.dataProvider.addItem(itemInput.text)"/>
  </mx:HBox>
</mx:Application>
```

ON the WEB   The code in Listing 17.2 is available in the Web site files as `ListWithHardCoded` `Array.mxml` in the `chapter17` project.

Using dynamic data providers

Data retrieved from an external source, such as the results of a remote server call through the Remote Procedure Call (RPC) components, or data retrieved from a local database (for an AIR desktop application) is typically stored in an `ArrayCollection`. As described in Chapter 16, the `ArrayCollection` object is typically declared in ActionScript code with the `[Bindable]` metadata tag or in MXML code.

In ActionScript code, the declaration looks like this:

```
[Bindable]
private var myData:ArrayCollection = new ArrayCollection();
```

And in MXML, it looks like this:

```
<mx:ArrayCollection id="myData"/>
```

 Data objects that are declared in MXML are immediately instantiated and always bindable.

Regardless of how the `ArrayCollection` object is declared, by making it bindable, you make it possible to pass the data to a `List` control with a simple binding expression:

```
<mx:List id="sizeList" dataProvider="{myData}"/>
```

Using RPC components

You can choose to retrieve data dynamically from many sources, including the Flex framework components that are grouped together as the RPC classes. These classes are distinguished from each other by the data format they use to communicate with a remote server:

- `HTTPService`: This class sends simple HTTP requests to URLs that return data formatted as simple text or XML. For example, a call to an RSS feed from a blog or content-based Web site would be executed using the `HTTPService` class.

- `WebService`: This class retrieves data from a server with calls formatted in the industry-standard SOAP format.

- `RemoteObject`: This class sends and receives messages formatted in Action Message Format (AMF). This binary format is defined by Adobe and implemented in many of its server products, including LiveCycle Data Services, BlazeDS, and ColdFusion.

These components and their methodologies are described starting in Chapter 24. All, however, are capable of returning data sets in the form of `ArrayCollection` objects that are suitable for use as `List` control data providers.

TIP The AMF data format was published by Adobe Systems in 2007 to support development of independent application server products that are compatible with Flex-based and Flash-based applications.

Retrieving local data in AIR applications

If you're building an AIR-based desktop application, you can retrieve data from local XML files using the `File` and `FileStream` classes or from the local SQLite embedded database with classes such as `SQLConnection` and `SQLStatement`. These classes aren't designed to return data in the `ArrayCollection` format directly; you typically need to manually move data into your data objects with explicit ActionScript code.

Controlling List Item Labels

If a `List` control's data provider contains simple `String` values, these values are displayed on each item by default. If the data provider contains complex objects (either instances of the ActionScript `Object` class or of your own custom value object classes), you can determine the text labels that are displayed in a `List` control's items using one of these strategies:

- The `labelField` property lets you point to a specific named property of each object whose values should be displayed.

- The `labelFunction` property lets you customize each item's label with your own ActionScript code.

Using the labelField property

Most `List` controls support the `labelField` property. This property allows you to indicate which of the named properties of data items in the control's data provider is displayed at runtime.

The default value of `labelField` is `label`. As a result, if the data provider's objects have a property named `label`, that property's value is displayed. In the following code, the `stateData` `Array` contains data objects with a `label` property. The `List` control displays the `label` property's value on each of its items:

```
<mx:Array id="stateData">
  <mx:Object>
    <mx:label>CA</mx:label>
    <mx:capitol>Sacramento</mx:capitol>
  </mx:Object>
  <mx:Object>
    <mx:label>OR</mx:label>
    <mx:capitol>Salem</mx:capitol>
  </mx:Object>
</mx:Array>
<mx:List id="stateList" dataProvider="{stateData}"/>
```

More commonly, the complex objects in the `ArrayCollection` have names that are determined by the structure of a database table, XML file, value object, or other existing data source. If you forget to set the `labelField` property on a `List` control that displays complex data objects, the control displays labels consisting of a set of [ ] characters wrapped around the word `object` and the object's data type. If the data item is cast as an ActionScript Object, the result looks like this:

```
[object Object]
```

As shown in Figure 17.2, the results aren't particularly useful, even when working with a value object class.

FIGURE 17.2

A List control displaying a complex data object with no labelField setting

To fix this behavior, you explicitly set the List control's labelField to the property you want to display:

```
<mx:Array id="stateData">
  <vo:StateVO>
    <vo:state>CA</vo:state>
    <vo:capitol>Sacramento</vo:capitol>
  </vo:StateVO>
  <vo:StateVO>
    <vo:state>OR</vo:state>
    <vo:capitol>Salem</vo:capitol>
  </vo:StateVO>
</mx:Array>
<mx:List id="stateList" dataProvider="{stateData}"
  labelField="state"/>
```

Figure 17.3 shows the same List control, this time displaying the value of the property named in the control's labelField property.

FIGURE 17.3

A List control displaying a complex data object with the labelField set to one of the properties of the data provider's complex data objects

The application in Listing 17.3 uses the List control's labelField property to determine which property value of each data object is displayed at runtime.

LISTING 17.3

Using the labelField property

```xml
<?xml version="1.0" encoding="utf-8"?>
<mx:Application xmlns:mx="http://www.adobe.com/2006/mxml"
   xmlns:vo="vo.*">
  <mx:Array id="stateData">
    <vo:StateVO>
      <vo:state>CA</vo:state>
      <vo:capitol>Sacramento</vo:capitol>
    </vo:StateVO>
    <vo:StateVO>
      <vo:state>OR</vo:state>
      <vo:capitol>Salem</vo:capitol>
    </vo:StateVO>
    <vo:StateVO>
      <vo:state>WA</vo:state>
      <vo:capitol>Washington</vo:capitol>
    </vo:StateVO>
  </mx:Array>
  <mx:List id="stateList" width="200"
    dataProvider="{stateData}" labelField="capitol"/>
</mx:Application>
```

ON the WEB   The code in Listing 17.3 is available in the Web site files as `UsingLabelField.mxml` in the `chapter17` project.

Using the labelFunction property

Most `List` controls implement the `labelFunction` property to allow you to customize the label that appears on each of the control's items at `runtime`. The `labelFunction` property points to the name of a function that follows a specific signature:

```
[access modifier] function [functionName](item:Object):String
```

The access modifier for a custom label function can be anything you like, although when you're calling the function from within the same application or component in which it's defined, the access modifier is typically set to private because it's most often used only from within. The name of the function's only argument (`item` in the example syntax) can be anything you like, but it should be typed as either an Object or a custom class implementing the Value Object design pattern, depending on what type of data is stored in your `List`'s `dataProvider` collection. And the function always returns a String, because its purpose is to generate a label for the `List` control's visual items.

At runtime, the `List` control calls the named function each time it needs to render an item visually. It passes the current data object to the custom function as its item argument and then displays the returned `String` value. This is an example of a function that's compatible with the `labelFunction` architecture:

```
private function getStateLabel(item:StateVO):String
{
   return item.capitol + ", " + item.state;
}
```

The application in Listing 17.4 displays a `List` control where each visual item's label is generated by the custom `getStateLabel()` function.

LISTING 17.4

Using the labelFunction property

```xml
<?xml version="1.0" encoding="utf-8"?>
<mx:Application xmlns:mx="http://www.adobe.com/2006/mxml"
   xmlns:vo="vo.*">
  <mx:Script>
    <![CDATA[
      import vo.StateVO;
      private function getStateLabel(item:StateVO):String
      {
        return item.capitol + ", " + item.state;
      }
```

continued

LISTING 17.4   *(continued)*

```
    ]]>
  </mx:Script>
  <mx:Array id="stateData">
    <vo:StateVO>
      <vo:state>CA</vo:state>
      <vo:capitol>Sacramento</vo:capitol>
    </vo:StateVO>
    <vo:StateVO>
      <vo:state>OR</vo:state>
      <vo:capitol>Salem</vo:capitol>
    </vo:StateVO>
    <vo:StateVO>
      <vo:state>WA</vo:state>
      <vo:capitol>Washington</vo:capitol>
    </vo:StateVO>
  </mx:Array>
  <mx:List id="stateList" width="200"
    dataProvider="{stateData}" labelFunction="getStateLabel"/>
</mx:Application>
```

ON the WEB   The code in Listing 17.4 is available in the Web site files as `UsingLabelField.mxml` in the `chapter17` project.

The resulting application is shown in Figure 17.4. Notice that each of the List control's labels is generated using both of the data object's named properties, concatenated with literal strings to separate the values.

FIGURE 17.4

A List control displaying `String` values calculated in a `labelFunction`

> **TIP** The `DataGrid` component doesn't implement the `labelField` or `labelFunction` properties directly. Instead, these properties are implemented in the `DataGridColumn` component so you can easily customize the presentation of individual columns.

List Control Events and Properties

All `List` controls support these events to notify you of user actions and other important updates to a control:

- `change`: Notifies you that the user has selected an item using either a mouse or keyboard gesture

- `dataChange`: Notifies you that the content of the control's data property has changes, which typically is relevant when the control is used in a custom item renderer or item editor

- `itemClick`: Notifies you that an item in the list control has been clicked

- `itemDoubleClick`: Notifies you that the user double-clicked on an item in the `List` control when the `doubleClickEnabled` property is set to `true`

- `itemRollOut`: Notifies you that the mouse pointer moved out of an item in the `List` control

- `itemRollOver`: Notifies you that the mouse pointer moved over an item in the `List` control

`List` controls also support these properties that can be used to detect which data the user currently has selected:

- `allowMultipleSelections:Boolean`: When set to `true`, this allows the user to select more than one item at a time by holding down Ctrl while clicking items.

- `selectedIndex:int`: This is the numeric index of the currently selected item.

- `selectedIndices:Array`: This is an array of indices of the currently selected items, when the `List` control's `allowMultipleSelection` property is set to `true`.

- `selectedItem:Object`: This is the data object underlying the `List` control's currently selected row or cell.

- `selectedItems:Array`: This is an array of currently selected objects, when the `List` control's `allowMultipleSelection` property is set to `true`.

- `doubleClickEnabled:Boolean`: When this property is set to `true` , the `List` control detects double clicks on its items and dispatches a `doubleClick` event.

In addition, each `List` control supports unique events and properties designed for that control's specific purpose and capabilities.

The `ComboBox` control does not support the `allowMultipleSelection`, `selectedIndices`, or `selectedItems` properties. Because it uses a drop-down interface to present its list, the user can select only one data item at a time.

Handling User Data Selections

When a user selects items in a `List` control, he's indicating that he wants to use the selected item's underlying data. When this occurs, the `List` control dispatches a `change` event. After this event occurs, you can use the control's `selectedItem` and `selectedIndex` properties to detect which item has been selected.

Using the change event

The `change` event is implemented in all `List` controls. It dispatches an event object typed as `mx.events.ListEvent`, which has a `rowIndex` property that indicates by index which data item was selected by the user.

You can detect which data item was clicked by the user by using the event object's `rowIndex` property and passing it to the `getItemAt()` method of the `ArrayCollection` data provider:

```
changeMessage = "You clicked on " +
  event.target.dataProvider.getItemAt(event.rowIndex);
```

This technique notifies you that the user clicked an item, but it doesn't always indicate that the item returned in the expression `event.target.dataProvider.getItemAt(event.rowIndex)` is currently selected. In most `List` controls, the user can hold down Ctrl and click to deselect an item, in which case you get a `change` event that can't be distinguished from the event that occurs when selecting an item.

Using the selectedItem property

A better approach is to use the `List` control's `selectedItem` property, which always returns a reference to the currently selected item. In the event the user has deselected all items in a `List` control, the `selectedItem` property returns `null`:

```
if (event.target.selectedItem == null)
{
  changeMessage = "None selected";
}
else
{
  changeMessage = "You selected " + event.target.selectedItem;
}
```

The application in Listing 17.5 uses a List control and a change event listener. Each time the change event is dispatched by the List control, an event handler function inspects the control's selectedItem and displays a message indicating which item (if any) is currently selected.

LISTING 17.5

Using the change event and selectedItem property

```
<?xml version="1.0" encoding="utf-8"?>
<mx:Application xmlns:mx="http://www.adobe.com/2006/mxml">
  <mx:Script>
    <![CDATA[
      [Bindable]
      private var changeMessage:String="None selected";
      private function changeHandler(event:Event):void
      {
        if (event.target.selectedItem == null)
        {
          changeMessage = "None selected";
        }
        else
        {
          changeMessage = "You selected " + event.target.selectedItem;
        }
      }
    ]]>
  </mx:Script>
  <mx:Array id="myData">
    <mx:String>Small</mx:String>
    <mx:String>Medium</mx:String>
    <mx:String>Large</mx:String>
  </mx:Array>
  <mx:List id="sizeList" width="200" dataProvider="{myData}"
    change="changeHandler(event)"/>
  <mx:Label text="{changeMessage}" fontSize="12"/>
</mx:Application>
```

ON the WEB   The code in Listing 17.5 is available in the Web site files as **ChangeEventDemo.mxml** in the **chapter17** project.

When testing this application, try holding down Ctrl and clicking an item that's already selected. You should see the message "None selected" displayed, because the control's selectedItem property now returns null.

Using the selectedIndex property

All List controls implement the selectedIndex property, which returns the index position of the control's currently selected item. Because all indexing in ActionScript starts at 0, if the first item is selected the selectedIndex property returns 1, the second returns 2, and so on. When you use a List or ComboBox control in a data entry form, you can place a data item as the first item in a list that indicates that the user is selecting all options:

```
<mx:ComboBox id="categoryList" change="changeHandler(event)">
  <mx:dataProvider>
    <mx:String>All Categories</mx:String>
    <mx:String>Comedy</mx:String>
    <mx:String>Drama</mx:String>
    <mx:String>Action</mx:String>
    <mx:String>Horror</mx:String>
  </mx:dataProvider>
</mx:ComboBox>
```

The following code would detect whether the user has selected the first item, indicating she wants all categories or a specific category:

```
private function changeHandler(event:Event):void
{
  if (categoryList.selectedIndex == 0)
  {
    Alert.show("You selected all categories", "Everything!");
  }
  else
  {
    Alert.show("You selected " + categoryList.selectedItem,
      "One Thing!");
  }
}
```

If no items are currently selected in a List control, the selectedIndex property returns a value of -1. This is particularly useful when you want to detect a state where the user hasn't yet selected a value from a List or DataGrid control:

```
private function changeHandler(event:Event):void
{
  if (categoryList.selectedIndex == -1)
  {
    Alert.show("You haven't selected anything!", "Nothin!");
  }
  else
  {
    Alert.show("You selected " + categoryList.selectedItem,
      "One Thing!");
  }
}
```

When using a ComboBox with its editable property set to the default value of false, its selectedIndex property never returns -1, because some item is always selected. When you set editable to true and the user types a value into the TextInput portion of the control at runtime, selectedIndex returns -1 to indicate the user has provided a custom value.

Selecting complex data objects

When a List control's data provider is a collection of complex objects instead of simple values, you can refer to selected data objects' named properties using either dot syntax or array-style syntax. Dot syntax is more common, because, especially when working with classes that implement the Value Object design pattern, they allow Flex Builder and the compiler to validate property names and provide code completion.

For example, when a user selects an item that represents a complex data object from a List control, you should first cast the control's selectedItem property as the appropriate ActionScript class. You can then refer to the object's named properties and gain the benefit of Flex Builder's and the compiler's syntax checking and code completion tools:

```
var selectedState:StateVO = stateList.selectedItem as StateVO;
var selectedCapitol = selectedState.capitol;
```

If you prefer, you can use array-style syntax to refer to a data object's named properties:

```
var selectedCapitol = stateList.selectedItem["capitol"];
```

This syntax allows you to use variables containing the names of the properties. The following code would have the same functional result as the other preceding examples:

```
var fieldName:String = "capitol";
var selectedCapitol = stateList.selectedItem[fieldName];
```

Particularly when using data model classes that implement the Value Object design pattern, you may want to declare a bindable instance of the class to store the most recently selected data item. This StateVO value object class contains two properties, both of which are bindable due to the use of the [Bindable] metadata tag before the class declaration:

```
package vo
{
  [Bindable]
  public class StateVO
  {
    public var state:String;
    public var capitol:String;
    public function StateVO()
    {
    }
  }
}
```

The application in Listing 17.6 uses a ComboBox with a data provider containing multiple instances of a value object class. Upon application startup, and then again when the user selects an item from the control, a reference to the currently selected data item is saved to the selectedState variable.

Notice that this variable is marked as bindable, and its internal [Bindable] tag also marks its properties as bindable. Both levels of "bindability" are required in order for the Label controls to successfully display the selected object's properties whenever the user selects new data.

LISTING 17.6

Selecting complex data objects

```
<?xml version="1.0" encoding="utf-8"?>
<mx:Application xmlns:mx="http://www.adobe.com/2006/mxml"
   layout="vertical"
  xmlns:vo="vo.*" creationComplete="setSelectedState()">
  <mx:Script>
    <![CDATA[
      import vo.StateVO;
      [Bindable]
      private var selectedState:StateVO;
      private function setSelectedState():void
      {
        selectedState=stateList.selectedItem as StateVO;
      }
    ]]>
  </mx:Script>
  <mx:Array id="stateData">
    <vo:StateVO>
      <vo:state>CA</vo:state>
      <vo:capitol>Sacramento</vo:capitol>
    </vo:StateVO>
    <vo:StateVO>
      <vo:state>OR</vo:state>
      <vo:capitol>Salem</vo:capitol>
    </vo:StateVO>
    <vo:StateVO>
      <vo:state>WA</vo:state>
      <vo:capitol>Washington</vo:capitol>
    </vo:StateVO>
  </mx:Array>
  <mx:ComboBox id="stateList"
    dataProvider="{stateData}"
    labelField="capitol"
    change="setSelectedState()"/>
  <mx:Label text="Selected State Information:"/>
  <mx:Label text="State: {selectedState.state}"/>
  <mx:Label text="Capitol: {selectedState.capitol}"/>
</mx:Application>
```

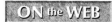 The code in Listing 17.6 is available in the Web site files as
`SelectingComplexObjects.mxml` in the `chapter17` project.

Using Custom Item Renderers

By default, `List` controls display simple strings in their visual items. As described previously, you can customize the string that's displayed with the control's `labelField` and `labelFunction` properties, but if you want to create a more complex display, you need to use a custom item renderer.

All `List` controls allow you to declare both item renderers and item editors. The differences between renderers and editors can be described as follows:

- Item renderers primarily display information, while item editors allow the user to modify the data that's stored in the `List` control's data provider.

- Item renderers display in every item of the `List` control regardless of the user's interactions with the control. Item editors are displayed only when the user clicks to start editing the item.

- Item renderers also can be marked as editors. In this case, they're still displayed on every item of List control like a normal item renderer. But, like an item editor, they allow the user to modify the data in the `List` control's data provider.

NOTE The use of custom item renderers is described in this chapter, because they can be used with all `List` controls. Custom item editors are described in Chapter 18 in the section about the `DataGrid` control.

You declare a `List` control's custom item renderer as a visual component that you want the control to instantiate each time it needs to render an item visually. Each of the `List` controls has a default item renderer class that it assigns to its `itemRenderer` property. The default `itemRenderer` class is `mx.controls.listClasses.ListItemRenderer`; this class is responsible for displaying simple string values as labels. When you declare a custom renderer, you override this default selection and have the freedom to create much more complex presentations.

You can declare custom item renderers in these ways:

- **Drop-in renderers** are visual components that you assign to a `List` control without any changes to the renderer component's default property or style settings.

- **Inline renderers** are components you define and nest within an MXML declaration of the `List` control.

- **Component renderers** are separate visual components that you define as MXML components or ActionScript classes and assign to the `List` control's `itemRenderer` property in an MXML declaration. You also can assign a component renderer at runtime with ActionScript code by using the `mx.core.ClassFactory` class (described below).

Using drop-in item renderers

A drop-in renderer is a visual component that you assign to the List control's itemRenderer or itemEditor properties using its complete package and class name. A limited number of components implement the IDropInListItemRenderer interface, making them eligible for this use. They include:

- Button
- CheckBox
- DateField
- Image
- Label
- NumericStepper
- Text
- TextArea
- TextInput

At runtime, for each item the List control renders, it creates an instance of the visual component you name as the renderer and passes data to the default property for that component. For example, if you use an Image component as your custom renderer, the data is passed to the control's source property. The Label, Text, TextArea, and TextInput controls have a default property of text, and each of the other controls has its own unique property.

If a List control's data provider contains String values, each containing the location of a graphic image you want to display instead of a label, you assign the itemRenderer using the fully qualified name of the component's equivalent ActionScript class:

```
<mx:List id="answerList" dataProvider="{answerData}"
    itemRenderer="mx.controls.Image"/>
```

CAUTION   When assigning a drop-in or a component item renderer, you must include the entire package and class name in the itemRenderer or itemEditor declaration. Including an import statement for the class you're using as the renderer does not eliminate this requirement.

The application in Listing 17.7 uses an ArrayCollection of String values, each containing the name of an image file in the project's source root. The List control's variableRowHeight property is set to true, allowing each row of the control to adjust to the image it displays.

LISTING 17.7

Using a drop-in item renderer

```xml
<?xml version="1.0" encoding="utf-8"?>
<mx:Application xmlns:mx="http://www.adobe.com/2006/mxml"
  backgroundColor="#EEEEEE">

  <mx:ArrayCollection id="answerData">
    <mx:String>assets/yesImage.png</mx:String>
    <mx:String>assets/noImage.png</mx:String>
    <mx:String>assets/maybeImage.png</mx:String>
  </mx:ArrayCollection>

  <mx:List id="answerList" dataProvider="{answerData}"
    itemRenderer="mx.controls.Image"
    rowCount="{answerData.length}"
    variableRowHeight="true"
    width="80" height="140"/>

</mx:Application>
```

ON the WEB The code in Listing 17.7 is available in the Web site files as `DropInRenderer.mxml` in the `chapter17` project.

Figure 17.5 shows the resulting application. Its List control displays the images based on the values in the control's data provider.

FIGURE 17.5

A List control with a drop-in item renderer

Drop-in item renderers work effectively with both single-column controls such as the `List` and `ComboBox` and with `DataGridColumn` components in the context of a `DataGrid`. Drop-in item editors can't be used very effectively in single-column controls, because with the drop-in architecture you don't have the ability to set object properties and override default behaviors. The use of drop-in item editors is described in Chapter 18.

You can use the `labelFunction` and `labelField` properties to affect the string that is passed to the drop-in renderers. For example, this function designed for use with `labelFunction` adds a URL path to an image reference:

```
private function doIt(item:Object):String
{
  return "http://www.myUrl.com/" + item as String;
}
```

Using inline renderers and editors

An inline renderer is an MXML component that you nest with the declaration of the `List` control. You first nest a `<mx:itemRenderer>` or `<mx:itemEditor>` child element with the `List` control's MXML tags, and then within that control, you nest a set of `<mx:Component>` tags. Finally, within the `<mx:Component>` tags, you nest the control or container from which you want to extend the custom component.

If the custom component you want to use as a custom renderer is extended from the `VBox` container, the structure of a `List` control's `itemRenderer` declaration looks like this:

```
<mx:List id="myList" dataProvider="{myData}">
  <mx:itemRenderer>
    <mx:Component>
      <mx:VBox>
      ... nested components ...
      </mx:VBox>
    </mx:Component>
  </mx:itemRenderer>
</mx:List>
```

When you create an inline item renderer, in object-oriented terms it's a local anonymous class. Local anonymous classes have the benefit of being declared within the context of their use, in this case within the `List` control for which it's designed. The drawback of using an anonymous class is that it can't be reused in a different context.

The `<mx:Component>` declaration is a compiler tag and doesn't represent a specific ActionScript class. Its purpose is to create a new component scope within an MXML file. Variables declared within the `<mx:Component>` tag set are local to the custom component and, unless declared public, aren't accessible to the containing application or component. Also, within the scope of the `<mx:Component>` tag set, the expression `this` refers to the current instance of the custom component and not to the application or containing component.

Every visual component in the Flex framework has a bindable `data` property designed for use in the custom item renderer architecture. At runtime, the `List` control creates an instance of the custom component for each of its items and passes the data provider's current data item to the component instance's `data` property.

Within the component code, you can refer to the current data item in a binding expression to use its information. In the application in Listing 17.8, the `List` control displays the same image as before, but this time the image location is determined in the custom item renderer by including a literal string in the Image control declaration.

LISTIN 17.8

Using an inline renderer

```
<?xml version="1.0" encoding="utf-8"?>
<mx:Application xmlns:mx="http://www.adobe.com/2006/mxml"
  backgroundColor="#EEEEEE">
  <mx:ArrayCollection id="answerData">
   <mx:String>yesImage.png</mx:String>
   <mx:String>noImage.png</mx:String>
   <mx:String>maybeImage.png</mx:String>
  </mx:ArrayCollection>
  <mx:List id="myList" dataProvider="{answerData}"
    rowCount="{answerData.length}"
    variableRowHeight="true"
    width="80" height="140">
    <mx:itemRenderer>
      <mx:Component>
        <mx:Image source="assets/{data}"/>
      </mx:Component>
    </mx:itemRenderer>
  </mx:List>
</mx:Application>
```

ON the WEB The code in Listing 17.8 is available in the Web site files as `InlineRenderer.mxml` in the `chapter17` project.

Using an inline or component renderer also makes working with data providers containing complex objects easier. The `List` control's `data` property is data typed as an ActionScript `Object` and is compatible with any sort of data object that might be passed from the `List` control's data provider. For example, if the data object has an `imageSource` property, the custom item renderer can use that property in a binding expression to pass values to its nested visual controls:

```
<mx:Image source="imageLocation/{data.imageSource}"/>
```

In the application in Listing 17.9, the List control's data provider contains objects with value and imageSource properties. The Image component used as the custom item renderer receives its source from the data object's imageSource property through a binding expression. The Label control at the bottom of the application displays the value property of the List control's currently selected data object through a binding expression of myList.selectedItem.value.

LISTING 17.9

Using complex data objects in a custom item renderer

```
<?xml version="1.0" encoding="utf-8"?>
<mx:Application xmlns:mx="http://www.adobe.com/2006/mxml"
  backgroundColor="#EEEEEE">

 <mx:ArrayCollection id="answerData">
   <mx:Object>
     <mx:value>Yes</mx:value>
     <mx:imageSource>yesImage.png</mx:imageSource>
   </mx:Object>
   <mx:Object>
     <mx:value>No</mx:value>
     <mx:imageSource>noImage.png</mx:imageSource>
   </mx:Object>
   <mx:Object>
     <mx:value>Maybe</mx:value>
     <mx:imageSource>maybeImage.png</mx:imageSource>
   </mx:Object>
 </mx:ArrayCollection>

  <mx:List id="myList" dataProvider="{answerData}"
    rowCount="{answerData.length}"
    variableRowHeight="true"
    width="80" height="140">
    <mx:itemRenderer>
      <mx:Component>
        <mx:Image source="assets/{data.imageSource}"/>
      </mx:Component>
    </mx:itemRenderer>
  </mx:List>

  <mx:Label text="{myList.selectedItem.value}"
    fontSize="14"/>

</mx:Application>
```

The code in Listing 17.9 is available in the Web site files as `InlineRendererComplexObjects.mxml` in the chapter17 project.

TIP You cannot create an empty `<mx:Component>` tag set; it must have a single nested child element indicating which visual component you're extending. The content of an inline component can include ActionScript code, `<mx:Binding>`, `<mx:Model>`, and `<mx:State>` tags, and pretty much anything else you might declare in a custom component in a separate MXML file.

Using component item renderers

A component item renderer is a separate class that can be created as either an MXML component or an ActionScript class that extends an existing visual component from the Flex framework. As with all visual components, the custom component has the same data property as was described in the previous section on inline components. At runtime, the List control creates an instance of the named component for each item it needs to render and passes the data provider's current data object to the component instance's data property.

NOTE This chapter describes how to create custom components with MXML. For details of creating components in ActionScript, see the product documentation.

You create item renderers as MXML components in the same manner as any other component. If you're using Flex Builder, you can use the New MXML Component wizard to create an MXML component source code file.

As with any MXML component, its root element is the visual component that you want your custom component to extend. The objects nested within the component's root element can use the data object and its named properties (determined by the List control's data provider) to display information dynamically.

TIP You should create custom components in subfolders of the Flex project's source root folder and give the subfolders descriptive names reflecting the use of the components they contain. For example, in the sample application described in this section, the custom components are stored in a `renderers` subfolder. Although it works technically to create custom components directly in the project's source root folder, this practice can create file management and application maintenance issues.

The custom component in Listing 17.10 extends the VBox container and contains an Image and a Label component. It uses its data property to set the nested object's properties through binding expressions.

LISTING 17.10

A custom item renderer component built with MXML

```
<?xml version="1.0" encoding="utf-8"?>
<mx:VBox xmlns:mx="http://www.adobe.com/2006/mxml"
  horizontalAlign="center"
  verticalScrollPolicy="off"
  horizontalScrollPolicy="off">
  <mx:Image source="assets/{data.imageSource}"/>
  <mx:Label text="{data.value}"/>
</mx:VBox>
```

ON the WEB The code in Listing 17.10 is available in the Web site files as `renderers/Image Renderer.mxml` in the `chapter17` project.

TIP A `List` control commonly "squeezes" a custom renderer component's available space and causes it to generate unwanted scrollbars. In the component in Listing 17.10, the component's `verticalScrollPolicy` and `horizontalScrollPolicy` properties are set to `off` to suppress scrollbars that might otherwise appear.

You use the custom renderer component with the same syntax as a drop-in renderer, supplying the fully qualified name and path of the component in the `List` control's `itemRenderer` or `itemEditor` property:

```
<mx:List id="myList" dataProvider="{answerData}"
    itemRenderer="renderers.ImageRenderer"/>
```

TIP When you provide the name of the custom renderer class to the `List` control, it is not a binding expression, and the class name isn't wrapped in braces (`{}`). You're providing the class definition, in a similar way to how an effect class is passed to a trigger. Instances of classes are wrapped in binding expressions; class definitions are passed solely by name without binding syntax.

The application in Listing 17.11 uses the custom component renderer to display all of each data object's values.

LISTING 17.11

Using a custom component renderer

```
<?xml version="1.0" encoding="utf-8"?>
<mx:Application xmlns:mx="http://www.adobe.com/2006/mxml"
  backgroundColor="#EEEEEE">
  <mx:ArrayCollection id="answerData">
   <mx:Object>
     <mx:value>Yes</mx:value>
```

```
        <mx:imageSource>yesImage.png</mx:imageSource>
     </mx:Object>
     <mx:Object>
        <mx:value>No</mx:value>
        <mx:imageSource>noImage.png</mx:imageSource>
     </mx:Object>
     <mx:Object>
        <mx:value>Maybe</mx:value>
        <mx:imageSource>maybeImage.png</mx:imageSource>
     </mx:Object>
  </mx:ArrayCollection>
  <mx:List id="myList" dataProvider="{answerData}"
     itemRenderer="renderers.ImageRenderer"
     rowCount="{answerData.length}"
     variableRowHeight="true"
     width="100" height="220"/>
  <mx:Label text="{myList.selectedItem.value}"
     fontSize="14"/>
</mx:Application>
```

ON the WEB The code in Listing 17.11 is available in the Web site files as `ComponentRenderer.mxml` in the **chapter17** project.

Figure 17.6 shows the completed application. Each visual item in the List displays both the Image and the Label, each populated with data from the current data object.

FIGURE 17.6

Using a component renderer with multiple nested visual components

Summary

In this chapter, I described how to use the basic functions of List controls. You learned the following:

- A List control presents data to the user and allows him make data selections with mouse or keyboard gestures.

- All the List controls use a common set of properties and events to determine their presentation and behavior.

- The List controls include the List, ComboBox, DataGrid, TileList, HorizontalList, Tree, AdvancedDataGrid, and OLAPDataGrid controls.

- Controls designed exclusively for use with AIR applications populate their data with information from the local client file system.

- You handle user selections with the change event and the selectedItem and selectedIndex properties.

- You can customize the labels presented in List control items with the labelField and labelFunction properties.

- Custom item renderers can be used with all List controls to create a more complex visual presentation.

- Custom item renderers can be declared using the drop-in, inline, or component architectures.

Chapter 18

Using Advanced List Controls

All list controls are not created equal. The two simplest list controls — the List and the ComboBox — display a single column of values and support the common functionality of custom labels, item renderers, and so on. But the ComboBox is really a compound control that allows the users to enter their own arbitrary values.

More complex list controls — such as the family of DataGrid components, the Tree control, and the TileList and HorizontalList — have their own unique capabilities. And as described briefly in Chapter 17, the AIR-based list controls have the ability to populate data from the local file system.

In Chapter 17, I described functionality that's common to all list controls, from the most fundamental to the most advanced. In this chapter, I describe the unique capabilities of specific data-driven controls, starting with the ComboBox and working up to the TileList, HorizontalList, and DataGrid.

ON the WEB To use the sample code for this chapter, import the chapter18.zip project from the Web site files into any folder on your disk.

Using the ComboBox Control

The ComboBox control is most like the basic List control in that it displays items in a single column. In terms of class inheritance, the two controls are related as cousins with a common ancestor. Figure 18.1 shows the two controls' direct superclass, up to their common UIComponent superclass.

FIGURE 18.1

The List and ComboBox inheritance hierarchies

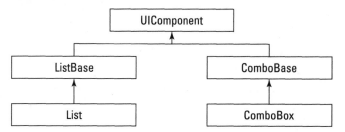

Using an editable ComboBox

The ComboBox control appears at first glance to be a simple drop-down list component. Its name, however, indicates that there's more to its capabilities. This component is actually a compound control that includes both a List and a TextInput.

The ComboBox control's nested TextInput isn't visible by default; instead, it appears only when the control's editable property is set to true. Used in this way, the user has an option of either selecting an item from the control's List or typing an arbitrary String value into the control.

When you set the control's editable property to true, you also have the option to set its prompt property. This property displays an initial value in the control's TextInput, allowing you to give the user a hint about what he's supposed to do. The following code declares a ComboBox with editable set to true and prompt set to a string that prompts the user accordingly:

> **TIP** The prompt property can be used even if the ComboBox isn't editable. When you set prompt to a value other than null, the ComboBox object's selectedIndex returns _1 and its selectedItem returns null. Once the user selects an item, selectedItem and selectedIndex reflect the currently selected item and its position in the ArrayCollection being used as the control's dataProvider.

```
<mx:ComboBox id="sizeCB" dataProvider="{sizeData}"
  prompt="Select an item" editable="true"/>
```

Figure 18.2 shows the resulting control displaying an initial prompt in the TextInput that appears as a result of the editable property being set to true.

FIGURE 18.2

An editable ComboBox

As with the List control, when the user selects an item from a ComboBox control's list, the selectedItem and selectedIndex properties point respectively to the selected data object and its ordinal position within the control's data provider. When the user types a value into the TextInput portion of the control, however, the control's properties are set as follows:

- selectedItem returns null.
- selectedIndex returns –1.
- prompt returns the user-entered value.
- text also returns the user-entered value.

TIP

While the ComboBox control's prompt and text properties return the same value, only the text property is bindable. If you try to use prompt in a binding expression, you get a compiler error indicating that the binding won't update at runtime if the property changes.

The application in Listing 18.1 uses a ComboBox with a data provider containing simple String values. The Label controls use binding expressions to display the control's current text, selectedIndex, and selectedItem properties.

LISTING 18.1

Using an editable ComboBox

```
<?xml version="1.0" encoding="utf-8"?>
<mx:Application xmlns:mx="http://www.adobe.com/2006/mxml"
  backgroundColor="#EEEEEE">
  <mx:Style>
    ComboBox, TextInput, Label { font-size:12 }
  </mx:Style>
  <mx:ArrayCollection id="sizeData">
    <mx:String>Small</mx:String>
```

continued

LISTING 18.1   (continued)

```
        <mx:String>Medium</mx:String>
        <mx:String>Large</mx:String>
    </mx:ArrayCollection>
    <mx:Label text="selectedIndex: {sizeCB.selectedIndex}"/>
    <mx:Label text="selectedItem: {sizeCB.selectedItem}"/>
    <mx:Label text="Text: {sizeCB.text}"/>
    <mx:ComboBox id="sizeCB" dataProvider="{sizeData}"
        prompt="Select an item" editable="true"/>
</mx:Application>
```

ON the WEB   The code in Listing 18.1 is available in the Web site files as `EditableComboBox.mxml` in the `chapter18` project.

Figure 18.3 shows the application in two states. The version on the left shows the control's values when an item is selected from the list, while the version on the right shows its values when the user has typed in an arbitrary value.

FIGURE 18.3

A ComboBox being used in two different ways

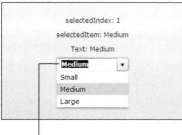

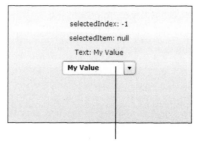

Selecting from the list   Typing in a value

Using a bindable ComboBox

The ComboBox control has a particular weakness in that you can't easily set its initial value when working with a data provider containing complex objects. In HTML code, it's common to set a `<select>` control's currently selected item by looping through the `<option>` tags and matching a property of the data set to values of the options. For example, in ColdFusion the classic code to accomplish this task looks like this:

```
<select name="sizeList" size="1">
  <cfloop query="availableOptions">
```

```
      <option value="#myData.recordid#"
        <cfif availableOptions.recordid IS currentDataRow.recordid>
          selected="selected"
        </cfif>
      >#availableOptions.labelField#</option>
    </cfloop>
  </select>
```

Each application server language that generates HTML code dynamically has its own unique way of accomplishing this task (and in many cases the code is considerably simpler than in this example), but the goal is always to generate only one <option> tag within the <select> tag set with an attribute of selected="selected".

The ComboBox control doesn't provide this capability directly. Assume that the data provider for a ComboBox contains complex objects with named properties, as in this example:

```
  <mx:Array id="stateData" labelField="capitol">
    <vo:StateVO>
      <vo:state>CA</vo:state>
      <vo:capitol>Sacramento</vo:capitol>
    </vo:StateVO>
    <vo:StateVO>
      <vo:state>OR</vo:state>
      <vo:capitol>Salem</vo:capitol>
    </vo:StateVO>
    <vo:StateVO>
      <vo:state>WA</vo:state>
      <vo:capitol>Olympia</vo:capitol>
    </vo:StateVO>
  </mx:Array>
```

If you want the ComboBox to show that one of its data items is selected based on a value that you pass in, you have to use a custom component that adds this feature. Fortunately, the work has been done for you if you know where to find it.

The ColdFusion Extensions for Flex Builder, which you can install with the initial Flex Builder installation or at a later time, have a feature named the ColdFusion/Flex Application Wizard. This feature generates a complete Flex/ColdFusion data entry application based on the structure of an existing database table structure. The generated application includes both BindableComboBox and BindableList custom components that are designed to solve this specific issue.

Listing 18.2 shows an application that uses the custom BindableComboBox component. The customized version of the component overrides the superclass's selectedItem property, allowing you to pass in any value instead of the actual object you want to select. Whenever the selectedItem you pass in changes, it's compared to a property of the existing data provider's objects. You indicate which named property of the data provider's objects you want to compare with the component's valueField property.

LISTING 18.2

Using a custom bindable ComboBox component

```xml
<?xml version="1.0" encoding="utf-8"?>
<mx:Application xmlns:mx="http://www.adobe.com/2006/mxml"
  layout="horizontal" xmlns:vo="vo.*"
  xmlns:components="com.adobe.components.*">
  <mx:Array id="stateData">
    <vo:StateVO>
      <vo:state>CA</vo:state>
      <vo:capitol>Sacramento</vo:capitol>
    </vo:StateVO>
    <vo:StateVO>
      <vo:state>OR</vo:state>
      <vo:capitol>Salem</vo:capitol>
    </vo:StateVO>
    <vo:StateVO>
      <vo:state>WA</vo:state>
      <vo:capitol>Olympia</vo:capitol>
    </vo:StateVO>
  </mx:Array>
  <mx:Panel id="listPanel" title="List" width="200">
    <mx:List id="stateList" dataProvider="{stateData}"
      labelField="capitol" width="100%"/>
  </mx:Panel>
  <mx:Panel title="ComboBox"
    width="{listPanel.width}" height="{listPanel.height}">
    <components:BindableComboBox id="stateCB"
      dataProvider="{stateData}"
      valueField="state"
      selectedItem="{stateList.selectedItem.state}"
      labelField="capitol"/>
    <mx:Label text="State: {stateCB.selectedItem.state}"/>
    <mx:Label text="Capitol: {stateCB.selectedItem.capitol}"/>
  </mx:Panel>
</mx:Application>
```

ON the WEB The code in Listing 18.2 is available in the Web site files as `UsingBindable`
`ComboBox.mxml` in the `chapter18` project. The application also uses the
`StateVO.as` value object class in the project source root's `vo` folder and the `Bindable`
`ComboBox.mxml` file in the `com/adobe/components` folder.

 The `BindableComboBox` and `BindableList` components that you generate with the ColdFusion/Flex Application Wizard were created by Dean Harmon and Mike Nimer.

The application is shown in Figure 18.4. The `List` control on the left displays all the data set's objects. The currently selected item's state property is passed to the custom `BindableComboBox` on the right through a binding expression; as a result, the two controls are synchronized.

FIGURE 18.4

Using the `BindableComboBox` control

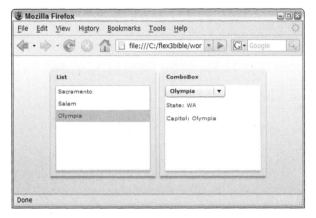

Using the DataGrid Control

The `DataGrid` control is one of the most popular controls in the Flex framework. It's designed to present relational data in the form of rows and columns to the user, and allow the user to easily scroll through and select data. In addition, the `DataGrid` can be made editable, allowing the user to edit multiple rows of data in batches instead of having to navigate to a data entry form interface for each row he wants to modify.

In terms of inheritance hierarchy, the `DataGrid` is directly extended from the `ListBase` class; as a result, it shares most of the events and properties of the `List` component. Figure 18.6 shows the inheritance tree of the `DataGrid`. The `FileSystemDataGrid` (used in AIR applications) and the `PrintDataGrid` (optimized for printing) are extended from `DataGrid` and inherit all its behaviors.

FIGURE 18.5

The `DataGrid` inheritance hierarchy

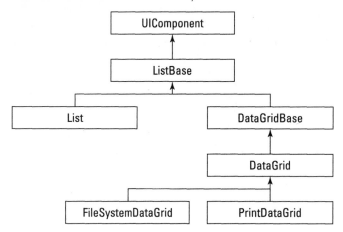

The `DataGrid` control has these built-in features:

- It displays multiple columns, each dedicated to displaying one named property of its data provider's data items.

- It displays column headers, which you can customize with simple strings or complex displays.

- The data display is sortable by the user when she clicks a column heading. This actually results in sorting the `DataGrid` object's underlying data collection.

- The user can change the order of the columns by clicking and dragging the columns.

- The user can resize columns by clicking and dragging the borders between the columns.

- Data is displayed in rows with alternating row colors.

- Scrolling through large amounts of data is supported through an architecture known as deferred instantiation.

- When integrated with Adobe's LiveCycle Data Services or a similar application server that supports the Data Management Service architecture, you can easily enable paging through large amounts of server-side data without overwhelming Flash Player memory.

- You can lock rows and columns to prevent scrolling.

> **TIP**   When you provide data to a `DataGrid` control, it should always be in the form of an `ArrayCollection` containing complex objects. The objects should have named properties that in turn contain either simple values that can be directly displaying in the `DataGrid` controls columns and or that can be used by item renderer components to create customized displays. Because the purpose of a `DataGrid` is to display more than a single column, it doesn't make sense to provide it with an `ArrayCollection` containing simple string values.

Customizing DataGrid display

The DataGrid control provides many features that allow you to customize how it's displayed:

- The height and width can be set in absolute pixels or percentage of available space.

- The rowCount property can determine the control's height based on the number of rows you display.

- The alternatingItemColors style is set to an Array of colors. When set with two colors, the items' backgrounds alternate between them. If you set this style to an Array with more than two colors, the items loop through the colors and display them in order of declaration.

- The columns property determines which columns are displayed to the user.

In this section, I describe some of the techniques that are most commonly used in customizing the DataGrid control.

Default columns display

By default, the DataGrid control generates columns for its data provider based on the property names of the first object in the data set.

> **NOTE** Ideally, all the data objects in a data collection have the same number of properties and identical names. When you allow the DataGrid to generate its columns automatically, it does so based only on the properties in the first item of the dataProvider.

In the following XML structure, each data object has eight properties, named (in order of declaration) contactid, firstname, lastname, streetaddress, city, state, email, and phone:

```
<?xml version="1.0"?>
<contacts>
  <row>
    <contactid>1</contactid>
    <firstname>Brad</firstname>
    <lastname>Lang</lastname>
    <streetaddress>3004 Buckhannan Avenue</streetaddress>
    <city>Syracuse</city>
    <state>NY</state>
    <email>Brad.C.Lang@trashymail.com</email>
    <phone>315-449-9420</phone>
  </row>
  <row>
    <contactid>2</contactid>
    <firstname>Kevin</firstname>
    <lastname>Mount</lastname>
    <streetaddress>341 Private Lane</streetaddress>
    <city>Montgomery</city>
```

```
        <state>GA</state>
        <email>Kevin.J.Mount@trashymail.com</email>
        <phone>229-329-4001</phone>
    </row>
    ... additional <row> elements ...
</contacts>
```

WEB RESOURCE The contact information used in this section of the book and elsewhere is fake! If you need fake data with which to test and benchmark your application, try the Web site at `www.fakenamegenerator.com`. You can order large amounts of fake data (up to 40,000 fake names at a time) in a variety of data formats. The only cost for this service comes up if you need it in a hurry.

As with the `List` and `ComboBox` controls, you pass data into the `DataGrid` with the `dataProvider` property. The application in Listing 18.3 uses code that embeds data from the XML file with the `<mx:Model>` tag and wraps it in an `ArrayCollection`. The data is then passed to the `DataGrid` with a binding expression.

LISTING 18.3

Default DataGrid column generation

```xml
<?xml version="1.0" encoding="utf-8"?>
<mx:Application xmlns:mx="http://www.adobe.com/2006/mxml" >
  <mx:Model id="contactData" source="data/contacts.xml"/>
  <mx:ArrayCollection id="contactAC" source="{contactData.row}"/>
  <mx:DataGrid id="contactGrid" dataProvider="{contactAC}"/>
</mx:Application>
```

ON the WEB The code in Listing 18.3 is available in the Web site files as `DataGridDefault Columns.mxml` in the `chapter18` project.

At runtime, the `DataGrid` examines the first data object in its `dataProvider` and then generates one column for each of the data object's named properties. The columns are arranged in alphabetical order, rather than the order in which the properties are declared in the XML file. (The data objects are cast as instances of the ActionScript `Object` class, which doesn't maintain its properties in any specific order.)

Figure 18.6 shows the resulting display, with the `DataGrid` showing all eight available columns of data.

FIGURE 18.6

A DataGrid with default column display

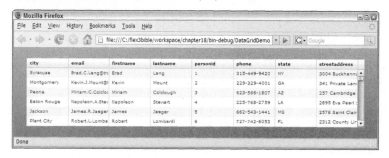

Controlling column display

You determine the number and order of columns displayed by the DataGrid with its columns property. The columns property must be an Array of DataGridColumn instances, typically declared like this:

```
<mx:DataGrid id="contactGrid" dataProvider="{contactAC}">
  <mx:columns>
    <mx:DataGridColumn ... property settings.../>
    <mx:DataGridColumn ... property settings.../>
  </mx:columns>
</mx:DataGrid>
```

The DataGridColumn control determines how each individual column is displayed. Its key properties include:

- dataField:String: This is the name of the property you want the column to display. This value is case-sensitive and must exactly match the property names of the data provider's items.

- headerText:String: This is the string value you want to display in the column header.

- width:Number: This is the width of the column in absolute pixels. (You cannot set a column's width based on a percentage of available space in the DataGrid without doing some calculations at runtime.)

This DataGridColumn declaration creates a column that displays each data object's firstname property, displays header text of "First Name", and has an explicit width of 100 pixels:

```
<mx:DataGridColumn dataField="firstname"
  headerText="First Name" width="100"/>
```

Columns are displayed in the order of their declaration: The first `DataGridColumn` is leftmost in the `DataGrid` display, the second is to its right, and so on. The application in Listing 18.4 declares a `DataGrid` with three columns displaying the data provider's `firstname`, `lastname`, and `email` properties.

LISTING 18.4

A DataGrid with explicit column settings

```xml
<?xml version="1.0" encoding="utf-8"?>
<mx:Application xmlns:mx="http://www.adobe.com/2006/mxml">
  <mx:Model id="contactData" source="data/contacts.xml"/>
  <mx:ArrayCollection id="contactAC" source="{contactData.row}"/>
  <mx:DataGrid id="contactGrid" dataProvider="{contactAC}">
    <mx:columns>
      <mx:DataGridColumn dataField="firstname" headerText="First Name"
        width="100"/>
      <mx:DataGridColumn dataField="lastname" headerText="Last Name"
        width="100"/>
      <mx:DataGridColumn dataField="email" headerText="Email Address"
        width="250"/>
    </mx:columns>
  </mx:DataGrid>
</mx:Application>
```

ON the WEB   The code in Listing 18.4 is available in the Web site files as `DataGridDefault Columns.mxml` in the `chapter18` project.

Figure 18.7 shows the resulting application, with three columns of data displayed in the order of their declaration in the `DataGrid` control's `columns` property.

FIGURE 18.7

A `DataGrid` with explicit columns

> **TIP** Even though only certain columns are displayed to the user, the `DataGrid` control's
> `selectedItem` property still refers to the complete data object represented by the
> currently selected row. In many data-oriented applications, you don't display the values of each row's
> unique identifiers (primary keys in database parlance) to the user. That information, however, is
> always available. In the application in Listing 18.7, for example, the expression `contactGrid`
> `.selectedItem.contactid` would refer to the unique identifier for the currently selected
> data item.

> **TIP** If you specify a column's property by setting `dataField`, that will be the property that
> the column sorts on when you click the header. If you don't specify a property (which is
> possible if you use a renderer or `labelFunction` to render a column's cells), then that row isn't
> automatically sortable.

Generating custom labels with DataGrid columns

In Chapter 17, I described how to use the `labelFunction` property with the `List` and
`ComboBox` controls. This property also is implemented in the `DataGridColumn` component,
but the function you create to format that column's labels has a slightly different signature.

As a reminder, the signature for a custom function compatible with the `List` and `ComboBox` controls looks like this:

```
private function getFormattedLabel(item:Object):String
```

When the function is assigned to a `DataGridColumn`, the function signature changes to:

```
private function getFormattedLabel(item:Object,
   column:DataGridColumn):String
```

The difference is the addition of the function's second argument, which is a reference to the
`DataGridColumn` object that calls the function at runtime.

In the data set used in this chapter, each data item has a `phone` property formatted with hyphens:

```
315-555-9420
```

If, instead, you want to format the phone number with parentheses around the area code, you
might declare an instance of the `PhoneFormatter` class:

```
<mx:PhoneFormatter id="formatter"/>
```

Then create the custom formatting function:

```
private function getPhoneLabel(item:Object,
   column:DataGridColumn):String
{
}
```

The `PhoneFormatter` requires a value that can be parsed as a number, so within the formatting function, you first strip the hyphen characters from the data item's value. You can do this in a couple of ways; the following code uses a regular expression and replaces all instances of the hyphen character with a blank string:

```
var pattern:RegExp = /-/g;
var phoneValue:String = item.phone.replace(pattern, "");
```

Finally, return the formatted value by passing the resulting expression to the `PhoneFormatter` object's `format()` method:

```
return formatter.format(phoneValue);
```

Listing 18.5 shows the complete application with a `DataGridColumn` that displays each contact's phone number with the format (315) 555-9420.

LISTING 18.5

Using a custom formatting function in a DataGridColumn

```
<?xml version="1.0" encoding="utf-8"?>
<mx:Application xmlns:mx="http://www.adobe.com/2006/mxml">
  <mx:Script>
    <![CDATA[
      import mx.controls.dataGridClasses.DataGridColumn;
      private function getPhoneLabel(item:Object,
        column:DataGridColumn):String
      {
        /*The regular expression consists of a hyphen
          (the value being replaced) and the /g global flag
          to replace ALL instances of the hyphen
        */
        var pattern:RegExp = /-/g;
        var phoneValue:String = item.phone.replace(pattern, "");
        return formatter.format(phoneValue);
      }
    ]]>
  </mx:Script>
  <mx:Model id="contactData" source="data/contacts.xml"/>
  <mx:ArrayCollection id="contactAC" source="{contactData.row}"/>
  <mx:PhoneFormatter id="formatter"/>
  <mx:DataGrid id="contactGrid" dataProvider="{contactAC}">
    <mx:columns>
      <mx:DataGridColumn dataField="firstname" headerText="First Name"
        width="100"/>
      <mx:DataGridColumn dataField="lastname" headerText="Last Name"
        width="100"/>
      <mx:DataGridColumn dataField="email" headerText="Email Address"
```

```
          width="250"/>
     <mx:DataGridColumn dataField="phone" headerText="Phone Number"
          width="150" labelFunction="getPhoneLabel"/>
   </mx:columns>
  </mx:DataGrid>
</mx:Application>
```

Figure 18.8 shows the resulting application with formatted phone numbers in the last column of the DataGrid control.

FIGURE 18.8

A DataGridColumn with custom label formatting

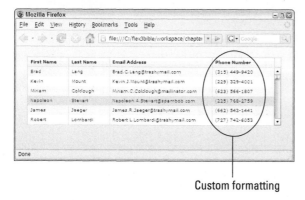

Custom formatting

Using a dynamic data field

As described previously, the custom formatting function for a DataGridColumn requires an argument that references the DataGridColumn that is calling the function. The purpose of this argument is to allow you to determine the data field of the current data item dynamically.

For example, if the data provider's data items have phone values in two different properties and you want to format them both with the same logic, you can identify the property you want to format with the array-style expression item[column.dataField]. The dataField property of the DataGridColumn returns the name of the property currently being processed, so you need only one custom function to format as many data properties as needed:

```
private function getPhoneLabel(item:Object,
     column:DataGridColumn):String
{
```

```
    var dataValue:String = item[column.dataField];
    var pattern:RegExp = /-/g;
    var phoneValue:String = dataValue.replace(pattern, "");
    return formatter.format(phoneValue);
}
```

Debugging a custom formatting function

It can be instructive to add a `trace()` statement to the body of a custom formatting function. As you scroll up and down in a `DataGrid`, each time the data grid column has to be formatted, the trace statement in the custom function is executed:

```
private function getPhoneLabel(item:Object,
  column:DataGridColumn):String
{
  var dataValue:String = item[column.dataField];
  var pattern:RegExp = /-/g;
  var phoneValue:String = item.phone.replace(pattern, "");
  trace("original value: " + dataValue + ", " +
    "formatted value: " +   formatter.format(phoneValue));
  return formatter.format(phoneValue);
}
```

Figure 18.9 shows the resulting output in Flex Builder's Console view when the application is run in debug mode. The Console view displays the trace statements continuously as you scroll up and down in the `DataGrid`.

FIGURE 18.9

Debugging a custom formatting function

```
 Problems  Console
DataGridDebugFormatting [Flex Application] file:/C:/flex3bible/workspace/chapter18/bin-debug/DataGridDebugFormat
[SWF] C:\flex3bible\workspace\chapter18\bin-debug\DataGridDebugFormatting.swf - 1
261,444 bytes after decompression
original value: 315-449-9420, formatted value: (315) 449-9420
original value: 315-449-9420, formatted value: (315) 449-9420
original value: 229-329-4001, formatted value: (229) 329-4001
original value: 623-566-1807, formatted value: (623) 566-1807
original value: 225-768-2759, formatted value: (225) 768-2759
original value: 662-543-1441, formatted value: (662) 543-1441
original value: 727-742-6053, formatted value: (727) 742-6053
original value: 315-449-9420, formatted value: (315) 449-9420
original value: 229-329-4001, formatted value: (229) 329-4001
original value: 623-566-1807, formatted value: (623) 566-1807
original value: 225-768-2759, formatted value: (225) 768-2759
original value: 662-543-1441, formatted value: (662) 543-1441
original value: 727-742-6053, formatted value: (727) 742-6053
```

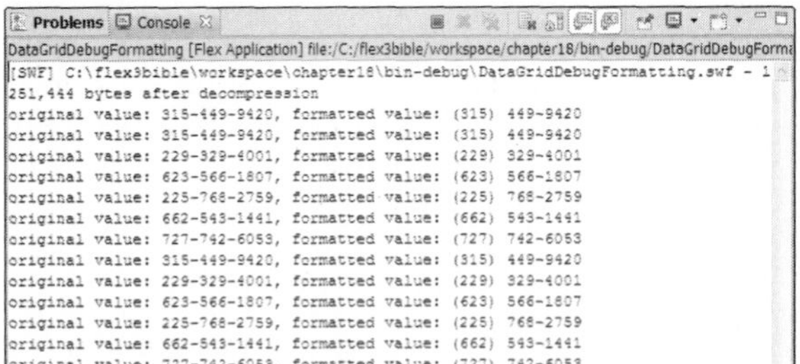

TIP One of the advantages of the `DataGrid` control is that it reuses its visual objects as you scroll. Unlike a `Repeater` control, which actually generates visual controls for every data item in its `dataProvider`, whether or not they'll be visible on the screen, the `DataGrid` simply populates existing visual controls with new data and creates the appearance of a smooth scrolling experience.

As a result, you can populate the DataGrid and other list controls with significant amounts of data without causing the Flash Player to bog down or overload its memory usage. When you run the application described previously with trace statements, try scrolling up and down. You'll notice that the function is called frequently as you scroll, and the existing visual objects are updated with new data.

Advanced Item Renderers and Editors

As described in Chapter 17, all list controls support the custom item renderer and editor architectures. In a DataGrid control, an item renderer or editor is used in a specific column, so the itemRenderer and itemEditor properties are implemented in the DataGridColumn component.

Just as with the List control, item renderer and editor components for the DataGridColumn can be declared in three ways:

- **Drop-in renderers** are visual components that you assign to a list control without any changes to the renderer component's default property or style settings.

- **Inline renderers** are components you define and nest within an MXML declaration of the list control.

- **Component renderers** are separate visual components that you define as MXML components or ActionScript classes and assign to the list control's itemRenderer property in an MXML declaration. You also can assign a component renderer at runtime with ActionScript code by using the mx.core.ClassFactory class (described below).

CROSS-REF For more information on the three types of item renderer declarations, see Chapter 17.

At runtime, the DataGridColumn creates an instance of the component and passes its data provider's current data item as the renderer object's data property. Within the custom component, whether declared inline or as a separate component, you use the data object's properties with either ActionScript statements or binding expressions to populate visual objects and create your custom presentation.

Using the dataChange event

In the following example, a DataGrid component displays contact information from the contacts.xml file. In the first column of the DataGrid, the contact's first and last names are displayed as a single concatenated string. This task can be easily handled with a custom label formatting function:

```
private function getNameLabel(item:Object,
  column:DataGridColumn):String
{
  return item.firstname + " " + item.lastname;
}
```

In the second column, the `DataGrid` will display the contact's full address, formatted as a single `Text` control using HTML markup for bold and other formatting. To handle this requirement, you can use the `dataChange` event to update a custom component's display at runtime. This event is dispatched within the custom component whenever the value of its data property is updated. You can respond to the event by explicitly updating the custom component's nested objects as needed.

The custom component in Listing 18.6 is extended from the `Text` component. When the component's `dataChange` event is dispatched, it responds by updating its own `htmlText` property with the `data` object's new property values.

LISTING 18.6

A custom component updating its display with the dataChange event

```
<?xml version="1.0" encoding="utf-8"?>
<mx:Text xmlns:mx="http://www.adobe.com/2006/mxml"
  dataChange="updateHTML()">

  <mx:Script>
    <![CDATA[

      private function updateHTML():void
      {
        htmlText = "<b>" + data.firstname + " " +
        data.lastname + "</b>\n" +
        data.streetaddress + "\n" +
        data.city + ", " + data.state + "\n" +
        "<b>Phone:</b> " + data.phone + "\n" +
        "<b>Email:</b> " + data.email + "\n";
      }
    ]]>
  </mx:Script>

</mx:Text>
```

ON the WEB   The code in Listing 18.6 is available in the Web site files as `AddressRenderer.mxml` in the `chapter18` project's `src/renderers` folder.

The application in Listing 18.7 uses the custom component as an item renderer to display complete formatted address information in the `DataGrid` control's second column. Notice that the `DataGrid` control's `selectable` property is set to `false`. This makes it easier for the user to select the custom component's text value for copying. Also, its `variableRowHeight` property is set to `true` to allow the `DataGrid` columns to adjust their height as needed.

LISTING 18.7

An application using a component item renderer

```
<?xml version="1.0" encoding="utf-8"?>
<mx:Application xmlns:mx="http://www.adobe.com/2006/mxml"
  backgroundColor="#EEEEEE">
  <mx:Script>
    <![CDATA[
      import mx.controls.dataGridClasses.DataGridColumn;
      private function getNameLabel(item:Object,
        column:DataGridColumn):String
      {
        return item.firstname + " " + item.lastname;
      }
    ]]>
  </mx:Script>
  <mx:Model id="contactData" source="data/contacts.xml"/>
  <mx:ArrayCollection id="contactAC" source="{contactData.row}"/>
  <mx:DataGrid id="contactGrid" dataProvider="{contactAC}"
    selectable="false" variableRowHeight="true" rowCount="5">
    <mx:columns>
      <mx:DataGridColumn dataField="firstname" headerText="Full Name"
          width="150" labelFunction="getNameLabel"/>
      <mx:DataGridColumn headerText="Address Info"
          width="350" itemRenderer="renderers.AddressRenderer"/>
    </mx:columns>
  </mx:DataGrid>
</mx:Application>
```

ON the WEB The code in Listing 18.7 is available in the Web site files as `DataGridCustom Renderer.mxml` in the `chapter18` project.

Figure 18.10 shows the resulting application, with each contact's full name in the left column and complete formatted address information in the right column. The user can select the text in the right column and then right-click (or Ctrl+click on the Mac) to copy the text with the pop-up context menu.

Using item editors

Like an item renderer, an item editor is a custom component that you display instead of the default label in a `DataGridColumn` cell. An item editor, however, is always an interactive control that allows the user to make changes to the data it represents. As with item renderers, you can declare an item editor using a drop-in, inline, and component syntax.

FIGURE 18.10

A custom item renderer using the `dataChange` event

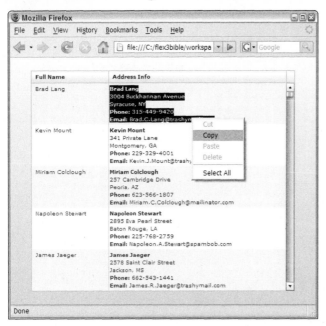

Before you can use an item editor, the `DataGrid` must have its `editable` property set to `true`. When you do this, the `DataGrid` automatically displays an item editor in any cell the user clicks. The default item editor is the `TextInput` control, so when the user clicks into an editable cell, he's presented with a `TextInput` that lets him change the data. When the user clicks or tabs out of the cell, the new data is saved to the `DataGrid` component's data provider in application memory.

When you set the `DataGrid` component's `editable` property to `true`, all its columns are automatically editable. Each `DataGridComponent` has an `editable` property as well; you stop editing of any particular column by setting its `editable` property to `false`.

In the following code, the `DataGrid` is editable, but editing is prevented in the `firstname` and `lastname` columns. As a result, only the data in the `phone` column can be changed by the user:

```
<mx:DataGrid id="contactGrid" dataProvider="{contactAC}"
  editable="true" selectable="false">
<mx:columns>
  <mx:DataGridColumn dataField="firstname" headerText="First
  Name"
    width="100" editable="false"/>
  <mx:DataGridColumn dataField="lastname" headerText="Last Name"
```

```
        width="100" editable="false"/>
    <mx:DataGridColumn dataField="phone" headerText="Phone"
        width="100"/>
  </mx:columns>
  </mx:DataGrid>
```

Figure 18.11 shows the resulting `DataGrid`. When the user clicks a cell in the phone column, a `TextInput` control appears to allow editing.

FIGURE 18.11

An editable `DataGrid` control with a default item editor

WARNING   If you apply a `labelFunction` to a column that's also editable and uses the default item editor, the user will be editing the value returned from the `labelFunction` and not the column's original data.

Using drop-in item editors

To use a component as a drop-in item editor, it must implement the `IDropInListItemRenderer` interface, and it must be interactive, allowing the user to make changes to data. Only a small number of components in the Flex class library qualify on both counts; they include:

- Button
- CheckBox
- DateField
- NumericStepper
- TextArea
- TextInput

To declare a drop-in editor in a DataGridColumn, you assign the component to the DataGridColumn component's itemEditor (if you want to see the component appear only when the user clicks a cell to edit it), or to its itemRenderer (if you want to see it appear on all rows). In either case, you assign the component by its fully qualified class name, including the package prefix:

```
<mx:DataGridColumn dataField="selected"
  itemEditor="mx.controls.CheckBox"
  ... remainder of declaration ...
/>
```

The details of each strategy are described in the following sections.

Using the itemEditor and editorDataField properties

When you declare an itemEditor for a DataGridColumn, you also have to set the DataGridColumn control's editorDataField property to indicate which field of the item editor component contains the value entered by the user. At runtime, the changed value is transferred back to the current data object's property (the property that's named as the DataGridColumn component's dataField).

For example, if you use a CheckBox control as an item editor, the editorDataField property should be set to selected. For a TextInput control, editorDataField should be set to text (the default), for a NumericStepper, it should be value, and so on.

When you set the itemEditor property to a named component, that component is instantiated only when the user clicks into the cell. For example, the following code indicates that a CheckBox control should appear only when the user clicks:

```
<mx:DataGridColumn dataField="selected"
  itemEditor="mx.controls.CheckBox"
  editorDataField="selected"
  headerText="" width="50"/>
```

Figure 8.12 shows the result: Unless the user has clicked a cell that's editable, the column's actual value is displayed as a label. When the user clicks in a cell, it displays the CheckBox control.

Using the rendererIsEditor property

If you want the item editor component to be displayed in every row of the DataGrid, follow these steps:

1. Assign the editor component DataGridColumn component's itemRenderer property instead of itemEditor.

2. Set the DataGridColumn component's editorIsRenderer property to true.

FIGURE 8.12

Using the `itemEditor` property

The following code causes the `CheckBox` control to appear in every row, regardless of whether the user has clicked into the cell:

```
<mx:DataGridColumn dataField="selected"
   itemRenderer="mx.controls.CheckBox"
   rendererIsEditor="true"
   editorDataField="selected"
   headerText="" width="50"/>
```

The application in Listing 18.8 uses an `itemRenderer` that is set with `rendererIsEditor` to true. The renderer is a drop-in component based on `mx.controls.CheckBox`. At application startup, the `initApp()` method loops through the `ArrayCollection` being used as the `DataGrid` component's data provider and adds a `selected` property to each object. That property is then both displayed and edited through the `CheckBox` that appears on every row.

> **TIP** Notice in Listing 18.8 that the `DataGrid` control's `selectable` property is set to false. This turns off the default selection and highlighting functionality of the `DataGrid` to let the user more easily click the `CheckBox` controls in the left column.

LISTING 18.8

Setting a renderer as an editor

```
<?xml version="1.0" encoding="utf-8"?>
<mx:Application xmlns:mx="http://www.adobe.com/2006/mxml"
  backgroundColor="#EEEEEE" creationComplete="initApp()">
  <mx:Script>
    <![CDATA[
```

continued

LISTING 18.8   *(continued)*

```
      private function initApp():void
      {
        //Add a selected property to each data object on startup
        for (var i:int=0;i < contactAC.length; i++)
        {
          var contact:Object = contactAC.getItemAt(i);
          contact.selected=false;
        }
      }
    ]]>
  </mx:Script>
  <mx:Model id="contactData" source="data/contacts.xml"/>
  <mx:ArrayCollection id="contactAC" source="{contactData.row}"/>
  <mx:DataGrid id="contactGrid" dataProvider="{contactAC}"
    editable="true" selectable="false">
    <mx:columns>
      <mx:DataGridColumn dataField="firstname" headerText="First Name"
        width="100" editable="false"/>
      <mx:DataGridColumn dataField="lastname" headerText="Last Name"
        width="100" editable="false"/>
      <mx:DataGridColumn dataField="phone" headerText="Phone"
        width="100"/>
    </mx:columns>
  </mx:DataGrid>
</mx:Application>
```

ON the WEB   The code in Listing 18.8 is available in the Web site files as `DataGridDropin Editor.mxml` in the `chapter18` project.

Figure 18.13 shows the resulting DataGrid with a CheckBox on every row. When the user clicks one of the CheckBox components, its `selected` value is saved to the appropriate data object's `selected` property.

TIP   When you allow the user to edit data through an editable `DataGrid`, changes are made to the data collection that's stored in client memory. If you want to save the data to a persistent data store on the server (or on the client, in the case of an AIR-based desktop application), you need to write code to transfer the changed data. If the persistent data store is on the server, you can accomplish this with the RPC components (`HTTPService`, `WebService`, or `RemoteObject`) or with the Data Management Service (if using LiveCycle Data Services). With a desktop-based application, you could use the local SQLite database that's embedded in the Adobe Integrated Runtime (AIR).

Using inline and component editors

As with custom renderers, you can declare custom item editor components with either inline syntax or as separate components. The benefits of using this syntax instead of drop-in components are that you're free to use any combination of visual controls and containers and you can override the components' default property and style settings.

FIGURE 18.13

A renderer displaying every row with `rendererIsEditor` set to `true`

For example, imagine that you wanted to use the `DateField` control as an item editor, but you modify its default behavior in some way. You might set its `editable` property to `true` to allow the user to enter a date directly (without having to pick it from the pop-up calendar control) or restrict its available dates:

```
<mx:DataGridColumn dataField="dob"
   editorDataField="selectedDate">
  <mx:itemEditor>
    <mx:Component>
      <mx:DateField maxYear="2000" editable="true"/>
    </mx:Component>
  </mx:itemEditor>
</mx:DataGridColumn>
```

Because the `DateField` component is declared with the `itemEditor` property, it's displayed only when the user clicks the cell containing the date value.

CROSS-REF The use of the `<mx:Component>` tag to define a separate component is described in Chapter 17's section about creating item renderers.

The application in Listing 18.9 shows the use of a `DateField` as an inline item editor. Upon application startup, the data is retrieved dynamically using an `HTTPService` component (described in Chapter 21). When the data is returned, the data objects in the `ArrayCollection` are transformed into instances of the `ContactVO` class. This is critical for this example, because the `ContactVO` class has a `dob` property typed as a `Date`, which makes it compatible with the `DateField` control that is then used as the property's editor in the `DataGrid`.

LISTING 18.9

Using an inline item editor

```xml
<?xml version="1.0" encoding="utf-8"?>
<mx:Application xmlns:mx="http://www.adobe.com/2006/mxml"
  backgroundColor="#EEEEEE" creationComplete="contactService.send()">
  <mx:Script>
    <![CDATA[
      import mx.controls.dataGridClasses.DataGridColumn;
      import mx.collections.ArrayCollection;
      import mx.rpc.events.ResultEvent;
      import vo.ContactVO;
      [Bindable]
      private var contactAC:ArrayCollection;
      private function resultHandler(event:ResultEvent):void
      {
        contactAC = event.result.contacts.row;
        for (var i:int=0; i<contactAC.length; i++)
        {
          var newContact:ContactVO =
            new ContactVO(contactAC.getItemAt(i));
          contactAC.setItemAt(newContact, i);
        }
      }
      private function getDateLabel(item:ContactVO,
        column:DataGridColumn):String
      {
        return dateFormatter.format(item.dob);
      }
    ]]>
  </mx:Script>
  <mx:DateFormatter id="dateFormatter" formatString="MM/DD/YYYY"/>
  <mx:HTTPService id="contactService"
    url="data/contactsWithDates.xml"
    result="resultHandler(event)"/>
  <mx:DataGrid id="contactGrid" dataProvider="{contactAC}" rowCount="5"
    editable="true">
    <mx:columns>
      <mx:DataGridColumn dataField="firstname" headerText="First Name"
        width="100"/>
      <mx:DataGridColumn dataField="lastname" headerText="Last Name"
        width="100"/>
      <mx:DataGridColumn dataField="dob" editorDataField="selectedDate"
        labelFunction="getDateLabel">
        <mx:itemEditor>
          <mx:Component>
            <mx:DateField maxYear="2000" editable="true"/>
          </mx:Component>
        </mx:itemEditor>
```

```
            </mx:DataGridColumn>
          </mx:columns>
       </mx:DataGrid>
    </mx:Application>
```

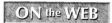 The code in Listing 18.9 is available in the Web site files as **DataGridInline Editor.mxml** in the **chapter18** project.

Figure 18.14 shows the resulting pop-up calendar control that's part of the DateField. When the user clicks the cell displaying the date, he sees the DateField; when he clicks the DateField control's button, the calendar control pops up. Because the DateField control's editable property is true, the user also can click into the TextInput portion of the DateField and type a value directly.

FIGURE 18.14

An itemEditor declared within inline syntax to allow custom properties and behaviors to be declared

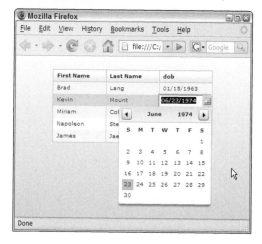

Using HorizontalList and TileList Controls

The HorizontalList and TileList controls share nearly all the behaviors and capabilities of the DataGrid and List controls:

- Data provided to a HorizontalList or TileList is typically displayed using a custom item renderer, declared either inline or as a separate component.
- The change event notifies you that the user has selected a data item.
- The selectedItem property returns a reference to the selected data item.

- The `allowMultipleSelection` property lets users select multiple data items by clicking while holding down Ctrl (or Cmd on the Mac) and Shift.

- As the user scrolls, existing visual objects are reused and their data is populated with the new data. As with the `DataGrid` control, this creates a smooth scrolling experience while allowing these controls to display large amounts of data without over-using Flash Player memory.

The difference between the `HorizontalList` and `TileList` controls has to do with their layout. As implied by their component names, the `HorizontalList` lays out cells in a single row, while the `TileList` lays out cells in a similar fashion to the Tile container, as a grid of objects in rows and columns.

The `TileList` and `HorizontalList` controls are almost always used with custom item renderers that determine the presentation of each of the list's cells. As with the other list controls, you declare the item renderer component with drop-in, inline, or component syntax.

The application in Listing 18.10 uses a `TileList` control and an inline renderer to display the contents of an XML file that refers to image files in the project's `assets` folder. The renderer component uses properties of each XML `<slide>` element to present an `Image` and a `Label` wrapped in a `VBox` container.

The `TileList` is wrapped inside a `Panel` container whose `status` property is bound to the caption property of the currently selected data item. The result is that the currently selected slide's caption is displayed in the `Panel` container's `status` area (on the right side of the header area).

LISTING 18.10

A TileList control presenting dynamic data

```
<?xml version="1.0" encoding="utf-8"?>
<mx:Application xmlns:mx="http://www.adobe.com/2006/mxml"
  backgroundColor="#EEEEEE" horizontalAlign="left">
  <mx:Model id="slideModel" source="data/slideshow.xml"/>
  <mx:ArrayCollection id="slideAC" source="{slideModel.slide}"/>
  <mx:Panel title="My Photos"
    height="100%" width="100%"
    paddingLeft="10" paddingRight="10"
    paddingTop="10" paddingBottom="10"
    status="{slideList.selectedItem.caption}">
    <mx:TileList id="slideList" dataProvider="{slideAC}"
      width="100%" height="100%" rowHeight="125" columnWidth="120">
      <mx:itemRenderer>
        <mx:Component>
          <mx:VBox horizontalScrollPolicy="off"
    verticalScrollPolicy="off"
            verticalAlign="middle" horizontalAlign="center">
            <mx:Image source="assets/thumbs/{data.source}"/>
            <mx:Label text="{data.caption}"/>
```

```
                </mx:VBox>
            </mx:Component>
          </mx:itemRenderer>
        </mx:TileList>
    </mx:Panel>
</mx:Application>
```

ON the WEB The code in Listing 18.10 is available in the Web site files as `TileListDemo.mxml` in the `chapter18` project.

Figure 18.15 shows the resulting application, with graphic images and their captions laid out in a grid-like format.

FIGURE 18.15

A `TileList` control displaying an inline item renderer

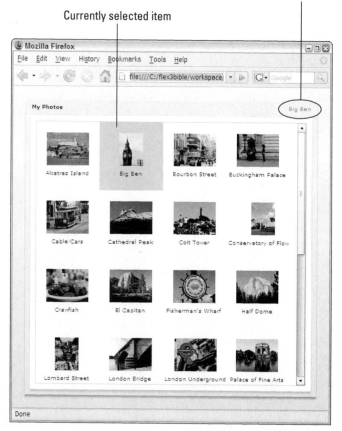

Status property bound to select item

Currently selected item

The HorizontalList control uses the same architecture, allowing the user to scroll sideways through content. In the application in Listing 18.11, the change event handler saves the current selectedItem to a bindable Object. When the item is selected, the VBox container at the bottom of the application becomes visible due to its use of a binding expression in its enabled property.

LISTING 18.11

Using the HorizontalList control

```
<?xml version="1.0" encoding="utf-8"?>
<mx:Application xmlns:mx="http://www.adobe.com/2006/mxml"
  backgroundColor="#EEEEEE" horizontalAlign="left">
  <mx:Model id="slideModel" source="data/slideshow.xml"/>
  <mx:ArrayCollection id="slideAC" source="{slideModel.slide}"/>
  <mx:Object id="currentImage"/>
  <mx:Panel title="My Photos" width="100%"
    paddingLeft="10" paddingRight="10"
    paddingTop="10" paddingBottom="10"
    status="{slideList.selectedItem.caption}" id="panel1">
    <mx:HorizontalList id="slideList" dataProvider="{slideAC}"
      width="100%" height="125" rowHeight="125" columnWidth="120"
      change="currentImage=event.target.selectedItem">
      <mx:itemRenderer>
        <mx:Component>
          <mx:VBox horizontalScrollPolicy="off"
  verticalScrollPolicy="off"
            verticalAlign="middle" horizontalAlign="center">
            <mx:Image source="assets/thumbs/{data.source}"/>
            <mx:Label text="{data.caption}"/>
          </mx:VBox>
        </mx:Component>
      </mx:itemRenderer>
    </mx:HorizontalList>
  </mx:Panel>
  <mx:Spacer height="50"/>
  <mx:VBox width="100%" horizontalAlign="center"
    visible="{slideList.selectedIndex != -1}">
    <mx:Image source="assets/{currentImage.source}"/>
    <mx:Label text="{currentImage.caption}" fontSize="12"
      fontWeight="bold"/>
  </mx:VBox>
</mx:Application>
```

ON the WEB The code in Listing 18.11 is available in the Web site files as HorizontalList Demo.mxml in the chapter18 project.

Figure 18.16 shows the resulting application, after an item has been selected from the HorizontalList control.

FIGURE 18.16

A HorizontalList control with selected information displayed in a detail region

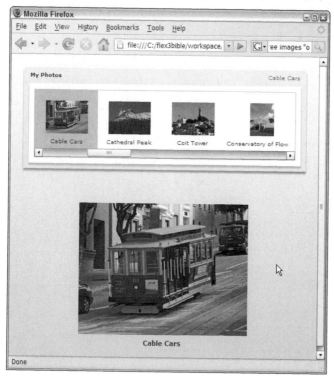

WEB RESOURCE The photos used in these examples are from the Web site www.pdphoto.org, dedicated to providing free public domain photos. Not all of their photos are completely free, but most are.

Using the AdvancedDataGrid Control

The AdvancedDataGrid control is an extended version of the DataGrid control that adds these features:

- Sorting by multiple columns
- Row- and column-based styling
- Display of hierarchical data with an embedded Tree component
- Dynamic grouping of "flat" data into a hierarchical display
- Grouping of multiple columns under a single heading
- Multi-column item renderers

Hierarchical data display

As with the DataGrid, the AdvancedDataGrid control's data provider is typically in the form of an ArrayCollection. To use the hierarchical data display feature, the objects in the data set should include at least one "grouping" property that can be used to collect and group data items based on their identical values in that property.

You can display data that is already in hierarchical form, such as the data created in this ActionScript code:

```
var employeeAC:ArrayCollection = new ArrayCollection();
employeeAC.source =
  [{department:"Shipping",
    children: [
      {firstname:"Kevin", lastname:"Mount"},
      {firstname:"Robert", lastname:"Lombardi"}]},
   {department:"Marketing",
    children: [
      {firstname:"Brad", lastname:"Lang"},
      {firstname:"James", lastname:"Jaeger"}]}]
  ];
```

Notice that the data is structured as an Array containing multiple Object instances, written in ActionScript shorthand notation. Each Object contains a department property designed as the grouping field and an Array named children that contains additional data objects.

You pass this type of data to the AdvancedDataGrid by first wrapping it in an instance of the HierarchicalData class. This class has a childrenField property that defines which field of each object is expected to contain child objects. Its default value is children, so the data described in the ActionScript code has the expected structure and field names already.

TIP The AdvancedDataGrid component handles XML-based data intuitively. Child XML nodes are rendered as nodes of the component's nested Tree control.

The columns property of the AdvancedDataGrid control should contain instances of the AdvancedDataGridColumn component. Its dataField and headerText properties behave just like the DataGridColumn, and its style allows you to specify the color and font on a per-column basis.

The application in Listing 18.12 uses a hierarchical data set and an AdvancedDataGrid to display grouped data.

LISTING 18.12

The AdvancedDataGrid control with hierarchical data

```
<?xml version="1.0" encoding="utf-8"?>
<mx:Application xmlns:mx="http://www.adobe.com/2006/mxml"
   layout="vertical"
  creationComplete="initData()">
  <mx:Script>
    <![CDATA[
      import mx.collections.ArrayCollection;
      [Bindable]
      private var employeeAC:ArrayCollection = new ArrayCollection();

      private function initData():void
      {
        employeeAC.source = [{department:"Shipping",
          children: [{firstname:"Kevin", lastname:"Mount"},
                     {firstname:"Robert", lastname:"Lombardi"}]},
        {department:"Marketing",
          children: [{firstname:"Brad", lastname:"Lang"},
                     {firstname:"James", lastname:"Jaeger"}]}
        ];
      }
    ]]>
  </mx:Script>
  <mx:AdvancedDataGrid id="employeeGrid">
    <mx:dataProvider>
      <mx:HierarchicalData source="{employeeAC}"/>
    </mx:dataProvider>
    <mx:columns>
      <mx:AdvancedDataGridColumn dataField="department"
        headerText="Department" fontWeight="bold"/>
      <mx:AdvancedDataGridColumn dataField="firstname"
        headerText="First Name"/>
      <mx:AdvancedDataGridColumn dataField="lastname"
        headerText="Last Name"/>
    </mx:columns>
  </mx:AdvancedDataGrid>
</mx:Application>
```

ON the WEB The code in Listing 18.12 is available in the Web site files as **AdvDataGridDemo.mxml** in the **chapter18** project.

The resulting application is shown in Figure 18.17. The user can click the grouped values in the leftmost column to expand the tree nodes and see the child rows.

FIGURE 18.17

The AdvancedDataGrid component

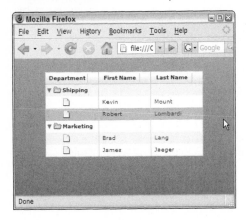

Grouping flat data

Flat data is typically defined as a conventional ArrayCollection containing rows and columns, such as you might import into a Flex application with a call to a database query. You can group this type of data structure in an AdvancedDataGrid control by wrapping it in a GroupingCollection object. This object contains one or more nested GroupingField objects that define which columns or properties you want to group on.

In MXML, you prepare the data like this:

```
<mx:GroupingCollection id="gc" source="{dataCollection}">
  <mx:grouping>
    <mx:Grouping>
      <mx:GroupingField name="department"/>
    </mx:Grouping>
  </mx:grouping>
</mx:GroupingCollection>
```

The GroupingCollection is then passed to the AdvancedDataGrid component's dataProvider. To make the GroupingCollection update its view, you must call its refresh() method. In the following code, the refresh() method is called when the grid component's initialize event is dispatched:

```
<mx:AdvancedDataGrid id="myAdvancedGrid"
  dataProvider="{gc}"
```

```
      initialize="gc.refresh()">
      ... column declarations ...
    </mx:AdvancedDataGrid>
```

The application in Listing 18.13 uses a flat data set from an XML file and groups it with the
GroupingCollection object.

LISTING 18.13

Grouping flat data with the GroupingCollection and AdvancedDataGrid

```
<?xml version="1.0" encoding="utf-8"?>
<mx:Application xmlns:mx="http://www.adobe.com/2006/mxml">
  <mx:Model id="empModel" source="data/employees.xml"/>
  <mx:ArrayCollection id="employeeAC" source="{empModel.row}"/>

  <mx:AdvancedDataGrid id="employeeGrid" initialize="gc.refresh()">
    <mx:dataProvider>
      <mx:GroupingCollection id="gc" source="{employeeAC}">
        <mx:grouping>
          <mx:Grouping>
            <mx:GroupingField name="department"/>
          </mx:Grouping>
        </mx:grouping>
      </mx:GroupingCollection>
    </mx:dataProvider>
    <mx:columns>
    <mx:AdvancedDataGridColumn dataField="department"
      headerText="Department" fontWeight="bold"/>
      <mx:AdvancedDataGridColumn dataField="firstname"
        headerText="First Name"/>
      <mx:AdvancedDataGridColumn dataField="lastname"
        headerText="Last Name"/>
    </mx:columns>
  </mx:AdvancedDataGrid>
</mx:Application>
```

ON the WEB   The code in Listing 18.13 is available in the Web site files as **AdvDataGrid**
             FlatData.mxml in the **chapter18** project.

Figure 18.18 shows the resulting application with two of the groups expanded to display their
child data items.

FIGURE 18.18

FIGURE 18.18

An AdvancedDataGrid with grouped data from a flat data provider

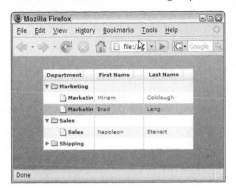

Summary

In this chapter, I described how to use advanced techniques with list controls. You learned the following:

- The ComboBox control's editable property produces a TextInput control into which the user can type an arbitrary String value, instead of selecting an item from the list.

- Bindable versions of the List and ComboBox controls are included with applications generated by the ColdFusion/Flex Application Wizard.

- A default DataGrid displays columns for each named property of the first data item in its data provider.

- You determine selection and order of column display in a DataGrid with the columns property, which in turn contains a set DataGridColumn objects declared in the order in which you want the columns displayed.

- The DataGridColumn component implements the labelFunction, itemRenderer, and itemEditor for customization of its appearance.

- The dataChange event can be used for customizing item renderer appearance at run-time with ActionScript code.

- Item editors can be declared to appear only on the current row with the itemEditor property or on every row with the itemRenderer and rendererIsEditor properties.

- The DataGridColumn component's editorDataField property should be set to the name of the item editor's property that contains data updated by the user.

- The TileList and HorizontalList controls display data in grid- or row-style layouts and use custom item renderers to determine the visual appearance of their cells.

- The AdvancedDataGrid component is available with the Data Visualization Components (part of Flex Builder Professional).

- The AdvancedDataGrid component can present hierarchical and flat data in groups, along with summaries and other advanced data display features.

Chapter 19

Using the Flex Charting Controls

The Flex Charting controls allow to you to represent numeric and statistical data visually in a graphical, interactive format. When presented in its raw form, numeric data can be difficult for users to interpret and grasp. When presented visually, in the form of pie charts, bar charts, and other graphical patterns, the data can be understood much more easily.

Consider the following visual presentations. The application in Figure 19.1 uses the following raw data, stored in an XML file:

```xml
<?xml version="1.0"?>
<data>
  <row>
    <fruit>Apples</fruit>
    <sales>34</sales>
  </row>
  <row>
    <fruit>Oranges</fruit>
    <sales>23</sales>
  </row>
  <row>
    <fruit>Pears</fruit>
    <sales>45</sales>
  </row>
</data>
```

Figure 19.1 shows the data display in a `DataGrid` and a `ColumnChart` control. The `DataGrid` shows the data in its raw form, while the chart makes the data more understandable to the user.

FIGURE 19.1

A data set displayed in a `DataGrid` and a `ColumnChart`

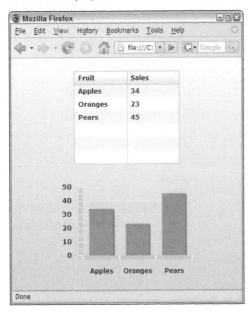

The data is clearly presented either way, but the graphical chart lets the user understand its meaning on a more intuitive level. Applications that make extensive use of charting controls are sometimes known as *dashboard* applications because, like a car's dashboard, they give the user a sense of the data with a quick glance.

NOTE The Flex Charting controls are included in the Flex Data Visualization components package and are part of the per-developer license for Flex Builder 3 Professional. Unlike in the Flex 2 product line, the charting components are not available under separate license: They're delivered only with Flex Builder 3 Professional. After you purchase a Flex Builder 3 license, you can include the charting controls in as many applications as you like without any ongoing royalties.

CAUTION You can test the charting components and other data visualization components (such as the `AdvancedDataGrid` control) in your Flex applications without a license, but they're displayed with a watermark in the background that prevents their use in a production application.

ON the WEB To use the sample code for this chapter, import the `chapter19.zip` project from the Web site files into any folder on your disk.

Understanding Flex's Types of Charts

The Flex Charting controls include nine distinct types of charts, each implemented as a particular Flex component. Each chart type requires data that's passed in with a component known as the *series class.*

> **TIP**
>
> *Data series* is another name for *data set.* A data series for a chart can be represented as an `Array` or an `ArrayCollection`; if you'll be making changes to the data at runtime, `ArrayCollection` is the usual choice.

The structure of a data series designed for use by a charting control is frequently determined by the structural requirements of chart type. A pie chart requires a simple set of data where each data item only requires one value. Data points for the candlestick chart require four values, representing each item's open, close, high, and low values. Check the documentation for each chart type to understand what kind of data structure it requires.

Table 19.1 describes the different types of charts in the Flex Charting controls. For each chart type, its Flex control name and matching series class are noted, along with a description of the chart type's characteristics.

TABLE 19.1

Flex Chart Types

Chart Type	Charting Component	Series Class	Characteristics
Area	`AreaChart`	`AreaSeries`	Similar to a line chart, but fills the area beneath the line with a fill pattern. Often used to represent a timeline with associated data.
Bar	`BarChart`	`BarSeries`	Presents data as a set of horizontal bars representing data levels across an x axis. Nearly identical in usage to the column chart, which presents data as vertical bars.
Bubble	`BubbleChart`	`BubbleSeries`	Represents data structures with three values for each data point: the x axis, the y axis, and the size of the symbol. Each data point is represented by a filled circle that covers some portion of the chart.
Candlestick	`CandleStick Chart`	`CandleStick Series`	Represents financial data with each data point representing high, low, opening, and closing values. All four values are required. To represent data points without the opening value, see the HighLowOpenClose chart type.
Column	`ColumnChart`	`ColumnSeries`	Presents data as a set of vertical bars representing data levels across a y axis. Nearly identical in usage to the bar chart, which presents data as horizontal bars.

continued

	TABLE 19.1	(continued)	
Chart Type	**Charting Component**	**Series Class**	**Characteristics**
HighLow OpenClose	HLOCChart	HLOCseries	Represents financial data with each data point representing high, low, opening, and closing values. The opening value is optional.
Line	LineChart	LineSeries	Represents data as a set of points connected with straight lines. Similar to an area chart in usage, but doesn't fill the area beneath the lines. Particularly useful for representing and comparing multiple related data series.
Pie	PieChart	PieSeries	A circular chart where each data point requires only one value. The aggregate of all data points should add up to 100 (or 100%), since the purpose of a pie chart is to show relative size of each "slice" of the pie. This component can also display a doughnut chart, with a hollow area in the center.
Plot	PlotChart	PlotSeries	A chart where each data item has three data points: x position, y position, and radius to determine the visible area covered by the data point. By default, data points for the first series are represented by a diamond graphic, the second by a circle, and the third by a square.

Declaring Chart Controls

You declare a chart control in the same manner as any other Flex visual control. You place it on the screen within a container; use the container's horizontal, vertical, or absolute layout to position the chart; and use either absolute pixel or percentage-based sizing to set its height and width.

> **TIP** Unlike images, charting controls do not have a concept of aspect ratio. If you set one dimension of a chart to a particular size, it doesn't have any effect on the other dimension: The chart's **height** and **width** properties are set independently.

As with all visual controls, charting controls can be declared in either MXML or ActionScript code. For example, a simple pie chart declared in MXML looks like this:

```
<mx:PieChart dataProvider="{salesData}"
  height="100%" width="100%">
  <mx:series>
    <mx:PieSeries field="sales" labelField="fruit"
      labelPosition="inside" explodeRadius=".05"/>
  </mx:series>
</mx:PieChart>
```

Figure 19.2 shows the resulting chart, displaying each data point as a wedge of the pie. The `explodeRadius` property, which has a range of possible values from 0 to 1, determines how much separation is displayed between each wedge of the pie.

FIGURE 19.2

A simple pie chart

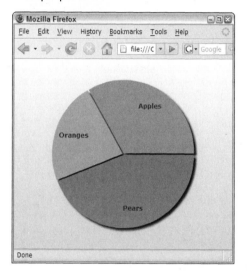

The same chart could be created with this ActionScript code:

```
import mx.charts.series.PieSeries;
import mx.charts.PieChart;
private function createChart():void
{
  var series:PieSeries = new PieSeries();
  series.field="sales";
  series.labelField="fruit";
  series.explodeRadius=.01;
  series.setStyle("labelPosition", "inside");
  var chart:PieChart = new PieChart();
  chart.visible=true;
  chart.dataProvider=salesData;
  chart.percentWidth=100;
  chart.percentHeight=100;
  chart.series=[series];
  addChild(chart)
}
```

As with many visual controls, the amount of ActionScript code required to create and display the chart is significantly more than the equivalent MXML, but developers should choose the coding style they prefer. There is no difference in function or performance between the two approaches.

Setting Chart Properties and Styles

Each chart type has its own individual requirements and unique behaviors that respond to its particular properties and styles. In this section, I describe the behaviors of each family of charts and how they respond to particular settings.

Using pie charts

As described previously, a pie chart is declared with the `PieChart` component, and its data is provided with the `PieSeries` class. Pie charts have these characteristics:

- A pie chart requires only a single data series. Unlike other, more complex charts, the pie chart is designed to show one set of data and illustrate the percentage of the total of the series' data points.

- Each data point is presented as a wedge of the pie.

- The fill colors of the pie wedges are set to default values that you can override.

- The pie wedges are presented with no default gap; you create gaps by applying various `explode` properties.

- Each wedge has a default drop shadow filter that you can remove or override.

Setting wedge labels

The wedge label is a string value that's displayed on or near each pie wedge. You control the label's position with the `DataSeries` class's `.labelPosition` style, which has these possible values:

- `none` (**default**): No label is displayed.

- `callout`: The label is displayed outside the pie with a line connecting it to its pie wedge.

- `inside`: The label is displayed inside its pie wedge.

- `insideWithCallout`: The label is displayed inside its pie wedge if it fits or outside with a callout connector if it doesn't.

- `outside`: The label is displayed outside the pie wedge, with added callout connectors where necessary.

You determine the value of the label with the `DataSeries` class's `labelField` or `labelFunction` property. The `labelField` behaves just like the same named property in list controls; you're naming a data property containing the value you want to display. This declaration would cause the raw value of each data item's sales property to be displayed inside the matching pie wedge:

```
labelField="sales" labelPosition="inside"
```

For more complex label presentations, you can use the labelFunction property to point to a function that's called at runtime to render each pie wedge. A custom label function for the PieSeries class requires four arguments:

- item:Object: The data item represented by the current pie wedge

- field:String: The name of the field being rendered

- index:Number: The ordinal position of the current data item in the chart's data provider

- percentValue:Number: The percent of the total value represented by the current pie wedge

This custom label function uses a NumberFormatter object to format both the sales value and the percentValue argument:

```
private function getWedgeLabel(item:Object, field:String,
  index:Number, percentValue:Number):String
{
  return item.fruit + ": $" + nf.format(item.sales) +
    " (" + nf.format(percentValue) + "%)";
}
```

As with the labelFunction property of the list controls, you set the property's value to the callback function's name:

```
<mx:PieSeries field="sales" labelFunction="getWedgeLabel"/>
```

The application in Listing 19.1 declares a custom label function suitable for use as a custom label function for the PieSeries class.

LISTING 19.1

A pie chart with a custom label function

```
<?xml version="1.0" encoding="utf-8"?>
<mx:Application xmlns:mx="http://www.adobe.com/2006/mxml"
  backgroundColor="#EEEEEE">
  <mx:Script>
    <![CDATA[
      private function getWedgeLabel(item:Object, field:String,
        index:Number, percentValue:Number):String
      {
        return item.fruit + ": $" + nf.format(item.sales) +
          " (" + nf.format(percentValue) + "%)";
      }
    ]]>
  </mx:Script>
```

continued

LISTING 19.1 *(continued)*

```
<mx:NumberFormatter id="nf" precision="0" rounding="nearest"/>
<mx:Model id="pieModel" source="data/PieData.xml"/>
<mx:ArrayCollection id="pieData" source="{pieModel.row}"/>
<mx:PieChart dataProvider="{pieData}" height="100%" width="100%">
  <mx:series>
    <mx:PieSeries field="sales" labelFunction="getWedgeLabel"
      labelPosition="callout" explodeRadius=".01"/>
  </mx:series>
</mx:PieChart>
</mx:Application>
```

ON the WEB The code in Listing 19.1 is available in the Web site files as `PieChartCustom Labels.mxml` in the `chapter19` project.

Figure 19.3 shows the resulting application with customized labels presented as callouts connected to their respective pie wedges.

FIGURE 19.3

A pie chart with customized labels

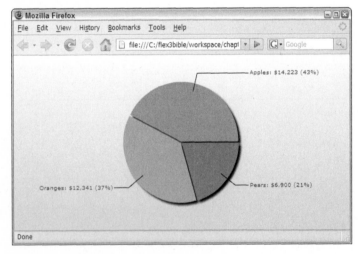

Exploding the pie

The pie chart has two methods for *exploding,* or *separating,* the wedges. The `explodeRadius` property, when set to a value greater than 0 (with a maximum of 1), pushes all wedges outward from the chart's center.

The following pie chart sets its `explodeRadius` property with a binding expression that references a slider's current value. As the user changes the slider, the pie wedges move farther apart:

```
<mx:PieChart dataProvider="{pieData}" height="100%" width="100%">
  <mx:series>
    <mx:PieSeries field="sales" labelField="sales"
      explodeRadius="{explodeSlider.value}"/>
  </mx:series>
</mx:PieChart>
<mx:Label text="Explode Radius: {explodeSlider.value}"/>
<mx:HSlider id="explodeSlider" minimum="0" maximum="1"
  snapInterval=".01"/>
```

Figure 19.4 shows the visual result: The pie wedges shrink and move apart as the value of `explodeRadius` increases.

FIGURE 19.4

Exploding the pie

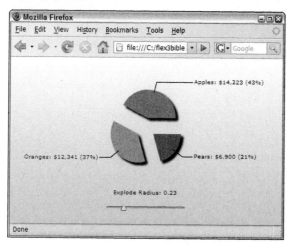

> **CAUTION** Setting `explodeRadius` to the maximum value of 1 causes the pie wedges to disappear.

You also can explode individual pie wedges with the `PieSeries` class's `perWedgeExplode Radius` property. This is set to an `Array` containing the same number of values as the series. As with `explodeRadius`, the values are set to a range from 0 to 1, with each of the values affecting only one of the pie wedges.

The application in Listing 19.2 explodes only one pie wedge, with its radius again bound to a slider control.

LISTING 19.2

Exploding one pie wedge

```
<?xml version="1.0" encoding="utf-8"?>
<mx:Application xmlns:mx="http://www.adobe.com/2006/mxml"
  backgroundColor="#EEEEEE">
  <mx:Script>
    <![CDATA[
      private function getWedgeLabel(item:Object, field:String,
        index:Number, percentValue:Number):String
      {
        return item.fruit + ": $" + nf.format(item.sales) +
          " (" + nf.format(percentValue) + "%)";
      }
    ]]>
  </mx:Script>
  <mx:NumberFormatter id="nf" precision="0" rounding="nearest"/>
  <mx:Model id="pieModel" source="data/PieData.xml"/>
  <mx:ArrayCollection id="pieData" source="{pieModel.row}"/>
  <mx:PieChart dataProvider="{pieData}"
    height="100%" width="100%">
    <mx:series>
      <mx:PieSeries field="sales" labelFunction="getWedgeLabel"
        labelPosition="callout"
        perWedgeExplodeRadius="{[0,0,explodeSlider.value]}"/>
    </mx:series>
  </mx:PieChart>
  <mx:Label text="Explode Radius: {explodeSlider.value}" fontSize="10"/>
  <mx:HSlider id="explodeSlider" minimum="0" maximum="1"
    snapInterval=".01"/>
</mx:Application>
```

ON the WEB   The code in Listing 19.2 is available in the Web site files as `PieExplode.mxml` in the `chapter19` project.

Figure 19.5 shows the result: One pie wedge is exploded from the rest of the chart.

Creating a doughnut chart

A doughnut chart is essentially a pie chart with a hole in the middle. You turn a pie into a dough-nut by setting the `PieChart` control's `centerRadius` property to a value greater than 0. The value is measured as the distance from the center of the chart to the inner edge of the wedges, as a percentage of the pie's total radius.

FIGURE 19.5

Exploding one pie wedge

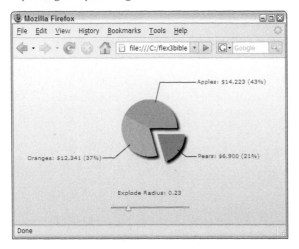

The application in Listing 19.3 generates a doughnut chart with a center radius that's 30 percent of the total pie radius.

LISTING 19.3

Displaying a doughnut chart

```
<?xml version="1.0" encoding="utf-8"?>
<mx:Application xmlns:mx="http://www.adobe.com/2006/mxml"
  backgroundColor="#EEEEEE">
  <mx:Model id="pieModel" source="data/PieData.xml"/>
  <mx:ArrayCollection id="pieData" source="{pieModel.row}"/>
  <mx:PieChart dataProvider="{pieData}"
    height="100%" width="100%" innerRadius=".3">
    <mx:series>
      <mx:PieSeries field="sales" labelField="fruit"
        labelPosition="inside"/>
    </mx:series>
  </mx:PieChart>
</mx:Application>
```

ON the WEB The code in Listing 19.3 is available in the Web site files as `DoughnutChart.mxml` in the `chapter19` project.

Figure 19.6 shows the result: a chart with a hole in the center.

FIGURE 19.6

A doughnut chart

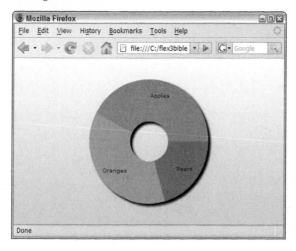

Using multiple data series

A pie chart declared with multiple data series displays its data as a set of concentric circles. When creating this type of chart, the PieChart doesn't need a dataProvider; instead, you assign a unique dataProvider to each PieSeries. When the chart is rendered, the first data series is displayed in the center of the pie, the second surrounds the first, and so on:

```
<mx:PieChart>
  <mx:series>
    <mx:PieSeries dataProvider="{pieData}" field="sales"
      labelPosition="none"/>
    <mx:PieSeries dataProvider="{pieData2}" field="sales"
      labelPosition="callout"/>
  </mx:series>
</mx:PieChart>
```

Notice that the first series (the inner circle) has its labelPosition style set to none, while the second (the outer circle) is set to callout. This results in a single label for each item, displayed outside the chart.

The application in Listing 19.4 declares a pie chart as a doughnut with two data series.

LISTING 19.4

A pie chart with two data series

```xml
<?xml version="1.0" encoding="utf-8"?>
<mx:Application xmlns:mx="http://www.adobe.com/2006/mxml"
  backgroundColor="#EEEEEE">
  <mx:Model id="pieModel" source="data/PieData.xml"/>
  <mx:ArrayCollection id="pieData" source="{pieModel.row}"/>
  <mx:Model id="pieModel2" source="data/PieData2.xml"/>
  <mx:ArrayCollection id="pieData2" source="{pieModel2.row}"/>
  <mx:PieChart height="100%" width="100%">
    <mx:series>
      <mx:PieSeries field="sales" labelField="fruit"
        dataProvider="{pieData}" labelPosition="none"/>
      <mx:PieSeries field="sales" labelField="fruit"
        dataProvider="{pieData2}" labelPosition="callout"/>
    </mx:series>
  </mx:PieChart>
</mx:Application>
```

ON the WEB   The code in Listing 19.4 is available in the Web site files as `PieChartMultiple Series.mxml` in the `chapter19` project.

Figure 19.7 shows the result: a pie chart with multiple data series displayed as concentric circles.

FIGURE 19.7

A pie chart with multiple data series

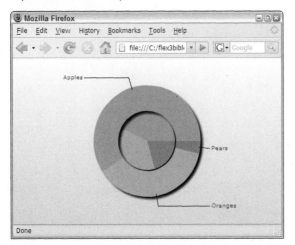

Controlling fill colors and backgrounds

You can override the fill colors of each wedge of a pie chart with the `fills` property of the
`PieSeries` class. This property is an `Array` containing objects that implement the `IFill`
interface. You can use these classes for this purpose:

- `BitMapFill`: Fills an object with a bitmap graphic
- `LinearGradient`: Fills an object with a linear gradient, defined as an `Array` of
  `GradientEntry` objects
- `RadialGradient`: Fills an object with a radial gradient, defined as an `Array` of
  `GradientEntry` objects
- `SolidColor`: Fills an object with a single solid color, defined by a hexadecimal color
  code or a named color that's recognized by the Flex compiler

To select solid fill colors for a pie chart, declare the `PieSeries` object's `fills` property as an
`<mx:fills>` tag set, and nest one `<mx:SolidColor>` declaration for each data element. The
following code sets three fill colors of red, green, and blue:

```
<mx:PieChart dataProvider="{pieData}">
  <mx:series>
    <mx:PieSeries field="sales" labelField="fruit"
      labelPosition="inside">
      <mx:fills>
        <mx:SolidColor color="#FF0000"/>
        <mx:SolidColor color="#00FF00 "/>
        <mx:SolidColor color="#0000FF "/>
      </mx:fills>
    </mx:PieSeries>
  </mx:series>
</mx:PieChart>
```

For a pie chart with more than one data series, you set each series individually, because each
instance of the `PieSeries` has its own `fills` property.

The application in Listing 19.5 selects colors of black, gray, and white for its three wedges. Figure 19.8
shows the finished pie chart.

LISTING 19.5

A pie chart with custom fill colors

```
<?xml version="1.0" encoding="utf-8"?>
<mx:Application xmlns:mx="http://www.adobe.com/2006/mxml"
  backgroundColor="#EEEEEE">
  <mx:Model id="pieModel" source="data/PieData.xml"/>
  <mx:ArrayCollection id="pieData" source="{pieModel.row}"/>
  <mx:PieChart height="100%" width="100%">
```

```
    <mx:series>
      <mx:PieSeries field="sales" labelField="fruit"
        dataProvider="{pieData}" labelPosition="callout">
        <mx:fills>
          <mx:SolidColor color="#000000"/>
          <mx:SolidColor color="#999999"/>
          <mx:SolidColor color="#FFFFFF"/>
        </mx:fills>
      </mx:PieSeries>
    </mx:series>
  </mx:PieChart>
</mx:Application>
```

ON the WEB   The code in Listing 19.5 is available in the Web site files as `PieSetFillColors.mxml` in the **chapter19** project.

FIGURE 19.8

A pie chart with black, gray, and white fill colors

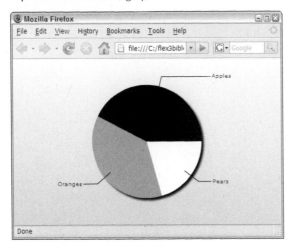

Using financial charts

The Flex framework contains two types of charts for use with financial data:

- **The candlestick chart** represents financial data as a series of candlesticks, each representing high, low, opening, and closing points for a data series.

- **The HighLowOpenClose (HLOC)** chart is similar but doesn't require opening values for its data series.

The data structure for these two charts is similar. Each data point should have values that can be assigned to these properties of the CandlestickSeries or HLOCSeries objects:

- **openField:** Represents the data item's opening value; optional for HLOC chart, and required for the candlestick chart
- **closeField:** Represents the data item's closing value; required for both charts
- **highField:** Represents the data item's high value; required for both charts
- **lowField:** Represents the data item's low value; required for both charts

The two charts differ in how they represent these values. As shown in Figure 19.9, the HLOC chart displays a vertical stroke for each data item showing the high and low values and two short strokes protruding from the main display. The stroke pointing to the left is the open value, and the stroke pointing to the right is the close value.

FIGURE 19.9

The icon for a HighLowOpenClose chart

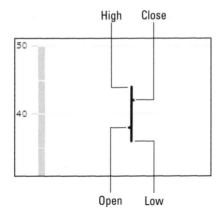

As shown in Figure 19.10, the candlestick chart displays a box indicating the high and low values as vertical lines, and the open and close values as a box. If the close value is higher than the open value, the box is filled; if the open value is higher, the box is empty.

FIGURE 19.10

Icons for the candlestick chart

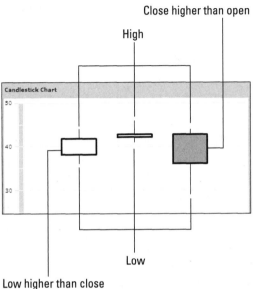

The application in Listing 19.6 shows a data set displayed in its raw form in a DataGrid and then rendered visually in a HighLowOpenClose and a candlestick chart.

LISTING 19.6

Data rendered in an HLOC and a candlestick chart

```
<?xml version="1.0" encoding="utf-8"?>
<mx:Application xmlns:mx="http://www.adobe.com/2006/mxml">
  <mx:Model id="financialModel" source="data/FinancialData.xml"/>
  <mx:ArrayCollection id="financialData" source="{financialModel.row}"/>
  <mx:DataGrid dataProvider="{financialData}" rowCount="3"/>
  <mx:HBox width="100%" height="100%">
    <mx:Panel title="HLOC Chart" height="100%" width="100%">
      <mx:HLOCChart dataProvider="{financialData}"
        height="100%" width="100%">
        <mx:horizontalAxis>
          <mx:LinearAxis minimum="-1" maximum="3" interval="1"/>
        </mx:horizontalAxis>
        <mx:series>
          <mx:HLOCSeries dataProvider="{financialData}"
```

continued

LISTING 19.6 *(continued)*

```
            highField="high" lowField="low"
            openField="open" closeField="close">
            <mx:stroke>
              <mx:Stroke color="black" weight="3"/>
            </mx:stroke>
            <mx:openTickStroke>
              <mx:Stroke color="black" weight="3"/>
            </mx:openTickStroke>
            <mx:closeTickStroke>
              <mx:Stroke color="black" weight="3"/>
            </mx:closeTickStroke>
          </mx:HLOCSeries>
        </mx:series>
      </mx:HLOCChart>
    </mx:Panel>
    <mx:Panel title="Candlestick Chart" height="100%" width="100%">
      <mx:CandlestickChart dataProvider="{financialData}"
        height="100%" width="100%">
        <mx:horizontalAxis>
          <mx:LinearAxis minimum="0" maximum="4" interval="1"/>
        </mx:horizontalAxis>
        <mx:series>
          <mx:CandlestickSeries dataProvider="{financialData}"
            highField="high" lowField="low"
            openField="open" closeField="close"
            xField="quarter">
            <mx:boxStroke>
              <mx:Stroke color="black" weight="3"/>
            </mx:boxStroke>
          </mx:CandlestickSeries>
        </mx:series>
      </mx:CandlestickChart>
    </mx:Panel>
  </mx:HBox>
</mx:Application>
```

> **ON the WEB** The code in Listing 19.6 is available in the Web site files as `FinancialCharts.mxml` in the `chapter19` project.

Figure 19.11 shows the resulting application, with the raw data displayed in the DataGrid and the two charts side by side.

The HLOC and candlestick charts, side by side

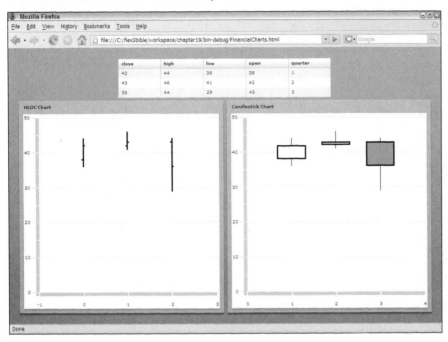

Using bar, column, line, and area charts

The bar, column, line, and area charts are all designed to render and compare values graphically along an x and a y axis. The data structure for all four of these charts is identical. Each requires one or more data series, each consisting of an `Array` or `ArrayCollection` of name/value pairs. As with the pie chart, the value should be numeric (a *chartable value*), but whereas the pie chart illustrates each value's percentage of the whole, these charts display values next to each for the purpose of comparison or trend analysis.

The data for a bar, column, line, or area chart series can be represented in ActionScript, MXML, or retrieved dynamically from an application server at runtime. A compatible data series, rendered in MXML, might look like this:

```
<?xml version="1.0"?>
<data>
  <row>
    <fruit>Apples</fruit>
    <sales>14223</sales>
  </row>
```

```
<row>
  <fruit>Oranges</fruit>
  <sales>12341</sales>
</row>
<row>
  <fruit>Pears</fruit>
  <sales>6900</sales>
</row>
</data>
```

Using bar and column charts

The bar and column charts are identical in their fundamental structure and purpose: They're used to compare values or show changes in values over time. As shown in Figure 19.12, these two charts are distinguished by the dimension in which they represent numeric values: The bar chart displays horizontal bars pushing out from the chart's left-inner border, while the column chart displays vertical columns rising from the chart's bottom-inner border.

FIGURE 19.12

A bar chart and a column chart representing the same data

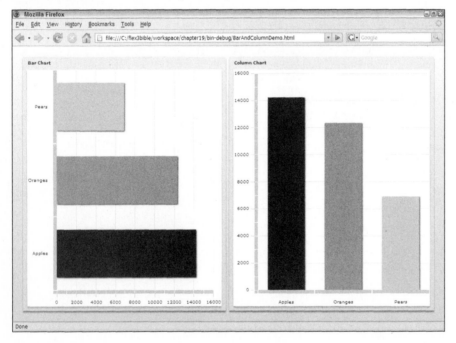

You declare a bar or column chart with much the same syntax as a pie chart, but you must include a declaration of one axis of the chart. For a bar chart, which uses the x axis to render its numeric values, you provide an explicit <mx:verticalAxis> declaration. Within the axis declaration, you declare an instance of one of these axis components:

- CategoryAxis: Treats alphanumeric values as category names along the axis
- LinearAxis: Treats numeric data points as a set of linear values along the axis
- LogAxis: Maps numerical values logarithmically along the axis
- DateTimeAxis: Lays out date/time values along the axis

TIP The DateTimeAxis plots values evenly across an access using a data set containing instances of the ActionScript Date class. It also can work with a set of string labels when you provide a custom parsing function to transform the strings into dates it can handle.

The following BarChart uses a set of categories (the names of fruit in the data set) as its vertical axis:

```
<mx:BarChart dataProvider="{salesData}">
  <mx:verticalAxis>
    <mx:CategoryAxis dataProvider="{salesData}"
      categoryField="fruit"/>
  </mx:verticalAxis>
  <mx:series>
    <mx:BarSeries xField="sales" yField="fruit"/>
  </mx:series>
</mx:BarChart>
```

The result, as shown in the bar chart in Figure 19.12, is to display the categorical data from the fruit field, named in the CategoryField property.

TIP The CategoryAxis component has its own dataProvider property and does not inherit this value from the BarChart or ColumnChart in which it's nested. Even when they share the same data, the data provider must be declared twice.

Similarly, the ColumnChart control needs a horizontalAxis declaration to indicate what values are displayed beneath the chart:

```
<mx:ColumnChart dataProvider="{salesData}">
  <mx:horizontalAxis>
    <mx:CategoryAxis dataProvider="{salesData}"
      categoryField="fruit"/>
  </mx:horizontalAxis>
  <mx:series>
    <mx:ColumnSeries xField="fruit" yField="sales"/>
  </mx:series>
</mx:ColumnChart>
```

Both the `ColumnChart` and `BarChart` controls implement these properties to determine which values are used on each axis of the chart:

- `xField`: The name of the property containing values for the x axis
- `yField`: The name of the property containing values for the y axis

The application in Listing 19.7 displays a bar chart and a column chart side by side, using the same data set.

LISTING 19.7

A bar and a column chart

```
<?xml version="1.0" encoding="utf-8"?>
<mx:Application xmlns:mx="http://www.adobe.com/2006/mxml"
  backgroundColor="#EEEEEE" layout="horizontal">
  <mx:Style>
    BarSeries, ColumnSeries {
      fills:#333333,#999999,#CCCCCC;
    }
  </mx:Style>
  <mx:Model id="salesModel" source="data/salesData.xml"/>
  <mx:ArrayCollection id="salesData" source="{salesModel.row}"/>
  <mx:Panel title="Bar Chart" height="100%" width="100%">
    <mx:BarChart dataProvider="{salesData}"
      height="100%" width="100%">
      <mx:verticalAxis>
        <mx:CategoryAxis dataProvider="{salesData}"
  categoryField="fruit"/>
      </mx:verticalAxis>
      <mx:series>
        <mx:BarSeries xField="sales" yField="fruit"/>
      </mx:series>
    </mx:BarChart>
  </mx:Panel>
  <mx:Panel title="Column Chart" height="100%" width="100%">
    <mx:ColumnChart dataProvider="{salesData}"
      height="100%" width="100%">
      <mx:horizontalAxis>
        <mx:CategoryAxis dataProvider="{salesData}"
  categoryField="fruit"/>
      </mx:horizontalAxis>
      <mx:series>
        <mx:ColumnSeries xField="fruit" yField="sales"/>
      </mx:series>
    </mx:ColumnChart>
  </mx:Panel>
</mx:Application>
```

ON the WEB   The code in Listing 19.7 is available in the Web site files as BarAndColumnDemo.mxml in the chapter19 project.

Using line and area charts

The line and area charts are nearly identical to each other in structure, with their primary visual difference lying in how they represent a trend visually. As shown in Figure 19.13, the area chart fills the area beneath the trend line with a fill color or bitmap, while the line chart leaves the area below the line blank.

As with the ColumnChart control, the LineChart and AreaChart require a horizontalAxis that determines what values are displayed below the chart, along the x axis:

```
<mx:LineChart dataProvider="{trendData}">
  <mx:horizontalAxis>
    <mx:CategoryAxis dataProvider="{trendData}"
      categoryField="quarter"/>
  </mx:horizontalAxis>
  <mx:series>
    <mx:LineSeries xField="quarter" yField="sales"/>
  </mx:series>
</mx:LineChart>
```

FIGURE 19.13

Line and area charts representing the same data

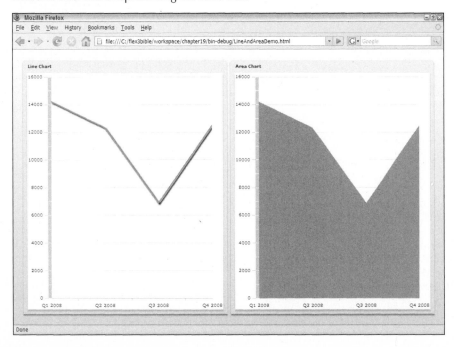

The application in Listing 19.8 displays a line chart and an area chart using the same data.

LISTING 19.8

Line and area charts

```xml
<?xml version="1.0" encoding="utf-8"?>
<mx:Application xmlns:mx="http://www.adobe.com/2006/mxml"
  backgroundColor="#EEEEEE" layout="horizontal">
  <mx:Style>
    LineSeries, AreaSeries {
      stroke-width:2;
      stroke-color:black;
      fills:#333333,#999999,#CCCCCC;
    }
  </mx:Style>
  <mx:Model id="trendModel" source="data/trendData.xml"/>
  <mx:ArrayCollection id="trendData" source="{trendModel.row}"/>
  <mx:Panel title="Line Chart" height="100%" width="100%">
    <mx:LineChart dataProvider="{trendData}"
      height="100%" width="100%">
      <mx:horizontalAxis>
        <mx:CategoryAxis dataProvider="{trendData}"
        categoryField="quarter"/>
      </mx:horizontalAxis>
      <mx:series>
        <mx:LineSeries xField="quarter" yField="sales"/>
      </mx:series>
    </mx:LineChart>
  </mx:Panel>
  <mx:Panel title="Area Chart" height="100%" width="100%">
    <mx:AreaChart dataProvider="{trendData}"
      height="100%" width="100%">
      <mx:horizontalAxis>
        <mx:CategoryAxis dataProvider="{trendData}"
          categoryField="quarter"/>
      </mx:horizontalAxis>
      <mx:series>
        <mx:AreaSeries xField="quarter" yField="sales"/>
      </mx:series>
    </mx:AreaChart>
  </mx:Panel>
</mx:Application>
```

ON the WEB   The application in Listing 19.8 is available in the Web site files as `LineAndAreaDemo.mxml` in the `chapter19` project.

Both the LineSeries and AreaSeries components can adjust the shape of their lines based on their form property. As displayed in Figure 19.13, the form property has these possible values:

- segment **(the default)**: Draws straight lines to connect data points
- step: Draws horizontal and then vertical lines to connect data points
- reverseStep: Draws vertical and then horizontal lines to connect data points
- vertical: Draws vertical lines from the y coordinate of the current point to the y coordinate of the next point
- horizontal: Draws vertical lines from the x coordinate of the current point to the x coordinate of the next point
- curve: Draws curves between data points

Figure 19.14 shows the six different forms of line charts.

FIGURE 19.14

The different forms of line charts

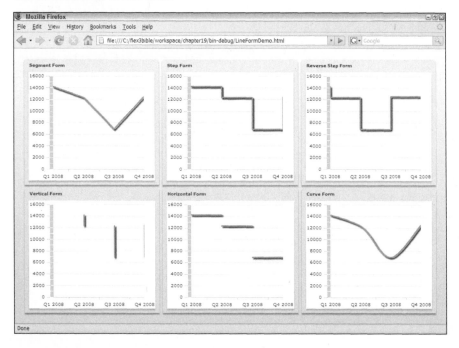

ON the WEB The application shown in Figure 19.13 is available in the Web site files as LineFormDemo.mxml in the chapter19 project.

Summary

In this chapter, I described how to use the Flex Charting controls to display data graphically in a Flex application. You learned the following:

- The Flex Charting controls are part of the Data Visualization Components and are included with a license for Flex Builder 3 Professional.

- There are nine types of charts.

- You can determine the visual presentation of a chart by setting its data, properties, and styles.

- Pie charts also can be displayed as doughnut charts with hollow centers.

- The HighLowOpenClose (HLOC) and candlestick charts are designed to show financial information.

- The bar, column, line, and area charts are designed to show comparative or trend data.

Chapter 20

Working with
Data Entry Forms

When you start to integrate data into a Flex application, you have to solve the problem of how to get data into the Flex runtime environment. As shown in earlier chapters, data can be embedded into the application using hard-coded MXML or ActionScript, or by integrating data into the application with the `<mx:Model>` tag. These strategies, however, only work for data that's both small and static.

For existing data that's retrieved from a server-based resource, such as a database or an XML file, you can use Remote Procedure Call (RPC) components such as `HTTPService` (Chapter 21), `WebService` (Chapter 23), and `RemoteObject` (Chapters 24, 27, and 28).

And then there's data that comes from the user. Unless an application is used exclusively with static data or content retrieved from a server at runtime, a data-centric application must collect data from the user. In this chapter, I describe the use of the following tools for building data entry form components:

- The `Form`, `FormHeading`, and `FormItem` components for laying out a data entry form

- `Validator` components to validate a user's data entry

- Custom value object and event classes to share data with the rest of the application

This chapter also includes tutorials that allow you to integrate many of the techniques described in preceding chapters, including the use of containers and controls (Chapter 8 and Chapter 9), creating custom MXML components (Chapter 5), modeling data with custom ActionScript classes (Chapter 16), and creating and dispatching custom event objects (Chapter 7).

587

 To use the sample code for this chapter, import the `chapter20.zip` project from the Web site files into any folder on your disk.

Using the Form Container

The `Form` component is a layout container that's responsible for laying out `Form` controls and labels in an intuitive, consistent manner.

TIP Unlike the HTML `<form>` element, which collects data and posts it to a server-based resource with an HTTP request, the Flex framework's `Form` container does not handle application navigation or packaging of data collected from the user. Instead, you (the developer) are responsible for declaring data collection objects and sharing them with the application. The `Form` container is never directly responsible for application navigation in Flex; this is handled with the `ViewStack` and related navigator containers.

As with all containers in the Flex framework, the `Form` can be declared inline in an application or component, or used as the superclass for a custom component. The `Form` container's background and border style settings are fully transparent by default, but you can modify these styles just as you can with the `Box` containers. This `Form`, for example, has a light gray background and a solid two-pixel wide border:

```
<mx:Form backgroundColor="#CCCCCC" borderStyle="solid" >
  ... nested components ...
</mx:Form>
```

You can nest any visual components within a `Form`, and they lay out in a single column stacked vertically, just like with the `VBox` container. But the following components have special behaviors when nested within a `Form` container:

- `FormItem`: Use this special container to nest the `Form`'s controls. Controls are stacked in a single column placed on the right side of the `Form`.
- `FormHeading`: This label-style control automatically aligns above the controls column.

Every `Form` container with these elements has two columns. Each nested `FormItem` container has a label property. All labels in the `FormItem` containers within a single `Form` are automatically right-aligned with each other and stacked in a single column placed on the left side of the form.

The following code declares a `Form` container with two columns, one on the left for labels and the other on the right for controls. The `FormItem` containers are nested within the `Form` and are declared in the order of their vertical presentation. The `FormHeading` control displays its label value left-aligned above the column containing the controls.

```
<mx:Form backgroundColor="#CCCCCC" borderStyle="solid"
  borderThickness="2" verticalCenter="0" horizontalCenter="0">
  <mx:FormHeading label="My Custom Form"/>
  <mx:FormItem label="First Name:">
```

```
      <mx:TextInput id="firstNameInput"/>
    </mx:FormItem>
    <mx:FormItem label="Last Name:">
      <mx:TextInput id="lastNameInput"/>
    </mx:FormItem>
  </mx:Form>
```

Figure 20.1 shows the resulting form, with two TextInput controls and a Button control displayed in a single column.

FIGURE 20.1

A simple data entry form

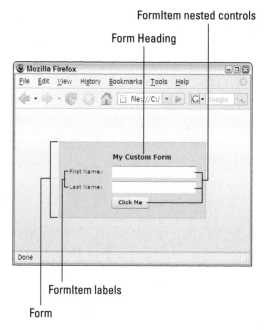

Using the FormHeading control

The FormHeading control is optional; it displays a label that's aligned with the controls that are wrapped in FormItem containers. It has these default style settings that make it display in a larger font than the Label or Text controls:

- fontSize is set to a default of 12 pixels (compared to 10 pixels for other text controls)
- fontWeight is set to a default of bold (compared to normal for other text controls)

You can use as many `FormHeading` objects as you like. For example, in a multi-part form, you might add a `FormHeading` at the top of each section:

```
<mx:Form>
  <mx:FormHeading label="Your Personal Information"/>
  <mx:FormItem label="First Name:">
    <mx:TextInput id="firstNameInput"/>
  </mx:FormItem>
  <mx:FormItem label="Last Name:">
    <mx:TextInput id="lastNameInput"/>
  </mx:FormItem>
  <mx:FormHeading label="Your Address"/>
  <mx:FormItem label="Address:">
    <mx:TextInput id="address1Input"/>
    <mx:TextInput id="address2Input"/>
  </mx:FormItem>
  <mx:FormItem label="City/State/Zip:" direction="horizontal">
    <mx:TextInput id="cityInput"/>
    <mx:TextInput id="stateInput"/>
    <mx:TextInput id="zipInput"/>
  </mx:FormItem>
  <mx:FormItem>
    <mx:Button label="Save Information"/>
  </mx:FormItem>
</mx:Form>
```

Figure 20.2 shows the resulting application, with `FormHeading` controls above each section of the data entry form.

Some developers prefer not to use the `FormHeading`, instead wrapping the `Form` container in a `Panel`. The `Panel` container's title is then used to display a heading, and the `FormHeading` isn't necessary:

```
<mx:Panel title="My Custom Form">
  <mx:Form>
    <mx:FormItem label="First Name:">
      <mx:TextInput id="firstNameInput"/>
    </mx:FormItem>
    <mx:FormItem label="Last Name:">
      <mx:TextInput id="lastNameInput"/>
    </mx:FormItem>
  </mx:Form>
  <mx:ControlBar>
    <mx:Button label="Click Me"/>
  </mx:ControlBar>
</mx:Panel>
```

Figure 20.3 shows the resulting application. The `Form` is wrapped inside a `Panel`, and the `Button` is displayed in the `ControlBar` container at the bottom of the form.

FIGURE 20.2

Using multiple `FormHeading` controls

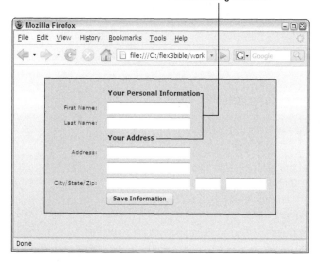

FIGURE 20.3

A `Form` wrapped inside a `Panel`

> **TIP** Notice that in the preceding code, the `Button` isn't inside the `Form` container. In HTML, this would have a negative effect; if an HTML submit button isn't inside the `<form>` element, clicking it doesn't have the desired effect of sending a new request to the server. In Flex, you handle the `Button` control's click event with explicit ActionScript statements. There is no built-in "submit" action as there is in HTML, so it simply doesn't matter whether the `Button` is nested in the `Form` container.

Using the FormItem container

The FormItem container is nested within a Form container and in turn contains one or more data entry Form controls. The container's label property is used to set a string value that is displayed in the Form container's left column.

Controlling label alignment

By default, the labels in a Form container are right-aligned. If you want to change their alignment to right or center, follow these steps:

1. Create a style selector for the FormItem container.

2. Within the selector, assign the labelStyleName style to an arbitrary style name.

3. Declare the style name selector with text-align set to the new alignment value.

The following <mx:Style> tag set handles each of these tasks:

```
<mx:Style>
  .rightAlignedLabels {
    text-align: left;
  }
  FormItem {
    labelStyleName:rightAlignedLabels;
  }
</mx:Style>
```

Figure 20.4 shows the visual result. The labels within the Form container's left column are now left-aligned.

FIGURE 20.4

A form with left-aligned labels and horizontal layout

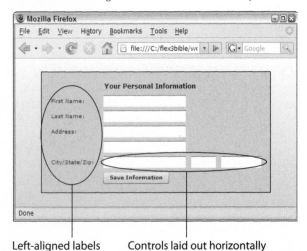

Left-aligned labels   Controls laid out horizontally

Controlling FormItem layout

Controls within the `FormItem` container are stacked vertically by default. You can change the layout rules for any particular `FormItem` container by setting its `direction` property to `horizontal`. The following code causes the three `TextInput` controls to lay out side by side, instead of being stacked on top of each other:

```
<mx:FormItem label="City/State/Zip:" direction="horizontal">
  <mx:TextInput id="cityInput"/>
  <mx:TextInput id="stateInput"/>
  <mx:TextInput id="zipInput"/>
</mx:FormItem>
```

The form displayed in Figure 20.4 shows the result: The three `TextInput` controls are laid out side by side instead of being stacked vertically.

CAUTION If a `FormItem` container with its `direction` set to `horizontal` has its width restricted to a point where there isn't room for all its nested controls, it "wraps" the controls to the next line. The solution is to widen the `FormItem` container.

Setting a default button

In most Web browsers, when the cursor is in an HTML form's text field and the user presses Enter or Return, the first "submit" button behaves as though the user has clicked it. This is known as *default button* behavior and is automatic in those browsers that support it.

The Flex `Form` container does not have an automatic default button, but you can create the behavior by setting the `Form` container's `defaultButton` property. This property is designed to refer to a `Button` object somewhere in the current application or component; you set it with a binding expression that refers to the target `Button` object by its `id`.

Setting a default button in Flex causes these behaviors:

■ When any control in the `Form` container has focus, the default button shows a colored glow indicating that pressing Enter or Return is the same as clicking the button.

■ When the user presses Enter or Return, the `Button` object's `click` event is dispatched.

The application in Listing 20.1 has a simple `Form` container with its `defaultButton` property set to a `Button` control with an `id` of `saveButton`. The user can click the button or press Enter or Return with the cursor in a `TextInput` control; either way, the `Button` object's `click` event is dispatched. Figure 20.5 shows the result.

LISTING 20.1

A Form with a default button

```
<?xml version="1.0" encoding="utf-8"?>
<mx:Application xmlns:mx="http://www.adobe.com/2006/mxml"
    layout="vertical"
  backgroundColor="#EEEEEE">
  <mx:Script>
    <![CDATA[
      import mx.controls.Alert;
      private function clickHandler(event:MouseEvent):void
      {
        Alert.show("You clicked the button", "Click Handler");
      }
    ]]>
  </mx:Script>
  <mx:Style source="styles.css"/>
  <mx:Form defaultButton="{saveButton}">
    <mx:FormHeading label="Your Personal Information"/>
    <mx:FormItem label="First Name:">
      <mx:TextInput id="firstNameInput"/>
    </mx:FormItem>
    <mx:FormItem label="Last Name:">
      <mx:TextInput id="lastNameInput"/>
    </mx:FormItem>
    <mx:FormItem>
      <mx:Button id="saveButton"
        label="Save Information"
        click="clickHandler(event)"/>
    </mx:FormItem>
  </mx:Form>
</mx:Application>
```

> **ON the WEB**   The code in Listing 20.1 is available in the Web site files as `FormDefaultButton.mxml` in the `chapter20` project.

> **TIP**   The default button does not have to be nested inside the `Form` container. The `defaultButton` property references the button object by its `id`, so as long as the button control is "in scope" the default button behavior works as expected. This is particularly important when placing a `Button` object in a `ControlBar` or other container to set its position outside the `Form` container.

FIGURE 20.5

Setting the default button in a Form container

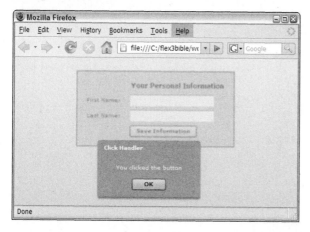

Using Custom Form Components

Data entry forms can be designed as fully encapsulated components that handle all the normal tasks of data entry:

- Presentation of a data entry interface
- Collection and validation of data entered by the user
- Sharing of data with the rest of the application with custom value object and event classes

In this section, I describe the steps to create and use a custom Form component.

Creating a custom Form component

You can create a custom Form component as an MXML component with a Form as its root element. Flex Builder 3 does a particularly nice job of helping you lay out Form components in Design view. Try these steps to create a simple Form component:

1. Open the chapter20 project from the Web site files. Notice that the project's source root folder has a subfolder named forms.

2. Right-click (Ctrl+click on the Mac) the forms subfolder.

3. Select New ➪ MXML Component from the context menu.

4. In the New MXML Component wizard, set these properties (shown in Figure 20.6):

   ▧ `Filename:LoginForm.mxml`

   ▧ Based on: Form

   ▧ Width: [blank value]

   ▧ Height: [blank value]

FIGURE 20.6

Creating a `Form` component with the New MXML Component wizard

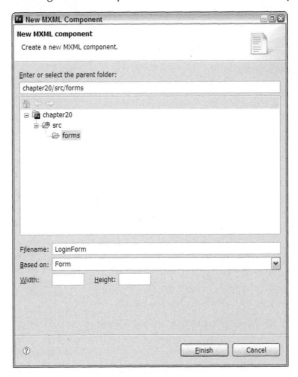

5. Click Finish to create the new component.

   The new component should appear in Flex Builder.

6. If the component opens in Design view, click Source to switch to Source view.

The beginning code for the Form component looks like this:

```
<?xml version="1.0" encoding="utf-8"?>
<mx:Form xmlns:mx="http://www.adobe.com/2006/mxml">

</mx:Form>
```

Switch to Design view to see the beginning Form component presentation, shown in Figure 20.7.

FIGURE 20.7

A beginning Form component

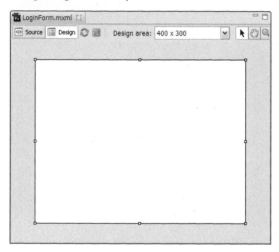

Adding controls to a Form component

When building a Form component, Flex Builder's Design view lets you easily drag and drop the objects you want to use from the Components view. Each time you add a control to a Form container, Design view automatically wraps the control in a new FormItem container. You can then set the FormItem container's label property, drag its handles to resize it, set other properties and styles in the Flex Properties view, and otherwise customize the control's appearance and behavior.

Follow these steps to add data entry form controls to the LoginForm component that was described in the preceding section:

1. Open the LoginForm.mxml file in Design view.

2. Locate the TextInput control in the Components view.

3. Drag the control into the editor region, and drop it anywhere.

As shown in Figure 20.8, you should see that the `TextInput` control is wrapped in a `FormItem` container automatically, with a default `label` property of `Label`.

FIGURE 20.8

A `TextInput` control wrapped in a `FormItem` container with the default label

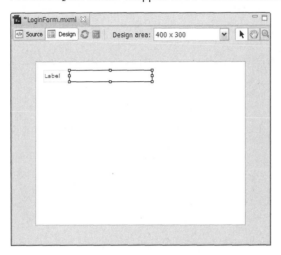

4. Double-click the `FormItem` container's label region. When the label turns into an input control, type the label **Email Address:**.

5. Click the new `TextInput` control in Design view.

6. In the Flex Properties view, change the `TextInput` control's `id` to **emailInput**.

7. Drag another `TextInput` control from the Components view into the form.

CAUTION   To ensure that a new `FormItem` container is wrapped around the new control, make sure the blue insertion line that's displayed during the drag-and-drop operation is as wide as the existing `FormItem` container (shown in Figure 20.9). If it's the size of the `TextInput` control when you release the mouse button, the new `TextInput` control will be dropped into the existing `FormItem` container.

8. Double-click the label of the new `FormItem` container, and change it to **Password:**.

9. Change the new `TextInput` control's `id` to **passwordInput**.

10. Drag a `Button` control into the `Form`, and place it below the existing `FormItem` container, in its own container.

11. Double-click the new `Button` control, and change its label to **Log In**.

12. Double-click the label of the new `FormItem` container, and change it to a blank string.

    The component should now appear as it does in Figure 20.9.

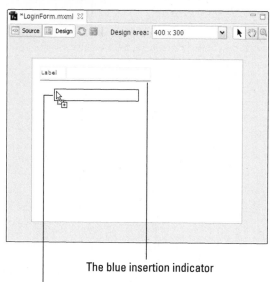

FIGURE 20.9

The Form component in its current state

The blue insertion indicator

Dragging the component from the Components view

13. Switch to Source view.

The Form component's source code should now look like this:

```xml
<?xml version="1.0" encoding="utf-8"?>
<mx:Form xmlns:mx="http://www.adobe.com/2006/mxml">
  <mx:FormItem label="Email Address:">
    <mx:TextInput id="emailInput"/>
  </mx:FormItem>
  <mx:FormItem label="Password:">
    <mx:TextInput id="passwordInput"/>
  </mx:FormItem>
  <mx:FormItem>
    <mx:Button label="Log In"/>
  </mx:FormItem>
</mx:Form>
```

> **TIP**
>
> When creating a **Form** component in Design view, it's easy to accidentally change the **id** property of the **FormItem** container instead of its nested component. The purpose of the **id** is to allow you to easily collect data from the **Form** controls when the user clicks the button or otherwise indicates that data entry is complete. You care about the data in the controls, not any data that might be associated with the **FormItem** containers.

Validating Data Entry

When a user enters data into any database application, you typically want to ensure that it matches specific criteria before sending it to the server or saving it into a persistent data store. Flex provides a set of ActionScript classes in the mx.validators package that are designed for this purpose. Each of the following classes validates a particular data type:

- CreditCardValidator: Checks that a string has the correct length and prefix, and passes Luhn mod10 algorithm for the specified card type

WEB RESOURCE For more information on the Luhn mod10 algorithm, visit this entry at Wikipedia: http://en.wikipedia.org/wiki/Luhn_algorithm.

- CurrencyValidator: Checks that String matches a valid currency pattern; can be customized for particular locales and other specific rules
- DateValidator: Checks that a Date, String, or Object contains a valid Date; can be customized for particular date ranges
- EmailValidator: Checks that a String follows the common pattern of an e-mail address
- NumberValidator: Checks that a value is a Number or a String that can be parsed as a number; can be customized for particular numeric ranges and other rules
- PhoneNumberValidator: Checks that a value matches a valid phone number pattern; can be customized for particular locales and other specific rules
- RegExpValidator: Checks that a String matches a regular expression
- SocialSecurityValidator: Checks that a String matches a valid social security number pattern
- StringValidator: Checks for String values that match your specific criteria, including minimum and maximum length
- ZipCodeValidator: Checks that a String matches a valid ZIP code pattern

All validator classes are extended from mx.validators.Validator, so they're all used with a common pattern.

Creating a validator object

You can create validator objects with either MXML or ActionScript. Each validator object is assigned to a single control and implements these required properties that determine its behavior at runtime:

- source: A reference to the data entry control being validated
- property: The name of the source object's property that contains the value to be validated

For example, assume your data entry form includes this `TextInput` control that you want to validate as an e-mail address:

```
<mx:TextInput id="emailInput"/>
```

The validator object declaration for this control would minimally include the source, referencing the `TextInput` control's `id` in a binding expression, and the property, referencing the input control's text property as a string:

```
<mx:EmailValidator id="myValidator"
    source="{emailInput}" property="text"/>
```

The equivalent functionality in ActionScript looks like this:

```
import mx.validators.EmailValidator;
private function initApp():void
{
  var myValidator:EmailValidator = new EmailValidator;
  myValidator.source = emailInput;
  myValidator.property = "text";
}
```

Controlling validation with trigger events

By default, validation occurs either when the user makes a change to a control's value or when he simply clicks or tabs into the control to give it focus and then clicks or tabs again to remove focus. This automatic validation is controlled by these two properties that are shared by all validator classes:

- `trigger`: A reference that points to an object that will trigger validation
- `triggerEvent`: A String containing the name of the event that will trigger validation

Validation happens automatically when a control loses focus because the validator object's trigger property defaults to the value of its source property (the control being validated) and `triggerEvent` defaults to the `valueCommitted` event. Normally, this event occurs when a change is made or the control simply loses focus.

You can change when validation occurs by changing these properties' values. For example, in an application where you want all controls to be validated when the user clicks a button, you would follow these steps:

1. Add a unique `id` to the `Button` control you want to use as the trigger.
2. Set each validator object's `trigger` property to the `Button` control's `id` in a binding expression.
3. Set each validator object's `triggerEvent` property to the event name `click`.

Follow these steps to add automatic validation to the `LoginForm` component you created in previous sections of this chapter:

1. Open `LoginForm.mxml` in Source view.

2. Locate the `Button` control with a label of `Log In`, and add an `id` of `loginButton`.

3. After the `<mx:Form>` start tag, declare an `EmailValidator` object with MXML code. Set its `id` to `emailValidator`, `source` to the `emailInput` control, `property` to `text`, `trigger` to `loginButton`, and `triggerEvent` to `click`:

```
<mx:EmailValidator id="emailValidator"
  source="{emailInput}" property="text"
  trigger="{loginButton}" triggerEvent="click"/>
```

4. Add a `StringValidator` object with an `id` of `passwordValidator`. Set its `source` to `passwordInput` and all other properties exactly like the first validator object:

```
<mx:StringValidator id="passwordValidator"
  source="{passwordInput}" property="text"
  trigger="{loginButton}" triggerEvent="click"/>
```

The `Form` component in Listing 20.2 uses identical `trigger` and `triggerEvent` properties to automatically trigger two different validator objects when a `Button` control is clicked.

LISTING 20.2

A Form component using automatic validation

```
<?xml version="1.0" encoding="utf-8"?>
<mx:Form xmlns:mx="http://www.adobe.com/2006/mxml">
  <mx:EmailValidator id="emailValidator"
    source="{emailInput}" property="text"
    trigger="{loginButton" triggerEvent="click"/>
  <mx:StringValidator id="passwordValidator"
    source="{passwordInput}" property="text"
    trigger="{loginButton" triggerEvent="click"/>
  <mx:FormItem label="Email Address:">
    <mx:TextInput id="emailInput"/>
  </mx:FormItem>
  <mx:FormItem label="Password:">
    <mx:TextInput id="passwordInput"/>
  </mx:FormItem>
  <mx:FormItem>
    <mx:Button id="loginButton" label="Log In"/>
  </mx:FormItem>
</mx:Form>
```

ON the WEB   The code in Listing 20.2 is available in the Web site files as `LoginFormAuto Validation.mxml` in the `src/forms` folder of the `chapter20` project.

To see the effect of this form, follow these steps to create a new application and incorporate the Form component:

1. Create a new MXML application named `ValidationDemo.mxml`.

2. In Source view, set these properties in the `<mx:Application>` start tag:

   - backgroundColor="#EEEEEE"
   - layout="absolute"

3. Add an instance of the new `LoginForm` component. Set its `id` property to `loginForm`. As you type, Flex Builder should add the required custom `forms` namespace prefix for the `forms` folder to the `<mx:Application>` tag.

4. Set the `LoginForm` object's `x` and `y` properties to 10 pixels each. The application code should appear as follows:

```
<?xml version="1.0" encoding="utf-8"?>
<mx:Application xmlns:mx="http://www.adobe.com/2006/mxml"
  backgroundColor="#EEEEEE" layout="absolute"
  xmlns:forms="forms.*">
  <forms:LoginForm id="loginForm" x="10" y="10"/>
</mx:Application>
```

5. Run the application in a browser.

6. Click the `LoginForm`'s Log In button to trigger validation.

At runtime, as the user clicks the button to trigger validation, each of the validator objects examines the named property of its `source` data entry control. If validation rules pass, the user sees no feedback. If a validation rule is broken, the source control displays a red border to the user. When the user moves the cursor over the control, he sees a pop-up window displaying the error message, as shown in Figure 20.10.

FIGURE 20.10

A form displaying a validation error message

Controlling validation with ActionScript

Trigger-based validation lets the user know he has entered invalid values, but doesn't give you (as the developer) an opportunity to handle the situation and decide whether to continue with form processing or cancel processing and display an error. In the above examples, if we were to execute a function on the button's `click` event, that function would execute regardless of whether the validation passed.

For most `Form` components, triggering validation with ActionScript code allows you to find out immediately whether all your validations have passed and to take appropriate action.

Disabling validation trigger events

When you use programmatic validation, you typically disable the automatic validation that results from using the `trigger` and `triggerEvent` properties. You accomplish this by removing the validator object's `trigger` property and setting `triggerEvent` to a blank String:

```
<mx:EmailValidator id="emailValidator"
    source="{emailInput}" property="text"
    triggerEvent=""/>
```

Because no event can be dispatched that would have a blank string for its event name, this results in disabling any event-based validation.

Triggering individual validator objects with ActionScript

To programmatically trigger validation on a single validator object, call the object's `validate()` method. This method returns an instance of the `ValidationResultEvent` event class:

```
var validObj:ValidationResultEvent =
  emailValidator.validate();
```

As with all event classes, `ValidationResultEvent` has a `type` property. You determine whether validation has succeeded by comparing the event object's `type` to event object constants named `VALID` and `INVALID`. For example, this conditional ActionScript block would execute only if the validation is passed:

```
if (validObj.type == ValidationResultEvent.VALID)
{
  ... process data ...
}
```

The version of the custom `Form` component in Listing 20.3 triggers validation programmatically on two separate validator objects and then evaluates both resulting event objects to determine whether the `Form`'s data is valid.

LISTING 20.3

A Form component with programmatic validation of one validator object at a time

```
<?xml version="1.0" encoding="utf-8"?>
<mx:Form xmlns:mx="http://www.adobe.com/2006/mxml">
  <mx:Script>
    <![CDATA[
      import mx.controls.Alert;
      import mx.events.ValidationResultEvent;
      private function isValid():Boolean
      {
        var emailObj:ValidationResultEvent = emailValidator.validate();
        var pwordObj:ValidationResultEvent = emailValidator.validate();
        if (emailObj.type == ValidationResultEvent.VALID &&
            pwordObj.type == ValidationResultEvent.VALID)
        {
          Alert.show("Data is valid", "Validation Logic");
          return true;
        }
        else
        {
          Alert.show("There are form errors", "Validation Logic");
          return false;
        }
      }
    ]]>
  </mx:Script>

  <mx:EmailValidator id="emailValidator"
    source="{emailInput}" property="text"
 triggerEvent=""/>
  <mx:StringValidator id="passwordValidator"
    source="{passwordInput}" property="text"
 triggerEvent=""/>

  <mx:FormItem label="Email Address:">
    <mx:TextInput id="emailInput"/>
  </mx:FormItem>
  <mx:FormItem label="Password:">
    <mx:TextInput id="passwordInput"/>
  </mx:FormItem>
  <mx:FormItem>
    <mx:Button id="loginButton" label="Log In"/>
  </mx:FormItem>

</mx:Form>
```

Triggering multiple validator objects with ActionScript

As a data entry form becomes more complex, with additional controls and validators, the coding style described in the preceding section can be cumbersome. An alternative approach is to use the Validator class's static `validateAll()` method to trigger multiple validator objects simultaneously.

To use this approach, call the `validateAll()` method and pass in an `Array` of validator objects:

```
var arInvalid:Array = Validator.validateAll(
   [emailValidator, passwordValidator]);
```

The `validateAll()` method returns an `Array` containing `ValidationResultEvent` objects only for those validator objects that fail validation. If the `Array` has no items, this means that all validators passed their validation rules. The following code evaluates the returned `Array`:

```
if (arInvalid.length == 0)
{
   Alert.show("Data is valid", "Validation Logic");
   return true;
}
```

Try these steps to add programmatic validation of multiple validator objects to the `LoginForm` component described in previous sections:

1. Open `LoginForm.mxml` in Source view.

2. For both of the existing validator objects, remove their `trigger` property and set their `triggerEvent` to a blank string:

   ```
   <mx:EmailValidator id="emailValidator"
      source="{emailInput}" property="text" triggerEvent=""/>
   <mx:StringValidator id="passwordValidator"
      source="{passwordInput}" property="text" triggerEvent=""/>
   ```

3. Add an `<mx:Script>` tag set just below the `<mx:Form>` start tag.

4. Create a new private function named `isValid()` that accepts no arguments and returns `void`.

5. Within the function body, use the `Validator.validateAll()` method to trigger both the `emailValidator` and the `passwordValidator` objects:

   ```
   var arInvalid:Array = Validator.validateAll(
      [emailValidator, passwordValidator]);
   ```

   As you type the code, Flex Builder might automatically add an import statement for the `Validator` class. If this doesn't happen, add this import statement above the `isValid()` function:

   ```
   import mx.validators.Validator;
   ```

6. Add the following code after the call to `validateAll()` to evaluate whether validation rules were passed:

```
if (arInvalid.length == 0)
{
  Alert.show("Data is valid", "Validation Logic");
  return true;
}
else
{
  Alert.show("There are form errors", "Validation Logic");
  return false;
}
```

7. Locate the `Button` control with the `Log In` label, and add a `click` event handler that calls the `isValid()` method:

```
<mx:Button id="loginButton" label="Log In"
click="isValid()"/>
```

8. Save the `Form` component file, and open `ValidatorDemo.mxml`, the application that was created in a preceding exercise.

9. Run the application, and try clicking the form button to trigger validation.

As shown in Figure 20.11, you should see that validation is triggered and a pop-up window produced by the Alert class is displayed. After clicking OK to clear the pop-up window, a validation error message is displayed when you move the cursor over any control with a red border.

> **TIP** The `target` of the `ValidationResultEvent` objects in the array refer back to the validator that failed. You can then refer to the validator object's `source` property to get a reference to the control that was validated

FIGURE 20.11

Results of validation with ActionScript

Controlling validation rules and error messages

Each validator class has a set of validation rules and equivalent error messages that are displayed when the rules are broken. One of these rules, named `required`, is implemented on the `Validator` superclass and is therefore used for all validator objects.

The required rule is a `Boolean` value that defaults to `true`. As a result, when you apply a validator object to a `Form` control, you're automatically indicating that the control's value can't be left blank. When this rule is broken, the value of the validator object's `requiredFieldError` property is displayed in the pop-up error message. The default error message for the `requiredFieldError` (in the U.S. English locale) is "This field is required." You can customize the error message by setting the appropriate property:

```
<mx:EmailValidator id="emailValidator"
  source="{emailInput}" property="text" triggerEvent=""
  requiredFieldError="Email address can't be left blank"/>
<mx:StringValidator id="passwordValidator"
  source="{passwordInput}" property="text" triggerEvent=""
  requiredFieldError="Password can't be left blank"/>
```

Each of the two validator objects now has its own distinct error message. As shown in Figure 20.12, the user gets better, more specific feedback when he makes a data entry error.

FIGURE 20.12

A customized validation error message

Table 20.1 describes some commonly used validation rules and equivalent error message properties. This is not an exhaustive list; see the product documentation for a complete list of validation rules and their equivalent error message property names.

TABLE 20.1

Examples of Validation Rules and Error Messages

Rule Name	Values	Error Name	Implemented By
required	Boolean	requiredFieldError	All validator classes
minLength	Numeric	tooShortError	StringValidator
maxLength	Numeric	tooLongError	StringValidator
domain	real | int	integerError	NumberValidator
minValue CurrencyValidator	Numeric	lowerThanMinError	NumberValidator,
maxValue CurrencyValidator	Numeric	exceedsMaxError	NumberValidator,
[automatic validation for NumberValidator, CurrencyValidator, and DateValidator]	n/a	invalidCharError	NumberValidator, CurrencyValidator
[Automatic validation for EmailValidator]	n/a	invalidCharError, invalidDomainError, invalidIPDomainError, invalidPeriodsInDomainError, missingAtSignError, missingPeriodInDomainError, missingUsernameError, tooManyAtSignsError	EmailValidator
[Automatic validation for DateValidator]	n/a	wrongDayError, wrongLengthError, wrongMonthError, wrongYearError	DateValidator

Follow these steps to add custom error messages to the LoginForm component:

1. Open LoginForm.mxml in Source view.

2. Set the emailValidator object's requiredFieldError property to **Email address can't be left blank**.

3. Set the passwordValidator object's requiredFieldError property to **Password can't be left blank**.

   The code for the validator objects should now look like this:

   ```
   <mx:EmailValidator id="emailValidator"
     source="{emailInput}" property="text" triggerEvent=""
     requiredFieldError="Email address can't be left blank"/>
   ```

```
<mx:StringValidator id="passwordValidator"
  source="{passwordInput}" property="text" triggerEvent=""
  requiredFieldError="Password can't be left blank"/>
```

4. Save the Form component file, and open ValidatorDemo.mxml, the application that was created in a preceding exercise.

5. Run the application, and try clicking the form button to trigger validation.

You should see the custom error messages displayed for each of the Form controls.

Sharing Data with the Application

When you use data entry form components, you share data with the application with custom events. Each data entry form requires two custom ActionScript classes:

■ A value object class that models the Form's data

■ A custom event class that is dispatched from the Form component

CROSS-REF Detailed information about using custom event classes is available in Chapter 7. Detailed information on modeling data with the Value Object design pattern is available in Chapter 16.

Modeling Form data with a value object

To share data from a Form component, you first create an instance of a value object class and populate the object with data from the Form's controls. You can accomplish this with either MXML or ActionScript code.

Listing 20.4 shows a custom value object class with public properties for each of the Form component's controls.

LISTING 20.4

A custom ActionScript class that implements the Value Object design pattern

```
package vo
{
  [Bindable]
  public class LoginVO
  {
    public var email:String;
    public var password:String;

    public function LoginVO()
    {
```

```
        }
    }
}
```

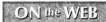 The code in Listing 20.4 is available in the Web site files as `LoginVO.as` in the `src/vo` folder of the `chapter20` project.

Populating value object data with MXML

To declare and populate the value object with data in MXML, declare the object and set each of its properties to one of the `Form` controls' values with binding expressions:

```
<vo:LoginVO id="formDataObj"
    email="{emailInput.text}"
    password="{passwordInput.text}"/>
```

At runtime, each of the value object's properties is populated when its matching `Form` control executes the binding expression.

CAUTION When working with value object properties that have complex data types such as a `Date`, the MXML approach has a liability: If the user never interacts with the `Form` control, the value in the declaration is never set. To handle this, you can set each property with a default value within the value object class:

```
public var myDateProperty:Date = new Date();
```

If you don't do this, in some cases the value object's property value ends up `null` (depending on how the user interacts with the form).

Populating value object data with ActionScript

You also can create and populate a value object with ActionScript code. This approach is sometimes preferred because you can examine values and take action based on various conditions. The code to create and populate the value object in ActionScript might look like this:

```
var loginObj:LoginVO = new LoginVO();
loginObj.email = emailInput.text;
loginObj.password = passwordInput.text;
```

Because data is being passed to the value object in ActionScript statements, you have the opportunity to further validate or modify data before sharing it with the rest of the application.

Dispatching a custom event

As described in Chapter 7, you create custom event classes to "wrap" and share particular types of data with the rest of the application. Because data from the `Form` controls is contained within a value object, you typically create a custom `Event` class with one public property data typed as the custom value object class.

The custom event class in Listing 20.5 has a single login property data typed as the LoginVO class. Notice that this event class sets its bubbles property by passing a value of true as the second argument in the super() constructor method call. Because it's a bubbling event, it also overrides the clone() method so that the event object can successfully be cloned during the bubbling process.

LISTING 20.5

A bubbling custom event object with a value object public property

```
package events
{
  import flash.events.Event;
  import vo.LoginVO;
  public class LoginEvent extends Event
  {
    public var login:LoginVO;
    public function LoginEvent(type:String, login:LoginVO)
    {
      super(type, true);
      this.login = login;
    }
    override public function clone():Event
    {
      return new LoginEvent(type, login);
    }
  }
}
```

ON the WEB   The code in Listing 20.5 is available in the Web site files as LoginEvent.as in the src/events folder of the chapter20 project.

To use this custom event and share data with the rest of the application, follow these steps in the Form component:

1. Declare an <mx:Metadata> tag set.

2. Declare an [Event] metadata tag for a custom event that uses the custom event class.

3. To share data with the rest of the application, add code that:

  a. Creates the value object and populates it with data

  b. Creates the custom event object and populates its public property with the value object

  c. Dispatches the custom event object

Follow these steps to complete the custom Form component:

1. Open the LoginForm.mxml file in Design view.

2. After the <mx:Form> start tag, add an <mx:Metadata> tag set.

3. Within the <mx:Metadata> tag set, declare a custom event with a name of login and a type of events.LoginEvent:

```
<mx:Metadata>
  [Event(name="login", type="events.LoginEvent")]
</mx:Metadata>
```

4. In the <mx:Script> section, create a new private function named clickHandler() that accepts an event argument typed as MouseEvent and returns void:

```
private function clickHandler(event:MouseEvent):void
{
}
```

5. Within the new function, add a conditional evaluation that executes the isValid() function:

```
if (isValid())
{
}
```

6. Within the conditional block, add the following code to create and populate the value object with data:

```
var loginObj:LoginVO = new LoginVO();
loginObj.email = emailInput.text;
loginObj.password = passwordInput.text;
```

7. Add code to create the custom event object, set its login property to the value object, and dispatch the event:

```
var e:LoginEvent = new LoginEvent("login", loginObj);
dispatchEvent(e);
```

8. In the isValid() function, comment out or delete the code that displays an Alert pop-up window.

9. Locate the button control, and change its click event listener to call the clickHandler() method and pass the event object:

```
<mx:Button id="loginButton" label="Log In"
  click="clickHandler(event)"/>
```

10. Save the LoginForm component.

Listing 20.6 shows the completed Form component with validation and data sharing through a custom event and a value object.

LISTING 20.6

A completed Form component with validation and data sharing

```xml
<?xml version="1.0" encoding="utf-8"?>
<mx:Form xmlns:mx="http://www.adobe.com/2006/mxml" xmlns:vo="vo.*">
  <mx:Metadata>
    [Event(name="login", type="events.LoginEvent")]
  </mx:Metadata>
  <mx:Script>
    <![CDATA[
      import vo.LoginVO;
      import events.LoginEvent;
      import mx.validators.Validator;
      import mx.controls.Alert;
      private function isValid():Boolean
      {
        var arInvalid:Array = Validator.validateAll(
          [emailValidator, passwordValidator]);
        if (arInvalid.length == 0)
        {
          return true;
        }
        else
        {
          Alert.show("There are form errors", "Validation Logic");
          return false;
        }
      }
      private function clickHandler(event:MouseEvent):void
      {
        if (isValid())
        {
          var loginObj:LoginVO = new LoginVO();
          loginObj.email = emailInput.text;
          loginObj.password = passwordInput.text;
          var e:LoginEvent = new LoginEvent("login", loginObj);
          dispatchEvent(e);
        }
      }
    ]]>
  </mx:Script>
  <mx:EmailValidator id="emailValidator"
    source="{emailInput}" property="text" triggerEvent=""
    requiredFieldError="Email address can't be left blank"/>
  <mx:StringValidator id="passwordValidator"
    source="{passwordInput}" property="text" triggerEvent=""
    requiredFieldError="Password can't be left blank"/>
  <mx:FormItem label="Email Address:">
```

```
      <mx:TextInput id="emailInput"/>
   </mx:FormItem>
   <mx:FormItem label="Password:">
      <mx:TextInput id="passwordInput"/>
   </mx:FormItem>
   <mx:FormItem>
         <mx:Button id="loginButton" label="Log In"
            click="clickHandler(event)"/>
   </mx:FormItem>
</mx:Form>
```

ON the WEB The code in Listing 20.6 is available in the Web site files as `LoginForm`
`Complete.mxml` in the `src/forms` folder of the `chapter20` project.

The final step in the process is to handle the custom event from the application. Follow these steps
to integrate the `Form` component into a new MXML application:

1. Create a new MXML application named `FormComponentDemo.mxml`.

2. Set the application's `layout` property to `vertical` and its `id` to `myForm`.

3. Add an instance of the `LoginForm` control.

   The code so far should look like this:

   ```
   <?xml version="1.0" encoding="utf-8"?>
   <mx:Application xmlns:mx="http://www.adobe.com/2006/mxml"
      xmlns:forms="forms.*">
      <forms:LoginForm id="loginForm"/>
   </mx:Application>
   ```

4. Add an `<mx:Script>` tag set to the application:

   ```
   <mx:Script>
      <![CDATA[

      ]]>
   </mx:Script>
   ```

5. Within the Script section's CDATA block, add a bindable private variable named
   `myLogin`, typed as the `LoginVO` class. As you code, Flex Builder should add the
   required import statement:

   ```
   import vo.LoginVO;

   [Bindable]
   private var myLogin:LoginVO;
   ```

6. Add a private function named `loginHandler()` that receives an event argument
   typed as `LoginEvent` and returns `void`.

7. Within the private function, save the event object's login property to the bindable `myLogin` variable:

```
private function loginHandler(event:LoginEvent):void
{
  myLogin = event.login;
}
```

8. Add a `login` event listener to the `LoginForm` component instance that calls `loginHandler()` and passes the event object:

```
<forms:LoginForm id="loginForm" login="loginHandler(event)"/>
```

9. Add a `Label` control to the bottom of the application that displays the `myLogin` object's `email` property:

```
<mx:Label text="Email address: {myLogin.email}"/>
```

10. Add another `Label` control to the bottom of the application that displays the `myLogin` object's `password` property:

```
<mx:Label text="Password: {myLogin.password}"/>
```

11. Run the application, and test the `Form` control by entering valid data and clicking Log In.

   You should see that the value object is passed from the `Form` component to the application and its data is displayed in the `Label` controls as a result of their binding expressions.

Listing 20.7 show the completed application.

LISTING 20.7

An application using a custom Form component

```
<?xml version="1.0" encoding="utf-8"?>
<mx:Application xmlns:mx="http://www.adobe.com/2006/mxml"
  xmlns:forms="forms.*">
  <mx:Script>
    <![CDATA[
      import events.LoginEvent;
      import vo.LoginVO;
      [Bindable]
      private var myLogin:LoginVO;
      private function loginHandler(event:LoginEvent):void
      {
        myLogin = event.login;
      }
    ]]>
  </mx:Script>
  <forms:LoginForm id="loginForm" login="loginHandler(event)"/>
  <mx:Label text="Email address: {myLogin.email}"/>
  <mx:Label text="Password: {myLogin.password}"/>
</mx:Application>
```

ON the WEB   The code in Listing 20.7 is available in the Web site files as `FormComponentDemo`
`Complete.mxml` in the `src` folder of the `chapter20` project.

TIP   You can manually trigger the validation interface by setting any visual component's
`errorString` property to a non-blank `String`. When `errorString` is set to a non-
blank `String`, the visual component displays the same red border, and displays the property's value
in the same pop-up error display window when the mouse hovers over the component, as when validation errors are passed to a control by a validator class. You can also explicitly remove the validation
interface from a visual component by setting its `errorString` to a blank `String` or null.

Summary

In this chapter, I described how to build and use data entry form components in Flex applications.
You learned the following:

- The `Form` container lays out labels in one column and controls in another column.

- The `FormHeading` control is optional and displays a label aligned inside the Form container's controls column.

- The `FormItem` container is nested within the `Form` container.

- The label properties of all `FormItem` containers within the `Form` are right-aligned by
  default, but they can be adjusted to center or left alignment with the use of CSS rules.

- The `FormItem` container can nest multiple controls that are stacked vertically by default.

- Flex Builder's Design view helps you quickly create `Form` components by adding
  `FormItem` containers to controls as they're dragged from the Components view.

- Data validation is handled with validator objects.

- You can trigger validation with trigger events or explicit ActionScript code.

- `Form` components share data with the rest of the application with custom value object
  and event classes.

Chapter 21

Working with HTTPService and XML

pplications built with the Flex framework are commonly both dynamic and data-centric: They use, present, and allow users to modify data that's imported at runtime from a server-based data store (or, in the case of desktop applications running on AIR, a local database).

Flash Player and the Adobe Integrated Runtime don't have the ability to communicate directly with server-based data storage applications such as database and LDAP servers. Instead, they're designed to communicate with *middleware* application servers using a variety of protocols.

The Flex framework includes three Remote Procedure Call (RPC) components that allow you to integrate your Flex applications with common application server products. Of these, the HTTPService component has the most flexibility in terms of the format of messages that are exchanged between the client and server at runtime. Unlike the other RPC components, you can use the HTTPService component with any application server, because it exchanges data in the form of simple HTTP parameters and XML of any flavor.

In this chapter, I describe the use of the HTTPService component to retrieve data from a Web server at runtime. I also cover how to send data from a Flex application to a dynamic application server using HTTP requests that are similar to those that are sent from a Web browser using a hyperlink or a data entry form.

ON the WEB To use the sample code for this chapter, import the chapter21.zip Flex project archive file from the Web site files into your Flex Builder workspace.

IN THIS CHAPTER

Understanding RPC and REST Web services

Understanding HTTP communications

Using the HTTPService control

Retrieving data at runtime

Parsing XML formatted data

Passing parameters to an application server

Working with Flash Player security

Using RPC and REST Architectures

RPC and REST are acronyms that represent architectural styles. Unlike SOAP and AMF, which are implemented by the other RPC components, RPC and REST are more like design patterns: They describe ways in which successful Web-based applications have been designed in the past.

Understanding the Representational State Transfer architecture

REST stands for Representational State Transfer, and it represents a software architecture or design pattern that can be implemented with numerous client-based and server-based platforms for the Web. A "RESTful" architecture allows resources stored in a remote system to be retrieved by a local client system without necessarily requiring a remote dynamic application server.

According to Roy Fielding, who coined the term, REST is intended to "evoke an image of how a well-designed Web application behaves: a network of Web pages (a virtual state-machine), where the user progresses through an application by selecting links (state transitions), resulting in the next page (representing the next state of the application) being transferred to the user and rendered for their use." In short, a Web site that returns either Web pages or structured data in the form of XML pages based on requests to consistently formatted requests is RESTful.

REST architecture is marked by these characteristics and benefits:

- Data that is represented in some form is "pulled" from the server to the client. When implemented with HTTP, the request is sent from a Web browser and the response comes from a Web server.

- Requests are stateless and do not depend on data stored persistently in the server. When you add statefulness to HTTP request/response systems with cookies or other token architectures, the application becomes less RESTful.

- Caching is implemented to improve performance. In the context of a Flex application, the use of static XML files that can be cached by the underlying Web browser improves performance when the data is requested multiple times.

- A uniform interface is used to simplify programming. In the context of Flex, this is implemented through the use of standard HTTP requests.

- Named resources are identified and retrieved by their URL. When you add query string parameters in a POST request, the system becomes more like RPC and less like REST.

- Server-side code written according to the principles of REST is guaranteed to be compatible with any client-side application development platform that supports industry-standard HTTP and XML.

The HTTPService component can be used in a REST-style application because, like the Web browser, it can communicate with its requests formatted as simple URL.

WEB RESOURCE Detailed descriptions of the REST architecture are available at these Web sites: `http://www.xfront.com/REST-Web-Services.html` and `http:// en.wikipedia.org/wiki/Representational_State_Transfer`.

Understanding the Remote Procedure Call architecture

RPC represents a software architecture that lets a computer program in one operating environment cause functions (also known as methods, operations, or subroutines) to be executed in separate, remote operating environments. As described previously, Flex applications can participate in RPC relationships with remote application servers using multiple architectures and techniques.

RPC-style architectures are typically implemented in Flex with a dynamic Web server that can respond to complex HTTP requests. All three RPC components communicate with the server over the HTTP protocol; they differ, however, in the format of the messages that are exchanged between client and server:

- **The `RemoteObject` component**, described in Chapters 24 and 26, communicates with application servers using the binary Action Message Format (AMF).
- **The `WebService` component,** described in Chapter 23, makes requests to, and handles responses from, application servers that support the industry-standard SOAP message format.
- **The `HTTPService` component** makes standard HTTP requests to any Web server environment, including calls to both static and dynamic Web pages, and uses either plain text or any well-formed XML language as its message format.

The `RemoteObject` and `WebService` components are limited in the servers with which they can communicate:

- `RemoteObject` **requests** work only with servers that implement AMF, including ColdFusion, LiveCycle Data Services, and BlazeDS among Adobe products, and numerous third-party and open-source products that are designed to be installed on top of ASP.NET, PHP, and Java Enterprise Edition (also known as J2EE) application servers.
- `WebService` requests work only with servers that use the SOAP protocol, including ColdFusion, ASP.NET, and J2EE servers that include a SOAP Web service library such as Apache's AXIS.

In contrast, the `HTTPService` component can be used to create an RPC-style application that uses any application server, because the use of well-formed XML as a message format can be accomplished nearly universally.

All three RPC components can be used to implement an RPC-style software architecture, where functions are called from the server to retrieve and modify data. Whereas the `WebService` and `RemoteObject` components are always used to implement RPC, because they always call functions (called *operations* in Web services and *methods* in remote objects), the `HTTPService` component can be used to implement RPC, REST, or a hybrid of the two.

Declaring and Configuring HTTPService Objects

You can declare and configure an HTTPService object in either MXML or ActionScript code. For applications that communicate only with a single network resource, the MXML approach might be simpler and easier to implement. In more complex applications that use multiple network resources, ActionScript classes and methods that dynamically generate HTTPService objects as needed can be easier to create.

Creating an HTTPService object

The MXML syntax to create an HTTPService object looks like this:

```
<mx:HTTPService id="myService"
  url="data/contacts.xml"/>
```

As with all Flex components, the object's id property is used to identify it uniquely in the context of the current application or component. The url property (discussed in detail in the next section) can be set with either a literal String, as in this example, or with a binding expression if you want to be able to switch to a different network resource at runtime.

The equivalent ActionScript code looks like this:

```
import mx.rpc.http.HTTPService;
private var myService:HTTPService =
new HTTPService("data/contacts.xml");
```

Alternatively, you can declare the object first and then set its url in a separate statement:

```
private var myService:HTTPService = new HTTPService();
myService.url = "data/contacts.xml";
```

> **TIP**
>
> There are two HTTPService classes in the Flex framework's class library. The first, which is imported in the preceding example, is a member of the mx.rpc.http package and is used in ActionScript code. The other version of the HTTPService class is a subclass of the first and is a member of the mx.rpc.http.mxml package. This is the version you use when you instantiate the object with the <mx:HTTPService> tag.
>
> The versions are nearly identical with two significant differences: Only the MXML version implements the showBusyCursor property, which causes an animated cursor to be displayed for the duration of an HTTPService request/response cycle, and the concurrency property, which determines how multiple concurrent requests to the same network resource are handled.
>
> You can simulate the behavior of the showBusyCursor property in ActionScript with the CursorManager class's setBusyCursor() and removeBusyCursor() methods. Concurrency also can be managed explicitly in ActionScript; for example, HTTPService implements a cancel() method that allows you to cancel the most recent request, if any, prior to sending a new request.

TIP ActionScript-based declarations of `HTTPService` should be placed outside of any function declarations, so that the object is accessible from all functions in the current application or component.

Essential HTTPService properties

Whether you use the MXML or ActionScript approach, the `HTTPService` component implements these properties that determine where the request is made and what HTTP methods are used:

- `url:String`: The Web address to which the request is sent
- `method:String`: The HTTP method to be used
- `resultFormat:String`: The format in which the data should be returned
- `showBusyCursor:Boolean`: When `true`, causes an animated cursor to appear for the duration of the request/response cycle
- `concurrency:String`: A rule that determines how to handle multiple concurrent calls to the same network resource

The details of these properties are described in the following sections.

Setting the url property

The `url` property is set to the network address to which the HTTP service should be sent. For a Flex application designed for Web deployment, this can be either a relative or absolute address. For example, if the Flex application is retrieving a static XML file that's on the same server and within the same directory structure, the `url` could be set as follows:

```
myHTTPService.url = "data/contacts.xml";
```

The expression `data/contacts.xml` means that the XML file is in a `data` subfolder on the same server from which the Flex application downloads at runtime.

For desktop applications deployed with AIR, or for Web applications that need to retrieve data from a domain other than one from which the application is downloaded, you can set the `url` as an absolute address:

```
myHTTPService.url = "http://www.myserver.com/data/contacts.xml";
```

CAUTION If you need to retrieve content at runtime from a different domain, you may need to deal with Flash Player's cross-domain security constraint. See the information on using the cross-domain permissions file later in this chapter and how to use the Proxy Service that's included with LiveCycle Data Services and BlazeDS in Chapter 25.

The network resource to which you send an `HTTPService` request can be either a static text file or a dynamic application server page that generates a response upon demand. As long as the response is in a form that the `HTTPService` component is able to parse (usually a well-formed XML file), the response will be read and understood when it's received from the server.

Setting the method property

The `HTTPService` component's `method` property supports the following values:

- `GET` (the default)
- `POST`
- `PUT` (only with `AIR` or a `proxy service`)
- DELETE (only with AIR or a proxy service)
- `OPTIONS` (only with a proxy service)
- HEAD (only with a proxy service)
- `TRACE` (only with a proxy service)

In RPC-style applications, the `HTTPService` component is mostly used with the `GET` and `POST` methods, while REST-style approaches sometimes use `PUT` and `DELETE` requests.

CAUTION Flash Player 9 only supports HTTP requests with methods of **GET** and **POST**. Desktop applications deployed with AIR also can use the **PUT** and **DELETE** request methods. To use **PUT** and **DELETE** requests with a Web application, or any other request methods, you must send requests through a server-side proxy such as the Proxy Service provided by LiveCycle Data Services and BlazeDS (described in Chapter 24).

For example, Flex developers who use Ruby on Rails as their middleware layer sometimes follow a RESTful pattern where the `HTTPService` method determines what kind of data manipulation is being requested by the client application. Each of the following methods is treated as a "verb" that indicates what should be done with the data passed in the request:

- A `GET` **request** retrieves a representation of data without making any changes to the version in the server's persistent data store.
- A `POST` **request** results in creating a new data item in the server tier.
- A `PUT` **request** results in modifying existing data in the server tier.
- A `DELETE` **request** results in deleting existing data in the server tier.

WEB RESOURCE For more information on using a RESTful approach with Ruby on Rails, visit the Ruby documentation at `http://api.rubyonrails.org/classes/ActionController/Resources.html`. An article by Derek Wischusen on integrating HTTPService and Ruby on Rails is available at `www.adobe.com/devnet/flex/articles/flex2_rails_print.html`.

Setting the resultFormat property

The `resultFormat` property determines how data is exposed in the Flex application when it's received from the server. The possible values are listed here:

- `object` **(the default):** Well-formed XML is returned as a tree of ActionScript objects. When a single element exists in a particular level of the XML hierarchy with a particular name, it's returned as an instance of the `ObjectProxy` class; when multiple elements of the same name are returned, they're wrapped in an `ArrayCollection`.

- `array`: The top-level object is returned as the first item in an ActionScript `Array`.

- `xml`: Well-formed XML is returned as an ActionScript `XMLNode` object.

- `flashvars`: Data formatted as name/value pairs is parsed into an ActionScript `Object` with named properties. For example, the following `String` value is a well-formed `flashvars` value:

  `firstName=Joe&lastName=Smith`

  The resulting ActionScript `Object` would have two properties named `firstName` and `lastName`.

- `text`: The response is returned as a simple `String` value.

- `e4x`: The response is returned as an `XML` object that can be parsed and modified with EcmaScript for XML (E4X) syntax.

> **CROSS-REF** The use of E4X to parse well-formed XML is described in Chapter 22.

Setting the concurrency property

The concurrency property is implemented only with the MXML version of the `HTTPService` component and determines how the responses from multiple concurrent requests will be handled. The property's possible values are listed here:

- `multiple` **(the default):** Multiple responses are handled as they're received from the server, and it's up to you (the developer) to create a code pattern that lets you identify the responses for each request. The `AsyncToken` class, an instance of which is returned from the `send()` method, can be helpful in this circumstance.

- `single`: You can have only a single request active at any given time. Issuing another request before the last one was completed results in a runtime error.

- `last`: Issuing another request before the last one was completed results in canceling the first request.

The following code results in canceling any pending `HTTPService` requests when a new request is sent:

```
<mx:HTTPService id="myService"
  url="data/contacts.xml"/>
```

> **TIP** The `concurrency` property isn't implemented in the version of the `HTTPService` class typically used in ActionScript because, when using ActionScript, you commonly create a new `HTTPService` object for each new request.

Sending and Receiving Data

You send an HTTP request with the HTTPRequest object's send() method. For example, if you want to retrieve data upon application startup, you can call the send() method in the application's creationComplete event handler:

```
<mx:Application xmlns:mx="http://www.adobe.com/2006/mxml"
  creationComplete="myService.send()">
</mx:Application>
```

Alternatively, you can send the request upon a user event, such as the click event handler of a Button component:

```
<mx:Button label="Make request" click="service.send()"/>
```

> **NOTE** The send() method accepts an optional **parameters** argument typed as an **Object** that allows you to send parameters to dynamic application server pages. This technique is described briefly later in this chapter and in much greater detail in Chapter 28.

Understanding asynchronous communications

All the Flex framework's RPC components send and receive data asynchronously. This means that when you send a request, Flash Player's ActionScript Virtual Machine (AVM) doesn't pause in its code execution and wait for data to be returned. This architecture is similar to how a Web browser's XMLHttpRequest object handles JavaScript requests for data: Requests are sent, and the responses are handled through event listeners.

> **NOTE** For ColdFusion developers, Flex's **HTTPService** and ColdFusion's **<cfhttp>** tags behave differently. ColdFusion handles responses to its **<cfhttp>** command synchronously, meaning that it waits for data to be returned before going to the next line of code. Two major differences between the runtime environments account for this.
>
> First, ColdFusion pages are transient and stay in server memory only until they've generated and returned HTML to the requesting Web browser. Asynchronous operations require a runtime environment that stays in memory and can listen for a response. Also, ColdFusion is multi-threaded and can afford to allocate a thread to wait for a response. Flash Player is single-threaded; if it had to wait for a response, the application would have to suspend all other operations such as animations and user interactions until the data came back.

Handling HTTPService responses

You can handle the response from a server with two approaches:

■ With a binding expression that references returned data

■ With event listeners that execute ActionScript code when data is returned

Of these approaches, the binding expression is simpler and easier to code, but it gives much less flexibility and power in terms of how you handle the returned data. In contrast, the event listener architecture gives you the opportunity to debug, inspect, manipulate, and save returned data persistently.

Using a binding expression

The HTTPService component's lastResult property is a reference variable that gives you access to the data that's returned from the server. When the service object's resultFormat property is set to the default value of object and you retrieve well-formed XML, the expression myService.lastResult refers to an instance of the ObjectProxy class that represents the XML document.

The following code represents the contents of an XML file named contacts.xml:

```
<?xml version="1.0"?>
<contacts>
  <row>
    <contactid>1</contactid>
    <firstname>Brad</firstname>
    <lastname>Lang</lastname>
    <streetaddress>3004 Buckhannan Avenue</streetaddress>
    <city>Syracuse</city>
    <state>NY</state>
    <email>Brad.C.Lang@trashymail.com</email>
    <phone>315-449-9420</phone>
  </row>
  ... additional <row> elements ...
</contacts>
```

When an XML file is structured with multiple repeating elements of the same name, as is the case with the <row> element in this XML structure, the HTTPService components generates an ArrayCollection that "wraps" the data. To display the data from a DataGrid or other data visualization component, use a binding expression that starts with the HTTPService object's id and lastResult property, and then "walks" down the XML hierarchy to the repeating element name.

The following DataGrid component uses the content of the repeating <row> elements as its data provider:

```
<mx:DataGrid
    dataProvider="{contactService.lastResult.data.row}"/>
```

Try these steps in the chapter21 project:

1. Open contacts.xml file from the project's src/data folder.

    Notice that the XML file has a root element named <contacts> and repeating elements named <row>. Each <row> element has a consistent internal structure consisting of named properties for contactId, firstname, lastname, and so on.

2. Create a new MXML application named `HTTPServiceWithBindings.mxml`. Set its `layout` property to `vertical`.

3. With the new application open in Source view, add an `<HTTPService>` tag set between the `<mx:Application>` tags. Set its `id` to `contactService` and its `url` property to `data/contacts.xml`:

```
<mx:HTTPService id="contactService"
   url="data/contacts.xml"/>
```

4. Add an `<mx:Button>` component below the `<mx:HTTPService>` tag. Set its label to **Get Data** and its `click` event listener to call the `HTTPService` object's `send()` method:

```
<mx:Button label="Get Data" click="contactService.send()"/>
```

5. Add a `DataGrid` component below the `<mx:Button>` tag. Set its `dataProvider` to display the `HTTPService` component's returned data using a binding expression that references the XML file's repeating `<row>` elements:

```
<mx:DataGrid
   dataProvider="{contactService.lastResult.contacts.row}"/>
```

6. Run the application, and click the Get Data button to send the request.

As shown in Figure 21.1, you should see the XML file's data displayed in the `DataGrid`.

FIGURE 21.1

Data retrieved from the XML file and displayed in the `DataGrid`

The completed application is shown in Listing 21.1.

LISTING 21.1

Using a binding expression to display retrieved data

```
<?xml version="1.0" encoding="utf-8"?>
<mx:Application xmlns:mx="http://www.adobe.com/2006/mxml"
   layout="vertical">
```

```
    <mx:HTTPService id="contactService" url="data/contacts.xml"/>
    <mx:Button label="Get Data" click="contactService.send()"/>
    <mx:DataGrid dataProvider="{contactService.lastResult.contacts.row}"/>
</mx:Application>
```

ON the WEB   The code in Listing 21.1 is available in the Web site files as `HTTPWithBindings` `Complete.mxml` in the `src` folder of the `chapter21` project.

TIP   When you retrieve content from the local hard disk instead of a Web server, a file access runtime error might occur. To fix this issue, you can place the application in a local security sandbox and block network access. You do this by adding the following compiler argument to the Flex project's compiler arguments:

```
-use-network=false
```

Figure 21.2 shows the Flex Compiler section of the project properties screen with the additional ----use-network compiler argument.

FIGURE 21.2

Placing an application in the local sandbox to guarantee access to local files

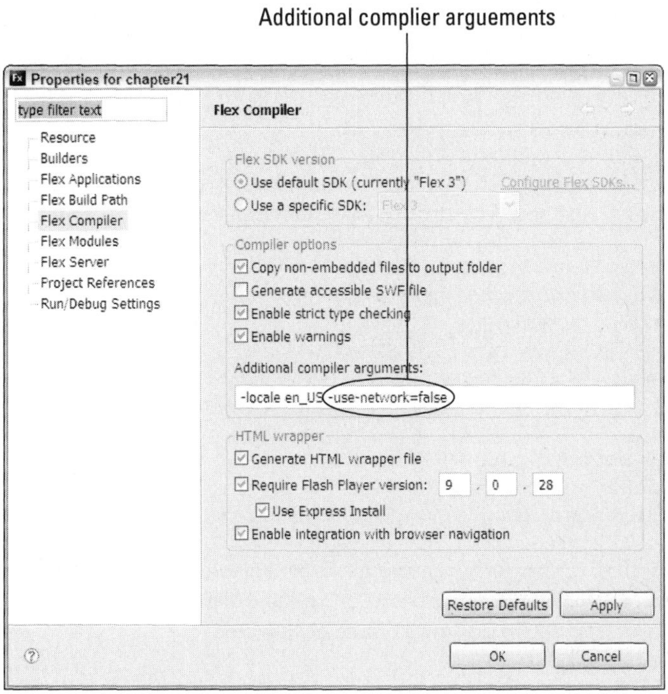

Additional complier arguements

Handling the result event

When data is returned from the remote server, the `HTTPService` object dispatches a `result` event, whose event object is typed as `mx.rpc.events.ResultEvent`. This `ResultEvent` class has a `result` property that refers to the returned data.

> **NOTE** The `ResultEvent` class also has a headers property that in theory should return the HTTP response headers from the Web server. In practice, this object frequently returns `null`.

To handle and save data using the `result` event, follow these steps:

1. Declare a bindable variable outside of any function that acts as a persistent reference to the returned data. If you're expecting a set of repeating data elements, cast the variable as an `ArrayCollection`:

   ```
   import mx.collections.ArrayCollection;
   [Bindable]
   private var myData:ArrayCollection
   ```

2. Create an event handler function that will be called when the event is dispatched. The function should receive a single event argument typed as `ResultEvent` and return `void`:

   ```
   private function resultHandler(event:ResultEvent):void
   {
   }
   ```

3. Within the event handler function, use the `event.result` expression to refer to the data that's returned from the server. Walk down the XML hierarchy to get to the repeating data elements, and return that expression to the bindable `ArrayCollection` variable:

   ```
   myData = event.result.contacts.row;
   ```

You can listen for the fault event with either an MXML attribute-based event listener or a call to the ActionScript `addEventListener()` method. The attribute-based event listener looks like this:

```
<mx:HTTPService id="contactService"
  url="http://localhost/contacts.xml"
  result="resultHandler(event)"/>
```

When using `addEventListener()` to create an event listener, you can designate the event name with the `String` value `result` or with the `ResultEvent` class's `RESULT` constant:

```
var myService:HTTPService = new HTTPService();
myService.url = "data/contacts.xml";
myService.addEventListener(ResultEvent.RESULT, resultHandler);
```

The application in Listing 21.2 retrieves a data set at runtime using an `HTTPService` object's `result` event. Data is saved to a persistent `ArrayCollection` variable that's been marked as `[Bindable]` and then displayed in a `DataGrid` using a binding expression.

LISTING 21.2

An application using the HTTPService component and a result event

```
<?xml version="1.0" encoding="utf-8"?>
<mx:Application xmlns:mx="http://www.adobe.com/2006/mxml">
  <mx:Script>
    <![CDATA[
      import mx.rpc.events.ResultEvent;
      import mx.collections.ArrayCollection;
      [Bindable]
      private var myData:ArrayCollection
      private function resultHandler(event:ResultEvent):void
      {
        myData = event.result.contacts.row;
      }
    ]]>
  </mx:Script>
  <mx:HTTPService id="contactService"
   url="http://localhost/contacts.xml"
    result="resultHandler(event)"/>
  <mx:Button label="Get Data" click="contactService.send()"/>
  <mx:DataGrid dataProvider="{contactService.lastResult.contacts.row}"/>
</mx:Application>
```

ON the WEB The code in Listing 21.2 is available in the Web site files as `HTTPResultEvent.mxml` in the `src` folder of the `chapter21` project.

TIP It may seem at first glance that the use of the `result` event simply takes more code than a binding expression. There are many advantages in this approach, however, that make the extra code worthwhile. By processing the returned data in an event handler function, you have the opportunity to debug or modify data when it's returned to the server, and the persistent variable lets you refer to the data at any later point.

It's also possible for a single service to return different data structures depending on which parameters are sent in the request. In this case, binding directly to the results isn't possible, because you have to extract data from the result with expression that can differ depending on the circumstance.

Handling the fault event

When an `HTTPService` request results in an error, the `HTTPRequest` object dispatches a `fault` event, whose event object is typed as `mx.rpc.events.FaultEvent`. This event object has a `fault` property typed as `mx.rpc.Fault`, which has these properties:

- `faultString:String`: The error message
- `faultCode:String`: A code that indicates the nature of the fault and whether it occurred in the client or server environment

- `faultDetail:String`: An additional message that sometimes contains useful information

- `message:String`: A string consisting of all the above values concatenated together with | characters used as separators

When you debug a `fault` event, you can easily see the structure of the `event` object. Figure 21.3 shows the Variables view during a debugging session showing the structure of the `FaultEvent` and `Fault` objects.

FIGURE 21.3

The Variables view displaying fault information during a debugging session

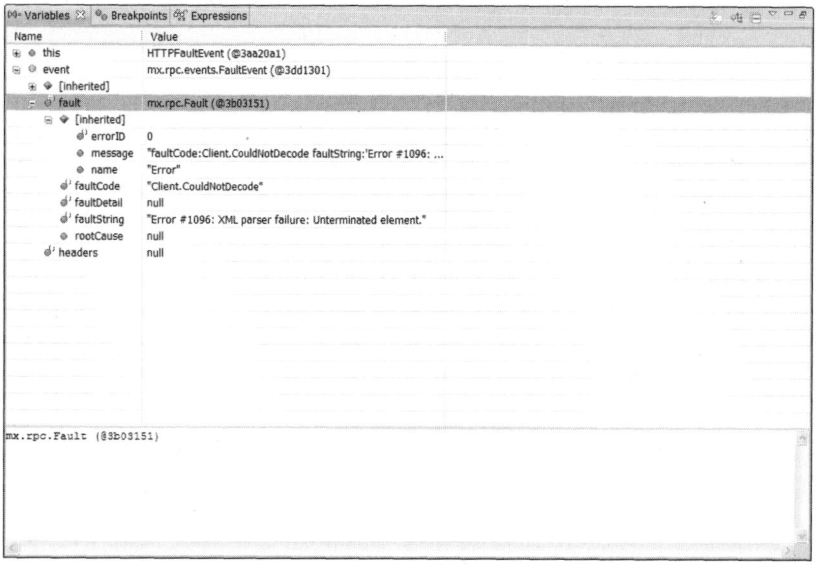

To handle a `fault` event, create an event handler function that receives an event argument typed as `FaultEvent`. Within the body of the function, you can deal with the fault however you like. This suppresses the ugly error message that appears in response to unhandled faults. The following code collects fault information from the event object and displays it to the user with an `Alert` pop-up window:

```
private function faultHandler(event:FaultEvent):void
{
   Alert.show(event.fault.faultString, event.fault.faultCode);
}
```

Figure 21.4 shows the resulting application with the `Alert` dialog box showing the user the `faultString` and `faultCode` values.

Displaying fault information to the user

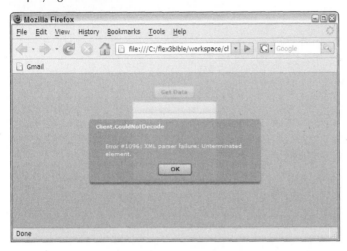

As with the `result` event, you can listen for the `fault` event with either an MXML attribute-based event listener or the `addEventListener()` method. The MXML attribute version looks like this:

```
<mx:HTTPService id="contactService"
  url="data/contactsMalformed.xml"
  result="resultHandler(event)"
  fault="faultHandler(event)"/>
```

When using `addEventListener()` to create an event listener, you can designate the event name with the `String` value `fault` or with the `FaultEvent` class's `FAULT` constant:

```
var myService:HTTPService = new HTTPService();
myService.url = "data/contacts.xml";
myService.addEventListener(ResultEvent.RESULT, resultHandler);
myService.addEventListener(FaultEvent.FAULT, faultHandler);
```

The application in Listing 21.3 shows the use of the `fault` event with an MXML-based event listener.

Using the fault event

```
<?xml version="1.0" encoding="utf-8"?>
<mx:Application xmlns:mx="http://www.adobe.com/2006/mxml">
  <mx:Script>
```

continued

LISTING 21.3 *(continued)*

```
    <![CDATA[
      import mx.controls.Alert;
      import mx.rpc.events.FaultEvent;
      import mx.rpc.events.ResultEvent;
      import mx.collections.ArrayCollection;
      [Bindable]
      private var myData:ArrayCollection
      private function resultHandler(event:ResultEvent):void
      {
        myData = event.result.contacts.row;
      }
      private function faultHandler(event:FaultEvent):void
      {
        Alert.show(event.fault.faultString, event.fault.faultCode);
      }
    ]]>
  </mx:Script>
  <mx:HTTPService id="contactService" url="data/contactsMalformed.xml"
    result="resultHandler(event)"
    fault="faultHandler(event)"/>
  <mx:Button label="Get Data" click="contactService.send()"/>
  <mx:DataGrid dataProvider="{contactService.lastResult.contacts.row}"/>
</mx:Application>
```

ON the WEB   The code in Listing 21.3 is available in the Web site files as `HTTPFaultEvent.mxml` in the `src` folder of the `chapter21` project.

TIP   All RPC components, including `HTTPService`, implement a `requestTimeout` property that sets a timeout value in terms of seconds. For example, if you set `requestTimeout` to a value of 10 and the server doesn't respond within 10 seconds, a `fault` event is dispatched.

TIP   The `result` and `fault` events work exactly the same for all RPC components and use the same set of event classes, `ResultEvent` and `FaultEvent`. The only significant difference lies in the structure of the data returned in a `result` event. For example, `HTTPService`, when used to retrieve XML, returns data as a set of objects or as an E4X-compatible `XML` object, depending on the value of its `resultFormat` property. In contrast, `WebService` and `RemoteObject` return data based on data types declared in metadata returned from the server. In all cases, though, you access the returned data by referencing the `ResultEvent` object's `result` property.

Working with ItemResponder and AsyncToken

Developers who prefer to work entirely with ActionScript to manage their service calls sometimes use a pattern that includes the Flex framework's `ItemResponder` and `AsyncToken` classes.

 The `ItemResponder` and `AsyncToken` classes work nearly exactly the same with all RPC components.

Using AsyncToken

The `AsyncToken` class is a dynamic object that allows you, the developer, to add arbitrary named properties to the object at runtime. Every request to an RPC component returns an instance of `AsyncToken` that stays in application memory for the duration of the RPC request. After making the request, you can add as many bits of information as you need to track the purpose of the request or other important details:

```
var token:AsyncToken = contactService.send();
token.myProp1 = "Any property value";
```

When a result event or fault event is dispatched, the `ResultEvent` or `FaultEvent` object provides a reference to the AsyncToken object you created through their token properties:

```
private function resultHandler(event:ResultEvent):void
{
  Alert.show("The value of property 1 is " +
    event.token.myProp1;
}
```

The `AsyncToken` object serves as a persistent repository of information about the request. You populate the object with information just after making the request, and retrieve it while handling the request's `result` or `fault` event.

Using ItemResponder

The `ItemResponder` class can be used instead of attribute-based event listeners or the `addEventListener()` method to handle and dispatch event objects to ActionScript event handler functions. To use `ItemResponder`, you first create custom event handler functions to handle an RPC request's `result` and `fault` events. Each event handler function receives an `AsyncToken` argument in addition to the expected event object. For example, the `result` handler function signature looks like this:

```
private function resultHandler(event:ResultEvent,
  token:AsyncToken):void
{
  ... handle returned data ...
}
```

The `fault` event handler function looks like this:

```
private function faultHandler(event:FaultEvent,
  token:AsyncToken):void
{
  ... handle fault ...
}
```

Before you make the RPC request, you create an instance of the `ItemResponder` class and pass references to the `result` and `fault` event handler functions as constructor method arguments:

```
var responder:ItemResponder =
  new ItemResponder(resultHandler,faultHandler);
```

 As with `addEventListener()`, you're passing the functions as objects, and not calling them directly, so you only pass the function names and not their complete calling syntax.

The next steps are to:

1. Make the RPC request and return an instance of AsyncToken.
2. Add the `ItemResponder` object to the `AsyncToken` object's array of responders with its addResponder() method.

```
var token:AsyncToken = contactService.send();
token.addResponder(responder);
```

When the asynchronous request is completed, the `AsyncToken` object calls the appropriate event handler function, depending on whether a `result` or `fault` event is dispatched by the RPC component. The event handler function receives both its event object and a reference to the `AsyncToken` object that called it.

The application in Listing 21.4 uses `ItemResponder` and `AsyncToken` objects to manage an asynchronous request and its result and fault events.

LISTING 21.4

Using ItemResponder and AsyncToken

```
<?xml version="1.0" encoding="utf-8"?>
<mx:Application xmlns:mx="http://www.adobe.com/2006/mxml">
  <mx:Script>
    <![CDATA[
      import mx.collections.ArrayCollection;
      import mx.collections.ItemResponder;
      import mx.controls.Alert;
      import mx.rpc.AsyncToken;
      import mx.rpc.events.FaultEvent;
      import mx.rpc.events.ResultEvent;
      import mx.rpc.http.HTTPService;
      [Bindable]
      private var myData:ArrayCollection
      private var contactService:HTTPService = new HTTPService();
      private function getData():void
      {
        contactService.url="data/contacts.xml";
```

```
        var responder:ItemResponder =
          new ItemResponder(resultHandler,faultHandler);
        var token:AsyncToken = contactService.send();
        token.addResponder(responder);
      }
      private function resultHandler(event:ResultEvent,
    token:AsyncToken):void
      {
        myData = event.result.contacts.row;
      }
      private function faultHandler(event:FaultEvent,
    token:AsyncToken):void
      {
        Alert.show(event.fault.faultString, event.fault.faultCode);
      }
    ]]>
  </mx:Script>

  <mx:Button label="Get Data" click="getData()"/>
  <mx:DataGrid dataProvider="{myData}"/>

</mx:Application>
```

ON the WEB The code in Listing 21.4 is available in the Web site files as `UsingItemResponder.mxml` in the `src` folder of the `chapter21` project.

TIP It's a common practice to create individual custom classes to manage each unique RPC request. Each custom class uses a common naming convention for both the function that creates and executes an RPC request, such as `execute()`, and its event handler methods, such as `resultHandler()` and `faultHandler()`. Known as the Command design pattern, this approach allows you to manage complex applications with dozens or thousands of unique server requests, and is at the heart of the Cairngorm microarchitecture that's used by developers of large Flex applications.

WEB RESOURCE Steven Webster provides an excellent description of the Command design pattern (in the context of the Cairngorm microarchitecture) in his six-part series on Cairngorm at `www.adobe.com/devnet/flex/articles/cairngorm_pt1.html`.

Working with Value Objects

XML-formatted data retrieved with the `HTTPService` component is always exposed as an `ArrayCollection` of `ObjectProxy` instances. If you prefer to work with strongly typed value object classes, you can create a simple set of code that transforms the `Object` instances into your value objects. This process has two steps:

■ Create a value object class with the appropriate properties. Set the value object class's constructor method to accept an optional argument typed as the ActionScript Object class. Within the constructor method, if the Object argument was passed in, transfer its property values to the equivalent properties in the current instance of the value object class:

```
public function Contact(data:Object = null)
{
  if (data != null)
  {
    this.contactid = Number(data.contactid);
    this.firstname = data.firstname;
    this.lastname = data.lastname;
    ... set additional properties ...
  }
}
```

■ At runtime, in the result event handler, loop through the ArrayCollection and create one new instance of the value object for each data item, and then replace the original object with the ArrayCollection class's setItemAt() method:

```
private function resultHandler(event:ResultEvent):void
{
  var obj:Contact;
  myData = event.result.contacts.row;
  for (var i:int=0; i<myData.length; i++)
  {
    obj = new Contact(myData.getItemAt(i));
    myData.setItemAt(obj, i);
  }
}
```

TIP Notice that the value object class's constructor method explicitly typecasts properties as necessary. This is a major benefit of creating the extra code to transfer data from generic instances of the Object class to strongly typed value objects: Data is correctly cast and easier to use in other code throughout the application.

The application in Listing 21.5 retrieves data from the server and then loops through the ArrayCollection to replace each generic Object with an equivalent value object.

LISTING 21.5

Using value objects with data from an HTTPService request

```
<?xml version="1.0" encoding="utf-8"?>
<mx:Application xmlns:mx="http://www.adobe.com/2006/mxml"
    layout="vertical">
  <mx:Script>
    <![CDATA[
      import vo.Contact;
```

```
      import mx.rpc.events.ResultEvent;
      import mx.collections.ArrayCollection;
      [Bindable]
      private var myData:ArrayCollection
      private function resultHandler(event:ResultEvent):void
      {
        var obj:Contact;
        myData = event.result.contacts.row;
        for (var i:int=0; i<myData.length; i++)
        {
          obj = new Contact(myData.getItemAt(i));
          myData.setItemAt(obj, i);
        }
      }
    ]]>
  </mx:Script>
  <mx:HTTPService id="contactService" url="data/contacts.xml"
    result="resultHandler(event)"/>
  <mx:Button label="Get Data" click="contactService.send()"/>
  <mx:DataGrid dataProvider="{myData}"/>
</mx:Application>
```

ON the WEB The code in Listing 21.5 is available in the Web site files as `HTTPValueObjects.mxml`
in the `src` folder of the `chapter21` project. The `Contact` value object class is defined
in `Contact.as` in the `src/vo` subfolder.

Passing Parameters to Server Pages

When you use the `HTTPService` component to make calls to dynamic pages that are managed by
an application server, you frequently need to pass parameters. The syntax for passing parameters is
the same regardless of whether you use the `HTTPService` component with `GET` or `POST` requests.

You can pass parameters in an `HTTPService` request in two ways:

- Named parameters that are packaged in an ActionScript `Object`
- Bound parameters that are set up in the `HTTPService` object declaration

Using named parameters

To pass parameters by name, first create an instance of an ActionScript `Object`. The `Object` class
is dynamic, meaning that you can add arbitrary named properties at runtime. Set each parameter
as a named property of the properties object, and then pass the properties object as the only argument in the object's `send()` method.

The ActionScript code to accomplish these tasks might look like this:

```
private function sendData():void
{
  var params:Object = new Object();
  params.firstname="Joe";
  params.lastname="Smith";
  contactService.send(params);
}
```

You also can use shorthand ActionScript code to create an object and pass it in a single statement:

```
private function sendData():void
{
  contactService.send({firstname:"Joe", lastname:"Smith"});
}
```

If the `HTTPService` object's `method` property is set to `GET`, the parameters are appended to the request URL. The first part of the resulting HTTP request would look like this:

```
GET /?firstname=Joe&lastname=Smith HTTP/1.1
```

In contrast, if the `HTTPService` object's `method` property is set to `POST`, the parameters are appended to the end of the HTTP request. The following is a literal `POST` request header sent from a Flex application hosted by Microsoft Internet Explorer 6:

```
POST / HTTP/1.1
Accept: */*
Accept-Language: en-US
Referer: file://C:\flex3bible\workspace\chapter21\
  bin-debug\HTTPSendParams.swf
x-flash-version: 9,0,115,0
Content-Type: application/x-www-form-urlencoded
Content-Length: 28
Accept-Encoding: gzip, deflate
User-Agent: Mozilla/4.0 (compatible; MSIE 6.0; Windows NT 5.1;
    SV1; .NET CLR 1.1.4322; .NET CLR 2.0.50727; .NET CLR
    3.0.04506.648; .NET CLR 3.5.21022)
Host: localhost
Connection: Keep-Alive
Cache-Control: no-cache

firstname=Joe&lastname=Smith
```

Using bound parameters

You can set up bound parameters in an `HTTPService` declaration so that named properties are sent with a consistent source. For example, assume that you've declared a bindable instance of a value object that stores current values:

```
[Bindable]
private var myContact:Contact;
```

If you know that the parameters you send with HTTPService always get their values from this
object, you can declare the relationship using binding expressions:

```
<mx:HTTPService id="contactService" url="myAppPage.php"
  result="resultHandler(event)">
  <mx:request>
    <firstname>{myContact.firstname}</firstname>
    <lastname>{myContact.lastname}</lastname>
  </mx:request>
</mx:HTTPService>
```

When you call the HTTPService object's send() method, the named parameters in the
<mx:request> tag set are sent with exactly the same HTTP request syntax as with the named
parameters syntax described previously.

 To fully demonstrate the use of **HTTPRequest** parameters, you need an application
server. Chapter 28 describes using this feature in greater detail in the context of PHP.

Handling Cross-Domain Policy Issues

When Flash Player is asked to make a request to a domain other than the one from which the current Flash document was downloaded, it needs to have permission from the target domain. This
issue frequently comes up when you're using data from a third-party data provider, but it also can
be relevant when you have two or more domains in a single organization.

Figure 21.5 describes the circumstance in which cross-domain permission is required. If a Flex
application downloaded from one domain makes an HTTP request to a different domain, Flash
Player automatically seeks cross-domain permission via a request for a cross-domain policy file
from the remote domain.

The goal of the cross-domain security constraint is to prevent malicious code from "taking over"
the user's Flash Player and making repeated requests to arbitrary Web-based resources.

TIP Cross-domain permission is required for all HTTP requests to remote domains, including
attempts to retrieve content with the **HTTPService** component, make remote procedure calls with the **WebService** and **RemoteObject** components, and download image or Flash
documents with the **Image** or **SWFLoader** components. The same restriction is applied to Flash documents that use the **URLLoader** or **XMLSocket** classes to connect to remote domains.

The cross-domain policy file is an XML file that is always named crossdomain.xml and placed
in the Web root of the remote domain. At runtime, when Flash Player determines that cross-domain
permission is required to execute a task, it tries to download this file from the remote domain's root
folder. If it finds the file, it parses it and looks for permissions that have been granted to the domain
from which the Flash document or Flex application was originally downloaded.

FIGURE 21.5

Cross-domain permission is required in this circumstance

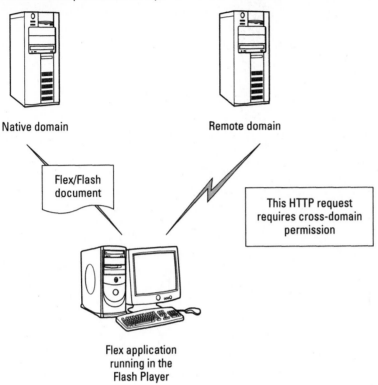

Native domain   Remote domain

Flex/Flash document

This HTTP request requires cross-domain permission

Flex application running in the Flash Player

The cross-domain policy file looks like this:

```
<?xml version="1.0"?>
<!DOCTYPE cross-domain-policy SYSTEM
  "http://www.adobe.com/xml/dtds/cross-domain-policy.dtd">
<cross-domain-policy>
  <allow-access-from domain="www.domain1.com" />
  <allow-access-from domain="domain2.com" />
  <allow-access-from domain="*.domain3.com" />
</cross-domain-policy>
```

Each `<allow-access-from>` element gives permission to Flash documents downloaded from the domain named in the domain attribute to make HTTP requests to the server on which the cross-domain file is stored.

Starting with Flash Player 7, the cross-domain policy rules enforce rules on a per-domain basis without regard for partial combinations of host names and domain names. So, for example, if a

Flex application is downloaded from a URL starting with mydomain.com and the cross-domain policy file has a declaration that allows access from www.mydomain.com, Flash Player does not consider permission to have been granted. The domain names must match exactly, and there is no DNS lookup for IP addresses.

Wildcard characters are supported, however. The following declaration would grant HTTP request permission to documents downloaded from mydomain.com, www.mydomain.com, and any other URL that ends with mydomain.com:

```
<allow-access-from domain="*.mydomain.com" />
```

WEB RESOURCE Complete information on creating a cross-domain security file, including how to handle requests to secure pages from a Flash document that was loaded from a non-secure Web page, is available on the Web at www.adobe.com/go/tn_14213.

Summary

In this chapter, I described how to use the HTTPService component to send and receive data over the Web. You learned the following:

- The Flex framework contains three RPC components: the RemoteObject, WebService, and HTTPService classes.

- Only the HTTPService component is completely portable among application servers, because it can use any XML or plain text format for its messages.

- You can declare an HTTPService object in either MXML or ActionScript.

- You handle data returned from an HTTPService request with either binding expressions or event handlers.

- The HTTPService component's method property determines what type of HTTP request is made.

- XML-formatted data is parsed automatically and delivered as either a tree of ActionScript Object instances or an E4X-compatible XML object.

- Parameters can be passed with either an Object that serves as a collection of name/value pairs or with bindings declared in MXML.

- Cross-domain constraint issues can be solved by placing a cross-domain policy file in the Web root of the remote domain.

Chapter 22

Managing XML with E4X

X ML has become a *lingua franca* for data exchange on the Web. When the XML standard was originally defined in 1998, its purpose was to define a common set of syntax rules that could be applied to multiple applications. XML isn't a language in itself, so much as it's a set of rules that define how markup languages designed for data representation should behave.

There have been a few attempts over the years to extend the XML recommendation and go beyond the original version 1.0, but each attempt has foundered. It's generally agreed that the rules of XML as they currently stand do what the standard should do, and each proposed addition has run into some sort of opposition.

The developer tools for working with XML, however, have continued to evolve. From the earliest XML processing APIs such as the Document Object Model (DOM) and the Simple API for XML (SAX), to more recent innovations such as JDOM for Java developers and the XML processing classes in the .NET framework, organizations that are responsible for creating programming languages and development platforms continue to improve the lot of developers who work with XML. The goal is always to make it as easy to parse and modify XML-formatted data as possible.

EcmaScript for XML (E4X) is one such toolkit. E4X was defined by Ecma International in the ECMA-357 standard and is implemented as a part of ActionScript 3. Any application running in Flash Player 9 or later has access to the E4X API and can use its simple syntax to parse, extract data from, and modify XML and XMLList objects stored in application memory.

In this chapter, I describe how to use E4X and ActionScript-based XML classes to parse and modify XML-formatted data in Flex applications.

TIP E4X also is implemented in other derivations of EcmaScript, including SpiderMonkey (the JavaScript engine that's embedded in the Gecko browser kernel) and Rhino (Mozilla's Java-based JavaScript engine).

ON the WEB To use the sample code for this chapter, import the `chapter22.zip` project from the Web site files into any folder on your disk.

Using XML Classes

Flash documents and Flex applications written with ActionScript 2 had access to an XML class that allowed the developer to extract data from an XML file or data packet. This object used Document Object Model (DOM) programming to extract information.

DOM-style programming has certain advantages: The coding style is implemented in many languages, so if you know how to code with DOM in one language, you can easily adapt your skills to another.

However, DOM programming tends to be verbose and require lots of extensive looping (loops within loops within loops) to get to the data you want.

Consider this XML content:

```
<?xml version="1.0"?>
<invoices>
  <invoice>
    <customer>Smith, Maria</customer>
    <items>
      <lineitem price="21.41" quantity="4">Widget</lineitem>
      <lineitem price="2.11" quantity="14">Mouse</lineitem>
      <lineitem price="8.88" quantity="3">Wrench</lineitem>
    </items>
  </invoice>
</invoices>
```

Using the old-style `XMLDocument` and `XMLNode` objects, you would first "walk" the XML tree to get a reference to the collection of elements you want to evaluate. Then, to locate a `<lineitem>` element with a particular text node (the item description), you'd loop through the elements and use conditional statements to evaluate each data item:

```
var arItems:Array=
  xmlDocument.firstChild.firstChild.childNodes[1].childNodes;
var arResult:Array = new Array();
for (var i:int=0; i<xInvoices.length; i++)
{
  var currentNode:XMLNode = arItems[i] as XMLNode;
  if (currentNode.attributes.price == '21.41')
  {
```

```
arResult.push(currentNode)
  }
}
```

With E4X you would first assign the XML file's root element to a new-style XML object. You can then extract the element representing the "Widget" with the simple expression:

```
var xResult:XMLList = xInvoices..lineitem.(@price=21.41);
```

This example makes clear that E4X offers a much more concise and readable syntax for finding and extracting data from an XML data structure.

> **TIP** The old **XML** class functionality was refactored into classes named **XMLNode** and **XMLDocument** in ActionScript 3. These are considered "legacy" classes that allow you to use DOM-style programming if you prefer. However, after developers understand and master the use of E4X to accomplish XML processing tasks, they usually don't go back.

In ActionScript 3, Flex developers can use the following XML classes to manage XML-formatted data at runtime:

- XML: A new version of the XML class that supports E4X expressions to parse and modify data at runtime. The XML class has only one root node.

- XMLList: A class representing an ordered set of XML objects. The XMLList class is similar to an Array in that it contains objects in fixed order. Also, like an Array, it doesn't have a complete API to manage, modify, and reliably execute bindings when its data changes at runtime.

- XMLListCollection: A "wrapper" class that manages an ArrayList. Just as the ArrayCollection provides sorting, filtering, and other advanced features for managing an Array, the XMLListCollection implements a powerful API that manages an XMLList and reliably executes bindings when its data changes at runtime.

The first step in using these classes is to create a new-style XML object.

Creating an XML object

The XML class represents a single XML node and can be created in a number of ways:

- With a hard-coded XML structure in an ActionScript statement
- With the MXML <mx:XML> tag
- By parsing an XML-formatted String value
- By retrieving XML-formatted data with the HTTPService component with its resultFormat property set to e4x

Declaring a hard-coded XML structure in ActionScript

You can declare an XML object and set its data in a single statement by using a value in the assignment statement structured as XML:

```
var sales:XML =
  <sales>
    <item type="apples" price="4.53" quantity="6"/>
    <item type="oranges" price="3.35" quantity="10"/>
    <item type="pears" price="5.16" quantity="3"/>
  </sales>;
```

 **TIP**   Notice that the XML structure isn't wrapped in quotes. When using an **XML** object, the data type is **XML**, not a **String** value, so quotation marks aren't required; in fact, using quotation marks would cause a syntax error.

 **TIP**   You can use binding expressions within attribute and element values to populate data into an XML structure at the moment of its creation.

The sales object in this example points to the XML structure's root element. The E4X expression that refers to the object's <item> elements is:

```
sales.item
```

Parsing an XML-formatted String value

If you have an XML-formatted string value that you've read from a server-based data source (for example, as a string stored in a database table column), you can transform the string into an XML object by passing the string value in a call to the XML class's constructor method.

For example, this code creates a well-formed XML data packet as a String variable (remember, because it's a String and not XML yet, you do need to use quotation marks):

```
var stringData:String = '<sales>' +
  '<item type="apples" price="4.53" quantity="6"/>' +
  '<item type="oranges" price="3.35" quantity="10"/>' +
  '<item type="pears" price="5.16" quantity="3"/>' +
  '</sales>';
```

To transform the stringData variable into an XML object that can be managed with E4X, declare the XML object with a call to its constructor method and pass the String as the only argument:

```
var xmlData:XML = new XML(stringData);
```

As with the first example, the XML object points to the XML document's root element, so the E4X expression xmlData.item refers to the set of <item> elements that are direct children of the root.

Declaring an XML object in MXML

The <mx:XML> tag declares an XML object using nested XML markup. The tag's format property is set either to xml to create a legacy XMLNode object or to e4x (the default) to create an XML object that can be managed with E4X expressions. The following code declares the XML object with this MXML syntax:

```
<mx:XML format="e4x" id="xmlData">
  <sales>
    <item type="apples" price="4.53" quantity="6"/>
    <item type="oranges" price="3.35" quantity="10"/>
    <item type="pears" price="5.16" quantity="3"/>
  </sales>
</mx:XML>
```

As with the version declared in ActionScript, the XML object's id is a reference to the root element (not an XML document), so the expression xmlData.item refers to the set of <item> elements that are direct children of the root.

Importing XML with HTTPService

The HTTPService component's resultFormat property can be set to e4x, causing the retrieved data to be represented as an XML object. The HTTPService object, for example, retrieves an external XML-formatted file:

```
<mx:HTTPService id="salesService"
  url="data/sales.xml"
  resultFormat="e4x"
  result="resultHandler(event)"/>
```

In the result event handler function, you capture the returned data by casting event.result as an XML object:

```
private var xmlData:XML;
private function resultHandler(event:ResultEvent):void
{
  xmlData = event.result as XML;
}
```

Again, the xmlData object refers to the root element of the retrieved XML document, not to the document itself.

Controlling parsing with XML properties

An XML object refers to a single XML element node, whether it's the XML document's root element or one of its children.

The XML class supports the following static properties that determine how it parses and exposes data to E4X expressions:

- ignoreComments: When true, this expression strips comments out of an XML string during the parsing process.

- `ignoreProcessingInstructions`: When `true`, this expression strips processing instructions out of an XML string during the parsing process.

- `ignoreWhitespace`: When `true`, this expression removes beginning and ending white space characters from text nodes during the parsing process.

To use any of these static properties, set their value before creating an `XML` object. For example, the following XML packet contains extra white space before and after the data.

```
<data>
   <firstname>Joe      </firstname>
</data>
```

By default, the extra white space is removed during parsing, because the `ignoreWhitespace` property is set to `true` by default. To preserve white space around text nodes, set `ignoreWhitespace` to `false` before creating the `XML` object:

```
XML.ignoreWhitespace = false;
var xmlData=<data>
   <firstname>Joe      </firstname>
</data>;
```

Now the E4X expression `xmlData.firstname` returns the value of the text node, and the extra spaces are preserved.

Using the XMLList class

The `XMLList` class is an ordered set of `XML` or `XMLList` objects. Like an ActionScript `Array`, it maintains the objects in the order of initial declaration or parsing, or in the most recent order based on changes you've made to the data through calls to object methods (or, in this case, E4X expressions).

You can create an `XMLList` object with an explicit MXML declaration that nests multiple `XML` nodes:

```
<mx:XMLList id="xList">
  <item type="apples" price="4.53" quantity="6"/>
  <item type="oranges" price="3.35" quantity="10"/>
  <item type="pears" price="5.16" quantity="3"/>
</mx:XMLList>
```

Or, if you already have an `XML` object in memory, you can use an E4X expression that refers to a set of elements. For example, if an `XML` object named `xmlData` contains two or more `<item>` child elements, the expression `xmlData.item` returns an `XMLList` object:

```
var xmlData:XML =
  <sales>
    <item type="apples" price="4.53" quantity="6"/>
    <item type="oranges" price="3.35" quantity="10"/>
    <item type="pears" price="5.16" quantity="3"/>
  </sales>;
var salesList:XMLList = xmlData.item;
```

This expression `xmlData.item` uses the dot (.) operator to navigate to the XML object's named child element. If only one element with the name (in this case, `item`) exists, the expression returns an XML object. When more the one element of the same name is found, the expression returns an XMLList.

> **TIP** When an `XMLList` contains only a single `XML` object, you can call any methods or properties of the XML class as though they were members of the `XMLList`. When the `XMLList` contains more than a single `XML` object, you can only call methods and properties implemented by the `XMLList` class.

Using the XMLListCollection class

The `XMLListCollection` class is a wrapper for the `XMLList`, in the same way the `ArrayCollection` wraps an `Array`. Like `ArrayCollection`, it extends the `ListCollectionView` superclass. As a result, it provides a rich API for storing, sorting, filtering, and modifying its contained data.

The `XMLListCollection` class's source property is typed as an `XMLList` (again like the `ArrayCollection` and `Array`), so you can instantiate and initialize an `XMLListCollection` object and associate it with an `XMLList` in a number of ways:

- Assign the `XMLList` to the `source` property after first instantiating the `XMLListCollection`:

  ```
  [Bindable]
  private var xCollection:XMLListCollection =
    new XMLListCollection();
  xCollection.source = xmlList;
  ```

- Pass the `XMLList` to the `XMLListCollection` constructor method:

  ```
  [Bindable]
  private var xCollection:XMLListCollection =
    new XMLListCollection(xmlList);
  ```

- Declare the `XMLListCollection` in MXML, and assign the `source` with an attribute and a binding expression:

  ```
  <mx:XMLListCollection id="xCollection" source="{xmlList}"/>
  ```

> **TIP** As with all MXML declarations, the MXML version of the object is automatically instantiated and made bindable. The ActionScript versions must be explicitly marked as bindable if you want to use binding expressions to update other components when the data changes at runtime.

In addition to the `ListCollectionView` API that allows you to add, update, and manipulate data at runtime, the `XMLListCollection` supports a small set of methods that are specifically designed to access hierarchical data. For example, the `attribute()` function allows you to search the `XMLList` for all nested `XML` child objects that share a named attribute. `XMLListCollection` also implements a `copy()` method that returns a "deep" copy of its `XMLList`.

TIP E4X expressions can be called only from an **XML** or **XMLList** object, not from an **XMLListCollection**. The **XMLListCollection** is typically used to represent the final result of an E4X expression and pass it to visual controls or other application components through bindings.

Using E4X Expressions

EcmaScript for XML (E4X) is an expression language that allows you to extract and manipulate data stored in XML objects with simple expressions. By using E4X, you can eliminate the significantly more verbose ActionScript code that would otherwise be required.

WEB RESOURCE   The specification for E4X is available at www.ecma-international.org/ publications/standards/Ecma-357.htm.

The examples in this section use the invoices.xml shown in Listing 22.1. This file uses a multi-level hierarchical data structure to represent simple invoice information.

LISTING 22.1

A file named invoices.xml representing a set of business invoices

```xml
<?xml version="1.0"?>
<invoices>
  <invoice>
    <customer>
      <firstname>Maria</firstname>
      <lastname>Smith</lastname>
    </customer>
    <items>
      <lineitem price="21.41" quantity="4">Widget</lineitem>
      <lineitem price="2.11" quantity="14">Mouse</lineitem>
      <lineitem price="8.88" quantity="3">Wrench</lineitem>
    </items>
  </invoice>
  <invoice>
    <customer>
      <firstname>John</firstname>
      <lastname>Jones</lastname>
    </customer>
    <items>
      <lineitem price="7.41" quantity="84">Mouse</lineitem>
      <lineitem price="0.91" quantity="184">Mousepad</lineitem>
    </items>
  </invoice>
</invoices>
```

ON the WEB The code in Listing 22.1 is available in the Web site files as `invoices.xml` in the `src/data` folder of the `chapter22` project.

NOTE   The structure of the sample XML file in Listing 22.1 intentionally mixes values represented in attributes and text nodes. A well-structured XML file would be more consistent; this one is designed to represent a varied set of parsing challenges.

Extracting data from XML objects

You can extract data from an XML object using an E4X expression that mixes various operators and data comparisons. In this section, I describe each operator and expression and provide code samples.

TIP   E4X expressions are a part of ActionScript and are 100 percent accurate only when used in their compiled form. Some programmers have tried to create a runtime E4X parser. For one such useful application, try Michael Labriola's E4XParser component, described at `www.adobe.com/devnet/flex/articles/e4x_print.html`. Use these with care and lots of testing, however; runtime E4X parsers don't handle all possible E4X expressions and occasionally return different results than when the same expression is evaluated in a compiled Flex application.

Using dot notation

As described previously, an ActionScript XML object that's been created from XML notation refers to the structure's root element, not to the XML document itself. If an `HTTPService` component imports the XML document in Listing 22.1 and passes the `ResultEvent` object to an event handler function, the expression `event.result` refers to the `<invoices>` element. You typically save the returned data to a variable typed as XML and then use E4X expressions to extract data as needed:

```
[Bindable]
private var xInvoices:XML;
private function resultHandler(event:ResultEvent):void
{
  xInvoices = event.result as XML;
}
```

Starting at the root element, you then "walk" down the XML hierarchy one level at a time using simple dot notation and element names. So, for example, this code extracts all elements named `<invoice>` that are child elements of the root:

```
xReturn = xInvoices.invoice;
```

The returned `XMLList` looks like this:

```
<invoice>
  <customer>
    <firstname>Maria</firstname>
    <lastname>Smith</lastname>
  </customer>
```

```
   <items>
     ... all <lineitem> elements ...
   </items>
 </invoice>
 <invoice>
   <customer>
     <firstname>John</firstname>
     <lastname>Jones</lastname>
   </customer>
   <items>
     ... all <lineitem> elements ...
   </items>
 </invoice>
```

Using array notation

When two or more elements have the same name at the same level of the XML hierarchy, you can refer to individual items as Array elements. As with all ActionScript array and index notation, indexing starts at 0. This statement extracts the second element named invoice:

```
xReturn = xInvoices.invoice[1];
```

The resulting XML object looks like this:

```
<invoice>
  <customer>
    <firstname>John</firstname>
    <lastname>Jones</lastname>
  </customer>
  <items>
    <lineitem price="7.41" quantity="84">Mouse</lineitem>
    <lineitem price="0.91" quantity="184">Mousepad</lineitem>
  </items>
</invoice>
```

After you've found an element using array notation, you can continue down the XML hierarchy with extended dot notation. This code extracts the customer element that's a child of the first invoice element:

```
xReturn = xInvoices.invoice[0].customer
```

The resulting XML object looks like this:

```
<customer>
  <firstname>Maria</firstname>
  <lastname>Smith</lastname>
</customer>
```

An E4X expression can return either an XML or XMLList object, depending on whether the expression returns a single node or more than one node. This can cause typecasting issues, because you can't use implicit coercion to automatically cast XML as XMLList, or vice versa.

The solution: Both classes are directly extended from the ActionScript Object class, so if you're using a single variable that will accept either type of result, cast it as Object:

```
var xReturn:Object;
```

The consequence of this approach is that as you code, you won't get as much assistance from Flex Builder and the compiler (in terms of code completion and compile-time syntax checking), but as long as you code correctly, everything works fine at runtime.

Using the descendant accessor operator

A single dot (.) causes the expression to look at direct child elements of the current XML object. You also can do a deep search of the XML hierarchy for elements by their names with the double-dot (..) descendant accessor operator. This allows you to search for all elements of the same name, regardless of their position or how many parent elements there are between the current element and the one you're looking for.

This code extracts all <customer> elements regardless of their position in the content:

```
xReturn = xInvoices..customer;
```

The resulting XMLList object looks like this:

```
<customer>
  <firstname>Maria</firstname>
  <lastname>Smith</lastname>
</customer>
<customer>
  <firstname>John</firstname>
  <lastname>Jones</lastname>
</customer>
```

TIP When an E4X expression doesn't find any results, it doesn't return null or undefined as you might expect. Instead, it returns an empty XMLList object. You can check whether you got results by calling the object's length() method and inspecting the result:

```
if (xReturn.length() == 0)
{
    errorMessage = "No XML nodes were found";
}
```

The length() method is implemented in both the XML and XMLList classes, so you can safely call it without knowing in advance which type of object you're working with.

Filtering XML data with predicate expressions

A predicate expression lets you filter data in an XML object, accomplishing tasks similar to the WHERE clause in an SQL statement. The predicate expression itself is an ActionScript comparison expression wrapped in parentheses. You append the predicate to the part of the E4X expression that indicates what data you want to return, separated with a dot operator.

This ActionScript extracts all <customer> elements that have a <lastname> matching the String value Jones:

```
xReturn = xInvoices..customer.(lastname=='Jones')
```

The resulting XML node looks like this:

```
<customer>
  <firstname>John</firstname>
  <lastname>Jones</lastname>
</customer>
```

CAUTION Notice that the predicate expression uses the ActionScript == equality operator, not the single equals (=) assignment operator. If you use the assignment operator in this expression, it results in changing all <lastname> elements' text nodes to Jones and returning them all as an XMLList.

You also can filter on values stored as text nodes in elements. For example, the XML structure sets <lineitem> descriptions as text nodes:

```
<items>
  <lineitem price="21.41" quantity="4">Widget</lineitem>
  <lineitem price="2.11" quantity="14">Mouse</lineitem>
  <lineitem price="8.88" quantity="3">Wrench</lineitem>
</items>
```

You can refer to an element's toString() method in a predicate expression to return the node value instead of the XML node itself and then compare the text node's value to any other value. This code extracts all <lineitem> elements whose text nodes equal the String value Mouse:

```
xReturn = xInvoices..lineitem.(toString()=='Mouse');
```

The result is an XMLList that looks like this:

```
<lineitem price="2.11" quantity="14">Mouse</lineitem>
<lineitem price="7.41" quantity="84">Mouse</lineitem>
```

You also can compare values to an element's attributes. You refer to attributes using the @ character as a prefix to the attribute's name. This command extracts all <lineitem> elements where the price is less than 8:

```
xReturn = xInvoices..lineitem.(@price < 8);
```

The result is an XMLList that looks like this:

```
<lineitem price="2.11" quantity="14">Mouse</lineitem>
<lineitem price="7.41" quantity="84">Mouse</lineitem>
<lineitem price="0.91" quantity="184">Mousepad</lineitem>
```

> **TIP**   When you compare values in an E4X expression, typecasting of literal numeric expressions depends on whether you wrap the expression in quotation marks. This version of the expression would execute a **String**-based filter, because the literal value is wrapped in quotation marks:

```
xReturn = xInvoices..lineitem.(@price < '8');
```

The resulting **XMLList** includes all **<lineitem>** elements where the first character of the price attribute comes before the character '8' in terms of alphanumeric sorting:

```
<lineitem price="21.41" quantity="4">Widget</lineitem>
<lineitem price="2.11" quantity="14">Mouse</lineitem>
<lineitem price="7.41" quantity="84">Mouse</lineitem>
<lineitem price="0.91" quantity="184">Mousepad</lineitem>
```

This pattern follows the JavaScript standard of typecasting literal values based on how they're expressed. A numeric literal with quotation marks is actually a **String**, while the same value without the quotation marks is a **Number**.

The application in Listing 22.2 tests each of the expressions described in this section and returns the result to a TextArea control. It uses an ActionScript helper class that contains all the expressions being tested.

LISTING 22.2

A demo application for testing E4X expressions

```
<?xml version="1.0" encoding="utf-8"?>
<mx:Application xmlns:mx="http://www.adobe.com/2006/mxml"
  layout="horizontal" creationComplete="initApp()">
  <mx:Script>
    <![CDATA[
      import helpers.E4XDemoHelper;
      import mx.rpc.events.ResultEvent;
      import mx.collections.ArrayCollection;
      [Bindable]
      private var acExpressions:ArrayCollection;
      [Bindable]
      private var xInvoices:XML;
      private function initApp():void
      {
        invoiceService.send();
        acExpressions = new ArrayCollection(
```

continued

LISTING 22.2   *(continued)*

```
        E4XDemoHelper.getExpressionsArray());
      XML.prettyIndent=2;
    }
    private function resultHandler(event:ResultEvent):void
    {
      xInvoices = event.result as XML;
    }
    private function evaluate():void
    {
      var xReturn:Object = E4XDemoHelper.evalE4X(
        xInvoices, expList.selectedIndex);
      if (xReturn.length() == 0)
      {
        resultString.text = "No XML nodes were found";
      }
      else
      {
        resultString.text = xReturn.toXMLString();
      }
    }
  ]]>
  </mx:Script>
  <mx:HTTPService id="invoiceService"
    url="data/invoices.xml" resultFormat="e4x"
    result="resultHandler(event)"/>
  <mx:VDividedBox width="50%" height="100%">
    <mx:Panel title="XML being searched:" width="100%" height="100%">
      <mx:TextArea width="100%" height="100%" editable="false"
        text="{xInvoices.toXMLString()}"/>
    </mx:Panel>
    <mx:Panel id="expListPanel" title="Select an E4X expression:"
      width="100%" height="100%" >
      <mx:List id="expList" dataProvider="{acExpressions}"
        width="100%" rowCount="{acExpressions.length}"
        change="evaluate()"/>
    </mx:Panel>
  </mx:VDividedBox>
  <mx:Panel title="Result as an XML String" height="100%"
width="100%">
    <mx:TextArea width="100%" height="100%" id="resultString"/>
  </mx:Panel>
</mx:Application>
```

ON the WEB   The code in Listing 22.3 is available in the Web site files as **E4XParsing.xml** in the **src** folder of the **chapter22** project.

The helper `E4XParsingHelper` class in Listing 22.3 contains all the test expressions in two forms: The `Array` of Strings is used by the demo application to display the expressions being evaluated, while the static `evalE4X()` method executes precompiled E4X expressions as requested by the user.

LISTING 22.3

The E4XParsingHelper class, containing all expressions being tested in the demo application

```
package helpers
{
  public class E4XParsingHelper
  {
    public var arExpressions:Array;
    public static function getExpressionsArray():Array
    {
      var arExpressions:Array = new Array();
      arExpressions.push("xInvoices.invoice");
      arExpressions.push("xInvoices.invoice[1]");
      arExpressions.push("xInvoices.invoice[0].customer");
      arExpressions.push("xInvoices..customer");
      arExpressions.push("xInvoices..customer.(lastname=='Jones')");
      arExpressions.push("xInvoices..lineitem.(toString()=='Mouse')");
      arExpressions.push("xInvoices..lineitem.(@price < 8)");
      arExpressions.push("xInvoices..lineitem.(@price < '8')");
      return arExpressions;
    }
    public static function evalE4X(xInvoices:XML, expIndex:int):Object
    {
      switch (expIndex)
      {
        case0: return xInvoices.invoice;
        case1: return xInvoices.invoice[1];
        case2: return xInvoices.invoice[0].customer;
        case3: return xInvoices..customer;
        case4: return xInvoices..customer.(lastname=='Jones');
        case5: return xInvoices..lineitem.(toString()=='Mouse');
        case6: return xInvoices..lineitem.(@price < 8);
        case7: return xInvoices..lineitem.(@price < '8');
        default: return new XMLList();
      }
    }
  }
}
```

ON the WEB   The code in Listing 22.3 is available in the Web site files as **E4XParsingHelper.as** in the **src/helpers** folder of the **chapter22** project.

TIP   You can add new test expressions to the helper class by adding a new item to the **Array** in the **getExpressionsArray()** method and adding an equivalent case statement in the **evalE4X()** method.

Modifying data in XML objects

E4X expressions also can be used to add, remove, and modify elements in an XML object. For example, if an XML object starts with a simple root element, it's a simple matter to add both elements and attributes, and to change the values of existing attributes and text nodes.

Changing existing values

You can change existing values in an XML object by using an E4X expression to identify one or more XML nodes and then assign a new value to them. For example, the XML structure that was used as a starting point in the preceding section has a root element with child <invoice> elements. Each invoice has customer.firstname and customer.lastname nodes.

The following code changes the firstname of the first invoice's customer to a new value of "Harry":

```
xInvoices.invoice[0].customer.firstname='Harry';
```

After modification, the <customer> element for the first <invoice> looks like this:

```
<customer>
  <firstname>Harry</firstname>
  <lastname>Smith</lastname>
</customer>
```

You also can modify existing attribute values by referring to the attribute name with the @ character as a prefix. This code changes the price attribute of the first <lineitem> in the first <invoice>:

```
xInvoices.invoice[0].items.lineitem[0].@price=12.50;
```

The <lineitem> element looks like this after the code has been executed:

```
<lineitem price="12.5" quantity="4">Widget</lineitem>
```

Notice that the String representation of the value is truncated to remove the trailing zero. That's because, with no quotation marks around the numeric value on the right side of the assignment operator, it's first evaluated as a Number and then saved as a String in the XML. You can force formatting of numeric values by wrapping quotation marks around the literal expression:

```
xInvoices.invoice[0].items.lineitem[0].@price='12.50';
```

The modified <lineitem> element now retains the formatting, as shown here:

```
<lineitem price="12.50" quantity="4">Widget</lineitem>
```

Adding elements and attributes

The same E4X syntax that modifies existing elements and attributes can be used to add new nodes. Simply put, if a node to which you refer in an assignment doesn't already exist, the assignment creates it.

This command adds a new `<city>` element to the first `<customer>` element and sets its value:

```
xInvoices.invoice[0].customer.city='Seattle';
```

After the code has been executed, the resulting `<customer>` element looks like this:

```
<customer>
  <firstname>Maria</firstname>
  <lastname>Smith</lastname>
  <city>Seattle</city>
</customer>
```

The same approach works with attributes. This command adds an `inStock` attribute to the first `<lineitem>` in the first invoice:

```
xInvoices.invoice[0].items.lineitem[0].@inStock=true
```

After the code is executed, the modified `<lineitem>` element looks like this:

```
<lineitem price="21.41" quantity="4"
   inStock="true">Widget</lineitem>
```

CAUTION You can make an assignment to only one XML object at a time. If the E4X expression on the left side of an assignment identifies more than one XML element, a runtime error occurs.

Deleting elements and attributes

The `delete` operator is used to remove data from an XML object at runtime. You start with the `delete` operator at the beginning of the statement and follow it with an E4X expression that identified the node you want to remove.

This command removes the second invoice in the XML object:

```
delete xInvoices.invoice[1];
```

In some cases, you can remove whole sets of elements. This command empties the items element of the first invoice:

```
delete xInvoices.invoice[0].items.lineitem;
```

After the code is executed, the first `<invoice>` looks like this:

```
<invoice>
  <customer>
    <firstname>Maria</firstname>
```

```
      <lastname>Smith</lastname>
    </customer>
    <items/>
  </invoice>
```

Attributes also can be removed with the `delete` operator. This code removes the quantity attribute from the first `<lineitem>` in the first `<invoice>`.

```
delete xInvoices.invoice[0].items.lineitem[0].@quantity;
```

After the code is executed, the modified `<lineitem>` element looks like this:

```
<lineitem price="21.41">Widget</lineitem>
```

> **TIP**
>
> All E4X expressions that modify **XML** objects return a reference to the modified XML. For example, this statement both modifies an **XML** object and returns a reference to the modified data:

```
var xNew:XML = xInvoices.invoice[0].customer.city='Seattle';
```

The application in Listing 22.4 uses a helper class, `E4XChangingHelper`, to demonstrate each of the expressions described in this section.

LISTING 22.4

An application that demonstrates modifying data with E4X

```
<?xml version="1.0" encoding="utf-8"?>
<mx:Application xmlns:mx="http://www.adobe.com/2006/mxml"
  layout="horizontal" creationComplete="initApp()">
  <mx:Script>
    <![CDATA[
      import helpers.E4XChangingHelper;
      import mx.rpc.events.ResultEvent;
      import mx.collections.ArrayCollection;
      [Bindable]
      private var acExpressions:ArrayCollection;
      [Bindable]
      private var xInvoices:XML;
      private function initApp():void
      {
        invoiceService.send();
        acExpressions = new ArrayCollection(
          E4XChangingHelper.getExpressionsArray());
        XML.prettyIndent=2;
      }
      private function resultHandler(event:ResultEvent):void
      {
        xInvoices = event.result as XML;
```

```
      }
      private function evaluate():void
      {
        var tempXML:XML = new XML(xInvoices.toXMLString());
        E4XChangingHelper.evalE4X(tempXML, expList.selectedIndex);
        resultString.text = tempXML.toXMLString();
      }

      ]]>
    </mx:Script>
    <mx:HTTPService id="invoiceService"
      url="data/invoices.xml" resultFormat="e4x"
      result="resultHandler(event)"/>
    <mx:VDividedBox width="50%" height="100%">
      <mx:Panel title="XML being searched:" width="100%" height="100%">
        <mx:TextArea width="100%" height="100%" editable="false"
          text="{xInvoices.toXMLString()}"/>
      </mx:Panel>
      <mx:Panel id="expListPanel" title="Select an E4X expression:"
        width="100%" height="100%" >
        <mx:List id="expList" dataProvider="{acExpressions}"
          width="100%" rowCount="{acExpressions.length}"
          change="evaluate()"/>
      </mx:Panel>
    </mx:VDividedBox>
    <mx:Panel title="Result as an XML String" height="100%" width="50%">
      <mx:TextArea width="100%" height="100%" id="resultString"/>
    </mx:Panel>
</mx:Application>
```

ON the WEB The code in Listing 22.4 is available in the Web site files as **E4XChanging.mxml** in the **src** folder of the **chapter22** project.

The ActionScript helper class in Listing 22.5 contains all the expressions that the application is designed to evaluate.

LISTING 22.5

A helper class containing expressions for modifying XML data

```
package helpers
{
  public class E4XChangingHelper
  {
    public var arExpressions:Array;
    public static function getExpressionsArray():Array
```

continued

LISTING 22.5   *(continued)*

```
  {
     var arExpressions:Array = new Array();

arExpressions.push("xInvoices.invoice[0].customer.firstname='Harry'")
;
     arExpressions.push(
       "xInvoices.invoice[0].items.lineitem[0].@price=12.50");
     arExpressions.push(
       "xInvoices.invoice[0].items.lineitem[0].@price='12.50'");
     arExpressions.push(
       "xInvoices.invoice[0].customer.city='Seattle'");
     arExpressions.push(
       "xInvoices.invoice[0].items.lineitem[0].@inStock=true");
     arExpressions.push("delete xInvoices.invoice[1]");
     arExpressions.push("delete xInvoices.invoice[0].items.lineitem");
     arExpressions.push(
       "delete xInvoices.invoice[0].items.lineitem[0].@quantity");
     return arExpressions;
  }
  public static function evalE4X(xInvoices:XML, expIndex:int):void
  {
     switch (expIndex)
     {
       case 0:
         xInvoices.invoice[0].customer.firstname='Harry'; break;
       case 1:
         xInvoices.invoice[0].items.lineitem[0].@price=12.50; break;
       case 2:
         xInvoices.invoice[0].items.lineitem[0].@price='12.50'; break;
       case 3:
         xInvoices.invoice[0].customer.city='Seattle'; break;
       case 4:
         xInvoices.invoice[0].items.lineitem[0].@inStock=true; break;
       case 5:
         delete xInvoices.invoice[1]; break;
       case 6:
         delete xInvoices.invoice[0].items.lineitem; break;
       case 7:
         delete xInvoices.invoice[0].items.lineitem[0].@quantity;
         break;
     }
   }
  }
 }
}
```

ON the WEB   The code in Listing 22.5 is available in the Web site files as `E4XPChangingHelper.as` in the `src/helpers` folder of the `chapter22` project.

> **TIP**   You can add new test expressions to the helper class by adding a new item to the `Array` in the `getExpressionsArray()` method and adding an equivalent case statement in the `evalE4X()` method.

Working with Namespaces

XML namespaces constitute a simple way to distinguish and group element and attribute names as members of groups, essentially allowing for the usage of different "flavors" of XML in a single document. For example, MXML uses a default namespace to identify the MXML language to the Flex compiler (`http://www.adobe.com/2006/mxml`) and allows you to create your own custom namespaces to identify directories as packages containing classes and components, such as in the declaration `xmlns:forms="forms.*"`.

E4X allows you to incorporate namespace notation into expressions that identify elements for extraction or modification. There are two basic steps to using namespaces in E4X:

- Create a namespace object that represents a namespace in the XML content you're parsing or modifying.

- Refer to the namespace object as a prefix for the elements or attributes you want to locate.

The following XML packet uses three namespaces to distinguish elements that share a name:

```
private var xTravel:XML =
<travel
  xmlns:train="http://www.bardotech.com/train"
  xmlns:plane="http://www.bardotech.com/airplane"
  xmlns:car="http://www.bardotech.com/automobile">
  <journey>
    <train:traveltime>8 hours</train:traveltime>
    <plane:traveltime>1 hour</plane:traveltime>
    <car:traveltime>3 days</car:traveltime>
  </journey>
</travel>
```

To extract a `<traveltime>` element and distinguish it from the other elements of the same name, first declare namespace objects that are mapped to the namespaces in the XML data. You can do this in two ways.

If you want to identify namespaces by their URI, use the ActionScript's `namespace` keyword to create a namespace object by the URI:

```
private namespace train = "http://www.bardotech.com/train";
private namespace plane = "http://www.bardotech.com/airplane";
private namespace car = "http://www.bardotech.com/automobile";
```

Alternatively, if you want to identify namespaces by their prefixes as assigned in the XML structure, create variables typed as the Namespace class. Assign each namespace by calling the XML object's namespace() method and passing the selected namespace prefix:

```
private var train:Namespace = xTravel.namespace("train");
private var plane:Namespace = xTravel.namespace("plane");
private var car:Namespace = xTravel.namespace("car");
```

> **TIP**
>
> The Namespace class is a *top level* Flash Player class, meaning that it isn't a member of any particular package and can be used without requiring an import statement.

> **TIP**
>
> Notice that the names of the ActionScript namespace objects match the namespace prefixes in the XML content. This isn't technically necessary; as long as the namespace URI or prefix match, XML elements will be identified correctly. But consistency between data and code notation certainly doesn't hurt.

After the namespace objects have been declared, you can use them as element and attribute prefixes in E4X expressions. The namespace object's name is separated from the element or attribute name with the :: operator, to qualify the node as being a member of the selected namespace.

The following code extracts the <traveltime> element that's qualified with the airplane namespace:

```
traveltime = xTravel.journey.plane::traveltime;
```

The application in Listing 22.6 declares an XML structure and then allows the user to indicate which of the three <traveltime> values she wants to see.

LISTING 22.6

Using XML namespaces in E4X

```
<?xml version="1.0" encoding="utf-8"?>
<mx:Application xmlns:mx="http://www.adobe.com/2006/mxml"
  backgroundColor="#EEEEEE">
  <mx:Style>
    RadioButton, Label {
      font-size:10;
      font-weight:bold;
    }
  </mx:Style>
  <mx:Script>
    <![CDATA[
      [Bindable]
      private var travelTime:String="Choose a vehicle";
      private var xTravel:XML =
      <travel xmlns:train="http://www.bardotech.com/train"
        xmlns:plane="http://www.bardotech.com/airplane"
```

```
         xmlns:car="http://www.bardotech.com/automobile">
         <journey>
           <train:traveltime>8 hours</train:traveltime>
           <plane:traveltime>1 hour</plane:traveltime>
           <car:traveltime>3 days</car:traveltime>
         </journey>
       </travel>
       private var train:Namespace = xTravel.namespace("train");
       private var plane:Namespace = xTravel.namespace("plane");
       private var car:Namespace = xTravel.namespace("car");
       private function getTravelTime():void
       {
         var vehicle:String = vehicleGroup.selectedValue as String;
         switch (vehicle)
         {
           case "plane":
             travelTime = xTravel.journey.plane::traveltime;
             break;
           case "train":
             travelTime = xTravel.journey.train::traveltime;
             break;
           case "car":
             travelTime = xTravel.journey.car::traveltime;
         }
       }
     ]]>
   </mx:Script>
   <mx:Panel title="Select a vehicle" width="135"
     paddingBottom="5" paddingLeft="5" paddingRight="5" paddingTop="5">
     <mx:RadioButton label="Plane" value="plane"
         groupName="vehicleGroup"/>
     <mx:RadioButton label="Train" value="train"
         groupName="vehicleGroup"/>
     <mx:RadioButton label="Automobile" value="car"
         groupName="vehicleGroup"/>
     <mx:RadioButtonGroup id="vehicleGroup" itemClick="getTravelTime()"/>
     <mx:ControlBar>
       <mx:Label text="{travelTime}"/>
     </mx:ControlBar>
   </mx:Panel>
</mx:Application>
```

ON the WEB   The code in Listing 22.6 is available in the Web site files as **E4XWithNamespaces.mxml** in the **src** folder of the **chapter22** project.

Figure 22.1 shows the resulting application, displaying the results of an E4X expression with namespaces to the user.

FIGURE 22.1

An application using E4X with namespaces

Summary

In this chapter, I described how to use EcmaScript for XML to parse and modify data stored in XML objects in Flex application memory at runtime. You learned the following:

- E4X stands for EcmaScript for XML.

- E4X is a standard of Ecma International that is implemented in ActionScript 3 and in certain other languages and platforms.

- E4X allows you to parse, extract, and modify XML-based data at runtime with simple, concise expressions.

- E4X is a part of the compiled ActionScript language and is not designed for runtime evaluation of arbitrary expressions.

- Array-style syntax is combined with various operators to "walk" the XML hierarchy.

- The `delete` operator removes elements and attributes at runtime.

- XML with namespaces can be accurately parsed using namespace objects and the namespace qualification operator (`::`).

Part IV

Integrating Flex Applications with Application Servers and the Desktop

Chapter 23

Working with SOAP-Based Web Services

In Chapter 21, I described the use of the Flex `HTTPService` component to make requests and handle responses from Web resources formatted as arbitrary XML data structures. The strength of REST and generic XML is that you can create and use Web services that employ any arbitrary data structure. The potential weakness of this strategy is that each application must have specific knowledge of the particular XML structure being used.

SOAP-based Web services take a different approach: They employ industry-standard XML languages to format both messages and metadata. The SOAP language itself is used to format requests and responses between a client and a server, while WSDL (Web Services Description Language) is used to declare to Web service consumers the structure and capabilities of Web service operations.

The strength of SOAP-based Web services lies in their industry-level standardization and their ability to strongly data type parameter and return values in a way that RESTful operations typically can't.

SOAP servers and clients are designed to be interoperable, so that you can easily call functions (known in SOAP as *operations*) from objects on remote servers without knowing what platform is hosting the service or what programming language was used to develop it, because many support SOAP. And, as data is passed between client and server, its data types are maintained as long as both tiers of the application use compatible types.

> **TIP** The term SOAP started as an acronym for Simple Object Access Protocol. Starting with version 1.2, it became simply SOAP.

WEB RESOURCE The SOAP and WSDL recommendations are managed by the World Wide Web Consortium (W3C), which also manages the recommendations for XML, HTML, and HTTP. The most recent recommendations are available at www.w3.org/TR/soap and www.w3.org/TR/wsdl.

For a history of SOAP, check out Dave Winer's "Dave's History of SOAP" at www.xmlrpc.com/stories/storyReader$555 and Don Box's "A Brief History of SOAP" at http://web services.xml.com/pub/a/ws/2001/04/04/soap.html.

ON the WEB To use the sample code for this chapter, import the chapter23.zip project from the Web site files into any folder on your disk. The sample Web service files are built in the CFML programming language for use with Adobe ColdFusion and should work with either ColdFusion 7 or 8. You can download the free developer edition of ColdFusion from www.adobe.com/products/coldfusion.

Understanding SOAP

SOAP is an XML language that's used to format messages sent between clients and servers in RPC-style applications. Its purpose is to allow client applications to call functions of remote objects that are defined and hosted in a server-based environment.

When a remote operation is called from a SOAP client application, the request message is encoded in the SOAP language as an XML package with a root element named <Envelope>. The following SOAP packet was generated by a Flex application calling a remote operation named helloWorld:

```
<SOAP-ENV:Envelope
 xmlns:SOAP-ENV="http://schemas.xmlsoap.org/soap/envelope/"
 xmlns:xsd="http://www.w3.org/2001/XMLSchema"
 xmlns:xsi="http://www.w3.org/2001/XMLSchema-instance">
  <SOAP-ENV:Body
   SOAP-ENV:encodingStyle=
     "http://schemas.xmlsoap.org/soap/encoding/">
    <intf:helloWorld xmlns:intf="http://flex3bible"/>
  </SOAP-ENV:Body>
</SOAP-ENV:Envelope>
```

When the response comes back from the server, it's encoded in the same XML language. This SOAP response was generated by a Web service written in CFML (ColdFusion Markup Language) and hosted by ColdFusion 8:

```
<?xml version="1.0" encoding="utf-8"?>
<soapenv:Envelope
  xmlns:soapenv="http://schemas.xmlsoap.org/soap/envelope/"
  xmlns:xsd="http://www.w3.org/2001/XMLSchema"
  xmlns:xsi="http://www.w3.org/2001/XMLSchema-instance">
 <soapenv:Body>
  <ns1:helloWorldResponse
```

```
soapenv:encodingStyle="http://schemas.xmlsoap.org/soap/
encoding/"
xmlns:ns1="http://flex3bible">
<helloWorldReturn
  xsi:type="xsd:string">Hello World</helloWorldReturn>
</ns1:helloWorldResponse>
</soapenv:Body>
</soapenv:Envelope>
```

If you compare the outgoing and incoming SOAP data packets, you'll see that they use the same XML namespace, `http://schemas.xmlsoap.org/soap/envelope/`, to define the elements and attributes of the SOAP language. They differ in certain minor details, such as the capitalization of namespace prefixes (Flex uses `SOAP-ENV`, while ColdFusion uses `soap-env`), but they agree on the important elements of Web-based communications.

The magic of SOAP, however, is that the developer doesn't need to know these details. SOAP-based client and server software is responsible for creating an abstraction layer that allows the developer to make calls to remote operations using code that's only minimally different from that used to call local methods.

A SOAP-based Web service can be built with many different programming languages and hosted on many operating systems. To host a service, you need an application server that knows how to read and write SOAP message packets. Similarly, the client application uses an implementation of SOAP that handles the serialization and deserialization of the SOAP message packets as data is sent and received.

Some SOAP-based software packages implement both server and client functionality. For example, Apache's Axis is a popular Java-based implementation of SOAP that implements client and server functionality and can be used freely with any Java-based application. Other implementations, such as the Flex framework's `WebService` component, include only a SOAP client.

This chapter describes how to use the `WebService` component to make calls to SOAP-based Web services. While the examples in this chapter are written against a Web service built and hosted in Adobe ColdFusion, Flex applications are interoperable with many SOAP server implementations, including these:

- Microsoft ASP.NET implements SOAP as a feature named XML Web Services.

- Apache AXIS includes implementations of SOAP for client-side and server-side Java-based applications on most operating systems.

- Adobe ColdFusion (used in this chapter) implements SOAP as an option for calling ColdFusion Component (CFC) functions and uses the `<cfinvoke>` command to call functions from most SOAP servers. The most recent version, ColdFusion 8, runs on Windows, Mac OS X, Linux, Solaris, and AIX.

- Many open-source and built-in implementations of SOAP also are available for various scripting languages, including PHP, Python, and Ruby.

CROSS-REF   With so many available options for building and deploying SOAP-based Web services, the process of creating a Web service in each of these software packages is beyond the scope of this book. However, detailed information on creating XML Web Services in ASP.NET is included in Chapter 28.

TIP   Whenever possible, most developers prefer to use the `RemoteObject` component to integrate Flex applications with ColdFusion, Java-based applications like LiveCycle Data Services and BlazeDS, and other non-Adobe products such as OpenAMF, AMFPHP, and WebOrb that support the Remoting Service architecture and binary AMF. This is primarily due to the performance advantage you get out of AMF. SOAP, while a strongly data typed messaging format, is pure text and generates much larger data packets than AMF-enabled architectures. Web service integration tends to be used for integration with third-party data vendors who support the SOAP standard or with application servers with particularly strong SOAP support, such as ASP.NET.

Understanding WSDL

Web Services Description Language (WSDL) is an XML language that's used to declare to Web service consumers the structure and capabilities of Web service operations. In order to consume a Web service, a Flex application must be able to read and parse a WSDL file at runtime that tells the WebService component everything it needs to know in order to successfully call the service's operations.

WSDL is a somewhat complex language, but many SOAP server implementations, including Apache Axis, ASP.NET's XML Web Services, and ColdFusion 8, can dynamically generate a WSDL file for a native class exposed as a Web service in response to an HTTP request from a client application. For all these application servers, you generate a WSDL file by sending an HTTP request from a client application to the service URL and appending a query string variable named `wsdl`.

Take as an example a ColdFusion Component (CFC) named `SoapService.cfc` that's designed to be called as a Web service. If the CFC is stored in a subfolder of the Web root named `services`, and ColdFusion is installed on your local server and connected to a Web server running on the default port 80, the CFC's URL would be:

```
http://localhost/services/SoapService.cfc
```

To generate the WSDL file, append a query string parameter named `wsdl`:

```
http://localhost/services/SoapService.cfc?wsdl
```

ColdFusion responds by generating the WSDL content and returning it to the requesting application. Similar patterns are used by other common SOAP server applications. This is an example of a WSDL URI for Apache Axis:

```
http://localhost/myJEEApp/services/MyWebService?wsdl
```

And this is an example for ASP.NET:

```
http://localhost/myDotNetApp/MyWebService.asmx?wsdl
```

TIP   The address of the WSDL document on the Web is referred to in Flex Builder and the Flex documentation as the WSDL URI (Uniform Resource Identifier).

WEB RESOURCE   The WSDL language is managed by the W3C. The current recommendation is available at www.w3.org/TR/wsdl.

WSDL is standardized across vendors and application servers, and usually looks pretty much the same regardless of its generating server software. The following sample WSDL page was generated by ColdFusion for a CFC with a single `helloWorld()` operation:

```xml
<?xml version="1.0" encoding="UTF-8"?>
<wsdl:definitions targetNamespace="http://flex3bible"
  xmlns:apachesoap="http://xml.apache.org/xml-soap"
  xmlns:impl="http://flex3bible" xmlns:intf="http://flex3bible"
  xmlns:soapenc="http://schemas.xmlsoap.org/soap/encoding/"
  xmlns:tns1="http://rpc.xml.coldfusion"
  xmlns:wsdl="http://schemas.xmlsoap.org/wsdl/"
  xmlns:wsdlsoap="http://schemas.xmlsoap.org/wsdl/soap/"
  xmlns:xsd="http://www.w3.org/2001/XMLSchema">
<!--WSDL created by ColdFusion version 8,0,0,176276-->
 <wsdl:types>
  <schema targetNamespace="http://rpc.xml.coldfusion"
    xmlns="http://www.w3.org/2001/XMLSchema">
   <import
   namespace="http://schemas.xmlsoap.org/soap/encoding/"/>
   <complexType name="CFCInvocationException">
    <sequence/>
   </complexType>
  </schema>
 </wsdl:types>
<wsdl:message name="CFCInvocationException">
   <wsdl:part name="fault" type="tns1:CFCInvocationException"/>
 </wsdl:message>
 <wsdl:message name="helloWorldResponse">
   <wsdl:part name="helloWorldReturn" type="xsd:string"/>
 </wsdl:message>
 <wsdl:message name="helloWorldRequest">
 </wsdl:message>
 <wsdl:portType name="SoapService">
    <wsdl:operation name="helloWorld">
       <wsdl:input message="impl:helloWorldRequest"
         name="helloWorldRequest"/>
       <wsdl:output message="impl:helloWorldResponse"
         name="helloWorldResponse"/>
       <wsdl:fault message="impl:CFCInvocationException"
         name="CFCInvocationException"/>
      </wsdl:operation>
   </wsdl:portType>
   <wsdl:binding name="SoapService.cfcSoapBinding"
     type="impl:SoapService">
```

```
<wsdlsoap:binding style="rpc"
  transport="http://schemas.xmlsoap.org/soap/http"/>
  <wsdl:operation name="helloWorld">
    <wsdlsoap:operation soapAction=""/>
    <wsdl:input name="helloWorldRequest">
      <wsdlsoap:body

encodingStyle="http://schemas.xmlsoap.org/soap/encoding/"
        namespace="http://flex3bible" use="encoded"/>
    </wsdl:input>
    <wsdl:output name="helloWorldResponse">
      <wsdlsoap:body

encodingStyle="http://schemas.xmlsoap.org/soap/encoding/"
        namespace="http://flex3bible" use="encoded"/>
    </wsdl:output>
    <wsdl:fault name="CFCInvocationException">
      <wsdlsoap:fault

encodingStyle="http://schemas.xmlsoap.org/soap/encoding/"
        name="CFCInvocationException"
        namespace="http://flex3bible" use="encoded"/>
    </wsdl:fault>
  </wsdl:operation>
</wsdl:binding>
<wsdl:service name="SoapServiceService">
<wsdl:documentation
xmlns:wsdl="http://schemas.xmlsoap.org/wsdl/">
  A ColdFusion web service built as a CFC
</wsdl:documentation>
<wsdl:port binding="impl:SoapService.cfcSoapBinding"
  name="SoapService.cfc">
<wsdlsoap:address

location="http://localhost:8500/flex3bible/SoapService.cfc"/>
  </wsdl:port>
</wsdl:service>
</wsdl:definitions>
```

The details of the WSDL language are beyond the scope of this book, but one thing is clear from this example: WSDL isn't designed to be human readable (at least without serious study). Its purpose is to inform a software-based Web service consumer (in this case, a Flex client application) about a service's metadata. It includes detailed information about an operation's name, what parameters and data types the operation expects, what type of data is returned in the operation's response, and where the request to call the operation should be sent at runtime.

WEB RESOURCE You can find many tutorials on WSDL on the Web. For one that's concise and to the point, check out http://msdn2.microsoft.com/en-us/library/ms996486.aspx.

Using the WebService Component

In this section, I describe how to use the `WebService` component to make calls to Web service functions and handle the resulting data. The sample applications call Web services written in CFML and hosted on ColdFusion 8, so if you want to run the sample applications on your own system, you'll first need to download and install ColdFusion 8 from Adobe Systems.

Installing ColdFusion 8

ColdFusion 8 is available for download from `www.adobe.com/products/coldfusion/` and can be installed and run in "developer" mode on your local system without any license fees. Versions are available for Windows, Mac OS X, and other operating systems.

> **TIP** The Web service examples in this chapter don't have any database dependencies, so they should run successfully on any of ColdFusion's supported operating systems.

After installing ColdFusion, create a folder under the server's Web root named `flex3bible`. (The default Web root folder in this environment is `C:\ColdFusion8\wwwroot` on Windows and `/Applications/ColdFusion8/wwwroot` on Mac OS X.)

Then extract the files from `ColdFusionServices.zip` in the `chaper23` project into this new folder.

> **TIP** The Flex application examples for this chapter assume that ColdFusion has been installed with the "development" Web server, which runs with port 8500. A request to the CFC in this environment would be sent to `http://localhost:8500/flex3bible/ SoapService.cfc?wsdl`. If you have the Web service component installed in another folder or if ColdFusion is running on another port, just modify the example applications as necessary to point to the correct port and location.

Creating a WebService object

As with the `HTTPService` component that was described in Chapter 21, the `WebService` component can be instantiated with either MXML or ActionScript code. The component's `wsdl` property is a `String` value that contains the URL from which the service's WSDL can be retrieved at runtime.

To create a `WebService` object in MXML, declare it with a unique `id` and set its `wsdl` property as in this example:

```
<mx:WebService id="myService"
  wsdl="http://localhost:8500/flex3bible/SoapService.cfc?wsdl"/>
```

> **TIP** As with the `HTTPService` component, if a Web-based Flex application and a Web service it calls are hosted in the same domain, you can use a relative URL in the `wsdl` property. In this example, you could shorten the `wsdl` property to `/flex3bible/SoapService.cfc?wsdl`.

To declare a `WebService` object in ActionScript, you can create the object and then set its `wsdl` property in a separate statement:

```
var myService:WebService = new WebService();
myService.wsdl =
   "http://localhost:8500/flex3bible/SoapService.cfc?wsdl"
```

Alternatively, you can pass the `wsdl` location into the `WebService` constructor method:

```
var myService:WebService = new WebService(
   "http://localhost:8500/flex3bible/SoapService.cfc?wsdl");
```

Loading the WSDL content

When you use MXML to declare a `WebService` object, it requests and downloads the WSDL content from the `wsdl` location upon object construction (usually as the application starts up). When using ActionScript code to declare the `WebService` object, you have to explicitly load the WSDL content by calling the object's `loadWSDL()` method. If the `wsdl` property is already set, you can call `loadWSDL()` without any arguments:

```
var myService:WebService = new WebService(
   "http://localhost:8500/flex3bible/SoapService.cfc?wsdl");
myService.loadWSDL();
```

Another approach is to pass the `wsdl` location into `loadWSDL()` and handle both tasks at the same time:

```
var myService:WebService = new WebService();
myService.loadWSDL(
   "http://localhost:8500/flex3bible/SoapService.cfc?wsdl");
```

Handling the load event

Whether you use ActionScript or MXML to declare a `WebService` object, it dispatches an event named `load` when the WSDL content has been successfully retrieved and parsed. The `WebService` object can make calls to Web service operations only after this task is complete, so it's common to make initial calls to Web service operations upon the `load` event being dispatched. In MXML, the code to make an initial call when the `WebService` component is ready looks like this:

```
<mx:WebService id="myService"
   wsdl="http://localhost:8500/flex3bible/SoapService.cfc?wsdl"
   load="myService.helloWorld()"/>
```

You also can use `addEventListener()` to handle the `load` event and make an initial call to the Web service operation:

```
import mx.rpc.soap.LoadEvent;
private function initApp():void
{
```

```
    myService.addEventListener(LoadEvent.LOAD, callService);
}
private function callService(event:LoadEvent):void
{
 myService.helloWorld();
}
```

> **TIP** The `LoadEvent` class implements a document property typed as `XMLDocument` that represents the WSDL document that was loaded from the server. This is a legacy XML object that you can parse with DOM-style programming. In highly dynamic applications, the `document` property allows you to parse and present options to users for calling Web service operations without having to hard code the operation names in your Flex application.

> **TIP** You also can make initial calls to Web service operations from the `Application` component's life cycle events, such as `initialize` or `creationComplete`. If these events are dispatched before the `WebService` component has successfully read its WSDL content, your pending calls are placed in a queue. When the `load` event is dispatched, queued calls are sent to the Web service provider automatically.

Handling Web service results

As with the `HTTPService` component, Web service requests and responses are handled asynchronously. This means that when you send a request, Flash Player's ActionScript Virtual Machine (AVM) doesn't pause in its code execution and wait for data to be returned. Instead, you call the Web service operation and then use either binding expressions or event listeners to handle and process the returned data.

Using binding expressions

A binding expression can be used to pass data returned from a call to a Web service operation to a visual control or other component that's capable of acting as a binding destination. A binding expression for a Web service operation consists of three parts, separated with dots:

- The `WebService` object's unique `id` or variable name
- The name of the Web service operation
- The `lastResult` property

Using the previous example, where the `WebService` object has an `id` of `myService` and the Web service operation is named `helloWorld()`, the binding expression to pass returned data to a Flex component would be:

```
myService.helloWorld.lastResult
```

> **CAUTION** The operation name is used to create a temporary instance of the `Operation` class that, in turn, implements the `lastResult` property. There are a number of versions of this class, including versions for `SOAP` and `Remoting`, and within each of these categories are separate versions for use with `WebService` objects declared in ActionScript and in MXML.

The application in Listing 23.1 uses binding expressions to handle and display both a simple String returned from the Web service's `helloWorld()` operation and an `ArrayCollection` returned from the service's `getAllContacts()` operation.

LISTING 23.1

Handling Web service results with binding expressions

```
<?xml version="1.0" encoding="utf-8"?>
<mx:Application xmlns:mx="http://www.adobe.com/2006/mxml">

  <mx:WebService id="myService"
    wsdl="http://localhost:8500/flex3bible/SoapService.cfc?wsdl"/>

  <mx:Button label="Get String" click="myService.helloWorld()"/>
  <mx:Label text="{myService.helloWorld.lastResult}" fontSize="12"/>

  <mx:Button label="Get Data" click="myService.getAllContacts()"/>
  <mx:DataGrid dataProvider="{myService.getAllContacts.lastResult}">
    <mx:columns>
      <mx:DataGridColumn dataField="firstName" headerText="First Name"/>
      <mx:DataGridColumn dataField="lastName" headerText="Last Name"/>
    </mx:columns>
  </mx:DataGrid>

</mx:Application>
```

ON the WEB The code in Listing 23.1 is available in the Web site files as `WebServiceWith` `Bindings.mxml` in the `src` folder of the `chapter23` project.

Figure 23.1 shows the resulting application, displaying a simple string and a complex data set returned from the Web service.

Using the result event

As with the `HTTPService` component, you can handle results of a call to a Web service operation with the `WebService` component's result event. This event dispatches an event object typed as `mx.rpc.events.ResultEvent`, the same event object that's used by `HTTPService` and `RemoteObject`. The event object's `result` property references the returned data.

FIGURE 23.1

Displaying Web service results

To handle and save data using the `result` event, follow these steps:

1. Declare a bindable variable outside of any functions that acts as a persistent reference to the returned data. Cast the variable's type depending on what you expect to be returned by the Web service operation. For example, if the data type declared in the WSDL document is `soapenc:Array` or is a custom type derived from that type (such as ColdFusion's `impl:ArrayOf_xsd_anyType`), the `WebService` component casts the returned data as an `ArrayCollection`.

```
import mx.collections.ArrayCollection;
[Bindable]
private var myData:ArrayCollection
```

2. Create an event handler function that will be called when the event is dispatched. The function should receive a single event argument typed as `ResultEvent` and return `void`:

```
private function resultHandler(event:ResultEvent):void
{
}
```

3. Within the event handler function, use the `event.result` expression to refer to the data that's returned from the server. Unlike with the `HTTPService` component, where you have to walk down the XML hierarchy to get to the returned data, the expression `event.result` returns a strongly typed `ArrayCollection` and can be passed directly to the persistent variable:

```
myData = event.result as ArrayCollection;
```

TIP Notice that when passing the value of `event.result` directly to a variable, you have to explicitly declare the type of the returned data using the ActionScript `as` operator. `ResultEvent.result` is typed in the API as an `Object`; explicit casting tells both the compiler and Flex Builder's code syntax checker that the data is expected to arrive already formatted as an `ArrayCollection`.

You can listen for the result event with either an MXML attribute-based event listener or a call to the ActionScript `addEventListener()` method. The attribute-based event listener looks like this:

```
<mx:WebService id="myService"
   wsdl="http://localhost:8500/flex3bible/SoapService.cfc?wsdl"
   result="resultHandler(event)"/>
```

When using `addEventListener()` to create an event listener, you can designate the event name with the String value result or with the `ResultEvent` class's `RESULT` constant:

```
var myService:WebService = new WebService();
myService.loadWSDL(
   "http://localhost:8500/flex3bible/SoapService.cfc?wsdl");
myService.addEventListener(ResultEvent.RESULT, resultHandler);
myService.callMethod();
```

Listing 23.2 uses a `result` event handler function to capture and save data that's been returned from a Web service operation.

LISTING 23.2

Using a WebService component with a result event handler function

```
<?xml version="1.0" encoding="utf-8"?>
<mx:Application xmlns:mx="http://www.adobe.com/2006/mxml">
  <mx:Script>
    <![CDATA[
      import mx.collections.ArrayCollection;
      import mx.rpc.events.ResultEvent;

      [Bindable]
      private var contactData:ArrayCollection;

      private function resultHandler(event:ResultEvent):void
      {
        contactData = event.result as ArrayCollection;
      }
    ]]>
  </mx:Script>
  <mx:WebService id="myService"
```

```
    wsdl="http://localhost:8500/flex3bible/SoapService.cfc?wsdl"
    result="resultHandler(event)"/>
  <mx:Button label="Get Data" click="myService.getAllContacts()"/>
  <mx:DataGrid dataProvider="{contactData}">
    <mx:columns>
      <mx:DataGridColumn dataField="firstName" headerText="First Name"/>
      <mx:DataGridColumn dataField="lastName" headerText="Last Name"/>
    </mx:columns>
  </mx:DataGrid>
</mx:Application>
```

ON the WEB   The code in Listing 23.2 is available in the Web site files as `WebServiceResult`
`Event.mxml` in the `src` folder of the `chapter23` project.

Handling fault events

When a call to a Web service operation fails, the `WebService` object dispatches a `fault` event.
Just like the `HTTPService` and `RemoteObject` components, the event object is typed
as `mx.rpc.events.FaultEvent`. This event object has a `fault` property typed as
`mx.rpc.Fault`, which has these properties:

- `faultString:String`: The error message

- `faultCode:String`: A code that indicates the nature of the fault and whether it
  occurred in the client or server environment

- `faultDetail:String`: An additional message that sometimes contains useful
  information

- `message:String`: A string consisting of all of the above values concatenated together
  with | characters used as separators

To handle a `fault` event, create an event handler function that receives an event argument typed
as `FaultEvent`. Within the body of the function, you can deal with the fault however you like.
This code collects fault information from the event object and displays it to the user with an
`Alert` pop-up window:

```
    private function faultHandler(event:FaultEvent):void
    {
        Alert.show(event.fault.faultString, event.fault.faultCode);
    }
```

The application in Listing 23.3 generates a fault by calling a non-existent operation from the Web
service.

LISTING 23.3

Using the fault event

```xml
<?xml version="1.0" encoding="utf-8"?>
<mx:Application xmlns:mx="http://www.adobe.com/2006/mxml">
  <mx:Script>
    <![CDATA[
      import mx.controls.Alert;
      import mx.rpc.events.FaultEvent;
      import mx.collections.ArrayCollection;
      import mx.rpc.events.ResultEvent;
      [Bindable]
      private var contactData:ArrayCollection;
      private function resultHandler(event:ResultEvent):void
      {
        contactData = event.result as ArrayCollection;
      }
      private function faultHandler(event:FaultEvent):void
      {
        Alert.show(event.fault.faultString, event.fault.faultCode);
      }
    ]]>
  </mx:Script>
  <mx:WebService id="myService"
    wsdl="http://localhost:8500/flex3bible/SoapService.cfc?wsdl"
    result="resultHandler(event)"
    fault="faultHandler(event)"/>
  <mx:Button label="Get Data" click="myService.noSuchMethod()"/>
</mx:Application>
```

ON the WEB   The code in Listing 23.3 is available in the Web site files as `WebServiceFault` `Event.mxml` in the `src` folder of the `chapter23` project.

As shown in Figure 23.2, the application responds by displaying the fault information in a pop-up window produced by the `Alert` class.

TIP   Just as with the `HTTPService` component, you also can use the `ItemResponder` and `AsyncToken` classes to handle result and fault events from a call to a `WebService` operation. Each call to an operation returns an `AsyncToken` object, to which you can add a responder object with its `addResponder()` method. See Chapter 21 for more details about this approach to handling RPC events.

FIGURE 23.2

Responding to a `fault` event

Handling events of multiple operations

When a Flex application needs to handle result and fault events from more than one operation of a single Web service, you need to distinguish which event handler method will be used for the results of each operation call. You can handle this requirement with either ActionScript or MXML code.

To set up an event listener for a single method in ActionScript, call `addEventListener()` as a method of an `Operation` object either before or after making a call to the Web service operation. The following code calls a Web service's `getAllContacts()` operation, and then dispatches its `result` event to an event handler function named `resultHandler()`:

```
myService.getAllContacts();
myService.getAllContacts.addEventListener(
   ResultEvent.RESULT, resultHandler);
```

Because `addEventListener()` is called as a member of the operation, not the `WebService` object itself, the event listener is active only for that particular operation.

To set up a similar architecture with MXML, declare the `WebService` component as a paired `<mx:WebService>` tag set. Within the tags, nest multiple `<mx:operation>` tags, each representing an operation you want to call. The `<mx:operation>` tag is an instruction to the compiler, rather than an instance of an ActionScript class. Its purpose is to configure a single operation with its own unique event handlers.

The following MXML code declares an instance of the WebService component with distinct result event listeners for each of two operations. Because the two operations return different types of data, it's important that they each have their own event handler functions:

```
<mx:WebService id="myService"
  wsdl="http://localhost:8500/flex3bible/SoapService.cfc?wsdl"
  result="contactsResultHandler(event)">
  <mx:operation name="getAllContacts"
    result="contactsResultHandler(event)"/>
  <mx:operation name="helloWorld"
    result="helloWorldHandler(event)"/>
</mx:WebService>
```

The application in Listing 23.4 declares MXML-based result event handlers for each of two Web service operations. The fault event handler is declared in the <mx:WebService> tag and is used by both of the service's operations.

LISTING 23.4

Handling events with multiple Web service operations

```
<?xml version="1.0" encoding="utf-8"?>
<mx:Application xmlns:mx="http://www.adobe.com/2006/mxml">
  <mx:Script>
    <![CDATA[
      import mx.controls.Alert;
      import mx.rpc.events.FaultEvent;
      import mx.collections.ArrayCollection;
      import mx.rpc.events.ResultEvent;
      [Bindable]
      private var contactData:ArrayCollection;
      [Bindable]
      private var helloData:String;
      private function contactsResultHandler(event:ResultEvent):void
      {
        contactData = event.result as ArrayCollection;
      }
      private function helloResultHandler(event:ResultEvent):void
      {
        helloData = event.result as String;
      }
      private function faultHandler(event:FaultEvent):void
      {
        Alert.show(event.fault.faultString, event.fault.faultCode);
      }
    ]]>
  </mx:Script>
  <mx:WebService id="myService"
```

```
  wsdl="http://localhost:8500/flex3bible/SoapService.cfc?wsdl"
  fault="faultHandler(event)">
  <mx:operation name="getAllContacts"
    result="contactsResultHandler(event)"/>
  <mx:operation name="helloWorld"
    result="helloResultHandler(event)"/>
</mx:WebService>
<mx:Button label="Get String" click="myService.helloWorld()"/>
<mx:Label text="{helloData}" fontSize="12"/>
<mx:Button label="Get Data" click="myService.getAllContacts()"/>
<mx:DataGrid dataProvider="{contactData}">
  <mx:columns>
    <mx:DataGridColumn dataField="firstName" headerText="First Name"/>
    <mx:DataGridColumn dataField="lastName" headerText="Last Name"/>
  </mx:columns>
</mx:DataGrid>
</mx:Application>
```

ON the WEB The code in Listing 23.4 is available in the Web site files as `WebServiceMultiple Operations.mxml` in the `src` folder of the `chapter23` project.

Passing parameters to Web service operations

You can pass parameters to Web service operations in two different ways:

- Explicit parameters, passed in the order in which they're declared in the service's WSDL description
- Bound parameters, set up in an MXML `<mx:WebService>` declaration

Using explicit parameters

To pass explicit parameters to a Web service operation, you must know the order in which they're declared in the server-side code. If you don't have explicit documentation, you can find this information in the Web service's WSDL metadata description.

For example, the ColdFusion Web service has an operation named `getFilteredContacts()` that lets you search for data by the data set's `firstname` and `lastname` columns. In a Web service's WSDL description, each incoming and outgoing packet is described as a "message." The incoming message for the `getFilteredContacts()` operation looks like this:

```
<wsdl:message name="getFilteredContactsRequest">
  <wsdl:part name="firstname" type="xsd:string"/>
  <wsdl:part name="lastname" type="xsd:string"/>
</wsdl:message>
```

To pass explicit parameters, call the Web service operation just like an ActionScript function. Match the order of the parameters exactly as you see them in the WSDL description. This code passes two values taken directly from the text properties of two `TextInput` controls as parameters of the `getFilteredContacts()` operation:

```
myService.getFilteredContacts(fnameInput.text, lnameInput.text);
```

The Web service will use the parameter values as needed to perform its functionality. In this case, the values are examined, and if they're not blank strings, the service filters the data before returning it to the Flex client.

Using bound parameters

You set up bound parameters by name and nest them within a pair of `<mx:request>` tags, which in turn are nested in a pair of `<mx:operation>` tags. Each parameter is expressed as an XML tag set where the element name matches the name of the parameter, as shown in the WSDL. This declaration includes a set of bindings that pass values directly from the `TextInput` controls to the Web service operations as parameters:

```
<mx:WebService id="myService"
  wsdl="http://localhost:8500/flex3bible/SoapService.cfc?wsdl"
  result="resultHandler(event)">
  <mx:operation name="getFilteredContacts">
    <mx:request>
      <firstname>{fnameInput.text}</firstname>
      <lastname>{lnameInput.text}</lastname>
    </mx:request>
  </mx:operation>
</mx:WebService>
```

When you call the Web service operation, you now must treat it as an operation object. Instead of calling the method directly, call the operation's `send()` method:

```
myService.getFilteredContacts.send();
```

> **TIP** Either explicit or bound parameters can be used effectively in Flex applications. I tend to use explicit parameters because, especially when calling an operation from different parts of an application, it makes it obvious where the parameters' values are coming from.

Figure 23.3 shows an application that uses server-side filtering through a call to a Web service.

> **ON the WEB** Applications that pass parameters to a Web service operation are available in the Web site files as `WebServiceExplicitParams.mxml` and `WebServiceBoundParams.mxml` in the `src` folder of the `chapter23` project.

FIGURE 23.3

Passing parameters to a Web service operation

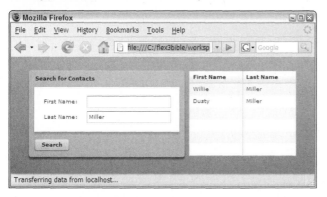

Using Web Service Introspection

Flex Builder 3 includes a new feature that allows you to examine the WSDL description of a Web service and generate ActionScript proxy classes that you can then use at runtime. When you "import" a Web service, you're allowing Flex Builder to help you create a more maintainable coding pattern that has these benefits:

- Your code makes calls to local proxy methods instead of calling operations directly from the Web service. As a result, Flex Builder and the Flex compiler can do a better job with code completion and compile-time syntax checking.

- Local proxy methods are structured with required arguments. As a result, you get better code hints and completion.

- Returned data is strongly typed, with data types determined by the Web service's WSDL description.

- If a Web service operation uses a complex value object either as a parameter or a return value, a local proxy class is generated to match the operation's requirements. At runtime, data is delivered already "wrapped" in the strongly typed value objects, reducing the amount of code you have to write.

Importing a Web service

When you import a Web service, Flex Builder creates a set of ActionScript proxy classes that you call instead of the native `WebService` object. In order to import a Web service, you must know its `WSDL` location.

1. From the Flex Builder menu, select Data ➪ Import Web Service (WSDL).

2. As shown in Figure 23.4, select a source folder in which the generated proxy classes should be created and click Next.

FIGURE 23.4

Selecting a source folder

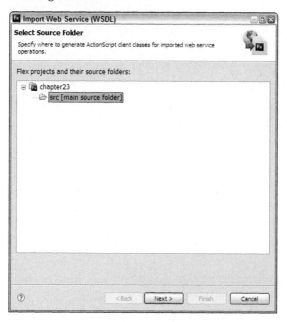

TIP   You should always select a project's source root folder or another location that's part of the project build path. The generated classes are created in a subdirectory structure underneath this location.

3. In the next screen, shown in Figure 23.5, enter the location of the Web service's WSDL file (its URI) and click Next.

TIP   The option to use a "destination" is enabled only if you create a Flex project that's configured to work with LiveCycle Data Services or BlazeDS. More information about this option is available in Chapter 25, in the section about the Proxy Service.

FIGURE 23.5

Selecting the WSDL URI

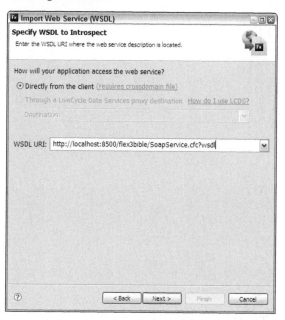

4. The final screen, shown in Figure 23.6, offers a number of configuration options:

   ▪ The Service and Port are selected automatically based on the contents of the Web service's WSDL file.

   ▪ The service's operations are listed, and are all selected by default. You can deselect operations for which you don't want to generate proxy code.

   ▪ The Package in which the generated code will be created defaults to a value of `generated.webservices`. You can change this to any other package you prefer.

   ▪ The Main class is the name of the ActionScript proxy class that will be generated. You can name this anything you like. It defaults to the name of the Web service with `Service` appended to the end.

FIGURE 23.6

Configuring code generation

When a Web service already has the word `Service` in its name, you'll see something like `SoapServiceService` as the default. There's no problem with removing the extra `Service` and setting the proxy class's name to the same value as the Web service's name. Alternatively, you can replace the last `Service` with the word `Proxy` to create an ActionScript class named, in this case, `SoapServiceProxy`. In the following examples, the generated ActionScript proxy class for the ColdFusion SoapService is `SoapServiceProxy`, located in the default package and subfolder structure `generated.webservices`.

Managing Web services

After importing a Web service, your Flex project source root has a new subfolder structure matching the package you selected for code generation. The folder contains the primary proxy class, such as `SoapServiceProxy`, plus many other supporting ActionScript classes, as shown in Figure 23.7.

In addition, a copy of the service's WSDL file is saved to a `.wsdl/general` subfolder of the project root; this file is not part of the source code and is saved to support Flex Builder's Web service management tools. This copy of the WSDL can be helpful if you need to look at the service's description and don't want to go back to the server.

You can open the Manage Web Services dialog box by selecting Data ⇨ Manage Web Services from the Flex Builder menu. As shown in Figure 23.8, the dialog box displays all currently imported Web services.

FIGURE 23.7

The Flex Navigator view displaying generated ActionScript proxy classes

FIGURE 23.8

Managing Web services

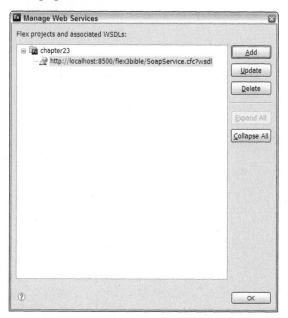

The Manage Web Services dialog box supports these options:

- **Click Add** to import a new Web service. This takes you to the first screen of the Import Web Service (WSDL) wizard.

- **Select a Web service, and click Update** to modify the currently generated code. This takes you to the Configure Code Generation screen of the Import Web Service (WSDL) wizard.

- **Select a Web service, and click Delete** to remove the proxy WSDL file and all the Web service's generated classes. This operation is permanent; deleted files can't be easily recovered.

Using generated Web service proxy classes

Each Web service operation that you select for import is represented within the primary proxy class by an ActionScript method of the same name and signature, and a custom `result` event that's dispatched when the operation's data is returned from the server. Each operation also is represented by custom request and event classes that have strong data typing based on the operation's WSDL definition.

Creating a proxy class instance

To use the proxy classes, start by creating an instance of the primary proxy class. You can create an instance of the proxy class in either MXML or ActionScript. The following code creates an instance of the proxy class and assigns it a unique `id`:

```
<webservices:SoapServiceProxy id="myService"/>
```

In this example, the `webservices` namespace prefix is bound to the location of the generated ActionScript code with a custom namespace declaration in the `<mx:Application>` root element:

```
<mx:Application xmlns:mx="http://www.adobe.com/2006/mxml"
    xmlns:webservices="generated.webservices.*">
```

You also can choose to instantiate the proxy class with ActionScript:

```
import generated.webservices.SoapServiceProxy;
[Bindable]
private var myService:SoapServiceProxy = new SoapServiceProxy();
```

> **TIP**   In this example, the `[Bindable]` metadata tag ensures that any bindings to the proxy class's properties are executed when their values change at runtime. If you use event handlers only to process returned data, not binding expressions, the `[Bindable]` tag isn't necessary.

Calling a Web service operation

After the proxy class has been instantiated, you call the Web service operation by calling the equivalent method of the proxy class. For example, the `getAllContacts()` operation is represented in the generated proxy class with this method:

```
public function getAllContacts():AsyncToken
{
  var _internal_token:AsyncToken = _baseService.getAllContacts();
  _internal_token.addEventListener("result",_
    getAllContacts_populate_results);
  _internal_token.addEventListener("fault",throwFault);
  return _internal_token;
}
```

The following code calls the remote operation by calling the equivalent proxy class method:

```
myService.getAllContacts()
```

Passing parameters

As when calling Web service operations directly, you can pass parameters with either explicit or bound notation. Explicit parameters are enforced by the proxy method signature, which uses the WSDL description to generate a set of required arguments:

```
public function getFilteredContacts(firstname:String,
  lastname:String):AsyncToken
{
  ... function body ...
}
```

As when calling the operation directly, you pass values into the proxy method in the order of their declaration. For example, in the application that requests filtered data from the server, this code would pass values from visual controls into the proxy method:

```
myService.getFilteredContacts(fnameInput.text, lnameInput.text);
```

The code looks exactly the same as when calling the operation directly, but you gain the advantage of compiler-level enforcement of the method signature.

If you prefer to use bound parameters, you can use the custom request object for the selected method. For example, when you import the getFilteredContacts() operation, a custom request object is created named GetFilteredContacts_request. This is passed to the proxy class as its custom getFilteredContacts_request_var property. The custom request object has properties matching the Web service operation parameters by name.

This code uses bound parameter syntax to pass values to the proxy service:

```
<webservices:SoapServiceProxy id="myService">
  <webservices:getFilteredContacts_request_var>
    <webservices:GetFilteredContacts_request
      firstname="{fnameInput.text}"
      lastname="{lnameInput.text}"/>
  </webservices:getFilteredContacts_request_var>
</webservices:SoapServiceProxy>
```

To support sending a request with bound parameters at runtime, the proxy class has custom send() methods for each imported operation. This code sends the operation request with the bound parameters:

```
myService.getFilteredContacts_send();
```

Handling returned data with binding expressions

The proxy class has a custom bindable lastResult property for each imported operation. For example, data returned from the getFilteredContacts() operation is represented in the proxy class by a property named getFilteredContents_lastResult. The property's data type is declared based on the operation's WSDL description. In contrast to working with the weakly typed WebService.operation.lastResult property, the result data is already typed correctly.

This DataGrid component displays the results of a call to the proxied getFilteredContacts() operation:

```
<mx:DataGrid
  dataProvider="{myService.getFilteredContacts_lastResult}"/>
```

The application in Listing 23.5 uses bindings for both Web service operation parameters and to display the operation's returned results.

LISTING 23.5

Using generated Web service proxy classes with parameter and result bindings

```
<?xml version="1.0" encoding="utf-8"?>
<mx:Application xmlns:mx="http://www.adobe.com/2006/mxml"
  layout="horizontal" xmlns:webservices="generated.webservices.*">
  <webservices:SoapServiceProxy id="myService">
    <webservices:getFilteredContacts_request_var>
      <webservices:GetFilteredContacts_request
        firstname="{fnameInput.text}"
        lastname="{lnameInput.text}"/>
    </webservices:getFilteredContacts_request_var>
  </webservices:SoapServiceProxy>
  <mx:Panel title="Search for Contacts" id="searchPanel">
    <mx:Form>
      <mx:FormItem label="First Name:">
        <mx:TextInput id="fnameInput"/>
      </mx:FormItem>
      <mx:FormItem label="Last Name:">
        <mx:TextInput id="lnameInput"/>
      </mx:FormItem>
    </mx:Form>
    <mx:ControlBar>
      <mx:Button label="Search"
```

```
            click="myService.getFilteredContacts_send()"/>
      </mx:ControlBar>
   </mx:Panel>
   <mx:DataGrid
     dataProvider="{myService.getFilteredContacts_lastResult}">
      <mx:columns>
         <mx:DataGridColumn dataField="firstName" headerText="First Name"/>
         <mx:DataGridColumn dataField="lastName" headerText="Last Name"/>
      </mx:columns>
   </mx:DataGrid>

</mx:Application>
```

> **ON the WEB** The code in Listing 23.5 is available in the Web site files as `WebServiceProxyWith` `Bindings.mxml` in the `src` folder of the `chapter23` project.

Listening for custom result events

The proxy class includes a custom `result` event for each imported operation. For example, the `getFilteredContacts()` operation dispatches an event named `GetFilteredContacts_result`. If you're declaring the proxy object in MXML, you can declare an attribute-based event listener:

```
<webservices:SoapServiceProxy id="myService"
  GetFilteredContacts_result="resultHandler(event)"/>
```

If you prefer to use ActionScript, you can use customized `addEventListener()` functions that are generated in the proxy class for each imported operation. This code declares an event listener for the `getFilteredContacts()` operation:

```
myService.addgetFilteredContactsEventListener(resultHandler);
```

> **TIP** Notice that the customized version of the `addEventListener()` method doesn't require an event name. Because you've already indicated by the use of the custom method which operation's `result` event you're listening for, you only need to pass in the name of the event handler function.

> **TIP** The proxy class declares a single `fault` event that's used by all the Web service's operations. Like the standard `WebService` component's `fault` event, it generates an event object typed as the `FaultEvent` class.

Handling custom result events

Each imported operation's custom `result` event object is typed as a custom event class that's also generated during the import process. For example, the custom event class for the `getFilteredContacts()` operation is named `GetFilteredContactsResultEvent`; its `result` property, like the custom `lastResult` proxy class property described in the previous section about handling results with binding expressions, is declared based on the operation's WSDL description.

This custom event handler function uses a single event argument typed as the imported service's custom event class:

```
private function resultHandler(
  event:GetFilteredContactsResultEvent):void
{
  contactData = event.result;
}
```

The application in Listing 23.6 uses ActionScript code to set up event listeners, call an operation's proxy method with explicit parameters, and handle event results.

LISTING 23.6

Using generated Web service proxy classes with ActionScript

```
<?xml version="1.0" encoding="utf-8"?>
<mx:Application xmlns:mx="http://www.adobe.com/2006/mxml"
  layout="horizontal" xmlns:webservices="generated.webservices.*"
  creationComplete="initApp()">
<mx:Script>
  <![CDATA[
    import mx.collections.ArrayCollection;
    import generated.webservices.GetFilteredContactsResultEvent;
    import generated.webservices.SoapServiceProxy;

    [Bindable]
    private var contactData:ArrayCollection;
    private var serviceProxy:SoapServiceProxy = new
SoapServiceProxy();

    private function initApp():void
    {
      serviceProxy.addgetFilteredContactsEventListener(resultHandler);
    }
    private function resultHandler(
      event:GetFilteredContactsResultEvent):void
    {
      contactData = event.result;
    }
    private function getContacts():void
    {
      serviceProxy.getFilteredContacts(fnameInput.text,
lnameInput.text);
    }
```

```
        ]]>
      </mx:Script>
      <mx:Panel title="Search for Contacts" id="searchPanel">
        <mx:Form>
          <mx:FormItem label="First Name:">
            <mx:TextInput id="fnameInput"/>
          </mx:FormItem>
          <mx:FormItem label="Last Name:">
            <mx:TextInput id="lnameInput"/>
          </mx:FormItem>
        </mx:Form>
        <mx:ControlBar>
          <mx:Button label="Search"
            click="getContacts()"/>
        </mx:ControlBar>
      </mx:Panel>
      <mx:DataGrid dataProvider="{contactData}">
        <mx:columns>
          <mx:DataGridColumn dataField="firstName" headerText="First Name"/>
          <mx:DataGridColumn dataField="lastName" headerText="Last Name"/>
        </mx:columns>
      </mx:DataGrid>
    </mx:Application>
```

ON the WEB   The code in Listing 23.6 is available in the Web site files as `WebServiceProxy` `WithAS.mxml` in the `src` folder of the `chapter23` project.

Summary

In this chapter, I described how to integrate Flex applications with SOAP-based Web services. You learned the following:

- SOAP is an XML-based industry-standard messaging format used in RPC-style applications.

- SOAP client and server software is designed to be interoperable across operating systems and programming languages.

- The Flex framework's `WebService` component encapsulates the process of sending and receiving SOAP-based messages.

- Like the other RPC components, the `WebService` component uses asynchronous communications.

- You can create and configure `WebService` objects in either MXML or ActionScript code.

- Flex Builder 3 can import Web services and generate proxy classes that you can call instead of the `WebService` component.

Chapter 24

Integrating Flex Applications with BlazeDS and Java

Flex was originally created by Macromedia in 2004 in the form of a server-based product. The Flex server incorporated the Flash Remoting technology that had been pioneered in ColdFusion and adapted its capabilities to work with Java-based classes stored in the server. Flex applications in their earliest incarnation were stored as source code on the server and compiled on demand when a browser made a request for the application's source code (its .mxml file). A command-line compiler was included for those developers who wanted to pre-build their applications prior to deployment. (Flex Builder 1 was a completely different product than the IDE used today and was based on the Dreamweaver code base. It was provided to developers as part of the Flex server license.)

When Flex 2 was released in 2006, the product line's client-side and server-side capabilities were separated. The Flex 2 SDK, including the client-side class library and the command-line tools, was made available as a no-royalty, no-license-fee product, and the new Flex Builder 2 was based on Eclipse and sold with fee-based, per-developer license The server-side functionality, including the Flash Remoting technology (now known as the Remoting Service) was packaged as Flex Data Services 2. In addition to the remoting tools that were included in Flex 1 and 1.5, Flex Data Services added services to support server-pushed communications for messaging and distributed database applications.

In 2007, Flex Data Services was renamed as LiveCycle Data Services, with the intent of strong integration with Adobe's existing LiveCycle product line. Some new features were added, such as server-side PDF generation, but the product's licensing and intended usage didn't change enormously. LiveCycle Data Services (referred to in this chapter as *LCDS*) remained the primary server-side solution for Flex developers who wanted to integrate their applications with Java-based application servers.

LiveCycle Data Services Features

LiveCycle Data Services includes many other features that aren't part of BlazeDS:

- The Data Management Service allows you to create applications with distributed data that's synchronized in real time between multiple clients and servers. This service also supports automated data paging, allowing you to use Flex data visualization components with large data sets without overloading Flash Player memory.

- RTMP (Real Time Messaging Protocol) allows you to build applications with highly scaled server-push messaging and distributed data.

- An agent process for Mercury QuickTestPro 9.1 enables Flex applications to be tested with Mercury QuickTest Professional, also known as HP QuickTest Professional since Mercury's acquisition by HP in 2006.

- Software clustering when using stateful services and non-HTTP channels, such as RTMP, ensures that Flex applications continue running in the event of server failure.

- You can generate template-driven PDF documents that include graphical assets from Flex applications, such as graphs and charts.

- For AIR developers, local data cache allows developers to cache client data requests and data changes to the local file system for later retrieval when an application resumes.

LiveCycle Data Services, in fact, is worthy of much more coverage than is possible in this book. For more information, see Adobe's Web site:

```
www.adobe.com/products/livecycle/dataservices
```

In February 2008, Adobe released BlazeDS, a free open-source implementation of many of LCDS's features. BlazeDS includes support for the Remoting Service, plus two of LCDS's other popular features, the Message Service and the Proxy Service. Unlike LCDS, which remains an enterprise-level product both in terms of scalability and pricing, BlazeDS can be used freely without any license fees or registration.

The point of all this history is that features that were available only in an enterprise-level server product upon the initial release of Flex are now available at zero cost to any organization or individual who wants to learn how to use them. In this chapter, I describe how to get and install BlazeDS, and how to use two of its features, the Proxy Service and the Remoting Service. In Chapter 25, I describe how to use the Message Service to share data between Flex applications and other messaging clients in real time.

ON the WEB   To use the sample code for this chapter, download `chapter24.zip` from the Web site.

The Web site .zip file for this and following chapters are not built as Flex project archive files. Follow the instructions later in this chapter to create a Flex project for use with LiveCycle Data Services or BlazeDS and install the various project assets to the client and server.

Using BlazeDS

BlazeDS is an open-source, freely available implementation of Java-based server-side functionality that's designed to deliver data and process messages from Flex applications at runtime. It includes the following features that are shared with LiveCycle Data Services:

- **The Proxy Service** supports proxying of HTTP requests and responses between Flex applications and remote servers. This service typically is used when direct communication between clients and servers is restricted due to cross-domain security issues.

- **The Remoting Service** is a server-side gateway that allows Flex applications to call methods of server-side Java classes using binary AMF (Action Message Format).

- **The Message Service** supports collaboration between Flex applications through a hub-and-spokes messaging architecture. Flex applications send messages to BlazeDS, and BlazeDS broadcasts the messages to other connected clients.

Understanding supported platforms

BlazeDS is supported on the following operating systems:

- Windows 2000, 2003, x86, and x64

- Red Hat Enterprise Linux AS 4, x86, and x64

- Red Hat Enterprise Linux Server, Advanced Platform 5, x86, and x64

- SUSE Linux Enterprise Server 9, 10, x86, and x64

- Solaris 9, 10 SPARC

 **Although not officially supported or noted in the product documentation, the first distribution of BlazeDS appears to work just fine on Mac OS X.**

BlazeDS can be installed on and hosted with many Java Enterprise Edition application servers, including:

- Apache Tomcat 6 (included in the BlazeDS turnkey distribution)

- JBoss

- IBM WebSphere

- BEA WebLogic

- Adobe JRun

BlazeDS requires a Java Development Kit installation, with a minimum required version of JDK 5. The turnkey distribution that includes Tomcat 6 does not include a JDK. On a Windows-based development or server system, you must download and install the JDK (most likely from Sun Microsystems) before running Tomcat.

The End of JRun

In late 2007, Adobe announced that it would discontinue new feature development for JRun, its own Java Enterprise Edition application server. The packaging of BlazeDS with Tomcat instead of JRun represents Adobe's first move away from JRun, which has been the default application server for Flex/LiveCycle Data Services, ColdFusion, and many other server-based products.

While JRun was one of the first Java servlet container applications, its lack of market share and the availability of free Java-based application servers such as Tomcat and JBoss drove the decision to move to other products. If you already use and are happy with JRun, there's no reason to stop using it, but as the Java-based application server market continues to evolve, JRun will eventually become a less compelling choice.

Getting started with BlazeDS

BlazeDS is hosted at Adobe's Open Source Web site and can be downloaded from `http://opensource.adobe.com/blazeds`. In addition to product downloads, this page includes links to the product's release notes, bug database, support forums, and developer documentation. As an open-source project, Adobe welcomes submissions of proposed patches for the product.

Downloading BlazeDS

Multiple download options are available for BlazeDS:

- The release builds are binary distributions that have been tested and declared stable and ready for production use.

- The nightly builds are binary distributions that are built with all the latest features and source code but haven't been fully tested.

- The product source code for the most recent release build is available for download as an archive file in .zip format.

- The latest product source code can be checked out from the source repository using any Subversion client. This source code is not tested or certified. As the product page says:

  "The Subversion repository should only be used if you want to be on the bleeding-edge of the development effort. The code contained in them may fail to work, or it may even eat your hard drive."

For the purposes of this chapter, I'll assume you're opting for safety and reliability and want to download a release build. (This is in contrast to the adventure and excitement that attend the nightly builds or the source code repository.) Two versions of the release build are available:

- A **turnkey** distribution that includes a preconfigured copy of Tomcat 6
- A **binary** distribution that includes WAR (Web Application Archive) files that can be deployed on any supported application server.

To download the turnkey distribution, follow these steps:

1. In any Web browser, navigate to `http://opensource.adobe.com/blazeds`.
2. Click Download BlazeDS now.
3. Review the Terms of Use.
4. If you accept the Terms of Use, click Download the latest BlazeDS Release builds.
5. Click Download the BlazeDS turnkey.

The turnkey distribution is delivered in a .zip file; the most recent release as of this writing was a file named `blazeds_turnkey_3-0-0-544.zip`. The .zip file can be extracted to any folder on your hard disk. If you want to match the Windows configuration used in this chapter's sample code, extract the files to a new folder named `C:\blazeds`. If you're working on Mac OS X or another operating system, extract the files to any location and then adapt the instructions throughout this chapter to your custom BlazeDS location.

The turnkey installation includes three complete instances of BlazeDS. Each BlazeDS instance is included as a WAR file in the installation folder root and also is extracted as a working application in the Tomcat server's `webapps` folder:

- `blazeds.war` contains a starting copy of BlazeDS. To start a new BlazeDS installation, deploy `blazeds.war` to your application server. The same application is included in the turnkey installation in the `webapps/blazeds` folder.

- `samples.war` contains a completed BlazeDS instance with deployed release builds of the sample applications, required configurations, and documentation. The same application is included in the turnkey installation in the `webapps/samles` folder.

- `ds-console.war` contains a management console application that makes calls to a Remoting Service destination to provide runtime information about various service activities. The same application is included in the turnkey installation in the `webapps/ds-console` folder.

To create a new BlazeDS installation on Tomcat, copy `blazeds.war` to a filename of your choosing, such as `myblazeds.war`. Then copy the new version of the file to Tomcat's `webapps` folder. Tomcat detects the presence of the new file and extracts it to a new context root with the same name.

Starting BlazeDS in Windows

To start the Tomcat server in Windows, you first must have installed a Java Development Kit. The server requires an environment variable named `JAVA_HOME` that points to the root folder of the JDK.

WEB RESOURCE You can download a free copy of the Java Development Kit from Sun Microsystems at `http://java.sun.com`.

Assuming you have a release of Sun's JDK5 installed on your system, follow these steps to start Tomcat in Windows:

1. Open a command window.

   ■ In Windows XP, click Start and choose Run. Then type `cmd`, and click OK.

   ■ In Windows Vista, open the Windows Start menu. Click into Start Search, type `cmd`, and press Enter.

2. Switch to the BlazeDS folder's `tomcat/bin` subfolder:

   ```
   cd \blazeds\tomcat\bin
   ```

3. Set the `JAVA_HOME` environment variable to point to your JDK's root folder. This command assumes that JDK version 1.5.15 is installed on your system in the default location:

   ```
   set JAVA_HOME=\Program Files\Java\jdk1.5.0_15
   ```

4. Type `startup`, and press Enter to run `Startup.bat` from the current folder.

As shown in Figure 24.1, Tomcat starts in a separate command window.

FIGURE 24.1

The Tomcat server running in a separate command window

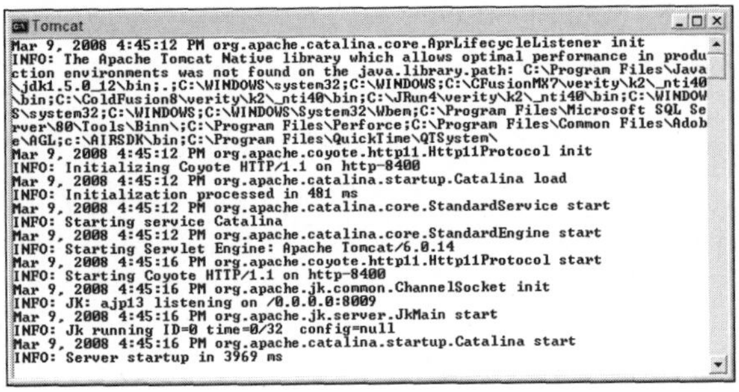

To shut down Tomcat in Windows, use either of these methods:

■ Close the command window in which it's running as an application.

■ Return to the original command window, and run the `shutdown.bat` batch file.

Starting BlazeDS on Mac OS X

As mentioned previously, BlazeDS and LCDS aren't officially supported on Mac OS X, but many developers use Mac systems as their primary development platform. Mac OS X comes equipped with an instance of the Java Development Kit, so unless your system has been otherwise configured, you shouldn't have to download and install the JDK. Just extract the turnkey distribution into any folder on your hard disk, and you should be ready to get started.

Follow these steps to start the version of Tomcat included with the turnkey distribution of BlazeDS on Mac OS X:

1. Open Terminal from `/Applications/Utilities`.

2. Switch to `tomcat/bin` in the folder in which you extracted the turnkey distribution. Assuming you extracted the distribution into `/Applications/blazeds`, this command would switch to the Tomcat server's `bin` folder:

    ```
    cd /Applications/blazeds/tomcat/bin
    ```

3. Start Tomcat with this command:

    ```
    ./startup.sh
    ```

4. To stop Tomcat when you're finished, use this command in Terminal:

    ```
    ./shutdown.sh
    ```

Starting the sample database

The turnkey distribution of BlazeDS includes an HSQLDB database that's designed to run as a separate process. Before using any of the sample applications that are included with BlazeDS, you must start the database process.

In Windows, follow these steps to start the sample database:

1. Open a separate command window.

2. Switch to the `sampledb` folder under the BlazeDS root folder, and run the `startdb.bat` batch file:

    ```
    cd \blazeds\sampledb
    startdb
    ```

The database runs as long as you keep the command window open. When you close the command window, the database shuts down.

On Mac OS X, follow these steps:

1. Open a new Terminal window.

2. Switch to the `sampledb` folder under the BlazeDS root folder, and run `startdb.sh` from the current folder:

    ```
    cd /Applications/blazeds/sampledb
    ./startdb.sh
    ```

As with Windows, the database runs only as long as you keep the window open. To shut down the database, press Ctrl+C or shut down Terminal.

Using the samples application

The turnkey distribution includes a complete instance of BlazeDS that contains many sample applications. Each sample application includes complete source code to communicate with the sample database where necessary.

The copy of Tomcat that's included with the turnkey distribution is configured to run on port 8400 (not on port 8080 as a version of Tomcat downloaded directly from Apache might be). The samples application is stored in the Tomcat server's `webapps` folder under context root of `/samples`. To explore the sample applications from a browser, navigate to this URL in any Web browser:

```
http://localhost:8400/samples
```

As shown in Figure 24.2, the `samples` application's home page includes links to each of the applications. They include excellent examples of using the Message Service and Remoting Service to build complete Internet-enabled Flex applications with Java-based server resources.

FIGURE 24.2

The BlazeDS `samples` application's home page

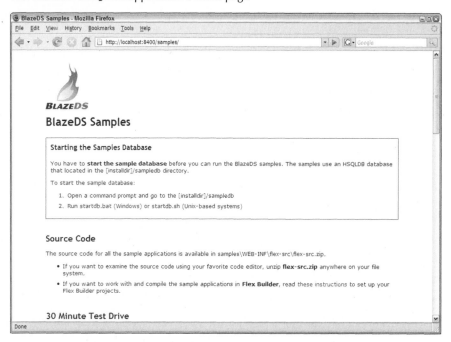

TIP   The sample applications are delivered as release builds; the folders from which they're executed don't contain Flex application source code. Instead, the Flex source code for all sample applications is delivered in a .zip file in the samples application as `WEB-INF/flex-src/flex-src.zip`.

Creating Flex Projects for Use with BlazeDS

When you create a new Flex project that will communicate with resources hosted by BlazeDS at run-time, Flex Builder allows you to add special configuration options that automate much of the creation and deployment of the Flex application. The Java server options in the initial release of Flex Builder 3 are labeled for LiveCycle Data Services, but they work equally well for a BlazeDS installation.

ON the WEB   The sample files for this chapter are in `chapter24.zip` on the Web site. Unlike the sample files for other chapters, this is not a Flex project archive, but rather a simple archive designed to be extracted after the project has been created.

Follow these steps to create a new Flex project for deployment with BlazeDS:

1. Select File ⇨ New ⇨ Flex Project from the Flex Builder menu.

2. Set the project name to **chapter24**.

3. Use the default project location, which should be a folder named `chapter24` under the current workspace. (Assuming you are compiling locally, rather than using the SDK on the server to compile the application upon request, you can place the project anywhere on your hard disk.)

4. Set the Application type to **Web application**.

5. Set the Application server type to **J2EE**.

6. Select **Use remote object access service** and **LiveCycle Data Services**.

7. If you see an option labeled "Create combined Java/Flex project using WTP," deselect it.

8. Click Next.

TIP   The option labeled "Create combined Java/Flex project using WTP" appears only if you've installed the Web Tools Platform project as an Eclipse plug-in. If you don't see these options, it just means that you haven't installed this additional plug-in. The WTP tools provide support for advanced Java constructs and allow developers to work with Flex and Java in a combined environment. More information about the WTP project is available at `www.eclipse.org/webtools/`.

9. The Server location defaults to a default installation of LiveCycle Data Services. As shown in Figure 24.3, deselect the option labeled "Use default location for local LiveCycle Data Services server" and set the Server location to the correct location of BlazeDS. For a default installation in Windows, set the properties as follows:

   ▪ Root folder: `c:\blazeds\tomcat\webapps\blazeds`

   ▪ Root URL: `http://localhost:8400/blazeds`

   ▪ Context root: `/blazeds`

FIGURE 24.3

Setting the location of BlazeDS

10. Check to be sure that BlazeDS is currently running. Then click Validate Configuration to verify that the Web root folder and root URL are valid.

11. Accept all other default values, and click Next.

12. Set the Main application filename to `HelloFromBlazeDS.mxml`.

13. Click Finish to create the application and project.

14. If you want to use the sample files from the Web site, extract `chapter24.zip` into the new project folder. This will result in overwriting your default Main application file and adding other required MXML and ActionScript source files.

15. Return to Flex Builder, and run the main application. As shown in Figure 24.4, the application should load from the BlazeDS URL of `http://localhost:8400/blazeds/HelloFromBlazeDS.html`.

FIGURE 24.4

Downloading and running the main application from BlazeDS

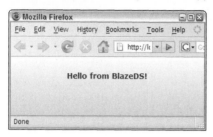

To use the server-side samples for this chapter, locate `blazedsFiles.zip` in the `chapter24` project. This archive file contains Java classes, updated configuration files, and other required resources for this chapter. Follow these steps to install the files before trying any of the chapter's applications:

1. If the application server that's hosting BlazeDS is currently running, shut it down.

2. Make backup copies of the following files in the BlazeDS `WEB-INF/flex` folder:

   ■ `services-config.xml`

   ■ `proxy-config.xml`

   ■ `remoting-config.xml`

3. Extract `blazedsfiles.zip` to the BlazeDS context root folder. If you're using the turnkey distribution in Windows with the recommended installation location, extract the files to:

   `C:\blazeds\tomcat\webapps\blazeds`

4. Restart Tomcat or whichever application server you're using.

CAUTION   On Mac OS X, when you extract ZIP archive files and you accept the prompt to over-write the folder, the entire folder is replaced, thus deleting any files already in place. Be careful not to replace the folder. Instead, replace the files when prompted.

Using the Proxy Service

The Proxy Service is one of BlazeDS's primary features. It allows you to use BlazeDS as a proxy for requests to servers in remote domains that would otherwise require the creation and placement of a cross-domain policy file.

As described in Chapter 21, when a Flex application (or, for that matter, any Flash document) makes an HTTP request, Flash Player first determines whether the domain of the request matches the domain from which the Flash document was downloaded. If the two domains don't match in any way, Flash Player makes a preliminary request for a file named `crossdomain.xml` that must be stored in the remote domain's Web root folder.

In many cases, it's difficult or impossible to get the cross-domain policy file where you need it. For example, if the content comes from a data syndication vendor, the vendor may be unaware of the need for, or unwilling to create and place, the cross-domain policy file. In this scenario, BlazeDS can help.

As shown in Figure 25.5, when you use the Proxy Service, requests from the `WebService` or `HTTPService` components are routed from the Flex application to BlazeDS at runtime. BlazeDS forwards the request to the remote domain. When the response from the remote domain is received, BlazeDS forwards the response back to the Flex client application.

FIGURE 25.5

The request to a remote domain is sent from the Flex application to BlazeDS when using the Proxy Service

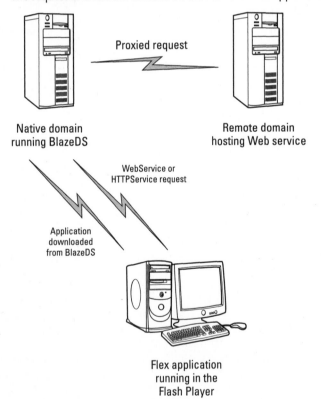

Proxied request

Native domain
running BlazeDS

Remote domain
hosting Web service

WebService or
HTTPService request

Application
downloaded
from BlazeDS

Flex application
running in the
Flash Player

Configuring the Proxy Service

The Proxy Service can proxy requests from the Flex framework's `WebService` and `HTTPService` components. You configure the service in nearly the same manner when creating a proxy for SOAP-based Web services or REST-style resources stored in on a remote domain.

The configuration files for LiveCycle Data Services and BlazeDS are stored in a folder under the application's context root folder named `WEB-INF/flex`. The turnkey installation's BlazeDS context root, the folder `WEB-INF/flex`, contains these files:

- `services-config.xml` is the primary configuration file that contains basic configurations and instructions to include all other files listed here.
- `remoting-config.xml` contains configurations for the Remoting Service.
- `messaging-config.xml` contains configurations for the Message Service.
- `proxy-config.xml` contains configurations for the Proxy Service.

> **TIP** The configuration folder for LiveCycle Data Services also includes the **data-management-config.xml** file with configurations for the Data Management Service.

The default `services-config.xml` file in a new BlazeDS installation contains these `<service-include>` elements that include the individual configuration files for each service:

```
<service-include file-path="remoting-config.xml" />
<service-include file-path="proxy-config.xml" />
<service-include file-path="messaging-config.xml" />
```

All configuration options for the Proxy Service should be placed in `proxy-config.xml`.

> **TIP** After making changes to any of the configuration files, you typically have to redeploy the BlazeDS instance. The deployment method differs between application servers. In Tomcat, you can force redeployment by making any small change to the context root's **web.xml** file (located in the **WEB-INF** folder) and saving it to disk. Tomcat is configured by default to listen for changes to this file and redeploy the context root when it notices that the file has been updated.

Using the default destination

A *destination* in the world of LiveCycle Data Services and BlazeDS is a resource hosted by the application server to which requests can be sent from a Flex application. A Proxy Service destination gives permission to BlazeDS to proxy a request and, in some cases, defines an alias that can be used in the Flex application instead of the actual URL where the Web resource is stored.

There are two kinds of Proxy Service destinations:

- The default destination supports proxying `HTTPService` requests to multiple resources through the use of dynamic URL declarations and wildcard characters.
- Named destinations create aliases that can be used by both `HTTPService` and `WebService` in a Flex application instead of the actual resource `url` or `wsdl` settings.

The default destination is defined by a reserved id of DefaultHTTP. The initial contents of proxy-config.xml, shown in Listing 24.1, includes the default destination but doesn't attach it to any URL patterns.

LISTING 24.1

The default contents of proxy-config.xml

```xml
<?xml version="1.0" encoding="UTF-8"?>
<service id="proxy-service"
  class="flex.messaging.services.HTTPProxyService">
  <properties>
    <connection-manager>
      <max-total-connections>100</max-total-connections>
      <default-max-connections-per-host>2</default-max-connections-per-
  host>
    </connection-manager>
    <allow-lax-ssl>true</allow-lax-ssl>
  </properties>
  <adapters>
    <adapter-definition id="http-proxy"
      class="flex.messaging.services.http.HTTPProxyAdapter"
  default="true"/>
    <adapter-definition id="soap-proxy"
      class="flex.messaging.services.http.SOAPProxyAdapter"/>
  </adapters>
  <default-channels>
    <channel ref="my-amf"/>
  </default-channels>
  <destination id="DefaultHTTP">
  </destination>
</service>
```

CAUTION   The default destination's id of DefaultHTTP is case-sensitive. If you spell it in the configuration file with all uppercase or lowercase letters, or with a different mixed case, it isn't recognized by BlazeDS.

The default destination can include one or more <dynamic-url> elements nested within a <properties> element. Each <dynamic-url> element declares a URL pattern that gives permission for requests that match the pattern to use the Proxy Service.

The following version of the default destination allows proxying of requests to resources on two different Web sites:

```
<destination id="DefaultHTTP">
  <properties>
    <dynamic-url>http://www.remotedomain.com/*</dynamic-url>
    <dynamic-url>http://www.anotherdomain.com/*</dynamic-url>
  </properties>
</destination>
```

You also can give global permission to the Proxy Service to proxy requests to any site with a <dynamic-url> element set to the * wildcard character:

```
<destination id="DefaultHTTP">
  <properties>
    <dynamic-url>*</dynamic-url>
  <properties>
</destination>
```

CAUTION   You should give global Proxy Service permission only in an environment where you're sure that only your applications can make requests to BlazeDS. The default destination is delivered without any `<dynamic-url>` permissions, because this sort of declaration can create a security risk.

After you've declared the default destination, any HTTPService component can use the Proxy Service by setting its useProxy property to true. As long as the component's url or wsdl value matches at least one of the <dynamic-url> declarations, the Proxy Service will route the request as needed.

This HTTPService component, for example, uses a proxy to make a request for an XML file on a remote domain that's been given permission in the default destination:

```
<mx:HTTPService id="myHTTPService"
  url="http://www.remotedomain.com/somedata.xml"
  result="resultHandler(event)"
  fault="faultHandler(event)"
  useProxy="true"/>
```

TIP   In order to use the Proxy Service with the default configuration, a Web-based Flex application should be downloaded from BlazeDS at runtime. The application then automatically sends its requests back to the server from which it was downloaded.

TIP   Desktop Flex applications deployed with AIR don't need to use the Proxy Service. These applications aren't downloaded from the Web at runtime, so they aren't subject to the rules of the Web security sandbox and can make runtime requests directly to any domain.

The application in Listing 24.2 uses a proxied request for data in an XML file stored on the server.

LISTING 24.2

A Flex application using the Proxy Service

```
<?xml version="1.0" encoding="utf-8"?>
<mx:Application xmlns:mx="http://www.adobe.com/2006/mxml"
   layout="vertical">
  <mx:Script>
    <![CDATA[
      import mx.controls.Alert;
      import mx.rpc.events.FaultEvent;
      import mx.rpc.events.ResultEvent;
      import mx.collections.ArrayCollection;
      [Bindable]
      private var myData:ArrayCollection
      private function resultHandler(event:ResultEvent):void
      {
        myData = event.result.contacts.row;
      }
      private function faultHandler(event:FaultEvent):void
      {
        Alert.show(event.fault.faultString, event.fault.faultCode);
      }
    ]]>
  </mx:Script>
  <mx:HTTPService id="contactService"
    url="http://127.0.0.1:8400/blazeds/flex3bible/data/contacts.xml"
    result="resultHandler(event)"
    fault="faultHandler(event)"/>
  <mx:Button label="Get Data" click="contactService.send()"/>
  <mx:DataGrid dataProvider="{myData}"/>
</mx:Application>
```

ON the WEB   The code in Listing 24.2 is available in the Web site files as **DefaultProxy Destination.mxml** in the **src** folder of the **chapter24** project.

When you run the application in its current state, it correctly downloads and displays the requested data. If you remove the HTTPService component's useProxy property or set it to false, the request fails, because the domain of the XML file and the domain from which the application is downloaded don't match. The result is a security fault, as shown in Figure 24.6.

TIP   In the example in Listing 24.2, the HTTPService request triggers a cross-domain security violation, because the application is downloaded from http://localhost, while the HTTPService component's url property refers to http://127.0.0.1. While these two ways of representing the localhost domain are technically the same, Flash Player doesn't have any way of knowing it. Flash Player cannot match IP addresses to their DNS equivalents and doesn't even try.

FIGURE 24.6

A Flex application displaying a security fault

Using named destinations

A named Proxy Service destination uses an `id` other than `DefaultHTTP`. You can use a named destination in two ways:

- When the named destination contains a nested `<url>` element, it represents an alias for a single Web resource. The destination `id` can then be referred to in the Flex application instead of the actual `url`.

- When the named destination contains one or more nested `<dynamic-url>` elements, it can proxy multiple Web resources.

To create a named destination for `HTTPService` that serves as an alias for a single Web resource, add a single `<url>` element nested within the destination's `<properties>` element. Set the `<url>` element's text value to the explicit address of the Web resource. The following declaration creates a destination with an `id` of `contactsXML` that points to the location of the data in the remote domain:

```
<destination id="contactsXML">
  <properties>
    <url>
    http://127.0.0.1:8400/blazeds/flex3bible/data/contacts.xml
    </url>
  </properties>
</destination>
```

In the Flex application, set the `HTTPService` object's `destination` property to the id you configured in BlazeDS:

```
<mx:HTTPService id="contactService"
  destination="contactsXML"
  result="resultHandler(event)"
  fault="faultHandler(event)"/>
```

> **TIP**   When you set the `destination` property of a `WebService` or `HTTPService` object, its `useProxy` property is set to `true` automatically. Setting a `destination` and then setting `useProxy` to `false` wouldn't make any sense, because the `destination` refers to a Proxy Service resource on the server.

Try these steps to use a destination that's already been created in `proxy-config.xml`:

1. Open `DefaultProxyDestination.mxml`.

2. Select File ⇨ Save As... from the Flex Builder menu, and name the new file `NamedProxyDestination.mxml`.

3. Locate the `<mx:HTTPService>` tag.

4. Remove the `url` and `useProxy` properties.

5. Add a `destination` property set to **contactsXML**. The `HTTPService` declaration should look like this:

```
<mx:HTTPService id="contactService"
  destination="contactsXML"
  result="resultHandler(event)"
  fault="faultHandler(event)"/>
```

6. Run the new version of the application, and test retrieving data from the server.

The proxied request should be completed successfully.

> **ON the WEB**   The completed code for this exercise is available in the Web site files as `NamedProxy DestinationComplete.mxml` in the `src` folder of the `chapter24` project.

You also can include `<dynamic-url>` elements in a named destination, either along with or instead of the `<url>` element. This declaration uses the same destination and a dynamic `url`:

```
<destination id="contactsXML">
  <properties>
    <dynamic-url>http://localhost:8400/blazeds/*</dynamic-url>
  </properties>
</destination>
```

To use a dynamic `url` in a named destination, set the `HTTPService` or `WebService` object's `destination` and `url` properties. The `url` should match the pattern in the dynamic `url` in the `destination` that's defined on the server:

```
<mx:HTTPService id="contactService"
  destination="contactsXML"

  url="http://127.0.0.1:8400/blazeds/flex3bible/data/contacts.xm
  l"
  result="resultHandler(event)"
  fault="faultHandler(event)"/>
```

To use the Proxy Service with the Flex framework's `WebService` component, declare a named destination that uses an adapter named `soap-proxy`. Declare a nested `<soap>` property that points to the endpoint URI where service requests should be sent and, optionally, a `<wsdl>` element that indicates the location of the service's WSDL service description:

```
<destination id="contactsWS">
  <adapter ref="soap-proxy"/>
  <properties>
    <wsdl>/myapp/services/contactService?wsdl</wsdl>
    <soap>/myapp/services/contactService</soap>
  </properties>
</destination>
```

The `WebService` object in the Flex application then declares just the `destination` and sends requests to execute service operations to BlazeDS:

```
<mx:WebService id="myService"
  destination="contactsWS"
  result="resultHandler(event)"
  fault="faultHandler(event)"/>
```

Using the Remoting Service

The Remoting Service allows you to execute public methods of server-side Java classes hosted by LiveCycle Data Services or BlazeDS. The Flex application uses the `RemoteObject` component to execute the calls and handle results returned from the remote server.

The `RemoteObject` component is one of the Flex framework's three RPC components. The other two, the `WebService` and `HTTPService` components, have been described previously. Like these two, the `RemoteObject` component makes calls asynchronously and handles returned results with either binding expressions or event handlers.

The Remoting Service on the server and the `RemoteObject` component on the client use a binary format to transfer data back and forth. This format, AMF (Action Message Format), was originally created for ColdFusion's Flash Remoting technology and was then adapted for use with Java classes in Flex Data Services, LiveCycle Data Services, and now BlazeDS. Because this format is binary, the result is smaller data bundles and there is no need for resource-intensive XML parsing. In most cases, the result is better speed and performance.

AMF Documentation

In the past, a number of individuals and organizations reverse-engineered AMF to create open-source or commercial server implementations that are compatible with Flex applications. OpenAMF (`http://sourceforge.net/projects/openamf/`), Red5 (`http://osflash.org/red5`), AMFPHP (`www.amfphp.org`), and WebOrb (`www.themidnightcoders.com/weborb/java/`) all represent potential alternatives to Adobe's own products for providing AMF-based messaging with Java-based application servers.

In February 2008, Adobe Systems publicly documented both AMF0 and AMF3 so that organizations that had previously implemented AMF-capable servers could verify that their work matched the protocol exactly and to allow new participants in the world of Flex development to get it right the first time.

The AMF documentation is currently available from these links:

AMF0:
```
http://opensource.adobe.com/wiki/download/attachments/1114283/
amf0_spec_121207.pdf?version=1
```

AMF3:
```
http://opensource.adobe.com/wiki/download/attachments/1114283/
amf3_spec_121207.pdf?version=1
```

> **TIP**   There are two versions of AMF. The first version, now known as AMF0, was originally supported in earlier versions of ColdFusion and Flex 1.x. The newer version, known as AMF3, is supported by the current versions of ColdFusion, LiveCycle Data Services, and BlazeDS. Flex 3 applications make requests in AMF3 by default, but they can be configured to communicate in AMF0 when required.

Creating and exposing Java classes

The `RemoteObject` component can call public methods of any basic Java class that's been hosted and configured in LiveCycle Data Services or BlazeDS. (For convenience, I'll refer exclusively to BlazeDS for the rest of this chapter, but the functionality and techniques are exactly the same for LiveCycle Data Services.)

You need to follow two steps when making the Java methods available:

1. Create and compile a Java class, and place in the BlazeDS classpath.
2. Create a destination that points to the Java class on the server.

Any plain old Java Object (sometimes known as a "POJO") can be used through the Remoting Service. Classes written in other common Java design patterns, such as servlets and Enterprise Java Beans (EJBs), can't be called directly through the Remoting Service. If you have existing functionality already built in these formats, though, it's a fairly easy task to create a POJO to call from Flex that in turn makes calls on the server to existing functions.

Follow these rules for creating Java classes for use with the Remoting Service:

- All classes must be in the BlazeDS classpath.

    - For individual classes, you can accomplish this by placing them in BlazeDS's `WEB-INF/classes` folder. As with all Java Enterprise Edition applications, classes placed in this folder are automatically available to the application.

    - For classes stored in JAR (Java Archive) files, the JAR file can be placed in BlazeDS's `WEB-INF/lib` folder. As with all Java Enterprise Edition applications, archive files placed in this folder are automatically added to the classpath when the application is started.

- The Java class must have a no-arguments constructor method or no explicit constructor methods at all. At runtime, the Remoting Service gateway creates an instance of the Java class (static methods aren't supported). It assumes the presence of a constructor method that can be called with no arguments:

```
public ROService()
{
  System.out.println("constructor method called");
}
```

    If you create a class with no explicit constructor method, the Java compiler adds the no-arguments constructor for you. If there's at least one constructor method with arguments, though, you're responsible for creating the alternative constructor method with no arguments.

- All methods must be explicitly marked as `public`. Java allows you to drop the access modifier from a method declaration, but these methods aren't available to the Remoting Service. This simple Java-based method is suitable for use by the Remoting Service:

```
public String helloWorld()
{
  return "Hello from the world of Java!";
}
```

- You can't use a small set of reserved method names. These methods are used by the gateway library at runtime; if your class implements any of these method names, conflicts can result:

    - `addHeader()`
    - `addProperty()`
    - `clearUsernamePassword()`
    - `deleteHeader()`
    - `hasOwnProperty()`
    - `isPropertyEnumerable()`
    - `isPrototypeOf()`
    - `registerClass()`
    - `setUsernamePassword()`

- ▦ toLocaleString()
- ▦ toString()
- ▦ unwatch()
- ▦ valueOf()
- ▦ watch()

- ■ Method names should not start with an underscore (_) character.

Listing 24.3 shows the source code for a Java class named ROService in the flex3Bible package. It has an explicit no-arguments constructor method and a single method that returns a String value.

LISTING 24.3

A Java class suitable for use with the Remoting Service

```
package flex3Bible;
public class ROService
{
  public ROService() {
  }
  public String helloWorld() {
    return "Hello from the world of Java";
  }
  public List getArray() {
    Map stateObj;
    List ar = new ArrayList();
    stateObj = new HashMap();
    stateObj.put("capital", "Sacramento");
    stateObj.put("name", "California");
    ar.add(stateObj);
    stateObj = new HashMap();
    stateObj.put("capital", "Olympia");
    stateObj.put("name", "Washington");
    ar.add(stateObj);
    stateObj = new HashMap();
    stateObj.put("capital", "Salem");
    stateObj.put("name", "Oregon");
    ar.add(stateObj);
    return ar;
  }
  public String concatValues(String val1, String val2) {
    return "You passed values " + val1 +
      " and " + val2;
  }
```

```
public String setContact(Contact myContact) {
  return "Contact sent from server: " + myContact.getFirstName() + " "
 +
    myContact.getLastName();
}
public Contact getContact(String val1, String val2) {
  Contact myContact = new Contact();
  myContact.setFirstName(val1);
  myContact.setLastName(val2);
  return myContact;
}
}
```

ON the WEB The source code in Listing 24.3 is available in the Web site files as `ROService.java` in the BlazeDS `WEB-INF/src` folder. The compiled version of the class is stored in BlazeDS `WEB-INF/classes` folder.

TIP The no-arguments constructor method in Listing 24.3 isn't required as long as the class doesn't have any other constructor methods.

Configuring Remoting Service destinations

Each Java class you want to call from a Flex application with the Remoting Service must be configured as a destination in the BlazeDS configuration files. Remoting Service destinations are defined in `remoting-config.xml` in the BlazeDS `WEB-INF/flex` folder.

The default `remoting-config.xml` that's delivered with a fresh BlazeDS installation looks like this:

```
<?xml version="1.0" encoding="UTF-8"?>
<service id="remoting-service"
  class="flex.messaging.services.RemotingService">
  <adapters>
    <adapter-definition id="java-object"

  class="flex.messaging.services.remoting.adapters.JavaAdapter"
      default="true"/>
  </adapters>
  <default-channels>
    <channel ref="my-amf"/>
  </default-channels>
</service>
```

The `<channel>` element toward the bottom of the file indicates that Remoting Service communications are handled by default with AMF. The `my-amf` channel is defined in `services-config.xml` in the same folder and looks like this:

```
<channel-definition id="my-amf"
  class="mx.messaging.channels.AMFChannel">
  <endpoint url="http://{server.name}:{server.port}/
    {context.root}/messagebroker/amf"
    class="flex.messaging.endpoints.AMFEndpoint"/>
</channel-definition>
```

Notice that the `<endpoint>` element includes dynamic expressions (wrapped in curly braces) that refer to the server, port, and context root from which the application is downloaded at runtime. This is how the Flex application knows which server should receive requests for remote object method calls.

Each Java class you want to call from Flex must be configured as a destination. Each destination is declared as a child of the configuration file's `<service>` root element and looks like this in its simplest form:

```
<destination id="helloClass">
  <properties>
    <source>flex3Bible.ROService</source>
    <scope>application</scope>
  </properties>
</destination>
```

The `<destination>` element's `id` property is an arbitrary value that you use in the Flex application to refer to this class as a remote object. Within the `<properties>` element, you declare these two values:

- The `<source>` element is required and is set to the fully qualified name and package of the Java class that contains methods you want to call.

- The `<scope>` element is optional and is set to one these three values:

  - `application` means that a single instance of the Java class is constructed as BlazeDS starts up and is shared by all users and requests.

  - `session` means that a new instance of the Java class is constructed for each new browser session. As each user sends new requests, the session instances are tracked (via the host JEE application server's session management) with cookies that are automatically generated and tracked by BlazeDS and the hosting application server.

  - `request` (the default) means that a new instance of the Java class is constructed for each call to any of the class's methods.

> **TIP**   All other things being equal, you achieve the best performance and most efficient memory usage on the server with `<scope>` set to `application`. The only reason to use the default setting of `request` is if the Java class has code that can't be called safely by concurrent requests from multiple clients.

Using the RemoteObject Component

The Flex framework's `RemoteObject` component is used to represent a server-side Java class containing public methods you want to call from a Flex application. Just as the `HTTPService` component sends and receives requests with generic XML-formatted messages and the `WebService` component does with SOAP, the `RemoteObject` component makes requests and handles responses using the HTTP communication protocol.

The big difference with `RemoteObject` is the message format: Because AMF is binary, instead of the text-based XML languages used by the `WebService` and `HTTPService` components, messages formatted in AMF are a fraction of the size generated by the other RPC components. As a result, communication is faster, less network bandwidth is used, and larger data packets can be transferred between client and server.

Instantiating the RemoteObject component

As with the `HTTPService` and `WebService` components, you can instantiate `RemoteObject` in MXML or ActionScript code. When used with BlazeDS, you instantiate the object and set its destination property.

This MXML code creates an instance of the `RemoteObject` component that points to a server-side destination:

```
<mx:RemoteObject id="roHello" destination="helloClass"/>
```

The equivalent code in ActionScript looks like this:

```
import mx.rpc.remoting.RemoteObject;
private var roHello:RemoteObject = new RemoteObject("roHello");
```

Alternatively, you can first declare the object and then set its `destination`:

```
var roHello:RemoteObject = new RemoteObject();
roHello.destination = "roHello";
```

Calling remote methods

You call public methods of server-side Java classes as though they were local methods of the `RemoteObject`. For example, the Java class in Listing 24.3 has a public method named `helloWorld()` that returns a simple `String`. As with local functions, you can call the remote method upon any application event. For example, this code calls the server-side `helloWorld()` method upon a `Button` component's `click` event:

```
<mx:Button label="Click to say hello"
  click="roHello.helloWorld()"/>
```

You also can call a remote method by calling the `RemoteObject` object's `getOperation()` method to create an instance of the `Operation` class. The following code creates the `Operation` object and then calls its `send()` method to call the remote method:

```
import mx.rpc.remoting.mxml.Operation;
private function callIt():void
{
  var op:Operation = roHello.getOperation("helloWorld") as
   Operation;
  op.send();
}
```

This technique allows you to determine which remote method will be called at runtime, instead of having to hard code the method name.

Handling RemoteObject results

As with the other RPC components, you can handle data returned from a call to a remote method with binding expressions or event handlers. Binding expressions take less code and are easy to create, while an event handler gives you much more flexibility in how you receive, process, and save data to application memory.

Using binding expressions

A binding expression used to pass returned data to application components consists of three parts, separated with dots:

- The `RemoteObject` instance's `id`
- The remote method name
- The `lastResult` property

At runtime, the method is created as an Operation object that's a member of the `RemoteObject` instance with an `id` that matches the method's name. The Operation object's `lastResult` property is populated with data when it's received from the server.

The `lastResult` property is typed as an ActionScript `Object`, but at runtime its native type is determined by what type of data was returned from the server. A `String` returned from Java is translated into an ActionScript `String` value, so a binding expression that handles the value returned from the simple `helloWorld()` method can be used to pass the returned value to a `Label` or other text display control.

The application in Listing 24.4 calls the remote `helloWorld()` method and displays its returned data in a `Label` control with a binding expression in its text property.

Handling returned data with a binding expression

```xml
<?xml version="1.0" encoding="utf-8"?>
<mx:Application xmlns:mx="http://www.adobe.com/2006/mxml"
  backgroundColor="#EEEEEE">

  <mx:RemoteObject id="roHello" destination="helloClass"/>

  <mx:Label text="Hello from BlazeDS!" fontSize="14" fontWeight="bold"/>

  <mx:Button label="Click to say hello" click="roHello.helloWorld()"/>

  <mx:Label text="{roHello.helloWorld.lastResult}"
    fontSize="14" fontWeight="bold"/>

</mx:Application>
```

ON the WEB   The code in Listing 24.4 is available in the Web site files as `ROWithBindings.mxml` in the `src` folder of the `chapter24` project.

Using the result event

As with the other RPC components, you can handle results of a call to a remote method with the `RemoteObject` component's `result` event in an identical fashion. This event dispatches an event object typed as `mx.rpc.events.ResultEvent`, the same event object that's used by the other RPC components `HTTPService` and `RemoteObject`. The event object's `result` property references the returned data.

To handle and save data using the `result` event, follow these steps:

1. Declare a bindable variable outside of any functions that acts as a persistent reference to the returned data. Cast the variable's type depending on what you expect to be returned by the remote method. For example, if the data returned by the remote Java-based method is typed as a primitive array or an implementation of the Java `List` interface, the `RemoteObject` component casts the returned data as an `ArrayCollection`:

```
import mx.collections.ArrayCollection;
[Bindable]
private var myData:ArrayCollection
```

2. Create an event handler function that will be called when the event is dispatched. The function should receive a single event argument typed as `ResultEvent` and return `void`:

```
private function resultHandler(event:ResultEvent):void
{
}
```

3. Within the event handler function, use the `event.result` expression to refer to the data that's returned from the server. Just as with the `WebService` component, `ResultEvent.result` is typed as an `Object`. Because the expression's native type differs depending on what's returned by the remote method, you typically have to explicitly cast the returned data. This code expects the remote method to return an `ArrayCollection`:

```
myData = event.result as ArrayCollection;
```

You can listen for the `result` event with either an MXML attribute-based event listener or a call to the ActionScript `addEventListener()` method. The attribute-based event listener looks like this:

```
<mx:RemoteObject id="roHello" destination="helloClass"
   result="resultHandler(event)"/>
```

When using `addEventListener()` to create an event listener, you can designate the event name with the `String` value result or with the `ResultEvent` class's RESULT constant:

```
var roHello:RemoteObject = new RemoteObject("helloClass");
roHello.addEventListener(ResultEvent.RESULT, resultHandler);
roHello.helloWorld();
```

Listing 24.5 uses a `result` event handler function to capture and save data that's been returned from a remote method.

LISTING 24.5

Handling returned data with the result event

```
<?xml version="1.0" encoding="utf-8"?>
<mx:Application xmlns:mx="http://www.adobe.com/2006/mxml"
  backgroundColor="#EEEEEE">
  <mx:Script>
    <![CDATA[
      import mx.collections.ArrayCollection;
      import mx.rpc.events.ResultEvent;
      [Bindable]
      private var statesData:ArrayCollection;
      private function resultHandler(event:ResultEvent):void
      {
        statesData = event.result as ArrayCollection;
      }
    ]]>
  </mx:Script>
  <mx:RemoteObject id="roHello" destination="helloClass"
    result="resultHandler(event)"/>
  <mx:Button label="Get Array" click="roHello.getArray()"/>
  <mx:DataGrid dataProvider="{statesData}"/>
</mx:Application>
```

ON the WEB The code in Listing 24.5 is available in the Web site files as `ROResultEvent.mxml` in the `src` folder of the `chapter24` project.

TIP As with the other RPC components, exceptions that occur during execution of remote methods generate a `fault` event. The code to handle faults is exactly the same as with the other RPC components. For full description and some code examples, see Chapter 21 and Chapter 23.

TIP As with the `HTTPService` and `WebService` components, you can dispatch `result` and `fault` event objects to ActionScript event hander functions using the `ItemResponder` and `AsyncToken` classes. See Chapter 21 for details.

Working with multiple methods

When you need to call more than one method of a Java class on the server, you have to distinguish which event handler function should be called for each of them. You do this in MXML with the `<mx:method >` compiler tag, which is nested within a `<mx:RemoteObject>` tag set. Each `<mx:method >` tag represents a remote Java method and can declare its own distinct result and event handlers.

The Java class in Listing 24.6 has a number of different methods. Its `helloWorld()` method returns a `String`, `getArray()` returns a `List`, and so on.

LISTING 24.6

The Java class with methods being called from Flex

```java
package flex3Bible;
import java.util.ArrayList;
import java.util.HashMap;
import java.util.List;
import java.util.Map;
public class ROService {
  public String helloWorld()
  {
    return "Hello from the world of Java";
  }
  public List getArray()
  {
    Map stateObj;
    List ar = new ArrayList();
    stateObj = new HashMap();
    stateObj.put("capital", "Sacramento");
    stateObj.put("name", "California");
    ar.add(stateObj);
    stateObj = new HashMap();
    stateObj.put("capital", "Olympia");
    stateObj.put("name", "Washington");
```

```
      ar.add(stateObj);
      stateObj = new HashMap();
      stateObj.put("capital", "Salem");
      stateObj.put("name", "Oregon");
      ar.add(stateObj);
      return ar;
   }
   public String concatValues(String val1, String val2)
   {
      return "You passed values " + val1 +
         " and " + val2;
   }
   public String handleObject(Contact myContact)
   {
      return "You Contact # " + myContact.getContactId() + ": " +
         myContact.getFirstName() + " " + myContact.getLastName();
   }
}
```

ON the WEB   The code in Listing 24.6 is available in the Web site files as `ROService.java` in the BlazeDS application's `WEB-INF/src/flex3Bible` folder. The compiled version of the class is stored in `WEB-INF/classes`.

A Flex application that needs to call more than one of these methods would use the `<mx:method>` tag as in the following example:

```
<mx:RemoteObject id="roHello" destination="helloClass"
   result="arrayHandler(event)">
   <mx:method name="helloWorld" result="helloHandler(event)"/>
   <mx:method name="getArray" result="arrayHandler(event)"/>
</mx:RemoteObject>
```

Each method's custom event handler function would then expect the appropriate type of data to be returned from its remote method.

The application in Listing 24.7 handles the `result` events of multiple remote methods using an MXML declaration.

LISTING 24.7

Handling multiple remote methods' result events

```
<?xml version="1.0" encoding="utf-8"?>
<mx:Application xmlns:mx="http://www.adobe.com/2006/mxml"
   backgroundColor="#EEEEEE">
   <mx:Script>
     <![CDATA[
```

```
    import mx.collections.ArrayCollection;
    import mx.rpc.events.ResultEvent;

    [Bindable]
    private var statesData:ArrayCollection;
    [Bindable]
    private var helloString:String;

    private function arrayHandler(event:ResultEvent):void
    {
      statesData = event.result as ArrayCollection;
    }
    private function helloHandler(event:ResultEvent):void
    {
      helloString = event.result as String;
    }
  ]]>
  </mx:Script>
  <mx:RemoteObject id="roHello" destination="helloClass"
    result="arrayHandler(event)">
    <mx:method name="helloWorld" result="helloHandler(event)"/>
    <mx:method name="getArray" result="arrayHandler(event)"/>
  </mx:RemoteObject>
  <mx:Button label="Get String" click="roHello.helloWorld()"/>
  <mx:Label text="{helloString}" fontSize="14"/>
  <mx:Button label="Get Array" click="roHello.getArray()"/>
  <mx:DataGrid dataProvider="{statesData}"/>
</mx:Application>
```

ON the WEB   The code in Listing 24.7 is available as ROMultipleMethods.mxml in the src folder of the chapter24.zip file.

Passing arguments to remote methods

As with WebService operation parameters, you can pass arguments to remote methods using either explicit or bound argument notation. Explicit notation means that arguments are passed in the same order in which they're declared in the Java method.

This Java method, for example, requires two String arguments and returns a concatenated String:

```
    public String concatValues(String val1, String val2)
    {
      return "You passed values " + val1 +     " and " + val2;
    }
```

The following ActionScript code passes arguments to this remote method with explicit syntax:

```
    roHello.concatValues(fnameInput.text, lnameInput.text);
```

731

You also can use bound argument notation with XML elements for each argument wrapped in an `<mx:arguments>` tag set. This code binds the `concatValues()` method's two arguments to values gathered from `TextInput` controls:

```
<mx:RemoteObject id="roHello" destination="helloClass">
  <mx:method name="concatValues">
    <mx:arguments>
      <val1>{fnameInput.text}</val1>
      <val2>{lnameInput.text}</val2>
    </mx:arguments>
  </mx:method>
</mx:RemoteObject>
```

To call the method with the bound arguments, call the operation's `send()` method without any explicit arguments:

```
roHello.concatValues.send()
```

CAUTION You cannot pass arguments by name to Java-based remote methods using the Remoting Service. Although the bound arguments syntax makes it look like arguments are being matched by their names, in fact they're passed and received in the order of declaration in the Flex application and the Java method. It may seem odd, but in bound notation with Java, the names of the argument elements don't matter at all.

The application in Listing 24.8 passes explicit arguments to a remote method on the server and displays the returned result with a binding expression.

LISTING 24.8

Passing arguments using explicit notation

```
<?xml version="1.0" encoding="utf-8"?>
<mx:Application xmlns:mx="http://www.adobe.com/2006/mxml"
  backgroundColor="#EEEEEE">
  <mx:RemoteObject id="roHello" destination="helloClass"/>
  <mx:Form>
    <mx:FormItem label="First Name:">
      <mx:TextInput id="fnameInput"/>
    </mx:FormItem>
    <mx:FormItem label="Last Name:">
      <mx:TextInput id="lnameInput"/>
      <mx:Button label="Send Args"
        click="roHello.concatValues(fnameInput.text, lnameInput.text)"/>
    </mx:FormItem>
  </mx:Form>
  <mx:Label text="{roHello.concatValues.lastResult}"
    fontSize="14" fontWeight="bold"/>
</mx:Application>
```

ON the WEB The code in Listing 24.8 is available as `ROExplicitArgs.mxml` in the `src` folder of the `chapter24.zip` file. Another file named `ROBoundArgs.mxml`, not shown here, demonstrates the use of bound arguments.

Passing data between ActionScript and Java

Data passed from a Flex application to a Java class with the Remoting Service is serialized, or transformed, from ActionScript data types to their equivalent types in Java. When data is returned from Java to Flex, a similar serialization occurs.

Table 24.1 describes how data is serialized from ActionScript to Java and back again.

TABLE 24.1

ActionScript to Java Data Serialization

ActionScript	To Java	Back to ActionScript
Array (dense, meaning there are no "holes" in the indexing)	List	ArrayCollection
Array (sparse, meaning there is at least one gap in the indexing, or associative with non-numeric keys)	Map	Object
ArrayCollection	List	ArrayCollection
Boolean	java.lang.Boolean	Boolean
Date	java.util.Date	
int/uint	java.lang.Integer	int
null	null	null
Number	java.lang.Double	Number
Object	java.util.Map	Object
String	java.lang.String	String
undefined	null	null
XML	org.w3c.dom.Document	XML

Notice that data moved in both directions doesn't always survive the round trip with the same data type as it had at the beginning. For example, a "sparse" ActionScript `Array` is serialized as a Java implementation of the `Map` interface. When the same data is returned from Java to ActionScript, it arrives as an ActionScript `Object` instead of an `Array`.

There are additional data conversions when returning data from Java to a Flex application. For example, both the Java `Calendar` and `Date` objects become instances of an ActionScript `Date`. All non-integer Java data types, such as `Double`, `Long`, and `Float` are mapped to an ActionScript

Number. And numeric Java types that don't fit the precision limitations of the ActionScript Number type, such as `BigInteger` and `BigDecimal`, are mapped to an ActionScript `String`.

Using value object classes

When passing data between a Flex client application and a Java-based server, data objects are typically built using the Value Object design pattern. This pattern ensures that data is serialized in a precise manner and avoids the uncertainties of automatic object serialization described in the previous section.

> **TIP** The Value Object design pattern is known in various Flex and Java documentation sources as the Transfer Object and Data Transfer Object pattern. The different names are all used to refer to the same pattern: a class that contains data for a single instance of a data entity.

The Java version of the value object is written with classic bean-style syntax. Each value is declared as a private field of the class and has its values set at runtime with public `set` and `get` accessor methods.

The Java class in Listing 24.9 has three private fields with matching accessor methods and is suitable for use in a Flex application.

LISTING 24.9

A Java-based value object class

```java
package flex3Bible;
public class Contact {
  private int contactId;
  private String firstName;
  private String lastName;
  public int getContactId() {
    return contactId;
  }
  public void setContactId(int contactId) {
    this.contactId = contactId;
  }
  public String getFirstName() {
    return firstName;
  }
  public void setFirstName(String firstName) {
    this.firstName = firstName;
  }
  public String getLastName() {
    return lastName;
  }
  public void setLastName(String lastName) {
    this.lastName = lastName;
  }
}
```

ON the WEB The code in Listing 24.9 is available in the Web site files as `Contact.java` in the BlazeDS application's `WEB-INF/src/flex3Bible` folder. The compiled version of the class is stored in `WEB-INF/classes`.

To pass this object to a Java-based remote method, create a matching ActionScript class. The ActionScript version's properties must match the Java class in both name and data type.

TIP Although this example uses public properties for brevity, you also can choose to use private properties with explicit `set` and `get` accessor methods.

The ActionScript class requires a `[RemoteClass]` metadata tag with an alias attribute describing the fully qualified name and package of the matching Java class:

```
[RemoteClass(alias="flex3Bible.Contact")]
```

This is a two-way mapping: When an ActionScript version of the object is sent to the server, the Remoting Service gateway creates a Java-based version and passes the received object's property values to the server-side version. Similarly, if a Java-based remote method returns instances of the server-side version, client-side versions are created automatically and their property values set to the values received from the server.

The ActionScript class in Listing 24.10 declares the same set of values as public properties and maps itself to the server's version with the `[RemoteClass]` metadata tag.

LISTING 24.10

An ActionScript value object class for use with the Remoting Service

```
package vo
{
  [Bindable]
  [RemoteClass(alias="flex3Bible.Contact")]
  public class Contact
  {
    public var contactId:int;
    public var firstName:String;
    public var lastName:String;
    public function Contact()
    {
    }
  }
}
```

ON the WEB The code in Listing 24.10 is available as `Contact.as` in the `src/vo` folder of the `chapter24.zip` file.

> **TIP**   Both the Java and ActionScript versions of the value object class must have either a no-arguments constructor method or none at all. In both cases, if the compiler doesn't find an explicit constructor method, it creates a no-arguments version in the compiled class automatically. Both the client and server assume the presence of the no-arguments constructor method when instantiating the matching value objects.

> **TIP**   If you're a Java developer who has a congenital distrust of public properties, you can define your ActionScript value object classes with implicit getter and setter accessor methods and private properties. This syntax is described in Chapter 16.

The Flex application in Listing 24.11 sends and receives value object classes. When it sends an ActionScript value object to the server, the Java method extracts the received object's properties and returns a concatenated value. When the Flex application sends two `String` values, the server's method builds a strongly typed value object and returns it to Flex.

LISTING 24.11

Sending and receiving strongly typed value object classes

```
<?xml version="1.0" encoding="utf-8"?>
<mx:Application xmlns:mx="http://www.adobe.com/2006/mxml"
  backgroundColor="#EEEEEE">

  <mx:Script>
    <![CDATA[
      import mx.controls.Alert;
      import mx.rpc.events.ResultEvent;
      import vo.Contact;
      [Bindable]
      private var myContact:Contact;
      private function setContact():void
      {
        myContact = new Contact();
        myContact.firstName = fnameInput.text;
        myContact.lastName = lnameInput.text;
        roHello.setContact(myContact);
      }
      private function getContact():void
      {
        roHello.getContact(fnameInput.text, lnameInput.text);
      }
      private function setHandler(event:ResultEvent):void
      {
        Alert.show(event.result as String, "Received String");
      }
      private function getHandler(event:ResultEvent):void
      {
        myContact = event.result as Contact;
        Alert.show("Contact VO received from server: " +
          myContact.firstName + " " + myContact.lastName,
```

```
                     "Received Contact value object");
      }
    ]]>
  </mx:Script>
  <mx:RemoteObject id="roHello" destination="helloClass">
    <mx:method name="setContact" result="setHandler(event)"/>
    <mx:method name="getContact" result="getHandler(event)"/>
  </mx:RemoteObject>
  <mx:Form>
    <mx:FormItem label="First Name:">
      <mx:TextInput id="fnameInput"/>
    </mx:FormItem>
    <mx:FormItem label="Last Name:">
      <mx:TextInput id="lnameInput"/>
    </mx:FormItem>
    <mx:ControlBar>
      <mx:Button label="Send Object" click="setContact()"/>
      <mx:Button label="Receive Object" click="getContact()"/>
    </mx:ControlBar>
  </mx:Form>
</mx:Application>
```

ON the WEB   The code in Listing 24.11 is available as `ROPassVO.mxml` in the `src` folder of the `chapter24.zip` file.

NOTE   The source code for the Java service class called from the Flex application in Listing 24.11 is shown in Listing 24.3.

Summary

In this chapter, I described how to integrate Flex client applications with Java Enterprise Edition application servers using BlazeDS. You learned the following:

- BlazeDS is a freely available, open-source implementation of the most popular features of LiveCycle Data Services.

- BlazeDS supports the Proxy Service, Remoting Service, and Message Service.

- The Proxy Service routes HTTP requests to remote domains, eliminating the need for cross-domain policy files.

- The Remoting Service allows Flex client applications to call remote methods of a Java-based class hosted by BlazeDS.

- The Remoting Service sends and receives messages in AMF, a binary format that results in much smaller messages than those that are encoded in XML and SOAP.

- The Flex framework's `RemoteObject` component is one of the three RPC components, along with `WebService` and `HTTPService`.

- Data can be sent and received between client and server as simple values or as strongly typed value objects.

Chapter 25

Using the Message Service with BlazeDS

When Flex Data Services 2 was first released, one of its most compelling new features was known as the Flex Message Service. This service allowed developers to create applications where data and information were shared instantly between multiple connected client applications, without having to program with low-level socket-style APIs.

With the renaming of Flex Data Services as LiveCycle Data Services, this server-based function became known simply as the Message Service (or, when referred to in the context of BlazeDS, the BlazeDS Message Service). Using this service, Flex client applications send messages to a destination on the server; the server then distributes the messages to other connected clients over a supported communication protocol.

LiveCycle Data Services (referred to here simply as LCDS) supports Real Time Messaging Protocol (RTMP), a protocol that implements true server-push capability. When LCDS Message Service destinations use an RTMP channel, data is pushed from the server to connected clients instantly (or as close as possible given available network and server resources). BlazeDS, the free open-source implementation of LCDS features, doesn't include the RTMP protocol, but adds the ability to define long-polling and streaming channels based on HTTP that allow you to create a messaging architecture that's very close to real time.

In this chapter, I describe how to use the Flex framework and BlazeDS to create and deploy an application that shares messages between multiple connected clients.

ON the WEB To use the sample code for this chapter, download `chapter25.zip` from the Web site. Follow the instructions later in this chapter to create a Flex project for use with BlazeDS and install the various project components to the client and server.

CROSS-REF Installation and setup of BlazeDS are described in Chapter 24.

Understanding the Message Service

The Message Service implements "publish/subscribe" messaging. Each client application that wants to participate in a messaging system can act as a *producer* that can publish messages and as a *consumer* that subscribes to a server-based destination. Messages are then distributed from the server to multiple connected clients using AMF-based encoding.

Client applications that participate in a messaging system aren't always built in Flex. The Message Service includes Java classes that serve as *adapters*. In addition to its default ActionScript adapter that allows sharing of messages between multiple connected Flex-based applications, BlazeDS includes these two specialized adapters:

- **The JMS adapter** supports integration between Flex client applications and Java-based environments that use the Java Message Service (JMS).
- **The ColdFusion Event Gateway Adapter** supports integration between Flex client applications and Web applications hosted by Adobe ColdFusion Enterprise.

The diagram in Figure 25.1 shows how messages travel between clients, using a BlazeDS or LCDS application running on a Java Enterprise Edition application server.

NOTE Unlike messaging systems that allow clients to create peer-to-peer connections, the Message Service always uses the server as a messaging hub. Clients always send messages to the server, and the server distributes messages as configured. As a result, you can achieve a high level of security through server-based configuration.

FIGURE 25.1

Messages traveling between Flex client applications using the Message Service

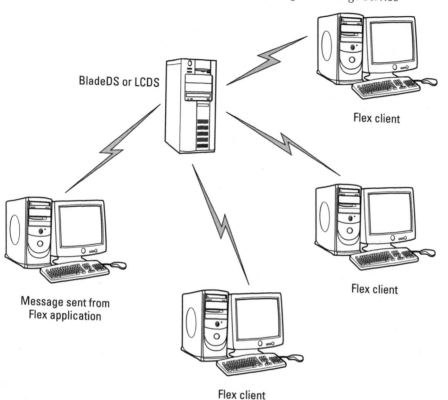

BladeDS or LCDS

Flex client

Message sent from
Flex application

Flex client

Flex client

Configuring Messaging on the Server

Applications send and receive messages through server-based destinations. As with the Proxy Service and the Remoting Service that were described in Chapters 23 and 24, you configure the Message Service by defining adapters, channels, and destinations in the server application's configuration files. As delivered in the starting BlazeDS application, `blazeds.war`, the primary configuration file, named `services-config.xml`, contains channel definitions. An included file named `messaging-config.xml` contains adapter and destination definitions for messaging.

Configuring channels for messaging

A channel definition includes information about the communication protocol, how messages are formatted, the location where messages are sent from the client at runtime (the endpoint), and whether messages are encrypted with SSL. BlazeDS supports the following types of channels for use with the Message Service:

■ **AMF with simple polling:** In this approach, the client makes a periodic request to the server for pending messages. The period between requests is configurable in the channel definition. The default services configuration file includes a channel with an id of my-polling-amf that looks like this:

```
<channel-definition id="my-polling-amf"
    class="mx.messaging.channels.AMFChannel">
  <endpoint
   url="http://{server.name}:{server.port}/{context.root}/
      messagebroker/amfpolling"
      class="flex.messaging.endpoints.AMFEndpoint"/>
  <properties>
     <polling-enabled>true</polling-enabled>
     <polling-interval-seconds>4</polling-interval-seconds>
  </properties>
</channel-definition>
```

The polling interval in this channel is set to 4 seconds; as a result, each client application makes a request every 4 seconds for pending messages, regardless of whether messaging activity has occurred.

■ **AMF with long polling:** This approach is similar to simple polling, but by setting the wait-interval-mills property to -1, you're telling the server to wait for requests indefinitely. With polling-interval-millis set to 0, the result is "almost real time" behavior. A channel that implements this sort of behavior looks like this:

```
<channel-definition id="my-long-polling-amf"
   class="mx.messaging.channels.AMFChannel">
   <endpoint url="http://servername:8100/contextroot/
      messagebroker/amf"
     class="flex.messaging.endpoints.AMFEndpoint"/>
   <properties>
      <polling-enabled>true</polling-enabled>
      <polling-interval-millis>0</polling-interval-millis>
      <wait-interval-millis>-1</wait-interval-millis>
      <max-waiting-poll-requests>0</max-waiting-poll-requests>
   </properties>
</channel-definition>
```

This strategy significantly reduces client wait times to receive messages, but scalability is limited by the number of available threads on the server. Each time a message is sent from the server to the client, the connection is closed to complete the communication. The client then immediately opens a new connection to wait for the next message.

■ **AMF with streaming:** A streaming channel uses different server-side Java classes than the polling channels and results in true "real time" messaging. A simple streaming channel looks like this in the configuration file:

```
<channel-definition id="my-streaming-amf"
  class="mx.messaging.channels.StreamingAMFChannel">
  <endpoint
   url="http://{server.name}:{server.port}/{context.root}/
     messagebroker/streamingamf"
    class="flex.messaging.endpoints.StreamingAMFEndpoint"/>
</channel-definition>
```

With this approach the client and server keep the HTTP connection open persistently, rather than closing and reopening it after every message. The result is instant message delivery to all connected clients, but there are some significant limitations.

All the AMF channel types used for messaging send and receive data between client and server as simple HTTP requests from the client. In the background, the server's servlet API uses blocking I/O, so with long polling and streaming you have to explicitly manage the number of concurrent connections to avoid overwhelming the server's available threads.

For example, when using an AMF streaming channel, each browser session can have only a single concurrent connection. (This can be changed in the channel configuration.) If you try to test a messaging application with multiple browser windows from a single browser application (for example, Firefox) on the same system, only the first copy of the application will successfully connect to the server. Application instances in additional browser windows will fail to connect because the maximum number of connections per browser session has been exceeded. You can solve this during testing by using multiple browser products (for example, both Internet Explorer and Firefox) or multiple computer systems.

> **TIP** One of the benefits of moving to LiveCycle Data Services from BlazeDS is support for RTMP (Real Time Messaging Protocol). This protocol, originally developed and delivered with Flash Media Server, supports true server-push and streaming communications. Unlike the HTTP streaming channel supported by BlazeDS, RTMP is capable of supporting thousands of concurrent connections and is limited only by available network and server resources.

The default services configuration file delivered with BlazeDS doesn't contain a streaming channel definition. If you'd like to use one in your development and testing, follow these steps:

1. Open `services-config.xml` from the BlazeDS `WEB-INF/flex` folder in any text editor.

2. Locate the `<channels>` start tag.

3. Add this `<channel>` element as a child of the `<channels>` tag set:

```
<channel-definition id="my-streaming-amf"
  class="mx.messaging.channels.StreamingAMFChannel">
  <endpoint
    url="http://{server.name}:{server.port}/{context.root}/
      messagebroker/streamingamf"
    class="flex.messaging.endpoints.StreamingAMFEndpoint"/>
</channel-definition>
```

4. Restart BlazeDS.

You can copy existing channel definitions from the version of `services-config.xml` that's included in the `samples` application.

Configuring messaging adaptors and destinations

You configure messaging destinations in the `messaging-config.xml` file in the BlazeDS `WEB-INF/flex` folder. The version of this file in the starting BlazeDS application (delivered as `blazeds.war`) looks like this:

```
<?xml version="1.0" encoding="UTF-8"?>
<service id="message-service"
  class="flex.messaging.services.MessageService">
  <adapters>
    <adapter-definition id="actionscript"
      class="flex.messaging.services.messaging.
        adapters.ActionScriptAdapter" default="true" />
    <!--
    <adapter-definition id="jms"

    class="flex.messaging.services.messaging.adapters.JMSAdapter"/
    >
    -->
  </adapters>
  <default-channels>
    <channel ref="my-polling-amf"/>
  </default-channels>
</service>
```

Configuring adaptors

An adaptor is a server-side Java class that manages how requests from a client are handled at run-time. The default `messaging-config.xml` file declares one adaptor with an `id` of `action-script` that manages messaging between Flex applications. It also includes a `jms` adaptor declaration that's used for integration with Java-based clients and is commented out in the default file.

Notice that the `actionscript` adaptor's `default` attribute is set to `true`. As a result, all messaging destinations without an explicit adapter use the `actionscript` adapter.

```
<adapter-definition id="actionscript"
   class="flex.messaging.services.messaging.
      adapters.ActionScriptAdapter" default="true" />
```

 **TIP**   If you want to integrate a messaging application with ColdFusion Enterprise, you must add this adaptor declaration:

```
<adapter-definition id="cfgateway"
   class="coldfusion.flex.CFEventGatewayAdapter"/>
```

The required Java class is included in the BlazeDS distribution, so this declaration just configures its use.

Configuring destinations

Each destination you configure is a hub for messages shared between multiple connected clients. To create a destination, add a `<destination>` child element of the `<service>` root with a unique `id`. To accept the default values for the adapter, channels, and all other properties, the destination configuration can be as simple as this:

```
<destination id="chat"/>
```

If you want to assign a particular channel to a destination, add a `<channels>` tag set and then declare one or more `<channel>` elements. If you declare more than one channel, they're used as a list in order or preference. The client always tries to use the first declared channel; in the event of any failure, it falls back to the second declared channel.

This destination uses the `my-streaming-amf` channel that was created in the preceding section as its first preference and adds the default `my-polling-amf` channel as a backup:

```
<destination id="chat">
   <channels>
      <channel ref="my-streaming-amf"/>
      <channel ref="my-polling-amf"/>
   <channels>
</destination>
```

If you're following the exercises in this chapter, follow these steps to configure three messaging destinations:

1. Open `messaging-config.xml` from the BlazeDS `WEB-INF/flex` folder in any text editor.

2. Add these destination definitions:
    ```
    <destination id="chat"/>
    <destination id="dashboard"/>
    ```

3. If you'd like to use the streaming channel described in the preceding section, change the `<default-channels>` element as follows:

```
<default-channels>
    <channel ref="my-streaming-amf"/>
</default-channels>
```

4. Save your changes, and restart BlazeDS.

Creating a Flex Messaging Application

A Flex application can participate in messaging both as a producer, sending messages, and as a consumer, receiving and processing them. In this section, I describe how to create a simple application that exchanges messages using a server-side messaging destination.

Creating a Flex project

When you create a project in Flex Builder that uses the Message Service, you can integrate the project with LiveCycle Data Services or BlazeDS. The steps are the same as when using the Remoting Service; the project properties include the location of the Flex server, the location of the output folder where generated files are placed during the compilation process, and the URL where requests are made to download the application from the server for testing.

Follow these steps to create a Flex project for use with BlazeDS and the Message Service:

1. Select File ➪ New ➪ Flex Project from the Flex Builder menu.
2. Set the project name to **chapter25**.
3. Use the default project location, which should be a folder named `chapter25` under the current workspace.
4. Set the Application type to **Web application**.
5. Set the Application server type to **J2EE**.
6. Select **Use remote object access service** and **LiveCycle Data Services**.
7. If you see an option labeled "Create combined Java/Flex project using WTP," deselect it.
8. Click Next.
9. Set server location properties as follows:
    - Root folder: `c:\blazeds\tomcat\webapps\blazeds`
    - Root URL: `http://localhost:8400/blazeds`
    - Context root: `/blazeds`
10. Check to be sure that BlazeDS is currently running. Then click Validate Configuration to verify that the Web root folder and root URL are valid.

11. Accept all other default values, and click Next.

12. Accept the default Main application filename to `chapter25.mxml`.

13. Click Finish to create the application and project.

14. If you want to use the sample files from the Web site, extract `chapter25.zip` into the new project folder. This will result in overwriting your default Main application file and adding other required MXML and ActionScript source files.

15. Return to Flex Builder, and run the main application. The application should load from the BlazeDS URL of `http://localhost:8400/blazeds/chapter25.html`.

Sending messages

A Flex application sends messages using the Flex framework's `Producer` component. You can create an instance of a `Producer` using either MXML or ActionScript code. The most important property of the `Producer` is the `destination`, which is set to a server-side destination as configured in the services configuration files.

The MXML code to create an instance of a `Producer` and set its `destination` looks like this:

```
<mx:Producer id="myProducer" destination="chat"/>
```

CAUTION The value of the `destination` property must be set exactly as declared on the server and is case-sensitive.

If you prefer to create the `Producer` using ActionScript, be sure to declare the object outside any functions so it persists for the duration of the user's application session. Then set the `destination` property inside a function that you call upon application startup:

```
import mx.messaging.Producer;
private var myProducer:Producer = new Producer();
private function initApp():void
{
  myProducer.destination = "chat";
}
```

To send a message to the destination at runtime, create an instance of the `AsyncMessage` class. This class is designed to serve as a message envelope that contains data you want to transfer between clients.

You start by instantiating the object:

```
var message:AsyncMessage = new AsyncMessage();
```

The message object has two properties that can contain data:

- **The** body **property** is the primary message data and can refer to any ActionScript object, including complex collection objects such as `ArrayCollection` and `XMLListCollection`.

- The headers **property** is a dynamic Object that can contain arbitrary named header values that serve as message metadata. The Message Service automatically adds certain headers that have a prefix of DS; to be sure you're avoiding any naming collisions, be sure that any headers you add have your own unique prefix.

For example, in a simple chat application where you want to send both a message and the user name of the person who sent it, you might use the body as the primary message containers and then create a chatUser header with the user's information:

```
message.body = messageToSend;
message.headers.chatUser = userWhoSentIt;
```

A complete function that sends a message using data from a set of TextInput controls might look like this:

```
private function sendMessage():void
{
  var message:AsyncMessage = new AsyncMessage();
  message.body = msgInput.text;
  message.headers.chatUser = userInput.text;
  myProducer.send(message);
}
```

Receiving and processing messages

A Flex application uses the Flex framework's Consumer component to receive and process messages sent through the Message Service. As with the Producer, you can instantiate a Consumer using either MXML or ActionScript code. These steps are required in order to receive messages:

1. Set the Consumer object's destination property to a destination that's been configured on the server.

2. Call the Consumer object's subscribe() method upon application startup or whenever you want to start receiving messages.

3. Handle the Consumer object's message event to receive and process each message when it comes in.

The code to create a Consumer object, set its destination, and add an event listener in MXML looks like this:

```
<mx:Consumer id="myConsumer" destination="chat"
  message="messageHandler(event)"
```

If you prefer to create the Consumer in ActionScript, be sure to declare the object outside any functions so it persists for the lifetime of the user's application session. Then set its destination and add an event listener in a function that's called upon application startup or whenever you want to start receiving messages:

```
import mx.messaging.Consumer;
private var myConsumer:Consumer = new Consumer();
private function initApp():void
{
  myConsumer.destination = "chat";
  myConsumer.addEventListener(MessageEvent.MESSAGE,
   messageHandler);
}
```

Regardless of how you create a `Consumer`, it must explicitly subscribe to the messaging destination by calling its `subscribe()` method:

```
myConsumer.subscribe();
```

You can call `subscribe()` at application startup or whenever you want to start receiving messages.

When a message is received from the server, the `Consumer` dispatches a message event. The event object is typed as `mx.messaging.events.MessageEvent`. This event class has a message property that refers to an `AsyncMessage` object. This is essentially the same object that was created and sent by the `Producer` in the sending application.

To process the message, extract data as needed from the `AsyncMessage` object's body and headers properties. This event handler function extracts the `chatUser` header and the main message, stored in the object's body:

```
private function messageHandler(event:MessageEvent):void
{
  var chatUser:String = event.message.headers.chatUser;
  var msg:String = event.body as String;
  ... save or present data as needed ...
}
```

TIP Notice in the preceding code that the event object's body property is explicitly cast as String, while the headers item is referenced without explicit casting. This is because the compiler expects body to be an Object, and to assign its value to a variable typed as String it must be explicitly cast. In contrast, the arbitrarily named properties of the headers object don't have implicit typing, so you can pass their values to variables of any type without explicit casting.

The application in Listing 25.1 uses `Producer` and `Consumer` components to send and receive messages. The body of each message is a simple String value, and the `chatUser` header value is created from a value entered by the user. When the message arrives, the `messageHandler()` function presents its contents by formatting and adding it to a `TextArea` control.

LISTING 25.1

Sending and receiving simple messages

```
<?xml version="1.0" encoding="utf-8"?>
<mx:Application xmlns:mx="http://www.adobe.com/2006/mxml"
  creationComplete="myConsumer.subscribe();">
  <mx:Script>
    <![CDATA[
      import mx.controls.Alert;
      import mx.messaging.events.MessageEvent;
      import mx.messaging.messages.AsyncMessage;
      private function sendMessage():void
      {
        var message:AsyncMessage = new AsyncMessage();
        message.body = msgInput.text;
        message.headers.chatUser = userInput.text;
        myProducer.send(message);
        msgInput.text="";
        msgInput.setFocus();
      }
      private function messageHandler(event:MessageEvent):void
      {
        msgLog.text += event.message.headers.chatUser + ": " +
          event.message.body + "\n";
      }
    ]]>
  </mx:Script>
  <mx:Producer id="myProducer" destination="chat"/>
  <mx:Consumer id="myConsumer" destination="chat"
    message="messageHandler(event)"/>
  <mx:Panel title="Simple Chat" id="sendPanel">
    <mx:Form width="100%">
      <mx:FormItem label="User Name:">
        <mx:TextInput id="userInput"/>
      </mx:FormItem>
      <mx:FormItem label="Message:">
        <mx:TextInput id="msgInput" enter="sendMessage()"/>
      </mx:FormItem>
      <mx:FormItem>
        <mx:Button label="Send Message" click="sendMessage()"
          enabled="{userInput.text != '' &amp;&amp; msgInput.text !=
''}"/>
      </mx:FormItem>
    </mx:Form>
  </mx:Panel>
```

```
<mx:Panel title="Message Log" width="{sendPanel.width}">
  <mx:TextArea id="msgLog" editable="false" height="200"
width="100%"/>
</mx:Panel>
</mx:Application>
```

ON the WEB The code in Listing 25.1 is available in the Web site files as `SimpleChat.mxml` in the `src` folder of the `chapter25` project.

Figure 25.2 shows the finished application sending and receiving simple String values as messages.

FIGURE 25.2

A simple chat application using the Message Service

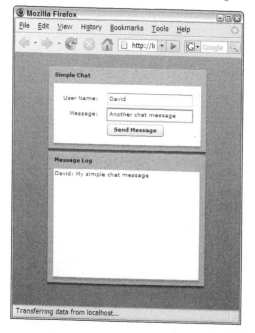

CAUTION If you want to test the application in more than one browser window and are using the `my-amf-streaming` channel, be sure to use a different browser product or different client system for each application session. If you have two copies of the application in different windows of the same browser product, and on the same client system, the second will fail to connect to the server.

Also, always completely close all browser windows between testing sessions to be sure you're starting a new browser session each time you test.

Sending and Receiving Complex Data

If you're using the Message Service's `actionscript` adapter and sharing data only between Flex client applications, the `AysncMessage` object's body property can refer to an instance of any ActionScript object. Unlike Java, where objects that can be serialized must be marked as such, in ActionScript all objects can be serialized. As long as both the sending and receiving application have included at least one reference to the class definition being used, the object can be deserialized upon receipt and made available to the receiving application in its native form.

The process for sending a complex message is exactly the same as for sending a simple value. After creating an `AsyncMessage` object, assign its body property to the object you want to send. Then, after assigning any headers you might need, send the message:

```
var message:AsyncMessage = new AsyncMessage();
message.body = acSales;
... assign headers if necessary ...
myProducer.send(message);
```

In the receiving application, the only difference in processing the message lies in how you typecast the received data. This version of the handler function for the `message` event assumes that the message object's body property refers to an `ArrayCollection` and explicitly casts it as such upon receipt:

```
private function messageHandler(event:MessageEvent):void
{
   acSales = event.message.body as ArrayCollection;
}
```

The application in Listing 25.2 uses an editable `DataGrid` to allow modifications to an `ArrayCollection` that in turn drives presentation of a pie chart. Each time a user on any connected client makes a change to his copy of the data, the `ArrayCollection` dispatches a `collectionChange` event. The application reacts by transmitting a message to all other connected clients containing the updated data object.

NOTE   Notice that the code in the `messageHandler()` function removes the `ArrayCollection` object's event listener, updates the data, and sets the event listener again. This ensures that the receiving application doesn't send a message when its data changes, causing a potential infinite loop between two copies of the application.

LISTING 25.2

Sending and receiving complex data

```
<?xml version="1.0" encoding="utf-8"?>
<mx:Application xmlns:mx="http://www.adobe.com/2006/mxml"
   layout="vertical"
  creationComplete="initApp()">
 <mx:Script>
   <![CDATA[
```

```
import mx.events.CollectionEvent;
import mx.messaging.messages.AsyncMessage;
import mx.messaging.events.MessageEvent;
import mx.collections.ArrayCollection;
[Bindable]
private var acSales:ArrayCollection = new ArrayCollection(
  [{name:"Popcorn", sales:65.00},
   {name:"Soda", sales:78.00},
   {name:"Candy", sales:32.00}]);
private function initApp():void
{
  myConsumer.subscribe();
  acSales.addEventListener(CollectionEvent.COLLECTION_CHANGE,
    syncClients);
}
private function messageHandler(event:MessageEvent):void
{
  acSales.removeEventListener(CollectionEvent.COLLECTION_CHANGE,
    syncClients);
  acSales = event.message.body as ArrayCollection;
  acSales.addEventListener(CollectionEvent.COLLECTION_CHANGE,
    syncClients);
}
private function syncClients(event:Event):void
{
  var message:AsyncMessage = new AsyncMessage();
  message.body = acSales;
  myProducer.send(message);
}
private function formatLabel(data:Object, field:String,
  index:Number, percentValue:Number):String
{
  return data.name + "\n" +
    cf.format(data.sales) + "\n(" +
    nf.format(percentValue) + "%)";
}
    ]]>
</mx:Script>
<mx:CurrencyFormatter id="cf" precision="2"/>
<mx:NumberFormatter id="nf" precision="1"/>
<mx:Producer id="myProducer" destination="dashboard"/>
<mx:Consumer id="myConsumer" destination="dashboard"
  message="messageHandler(event)"/>
<mx:Label text="Concession Sales" fontWeight="bold" fontSize="14"/>
<mx:PieChart id="chart" dataProvider="{acSales}"
  width="100%" height="100%">
  <mx:series>
    <mx:PieSeries field="sales" explodeRadius=".05"
      labelPosition="callout" labelFunction="formatLabel"
```

continued

LISTING 25.2   (continued)

```
          fontSize="12" fontWeight="bold"/>
    </mx:series>
  </mx:PieChart>
  <mx:DataGrid dataProvider="{acSales}" editable="true"
    rowCount="{acSales.length}">
    <mx:columns>
      <mx:DataGridColumn dataField="name" headerText="Product Name"
        editable="false"/>
      <mx:DataGridColumn dataField="sales" headerText="Sales"/>
    </mx:columns>
  </mx:DataGrid>
</mx:Application>
```

ON the WEB   The code in Listing 25.2 is available in the Web site files as `Dashboard.mxml` in the `src` folder of the `chapter25` project.

Figure 25.3 shows the resulting application, with a pie chart that's synchronized across multiple clients.

FIGURE 25.3

Synchronizing complex data with the Message Service

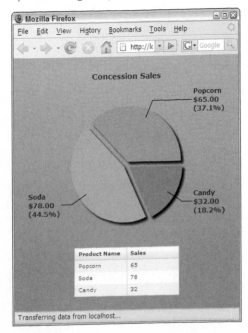

Filtering Messages on the Server

The Message Service supports these strategies for filtering messages on the server, so that a consumer application includes in its subscription information instructions to receive only messages that are of interest:

- The Consumer component's selector property filters messages based on values in message headers.

- The Producer and Consumer components implement a subtopic property that can be used to filter messages based on arbitrary topic names.

- The MultiTopicProducer and MultiTopicConsumer components allow you to send and receive messages that are filtered for multiple arbitrarily named topics.

In this section, I describe the use of the selector property and of subtopics with the Producer and Consumer components.

 When you filter messages either with the Consumer components selector property or with subtopics, the filtering always happens at the server.

Using the selector property

The selector property allows the Consumer to determine which messages are sent based on a Boolean evaluation. The syntax for a selector is based on SQL-style comparisons of header values to literal strings. This Consumer, for example, instructs the server to send messages only where their headers have a chatroom header with a value of "Room1":

```
<mx:Consumer id="myConsumer" destination="chat"
  message="messageHandler(event)"
  selector="chatRoom='Room1'/>
```

Using a selector to filter messages has these advantages:

- All Message Service destinations support use of the selector without any required additional configurations. In contrast, a destination must be specifically configured to support the use of subtopics.

- Complex Boolean expressions can be used with SQL-style syntax. For example, this selector examines two header values to determine whether messages should be shared with the current application:

  ```
  selector="chatRoom='Room1' AND chatUser='Joe'"
  ```

On the downside, selectors don't perform on the server as well as subtopics.

 If a Consumer has already subscribed and you change its selector property at runtime, it automatically unsubscribes and resubscribes with the new selector data.

Using subtopics

In order for a Flex application to use subtopics to filter messages, the server-side destination must be specifically configured to support the feature. In the services configuration file, you add an `<allow-subtopics>` element as a child of a `<server>` element within `<properties>` and set its value to `true`. This destination supports subtopics:

```
<destination id="chatrooms">
  <properties>
    <server>
      <allow-subtopics>true</allow-subtopics>
    </server>
  </properties>
</destination>
```

The `subtopic` property is set in both the `Producer` and the `Consumer`. When you set a `subtopic` in a `Producer`, the message that's sent to the server includes the subtopic information. When a `Consumer` subscribes to a destination, its `subtopic` is sent along with the subscription information. The server then sends messages to a `Consumer` only where the `subtopic` matches what the `Consumer` requested. If the `Consumer` doesn't define a subtopic, any messages sent from `Producer` objects with subtopics are not passed to that `Consumer`.

 If a `Consumer` has already subscribed and you change its `subtopic` at runtime, it automatically unsubscribes and resubscribes with the new `subtopic` value.

Follow these steps to modify your services configuration file and add a destination that supports subtopics:

1. Open `messaging-config.xml` from the BlazeDS `WEB-INF/flex` folder in any text editor.

2. Add this destination before the closing `</service>` tag:

```
<destination id="chatrooms">
  <properties>
    <server>
      <allow-subtopics>true</allow-subtopics>
    </server>
  .</properties>
</destination>
```

3. Save your changes, and restart BlazeDS.

The application in Listing 25.3 (the MXML code) and Listing 25.4 (the ActionScript code) uses subtopics to filter messages on the server, allowing sending applications to send messages only to a subset of connected clients.

NOTE This application uses a separate ActionScript file to demonstrate the use of scripting to implement all non-visual controls and event listeners. You could implement the same application with more MXML code and less ActionScript if you prefer.

LISTING 25.3

An application that filters messages with subtopics

```xml
<?xml version="1.0" encoding="utf-8"?>
<mx:Application xmlns:mx="http://www.adobe.com/2006/mxml"
  layout="vertical"
  creationComplete="initApp()">
  <mx:states>
    <mx:State name="loggedIn">
      <mx:RemoveChild target="{loginBox}"/>
      <mx:AddChild relativeTo="{appControlBar}" position="lastChild">
        <mx:HBox>
          <mx:Label text="Room:
  {currentRoom==null?'None':currentRoom}"/>
          <mx:Label text="User: {user}"/>
          <mx:Button label="Log Out" click="logout()"/>
        </mx:HBox>
      </mx:AddChild>
    </mx:State>
  </mx:states>
  <mx:Script source="ChatRooms.as"/>
  <mx:Style source="styles.css"/>
  <mx:ApplicationControlBar dock="true" id="appControlBar">
    <mx:Label text="My Chat Rooms" styleName="appHeading"/>
    <mx:Spacer width="100%"/>
    <mx:HBox id="loginBox">
      <mx:Label text="User name:"/>
      <mx:TextInput id="userInput" enter="login()" width="200"/>
      <mx:Button label="Log In" click="login()"/>
    </mx:HBox>
  </mx:ApplicationControlBar>
  <mx:HDividedBox width="100%" height="100%">
    <mx:VBox width="100%" height="100%">
      <mx:Panel height="100%" width="100%" title="Rooms">
        <mx:List id="roomList" dataProvider="{acRooms}"
          width="100%" height="100%"/>
        <mx:ControlBar>
          <mx:Button label="Change Room" click="changeChatRoom()"
            enabled="{roomList.selectedIndex != -1}"/>
        </mx:ControlBar>
      </mx:Panel>
    </mx:VBox>
    <mx:Panel width="100%" height="100%" id="chatPanel" title="Chat">
      <mx:TextArea id="msgLog" width="100%"  height="100%"
        editable="false"/>
      <mx:ControlBar>
```

continued

LISTING 25.3 *(continued)*

```
        <mx:TextInput id="msgInput" enter="send()" width="100%"/>
        <mx:Button label="Send" click="send()"/>
        <mx:Button label="Log Out" click="logout()"/>
      </mx:ControlBar>
    </mx:Panel>
  </mx:HDividedBox>
</mx:Application>
```

The code in Listing 25.3 is available in the Web site files as `ChatRooms.mxml` in the src folder of the `chapter25` project.

TIP   The following binding expression in Listing 25.3 uses a *ternary expression*, a syntax that's common to languages such as ActionScript, Java, and JavaScript:

```
    <mx:Label
      text="Room: {currentRoom==null?'None':currentRoom}"/>
```

A ternary expression is a shortened form of an `if` statement that includes three parts. The first part, before the `?` character, is a Boolean expression, frequently comparing two values. If the first part returns `true`, the ternary expression returns the second part of the expression (the part between the `?` and `:` characters). If the first part returns `false`, the ternary expression returns the third part (after the `:` character).

LISTING 25.4

The ActionScript code for the Chat Rooms application

```
import mx.collections.ArrayCollection;
import mx.controls.Alert;
import mx.messaging.Consumer;
import mx.messaging.Producer;
import mx.messaging.events.MessageEvent;
import mx.messaging.events.MessageFaultEvent;
import mx.messaging.messages.AsyncMessage;
[Bindable]
private var user:String;
[Bindable]
private var currentRoom:String;
[Bindable]
private var acRooms:ArrayCollection =
  new ArrayCollection(["Room 1", "Room 2"]);
private var myConsumer:Consumer = new Consumer();
private var myProducer:Producer = new Producer();
private function initApp():void
{
```

```
    myProducer.destination = "chatrooms";
    myProducer.addEventListener(MessageFaultEvent.FAULT, faultHandler);
    myConsumer.destination = "chatrooms";
    myConsumer.addEventListener(MessageEvent.MESSAGE, messageHandler);
    myConsumer.addEventListener(MessageFaultEvent.FAULT, faultHandler);
}
private function send():void
{
    var message:AsyncMessage = new AsyncMessage();
    message.body = msgInput.text;
    message.headers.user = user;
    myProducer.send(message);
    msgInput.text="";
    msgInput.setFocus();
}
private function messageHandler(event:MessageEvent):void
{
    msgLog.text += event.message.headers.user + ": " +
        event.message.body + "\n";
}
private function login():void
{
    user = userInput.text;
    myConsumer.subscribe();
    currentState = "loggedIn";
}
private function logout():void
{
    myConsumer.unsubscribe();
    msgLog.text="";
    currentState = "";
    currentRoom="";
    roomList.selectedIndex=-1;
}
private function changeChatRoom():void
{
    currentRoom = roomList.selectedItem as String;
    myProducer.subtopic = currentRoom;
    myConsumer.subtopic = currentRoom;
}
private function faultHandler(event:MessageFaultEvent):void
{
    Alert.show(event.faultString, event.faultCode);
}
```

ON the WEB   The code in Listing 25.4 is available in the Web site files as `ChatRooms.as` in the `src` folder of the `chapter25` project.

Figure 25.4 shows the resulting application sharing data only within a selected subtopic.

FIGURE 25.4

An application sending and receiving filtered messages using subtopics

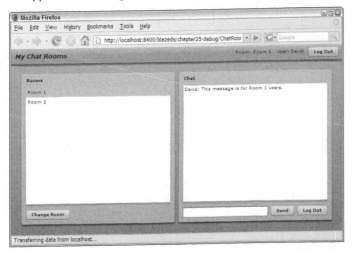

CAUTION   If you're using a streaming channel for this application, remember to use multiple browser products or client systems to successfully test messaging between multiple clients.

Tracing Messaging Traffic

As with all network communications between Flex clients and application servers, you can use the `TraceTarget` component to enable tracing of messaging traffic. Follow these steps to trace messaging:

1. Open any Flex application that uses the Message Service.

2. Add an `<mx:TraceTarget/>` tag as a child element of the application's root `<mx:Application>`.

3. Set any optional values that determine what metadata is included with each tracing message. For example, this declaration of the `TraceTarget` object would include date and time information:

   ```
   <mx:TraceTarget includeDate="true" includeTime="true"/>
   ```

4. Run the application in debug mode.

5. Watch Flex Builder's Console view to see the tracing output.

Figure 25.5 shows the resulting output in Flex Builder's Console view.

FIGURE 25.5

Tracing output from a messaging application

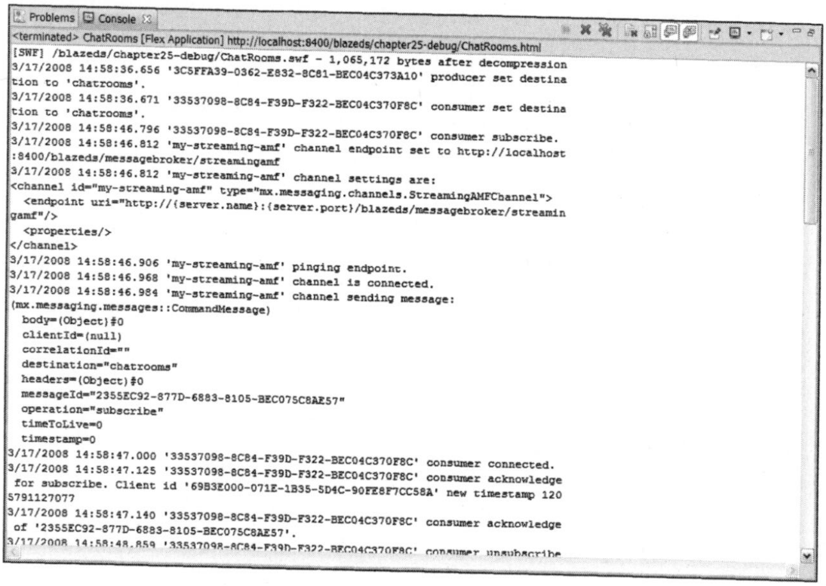

Summary

In this chapter, I described how to create and deploy Flex client applications that use the Message Service with BlazeDS. You learned the following:

- The Message Service is implemented in both LiveCycle Data Services and BlazeDS.
- The Message Service allows you to share data between multiple connected Flex applications in real time or "almost real time."
- Flex applications that use the Message Service can be integrated with other applications that are built in Java and ColdFusion.
- A Flex application sends messages using the Flex framework's Producer component.
- A Flex application receives and processes messages using the Flex framework's Consumer component.
- You can send and receive both simple and complex data.
- Messages can be filtered at the server with the Consumer component's selector property or with subtopics.
- You can turn on tracing of message traffic with the TraceTarget logger target.

Chapter 26

Integrating Flex Applications with ColdFusion

IN THIS CHAPTER

Understanding Flash Remoting and ColdFusion

Creating a Flex project for use with ColdFusion

Configuring Flash Remoting on the server

Creating CFCs for Flex

Calling CFC functions

Handling CFC function results

Passing arguments to CFC functions

Using value object classes

Working with RemoteObject faults

Flash Remoting, the technology that allows Flash-based documents to communicate with Web-based resources over a high-speed, binary protocol, was first introduced with ColdFusion MX (also known as ColdFusion version 6). In the early days of the technology, before the introduction of Flex, applications built in Flash MX and subsequent releases had the ability to make remote procedure calls to functions of ColdFusion components (CFCs) over a standard Web connection.

When Flex 1.0 was released, Flash Remoting was adapted for use with Java-based application servers that hosted Java-based classes. Flex client applications could make calls to Java-based methods just as easily as with ColdFusion using the feature first known as Remote Object Services, now known as the Remoting Service.

CROSS-REF The Java-based Remoting Service is described in Chapter 24.

Adobe ColdFusion 8 continues to offer built-in support for Flash Remoting with Flex-based and Flash-based client applications, and it adds the ability to integrate tightly with features that are unique to LiveCycle Data Services or BlazeDS. When ColdFusion is integrated with these Adobe products, you can build and deploy Flex applications that share messages in real time or near real time with ColdFusion-based resources using the Message Service, and you can use LiveCycle Data Services' Data Management Service to create applications that synchronize data between multiple connected clients and servers.

> **TIP**
>
> All the currently available ColdFusion features that support integration with Flex client applications were first introduced in ColdFusion version 7.02. With the exception of the event gateway used to integrate Flex applications with the Message Service, all the features described in this chapter work equally well with ColdFusion 7.02 or ColdFusion 8.

In this chapter, I describe how to use Flash Remoting to call ColdFusion component functions from Flex applications. In Chapter 27, I describe how to use the ColdFusion Extensions for Eclipse to interact with ColdFusion during development and generate server-side ColdFusion components for use with Flex/ColdFusion applications.

> **ON the WEB**
>
> To use the sample code for this chapter, download `chapter26.zip` from the Web site. Follow the instructions later in this chapter to create a Flex project for use with ColdFusion and install the various project components to the client and server.

Understanding Flash Remoting and ColdFusion 8

The feature known as the Remoting Service in LiveCycle Data Services and BlazeDS is known as Flash Remoting in ColdFusion. Flash Remoting allows you to directly make calls to functions of ColdFusion components using the Flex framework's `RemoteObject` component.

Calls from a Flex client application are sent directly to the ColdFusion server as HTTP requests encrypted in Action Message Format (AMF), and responses are returned from ColdFusion to the Flex application without any intermediate proxy or additional software. As shown in Figure 26.1, when using the `RemoteObject` component to call CFC methods, you don't need to install or integrate LiveCycle Data Services or BlazeDS.

FIGURE 26.1

Flash Remoting requests and responses travel directly from the Flex application to ColdFusion and back again.

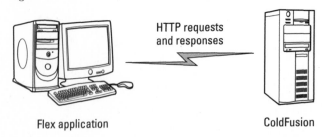

HTTP requests and responses

Flex application   ColdFusion

To call CFC functions from a Flex application, follow these steps:

1. Install Adobe ColdFusion or obtain access to a ColdFusion server. You can use either the Standard or Enterprise edition or, if you don't have a license, you can install ColdFusion locally as the Developer edition. This edition is free for development and testing and has some limitations, including allowing connections from only two browser clients during any particular session.

2. If using Flex Builder, optionally install the ColdFusion Extensions for Flex Builder.

3. Create ColdFusion components on the server with code you can call from a Flex application.

4. If using Flex Builder, create a Flex project that's integrated with your ColdFusion server installation.

5. Create and test Flex client code to call the CFC functions.

> **NOTE** The sample code and instructions in this chapter assume that ColdFusion 8 has been installed on a Windows-based development system using the development Web server running on port 8500. If your ColdFusion installation differs, adapt the instructions as needed.

Creating a Flex project for use with ColdFusion

When you create a new Flex project, you can add project properties that allow you to easily test your Flex application with the ColdFusion server. Follow these steps to create a new Flex project:

1. Select File ➪ New ➪ Flex Project from the Flex Builder menu.

2. On the first screen, set these properties, as shown in Figure 26.2:
   - Project name: **chapter26**
   - Use default location: **selected**
   - Application type: **Web application**
   - Application server type: **ColdFusion**
   - Use remote object access service: **selected**
   - ColdFusion Flash Remoting: **selected**

3. Click Next.

4. On the Configure ColdFusion Server screen, set the ColdFusion installation type and location. If you installed the server configuration to the default location in Windows, use these settings:
   - ColdFusion installation type: **Standalone**
   - Use default location for local ColdFusion server: **selected**
   - Use built-in ColdFusion web server: **selected**

FIGURE 26.2

Creating a new Flex project

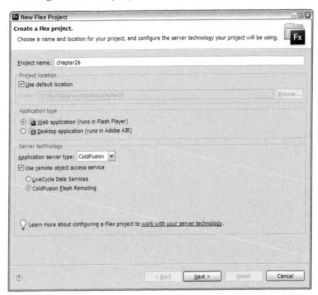

5. Click Validate Configuration to verify that your ColdFusion configuration settings are accurate.

> **NOTE** ColdFusion must be running in order to validate the configuration at this point. Flex Builder sends a test request to the ColdFusion server's Root URL to ensure that the server is reachable.

6. Set the Output folder to a location under the ColdFusion Root URL. This is the folder where the application's debug output files will be generated during the compilation process and from which you retrieve documents in the browser during testing. The default setting is a subfolder under the ColdFusion Web root whose name starts with the project name and ends with "-debug".

7. Click Next.

8. Accept the Main application filename of chapter26.mxml.

9. Click Finish to create the project and application.

10. Run the application.

You should see that the application is retrieved from the folder on the ColdFusion server using the server's root URL and the subfolder in which the output files are generated.

ON the WEB If you want to use the sample applications for this chapter from the Web site, follow these instructions: Extract the contents of `chapter26.zip` to the new project's root folder, locate `chapter26CFFiles.zip` in the project files, and extract those files to the ColdFusion server's Web root folder, such as `C:\ColdFusion8\wwwroot`. This creates a new subfolder named `flex3bible/chapter26` under the ColdFusion Web root.

Configuring Flash Remoting on the server

Just as with the Remoting Service on LiveCycle Data Services or BlazeDS, to use Flash Remoting from a Flex application, it must be configured on the server. When you install ColdFusion, a folder named `WEB-INF/flex` is created that contains a default set of configuration files.

TIP The `WEB-INF` folder is located under the ColdFusion Web root, as defined during the ColdFusion installation process. The actual location differs depending on ColdFusion's configuration.

The "server" configuration that includes a limited JRun server places `WEB-INF` under the installation folder's wwwroot subfolder. When the server configuration of ColdFusion is installed on Windows with the default location, the Flex configuration files are stored in `C:\ColdFusion8\wwwroot\WEB-INF\flex`. For the J2EE or multi-server configurations, `WEB-INF` is located under the ColdFusion "context root" folder. For example, when installed with the default location on Windows, the Flex configuration files are stored in `C:\JRun4\servers\cfusion\cfusion-ear\cfusion-war\WEB-INF\flex`.

Flash Remoting access is configured in one of two files in the `WEB-INF/flex` folder:

- If you install ColdFusion with the integrated LiveCycle Data Services, the primary services configuration file, `services-config.xml`, includes a file named `remoting-config.xml` that declares Flash Remoting configuration options.

- If you install ColdFusion without the integrated LiveCycle Data Services, a file named `service-config.xml` contains all Flex server configuration options, including Flash Remoting destination definitions.

ColdFusion includes a predefined Flash Remoting destination definition with an `id` of `ColdFusion` in either `services-config.xml` or `remoting-config.xml` that looks like this:

```
<destination id="ColdFusion">
  <channels>
    <channel ref="my-cfamf"/>
  </channels>
  <properties>
    <source>*</source>
    <!-- define the resolution rules and access level of
      the cfc being invoked -->
    <access>
      <!-- Use the ColdFusion mappings to find CFCs, by default
```

```
          only CFC files under your webroot can be found. -->
        <use-mappings>false</use-mappings>
        <!-- allow "public and remote" or just "remote" methods to
           be invoked -->
        <method-access-level>remote</method-access-level>
      </access>
      <property-case>
        <!-- cfc property names -->
        <force-cfc-lowercase>false</force-cfc-lowercase>
        <!-- Query column names -->
        <force-query-lowercase>false</force-query-lowercase>
        <!-- struct keys -->
        <force-struct-lowercase>false</force-struct-lowercase>
      </property-case>
    </properties>
  </destination>
```

These key destination properties are worth a detailed description:

- The `<channel>` is set to `my-cfamf`. This channel is defined in `services.config.xml`, and uses the `AMFChannel` class on the server to serialize and deserialize AMF-formatted messages between client and server. The services configuration file also defines a channel named `my-cfamf-secure` that can be used for encrypted communications over SSL.

- The `<source>` element is set to a wildcard value of `*`, meaning that the predefined ColdFusion destination can be used to call any CFC on the server. This is in contrast to the use of the Java-based Remoting Service with LCDS and BlazeDS, where each Java class must be configured with its own unique destination.

- The `<access>` element determines which functions can be called from the Flex application. The default setting of `remote` means that only functions whose access attribute is set to remote can be called from Flex.

- The settings in the `<property-case>` element determine whether property names are forced to lowercase as they're returned from ColdFusion to the Flex client application. Because ColdFusion is mostly case-insensitive, the names of CFC properties, structure properties, and query columns are automatically returned in uppercase. The code works fine, but it looks odd to the eye of a developer who's accustomed to object-oriented coding conventions, where property names always start with initial lowercase characters. If you want to change the default behavior, switch the value of the case properties to `true` to force lowercase names:

```
<property-case>
  <force-cfc-lowercase>true</force-cfc-lowercase>
  <force-query-lowercase>true</force-query-lowercase>
  <force-struct-lowercase>true</force-struct-lowercase>
</property-case>
```

The default `ColdFusion` destination is designed to be usable with its initial property settings. In most cases, you can start calling CFC functions from a Flex client application without changing any of the server-side configuration options.

Creating ColdFusion Components for Flex

The rules for creating ColdFusion components for use with a Flex application are very similar to those CFCs used as SOAP-based Web services:

- CFCs should be placed in a folder under the Web root. With additional configuration, you also can place CFCs in folders that are mapped through the ColdFusion administrator.

- CFC functions should have their access attribute set to remote. With additional configuration, you also can expose functions with their access set to public.

- Functions should return values with data types that are compatible with Flex applications.

NOTE A complete description of how to create and deploy ColdFusion components is beyond the scope of this chapter. For a good starting tutorial on this subject, see Ben Forta's article on the Adobe Developer Center Web site at:

```
www.adobe.com/devnet/coldfusion/articles/intro_cfcs.html
```

Table 26.1 describes the data types that can be returned from a CFC to a Flex application and how each value is translated into ActionScript variables when it's returned from a CFC function to a Flex client application.

TABLE 26.1

Data Conversion from ColdFusion to ActionScript

ColdFusion Data Type	ActionScript Data Type
String	String
Array	Array
Query	ArrayCollection
Struct	Object
CFC instance	Strongly typed value object
Date	Date
Numeric	Number
XML Object	XML Object

The returned data type is determined in a ColdFusion function by its returntype property. The CFC in Listing 26.1 shows a ColdFusion component with a helloWorld() function that declares a returntype of string:

LISTING 26.1

A simple ColdFusion component

```
<cfcomponent name="HelloService" output="false"
    hint="A ColdFusion Component for use in Flash Remoting">
  <cffunction name="helloWorld" returntype="string" access="remote">
    <cfreturn "Hello from a ColdFusion Component!"/>
  </cffunction>
</cfcomponent>
```

ON the WEB The code in Listing 26.1 is available in the Web site files as `HelloService.cfc` in the ColdFusion files of the `chapter26` project.

TIP Unlike the worlds of Java and ActionScript, ColdFusion Markup Language is mostly case-insensitive. As a result, `returntype` values of `string` and `String` mean the same thing.

The `returntype` attribute is also used by ColdFusion to verify that data being returned by a function is of the correct type. CFML (ColdFusion Markup Language) is a very loosely typed language, where simple values are generally stored as String values until being cast appropriately at runtime (a process sometimes known as "lazy evaluation"). But at runtime, ColdFusion can detect discrepancies between a declared `returntype` and the actual value being returned. This function, for example, would generate a server-side runtime error, because the value being returned can't be parsed as a number:

```
<cffunction name="getNumber" returntype="numeric"
   access="remote">
  <cfreturn "This is not a numeric value"/>
</cffunction>
```

This resulting server-side error would be exposed in the Flex client application as a `fault` event dispatched by the `RemoteObject` that made the remote call to the function.

Using CFCs with the RemoteObject Component

To call a CFC function from a Flex client application, you start by creating an instance of the `RemoteObject` component. This is the same RPC component that's used to integrate Flex applications with LiveCycle Data Services and BlazeDS, and the client-side code that's used to communicate with ColdFusion is almost exactly the same. If the source of the component is set to a wildcard in the server-side destination, you set the component's source property in the client-side `RemoteObject` declaration.

Setting the source property

The CFC is known to the Flex client application by its fully qualified name and location, declared with dot notation. This `String` value is passed to the `RemoteObject` component's `source` property to determine which component will be called on the server.

ColdFusion uses a naming pattern whereby CFCs are known by the name of the file in which the component is defined (without the file extension), prefixed with the names of the folders in which it's stored, starting at the Web root folder. Folder and component names are separated with dot characters, just like packages in Java. So, for example, a CFC that's defined in a file named `MyComponent.cfc` and stored in a subfolder under the ColdFusion Web root named `flex3bible/cfc` would be referred to from Flex as:

```
flex3bible.cfc.MyComponent
```

If you're working on a development server that has RDS, you can generate a CFC's documentation by navigating to the component from a Web browser. The documentation includes the exact string you need to set the component's source accurately in Flex. For example, you can browse to the `HelloService.cfc` file stored in the Web root folder's `flex3bible/chapter26` folder with this URL:

```
http://localhost:8500/flex3bible/chapter26/HelloService.cfc
```

 **If you have RDS security turned on in the ColdFusion administrator, you'll need to enter your RDS password to view the CFC's documentation.**

Figure 26.3 shows the resulting CFC documentation. The string value you use as the source attribute in Flex is displayed twice: once at the top of the documentation page and again in the hierarchy section.

Creating a RemoteObject instance

You can create an instance of the `RemoteObject` component that works with the `ColdFusion` destination in either MXML or ActionScript. In addition to the object's unique `id`, you set object's `destination` to the `id` of the destination on the server, named by default `ColdFusion`. The object's `source` attribute is set to the fully qualified name and location of the CFC, as described in the preceding section.

The code to create a `RemoteObject` and set its required properties in MXML looks like this:

```
<mx:RemoteObject id="helloService"
  destination="ColdFusion"
  source="flex3bible.chapter26.HelloService"/>
```

FIGURE 26.3

Automatically generated CFC documentation, including the component's fully qualified name and location

The component's source name and location

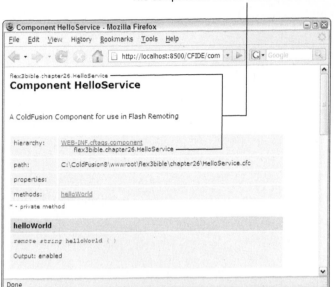

The code to create the same object in ActionScript looks like this:

```
import mx.rpc.remoting.RemoteObject;
var helloService:RemoteObject = new RemoteObject("ColdFusion");
helloService.source = "flex3bible.chapter26.HelloService";
```

After you've declared the `RemoteObject` and set its `source` and `destination` properties, you're ready to make runtime calls to remote CFC functions.

Calling CFC functions

You call CFC functions as though they were local methods of the `RemoteObject`. For example, the CFC in Listing 26.1 has a public method named `helloWorld()` that returns a simple `String`. As with local functions, you can call the remote method upon any application event. For example, this code calls the server-side `helloWorld()` method upon a `Button` component's `click` event:

```
<mx:Button label="Click to say hello"
  click="helloService.helloWorld()"/>
```

You also can call a CFC function by calling the RemoteObject component's getOperation() method to create an instance of the Operation class. The following code creates the Operation object and then calls its send() method to call the remote method:

```
import mx.rpc.remoting.mxml.Operation;
private function callIt():void
{
  var op:Operation = helloService.getOperation("helloWorld")
    as Operation;
  op.send();
}
```

This technique allows you to determine which remote method will be called at runtime, instead of having to hard code the method name.

Handling CFC Function Results

Calls to remote CFC functions are made asynchronously in Flex, so a call to a CFC function doesn't return data directly. Instead, as with the other RPC components, you handle the response with binding expressions or event handlers. Binding expressions require less code and are easy to create, while event handlers offer much more power and flexibility in how you receive, process, and save data to application memory.

Using binding expressions

A binding expression used to pass returned data to application components consists of three parts, separated with dots:

- The RemoteObject instance's id
- The CFC function name
- The lastResult property

At runtime, the method is created as an Operation object that's a member of the RemoteObject instance. The Operation object's lastResult property is populated with data when it's received from the server.

The lastResult property is explicitly typed as an ActionScript Object, but at runtime its native type is determined by the type of data that's returned from the server. A String returned from ColdFusion is translated into an ActionScript String value, so a binding expression that handles the value returned from the simple helloWorld() method can be used to pass the returned value to a Label or other text display control.

The application in Listing 26.2 calls the remote helloWorld() CFC function and displays its returned data in a Label control with a binding expression in its text property.

LISTING 26.2

Handling returned data with a binding expression

```xml
<?xml version="1.0" encoding="utf-8"?>
<mx:Application xmlns:mx="http://www.adobe.com/2006/mxml"
  backgroundColor="#EEEEEE">

  <mx:RemoteObject id="helloService"
    destination="ColdFusion"
    source="flex3bible.chapter26.HelloService"/>

  <mx:Button label="Hello World" click="helloService.helloWorld()"/>

  <mx:Label text="{helloService.helloWorld.lastResult}"
    fontSize="12"/>

</mx:Application>
```

ON the WEB   The code in Listing 26.2 is available in the Web site files as `ROWithBinding.mxml` in the `src` folder of the `chapter26` project.

Using the result event

As with other RPC components, you can handle results of a call to a CFC function with the `RemoteObject` component's `result` event. This event dispatches an event object typed as `mx.rpc.events.ResultEvent`, the same event object that's used by the other RPC components `HTTPService` and `RemoteObject`. The event object's `result` property references the returned data.

To handle and save data using the `result` event, follow these steps:

1. Declare a bindable variable outside of any functions that acts as a persistent reference to the returned data. Cast the variable's type depending on what you expect to be returned by the remote method. For example, if the data returned by the CFC function is typed as a Query, the `RemoteObject` component casts the returned data as an `ArrayCollection`. This code declares a bindable `ArrayCollection` variable:

   ```
   import mx.collections.ArrayCollection;
   [Bindable]
   private var myData:ArrayCollection
   ```

2. Create an event handler function that will be called when the event is dispatched. The function should receive a single event argument typed as `ResultEvent` and return `void`:

   ```
   private function resultHandler(event:ResultEvent):void
   {
   }
   ```

3. Within the event handler function, use the `event.result` expression to refer to the data that's returned from the server. Just as with the `WebService` component, `ResultEvent.result` is typed as an `Object`. Because the expression's native type differs depending on what's returned by the CFC function, you typically have to explicitly cast the returned data. This code expects the CFC function to return an `ArrayCollection`:

```
myData = event.result as ArrayCollection;
```

You can listen for the `result` event with either an MXML attribute-based event listener or a call to the ActionScript `addEventListener()` method. The attribute-based event listener looks like this:

```
<mx:RemoteObject id="myService" destination="helloClass"
  source="flex3bible.chapter26.ContactService"
  result="resultHandler(event)"/>
```

When using `addEventListener()` to create an event listener, you can designate the event name with the `String` value result, or with the `ResultEvent` class's RESULT static constant:

```
var contactService:RemoteObject = new RemoteObject("ColdFusion");
contactService.source =
    source="flex3bible.chapter26.ContactService";
contactService.addEventListener(ResultEvent.RESULT,
    resultHandler);
contactService.getAllContacts();
```

Listing 26.3 uses a `result` event handler function to capture and present data that's been returned from a CFC function.

LISTING 26.3

Handling results from a CFC function with a result event handler

```
<?xml version="1.0" encoding="utf-8"?>
<mx:Application xmlns:mx="http://www.adobe.com/2006/mxml"
  backgroundColor="#EEEEEE" creationComplete="initApp()"
  xmlns:view="view.*">
  <mx:Script>
    <![CDATA[
      import mx.collections.ArrayCollection;
      import mx.rpc.events.ResultEvent;
      import mx.rpc.remoting.RemoteObject;
      [Bindable]
      private var contactData:ArrayCollection;
      private var contactService:RemoteObject;
      private function initApp():void
      {
```

```
            contactService = new RemoteObject("ColdFusion");
            contactService.source = "flex3bible.chapter26.ContactService";
            contactService.addEventListener(ResultEvent.RESULT,
    resultHandler);
        }
        private function resultHandler(event:ResultEvent):void
        {
          contactData = event.result as ArrayCollection;
        }
      ]]>
    </mx:Script>
    <mx:Button label="Hello World"
      click="contactService.getAllContacts()"/>
    <view:ContactsGrid dataProvider="{contactData}"/>
</mx:Application>
```

ON the WEB   The code in Listing 26.3 is available in the Web site files as `ROResultHandler.mxml` in the `src` folder of the `chapter26` project. The custom `DataGrid` component that displays data in this and other applications in this chapter is defined as a custom MXML component named `ContactsGrid.mxml` in the project's `src/view` folder.

Listing 26.4 shows the code for the CFC that's called by this and other applications in this section. Notice that the `Query` object is created manually in ColdFusion code, rather than being generated with a `<cfquery>` command. As a result, the case of the column names is controlled by this call to the ColdFusion `QueryNew()` function, rather than being derived from a database query's metadata:

```
        <cfset var
            qContacts=queryNew('contactId,firstname,lastname,city')>
```

LISTING 26.4

A CFC returning a Query object

```
<cfcomponent name="ContactService"
  hint="Delivers Contact data from an XML file to a Flex application">
  <cfapplication name="flex3BibleChapter26" sessionManagement="true">
  <!--- Initialize data set in memory if it doesn't already exist --->
  <cfif not structKeyExists(session, "qContacts")>
    <cfset createDataSet()>
  </cfif>

  <!--- Returns all data from a query object --->
  <cffunction name="getAllContacts" returntype="query" access="remote">
    <cfreturn session.qContacts>
  </cffunction>
  <!--- Returns filtered data using query of query --->
```

```
<cffunction name="getFilteredContacts" returnType="query"
 access="remote">
  <cfargument name="firstname" type="string" required="true">
  <cfargument name="lastname" type="string" required="true">
  <cfset var qFiltered="">
  <cfquery dbtype="query" name="qFiltered">
    SELECT * FROM session.qContacts
    WHERE 0=0
    <cfif len(trim(firstname))>
      AND firstname LIKE '%#trim(arguments.firstname)#%'
    </cfif>
    <cfif len(trim(lastname))>
      AND lastname LIKE '%#trim(arguments.lastname)#%'
    </cfif>
  </cfquery>
  <cfreturn qFiltered>
</cffunction>
<!--- Returns the total count of Contacts --->
<cffunction name="getContactCount" returntype="numeric"
 access="remote">
  <cfreturn session.qContacts.recordCount>
</cffunction>
<!--- Called to create a query object from an XML file --->
<cffunction name="createDataSet" returntype="void" access="private">
  <cfset var strContacts="">
  <cfset var xContacts="">
  <cfset var i="">
  <cfset var qContacts=queryNew('contactId,firstname,lastname,city')>
  <cffile action="read" file="#expandPath('data/contacts.xml')#"
    variable="strContacts">
  <cfset xContacts=xmlParse(strContacts)>
  <cfloop from="1" to="#arrayLen(xContacts.contacts.row)#" index="i">
    <cfset QueryAddRow(qContacts)>
    <cfset qContacts.firstname[i]=xContacts.contacts.row[i]
      .firstname.xmltext>
    <cfset qContacts.lastname[i]=xContacts.contacts.row[i].
      lastname.xmltext>
    <cfset qContacts.contactId[i]=xContacts.contacts.row[i].
      contactId.xmltext>
    <cfset qContacts.city[i]=xContacts.contacts.row[i].city.xmltext>
  </cfloop>
  <cfset session.qContacts=qContacts>
</cffunction>
</cfcomponent>
```

ON the WEB The code in Listing 26.4 is available in the Web site files as `ContactService.cfc` in the ColdFusion files of the `chapter26` project.

Handling results from multiple CFC functions

When you need to call more than one function from a CFC, you have to distinguish which event handler function should be called for each of them. You do this in MXML with the <mx:method > compiler tag, which is nested within a <mx:RemoteObject> tag set. Each <mx:method > tag represents a CFC function and can declare its own distinct result and fault event handlers.

The CFC in Listing 26.4, for example, has a function named getContactCount() that returns a numeric value and a function named getAllContacts() that returns a Query object (translated to an ArrayCollection in the Flex application). To handle each function's result event with its own distinct event handler function, you create the functions and then declare the <mx:method> tags as follows:

```
<mx:RemoteObject id="contactService"
  destination="ColdFusion"
  source="flex3bible.chapter26.ContactService">
  <mx:method name="getContactCount"
   result="countHandler(event)"/>
  <mx:method name="getAllContacts" result="dataHandler(event)"/>
</mx:RemoteObject>
```

The application in Listing 26.5 calls getContactCount() upon application startup to inform the user how many data items are available on the server. The call to getAllContacts() to actually retrieve the data is made only when the user clicks Get Contact Data.

LISTING 26.5

Handling result events from multiple CFC functions

```
<?xml version="1.0" encoding="utf-8"?>
<mx:Application xmlns:mx="http://www.adobe.com/2006/mxml"
  xmlns:view="view.*" backgroundColor="#EEEEEE"
  creationComplete="contactService.getContactCount()">
  <mx:Script>
    <![CDATA[
      import mx.collections.ArrayCollection;
      import mx.rpc.events.ResultEvent;
      [Bindable]
      private var recordCount:Number;
      [Bindable]
      private var contactData:ArrayCollection;
      private function countHandler(event:ResultEvent):void
      {
        recordCount = event.result as Number;
      }
      private function dataHandler(event:ResultEvent):void
      {
        contactData = event.result as ArrayCollection;
```

```
      }
   ]]>
</mx:Script>
<mx:RemoteObject id="contactService"
   destination="ColdFusion"
   source="flex3bible.chapter26.ContactService">
   <mx:method name="getContactCount" result="countHandler(event)"/>
   <mx:method name="getAllContacts" result="dataHandler(event)"/>
</mx:RemoteObject>
<mx:Label
   text="There are {recordCount} Contacts available on the server"/>
<mx:Button label="Get Contact Data"
   click="contactService.getAllContacts()"/>
<view:ContactsGrid dataProvider="{contactData}"/>
</mx:Application>
```

ON the WEB The code in Listing 26.5 is available in the Web site files as
`ROMultipleFunctions.mxml` in the `src` folder of the `chapter26` project.

Figure 26.4 shows the resulting application. The `Label` at the top of the application displays the
`getContactCount()` results immediately upon application startup, while the actual data is displayed only when the user requests it from the server.

FIGURE 26.4

An application using two different functions of a single CFC

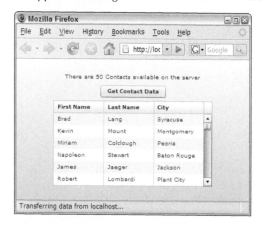

TIP As with other RPC components, you can also handle `result` and `fault` events using
the `ItemResponder` and `AsyncToken` classes. For a description of this pattern and
sample code, see Chapter 21.

Passing Arguments to CFC Functions

You can pass arguments to CFC functions in three different ways:

- Explicit arguments are passed in the order in which they're declared in the CFC function
- Bound arguments are declared with MXML code and bound to data sources in the Flex application
- Named arguments are wrapped in an ActionScript Object and are passed as though the CFC function expects only a single argument.

Using explicit arguments

Explicit arguments are passed in the same order in which they're declared in the CFC function. The CFC's getFilteredContacts() function declares two required arguments:

```
<cffunction name="getFilteredContacts" returnType="query"
   access="remote">
   <cfargument name="firstname" type="string" required="true">
   <cfargument name="lastname" type="string" required="true">
   ... function body ...
</cffunction>
```

Using explicit arguments, you pass values that match the expected data types. This code sends the data in the same order in which they're declared:

```
contactService.getFilteredContacts(fnameInput.text,
   lnameInput.text);
```

TIP   It's also possible to pass arguments explicitly with the `Operation` class's `send()` method. The following syntax allows you to pass remote CFC function names as strings or variables, passed into the `RemoteObject` component's `getOperation()` method:

```
contactService.getOperation("getFilteredContacts").send(
   fnameInput.text, lnameInput.text);
```

This calling syntax also works with the `WebService` component.

Using bound arguments

Bound arguments are declared in MXML and then passed through a call to the `RemoteObject` component's `send()` method. Just as when using the `RemoteObject` component to call Java-based methods in classes hosted by BlazeDS, you use bound argument notation with XML elements for each argument wrapped in an `<mx:arguments>` tag set. This code binds the `getFilteredContacts()` method's two arguments to values gathered from `TextInput` controls:

```
<mx:RemoteObject id="contactService" destination="ColdFusion"
  source="flex3bible.chapter26.ContactService">
  <mx:method name="getFilteredContacts">
    <mx:arguments>
      <firstname>{fnameInput.text}</firstname >
      <lastname>{lnameInput.text}</lastname>
    </mx:arguments>
  </mx:method>
</mx:RemoteObject>
```

To call the method with the bound arguments, call the operation's send() method without any explicit arguments:

```
contactService.getFilteredContacts.send()
```

> **TIP** When using bound arguments with CFC functions, the arguments are matched by name, not by the order of declaration in the client-side code. This behavior is different from Java-based methods and arguments, where bound arguments are sent in the order in which they're declared, and the XML element names are ignored.

Using named arguments

You can match CFC function arguments by name by wrapping them in an ActionScript Object. Each property has a name and a value; the name of the Object property must match the name of the CFC function argument.

This code creates an Object and attaches argument values by name:

```
var args:Object = new Object();
args.firstname = fnameInput.text;
args.lastname = lnameInput.text;
contactService.getFilteredContacts(args);
```

You also can write the same code using shorthand Object notation:

```
contactService.getFilteredContacts(
  {firstname:fnameInput.text, lastname:lnameInput.text});
```

> **TIP** This behavior is sometimes confusing to ColdFusion developers who first encounter it, because it means that you can't pass an anonymous Object as an argument to a CFC function and expect it to arrive intact as a ColdFusion structure. The Object is always broken down into its named properties, and then the individual properties are passed to the CFC function. If you need to pass a structure argument to a CFC function, you have to wrap it in another Object and pass it by name:

```
myService.myFunction({myArgumentName:myObject});
```

The named arguments behavior in Flex is very similar to ColdFusion's own `argumentCollection` attribute, which can be used to pass a structure of named arguments to functions from CFML code. This CFML code calls a CFC function and passes a structure in very much the same way:

```
<cfset stArgs=structNew()>
<cfset stArgs.firstname="firstnameValue">
<cfset stArgs.lastname="lastnameValue">
<cfinvoke component="flex3bible.chapter26.ContactService"
   argumentCollection="#stArgs#" returnVariable="qContacts"/>
```

The application in Listing 26.6 uses named arguments wrapped in an ActionScript `Object`.

LISTING 26.6

An application passing named arguments to a CFC function

```xml
<?xml version="1.0" encoding="utf-8"?>
<mx:Application xmlns:mx="http://www.adobe.com/2006/mxml"
  backgroundColor="#EEEEEE" xmlns:view="view.*">
  <mx:Script>
    <![CDATA[
      private function getContacts():void
      {
        var args:Object = new Object();
        args.firstname = fnameInput.text;
        args.lastname = lnameInput.text;
        contactService.getFilteredContacts(args);
      }
    ]]>
  </mx:Script>
  <mx:RemoteObject id="contactService" destination="ColdFusion"
    source="flex3bible.chapter26.ContactService"/>
  <mx:Form>
    <mx:FormItem label="First Name:">
      <mx:TextInput id="fnameInput"/>
    </mx:FormItem>
    <mx:FormItem label="Last Name:">
      <mx:TextInput id="lnameInput"/>
      <mx:Button label="Get Filtered Data" click="getContacts()"/>
    </mx:FormItem>
  </mx:Form>
  <view:ContactsGrid
    dataProvider="{contactService.getFilteredContacts.lastResult}"/>
</mx:Application>
```

ON the WEB   The code in Listing 26.6 is available in the Web site files as `RONamedArgs.mxml` in the `src` folder of the `chapter26` project. Examples of the same application using explicit and bound arguments are in `ROExplicitArgs.mxml` and `ROBoundArgs.mxml`, respectively.

Using Value Object Classes

When passing data between a Flex client application and ColdFusion, you can build both client-side and server-side data objects using the Value Object design pattern. The Flex version is built as an ActionScript class, while the ColdFusion version is built as a CFC. At runtime, you can pass strongly typed value objects between the client and server tiers of your application, and the Flex application and the Flash Remoting gateway automatically transfer data between the objects based on a mapping that you provide in the code.

> **TIP**   The Value Object design pattern is also known in various industry documentation sources as the Transfer Object and Data Transfer Object pattern. The different names are all used to refer to the same pattern: a class that contains data for a single instance of a data entity.

Creating a ColdFusion value object

The ColdFusion version of a value object is written as a simple CFC. The `<cfcomponent>` start tag requires an `alias` attribute that's set to the fully qualified name and location of the CFC:

```
<cfcomponent output="false" alias="flex3Bible.chapter26.Contact">
   ... component body ...
</cfcomponent>
```

Each named property is declared after the `<cfcomponent>` start tag using the `<cfproperty>` tag. Each property has a name and a type to indicate how it will be exchanged with Flex. The following `<cfproperty>` tags declare one `numeric` and two `string` properties:

```
<cfproperty name="contactId" type="numeric" default="0">
<cfproperty name="firstname" type="string" default="">
<cfproperty name="lastname" type="string" default="">
```

> **TIP**   The `<cfproperty>` tag, which in conventional ColdFusion code is used only to generate CFC documentation, controls the name and case of the property name when it's exchanged with the Flex application at runtime. This overrides the settings in the configuration files that control the case of property names.

The `<cfproperty>` tag's `default` attribute is used to generate CFC documentation and doesn't actually set default values when the CFC is instantiated in ColdFusion. Instead, you typically add code outside any function definitions that set the properties' default values upon instantiation:

```
<cfscript>
   this.contactId = 0;
   this.firstname = "";
   this.lastname = "";
</cfscript>
```

The CFC in Listing 26.7 is a value object that declares four properties of a `Contact` value object and sets their initial values upon instantiation.

LISTING 26.7

A simple value object CFC

```
<cfcomponent output="false" alias="flex3Bible.chapter26.Contact">
  <cfproperty name="contactId" type="numeric" default="0">
  <cfproperty name="firstname" type="string" default="">
  <cfproperty name="lastname" type="string" default="">
  <cfproperty name="city" type="string" default="">
  <cfscript>
    this.contactId = 0;
    this.firstname = "";
    this.lastname = "";
    this.city = ""
  </cfscript>
</cfcomponent>
```

> **ON the WEB**
> The code in Listing 26.7 is available in the Web site files as `Contact.cfm` in the ColdFusion files of the `chapter26` project.

Creating an ActionScript value object

The Flex client application uses an ActionScript version of the value object built as an ActionScript class. The class requires a `[RemoteClass]` metadata tag with an `alias` attribute that describes the fully qualified name and location of the matching CFC:

> `[RemoteClass(alias="flex3Bible.chapter26.Contact")]`

This is a two-way mapping: When an ActionScript version of the object is sent to ColdFusion, the Flash Remoting gateway creates an instance of the CFC and passes the received object's property values to the server-side version. Similarly, if a CFC function returns instances of the server-side version, client-side versions are created automatically and their property values set to the values received from the server.

> **CAUTION**
> The `alias` attributes of the `[RemoteClass]` metadata tag on the client and the `<cfcomponent>` tag on the server must match exactly and are case-sensitive.

The ActionScript class in Listing 26.8 declares the same set of values as public properties and maps itself to the server's version with the `[RemoteClass]` metadata tag.

LISTING 26.8

An ActionScript value object class

```
package vo
{
  [Bindable]
  [RemoteClass(alias="flex3Bible.chapter26.Contact")]
  public class Contact
  {
    public var contactId:int;
    public var firstname:String;
    public var lastname:String;
    public var city:String;
    public function Contact()
    {
    }
  }
}
```

ON the WEB The code in Listing 26.8 is available in the Web site files as `Contact.as` in the `src/vo` folder in the `chapter26` project.

Returning value objects from ColdFusion to Flex

After you've built versions of the value object in both ColdFusion and ActionScript and provided the appropriate mappings, a CFC function has the ability to return either individual value object instances or collections of value objects wrapped into arrays. This CFC function creates an instance of the Contact value object and returns it to Flex:

```
<cffunction name="getContactVO" access="remote"
  returntype="flex3Bible.chapter26.Contact">
  <cfset contact=createObject("component",
    "flex3Bible.chapter26.Contact")>
  <cfset contact.contactId = 1 >
  <cfset contact.firstname = "David">
  <cfset contact.lastname = "Gassner">
  <cfset contact.city = "Seattle">
  <cfreturn contact>
</cffunction>
```

Notice that the function's `returntype` attribute is set to the fully qualified name and location of the value object CFC.

The CFC in Listing 26.9 extends the original CFC and uses its data, but transforms the query object into an array of strongly typed value objects before returning it to Flex. Notice that this time the CFC function's `returntype` attribute is set to an array of CFC instances, rather than the usual generic `array` notation.

785

LISTING 26.9

A CFC function returning an array of value objects

```
<cfcomponent name="ContactServiceWithVO"
  hint="Delivers Contact data as an array of value objects"
  extends="ContactService">
  <cfapplication name="flex3BibleChapter26" sessionManagement="true">
  <cfif not structKeyExists(session, "qContacts")>
    <cfset createDataSet()>
  </cfif>
  <!--- Returns all data as an array of structures --->
  <cffunction name="getContactsAsArray" access="remote"
    returntype="flex3Bible.chapter26.Contact[]">
    <cfset var contact="">
    <cfset var arReturn=arrayNew(1)>
    <cfloop query="session.qContacts">
      <cfset contact=createObject("component",
        "flex3Bible.chapter26.Contact")>
      <cfset contact.contactId = session.qContacts.contactId>
      <cfset contact.firstname = session.qContacts.firstname>
      <cfset contact.lastname = session.qContacts.lastname>
      <cfset contact.city = session.qContacts.city>
      <cfset arrayAppend(arReturn, contact)>
    </cfloop>
    <cfreturn arReturn>
  </cffunction>
</cfcomponent>
```

ON the WEB   The code in Listing 26.9 is available in the Web site files as `ContactServiceWithVO.cfc` in the ColdFusion files of the `chapter26` project.

Receiving value objects from ColdFusion

In order to receive value objects from a CFC function and have them automatically transformed into instances of the ActionScript value object, the Flex application must contain at least one reference to the ActionScript class. The reference can be a declared instance of the class or a call to any static properties or methods. This ensures that the class, which contains the `[RemoteClass]` metadata tag, is compiled into the application and is available at runtime.

CAUTION   It isn't enough to just import the value object class in the Flex application; you have to declare at least one instance. The purpose of importing a class is to inform the Flex compiler of the class's existence, but the compiler doesn't include the class definition in the binary version of the application unless at least one instance of the class is declared, or there's a reference to one of its static members.

The Flex application in Listing 26.10 receives the `Array` of value objects and processes them in an event handler. Notice the MXML `<vo:Contact/>` declaration that ensures the mapping of the value object classes is included in the compiled application.

> **TIP**
>
> When a CFC function returns a ColdFusion `array`, it's received in Flex as an ActionScript `Array`, not an `ArrayCollection`. In this application, the `result` event handler expects an `Array` and assigns it to the `source` of the already-instantiated `ArrayCollection`:
>
> ```
> contactData.source = event.result as Array;
> ```

LISTING 26.10

Receiving an Array of strongly typed value objects

```
<?xml version="1.0" encoding="utf-8"?>
<mx:Application xmlns:mx="http://www.adobe.com/2006/mxml"
  backgroundColor="#EEEEEE" creationComplete="initApp()"
  xmlns:view="view.*" xmlns:vo="vo.*">
  <mx:Script>
    <![CDATA[
      import mx.controls.Alert;
      import mx.collections.ArrayCollection;
      import mx.rpc.events.ResultEvent;
      import mx.rpc.remoting.RemoteObject;
      [Bindable]
      private var contactData:ArrayCollection = new ArrayCollection();
      private var contactService:RemoteObject;
      private function initApp():void
      {
        contactService = new RemoteObject("ColdFusion");
        contactService.source =
  "flex3bible.chapter26.ContactServiceWithVO";
        contactService.addEventListener(ResultEvent.RESULT,
  resultHandler);
      }
      private function resultHandler(event:ResultEvent):void
      {
        contactData.source = event.result as Array;
      }
    ]]>
  </mx:Script>
  <vo:Contact/>
  <mx:Button label="Get Contacts"
    click="contactService.getContactsAsArray()"/>
  <view:ContactsGrid dataProvider="{contactData}"/>
</mx:Application>
```

ON the WEB   The code in Listing 26.10 is available in the Web site files as
RoReceiveValueObjects.mxml in the src folder of the chapter26 project.

Passing value object arguments to CFC functions

Value objects also can be passed from a Flex client application to a CFC function. The CFC function should have declared an argument typed as the ColdFusion version of the value object. This CFC function receives an instance of the Contact value object CFC and returns a concatenated string built from its properties:

```
<cffunction name="parseContact" access="remote">'
  <cfargument name="contactVO"
   type="flex3Bible.chapter26.Contact"
    required="true">
  <cfreturn "Contact received: " + contactVO.firstname +
    " " + contactVO.lastname>
</cffunction>
```

To pass a value object argument to the CFC function from Flex, create an instance of the ActionScript version of the object and set its properties. Then pass the value object to the function using any of the argument-passing strategies described previously.

The application in Listing 26.11 passes an instance of the ActionScript value object to a CFC function that extracts its properties and returns a concatenated string.

LISTIN 26.11

Passing a value object to a CFC function

```
<?xml version="1.0" encoding="utf-8"?>
<mx:Application xmlns:mx="http://www.adobe.com/2006/mxml"
  backgroundColor="#EEEEEE">
  <mx:Script>
    <![CDATA[
      import vo.Contact;
      private function passArgument():void
      {
        var newContact:Contact = new Contact();
        newContact.firstname = fnameInput.text;
        newContact.lastname = lnameInput.text;
        contactService.parseContact(newContact);
      }
    ]]>
  </mx:Script>
  <mx:RemoteObject id="contactService" destination="ColdFusion"
    source="flex3bible.chapter26.ContactServiceWithVO"/>
  <mx:Panel title="Enter Contact Information">
```

```
<mx:Form>
  <mx:FormItem label="First Name:">
    <mx:TextInput id="fnameInput"/>
  </mx:FormItem>
  <mx:FormItem label="Last Name:">
    <mx:TextInput id="lnameInput"/>
    <mx:Button label="Pass Argument" click="passArgument()"/>
  </mx:FormItem>
</mx:Form>
</mx:Panel>
<mx:Label text="{contactService.parseContact.lastResult}"
  fontSize="12"/>
</mx:Application>
```

ON the WEB   The code in Listing 26.11 is available in the Web site files as `ROPassVOArg.mxml` in the `src` folder of the `chapter26` project.

Working with RemoteObject Faults

When an exception occurs during a call to a CFC function, the `RemoteObject` dispatches a `fault` event. The event object is typed as `mx.rpc.events.FaultEvent` and contains a fault property typed as `mx.rpc.Fault`. This object in turn has `String` properties named `faultCode`, `faultString`, and `faultDetail`. The values of these properties differ depending on the nature of the error, and in the case of `faultDetail` they sometimes don't contain useful information.

Handling the fault event

As with all events, you can create an event listener with either MXML or ActionScript code. The MXML attribute-based event listener looks like this:

```
<mx:RemoteObject id="contactService" destination="ColdFusion"
  source="flex3bible.chapter26.ContactServiceWithVO"
  fault="faultHandler(event)"/>
```

To create an event listener in ActionScript code, call the `RemoteObject` component's `addEventListener()` method and declare the event name using the `FaultEvent.FAULT` constant:

```
faultService.addEventListener(FaultEvent.FAULT, faultHandler);
```

When the event handler function receives the event object, you can handle it in any way you like. Minimally, you might display the fault information to the user with a pop-up dialog box generated by the `Alert` class:

```
private function faultHandler(event:FaultEvent):void
{
    Alert.show(event.fault.faultString, event.fault.faultCode);
}
```

> **TIP**
> In ColdFusion 8, the value of the error message always has a prefix of "Unable to invoke CFC -". If you don't want to display this prefix, you have to parse the original error message from the value of the **faultString** property:

```
var errorMessage:String = event.fault.faultString;
errorMessage = errorMessage.substring(22,
    errorMessage.length);
Alert.show(errorMessage, event.fault.faultCode);
```

Generating custom exceptions from a CFC function

On the server, you can generate your own faults from a CFC function by calling the ColdFusion `<cfthrow>` command. These `<cfthrow>` commands' attributes are exposed in the Flex application's `FaultEvent.fault` object:

- The `message` attribute appears in the `fault` object's `faultString` property.
- The `errorcode` attribute appears in the `fault` object's `faultCode` property.

The CFC in Listing 26.12 implements a `throwCFCFault()` function that always generates a fault with `message` and `errorcode` attributes.

LISTING 26.12

A CFC function generating a server-side fault

```
<cfcomponent output="false">
  <cffunction name="throwCFCFault" returntype="String">
    <cfthrow message="An error message generated by a CFC function"
      errorcode="CFC Function Error">
    <cfreturn "A String">
  </cffunction>
</cfcomponent>
```

ON the WEB The code in Listing 26.12 is available in the Web site files as `FaultService.cfc` in the ColdFusion files of the `chapter26` project.

The Flex application in Listing 26.13 calls the CFC function to intentionally generate a fault and display its information in an `Alert` pop-up dialog box.

LISTING 26.13

A Flex application handling a server-side fault from a CFC function

```
<?xml version="1.0" encoding="utf-8"?>
<mx:Application xmlns:mx="http://www.adobe.com/2006/mxml"
  backgroundColor="#EEEEEE">
  <mx:Script>
    <![CDATA[
      import mx.controls.Alert;
      import mx.rpc.events.FaultEvent;
      import mx.rpc.events.ResultEvent;
      import mx.rpc.remoting.RemoteObject;
      [Bindable]
      private var returnString:String;
      private function resultHandler(event:ResultEvent):void
      {
       returnString = event.result as String;
      }
      private function faultHandler(event:FaultEvent):void
      {
        var errorMessage:String = event.fault.faultString;
        errorMessage = errorMessage.substring(22, errorMessage.length);
        Alert.show(errorMessage, event.fault.faultCode);       }
    ]]>
  </mx:Script>
  <mx:RemoteObject id="faultService" destination="ColdFusion"
    source="flex3bible.chapter26.FaultService"
    result="resultHandler(event)"
    fault="faultHandler(event)"/>
  <mx:Button label="Generate Fault"
   click="faultService.throwCFCFault()"/>
  <mx:Label text="{returnString}"/>
</mx:Application>
```

ON the WEB The code in Listing 26.13 is available in the Web site files as `ROFaultHandler.mxml` in the `src` folder of the `chapter26` project.

Summary

In this chapter, I described how to integrate Flex client applications with Adobe ColdFusion 8 using Flash Remoting and the Flex framework's RemoteObject component. You learned the following:

- Flash Remoting was originally introduced with ColdFusion MX and was adapted for use in LiveCycle Data Services and Blaze as the Remoting Service.

- Flash Remoting allows you to call functions of ColdFusion components (CFCs) from a ColdFusion server.

- Remote function calls and responses are encrypted in AMF, a binary message format that's significantly smaller and faster than XML.

- Data can be exchanged between the Flex client and a CFC function based on documented data type mappings.

- Calls to CFC functions are asynchronous.

- CFC function results can be handled with binding expressions or by handling the RemoteObject component's result event.

- Arguments can be passed to CFC functions using explicit, named, or bound argument syntax.

- Strongly typed value objects can be created in both ActionScript and ColdFusion and exchanged automatically between client and server at runtime.

- Exceptions are handled as Flex application faults using the RemoteObject component's fault event.

- Custom exceptions can be generated in ColdFusion and handled in a Flex client application.

Chapter 27

Using the ColdFusion Extensions for Flex Builder

When you install Adobe Flex Builder 3, you also can install additional plug-ins that support application development with additional technologies. The first of these, the ColdFusion Extensions for Flex Builder, includes a set of development tools that increase productivity and reduce application development time for developers using ColdFusion as their Flex application's middleware layer.

TIP The other additional plug-in that's included with Flex Builder, JSEclipse, supports programming in JavaScript and is included primarily for developers who use Flex Builder and Eclipse to build HTML-based AIR applications.

The ColdFusion Extensions for Flex Builder are built in part around Remote Development Service (RDS), a technology that was originally created by Allaire and integrated into ColdFusion Studio. RDS allows developers to connect from their development environments to ColdFusion on the server and expose information about the server's data sources and file system.

In their last incarnation, ColdFusion Studio and Homesite were merged to become Homesite+. Because many ColdFusion developers continue to use Homesite+, Adobe still sells the product and releases product updates to support each new ColdFusion release.

RDS has also been a part of Dreamweaver since the acquisition of Allaire by Macromedia and the release of Dreamweaver MX. Some of Homesite's RDS-dependent features, however, were never re-created in Dreamweaver.

IN THIS CHAPTER

Understanding ColdFusion Extension features

Installing the ColdFusion Extensions for Flex Builder

Configuring RDS

Using the RDS Dataview

Using the Visual Query Builder

Generating code with the CFC value object wizard

Using generated code in a Flex application

For example, ColdFusion Studio's Visual Query Builder, which allows developers to create advanced SQL statements based on drag-and-drop operations in a visual interface, was never a part of Dreamweaver. This and other RDS-dependent features have been recreated in the ColdFusion Extensions.

In this chapter, I describe how to install and use the ColdFusion Extensions for Flex Builder to inspect server-side resources and generate valuable code for your Flex/ColdFusion application.

ON the WEB To use the sample code for this chapter, download `chapter27.zip` from the Web site. You must have the sample `cfartgallery` database and data source installed that comes with ColdFusion 8 for the code to work correctly.

If you want to follow along with the completed sample application for this chapter, follow these steps:

1. Create a new Flex project named **chapter27** that's integrated with your ColdFusion server, as described in Chapter 26.

2. Extract the contents of `chapter27.zip` to the project's root folder.

3. Locate the `chapter27CFFiles.zip` file from the project, and extract its files to the ColdFusion Web root folder (for example, `C:\ColdFusion8\wwwroot`). This creates a new subfolder structure named `flex3Bible/chpater27` that contains the sample application's generated CFCs.

4. To test the application, first make sure your ColdFusion server is running. Then run the Flex application named `UseActiveRecord.mxml`. You should see that the application displays a `DataGrid` with a list of `Artist` records and that you can add, update, and delete data as desired.

Understanding ColdFusion Extension Features

The ColdFusion Extensions for Flex Builder are installed as a single Eclipse plug-in and provide these features:

- **The Remote Development Service (RDS)** allows Flex Builder to communicate with ColdFusion during development to show you information about the ColdFusion server's data sources and file system.

- **The RDS Dataview** displays the ColdFusion server's data sources and each data source's tables. Each table or view's metadata can be displayed, including column names, data types, and maximum sizes.

- **The RDS Fileview** displays the server's file system and allows you to create new remote files and to create, rename, and delete remote folders.

- **The Visual Query Builder** allows you to build an advanced SQL statement using a visual interface.

- **The Services Browser** displays a list of the server's CFCs and their functions and properties.

- **The CFC Value Object wizard** generates server-side code suitable for being called from Flex applications over Flash Remoting.

- **The AS-CFC and CFC-AS Class wizards** generate value object classes on either the server or the client based on existing class definitions.

Installing the ColdFusion Extensions for Flex Builder

The ColdFusion Extensions for Flex Builder are delivered as an Eclipse plug-in that's included with Flex Builder 3. As shown in Figure 27.1, toward the end of the Flex Builder 3 installation process, you're prompted to install the ColdFusion Extensions.

FIGURE 27.1

ColdFusion Extensions installation integrated into the Flex Builder 3 installation

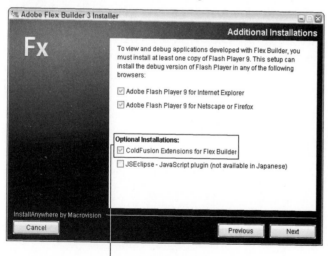

Installing the optional CF Extensions

If you've already installed Flex Builder 3 or Eclipse without the ColdFusion Extensions, you can install the plug-in using the Eclipse standard plug-in installation process. The plug-in is included in the Flex Builder installation as a file named `ColdFusion_Extensions_for_Eclipse.zip`, located in the Flex Builder installation folder under an `Installers` subfolder.

> **TIP**
> The ColdFusion Extensions plug-in can be installed into any copy of Eclipse, and it does not require either the Flex Builder standalone installation or the Flex Builder plug-in to already have been installed. You also can download the ColdFusion Extensions plug-in from Adobe's Web site at **www.adobe.com/support/coldfusion/downloads.html**. This version is known as the ColdFusion Extensions for Eclipse (rather than Flex Builder), but it has the same feature set.

Follow these steps to install the ColdFusion Extensions:

1. From the Flex Builder or Eclipse menu, select Help ➪ Software Updates ➪ Find and Install.

2. Select Search for new features to install, and click Next.

3. Click New Archived Site.

4. Browse and select `ColdFusion_Extensions_for_Eclipse.zip` from the `Installers` subfolder under the Flex Builder root installation folder (located by default on Windows in `C:\Program Files\Adobe\Flex Builder 3\Installers`).

5. As shown in Figure 27.2, you're prompted to assign a name to the plug-in installer as a Local Site.

FIGURE 27.2

Assigning a name to the plug-in installer

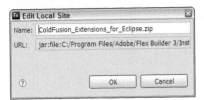

6. As shown in Figure 27.3, select the ColdFusion Extensions in the Search Results screen and click Next.

7. Follow the remaining prompts to complete the installation.

8. When prompted, restart Flex Builder to ensure that all plug-in features are immediately available.

FIGURE 27.3

Selecting the ColdFusion Extensions installer

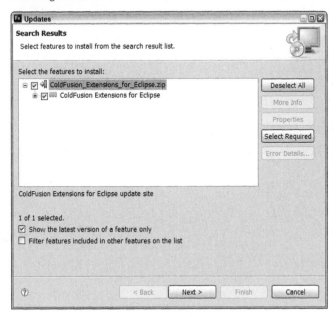

Configuring RDS Servers

Many features of the ColdFusion Extensions for Flex Builder require an RDS connection to a ColdFusion server. When you install ColdFusion 8, you're prompted to create two passwords, one for access to the ColdFusion Administrator application and one for RDS access. To connect to your ColdFusion development server from Eclipse, you need to know the server's RDS password.

> **TIP**
> If multiple-user security is enabled with ColdFusion's User Manager (a configuration option in ColdFusion Administrator), you may need both a username and an RDS password to connect to the server from Eclipse. If you're running a development server that isn't installed locally on your system, check with the administrator of your ColdFusion development server to find out what RDS credentials are required.

Follow these steps to open RDS Configuration in Eclipse:

1. Select Window ⇨ Preferences... from the Eclipse menu.

2. In the Preferences wizard, select Adobe ⇨ RDS Configuration.

    As shown in Figure 27.4, the RDS Configuration screen shows a preconfigured RDS server with a description of `localhost`. The default configuration assumes that you're using ColdFusion with the server configuration and the development Web server running on port 8500.

FIGURE 27.4

The default RDS `localhost` configuration

3. If ColdFusion is installed on your local development system, click the existing `local-host` server configuration and make any required changes to the server configuration for your ColdFusion installation. For example, if you're using the J2EE configuration, you may need to enter a value for the Context Root.

4. If you're working with a remote ColdFusion development server, click New and enter all the required connection information:

   ▦ Description: **Any descriptive string**

   ▦ Host Name: **The server's IP address or DNS host name**

   ▦ Port Number: **The port on which the ColdFusion server can be accessed**

   ▦ Context Root: **The context root of the ColdFusion application** (typically only required for J2EE configuration)

5. If you want to be able to connect to ColdFusion in each development session without having to enter an RDS password each time, enter your RDS authentication credentials and deselect the Prompt for Password option.

6. Click Test Connection. As shown in Figure 27.5, you should see a prompt indicating that Eclipse successfully connected to ColdFusion.

FIGURE 27.5

A successful connection from Eclipse to ColdFusion

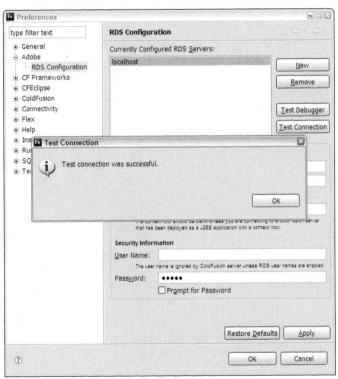

7. Click OK to save your RDS configuration settings.

Connecting to ColdFusion Data Sources

After you've successfully connected to an RDS server, you should be able to inspect the server's data sources and see your database's structure and contents from within Eclipse. Follow these steps to open the RDS Dataview:

   1. Select Window ⇨ Other Views... from the Eclipse menu.

   As shown in Figure 27.6, the Show View dialog box displays a tree of available Eclipse views for all installed plug-ins.

FIGURE 27.6

Selecting an Eclipse view

   2. Select ColdFusion ⇨ RDS Dataview.

TIP   RDS Dataview opens initially in the tabbed interface in Eclipse's bottom docking position. Because it displays its data in a tree control that expands vertically, it's a bit more useful if you drag it to the right docking position, as shown in Figure 27.7.

FIGURE 27.7

Repositioning the RDS Dataview

Click and drag to upper right to view its data

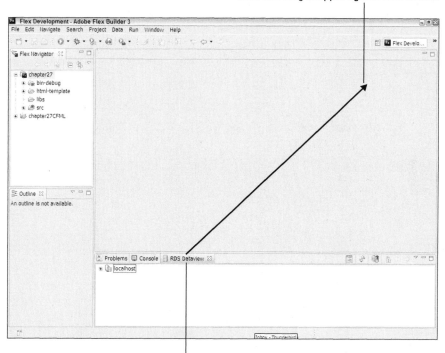

RDS Dataview initial position

Inspecting a data source

As shown in Figure 27.8, all of the ColdFusion server's data sources are displayed in the RDS Dataview. The RDS Dataview includes buttons at the top for these tasks:

- Show RDS Configuration dialog box
- Refresh active RDS server
- Open the RDS query viewer

Follow these instructions to inspect the `cfartgallery` data source that's automatically included in a new ColdFusion 8 installation:

1. Click the plus (+) icon next to the data source name to expand the data source. You should see items presenting the data source's Tables, Views, Synonyms, and System Tables.
2. Click to expand Tables.
3. Click to expand the structure of any database table.

FIGURE 27.8

RDS Dataview with an expanded data source

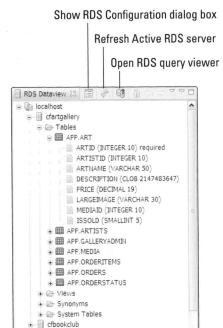

The descriptions and code samples in this chapter assume that example data sources initially installed with ColdFusion are available to you. If they've been removed from your ColdFusion installation, use any of your own data sources instead.

A *synonym* is an alias for the data source that tells the server how tables are described and where to find them. Not all databases support synonyms; for many databases, this section is empty.

Each database table's structure includes this information about each of the table's columns:

- Data type
- Column size (only meaningful with string-based columns)
- Whether the column requires values (usually known in the actual database structure as whether the column can be NULL)

TIP   With certain database drivers, ColdFusion returns table and column names through RDS in all uppercase strings. And some database drivers, such as the Apache Derby driver that's used to manage ColdFusion 8's sample data sources, add a schema prefix to all table names. For example, unless otherwise configured, Derby adds an APP prefix to the names of all database tables. You can change the schema prefix when the database is created, but you can't remove it entirely. There isn't much you can do about either the uppercase or the prefix phenomena, but they also don't hurt anything.

Viewing table data

You can view a table's data from within the RDS Dataview:

1. Right-click (Ctrl-click on the Mac) on the table that contains data you want to view.

2. Select Show Table Contents.

As shown in Figure 27.9, the RDS Query Viewer opens and displays the table's data.

CAUTION   When working with a table with large amounts of data, don't use this tool to display all the table data. Even though the RDS Query Viewer displays only the first 50 rows, the ColdFusion Extensions actually retrieve all the table's data into memory. With a very large data table, this can overwhelm Eclipse's memory and resources.

FIGURE 27.9

The RDS Query Viewer displaying data from a ColdFusion data source's table

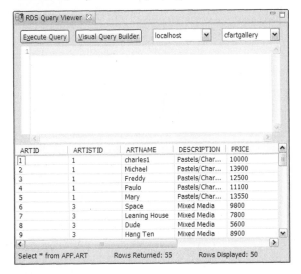

Using the Visual Query Builder

The Visual Query Builder allows you to generate complex SQL statements using a visual interface. Open the Query Builder from the RDS Query Viewer by clicking the Visual Query Builder button.

CAUTION The Visual Query Builder is available only in Windows and is not implemented in Mac OS X. When you view the RDS Query Viewer on a Mac, the Visual Query Builder button doesn't appear.

The Visual Query Builder is based on the same tool as implemented in ColdFusion Studio and Homesite+. After the Query Builder is open, you can take these actions:

- Add a table to the query in two ways:
  - Drag the table from the Tables list on the left.
  - Right-click the table, and select Add to Work Area.

- Remove a table from the query in two ways:
  - Right-click the table header, and select Remove Table from the context menu.
  - Click the table header to select it, and then press Delete.

- Create a join between two tables in two ways:
  - If two tables added to the work area have columns with identical names and compatible data types, a join between those columns is created automatically.
  - Drag from one table column to another to create a join.

- Remove or modify the behavior of a join:
  - Right-click the join icon between the tables. Use the context menu that appears (shown in Figure 27.10) to remove the join, change to an outer join, or change the join's comparison operator.

- Add a column to the query in two ways:
  - Double-click the column in a table's column list in the Tables work area.
  - Click an empty row in the Columns grid (between the Tables work area and the SQL panel at the bottom). Select a Table and a Column from the pull-down lists in that row.

- Set an AS operator to create a column alias:
  - Set an Alias in the appropriate row of the Columns grid.

- Add an ORDER BY clause:
  - Set the Sort Order and Sort Type for one or more selected table columns.

- Add a WHERE clause:
    - Select WHERE in the Condition, and add a Boolean expression in the Criteria of a selected column.

- Add a GROUP BY clause:
    - Select GROUP BY in the Condition. Any Boolean expression in the Criteria is translated as a HAVING clause.

FIGURE 27.10

Modifying a join in the Visual Query Builder

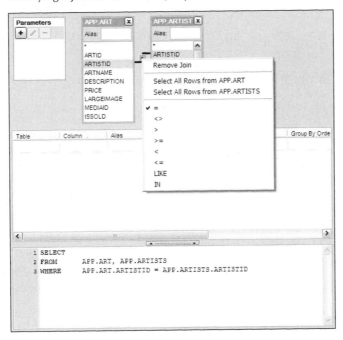

Figure 27.11 shows the Visual Query Builder with a completed SQL statement. Notice that the SQL content in the SQL pane at the bottom reflects choices made in the Tables pane on top and the Columns grid in the middle.

After an SQL statement is complete, you can test it by clicking Test Query at the bottom of the Visual Query Builder. As shown in Figure 27.12, the returned data is displayed in a pop-up window.

TIP   Unlike Homesite+, the ColdFusion Extensions' Visual Query Builder doesn't have the ability to save a query to disk either locally or on the server. It's up to the developer to copy the generated SQL code and use it in an appropriate ColdFusion <cfquery> command.

FIGURE 27.11

A completed SQL query

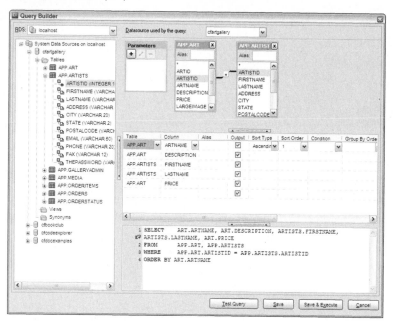

FIGURE 27.12

The returned data

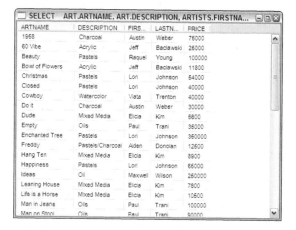

Using the CFC Value Object Wizard

The CFC Value Object wizard is one of the most valuable tools in the ColdFusion Extensions for Flex Builder. Its purpose is to generate server-side and client-side code that manages a database table through a ColdFusion data source. The server-side code, in the form of a set of ColdFusion Components, is designed to be easy to call from a Flex application through Flash Remoting.

The wizard creates CFCs based your selection from three available sets of design patterns:

- An Active Record component that includes both data representation (the value object) and database functionality in a single CFC

- Bean and DAO components that separate data representation in the bean (the value object) from database functionality in the DAO (Data Access Object)

- LiveCycle Data Services Assembler components that are designed to work with the LCDS Data Management Service

When creating a Flex/ColdFusion application that uses Flash Remoting to make asynchronous calls to remote CFC methods, you can choose between the Active Record and the Bean and DAO architectures. Both architectures include a "gateway" CFC that contains functions with their access attribute set to remote. These functions are designed to be called by the Flex framework's RemoteObject component at runtime.

> **TIP** My own preference is the Bean and DAO set of design patterns because, in my opinion, they create a better separation of functionality on the server. However, both approaches can be used to create a powerful multi-tier application that's easy to maintain.

With all three architectures, the wizard produces a server-side value object CFC that manages data for a single instance of the data entity represented by the selected database table. Optionally, the wizard also produces a client-side ActionScript value object class that's correctly mapped to the CFC. This allows you to easily pass data back and forth between client and server in your Flex application.

Preparing to use the CFC Value Object wizard

Before using the CFC Value Object wizard, you have to set up certain resources in your Flex project:

- The folder in which server-side ColdFusion code will be generated must be available in an Eclipse project definition that's currently open.

- The folder in which the client-side ActionScript value object class is generated must already exist.

The CFC folder can be in the current Flex project, or if you're using a separate project to manage your ColdFusion code, it can be in that project. In either case, the folder must be created and the project must be open before you start the wizard.

> **TIP** If you use the open source CFEclipse plug-in to create and maintain ColdFusion code, you can use a CFEclipse project to expose the CFC folder to the wizard.

If you're running the wizard on your own system, follow these steps to prepare your project:

1. Create a new subfolder in your Flex project's source root to accept the ActionScript value object class that will be created by the wizard. In the sample application for this chapter, a vo folder is created that contains the client-side value object classes.

2. If your ColdFusion folder isn't exposed in a separate Eclipse project, create a linked folder within the Flex project:

   a. Right-click (Ctrl-click on the Mac) on the project name in the Flex Navigator view.

   b. Select New ⇨ Folder from the context menu.

   c. In the New Folder dialog box, shown in Figure 27.13, set the Folder Name as any descriptive value. The name is used to identify the linked folder on disk and doesn't affect the folder's physical name. In the sample application, the linked folder name is "CFCode."

   d. Click Advanced to see the linking controls.

   e. Click Link to folder in the file system.

FIGURE 27.13
_____

Creating a linked folder for ColdFusion code generation

Create linked folder in this area

f. Click Browse and navigate to and select the folder within the ColdFusion web root where you want to create the server-side code. In the sample application, the linked folder is `flex3Bible/chapter27` under the ColdFusion web root.

g. Click Finish to create the linked folder.

The completed New Folder dialog is shown in Figure 27.13. Once these resources have been created, you're ready to run the wizard.

Running the CFC Value Object wizard

To run the CFC Value Object wizard, you first select a database table that the generated code will represent and manage. Follow these steps to open the wizard:

1. Open the RDS Dataview.

2. Open the selected data source's Tables list.

3. Right-click (Ctrl-click on the Mac) on the name of the table for which you want to generate code.

4. Select ColdFusion Wizards ➪ Create CFC from the context menu.

As shown in Figure 27.14, the CFC Value Object wizard opens and prompts you for code generation options.

The CFC Value Object wizard includes these options for both server- and client-side code generation:

■ The CFC Folder is the location where the CFCs are generated. You can click Browse to select the folder from currently open Eclipse projects. If you created a linked folder as described in the preceding section, select that folder.

■ The CFC Package Name is the subfolder structure of the CFC Folder relative to the ColdFusion Web root, set with dot syntax. For example, if your code is generated in a folder under the Web root named `myproject/cfc`, the package should be set to `mypackage.cfc`. In the sample application, the package was set as `flex3Bible.chapter27`.

> **CAUTION** The wizard doesn't have the ability to match the project's folders to the location of the ColdFusion Web root. You are responsible for setting the package name correctly.

■ The Primary Key is the column that serves as the primary key for the selected table. This value is usually set automatically by the wizard based on the data source's metadata.

■ If the primary key is an auto-incrementing numeric column, the option to allow the user to manage the primary key directly is deselected by default. If you want to provide primary key values from Flex client-side code, whether provided by the user or generated in ActionScript, select this option.

■ The CFC Type lets you select a set of design patterns. If you're creating an application with Flash Remoting, choose either Active Record or Bean CFC & DAO CFC.

FIGURE 27.14

The ColdFusion CFC Value Object wizard

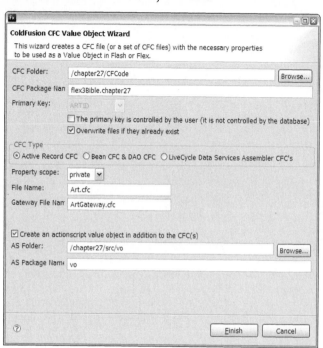

- The Property scope is set to either Public or Private and affects how the value object CFC manages its data properties. When set to Public, properties are declared in the ColdFusion `this` scope and can be read and written to by external ColdFusion code with simple dot syntax. When set to Private, properties are declared in the ColdFusion `variables` scope and are accessible only to external code through the value object CFC's `setter` and `getter` functions.

NOTE The selection of public or private properties applies only to the value object on the server. The ActionScript value object class is always created with public properties.

TIP In ColdFusion components, properties in the scope named `this` are analogous to ActionScript properties declared as `public`, while properties in the `variables` scope behave like ActionScript properties declared as `private`.

- The File names determine the names of the CFCs on the server. The default names always start with the name of the selected table as delivered by ColdFusion through RDS. The first is the name of the value object, and the others represent the gateway CFC, and if using the Bean & DAO patterns, the DAO CFC.

> **TIP** If table names are shown as all uppercase, the names of the CFCs default that way as well. To more closely model good object-oriented naming conventions, it's a good idea to customize the table names. For example, if a table name is all uppercase, such as ART, change it to initial-cap syntax, as in Art. And if a table name uses a plural expression, such as ARTISTS, I usually change the filenames to singular syntax, as in Artist. (The latter guideline is important because a value object class refers to a single instance of the data entity, never more than one.)

- The option at the bottom of the wizard, when selected, creates a client-side ActionScript value object that matches the value object CFC on the server. Its name always matches the CFC version, so you don't have to provide that in the wizard options. (For example, if your value object CFC is named Artist.cfc, the ActionScript version will be Artist.as.)

- The AS Folder is a folder within your Flex project where you want the ActionScript value object class to be generated. You can browse to select this folder from the Flex project, but it must have been created before you run the wizard.

- The AS Package Name is the folder's equivalent package.

> **CAUTION** In Flex Builder 3, the source root folder is to a project subfolder named src by default. The Value Object wizard doesn't exhibit awareness of this change, so if you browse to select a folder named vo within the source root, the wizard incorrectly sets the package to src.vo. Just change to the correct package name of vo before clicking Finish to generate the code.

After setting all options, click Finish to generate the CFCs and the ActionScript value object class. Depending on which set of design patterns you selected, within a few seconds a new value object, gateway, and, if selected, DAO CFCs are created for you.

> **CAUTION** The CFC Value Object Wizard is presented in a resizable pop-up window. If it's too small, certain data entry controls such as the CFC Type radio buttons may not be visible. If you don't see the controls described in this section, expand the size of the wizard pop-up window.

Understanding generated value object classes

In order to make the best use of the generated ActionScript and ColdFusion code, it's important to understand the code's patterns and its strengths and weaknesses. The generated code isn't a final product but instead is designed to be a starting point for your application's requirements. In some cases, the code requires immediate changes to be even functional; in others, only the developer can select and apply some recommended customizations.

Understanding the value object CFC

The value object CFC defines properties for each of the selected database table's columns. Each property has its data type and default value set to match the type of the table column. In addition, it implements functions to manage the data from ColdFusion code.

> **TIP** The value object CFC's functions aren't designed to be called directly from the Flex clients, so they all have their access property set to public rather than remote.

As described in Chapter 26, a value object CFC should have an `alias` attribute that declares the component's fully qualified name and location and `<cfproperty>` tags for each property that determine how property names and data types are exchanged with Flex at runtime. A generated value object CFC follows these rules closely, adding as many `<cfproperty>` tags as necessary at the top of the component:

```
<cfcomponent output="false" alias="flex3Bible.chapter27.Artist">
  <cfproperty name="ARTISTID" type="numeric" default="0">
  <cfproperty name="FIRSTNAME" type="string" default="">
  <cfproperty name="LASTNAME" type="string" default="">
  ... additional <cfproperty> tags as needed ...
</cfcomponent>
```

> **TIP** The `alias` is set based on the CFC package and filenames you set in the CFC wizard. If you need to change these values, you may decide to regenerate the code from scratch, because the `alias` is referred to in many other parts of the code.

The default values for each property are set in a `<cfscript>` section below the `<cfproperty>` tags. Because the code is outside any CFC functions, it's executed automatically upon object instantiation:

```
<cfscript>
  variables.ARTISTID = 0;
  variables.FIRSTNAME = "";
  variables.LASTNAME = "";
  ... additional default settings as needed ...
</cfscript>
```

In this example, the properties are declared in the `variables` scope because the Property scope was set to `Private` in the CFC wizard. If you select `Public`, the properties are instead created in the ColdFusion `this` scope.

Regardless of which design pattern is selected, the value object CFC implements explicit `setter` and `getter` functions for each of its properties. The `setter` function receives a value and passes it to the property, which the `getter` returns with the property's current value:

```
<cffunction name="getFirstName" output="false" access="public"
  returntype="any">
  <cfreturn variables.FirstName>
</cffunction>

<cffunction name="setFirstName" output="false" access="public"
  returntype="void">
  <cfargument name="val" required="true">
  <cfset variables.FirstName = arguments.val>
</cffunction>
```

The generated value object CFC implements an init() method that returns an instance of the component. When generated with the Active Record design pattern, init() accepts an optional id argument and then uses the component's load() method to create the component instance:

```
<cffunction name="init" output="false" returntype="Artist">
  <cfargument name="id" required="false">
  <cfscript>
    if( structKeyExists(arguments, "id") )
    {
      load(arguments.id);
    }
    return this;
  </cfscript>
</cffunction>
```

The load() method queries the database for the selected record, creates the value object, populates its properties from the database by calling the explicit setter functions, and returns the object:

```
<cffunction name="load" output="false" access="public"
  returntype="void">
  <cfargument name="id" required="true" >
  <cfset var qRead="">
  <cfquery name="qRead" datasource="cfartgallery">
    select ARTISTID, FIRSTNAME, LASTNAME, ADDRESS, CITY, STATE,
        POSTALCODE, EMAIL, PHONE, FAX, THEPASSWORD
    from APP.ARTISTS
    where ARTISTID = <cfqueryparam cfsqltype="CF_SQL_INTEGER"
     value="#arguments.id#" />
  </cfquery>

  <cfscript>
    setARTISTID(qRead.ARTISTID);
    setFIRSTNAME(qRead.FIRSTNAME);
    setLASTNAME(qRead.LASTNAME);
    ... more setter method calls ...
  </cfscript>
</cffunction>
```

The Bean & DAO version of the value object CFC is much simpler than the Active Record version, because it only represents data and doesn't interact with the database:

```
<cffunction name="init" output="false" returntype="Artist">
  <cfreturn this>
</cffunction>
```

That's all the non-property related, generated code for the Bean & DAO version of the value object CFC. Because database functionality in this pattern is isolated in a separate DAO CFC, no additional methods are implemented in the value object CFC. For a value object CFC generated with the Active Record pattern, however, additional functions manage creating, updating, and deleting of database rows.

The create() function uses the current object's properties and passes them to an SQL Insert command. If the option to allow generation of a primary key value from the client application wasn't selected in the Value Object wizard, an additional SQL statement is executed to discover the newly generated primary value from the database:

```
<cffunction name="create" output="false" access="private"
  returntype="void">
  <cfset var qCreate="">

  <cfset var local1=getFIRSTNAME()>
  <cfset var local2=getLASTNAME()>
  <cfset var local3=getADDRESS()>

  <cftransaction isolation="read_committed">
    <cfquery name="qCreate" datasource="cfartgallery">
    insert into APP.ARTISTS(FIRSTNAME, LASTNAME, ADDRESS)
    values (
      <cfqueryparam value="#local1#" cfsqltype="CF_SQL_VARCHAR"
    />,
      <cfqueryparam value="#local2#" cfsqltype="CF_SQL_VARCHAR"
    />,
      <cfqueryparam value="#local3#" cfsqltype="CF_SQL_VARCHAR"
    />
    )
    </cfquery>

    <!--- If your server has a better way to get the ID that is
    more
      reliable, use that instead --->
    <cfquery name="qGetID" datasource="cfartgallery">
    select ARTISTID
    from APP.ARTISTS
    where FIRSTNAME = <cfqueryparam value="#local1#"
      cfsqltype="CF_SQL_VARCHAR" />
      and LASTNAME = <cfqueryparam value="#local2#"
      cfsqltype="CF_SQL_VARCHAR" />
      and ADDRESS = <cfqueryparam value="#local3#" >
    order by ARTISTID desc
    </cfquery>
  </cftransaction>
  <cfset variables.ARTISTID = qGetID.ARTISTID>
</cffunction>
```

As noted in the code comment, the approach used to find the new primary key isn't really the right way to do it. This code queries for the new row by filtering on every column of the database table. Particularly when working with a large table with columns that don't have indices, this can result in very slow performance.

The problem is that the "correct" approach for discovering a newly assigned primary key is different for nearly every database platform. So, after generating the code with the Value Object wizard, you should modify the create() method to use the right SQL syntax for your database. Here are some examples:

- For a MySQL table with an auto-incrementing numeric primary key column, use the LAST_INSERT_ID() function to return the most recently generated primary key value:

```
<cfquery name="qGetID" datasource="cfartgallery">
  select LAST_INSERT_ID() as ARTISTID
</cfquery>
```

- In Apache Derby, the IDENTITY_VAL_LOCAL( ) function does the same job:

```
<cfquery name="qGetID" datasource=" cfartgallery">
  select IDENTITY_VAL_LOCAL() as ARTISTID
</cfquery>
```

- For Microsoft SQL Server, the IDENT_CURRENT() function returns the most recent identity value for a specific table:

```
<cfquery name="qGetID" datasource="cfartgallery">
  select IDENT_CURRENT('ARTISTS') as ARTISTID
</cfquery>
```

CAUTION In all cases, be sure to wrap both queries (the INSERT statement and the SELECT statement) in a set of <cftransaction> tags to ensure that other users can't create a new record between operations.

TIP SQL Server also supports the @@IDENTITY and SCOPE_IDENTITY() functions; see the SQL Server documentation for information on differences between these functions.

For other database applications, check the product documentation for the correct way to retrieve a dynamically generated primary key value.

TIP If your database table uses a non-numeric primary key, such as SQL Server's uniqueidentifier data type, it's typically better to indicate that the user will supply the primary key value when generating the value object CFC. Then modify the CFC's generated create() function to create the primary key before executing the INSERT statement. For example, this modified code generates a new unique identifier in the first statement by calling SQL Server's NEWID() function and then passes the resulting value in the INSERT statement to create a record:

```
<cfquery name="qGetID" datasource="cfartgallery">
  select NEWID() as ARTISTID
</cfquery>
<cfquery name="qCreate" datasource="cfartgallery">
  insert into ARTISTS(ARTISTID, FIRSTNAME, LASTNAME ...)
  values (<cfqueryparam value="#qGetID.ARTISTID#"
          cfsqltype="CF_SQL_VARCHAR" />,
      ... remaining column values ...
    )
</cfquery>
```

The CFC also implements an `update()` function that passes its current properties to an SQL UPDATE statement:

```
<cffunction name="update" output="false" access="private"
  returntype="void">
  <cfset var qUpdate="">

  <cfquery name="qUpdate" datasource="cfartgallery"
   result="status">
    update APP.ARTISTS
    set FIRSTNAME = <cfqueryparam value="#getFIRSTNAME()#"
       cfsqltype="CF_SQL_VARCHAR" />,
      LASTNAME = <cfqueryparam value="#getLASTNAME()#"
       cfsqltype="CF_SQL_VARCHAR" />,
      ADDRESS = <cfqueryparam value="#getADDRESS()#"
       cfsqltype="CF_SQL_VARCHAR" />
    ... remaining columns as needed ...
    where ARTISTID = <cfqueryparam value="#getARTISTID()#"
       cfsqltype="CF_SQL_INTEGER">
  </cfquery>
</cffunction>
```

The `update()` function is well built and doesn't require any modification. The same is true for the `delete()` function, which deletes a row from the database table based on a required `id` argument:

```
<cffunction name="delete" output="false" access="public"
  returntype="void">
  <cfset var qDelete="">

  <cfquery name="qDelete" datasource="cfartgallery"
   result="status">
    delete
    from APP.ARTISTS
    where ARTISTID = <cfqueryparam cfsqltype="CF_SQL_INTEGER"
    value="#getARTISTID()#" />
  </cfquery>
</cffunction>
```

If you decide to use the Bean & DAO design pattern, the `create()`, `update()`, and `delete()` functions are found in the DAO CFC, the object directly responsible for the data interaction. The recommendations in this section apply in the same manner: The `update()` function should be customized for your particular database, while the `update()` and `delete()` functions can be left as is.

Understanding the ActionScript value object class

The ActionScript value object class is generated in the Flex project and includes property settings as public properties. It also adds the `[RemoteClass]` metadata tag that provides the two-way mapping of the client-side and server-side value objects to each other:

```
package vo
{
  [RemoteClass(alias="flex3Bible.chapter27.Artist")]
  [Bindable]
  public class Artist
  {
    public var ARTISTID:Number = 0;
    public var FIRSTNAME:String = "";
    public var LASTNAME:String = "";
    ... additional property declarations ...

    public function Artist()
    {
    }
  }
}
```

The ActionScript value object class looks the same for either the Active Record or the Bean and DAO design patterns.

Using the gateway CFC

The gateway CFC is generated for both the Active Record and the Bean and DAO design patterns. In either case, the gateway CFC implements CFC functions that are designed to be called from Flex and have their access attributes set to remote.

The names of the functions implemented in the gateway CFC differ depending on which design pattern you select. Table 27.1 describes function names and their purpose.

TABLE 27.1

Gateway CFC Functions

Active Record CFC	Bean CFC and DAO CFC	Purpose
get()	getById()	Receives a required id argument, and returns a single value object instance.
save()	save()	Receives a required instance of the value object as an argument, and either updates or creates a database row. Returns a value object instance with new or updated data.
delete()	deleteById()	Receives a single id argument, and deletes a database row. See the note following this table about modifying the delete() function for the Active Record version of the gateway CFC.
getAll()	getAll()	Returns an array of strongly typed value objects.
getAllAsQuery()	getAllAsQuery()	Returns a ColdFusion query object, translated in Flex as an ArrayCollection of Object instances.

Modifying the save() function

The save() function in the Active Record version of the gateway CFC doesn't return a useful value as initially generated. It's designed to return the value of the value object's save() function, but that function doesn't return anything. This is the gateway CFC's save() function as initially generated:

```
<cffunction name="save" output="false" access="remote">
  <cfargument name="obj" required="true" />
  <cfreturn obj.save() />
</cffunction>
```

Instead, it's better to modify the function so that it returns the same object that's passed in as an argument. Because this object is strongly typed as the value object, and during the data row creation process, its primary key is populated with any new value, when you return it to the Flex client application, it contains any information generated by the server-side code. This is the same function after being modified:

```
<cffunction name="save" output="false" access="remote"
    returntype="flex3Bible.chapter27.Artist">
  <cfargument name="obj" required="true" type="Artist"/>
  <cfset obj.save()>
  <cfreturn obj/>
</cffunction>
```

Renaming the delete() function

For the most part, the names of the gateway CFC's functions don't matter; you just call them as named from the Flex client application as RemoteObject operations. In the case of the Active Record version's delete() method, however, the name of the function creates a problem. ActionScript 3 has a delete operator that's used to remove data items from an XMLList or XML object with E4X syntax. Normally you would try to use this code to call the function from the Flex application:

```
myRemoteObject.delete(myRowID);
```

Because of the collision between the reserved keyword delete and the CFC function name, a compiler error results and you can't compile or run the Flex application. The fix, however, is simple: After generating the CFCs with the CFC Value Object wizard, rename the gateway CFC's delete() function as deleteByID() (or any other name you prefer):

```
<cffunction name="deleteById" output="false" access="remote">
  <cfargument name="id" required="true" />
  <cfset var obj = get(arguments.id)>
  <cfset obj.delete()>
</cffunction>
```

Modifying the getAll() function

The gateway CFC's `getAll()` function returns an array of strongly typed value objects. Its logic seems sturdy at first: It starts by querying the primary key values for the entire table and then loops through the resulting query object to create one value object for each row:

```
<cffunction name="getAll" output="false" access="remote"
  returntype="flex3Bible.chapter27.Artist[]">
  <cfset var qRead="">
  <cfset var obj="">
  <cfset var ret=arrayNew(1)>

  <cfquery name="qRead" datasource="cfartgallery">
    select ARTISTID
    from APP.ARTISTS
  </cfquery>

  <cfloop query="qRead">
  <cfscript>
    obj = createObject("component",
   "Artist").init(qRead.ARTISTID);
    ArrayAppend(ret, obj);
  </cfscript>
  </cfloop>
  <cfreturn ret>
</cffunction>
```

On closer inspection though, it turns out this code needs some changes. Each time the value object CFC's `init()` method is called, another query is executed to retrieve the selected database row and build the value object. The result is that each call to `getAll()` results in one initial database query and then multiple subsequent queries for each database row. As a table gets larger, this code degrades quickly.

To fix this issue, change the `getAll()` method as follows:

1. Change the initial query to retrieve all required columns.
2. Change the code within the loop through the resulting query object. For each query row, create a new instance of the value object CFC by calling its `init()` function with no arguments.
3. Set the value object's properties as needed.
4. Add the value object to the array that's returned at the end of the function.

A modified version of the `getAll()` function might look like this:

```
<cffunction name="getAll" output="false" access="remote"
  returntype="flex3Bible.chapter27.Artist[]">
  <cfset var qRead="">
  <cfset var obj="">
  <cfset var ret=arrayNew(1)>
```

```
<cfquery name="qRead" datasource="cfartgallery">
  select *
  from APP.ARTISTS
</cfquery>

<cfloop query="qRead">
<cfscript>
  obj = createObject("component", "Artist").init();
  obj.setFIRSTNAME(qRead.FIRSTNAME);
  obj.setLASTNAME(qRead.LASTNAME);
  ... set additional properties ...
  ArrayAppend(ret, obj);
</cfscript>
</cfloop>
<cfreturn ret>
</cffunction>
```

The result of the modified code is that only a single query is needed to retrieve all required data from the server.

 The resulting `getAll()` function is still just a starting point for your application. You may want to add arguments, filtering, dynamic sorting, and other features as required.

Calling gateway CFC functions

To use the generated CFC code from a Flex client application, create an instance of the `RemoteObject` component and set its `source` to the fully qualified location of the gateway CFC:

```
<mx:RemoteObject id="artistService"
  destination="ColdFusion"
  source="flex3Bible.chapter27.ArtistGateway"/>
```

Then at runtime, call the gateway CFC's functions as needed. For example, this code calls the `getAll()` method to retrieve an array of value objects:

```
artistService.getAll();
```

To create or update a database record, pass an instance of the ActionScript value object to the gateway CFC's `save()` method. The logic on the server examines the value object's primary key value. If the primary key value is 0 (or a blank string if using a String-based primary key column), the server code calls the `create()` method; otherwise it calls the `update()` method.

```
artistService.save(myArtist);
```

And to delete a database record on the server, call the gateway CFC's `deleteById()` function and pass the unique `id` of the record you want to delete:

```
artistService.deleteById(artistGrid.selectedItem.ARTISTID);
```

The application in Listing 27.1 presents a simple user interface with a pop-up window data entry form for adding and updating database rows. The main application file declares an instance of the RemoteObject component with attribute-based event listeners for each of the gateway CFC's functions. Its logic is stored in a separate UseActiveRecord.as ActionScript file.

LISTING 27.1

A Flex application with a RemoteObject component pointing to the gateway CFC

```xml
<?xml version="1.0" encoding="utf-8"?>
<mx:Application xmlns:mx="http://www.adobe.com/2006/mxml"
  layout="vertical"
  creationComplete="initApp()">
  <mx:Script source="UseActiveRecord.as"/>
  <mx:RemoteObject id="artistService"
    destination="ColdFusion"
    source="flex3Bible.chapter27.ArtistGateway">
    <mx:method name="getAll" result="getAllHandler(event)"/>
    <mx:method name="save" result="saveHandler(event)"/>
    <mx:method name="deleteById" result="deleteHandler(event)"/>
  </mx:RemoteObject>
  <mx:Panel title="Artist List">
    <mx:DataGrid id="artistGrid" dataProvider="{acArtist}" width="300"
      doubleClickEnabled="true" doubleClick="editArtist()">
      <mx:columns>
        <mx:DataGridColumn dataField="FIRSTNAME" headerText="First
  Name"/>
        <mx:DataGridColumn dataField="LASTNAME" headerText="Last Name"/>
      </mx:columns>
    </mx:DataGrid>
    <mx:ControlBar>
      <mx:Button label="Add" click="addArtist()"/>
      <mx:Button label="Edit" enabled="{artistGrid.selectedIndex != -1}"
        click="editArtist()"/>
      <mx:Button label="Delete" enabled="{artistGrid.selectedIndex != -
  1}"
        click="deleteArtist()"/>
    </mx:ControlBar>
  </mx:Panel>
</mx:Application>
```

The code in Listing 27.1 is available in the Web site files as UseActiveRecord.mxml in the src folder of the chapter27 project.

The ActionScript file in Listing 27.2 contains the application's logic, including `result` event handler functions for each of the gateway CFC's functions.

LISTING 27.2

The ActionScript logic for the Artist application

```
import events.ArtistEvent;
import forms.ArtistForm;
import mx.collections.ArrayCollection;
import mx.controls.Alert;
import mx.managers.PopUpManager;
import mx.rpc.AsyncToken;
import mx.rpc.events.FaultEvent;
import mx.rpc.events.ResultEvent;
import vo.Artist;

[Bindable]
private var acArtist:ArrayCollection = new ArrayCollection;
private var artistPopupForm:ArtistForm = new ArtistForm();

private function initApp():void
{
  artistService.getAll();
  artistPopupForm.addEventListener("save", artistFormHandler);
  artistPopupForm.addEventListener("cancel", artistFormCancel);
}
private function getAllHandler(event:ResultEvent):void
{
  acArtist.source = event.result as Array;
}
private function addArtist():void
{
  artistPopupForm.artist = new Artist();
  PopUpManager.addPopUp(artistPopupForm, this, true);
  PopUpManager.centerPopUp(artistPopupForm);
}
private function editArtist():void
{
  artistPopupForm.artist = artistGrid.selectedItem as Artist;
  PopUpManager.addPopUp(artistPopupForm, this, true);
  PopUpManager.centerPopUp(artistPopupForm);
}
private function artistFormHandler(event:ArtistEvent):void
{
```

```
  PopUpManager.removePopUp(artistPopupForm);
  var token:AsyncToken = artistService.save(event.artist);
  if (event.artist.ARTISTID == 0)
  {
    token.action="create";
  }
  else
  {
    token.action="update";
  }
}
private function artistFormCancel(event:Event):void
{
  PopUpManager.removePopUp(artistPopupForm);
}
private function saveHandler(event:ResultEvent):void
{
  if (event.token.action == "create")
  {
    var artist:Artist = event.result as Artist;
    acArtist.addItem(artist);
    artistGrid.selectedItem = artist;
    artistGrid.scrollToIndex(artistGrid.selectedIndex);
    Alert.show("Artist was successfully added", "Artist Added");
  }
  else if (event.token.action == "update")
  {
    Alert.show("Artist was successfully updated", "Artist Updated");
  }
}
private function deleteArtist():void
{
  artistService.deleteById(artistGrid.selectedItem.ARTISTID);
}
private function deleteHandler(event:ResultEvent):void
{
  acArtist.removeItemAt(artistGrid.selectedIndex);
}
private function faultHandler(event:FaultEvent):void
{
  Alert.show(event.fault.faultString, event.fault.faultCode);
}
```

ON the WEB The code in Listing 27.1 is available in the Web site files as `UseActiveRecord.mxml` in the `src` folder of the `chapter27` project.

A conclusion about the CFC Value Object wizard

As you've seen, the code generated by the CFC Value Object wizard isn't perfect. But the changes that are typically required to make that code useful and dependable for Flex/ColdFusion applications is minimal, and they're always the same. For applications that interact with many database tables on the server, using this feature can significantly reduce server-side programming time and let you get to the fun part of Flex application development: creating a dynamic, compelling user interface that works exactly the same on the desktop or the Web.

Summary

In this chapter, I described how to use the ColdFusion Extensions for Flex Builder to inspect server-side resources and generate valuable code for your application. You learned the following:

- The ColdFusion Extensions are packaged and delivered with Flex Builder 3.

- You can install the ColdFusion Extensions either during the initial Flex Builder installation or afterward using the Eclipse's plug-in installation architecture.

- The Remote Development Service (RDS) lets you communicate with a ColdFusion server installation during development.

- RDS must be configured to connect to your ColdFusion server.

- The ColdFusion Extensions include the RDS Dataview and the RDS Fileview that let you inspect server-side data sources and file and directory information.

- The Visual Query Builder lets you generate complex SQL statements with a visual interface.

- The ColdFusion CFC Value Object wizard generates server-side and client-side code for database table management in a Flex application.

Chapter 28

Integrating Flex Applications with ASP.NET

Web application developers who are immersed in and accustomed to working with Microsoft's ASP.NET application server have good reason to want to stick with it. Beyond the advantage of leveraging existing knowledge, selecting ASP.NET as the middleware application server for a Flex-based application offers many benefits:

- A powerful implementation of a SOAP-based Web service provider
- The best possible integration with Microsoft's Windows operating system and SQL Server database platform
- A selection of programming languages in which you can develop your server-side logic and resources

In addition, the ASP.NET developer community is served by a large third-party market of components and development tools. When you need a component for integration with an ASP.NET Web site, you'll likely find it available for sale or for free somewhere in the .NET community.

As when working with Adobe ColdFusion, a developer can select from any of the three Flex RPC methodologies to retrieve data and call functions from the server. As with any middleware application server, if you know how to read and write XML-formatted data in ASP.NET, you can use the Flex framework's HTTPService component to exchange data in generic XML formats. And for those who are addicted to the performance available with the RemoteObject component and the AMF messaging format, there are implementations of AMF-based communications available as freely licensed open-source projects (Fluorine FX at www.fluorinefx.com) and commercial products (WebOrb at www.themidnightcoders.com).

The most commonly used RPC strategy with Flex and ASP.NET, however, is to use the `WebService` component to call remote operations hosted as SOAP-based Web services (known in ASP.NET as *XML Web Services*). This approach doesn't require any additional software purchases or installation, and it makes good use of one of ASP.NET's strengths in the application server market.

In this chapter, I describe how to build Web services in ASP.NET that are compatible with Flex client applications and how to use Flex Builder 3's new code generation features to generate ASP.NET Web service components. I then offer some tips on how to best leverage these server-side assets in your Flex application.

ON the WEB   To use the sample code for this chapter, download `chapter28.zip` from the Web site. This is not a Flex project archive file. Its use and installation are described later in this chapter.

CROSS-REF   Many details of using the Flex framework's `WebService` component are described in Chapter 23. This chapter focuses on details of the Web service architecture that are unique to ASP.NET.

Installing ASP.NET

ASP.NET can be installed either as a separate free download from Microsoft or as part of a development environment. The techniques described in this chapter are designed to work with .NET Framework version 2.0 or later. The most recent versions of Microsoft's .NET development tools deliver .NET Framework version 3.5.

TIP   To test your XML Web Services in .NET, you can either use Internet Information Services (IIS), the Web server software that's included with advanced Windows editions, or you can use the development Web server that's included with Microsoft's development tools. If you want to use IIS, be sure that the Web server is fully installed and tested prior to installing the .NET Framework. This ensures that the application server components are correctly integrated into the Web server.

You can download the .NET Framework installer from Microsoft's home page for ASP.NET at `www.asp.net`. From the home page, click the link for the .NET Framework. The Downloads page, shown in Figure 28.1, has links to download the Framework on its own or to download a complete Web development tool named Microsoft Visual Web Developer 2008 Express Edition.

CROSS-REF   The steps for downloading and installing Visual Web Developer 2008 are described later in this chapter.

To install the ASP.NET Framework on its own, download the .NET Framework installer as described in the previous section. For the most recent version of ASP.NET as of this writing, the file is named `dotNetFx35setup.exe`. Run the installer application to get started. As shown in Figure 28.2, the initial screen asks you to accept a license agreement and click Install.

The .NET Framework installation doesn't have any configurable options, and it runs unattended after the license agreement has been accepted. After completing the installation, you may be prompted to restart your system.

FIGURE 28.1

Getting the .NET Framework

The Framework alone

Visual Web Developer 2008 Express Edition

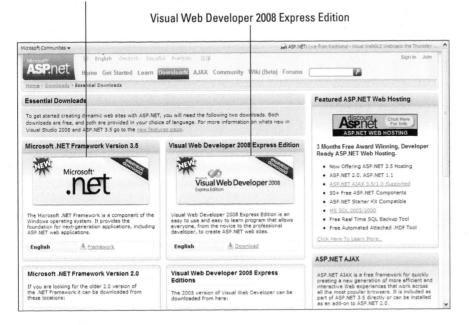

FIGURE 28.2

The .NET Framework installer

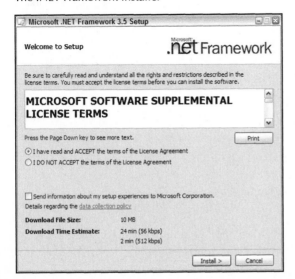

Creating an XML Web Service

You can create an XML Web Service with a variety of tools. As with ColdFusion, PHP, and other scripting environments, an XML Web Service is defined in a set of source code files. Like these other application server technologies, a Web service compiles "on request" on the ASP.NET application server, so you can define and deploy a Web service with nothing more than a simple text editor.

Most developers, however, prefer to use a development tool that handles the most common tasks automatically and frees their time for the creative side of application development. Available code generation tools include:

- Flex Builder 3, which can generate a .NET-based Web service based on the structure of a database table hosted by Microsoft SQL Server
- Visual Studio Professional
- Visual Web Developer Express Edition

Regardless of which tool you use, the syntax rules for creating the service are the same. In this section, I describe the most important aspects of any Web service hosted by ASP.NET.

Creating a gateway file

A SOAP-based Web service in ASP.NET typically consists of at least two source code files. The first is the Web service gateway file, which always has a file extension of `.asmx`. The purpose of this file is to listen for and respond to requests from Web service client applications. The Web service gateway file contains a `<%@ Web-Service %>` declaration that determines these properties of the Web service:

- The language in which the service is written
- The name of the .NET custom class that defines the Web service's operations

The code that implements the Web service can be hosted within the gateway file or, more commonly, is placed in a separate .NET class definition that's used as the `CodeBehind` component. When using this code architecture, you declare the name of the class containing the service implementation in the `WebService` declaration's `CodeBehind` attribute.

This Web service declaration defines itself as a .NET class named `HelloService` written in the C# programming language and indicates that the class implementation is in an external code module named `HelloService.cs`:

```
<%@ WebService Language="C#"
    CodeBehind="~/App_Code/HelloService.cs"
   Class="HelloService" %>
```

When the .NET class implementation is placed in a separate code module file, the gateway file doesn't require any additional code. This type of file is often referred to as a *stub,* because it represents the main application interface (in this case, a Web service waiting for client requests) but leaves all implementation details to a separate file.

You access a Web service from a Flex application by setting the `WebService` component's `wsdl` property to the gateway file location, with a `?wsdl` query string parameter. For example, if the previous code is in a file named `HelloService.asmx` in a `flex3bible` folder under the IIS Web root, the `wsdl` property might be set to:

```
http://www.myserver.com/flex3bible/HelloService.asmx?wsdl
```

The first time an HTTP request is made to the gateway file, the .NET compiler reads the gateway and any dependent files such as the code-behind module and compiles them into `.dll` files on the server. The Web service is then executed, and the generated WSDL content is returned to the client application.

Creating a code-behind module

A code-behind class is implemented as a standard .NET class with these required elements:

- All code libraries (known in .NET as *assemblies*) that are used in the class implementation are imported.

- Metadata tags declare the Web service's unique identifier and conformance rules.

- Class methods that are exposed as Web service operations are identified with metadata tags.

> **NOTE** The code samples throughout this chapter are implemented using C#. Both Flex Builder 3 and Visual Web Developer 2008 also are capable of generating Web service code in Visual Basic .NET. The choice between these two programming languages is purely a matter of developer preference. Developers with a background in C, Java, JavaScript, or ActionScript typically find C# to be easier to use, because its fundamental syntax is nearly the same as these other languages. Developers with a background in Basic may prefer to work in Visual Basic .NET. Both languages have access to the entire .NET Framework and its associated code libraries, so you should be able to create any required functionality in your own Web services with either language.

Using .NET assemblies

The code module has some required statements that identify particular .NET code libraries (or assemblies) and make them available to the .NET compiler. In C#, a using statement accomplishes the same task as an import statement in ActionScript or Java: It identifies and makes the designated code library available to the compiler.

A basic set of using statements in a Web service class that accesses might look like this:

```
using System;
using System.Data;
using System.Data.Common;
using System.Text;
using System.Web.Services;
```

Declaring the Web service namespace URI

The next bit of code in the code module is a [WebService] metadata tag that identifies the namespace URI (Universal Resource Identifier) for the service. In a new Web service that's generated by Visual Studio, Visual Web Developer, or Flex Builder, the [WebService] declaration sets a temporary URI:

```
[WebService(Namespace = "http://tempuri.org/")]
```

For a production Web service, you should always customize this URI to make it globally unique. You typically accomplish this with a URI that starts with your organization's Web domain and ends with a virtual directory structure that identifies the purpose of the Web service:

```
[WebService(Namespace = "http://www.bardotech.com/helloservice")]
```

> **TIP** As with all namespace URI strings, the Web service's namespace doesn't have to resolve to a URL. However, developers often use their organization's URL as the first part of a namespace to guarantee that the namespace is globally unique.

Setting conformance rules

In each Web service, ASP.NET allows you to declare the industry standards to which the service conforms. The most common standard used in .NET Web services is the WSI Basic Profile, defined by the Web Service Interoperability Organization (the WSI). This profile describes how service members such as operations and messages are described in WSDL, and how messages are encoded in the SOAP requests and responses. Because interoperability is critical to successful communication between SOAP clients and servers, declaring conformance in the service description provides assurance that the Web service can be accessed with requests formatted based on industry standards.

The [WebServiceBinding] metadata tag is typically placed after the [WebService] tag and declares conformance with the WSI Basic Profile version 1.1:

```
[WebServiceBinding(ConformsTo = WsiProfiles.BasicProfile1_1)]
```

> **TIP** The .NET WsiProfiles class has members that are implemented as static constants to reflect available profiles. In ASP.NET 3.5, the only 2 available values are BasicProfile1_1 and None. In October 2007, the WSI published a new Basic Profile 1.2 in working group approval draft form. Web services built in ASP.NET 3.5. do not claim conformance to the version of the basic profile.

Declaring the service class

The code-behind class should be declared as an extension of the .NET WebService class. In C#, this is accomplished by declaring the superclass after the class declaration, separated with a colon (:):

```
public class HelloService : System.Web.Services.WebService
{
  ... class implementation ...
}
```

Web service operations are then declared within the class implementation.

Declaring Web service operations

A Web service operation is declared as a method of the .NET class and prefixed with a [WebMethod] metadata tag. The following method returns a simple String value:

```
[WebMethod]
public string HelloWorld() {
  return "Hello World";
}
```

The method's return data type determines how the operation's data is received in the Flex client application. A .NET string value is translated into an ActionScript String, and so on.

The code-behind class in Listing 28.1 defines a single HelloWorld() Web service operation.

LISTING 28.1

A simple Hello World code-behind class for a .NET Web service

```
using System.Web.Services;

[WebService(Namespace = "http://www.bardotech.com/samples/hello/")]
[WebServiceBinding(ConformsTo = WsiProfiles.BasicProfile1_1)]
public class HelloService : WebService
{
  public HelloService () {
  }

  [WebMethod]
  public string HelloWorld() {
    return "Hello World";
  }

}
```

Generating a Web Service in Flex Builder 3

Flex Builder 3 has a feature that generates an ASP.NET Web service to manage data in a single database table hosted by Microsoft SQL Server. The code generation tool also generates a simple Flex application that serves as an example of how to make calls to the server.

To use the ASP.NET Web service generation tool, you must have the following software installed on, or available to, your development system:

- The .NET Framework, version 2.0 or later, must be installed locally.

- Microsoft SQL Server 2000 or later must be available to Flex Builder over a network connection.

> **TIP**
>
> Microsoft SQL Server 2005 Express is a free version of the database application that you can download from www.microsoft.com/express/download. This version of SQL Server is licensed for development and production use. Limitations include usage of only a single CPU, 1GB of RAM, and a maximum database size of 4GB. (You can install the Express edition on systems with more resources, but only one CPU and the maximum memory buffer will be used.)

Creating a Flex project with ASP.NET

The first step is to create a Flex project for use with ASP.NET. Follow these steps:

1. Select File ➪ New ➪ Flex Project from the Flex Builder menu.

2. As shown in Figure 28.3, set the project properties as follows:

   ▪ Project name: **chapter28**

   ▪ Project location: **Use default location**

   ▪ Application type: **Web application**

   ▪ Application server type: **ASP.NET**

FIGURE 28.3

Creating a Flex project for use with ASP.NET

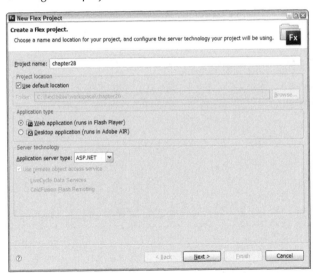

3. Click Next.

4. On the next screen, shown in Figure 28.4, indicate whether you want to use the ASP.NET Development Server or Internet Information Services (IIS). If you don't have IIS installed, select the development server. This results in deploying a simple Web server running on port 3000 with its Web root set to the Flex project's root folder.

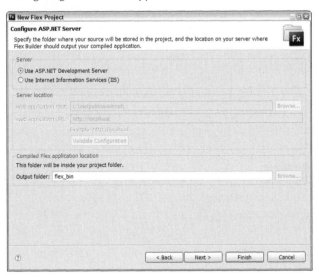

FIGURE 28.4

Configuring the ASP.NET application server

5. If you want to test your Web service with IIS, provide the Web application root defaulting to `C:\inetpub\wwwroot` and the Web application URL defaulting to `http://localhost`.

6. Set the output folder as follows:

   - If you're using the development server, create the output folder as a subfolder of the project root.

   - If you're using IIS, create the output folder as a subfolder of the IIS Web root.

7. Click Next.

8. Set the Main application filename, and click Finish to create the project and the main application file.

Creating an SQL Server database connection

Before generating Web service code, you first must define a database connection. You can define the connection either during the code generation process or as a separate task from the Data Source Explorer view.

TIP ASP.NET is certainly capable of communicating with database products other than SQL Server, but the Flex Builder 3 code generation wizard is designed to work only with databases hosted in Microsoft's own product. Similarly, the PHP code generation wizard (described in Chapter 29) works only with databases hosted by MySQL. In either case, if you want to use a database other than the one most commonly associated with each application server, you have to set up the database drivers and code the Web service manually.

 This example uses a sample database named Northwind that's provided by Microsoft for testing and evaluation of SQL Server. This database is compatible with SQL Server 2000 and 2005, and can be downloaded from:

```
http://msdn2.microsoft.com/en-us/library/aa276825.aspx
```

This Web page includes instructions for how to install the database using the provided SQL script.

Follow these steps to define a database connection:

1. Select Window ⇨ Other Views from the Flex Builder menu.

2. Select Connectivity ⇨ Data Source Explorer from the Show View dialog box, as shown in Figure 28.5.

FIGURE 28.5

Opening the Data Source Explorer

3. Right-click (Ctrl-click on the Mac) the Databases item in the Data Source Explorer view and select New... from the context menu, as shown in Figure 28.6.

FIGURE 28.6

Creating a new database connection

4. In the New Connection Profile screen, select Simple Microsoft SQL Server Connection and click Next.

5. In the Create Connection Profile screen, set the connection name to any descriptive string and click Next. For example, if you're using the Northwind database, set the connection name to **northwind**.

6. In the Simple SQL Server screen, shown in Figure 28.7, set the connection properties as follows:

   - Server Name: **The IP address or DNS name of the system hosting SQL Server**

   - Database Name: **The name of the database you want to use**

   - User Name: **The username to be used in authenticating your SQL Server connection**

   - Password: **The password to be used in authenticating your SQL Server connection**

7. Click Test Connection to make sure Flex Builder can connect to your SQL Server database.

8. Click Finish to create the connection and return to the Data Source Explorer view.

FIGURE 28.7

Setting database connection properties

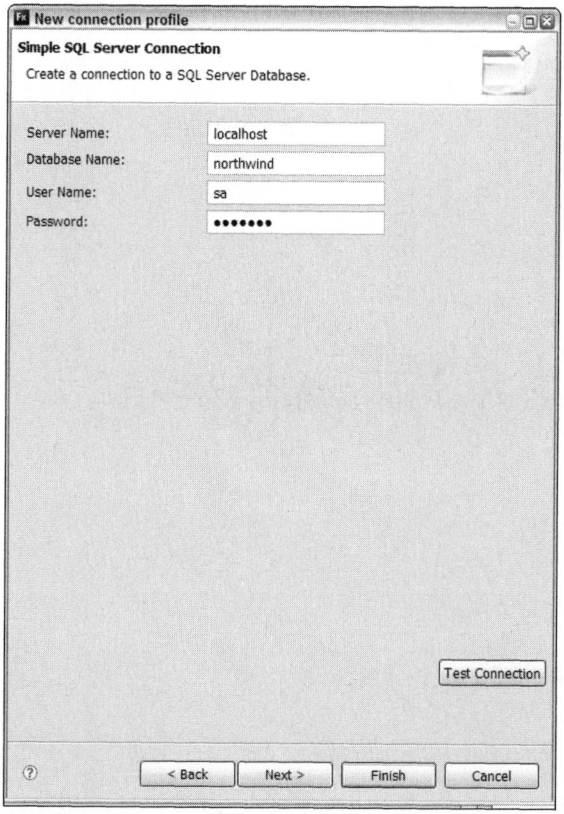

Generating a Flex/ASP.NET application

After you've created a database connection and have a database and table to work with, you're ready to use Flex Builder's application generator. Follow these steps:

1. Select Data ➪ Create Application from Database... from the Flex Builder menu.

2. In the Choose Data Source screen, shown in Figure 28.8, select a Connection and a Table. The Primary Key column should be selected automatically.

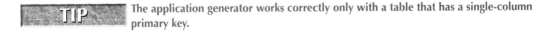 **TIP** You also can create a database connection from this point of the application generator. When working with an ASP.NET Flex project, you can only create a connection for Microsoft SQL Server.

FIGURE 28.8

Selecting a connection and a database table

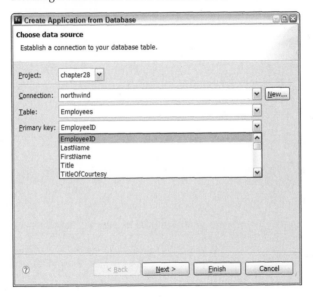

3. Click Next.

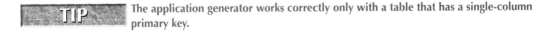 **TIP** The application generator works correctly only with a table that has a single-column primary key.

4. On the Generate Server-side Code screen, shown in Figure 28.9, set the .NET name of the Web service class; the default value is the name of the database table. Also select the programming language; the default is C#.

FIGURE 28.9

Selecting a server-side Web service class name and programming language

5. Click Next.

6. On the Generate client-side code screen, shown in Figure 28.10, select the columns you want to display in the Flex client application's default view. This screen also allows you to select these options:

  - Data types for each column default to the same type as the original column itself but can be reset in this screen.

  - The default view allows the user to filter on a single column; this screen allows you to select the filtering column.

7. Click Finish to generate the Flex client application and the server-side Web service.

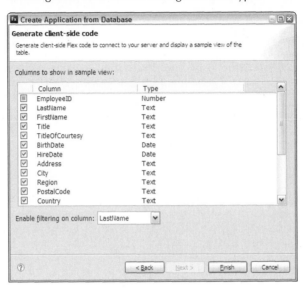

FIGURE 28.10

Selecting table columns and setting their data types

Understanding and using the generated code

The database application generator creates both a Flex client application and an XML Web Service. The Flex application is rudimentary at best and is designed primarily as a teaching tool that shows you how to define the location of the Web service and make calls to its operations. The Flex application is named for the data table it manages; for example, if you generate an application that manages a table named `Employees`, the Flex application source code file is named `Employees.mxml`.

The Web service code is spread across multiple files on the server, some in the Web root and others in a special subfolder named `/App_Code`. The Web root folder location is determined by your selection of a Web server in the project properties. If you're using IIS, the Web service is created in the Web root folder, while using the development Web server places the generated Web service in the Flex project root.

These are the files that are generated by Flex Builder:

- The Web service gateway file is created in the root folder with a file extension of `.asmx`. For example, if you selected a class name of `Employees` in the application generator wizard, the Web service gateway file is named `Employees.asmx`. The code in the gateway file looks like this:

```
<%@ WebService Language="C#"
  CodeBehind="~/App_Code/Employees.cs"
 Class="Employees" %>
```

- An application configuration file named `web.config` is also placed in the Web root folder. This specially named file is used to configure all ASP.NET applications and includes such configuration options as the database connection string, authentication mode, debug tracing, and others. For example, this section of the `web.config` file determines which SQL Server database is used at runtime:

```
<connectionStrings>
  <add connectionString="server=localhost;database=northwind;
    uid=sa;pwd=myAdminPassword" name="Northwind"
    providerName="System.Data.SqlClient"/>
</connectionStrings>
```

- A .NET class is created in the `App_Code` folder that manages the database connection at runtime. The class is named for the database connection, so if the connection is named `Northwind`, the database connection manager class source code file is named `Northwind.cs`. This class's most important method is named `OpenConnection()` and is called by the Web service class whenever it needs to communicate with the database:

```
public static DbConnection CreateConnection()
{
  try
  {
    DbConnection connection = Factory.CreateConnection();
    connection.ConnectionString = Settings.ConnectionString;
    connection.Open();
    return connection;
  }
  catch (Exception ex)
  {
    throw new DataException(String.Format(
      "Unable to connect to {0} database.", Settings.Name),
     ex);
  }
}
```

- The code-behind .NET class is created in the `App_Code` folder. Its name matches the name of the gateway class, but it has a file extension matching the programming language being used. For example, if you selected a class name of `Employees` and the C# programming language in the application generator wizard, the code-behind file is named `Employees.cs`. The code-behind class implements these public operations that you can call from a Flex application:

  - The `FindAll()` operation accepts arguments that determine filtering and order of the returned data. It returns a .NET `DataTable` object that's translated in Flex into an ActionScript `ArrayCollection`.

  - The `Update()` operation accepts one argument for each database table column and executes an SQL `UPDATE` statement on the server to modify the column values of a single table row. This operation doesn't return any value.

■ The Insert() operation accepts one argument for each database table column and executes an SQL INSERT statement on the server to add a single table row. This operation doesn't return any value.

■ The Remote() operation accepts a single argument as a value of the primary key column and executes a DELETE FROM statement on the server to remove the selected database row. This operation doesn't return any value.

A typical generated .NET class is shown in Listing 28.2.

LISTING 28.2

A generated .NET code-behind class for a Web service

```
using System;
using System.Data;
using System.Data.Common;
using System.Text;
using System.Web.Services;

[WebService(Namespace = "http://tempuri.org/")]
[WebServiceBinding(ConformsTo = WsiProfiles.BasicProfile1_1)]
public class Employees : WebService {

  private readonly string[] FieldNames = {"EmployeeID","LastName",

   "FirstName","Title","TitleOfCourtesy","BirthDate","HireDate","Address
   ",
    "City","Region","PostalCode","HomePhone"};

  [WebMethod]
  public DataTable FindAll(string City,string orderField, bool
   orderDesc)
  {
    try
    {
    StringBuilder sql = new StringBuilder(128);

    sql.Append("SELECT ");
    sql.Append(String.Join(",", FieldNames));
    sql.Append(" FROM Employees ");

    sql.Append("WHERE City LIKE @City ");

    if (!String.IsNullOrEmpty(orderField) &&
    Array.IndexOf(FieldNames, orderField) > -1)
    {
    sql.Append("ORDER BY " + orderField);
```

```
  if (orderDesc)
  {
    sql.Append(" DESC");
  }
  }

  using(DbConnection cnn = Northwind.CreateConnection())
  using(DbCommand command = cnn.CreateCommand())
  using(DbDataAdapter adapter = Northwind.Factory.CreateDataAdapter())
  {
  command.CommandText = sql.ToString();

  Northwind.CreateParameter(command, "@City", "%" + City + '%');

  DataTable result = new DataTable("Table0");
  adapter.SelectCommand = command;
  adapter.Fill(result);
  return result;
  }
}
  catch (Exception ex)
  {
  throw CreateSafeException(ex);
  }
}

[WebMethod]
public void Update(Decimal EmployeeID, string LastName, string
 FirstName,
  string Title, string TitleOfCourtesy, DateTime BirthDate,
  DateTime HireDate, string Address, string City, string Region,
  string PostalCode, string HomePhone)
{
try
{
  string sql = @"
    UPDATE Employees
    SET LastName=@LastName, FirstName=@FirstName, Title=@Title,
      TitleOfCourtesy=@TitleOfCourtesy, BirthDate=@BirthDate,
      HireDate=@HireDate, Address=@Address, City=@City,
 Region=@Region,
      PostalCode=@PostalCode, HomePhone=@HomePhone
    WHERE EmployeeID=@EmployeeID ";

  using(DbConnection cnn = Northwind.CreateConnection())
  using(DbCommand command = cnn.CreateCommand())
  {
```

continued

LISTING 28.2   *(continued)*

```
    command.CommandText = sql;
    Northwind.CreateParameter(command, "@EmployeeID", EmployeeID);
    Northwind.CreateParameter(command, "@LastName", LastName);
    ... additional parameters for all columns ...
    command.ExecuteNonQuery();
    }
}
catch (Exception ex)
{
  throw CreateSafeException(ex);
}
}


[WebMethod]
public void Insert(string LastName,string FirstName,string
 Title,string TitleOfCourtesy,DateTime BirthDate,DateTime
 HireDate,string Address,string City,string Region,string
 PostalCode,string HomePhone)
{
try
{
  string sql = @"INSERT INTO Employees (LastName, FirstName, Title,
    TitleOfCourtesy, BirthDate, HireDate, Address, City, Region,
    PostalCode, HomePhone)
   VALUES ( @LastName,@FirstName, @Title, @TitleOfCourtesy,
 @BirthDate,
    @HireDate, @Address, @City, @Region, @PostalCode, @HomePhone) ";

  using (DbConnection cnn = Northwind.CreateConnection())
  using (DbCommand command = cnn.CreateCommand())
  {
  command.CommandText = sql;

  Northwind.CreateParameter(command, "@LastName", LastName);
  Northwind.CreateParameter(command, "@FirstName", FirstName);
  ... additional parameters for all columns ...
  command.ExecuteNonQuery();
  }
}
catch (Exception ex)
{
  throw CreateSafeException(ex);
}
 }
```

```
[WebMethod]
public void Remove(Decimal EmployeeID)
{
try
{
  string sql = @"
    DELETE FROM  Employees
    WHERE  EmployeeID = @EmployeeID ";

  using (DbConnection cnn = Northwind.CreateConnection())
  using (DbCommand command = cnn.CreateCommand())
  {
  command.CommandText = sql;

  Northwind.CreateParameter(command, "@EmployeeID", EmployeeID);

  command.ExecuteNonQuery();
  }
}
catch (Exception ex)
{
  throw CreateSafeException(ex);
}
}

private Exception CreateSafeException(Exception ex)
{
  Context.Trace.Write("Exception",
  "An unexpected error occurred processing request", ex);
  return new Exception("An unexpected error occurred and
    has been logged.");
}

}
```

Building Web Services with Visual Web Developer 2008

Microsoft Visual Web Developer 2008 Express Edition is a free product that offers a subset of the features available in Visual Studio Professional. If you're just getting started building Web services and want to build your own from scratch, it can serve as a great entry point into the world of ASP.NET development.

The Web installer application for Visual Web Developer 2008 can be downloaded from Microsoft at:

```
http://www.microsoft.com/express/vwd/
```

 When you install Visual Web Developer 2008, the installer detects whether you already have the .NET Framework installed, and if not, includes the Framework installation.

When you download the installer application for Visual Web Developer 2008 from the Microsoft Web site, you get a file named `vnssetup.exe` that's about 2.5MB. When you run the installer, you'll see these prompts:

- According to the license for Visual Web Developer 2008 Express Edition, you can use the product without any license fees, but you must register for continued use beyond an initial 30-day evaluation period. Each time you start the product after installation, you'll be prompted to complete the registration process.

- During the installation, you're prompted to indicate whether you want to download and install Microsoft SQL Server 2005 Express Edition during the installation of Visual Web Developer.

- On the final installation screen, you're prompted to download the required installation files and start the installation. The installation files are then downloaded from Microsoft's Web site during the installation process.

CAUTION The installation download can be as large as 89MB, depending on whether you select the SQL Server Express installation.

 Microsoft also offers a downloadable DVD image that includes local installation files for all the Express edition software packages. This is an `.iso` file that's about 894MB and should be downloaded only with a high-speed Internet connection. You can find this file at `www.microsoft.com/express/download/#webInstall`.

Creating a Web service

Follow these steps to create a new Web service in Visual Web Developer 2008:

1. Select File ➪ New Web Site... from the Visual Web Developer menu.
2. Select ASP.NET Web Service from the Visual Studio installed templates, as shown in Figure 28.11.
3. Set the Location to File System, and choose a folder on your system where you want to create the Web site.
4. Select a Language from the options of Visual Basic or Visual C#.
5. Click OK to create the new Web service.

FIGURE 28.11

Creating a new Web service in Visual Web Developer 2008

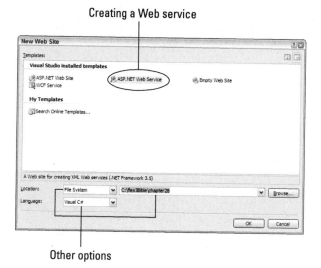

The initial site files include a gateway file named Service.asmx in the Web site root folder and a code-behind module named Service.cs for C# or Service.vb for Visual Basic. You should immediately customize the files as follows:

1. Rename the gateway file with a descriptive name. For example, if your service is designed to manage a database table named Employees, you might rename the gateway file EmployeesService.asmx.

2. Optionally, rename the code-behind class in the App_Code folder:

   a. Rename the file from the Solution Explorer panel in the upper-right corner of the application interface, as shown in Figure 28.12.

   b. Open the class source code file, and change both the name of the class in the class declaration and the name of its constructor method. You also can change the Web service's namespace URI to a value that incorporates your organization's domain and a string that describes the service. For example, you might change the [WebService] tag as follows:

```
[WebService(Namespace =
    "http://www.mycompany.com/EmployeeService")]
```

The modified class declaration and constructor method should look like this:

```
public class EmployeeService : System.Web.Services.WebService
{
  public EmployeeService () {
  }
```

```
[WebMethod]
public string HelloWorld() {
  return "Hello World";
  }
}
```

c. Return to the gateway file, and update both the `CodeBehind` and `Class` attributes to reflect the new name of the code-behind class:

```
<%@ WebService Language="C#"
  CodeBehind="~/App_Code/EmployeeService.cs"
  Class="EmployeeService" %>
```

FIGURE 28.12

The Solution Explorer with renamed service files

3. To test the Web service, select Debug ➪ Start without Debugging from the Visual Web Developer menu. This results in starting up the development Web server and opening a Web browser to view the Web service's preview page, as shown in Figure 28.13.

Configuring the development Web server

Visual Web Developer assigns an arbitrary port number to the development server. You can change this to a fixed port in the project properties, allowing you to predict where the Web service can be reached from a Flex client application.

FIGURE 28.13

The Web service preview page

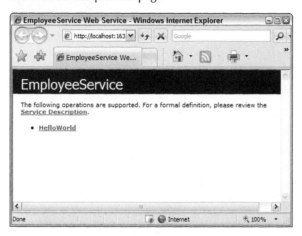

Follow these steps to change this configuration:

1. Click the project heading in the Solution Explorer.

2. Locate the Properties panel in the lower-right corner of the application interface. Change the Use dynamic ports option to `false`, as shown in Figure 28.14.

FIGURE 28.14

The Properties panel

3. Set the Port number to any port you want to use. (I commonly use port number 4567 for my custom development work, because I don't know of any existing Web or application servers that default to this port.)

Testing a Web service

The Web service preview page displays a link for each Web service operation. Click the link for an operation you want to test. The next page, shown in Figure 28.15, shows sample SOAP request and response packets for the selected operation and an Invoke button to run the operation in the Web browser.

FIGURE 28.15

The Web service operation testing page

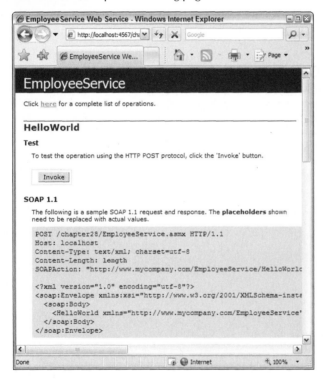

Click Invoke to run the operation. The returned data is displayed as an XML packet in the Web browser, shown in Figure 28.16.

FIGURE 28.16

The results of a Web service invocation

Exchanging Data with XML Web Services

When you use XML Web Services from a Flex application, you can use many of the same techniques described in previous chapters to create strongly typed value object classes and exchange them between the Flex client application and the Web service.

Setting up the sample files

Follow these instructions to set up a Flex Builder project:

ON the WEB The code samples in this section are available in the `chapter28.zip` file from the Web site. Follow the instructions in this section to set up a Flex Builder that allows you to examine and test the sample application files.

1. Create a new Flex Builder project with these properties on the initial screen:
   - Project name: **chapter28**
   - Use default location: **checked**
   - Application type: **Web application**
   - Application server type: **ASP.NET**
2. On the next screen, select the ASP.NET Development Server.
3. Accept the default output folder, and click Finish to create the project.
4. Extract the contents of `chapter28.zip` to the Flex project root folder.

After extracting the files, the Flex project contains Flex application source files in the `src` folder. The Web service gateway file, `EmployeeService.asmx`, is stored in the project's root folder, its code-behind class is in the `App_Code` folder, and a Microsoft Access version of the Northwind database is stored in the `App_Data` folder.

To test the Web service in the sample project and view its WSDL description, follow these steps:

1. Open `HelloWorld.mxml` from the project's `src` folder.

2. Run the application. The development Web server starts automatically and shows an icon in the system tray, as shown in Figure 28.17.

FIGURE 28.17

The development Web server icon in the system tray

3. Click Talk to .NET to make a call to the .NET Web service, as shown in Figure 28.18.

FIGURE 28.18

Calling the Web service

4. Navigate to this URL to view the Web service's WSDL description:

   `http://localhost:3000/chapter28/EmployeeService.asmx?wsdl`

Returning data from .NET

The approach used in the Web services generated by Flex Builder is fairly code-heavy, and you can enormously simplify your own Web service by coding it from scratch. In this section, I describe some recommended coding patterns that reduce the amount of Web service code and result in more maintainable applications.

When you return a data set from a Web service to a Flex application, you can either return a .NET `DataTable` object or an array of strongly typed value objects. Returning a `DataTable` takes a very small amount of code in ASP.NET and is transformed in Flex into an `ArrayCollection` of generic ActionScript Object instances. Returning an array of strongly typed value objects takes a bit more code on both the client and the server, but this allows you to follow many object-oriented best practices.

Returning a .NET DataSet

This Web service operation queries a table of a database and returns a DataSet (a collection of DataTable objects):

```
[WebMethod]
public DataSet getData()
{
   OleDbDataAdapter adpt =
     new OleDbDataAdapter("SELECT EmployeeID, FirstName, LastName
       FROM Employees", connString );
   DataSet ds = new DataSet();
   adpt.Fill(ds);
   return ds;
}
```

ON the WEB   The code for all Web service operations described in this section is available in the Web site files as **EmployeeService.cs** in the **App_Code** folder of the **chapter28** project.

When a DataSet is returned to Flex, it's received as an ActionScript Object. The actual data set is returned as an ArrayCollection property of the DataSet named Tables.Table.Rows. Each item in the ArrayCollection is an Object containing properties whose names match the names of the data set columns.

This event handler function saves the returned data from this Web service operation to a pre-declared ArrayCollection variable named myData:

```
[Bindable]
private var myData:ArrayCollection;
private function dataHandler(event:ResultEvent):void
{
   myData = event.result.Tables.Table.Rows;
}
```

This code is incredibly simple and returns usable data. If, however, you've used and experienced the benefits of using strongly typed value objects in Flex applications, you may want to receive your data in that form.

Returning an array of value objects

Web service operations built in .NET can return strongly typed value objects, but they're always received in Flex as generic ActionScript Object instances. Unlike the Remoting architecture with Java or ColdFusion, there's no built-in method with SOAP-based Web services for transforming server-side value objects into their client-side equivalents. (The [RemoteClass] tag doesn't work here.)

If you prefer to work with value objects, it's up to you to explicitly transform the returned generic Object instances into new instances of the client-side value object. To handle this task, create a constructor method in the client-side value object class that allows easy initialization of its properties from a generic ActionScript Object.

The ActionScript value object class in Listing 28.3 has a constructor method that receives an optional Object argument. If the argument is provided, its property values are passed to the new value object instance's properties.

LISTING 28.3

An ActionScript value object class designed for use with Web services

```
package vo
{
  [Bindable]
  public class Employee
  {
    public var employeeId:int=0;
    public var firstName:String="";
    public var lastName:String="";
    public function Employee(obj:Object = null)
    {
      if (obj != null)
      {
        this.employeeId = obj.EmployeeID;
        this.firstName = obj.FirstName;
        this.lastName = obj.LastName;
      }
    }
  }
}
```

ON the WEB The code in Listing 28.3 is available in the Web site files as `Employee.as` in the `src/vo` folder of the `chapter28` project.

TIP The capitalization of the `Object` property names received from .NET is determined by the spelling of the database table columns in the SQL statement that generates the data set. For example, this SQL statement would result in all properties being returned with their names in lowercase:

```
OleDbDataAdapter adpt = new OleDbDataAdapter(
  "SELECT employeeid, firstname, lastname FROM Employees",
  connString );
```

It's critical that you spell the property names from .NET exactly as they're spelled in the SQL code. Otherwise, the values aren't transferred from the .NET object to the ActionScript `object`.

The Flex application in Listing 28.4 receives the .NET array as an `ArrayCollection` of generic ActionScript `Object` instances. After saving the data to a pre-declared `ArrayCollection`, the event handler function loops through the data and transforms each object to an instance of the client-side value object. The result is an `ArrayCollection` of value objects that you can manage in your Flex application using the same strategies as when working with the Remoting architecture in ColdFusion and Java.

LISTING 28.4

Transforming `Object` **instances into value objects**

```
<?xml version="1.0" encoding="utf-8"?>
<mx:Application xmlns:mx="http://www.adobe.com/2006/mxml">
  <mx:Script>
    <![CDATA[
      import vo.Employee;
      import mx.collections.ArrayCollection;
      import mx.rpc.events.ResultEvent;

      [Bindable]
      private var myObjects:ArrayCollection;
      private function objectsHandler(event:ResultEvent):void
      {
        var currentEmployee:Employee;
        myObjects = event.result.Tables.Table.Rows as ArrayCollection;
        for (var i:int=0; i<myObjects.length; i++)
        {
          currentEmployee = new Employee(myObjects.getItemAt(i));
          myObjects.setItemAt(currentEmployee, i);
        }
      }
    ]]>
  </mx:Script>
  <mx:WebService id="dataService"
    wsdl="../EmployeeService.asmx?wsdl"
    result="objectsHandler(event)"/>
  <mx:Button label="Get Data" click="dataService.getData()"/>
  <mx:DataGrid dataProvider="{myObjects}"/>
</mx:Application>
```

ON the WEB   The code in Listing 28.4 is available in the Web site files as `GetArrayOfObjects.mxml` in the `src` folder of the `chapter28` project.

Passing value objects to .NET service operations

You can pass a strongly typed value object to a .NET Web service operation as long as you've set up the following code:

- A .NET version of the value object must be defined.
- The Web service operation must expect an argument with the value object class as its data type.
- The properties of the client-side and server-side value object classes must exactly match in name and have compatible data types.

You can declare a .NET value object class either in a separate class file or within the same source file in which the Web service's code-behind class is defined. The value object class can be declared with simple public properties:

```
public class Employee
{
  public int employeeId;
  public string lastName;
  public string firstName;
}
```

The client-side version of the class is the same as described in the previous section and shown in Listing 28.3. As described previously, the [RemoteClass] tag doesn't execute the same sort of two-way mapping in Web services as it does in Remoting. Instead, you depend on .NET to receive and transform the object.

The following Web service operation receives a value object argument:

```
[WebMethod]
public string handleObject(Employee obj)
{
  return "You sent me the employee " +
    obj.firstName + " " + obj.lastName;
}
```

As long as the argument object's properties match the .NET version of the class, as described previously, the .NET Web service architecture correctly deserializes the object into the local native version of the class.

The Flex application in Listing 28.5 passes a strongly typed value object to a .NET Web service and receives a response showing the values that were parsed from the object in the server-side code.

LISTING 28.5

A Web service operation passing a strongly typed value object to a .NET Web service

```
<?xml version="1.0" encoding="utf-8"?>
<mx:Application xmlns:mx="http://www.adobe.com/2006/mxml">
  <mx:Script>
    <![CDATA[
      import vo.Employee;
      private function sendObject():void
      {
        var obj:Employee = new Employee();
        obj.firstName = fnameInput.text;
        obj.lastName = lnameInput.text;
        dataService.handleObject(obj);
      }
    ]]>
  </mx:Script>
  <mx:WebService id="dataService"
    wsdl="../EmployeeService.asmx?wsdl"/>
  <mx:VBox width="800" borderStyle="solid" borderThickness="1"
    backgroundColor="#eeeeee">
    <mx:Label text="Sending Arguments" fontSize="14"/>
    <mx:HBox>
      <mx:Label text="Value 1:"/><mx:TextInput id="fnameInput"/>
    </mx:HBox>
    <mx:HBox>
      <mx:Label text="Value 2:"/><mx:TextInput id="lnameInput"/>
      <mx:Button label="Send Object" click="sendObject()"/>
    </mx:HBox>
    <mx:Label fontSize="12"
   text="{dataService.handleObject.lastResult}"/>
  </mx:VBox>
</mx:Application>
```

ON the WEB The code in Listing 28.5 is available in the Web site files as `SendObject.mxml` in the src folder of the `chapter28` project.

Summary

In this chapter, I described how to integrate Flex client applications with Microsoft ASP.NET using the .NET implementation of SOAP-based Web services. You learned the following:

- ASP.NET is a free application server that is included with many editions of Microsoft Windows.

- ASP.NET supports multiple programming languages and is strongly integrated with Internet Information Services and the Windows operating system.

- You can download and install ASP.NET from Microsoft's Web site.

- You can build XML Web Services with a variety of development environments, including Adobe Flex Builder 3, Microsoft Visual Web Developer 2008, and Microsoft Visual Studio.

- Flex Builder 3 can generate a complete Flex/ASP.NET application that manages data in a single database table hosted by Microsoft SQL Server.

- Microsoft Visual Web Developer 2008 is free and offers a subset of the features of Visual Studio Professional.

- Both Flex Builder 3 and Visual Web Developer offer a free development Web server that you can use to test your Web services.

- You can improve your application's maintainability by using strongly typed value objects built in ActionScript 3 on the client and in your choice of .NET programming languages on the server.

Chapter 29

Integrating Flex Applications with PHP

PHP has become one of the most widely used application scripting frameworks on the Web. Originally standing for *Personal Home Page,* PHP has evolved into a high-performance application server technology that's used both to dynamically generate Web pages and to provide a middleware layer for rich client applications such as those built with Flex.

> **TIP** The term *PHP* is used to refer to both the server technology and the programming language used to create dynamic Web functionality.

In addition to its core feature set, PHP has extensibility features that allow developers to create and add modules as needed. PEAR (PHP Extension and Application Repository), in the words of its creators, offers both a "structured library of open-source code for PHP users" and a "system for code distribution and package maintenance." It also encourages a standardized approach to formatting PHP code, including recommendations for indentation, identifier naming, and other issues that sometimes invite controversy between developers.

PHP is portable between operating systems. Binary distributions of PHP are available for these operating systems:

- AS/400
- Mac OS X
- Novell NetWare
- OS/2
- RISC OS
- SGI IRIX 6.5.x
- Solaris (SPARC, INTEL)
- Windows

IN THIS CHAPTER

Understanding PHP

Installing PHP with WAMP and MAMP

Creating a Flex project for use with PHP

Returning simple XML to Flex

Generating a Flex/PHP application with Flex Builder 3

Working with generated PHP services

Using Remoting and AMF with Flex and AMFPHP

PHP is also included in most distributions of Linux and is available in source format that allows you to customize and build your own PHP distributions.

In addition to all of these benefits, PHP is completely free. Because it's a free, open-source project managed by the PHP Group (www.php.net), you can download and use PHP on as many servers as you like without any registration or license fees.

There are many ways to integrate Flex applications with PHP, including these strategies:

- You can send and receive generic XML-formatted data using a RESTful architecture.
- You can use XML-RPC libraries that are delivered with PEAR (http://pear.php.net/package/XML_RPC).
- You can use a PHP implementation of SOAP-based Web services, such NuSOAP (http://dietrich.ganx4.com/nusoap) or PEAR (http://pear.php.net/package/SOAP).
- You can choose from a variety of Remoting and binary AMF of implementations, such as AMFPHP (described in more detail later in this chapter) or SabreAMF (http://osflash.org/sabreamf).

In this chapter, I describe how to integrate PHP with Flex applications using RESTful XML with HTTPService and AMF with RemoteObject.

ON the WEB   To use the sample code for this chapter, download chapter29.zip from the Web site. This is not a Flex project archive file. Its use and installation are described later in this chapter.

Installing PHP

You can install PHP in a number of ways. Developers who are new to PHP typically select from one of these options:

- If you already have a Web server and database installed, you can download the core PHP binary distribution for your operating system and then install it as a Web server module.
- If you don't have a Web server or database installed, you can download and install a free integrated software bundle package that includes the Apache Web server, PHP, and the MySQL database. Software bundles of note include:
  - WAMP for Windows
  - MAMP for Mac OS X

The easiest way to get started with PHP on Windows or Mac OS X is to select one of the integrated software bundles. Both WAMP and MAMP install quickly and easily to let you get started with development work as quickly as possible. In this section, I describe how to download and install WAMP for Windows and MAMP for Mac OS X.

Installing WAMP on Windows

WAMP is a free integrated software bundle for the Windows operating system that includes the Apache Web server, PHP, and the MySQL database. You can download the WAMP installer from:

    http://www.wampserver.com/en

Follow these steps to download the WAMP installer application:

1. Click Downloads from the Web site's home page.
2. Click Download on the Downloads page, as shown in Figure 29.1.

FIGURE 29.1

Selecting the Latest Release from the WAMP downloads page

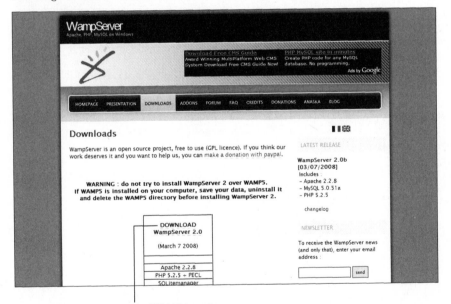

Click to download the WAMP installer

The installer application is in .exe form and can be run from any folder after downloading. When you start the installer application, you first see a warning, shown in Figure 29.2, indicating that if you have an older version of WAMP installed you should first uninstall it.

FIGURE 29.2

WAMP installer application warning dialog box

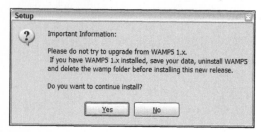

Follow the installer application's prompts to complete the installation. As shown in Figure 29.3, the installer sets the default destination folder to c:\wamp on your system's hard disk.

FIGURE 29.3

Setting the WAMP destination location

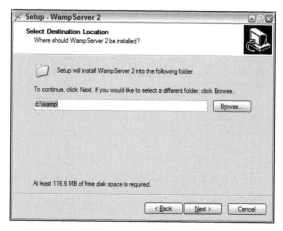

TIP The instructions in this chapter assume that you've accepted the default folder location of c:\wamp. If you've selected a different installation folder or are using PHP with a different configuration, adapt the instructions as necessary.

Managing WAMP servers

As shown in Figure 29.4, the WAMP installer creates an icon in the system tray that allows you to start and stop the Apache and MySQL servers and to navigate to key Web pages.

FIGURE 29.4

The WAMP system tray icon

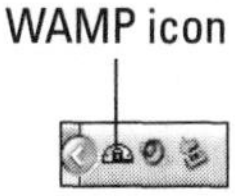

WAMP icon

Click the system tray icon to see the WAMP menu, shown in Figure 29.5.

FIGURE 29.5

The WAMP system menu

The WAMP menu offers these options under the Quick Admin heading (toward the bottom of the menu):

- Start All Services (includes both Apache and MySQL)
- Stop All Services
- Restart All Services

TIP You also can start and stop Apache and MySQL individually by navigating to the appropriate section of the menu. For example, to restart the Apache Web server, select Apache ⇨ Service ⇨ Restart Service from the WAMP menu.

The menu also offers quick links to these key Web pages:

- **Localhost** opens a Web browser to `http://localhost/` to view the WAMP server's home page, as shown in Figure 29.6.

- **phpMyAdmin** opens a Web browser to a Web-based application that manages MySQL databases.

- **SQLiteManager** opens a Web browser to a Web-based application that manages SQLite databases.

- **www directory** opens Windows Explorer to the WAMP Web root folder, which defaults to `c:\wamp\www`.

FIGURE 29.6

The WAMP server's home page

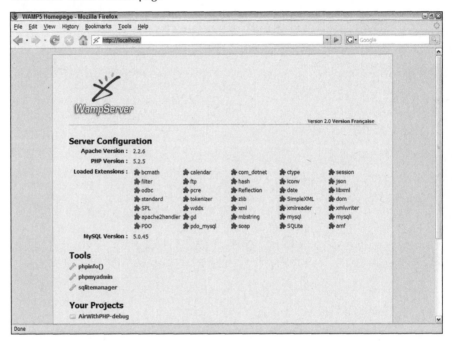

Installing MAMP on Mac OS X

MAMP offers the same integrated server functionality as WAMP, but it's designed for Mac OS X. You can download the MAMP installer from `www.mamp.info/en/index.php`. The installer is delivered as a .dmg file that you mount as a virtual drive on your Mac development system.

When you open the .dmg file, you're first prompted with the MAMP server's license agreement. Just as with WAMP, MAMP can be used freely according to the license terms. After accepting the license the installation screen appears, the installation screen appears, as shown in Figure 29.7.

Drag the MAMP folder icon to the `Applications` folder to complete the installation. The server installs into a folder on your Mac hard disk named `/Applications/MAMP`.

 The `MAMP Pro` folder installs the professional version of MAMP that includes additional enterprise-level features. This version of MAMP is installed with a fee-based license.

 The `How to upgrade.rtf` link opens a document describing how to upgrade from one version of MAMP to another.

FIGURE 29.7

The MAMP server's installation screen

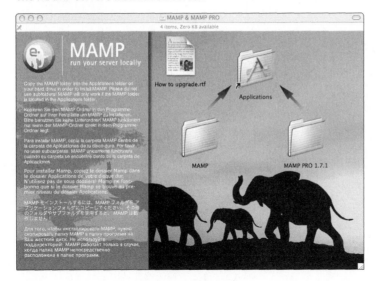

Managing MAMP servers

To start MAMP servers, open the `/Applications/MAMP` folder and run the MAMP application. Because starting servers requires administrative access, you're prompted for your Mac administrative Name and Password.

After entering your administrative credentials, the MAMP server starts and two windows open:

■ The MAMP application window, shown in Figure 29.8, includes tools for starting, stopping, and configuring Apache, PHP, and MySQL.

The MAMP application window

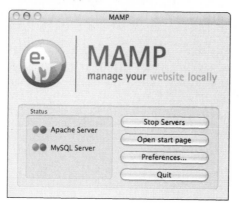

- A browser window opens to the MAMP server's home page, as shown in Figure 29.9. This page includes links to phpMyAdmin and SQLLiteManager.

The MAMP home page

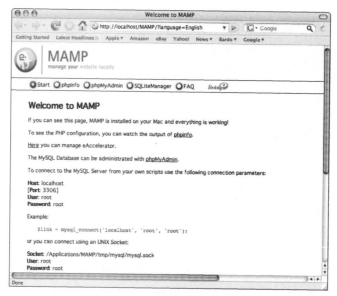

 When you close the MAMP application window, the Apache and MySQL servers both shut down.

When you first install MAMP, the Apache and MySQL servers run on custom ports, rather than their respective default ports of 80 and 3306. If you don't have other copies of Apache or MySQL running on your Mac development system, you can switch to the default ports.

If you're not sure whether the Apache Web server that's included with Mac OS X is currently running, follow these steps:

1. Open the Mac OS X System Preferences application.
2. Click Sharing under Internet & Network.
3. With the Services category selected, make sure the Personal Web Sharing option is unchecked. If it's checked, uncheck it or, with the option currently selected, click Stop.

Then follow these steps to configure the MAMP ports:

1. Click Preferences in the MAMP application window.
2. Click Ports in the Preferences toolbar.
3. Click the Set to default Apache and MySQL ports option, as shown in Figure 29.10.

FIGURE 29.10

Changing Apache and MySQL ports

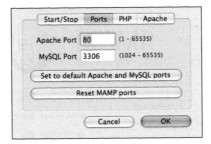

4. Click OK to accept the new port settings.
5. When prompted, enter your administrative password again to restart both servers.

You also can change the Apache Web root folder, which defaults to a subfolder name `htdocs` under the MAMP installation folder. For example, on a system that's used by more than one developer, you may want to set the document root folder to a new subfolder under your home directory, such as `/[UserName]/htdocs`. Follow these steps to set the Apache document root folder:

1. Click Preferences in the MAMP application window.
2. Click Apache in the Preferences toolbar.
3. Select a new document root folder, and click OK.
4. When prompted, enter your administrative password again to restart Apache.

Creating a Flex Project for Use with PHP

When you create a Flex project, you have the option to integrate the project with PHP and its hosting Web server. The steps are similar to those for integrating ColdFusion, described in Chapter 26, and ASP.NET, described in Chapter 28. The project includes properties that designate the disk location and testing URL for the PHP Web root folder. The debug version of the application is created in a folder under the PHP Web root. To test the Flex application, you download the application's HTML wrapper from the Web server, resulting in running the application from the Web server rather than from the local hard disk.

Follow these steps to create a Flex application that's integrated with your PHP installation:

1. Select File ➪ New ➪ Flex Project from the Flex Builder menu.

2. On the first screen of the New Flex Project wizard, shown in Figure 29.11, use these property settings:

   ▪ Project name: **chapter29**

   ▪ Project location: **Use the default location**

   ▪ Application type: **Web application**

   ▪ Server technology: **PHP**

FIGURE 29.11

The New Flex Project wizard creating a project for use with PHP

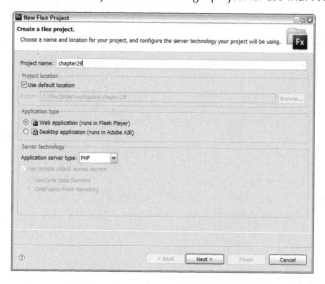

3. Click Next.

4. On the Configure PHP Server screen, shown in Figure 29.12, set the PHP server's Web root and Root URL. If you're using WAMP with the default installation settings, these properties are:

   ▦ Web root: `c:\wamp\www`

   ▦ Root URL: `http://localhost`

Configuring the PHP server

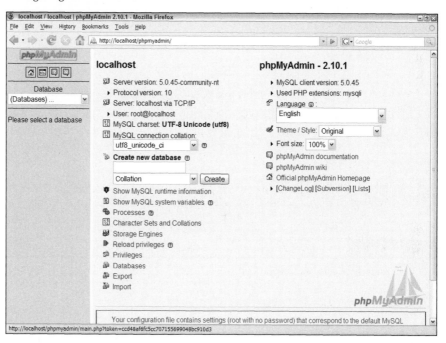

5. Make sure the Web server that hosts PHP is running, and then click Validate Configuration to ensure that Flex Builder can reach the Web server.

6. The output folder can be set to any location within the Web server's document root. The default output folder name starts with the project name and ends with `-debug` to indicate that the output folder contains the debug version of the application. For example, the default output folder in the `chapter29` project is placed under the PHP Web root with a name of `chapter29-debug`.

7. Click Next.

8. Select a Main application filename, and click Finish to create the project and main application.

When you create your PHP pages, they can be placed in the project's source root folder. During the compilation process, the PHP pages are recognized as application resources and copied to the project output folder from which they're called at runtime.

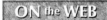 If you want to try the sample applications from this chapter, extract the files from the Web site's `chapter29.zip` file into the new Flex project's root folder.

Using PHP with HTTPService and XML

You can integrate Flex applications with PHP using the Flex framework's `HTTPService` component and PHP pages that generate structured XML-based content on the server. To return structured data from a PHP page, you can either generate your own XML content with conventional text concatenation, or you can use a more reliable approach that requires an external library to serialize XML packets.

Using the PHP SimpleXML extension

The PHP page in Listing 29.1 uses a PHP5 extension named SimpleXML to generate and return an XML-formatted response with literal values in each of the XML elements. The `header()` function is used to inform the client application that the content is being delivered with the `xml/text` content type.

WEB RESOURCE The documentation for the PHP SimpleXML extension is available on the Web at `http://us3.php.net/simplexml`.

LISTING 29.1

A PHP page that returns simple XML

```php
<?php
$xmlstr = <<<XML
<?xml version='1.0'?>
<vendors>
 <vendor>
  <name>You Grow 'em, We Mow 'em</name>
  <service>Lawn Mowing</service>
 </vendor>
 <vendor>
  <name>How High the Shingle</name>
  <service>Roofing</service>
 </vendor>
 <vendor>
  <name>Ma & Pa Kettle</name>
  <service>Cooking Supplies</service>
```

```
  </vendor>
</vendors>
XML;
header("Content-type: text/xml");
echo $xmlstr;
?>
```

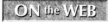 The code in Listing 29.1 is available in the Web site files as `ReturnSimpleXML.php` in the `src` folder of the `chapter29` project.

The SimpleXML extension used in Listing 29.1 isn't 100 percent bullet-proof because it doesn't know how to automatically replace XML reserved characters with their equivalent entity strings. For example, in the last `<vendor>` element in this packet, a literal ampersand (&) character is included in the `<name>` element:

```
<name>Ma & Pa Kettle</name>
```

A truly robust XML serializer would replace the ampersand with its equivalent entity:

```
<name>Ma &amp; Pa Kettle</name>
```

Many XML processors, including those that are embedded in the common Web browsers, fail to read this sort of content because it is assumed a character reference will follow the ampersand. The Flex framework's `HTTPService` component, however, survives this condition and, where necessary, replaces literal reserved characters with their equivalent aliases.

To request this XML-formatted content in a Flex application, use the Flex framework's `HTTPService` component. Set the `HTTPService` object's `url` property to the location of the PHP page:

```
<mx:HTTPService id="phpService"
  url="ReturnSimpleXML.php"/>
```

Retrieving XML data with HTTPService

Retrieving the data from the server is a simple matter of calling the `HTTPService` object's `send()` method and handling the returned results with a binding expression or a `result` event handler. The Flex application in Listing 29.2 retrieves the data in XML format from the PHP page and displays it in a `DataGrid` control.

 The code in Listing 29.2 is available in the Web site files as `GetSimpleXML.mxml` in the `src` folder of the `chapter29` project.

TIP If you prefer to parse the returned XML with E4X syntax, set the `HTTPService` component's `resultFormat` property to a value of `e4x`.

```
LISTING 29.2
```

Retrieving XML-formatted data from PHP

```
<?xml version="1.0" encoding="utf-8"?>
<mx:Application xmlns:mx="http://www.adobe.com/2006/mxml">
  <mx:Script>
    <![CDATA[
      import mx.collections.ArrayCollection;
      import mx.controls.Alert;
      import mx.rpc.events.ResultEvent;
      [Bindable]
      private var vendorData:ArrayCollection;

      private function resultHandler(event:ResultEvent):void
      {
        vendorData = event.result.vendors.vendor as ArrayCollection;
      }
    ]]>
  </mx:Script>
  <mx:HTTPService id="phpService"
    url="ReturnSimpleXML.php"
    result="resultHandler(event)"/>
  <mx:Button label="Get XML" click="phpService.send()"/>
  <mx:DataGrid dataProvider="{vendorData}" width="400"/>
</mx:Application>
```

Generating PHP Code with Flex Builder 3

As with ASP.NET, Flex Builder has a feature that can generate a complete client/server application that manages code in a single database table. Before using this feature, you must have first installed PHP and MySQL and created a database table structure.

Importing a database to MySQL

The project files for this chapter from the Web site include an SQL script that creates a new table and populates it with 100 rows of data. If you've installed WAMP or MAMP according to the instructions earlier in this chapter, follow these steps to create a MySQL data table and import its data:

1. Open phpMyAdmin in a Web browser:

   - If working on Windows, click the WAMP system tray icon and then select phpMyAdmin from the WAMP menu.

   - If working on Mac OS X, open the MAMP home page and click the phpMyAdmin link.

2. On the phpMyAdmin home page, as shown in Figure 29.13, enter **contacts** in the Create new database text field and click Create.

Creating a new MySQL database in phpMyAdmin

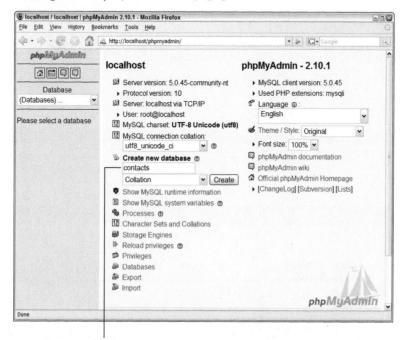

Enter new database name

3. On the Database administration screen, as shown in Figure 29.14, click Import.

4. From the Import screen, browse and select the file contacts.sql from the Flex project root folder (by default, in c:\flex3bible\workspace\chapter29).

5. Click Go to create the database table and import data.

FIGURE 29.14

Starting an Import operation in `phpMyAdmin`

Click to import data

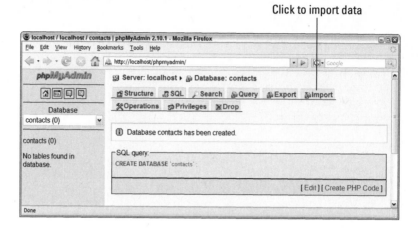

6. To verify that the import was successful, click the `person` table link on the left menu under the Database selector, as shown in Figure 29.15.

FIGURE 29.15

Selecting a database table in `phpMyAdmin`

7. In the Table administrative screen, click Browse.

You should see that the `contacts` database now has a `person` table with eight columns and 1,000 rows.

Creating a MySQL database connection

Before generating PHP and Flex client application code, you first must define a database connection. You can define the connection either during the code generation process or as a separate task from the Data Source Explorer view.

> **TIP**   PHP is certainly capable of communicating with database products other than MySQL, but the Flex Builder 3 code generation wizard for PHP is designed to work only with MySQL. Similarly, the ASP.NET code generation wizard (described in Chapter 28) works only with databases hosted by SQL Server. In either case, if you want to use a database other than the one most commonly associated with each application server, you must set up the database drivers and code the server-side code manually.

Follow these steps to define a MySQL database connection:

1. Select Window ⇨ Other Views from the Flex Builder menu.

2. Select Connectivity ⇨ Data Source Explorer from the Show View dialog box, as shown in Figure 29.16.

FIGURE 29.16

The Data Source Explorer view

---

3. Right-click (Ctrl-click on the Mac) the Databases item in the Data Source Explorer view, and select New... from the context menu.

4. In the New Connection Profile screen, select Simple MySQL Connection and click Next.

5. In the Create Connection Profile screen, set the connection name to any descriptive string and click Next. For example, if you're using a database named `contacts`, set the connection name to **contacts**.

> **TIP**   If you select the option to auto-connect when the wizard is finished or when the Data Source Explorer view opens, you'll be able to browse the database's table structures in the Data Source Explorer view without having to connect explicitly. If you didn't select this option while creating a connection, just right-click (or Ctrl+click on the Mac) on the connection in the Data Source Explorer view and click Connect for the same functionality. To change this or other options in an existing connection, right-click (or Ctrl+click on the Mac) on the connection in the Data Source Explorer view.

6. In the Simple SQL Server screen, shown in Figure 29.17, set the connection properties as follows:

- Server Name: **The IP address or DNS name of the system hosting MySQL**
- Database Name: **The name of the database you want to use**
- User Name: **The username to be used in authenticating your MySQL connection**
- Password: **The password to be used in authenticating your MySQL connection**

FIGURE 29.17

Configuring the MySQL data source

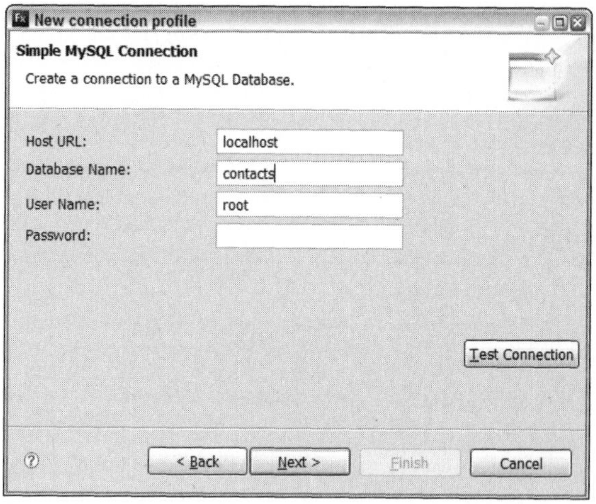

The MySQL administrative user is always named `root` upon first installation. The WAMP installer for Windows installs MySQL with the `root` user's password set to a blank string. The MAMP on Mac OS X sets the `root` user's password to `root`.

7. Click Test Connection to make sure Flex Builder can connect to your MySQL database.

8. Click Finish to create the connection and return to the Data Source Explorer view.

Generating a Flex/PHP application

After you've created a database connection and have a database and table to work with, you're ready to use Flex Builder's application generator.

Follow these steps to generate both client-side and server-side code:

1. Select Data ➪ Create Application from Database... from the Flex Builder menu.

2. In the Choose Data Source screen, shown in Figure 29.18, select a Connection and a Table. The Primary Key column should be selected automatically.

 You also can create a database connection from this point of the application generator. When working with a Flex/PHP project, you can create only a connection for MySQL.

FIGURE 29.18

Selecting a connection and a database table

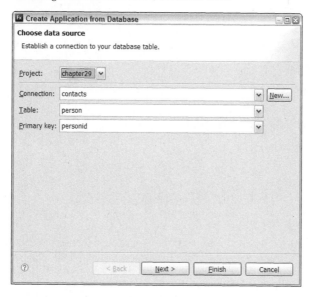

3. Click Next.

 The application generator works correctly only with a table that has a single-column primary key.

4. On the Generate server-side code screen, shown in Figure 29.19, set the PHP source folder to indicate where generated PHP code should be placed. The default target location is the project's output folder.

FIGURE 29.19

Selecting a server-side PHP source folder and filename

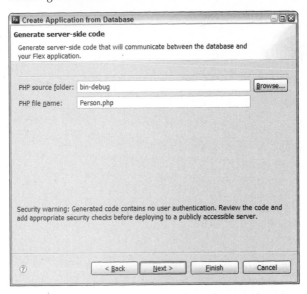

5. Set the PHP filename to indicate what to name the file that serves data to the Flex application. The default is the name of the database table with a file extension of .php.

6. Click Next.

7. On the Generate client-side code screen, shown in Figure 29.20, select the columns you want to display in the Flex client application's default view. This screen also allows you to select these options:

- Data types for each column default to the same type as the original column itself, but they can be reset in this screen.

- The default view allows the user to filter on a single column; this screen allows you to select the filtering column.

8. Click Finish to generate the Flex client application and the server-side PHP page and supporting files.

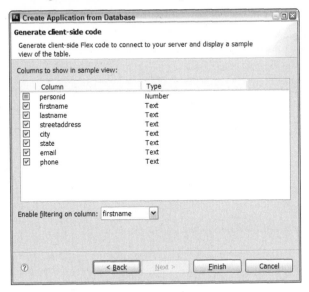

FIGURE 29.20

Selecting table columns and setting their data types

Understanding and using the generated code

The generated Flex/PHP application is designed to exchange data between client and server using the Flex framework's HTTPService component. The Flex application sends data to PHP as a standard HTTP GET request and receives well-formed XML in the response.

The client-side Flex application

The generated client-side application, as shown in Figure 29.21, displays data returned from PHP with a rudimentary set of views.

The application includes an editable DataGrid that displays and allows you to modify data, a TextInput control and Button that allow you to filter data using server-side SQL statements, and a very simple data entry form for adding new data.

The HTTPService object that communicates with PHP is declared and controlled in an ActionScript file named for the selected database table. For example, if the table is named person, the ActionScript file is named personScript.as. The location of the PHP page is declared in an included ActionScript file named for the selected table. The file for the person table is named personConfig.as.

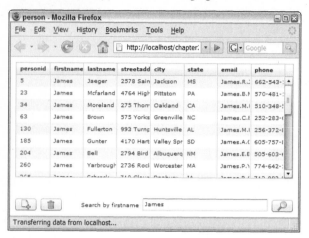

FIGURE 29.21

A generated Flex application exchanging data with PHP

The server-side PHP code

The more interesting and useful code is on the server in the Flex project's output folder. The PHP page to which requests are sent expects a request parameter named `method`. When a request is received, this PHP code evaluates the parameter and determines which of the PHP page's five methods should be executed:

```
switch (@$_REQUEST["method"]) {
  case "FindAll":
    $ret = findAll();
  break;
  case "Insert":
    $ret = insert();
  break;
  case "Update":
    $ret = update();
  break;
  case "Delete":
    $ret = delete();
  break;
  case "Count":
    $ret = rowCount();
  break;
```

The names of the method parameter's possible values are case-sensitive and must be passed exactly as shown in the preceding code.

TIP The generated PHP code is based on a set of template files in Flex Builder's installation folder under `plugins\com.adobe.flexbuilder.dbwizard_3.0.194161\`
`templates`. Within this folder, you'll find subfolders supporting the PHP, ASP.NET, and Java application wizards. The `php_rest/php` subfolder contains files that control the code generation for connections, database table management, and supporting functions. You should modify this code only if you have a strong understanding of PHP. And, of course, you should make backup copies just in case anything goes wrong.

To call the PHP page without using the generated Flex client application, pass named parameters as part of the `HTTPService` request. For example, this code creates a `params` object and populates its `method` property with a value of `Count` to call the PHP pages' `rowCount()` method:

```
var params:Object = new Object();
params.method="Count";
myHTTPService.send(params);
```

Returned data is serialized into XML using a PHP class named `XmlSerializer` that's delivered as part of the generated application. The following code in the generated PHP page is responsible for serializing the response into well-formed XML before returning it to the requesting client in the HTTP response:

```
$serializer = new XmlSerializer();
echo $serializer->serialize($ret);
```

TIP Unlike the PHP5 SimpleXML extension, the `XmlSerializer` class correctly replaces XML reserved characters with their equivalent extensions, guaranteeing that the XML returned by the class is truly well-formed and can be read successfully by any XML parser.

The `XmlSerializer` class always returns its data with a root element named `<response>` and a child element named `<data>` that in turn nests the returned data. For example, the XML packet returned from the `rowCount()` method looks like this:

```
<?xml version="1.0" encoding="ISO-8859-1"?>
<response>
  <data>1000</data>
  <metadata />
</response>
```

When repeating rows of data are returned, each row's data is nested within a `<row>` element that in turn is a child of `<data>`. The `<response>` element's child `<metadata>` element contains a `<totalrows>` element that indicates the number of available rows in the returned data set:

```
<?xml version="1.0" encoding="ISO-8859-1"?>
<response>
  <data>
    <row>
      <personid>1</personid>
      <firstname>Brad</firstname>
      <lastname>Lang</lastname>
      <streetaddress>3004 Buckhannan Avenue</streetaddress>
```

```
      <city>Syracuse</city>
      <state>NY</state>
      <email>Brad.C.Lang@trashymail.com</email>
      <phone>315-449-9420</phone>
    </row>
    ... additional rows ...
  </data>
  <metadata>
    <totalRows>1000</totalRows>
    <pageNum>0</pageNum>
  </metadata>
</response>
```

Because the XmlSerializer class is consistent in how it returns data, regardless of the selected database table's column names and data types, you can safely use the same basic code for each event handler function that receives and saves a reference to returned data:

```
[Bindable]
private var myData:ArrayCollection
private function resultHandler(event:ResultEvent):void
{
  myData = event.result.response.data.row as ArrayCollection
}
```

Inserting data

The generated PHP page implements this insert() function that uses parameters from the HTTP request to build and execute an SQL INSERT statement:

```
function insert() {
  global $conn;

  //build and execute the insert query
  $query_insert = sprintf("INSERT INTO `person`
    (firstname,lastname,streetaddress,
     city,state,email,phone)
  VALUES (%s,%s,%s,%s,%s,%s,%s)" ,
    GetSQLValueString($_REQUEST["firstname"], "text"), #
    GetSQLValueString($_REQUEST["lastname"], "text"), #
    ... additional columns as needed ...
  );
  $ok = mysql_query($query_insert);

  if ($ok) {
    // return the new entry, using the insert id
    $toret = array(
      "data" => array(
        array(
          "personid" => mysql_insert_id(),
          "firstname" => $_REQUEST["firstname"], #
```

```
            "lastname" => $_REQUEST["lastname"]
            ... additional columns as needed
        )
      ),
      "metadata" => array()
    );
  } else {
    // we had an error, return it
    $toret = array(
      "data" => array("error" => mysql_error()),
      "metadata" => array()
    );
  }
  return $toret;
}
```

Notice that the `insert()` function uses the value of the PHP `mysql_insert_id()` function to retrieve the newly assigned primary key value for the inserted row from MySQL. That value is then used to build an object that's returned to the requesting client application.

To call this function from Flex, create an `Object` with the method parameter set to `Insert`. Add one parameter for each database table column with the new value, and then pass the object to the `HTTPService` component's `send()` method:

```
var params:Object = new Object();
params.method="Insert";
params.firstname = fnameInput.text;
params.lastname = lnameInput.text;
... additional columns as necessary ...
myHTTPService.send(params);
```

Then, if you want to capture the newly assigned primary key, it will be available in the `HTTPService` component's `result` event object.

Updating data

The generated PHP page implements this `update()` function that uses parameters from the HTTP request to build and execute an SQL UPDATE statement:

```
function update() {
  global $conn;

  // check to see if the record actually exists in the database
  $query_recordset =
    sprintf("SELECT * FROM `person` WHERE personid = %s",
    GetSQLValueString($_REQUEST["personid"], "int") );
  $recordset = mysql_query($query_recordset, $conn);
  $num_rows = mysql_num_rows($recordset);

  if ($num_rows > 0) {
```

```
// build and execute the update query
$row_recordset = mysql_fetch_assoc($recordset);
$query_update = sprintf("UPDATE `person`
  SET firstname = %s,lastname = %s WHERE personid = %s",
  GetSQLValueString($_REQUEST["firstname"], "text"),
  GetSQLValueString($_REQUEST["lastname"], "text")
  GetSQLValueString($row_recordset["personid"], "int")
);
$ok = mysql_query($query_update);
if ($ok) {
  // return the updated entry
  $toret = array(
    "data" => array(
      array(
        "personid" => $row_recordset["personid"],
        "firstname" => $_REQUEST["firstname"], #
        "lastname" => $_REQUEST["lastname"] #
      )
    ),
    "metadata" => array()
  );
} else {
  // an update error, return it
  $toret = array(
    "data" => array("error" => mysql_error()),
    "metadata" => array()
  );
}
} else {
  $toret = array(
    "data" => array("error" => "No row found"),
    "metadata" => array()
  );
}
return $toret;
}
```

To call this function from Flex, create an Object with the method parameter set to Update. Add one parameter for each database table column, including the current primary key value, and then pass the object to the HTTPService component's send() method:

```
var params:Object = new Object();
params.method="Update";
params.personid = currentPrimaryKey;
params.firstname = fnameInput.text;
params.lastname = lnameInput.text;
... additional columns as necessary ...
myHTTPService.send(params);
```

Deleting data

The generated PHP page implements this `delete()` function that uses parameters from the HTTP request to build and execute an SQL DELETE statement:

```php
function delete() {
  global $conn;
  // check to see if the record actually exists in the database
  $query_recordset =
    sprintf("SELECT * FROM `person` WHERE personid = %s",
      GetSQLValueString($_REQUEST["personid"], "int") );
  $recordset = mysql_query($query_recordset, $conn);
  $num_rows = mysql_num_rows($recordset);
  if ($num_rows > 0) {
    $row_recordset = mysql_fetch_assoc($recordset);
    $query_delete = sprintf(
      "DELETE FROM `person` WHERE personid = %s",
      GetSQLValueString($row_recordset["personid"], "int"));
    $ok = mysql_query($query_delete);
    if ($ok) {
      // delete went through ok, return OK
      $toret = array(
        "data" => $row_recordset["personid"],
        "metadata" => array()
      );
    } else {
      $toret = array(
        "data" => array("error" => mysql_error()),
        "metadata" => array()
      );
    }
  } else {
    // no row found, return an error
    $toret = array(
      "data" => array("error" => "No row found"),
      "metadata" => array()
    );
  }
  return $toret;
}
```

To call this function from Flex, create an `Object` with the method parameter set to `Delete`. Add a parameter representing the record's current primary key value, and then pass the object to the `HTTPService` component's `send()` method:

```actionscript
var params:Object = new Object();
params.method="Delete";
params.personid = currentPrimaryKey;
myHTTPService.send(params);
```

Using PHP and Remoting with AMFPHP

A number of PHP-based implementations of the technology are variously known as the Remoting Service (in BlazeDS and LiveCycle Data Services) or Flash Remoting (in ColdFusion). They include:

- **AMFPHP:** A free, open-source project available at www.amfphp.org
- **SabreAMF:** A free, open-source project available at http://osflash.org/sabreamf
- **WebOrb:** A commercial implementation of Remoting for PHP, Java, ASP.NET, and Ruby on Rails that's available at www.themidnightcoders.com

Developers typically switch from using the HTTPService component and generic XML to an implementation of AMF when they want better performance in applications that exchange data with a server at runtime. As with Flash Remoting in ColdFusion, described in Chapter 26, and the Java-based Remoting Service in LiveCycle Data Services and BlazeDS, described in Chapter 24, messages that use binary AMF are significantly smaller than an equivalent message formatted in SOAP or generic XML. The result is faster exchange of data and decreased use of network resources.

The details of implementation on the server are different for each of these server-based software packages. Because AMFPHP is a bit easier to use than SabreAMF and is completely free for development and deployment (in contrast to the commercial WebOrb product), in this section I describe how to download and install AMFPHP and then how to build and deploy PHP classes for use with the Flex framework's RemoteObject component.

Installing AMFPHP

You can download the most recent version of AMFPHP from:

```
http://sourceforge.net/project/showfiles.php?group_id=72483#files
```

As of this writing, the most recently available download was version 1.9, beta 2. Download that or a more recent version from the AMFPHP downloads page. The files are delivered in a .zip archive file with a filename indicating the date of release. (For example, the archive file that was available at the time of this writing was named amfphp-1.9.beta.20080120.zip.) Then follow these brief steps to integrate the AMFPHP package into your PHP installation:

1. Extract the files to any location on your hard disk. The top-level folder is named the same as the archive file, without a .zip file extension. Within that folder, you'll find a folder named amfphp that contains the AMFPHP service manager and some other valuable tools.

2. Copy or move the amfphp folder to your Web server's document root folder. For example, if you've installed WAMP on Windows in the default installation location, copy the amfphp folder to c:\wamp\www.

3. To test the installation, make sure your Web server is running. Then open any Web browser, and navigate to the amfphp/browser folder under the Web root:

```
http://localhost/amfphp/browser/
```

As shown in Figure 29.22, you should see the AMFPHP Service Browser application displaying a tree control in the left panel.

The AMFPHP Service Browser

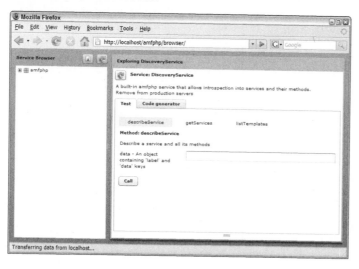

The Service Browser displays all the currently installed services and allows you to make calls to the service methods and see the results in a number of formats.

Creating an AMFPHP service in PHP

AMFPHP services are built as PHP classes that are placed in a services subfolder under the amfphp root folder. Functions declared as class members return values that are encoded in binary AMF for exchange with a client Flex application. Just as with any PHP file, you don't need to compile or otherwise prepare a PHP class to be called as a service. You just create the file in the correct location, and it's immediately ready for use.

The PHP class in Listing 29.3 implements a single sayHello() function that returns a string value to the client application.

LISTING 29.3

A Hello World PHP class that's compatible with AMFPHP

```php
<?php
class HelloWorld {
  function sayHello()
  {
    return "Hello Flex from PHP!";
  }
}
?>
```

ON the WEB   The code in Listing 29.3 is available in the Web site files as `HelloWorld.php` in the `amfphp/flex3bible/chapter29` folder of the `chapter29` project.

Follow these steps to install and test the `HelloWorld` class for use in AMFPHP:

1. Copy the contents of the `amfphp` folder of the `chapter29` project to the `amfphp` root folder's `services` subfolder. The `services` folder should now contain a `flex3bible` folder in which the `HelloWorld.php` file is stored. The service is now installed and ready for testing.

2. Open a Web browser, and navigate to the AMFPHP Service Browser application at:

   `http:/localhost/amfphp/browser`

   You should see a new item labeled `flexbible` in the tree control on the left.

3. Click the + icon next to the `flex3bible` item to expand it.

4. Click the tree control's `HelloWorld` item to select the service class and display its details.

   You should see the `sayHello()` method appear in the right panel with an associated button labeled Call.

5. Click Call to execute the service method, and then click the Results tab that appears.

As shown in Figure 29.23, the Service Browser now displays the data returned from the service method.

FIGURE 29.23

The AMFPHP Service Browser displaying returned data

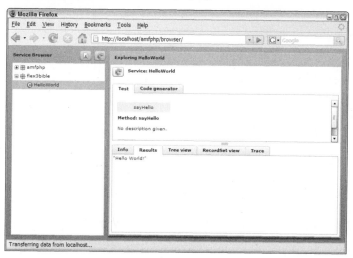

Configuring AMFPHP Remoting in Flex Builder

Before calling an AMFPHP service's methods with the RemoteObject component, you first need to create a services configuration file that defines an AMFPHP-based Remoting channel and create a Remoting destination that can be called from Flex.

> **TIP** The services configuration file can be placed anywhere on disk. Unlike when using the Remoting Service with BlazeDS and Java, the services configuration file isn't used by PHP: Its settings are used solely by the Flex compiler to provide information to the client application about the location and capabilities of the server-side destination.

The services configuration file in Listing 29.4 defines an AMF channel with an id of my-amfphp and a destination with an id of amfphp. The channel defines a hard-coded server location in its endpoint element's uri attribute of http://localhost/amfphp/gateway.php.

> **TIP** The gateway.php file is part of the AMFPHP installation and is configured in AMFPHP to receive and handle AMF-formatted requests from client applications.

LISTING 29.4

A services configuration file for use with AMFPHP

```
<services-config>
  <services>
    <service id="amfphp-flashremoting-service"
      class="flex.messaging.services.RemotingService"
      messageTypes="flex.messaging.messages.RemotingMessage">
      <destination id="amfphp">
        <channels>
          <channel ref="my-amfphp"/>
        </channels>
        <properties>
          <source>*</source>
        </properties>
      </destination>
    </service>
  </services>
  <channels>
    <channel-definition id="my-amfphp"
      class="mx.messaging.channels.AMFChannel">
      <endpoint uri="http://localhost/amfphp/gateway.php"
        class="flex.messaging.endpoints.AMFEndpoint"/>
    </channel-definition>
  </channels>
</services-config>
```

ON the WEB The code in Listing 29.4 is available in the Web site files as `services-config.xml` in the `src` folder of the `chapter29` project.

You provide the location of the services configuration file to the Flex compiler through a `-services` compiler argument. If the services configuration file is in the same folder as the Flex application files, you can provide only the filename; otherwise, you provide a relative or absolute folder location. The following `-services` argument assumes that the services configuration file is in the same folder as the application files:

```
-services services-config.xml
```

Follow these steps to configure the Flex project to use the services configuration file in the project's source root folder:

1. Select the Flex project in the Flex Navigator view.

2. Select Project ➪ Properties from the Flex Builder menu.

3. Select Flex Compiler from the categories list.

4. Add a -services argument to the Additional compiler arguments with the name of the services configuration file, services-config.xml, as shown in Figure 29.24

5. Click OK to save the new configuration.

Setting the Flex compiler to include new Remoting Services

Setting the services configuration file

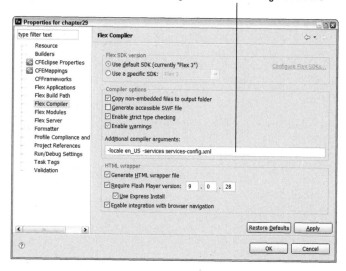

 All AMF service providers, including third-party products such as WebOrb, use the same basic process to configure AMF-based services.

Calling an AMFPHP service with RemoteObject

You call an AMFPHP service's methods using the RemoteObject component. The behavior and functionality of the RemoteObject component on the client is exactly the same as when using it with Java or ColdFusion.

CROSS-REF Because the client-side code for using the RemoteObject component is pretty much the same regardless of the language or platform on the server, many details of the client-side code aren't covered in this chapter. See Chapters 24 and 26 for more client-side code samples.

Whether you declare your RemoteObject instance in MXML or ActionScript, the object's destination property should be set to the destination id as defined in the services configuration file. The source is set to the name of the AMFPHP service class, with a package that's determined by the folder structure in which the class is stored.

The application in Listing 29.5 declares a `RemoteObject` component instance in MXML code and sets its source to the location of the `HelloWorld` service installed previously.

LISTING 29.5

A Flex application calling an AMFPHP service

```
<?xml version="1.0" encoding="utf-8"?>
<mx:Application xmlns:mx="http://www.adobe.com/2006/mxml">

  <mx:RemoteObject id="phpService"
    destination="amfphp"
    source="flex3bible.HelloWorld"/>
  <mx:Button label="Say Hello" click="phpService.sayHello()"/>
  <mx:Label text="{phpService.sayHello.lastResult}"/>

</mx:Application>
```

ON the WEB   The code in Listing 29.5 is available in the Web site files as `CallHelloService.mxml` in the `src` folder of the `chapter29` project.

Returning complex data from AMFPHP

You can return complex data from PHP either by manually constructing an array to return or by generating and returning a simple data set.

The PHP service class in Listing 29.6 executes a simple query and returns its data.

LISTING 29.6

Returning a simple data set from a PHP class

```
<?php
class DataManager {
  function returnResultset()
  {
    mysql_connect('localhost', 'root', '');
    mysql_select_db('contacts');
    return mysql_query(sprintf(
      "SELECT * FROM person ORDER BY lastname, firstname"));
  }
}
?>
```

The code in Listing 29.6 is available in the Web site files as **DataManager.php** in the AMFPHP files of the **chapter29** project.

When you call the service function, the query result is received in Flex as an `ArrayCollection`. The Flex application in Listing 29.7 calls the service function and uses debugging code to determine how much time elapses between sending the request and receiving the result. When you run the application in debug mode and send the request, a tracing message reports the time elapsed in Flex Builder's Console view.

LISTING 29.7

A Flex application receiving complex data

```
<?xml version="1.0" encoding="utf-8"?>
<mx:Application xmlns:mx="http://www.adobe.com/2006/mxml">
  <mx:Script>
    <![CDATA[
      import mx.collections.ArrayCollection;
      import mx.rpc.events.ResultEvent;
      [Bindable]
      private var myData:ArrayCollection;
      private var startTime:Number;
      private function sendRequest():void
      {
        startTime = (new Date()).getTime();
        phpService.getPersonData();
      }
      private function resultHandler(event:ResultEvent):void
      {
        var endTime:Number = (new Date()).getTime();
        trace("Time elapsed: " + (endTime - startTime));
        myData = event.result as ArrayCollection;
      }
    ]]>
  </mx:Script>
  <mx:RemoteObject id="phpService" destination="amfphp"
    source="flex3bible.DataManager" result="resultHandler(event)"/>
  <mx:Button label="Get Data" click="sendRequest()"/>
  <mx:DataGrid dataProvider="{myData}"/>
</mx:Application>
```

The code in Listing 29.7 is available in the Web site files as **GetComplexData.php** in the AMFPHP files of the **chapter29** project.

The PHP `mysql_query()` function returns a PHP `resource`, which is serialized to an ArrayCollection when returned to Flex. Table 29.1 describes how other PHP data types are serialized from ActionScript to PHP and back again.

TABLE 29.1

ActionScript to PHP Data Serialization

ActionScript	To PHP	Back to ActionScript
null	null	null
Boolean	boolean	Boolean
String	string	String
Date	float	Number
Array	array	Array
Object	associative array	Object
XML	string	String

WEB RESOURCE Many Flex/PHP developers have shared what they've learned about advanced integration of Flex and AMFPHP. These articles on the Web can be particularly helpful:

Flex, AMFPHP, and Value Objects (Renaun Erickson) at `http://renaun.com/blog/2006/07/25/70/`

Mapping VO's from Flex to PHP using AMFPHP (Victor Rubba) at `http://viconflex.blogspot.com/2007/04/mapping-vos-from-flex-to-php-using.html`

Using AMFPHP 1.9 with the Adobe Flex 2 SDK (Michael Ramirez) at `www.howtoforge.com/amfphp_adobe_flex2_sdk`

Summary

In this chapter, I described how to build Flex applications that are integrated with server-side code managed by PHP. You learned the following:

- PHP is an open-source, freely available application server that is compatible with many operating systems.

- PHP's scripting language doesn't require any compilation prior to being requested from a client application.

- To get started quickly with PHP, you can download and use free integrated software bundles named WAMP (for Windows) and MAMP (for Mac OS X) that include the Apache Web server, PHP, and MySQL.

- When you create a Flex project, you can associate it with your PHP installation.

- The PHP5 SimpleXML extension can create XML packets to return to a Flex application.

- Flex Builder 3 can generate complete client and server code to manage a MySQL database table with PHP code on the server.

- You can build your own client Flex application to work with the generated PHP code using the `HTTPService` component.

- Better network and data exchange performance can be achieved by using the `RemoteObject` component and PHP classes hosted by AMFPHP, a free, open-source project.

Chapter 30

Deploying Desktop Applications with AIR

A dobe's release of Flex 3 in February 2008 was tightly integrated with the release of the Adobe Integrated Runtime, known as AIR. Formerly known by its public code name, Apollo, AIR is Adobe's first step toward a universal runtime client that can run local applications on a variety of personal computer systems and other computing devices.

With AIR 1.0, Adobe has delivered the ability to deploy applications on for Windows and Mac OS X client systems, with a Linux version of the runtime in current development. Adobe's roadmap for AIR includes future versions for cell phones and other mobile devices, which eventually would allow AIR desktop applications to be deployed on a more truly universal basis.

> **TIP** As of this writing, an alpha version AIR for Linux was available on Adobe Labs at `http://labs.adobe.com/technologies/air`. New versions should appear on this Web page as they become available.

AIR applications can be built from many different kinds of assets, but each application's core asset is made up of either Flash-based content, built in either Flash CS3 or Flex 3, or HTML-based and JavaScript-based content. Regardless of which kind of asset is used as the application's core element, any AIR application can use and present HTML, Flash, Flex, or Acrobat PDF content.

> **TIP** The ability to present and manipulate Acrobat PDF content is dependent on the user having Acrobat Reader 8.1 or higher installed on their client system.

In this chapter, I describe the basics of creating and deploying a Flex-based desktop application with Flex Builder 3 and AIR.

 To use the sample code for this chapter, download `chapter30.zip` from the Web site. This is not a Flex project archive file. Its use and installation are described later in this chapter.

Understanding AIR Architecture

The Adobe Integrated Runtime is installed as a runtime library on your client system. Its purpose is to provide core runtime functionality that's needed by all AIR-based desktop applications, regardless of whether they're built in Flash, Flex, or HTML.

As shown in Figure 30.1, AIR includes a copy of both the Flash Player and a Web browser. In AIR 1.0, the included Flash Player is based on Flash Player 9, while the Web browser is an implementation of WebKit, an open-source Web browser engine.

FIGURE 30.1

Adobe Integrated Runtime architecture with Flex applications

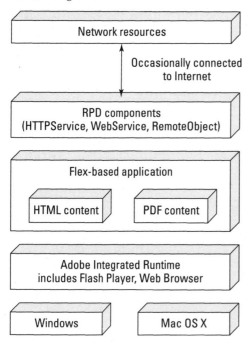

TIP   The WebKit Web browser engine is used as the kernel for the Safari browser on Mac OS X and the Konqueror browser that's available with the K desktop environment on Linux. The version that's used in AIR 1.0 is derived from the open-source version of WebKit that's available at `http://webkit.org`.

A desktop application deployed on AIR is delivered as an installable archive file with a file extension of .air. After installation, it runs as a local application that's native to the operating system, rather than as a Web-based application. As a result, desktop applications deployed on AIR aren't subject to the same security sandbox restrictions as a Web-based application that's downloaded and run on request from within a Web browser.

Because an AIR application's assets are made up of content that runs equally well on multiple operating systems without having to be rebuilt (Flash documents, HTML pages, JavaScript and CSS code, and Acrobat PDF documents), a single application can run on all supported operating systems without having to be recompiled.

Installing the Adobe Integrated Runtime

If you're using Flex Builder 3 to develop Flex applications, you don't necessarily have to install AIR on your development system, because Flex Builder includes all the tools you need to compile, test, and debug an AIR application. But to fully install a completed application, the runtime should be installed.

You can install the runtime in two ways:

- If you know you need AIR on your system, you can download the AIR installer from Adobe's Web site and install it on your system prior to installing any applications.

- When you install an AIR application that uses a seamless installation badge, the application installer detects whether the runtime is already installed and, if not, offers to include the runtime installation along with the application.

The seamless installation badge experience is described in a section at the end of this chapter. In this section, I describe how to download and install the correct version of AIR for your operating system.

Downloading the AIR installer

To download the AIR installer directly from Adobe, navigate to this URL:

```
http://get.adobe.com/air/
```

As shown in Figure 30.2, the Adobe Web page detects which operating system the request comes from and offers a download link for the appropriate version of the AIR installer.

 **TIP** You can download versions of AIR for other operating systems, or versions other than the most recent, from `http://get.adobe.com/air/otherversions`.

FIGURE 30.2

Download the AIR installer from Adobe

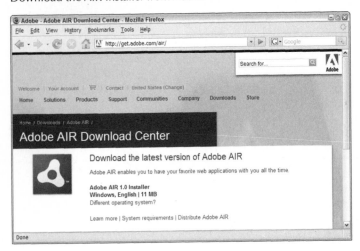

Installing and uninstalling AIR on Windows

The AIR 1.0 installer for Windows is delivered as an executable application that's approximately 11.2MB.

 **TIP** You must be logged into Windows as an administrative user to successfully install or uninstall AIR.

After downloading the installer application, follow these steps to install AIR:

1. Run the installer application, as shown in Figure 30.3.

2. Follow the prompts to complete the installation process.

No configuration options are available, so the installation completes from that point without any further requests for information. On a typical Windows installation, the runtime is installed into the following folder:

```
C:\Program Files\Common Files\Adobe AIR
```

Follow these steps to uninstall AIR on Windows:

1. Go to the Windows Control Panel.

2. Select Add or Remove Programs on Windows XP or Uninstall a program on Windows Vista.

3. Select the Adobe AIR entry.

4. Click Remove on Windows XP or Uninstall on Windows Vista.

5. When the Adobe AIR Setup dialog box appears, click Uninstall to remove AIR from your system.

CAUTION When you uninstall AIR from your system, any installed AIR applications are disabled. You can no longer run them or perform a clean uninstall process. If you want to permanently remove AIR and any dependent applications, you should uninstall the applications first, and run the AIR uninstaller afterward.

FIGURE 30.3

The AIR installer displaying the license agreement

Installing and uninstalling AIR on Mac OS X

The AIR 1.0 installer for Mac OS X is delivered as a DMG file that's approximately 16MB. After downloading the installer file, follow these steps to install AIR:

1. Open the DMG file.

2. Double-click the Adobe AIR Installer application.

3. After accepting the license agreement, enter your Mac administrator password and click OK to complete the installation.

As with installation on Windows, no configuration options are available, so the installation completes from that point with no further requests for information.

Follow these steps to uninstall AIR on Mac OS X:

1. Navigate to the `/Applications/Utilities` folder.

2. Locate and run the Adobe AIR Uninstaller application.

3. When the Adobe AIR Setup dialog box appears, click Uninstall to remove AIR from your system.

4. Enter your Mac administrator password, and click OK to uninstall AIR.

Creating a Flex Desktop Application

You can create and deploy a desktop application with Flex 3 using one of these strategies:

- If you're using the free Flex 3 SDK to build your Flex applications, you can use the free AIR SDK to package your applications for deployment.

- If you're using Flex Builder 3 to create your Flex applications, everything you need to package an AIR application is already included.

In this section, I describe the steps for building a Flex desktop application project with Flex Builder 3.

Creating a Flex desktop application project

When you create a new Flex project in Flex Builder, you have the option of setting the Application type to Desktop. All MXML applications in such a project are designated as desktop applications and are tested and deployed with AIR.

> **TIP** In Flex Builder 3, you can't deploy a single application to both the desktop and the Web. The selection of AIR-based or Web-based deployment is made at the project level, and after a project is configured as such, you can't change it without going back and rebuilding the project from scratch.
>
> If you do need to create a Flex application that's deployed with both architectures, consider creating three projects: one for the Web, one for the desktop, and one that's created as a Flex library project. The first two projects would have applications that are bare skeletons and get all their real functionality from components in the library project. Then, as you code and compile the library project, its assets are shared with the "real" project that contain and are responsible for building the Web and desktop applications.

Follow these steps to create a Flex project in Flex Builder 3 that's designed for the desktop:

1. Select File ➪ New ➪ Flex Project from the Flex Builder menu.

2. On the first screen of the New Flex Project wizard, shown in Figure 30.4, set these project properties:

   ▪ Project name: **chapter30**

   ▪ Project location: **Use default location**

   ▪ Application type: **Desktop application**

   ▪ Application server type: **None**

FIGURE 30.4

Creating a new Flex desktop application project

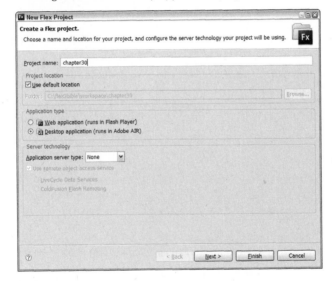

3. Click Next.

4. On the Configure Output screen, accept the default Output folder location and click Next.

5. On the final screen, shown in Figure 30.5, set the Main application filename to MyDesktopApp.mxml.

Setting the main application filename and the application id

6. Set the Application ID to com.mycompany.MyDesktopApp.

7. Click Finish to create the project and application.

   You should see a starting Flex application open in the Flex Builder editor with a root element of <mx:WindowedApplication>. In the Flex Navigator view, shown in Figure 30.6, you should see both the main application file and the XML-based application descriptor file MyDesktopApp-app.xml.

8. Set the <mx:WindowedApplication> start tag's layout property to vertical.

9. Add a Label control to the application with a text property of "Hello from AIR!":

   ```
   <mx:Label text="Hello from AIR!"/>
   ```

10. Save and run the application.

FIGURE 30.6

The contents of a new Flex desktop application project shown in the Flex Navigator view

As shown in Figure 30.7, the application runs in a native window, rather than within a Web browser.

FIGURE 30.7

The resulting "Hello World" AIR application

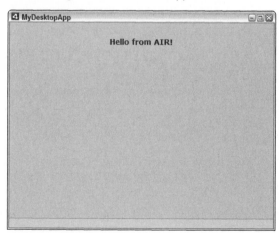

TIP The appearance of a basic Flex application differs depending on the hosting operating system. This screen shot was taken on Windows XP, so the window title bar, borders, and control icons have the look of a standard Windows XP window. The magic of AIR is that you don't have to recompile the application for different operating systems. When packaged with default settings in the application descriptor file, the version of AIR that's currently hosting the application at runtime controls the application window's look and feel.

Using the application descriptor file

The application descriptor file is in XML format and contains settings that are used by the AIR Developers Tool (ADT) and the AIR Debug Launcher (ADL) during packaging and testing of the application. When you create a new MXML application in a Flex desktop project, Flex Builder prompts you for both an application filename and an application id, and it creates both the application file and the application descriptor file at the same time.

> **TIP** A clean starting copy of an application descriptor file with all available options is included in the Flex Builder application as `descriptor-template.xml` in the Flex Builder installation folder's `sdks\3.0.0\templates\air` subfolder.

When you create a new Flex application in a desktop project, the following required properties are set in the default descriptor file:

- `id`: The application id is a string that uniquely identifies each AIR desktop application. To ensure that each application has an id that's globally unique, the id should start with a package-style reference based on your organization's reversed domain name, with the domain parts separated with dots. For example, if an organization's Web domain name is `coolstuff.com`, the id for its desktop applications would always start with `com.coolstuff`.

- `filename`: This is the name of the packaged application's installer file, without a file extension. When the application is packaged for installation, this value is appended with the .air file extension.

- `name`: This is the name of the application as known to its users. This can be any string and can include spaces and special characters.

- `version`: This is the version number of the application.

- `initialWindow/content`: This is the primary asset that's presented in the application's primary window. When working with the AIR SDK, this can be either a Flash .swf file or an HTML file. When working in Flex Builder, the `<content>` element initially contains a comment and is filled in during compilation and testing with the Flex application's compiled .swf filename.

The following starting application descriptor file contains only required elements, after commented-out elements and strings have been removed from the starting file you get in Flex Builder.

```
<?xml version="1.0" encoding="UTF-8"?>
<application xmlns="http://ns.adobe.com/air/application/1.0">
  <id>com.mycompany.MyDesktopApp</id>
  <filename>MyDesktopApp</filename>
  <name>MyDesktopApp</name>
  <version>v1</version>
  <initialWindow>
    <content>[This value will be overwritten by Flex Builder
      in the output app.xml]</content>
  </initialWindow>
</application>
```

TIP   The `<application>` element's xmlns namespace declaration is used to determine which version of AIR is required to run the application. The namespace shown in Listing 30.1 is for the final release of AIR 1.0. You can recognize application descriptor files that were created for the various public beta releases of AIR by their namespace declaration. For example, the namespace for the AIR public beta 3 looked like this:

```
<application
  xmlns="http://ns.adobe.com/air/application/1.0.M6">
</application>
```

You can include many other optional elements in the application descriptor file that affect the installation experience or the behavior and appearance of the application at runtime. As shown in Listing 30.1, the default application descriptor file includes comments above each element describing its purpose.

LISTING 30.1

The default application descriptor file with comments describing the purpose of each element

```
<?xml version="1.0" encoding="UTF-8"?>
<application xmlns="http://ns.adobe.com/air/application/1.0">
  <!-- The application identifier string, unique to this application.
    Required. -->
  <id>com.mycompany.MyDesktopApp</id>
  <!-- Used as the filename for the application. Required. -->
  <filename>MyDesktopApp</filename>
  <!-- The name that is displayed in the AIR application installer.
    Optional. -->
  <name>MyDesktopApp</name>
  <!-- An application version designator
    (such as "v1", "2.5", or "Alpha 1"). Required. -->
  <version>v1</version>
  <!-- Description, displayed in the AIR application installer.
    Optional. -->
  <!-- <description></description> -->
  <!-- Copyright information. Optional -->
  <!-- <copyright></copyright> -->
  <!-- Settings for the application's initial window. Required. -->
  <initialWindow>
    <!-- The main SWF or HTML file of the application. Required. -->
    <!-- Note: In Flex Builder, the SWF reference is set automatically.
    -->
    <content>[This value will be overwritten by Flex Builder
      in the output app.xml]</content>
    <!-- The title of the main window. Optional. -->
    <!-- <title></title> -->
    <!-- The type of system chrome to use (either "standard" or "none").
      Optional. Default standard. -->
```

continued

LISTING 30.1 *(continued)*

```
    <!-- <systemChrome></systemChrome> -->
    <!-- Whether the window is transparent. Only applicable when
      systemChrome is false. Optional. Default false. -->
    <!-- <transparent></transparent> -->
    <!-- Whether the window is initially visible. Optional.
      Default false. -->
    <!-- <visible></visible> -->
    <!-- Whether the user can minimize the window.
      Optional. Default true. -->
    <!-- <minimizable></minimizable> -->
    <!-- Whether the user can maximize the window.
      Optional. Default true. -->
    <!-- <maximizable></maximizable> -->
    <!-- Whether the user can resize the window.
      Optional. Default true. -->
    <!-- <resizable></resizable> -->
    <!-- The window's initial width. Optional. -->
    <!-- <width></width> -->
    <!-- The window's initial height. Optional. -->
    <!-- <height></height> -->
    <!-- The window's initial x position. Optional. -->
    <!-- <x></x> -->
    <!-- The window's initial y position. Optional. -->
    <!-- <y></y> -->
    <!-- The window's minimum size, specified as a width/height pair,
      such as "400 200". Optional. -->
    <!-- <minSize></minSize> -->
    <!-- The window's initial maximum size, specified as a width/height
      pair, such as "1600 1200". Optional. -->
    <!-- <maxSize></maxSize> -->
</initialWindow>
<!-- The subpath of the standard default installation location to use.
  Optional. -->
<!-- <installFolder></installFolder> -->
<!-- The subpath of the Windows Start/Programs menu to use. Optional.
  -->
<!-- <programMenuFolder></programMenuFolder> -->
<!-- The icon the system uses for the application. For at least one
  resolution, specify the path to a PNG file included in the AIR
  package.
  Optional. -->
<!-- <icon>
  <image16x16></image16x16>
  <image32x32></image32x32>
  <image48x48></image48x48>
  <image128x128></image128x128>
```

```
  </icon> -->
  <!-- Whether the application handles the update when a user double-
  clicks
    an update version of the AIR file (true), or the default AIR
    application
    installer handles the update (false).
  Optional. Default false. -->
  <!-- <customUpdateUI></customUpdateUI> -->
  <!-- Whether the application can be launched when the user clicks a
  link
    in a web browser. Optional. Default false. -->
  <!-- <allowBrowserInvocation></allowBrowserInvocation> -->
  <!-- Listing of file types for which the application can register.
    Optional. -->
  <!-- <fileTypes> -->
    <!-- Defines one file type. Optional. -->
    <!-- <fileType> -->
      <!-- The name that the system displays for the registered file
  type.
        Required. -->
      <!-- <name></name> -->
      <!-- The extension to register. Required. -->
      <!-- <extension></extension> -->
      <!-- The description of the file type. Optional. -->
      <!-- <description></description> -->
      <!-- The MIME type. Optional. -->
      <!-- <contentType></contentType> -->
      <!-- The icon to display for the file type. Optional. -->
      <!-- <icon>
        <image16x16></image16x16>
        <image32x32></image32x32>
        <image48x48></image48x48>
        <image128x128></image128x128>
      </icon> -->

    <!-- </fileType> -->
  <!-- </fileTypes> -->
</application>
```

Packaging a release version of an AIR application

When you package a release version of an AIR application, you create an AIR file (with a file extension of .air) that's delivered to the user as the application installer. When the user opens the .air file on a system where the Adobe Integrated Runtime has already been installed, the application installer is executed.

Follow these steps to package the application for installation and deployment:

1. With the application open in the Flex Builder editor, select File ⇨ Export ⇨ Release Build... from the menu.

2. In the Export Release Build wizard, shown in Figure 30.8, set these properties:

   ▪ Project: **The selected project.**

   ▪ Application: **The MXML application you want to package.**

   ▪ View Source: **Whether you want to allow the user to view the application's source code** (available when the user right-clicks on the application at runtime).

   ▪ Export to file: **The name of the generated .air file you want to build.** By default, this file is placed in the Flex project's root folder, but you can browse and select any other location within a currently open Eclipse project.

FIGURE 30.8

The Export Release Build wizard's initial screen

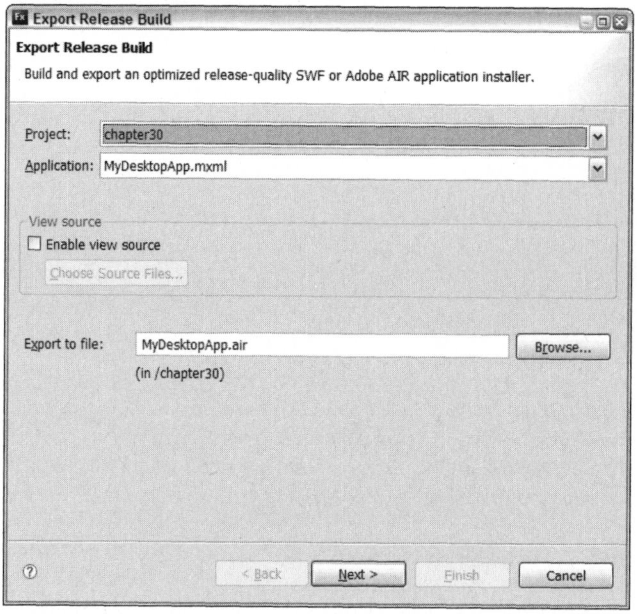

3. Click Next.

On the Digital Signature screen, shown in Figure 30.9, you can either export and sign the generated AIR file with a digital certificate or create an intermediate file with a file extension of .air that can be signed and completed in a secondary step.

FIGURE 30.9

Selecting a security certificate

TIP   To package any AIR application, you must provide a security certificate that certifies to the user who developed the application. For applications that are in testing or that are only deployed within an organization, you can generate a self-signed certificate from within Flex Builder. This certificate allows you to package and deploy the application, but because no recognized certificate authority will have authenticated your organization's identity, the resulting installer application indicates that the author of the application is "Unknown."

For an application that will be deployed to a public audience, you should always purchase a security certificate from a recognized certificate authority such as VeriSign (www.verisign.com) or Thawte (www.thawte.com). When you use this sort of publicly recognized certificate to package your AIR application, the resulting installer correctly displays your organization name as the application author.

CAUTION   Even an application that reports an unknown author has unrestricted access to the user's system. The purpose of the security certificate is to give the user an opportunity to accept or reject installation based on the author's identity, and doesn't stop bad applications from doing bad things.

If you don't have a security certificate, follow these steps to create a self-signed certificate for testing or internal use:

4.   Click Create on the Digital Signature screen.

5.   Enter the requested values on the Create Self-Signed Digital Certificate screen, shown in Figure 30.10. Items marked with an asterisk are required. In particular, you must provide a password that will then be required each time the certificate is used.

FIGURE 30.10

FIGURE 30.10

Creating a self-signed digital certificate

6. Select the name of your certificate file with a file extension of .p12, and click OK to create the certificate file.

   When you return to the Digital Signature screen, the certificate filename and password will already be filled in.

   If you already have a digital certificate file, just select the file and enter the certificate password.

7. Click Finish in the Digital Signature screen to create the AIR installer file.

   You should see that the application's AIR file is available in the project root folder and can be seen in the Flex Navigator view, as shown in Figure 30.11.

FIGURE 30.11

A packaged AIR application

Installing AIR applications

To install an AIR application on a desktop system that already has the runtime installed, just open the .air file that was generated in Flex Builder. From within Flex Builder, you can open the file by double-clicking it in the Flex Navigator view.

As shown in Figure 30.12, the initial installation screen displays the application's Publisher (displayed as "UNKNOWN" when the AIR file is built with a self-signed certificate) and the application's name as configured in the descriptor file.

FIGURE 30.12

An AIR installer's initial screen

After clicking Install on the initial screen, the confirmation screen, shown in Figure 30.13, displays the application name and the description as provided in the descriptor file. The installer also offers the user these options:

- Whether to include a shortcut icon for the application on the desktop
- Whether to start the application after installation is complete
- The application installation location, which defaults to C:\Program Files on Windows and /Applications on Mac OS X

> **TIP** On Windows, the application is installed in a subfolder of the selected location named for the application name. For example, the default location MyDesktopApp on Windows is a folder named C:\Program Files\MyDesktopApp. On Mac OS X, the application is installed as a single application package file in the selected location folder with a file extension of .app. For example, the default location of MyDeskTopApp on Mac is a single application file named /Applications/MyDesktopApp.app.

When the user clicks Continue, the application is installed on his system. If the option to start the application after installation is complete was selected, the application opens.

FIGURE 30.13

An AIR installer's confirmation screen

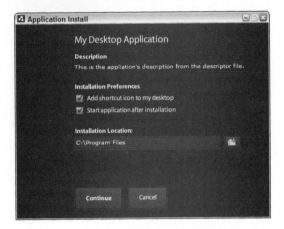

Uninstalling AIR applications

You uninstall an AIR desktop application in the same manner as most other native applications. Follow these steps on Windows:

1. Go to the Windows Control Panel.

2. Select Add or Remove Programs on Windows XP or Uninstall a program on Windows Vista.

3. Select the application entry.

4. Click Remove on Windows XP or Uninstall on Windows Vista.

5. When the Adobe AIR Setup dialog box appears, click Uninstall to remove AIR from your system.

To uninstall an AIR application on Mac OS X, just delete the application .app package file from the /Applications folder by dragging it into the trash.

 Running the .air installation package file after the application is installed also offers the uninstall option.

Flex Application Tips and Tricks with AIR

As described previously, the subject of developing Flex applications for desktop deployment with AIR is too large for a single chapter. There are, however, a few specific things you do a bit differently in a desktop application, and there are many Flex SDK features that are available only when you're developing for AIR. These include:

- Debugging AIR applications in Flex Builder
- Rendering and managing HTML-based and PDF-based content
- Using the `WindowedApplication` component as the application's root element
- Creating channels at runtime for communicating with Remoting gateways

In this section, I briefly describe some of these programming and development techniques.

ON the WEB   If you want to review the sample applications described in this section, extract the contents of the `chapter30.zip` file into the root folder of the `chapter30` Flex desktop application project. Each sample application includes both an application file and an application descriptor file.

Debugging AIR applications in Flex Builder

For the most part, debugging an AIR application in Flex Builder is just like debugging a Web-based Flex application. You have access to all the same debugging tools, including the `trace()` function, breakpoints, and the ability to inspect the values of application variables when the application is suspended.

When you run a Flex application from within Flex Builder in either standard or debug mode, Flex Builder uses ADL (AIR Debug Launcher) in the background. In some cases, ADL can stay in system memory with hidden windows even after an AIR application session has apparently been closed.

The symptom for this condition is that when you try to run or debug that or another application, Flex Builder simply does nothing. Because a debugging session is still in memory, Flex Builder can't start a new one.

Follow these steps to recover from this condition in Windows:

1. Open the Windows Task Manager.
2. In the Processes pane, locate and select the entry for `adl.exe`.
3. Click End Process to force ADL to shut down.
4. Close Task Manager, and return to Flex Builder.

On the Mac:

1. In the Apple menu, select Force Quit.

2. In the Force Quit dialog box, select adl and click the Force Quit button.

3. Close the Force Quit dialog box, and return to Flex Builder.

You should now be able to start your next AIR application session successfully. One common scenario that can result in this problem is when a runtime error occurs during execution of startup code. For example, if you make a call to a server-based resource from an application-level creationComplete event handler and an unhandled fault occurs, the application window might never become visible. If you're running the application in debug mode, you can commonly clear the ADL from memory by terminating the debugging session from within Flex Builder. When running in standard mode, however, the ADL can be left in memory with the window not yet visible.

To solve this issue, it's a good idea to explicitly set the application's initial windows as visible. In the application descriptor file, the <initialWindow> element's child <visible> property is commented out by default. Because this value defaults to false, if the window construction code never succeeds to a runtime error, you're left with an invisible window and ADL still in memory. To solve this, open the application's descriptor file, uncomment the <visible> element, and set its value to true:

```
<visible>true</visible>
```

Working with HTML-based content

The Flex framework offers two ways of creating a Web browser object within any application:

- The HTMLLoader class is extended from the Sprite class and can be used in any Flash or Flex application. Because this class doesn't extend from UIComponent, you can't add it to a Flex container with simple MXML code or by using the addChild() method.

- The HTML control is extended from UIComponent and can be instantiated with either MXML or ActionScript code.

The HTML control is quite a bit easier to use and provides the same functionality as HTMLLoader. Declaring an instance of the control results in a Web browser instance that can freely navigate to any location on the Web (assuming the client system is currently connected).

Instantiating the HTML control

As with all visual controls, the HTML control can be instantiated in MXML or ActionScript code. After it's been instantiated, its location property determines which Web page is displayed. This HTML object, for example, displays Adobe's home page and expands to fill all available space within the application:

```
<mx:HTML id="myHTML" width="100%" height="100%"
    location="http://www.adobe.com"/>
```

When you assign the HTML control's id property, you can then reset its location as needed from any ActionScript code. This statement resets the HTML control's location to the Wiley home page:

```
myHTML.location = "http://www.wiley.com";
```

The application in Listing 30.2 uses an HTTPService object to retrieve an RSS listing from a URL. When the user selects an item from the ComboBox that presents the RSS items, a bit of ActionScript code causes the HTML object to navigate to the selected Web page.

TIP

Because the structure of an RSS feed is consistent regardless of the data provider, this application should work with any RSS feed from any data provider.

LISTING 30.2

A Flex desktop application displaying Web pages from an RSS feed

```
<?xml version="1.0" encoding="utf-8"?>
<mx:WindowedApplication xmlns:mx="http://www.adobe.com/2006/mxml"
  creationComplete="photosXML.send()">
  <mx:Script>
    <![CDATA[
      import mx.controls.Alert;
      import mx.collections.ArrayCollection;
      import mx.rpc.events.FaultEvent;
      import mx.rpc.events.ResultEvent;
      private const feedURL:String =
  "http://www.wiley.com/WileyCDA/feed/RSS_WILEY2_ALLNEWTITLES.xml";
      [Bindable]
      private var feed:ArrayCollection;
      private function resultHandler(event:ResultEvent):void
      {
        feed = event.result.rss.channel.item as ArrayCollection;
        updateHTML();
      }
      private function faultHandler(event:FaultEvent):void
      {
        Alert.show(event.fault.faultString, event.fault.faultCode);
      }
      private function updateHTML():void
      {
       myHTML.location = feedSelector.selectedItem.link;
      }
    ]]>
```

continued

LISTING 30.2 *(continued)*

```
  </mx:Script>
  <mx:HTTPService id="photosXML" url="{feedURL}"
    result="resultHandler(event)" fault="faultHandler(event)"/>
  <mx:HBox width="100%">
    <mx:Label text="Select a new title:"/>
    <mx:ComboBox id="feedSelector" dataProvider="{feed}"
  labelField="title"
      width="400" change="updateHTML()"/>
  </mx:HBox>

  <mx:HTML id="myHTML" width="100%" height="100%"/>
</mx:WindowedApplication>
```

ON the WEB   The code in Listing 30.2 is available in the Web site files in the `chapter30` project as `NewTitlesReader.mxml`.

Figure 30.14 shows the completed application, displaying the contents of the RSS feed in the ComboBox and a currently selected Web page in the HTML component.

FIGURE 30.14

A simple RSS feed application displaying Web pages in an HTML component instance

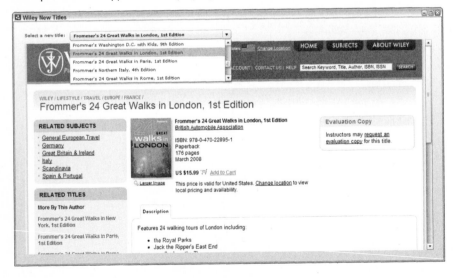

916

Navigating with the HTML control

In addition to the location property, the HTML control implements these methods that allow you to control navigation with ActionScript code:

- `historyBack()`: Navigates back one step in the control's history list.
- `historyForward()`: Navigates back one step in the control's history list.
- `historyGo(steps:int)`: Navigates the number of steps. The value of the `steps` argument can be positive to move forward or negative to move back.

Presenting Acrobat PDF documents

The HTML component also is used to present Acrobat PDF documents. As with Web pages, you simply set the HTML object's location to the document you want to present:

```
<mx:HTML id="myPDF" width="100%" height="100%"
    location="brochure.pdf"/>
```

Figure 30.15 shows an application with just the HTML object described in the previous code. Because the HTML object is the application's only visual object and its dimensions are set to 100 percent of available space, the Acrobat Reader interface fills the entire application and grows and shrinks whenever the application is resized.

FIGURE 30.15

Displaying an Acrobat PDF document in an AIR application

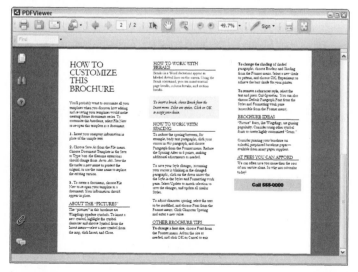

As described previously, the runtime doesn't include a copy of Acrobat Reader, but instead requires that this software package is already installed on the client system. You can find out whether the current client system is capable of displaying Acrobat PDF documents by evaluating the HTML control's static pdfCapability property. The property's value is matched to constants in a PDFCapability class with these values and meanings:

- STATUS_OK: Acrobat Reader 8.1 or later is installed.

- ERROR_INSTALLED_READER_NOT_FOUND: No version of Acrobat Reader is installed.

- ERROR_INSTALLED_READER_TOO_OLD: Acrobat Reader is installed, but it's older than version 8.1.

- ERROR_PREFERED_READER_TOO_OLD: Acrobat Reader 8.1 or later is installed, but another older version is viewed by the operating system as the preferred application for PDF documents.

The application in Listing 30.3 is a simple Web browser application. The application's navigate() function examines the file extension of a document requested by a client application. If the file extension is .pdf and Acrobat Reader 8.1 or later isn't detected, the application displays an error to the user.

LISTING 30.3

A simple Web browser application

```
<?xml version="1.0" encoding="utf-8"?>
<mx:WindowedApplication xmlns:mx="http://www.adobe.com/2006/mxml">

  <mx:Script>
    <![CDATA[
      import mx.controls.Alert;
      import mx.managers.CursorManager;
      [Bindable]
      private var myURL:String = "http://";
      private function navigate():void
      {
        myURL = urlInput.text;
        if (myURL.substr(0,4) != "http")
        {
          myURL = "http://" + myURL;
        }
        var fileExtension:String = myURL.substr(myURL.length-3, 3);
        if (fileExtension.toLowerCase() == "pdf" &&
            HTML.pdfCapability != HTMLPDFCapability.STATUS_OK)
        {
          Alert.show("This request requires Acrobat Reader 8.1 or
later",
            "Acrobat Error");
```

```
      }
      else
      {
        myHTML.location = myURL;
      }
    }
  ]]>
</mx:Script>
<mx:ApplicationControlBar dock="true">
  <mx:Label text="My AIR Web Browser" fontWeight="bold"
  fontSize="14"/>
  <mx:Spacer width="25"/>
  <mx:Label text="New URL:" fontWeight="bold" fontSize="10"/>
  <mx:TextInput id="urlInput" text="{myURL}" enter="navigate()"/>
  <mx:Button label="Go" click="navigate()"/>
</mx:ApplicationControlBar>
<mx:HTML id="myHTML" width="100%" height="100%" />
</mx:WindowedApplication>
```

ON the WEB The code in Listing 30.3 is available in the Web site files in the `chapter30` project as `AIRWebBrowser.mxml`.

Using the WindowedApplication component

Flex applications designed for desktop deployment typically use `<mx:WindowedApplication>` as the application root element. A beginning desktop application's code looks like this:

```
<?xml version="1.0" encoding="utf-8"?>
<mx:WindowedApplication xmlns:mx="http://www.adobe.com/2006/mxml"
  layout="absolute">
  ... add content here ...
</mx:WindowedApplication>
```

The `WindowedApplication` component is extended from `Application` and provides all the application-level functionality you expect from a typical Flex application. It also adds these capabilities that are unique to Flex desktop applications:

- Native menus can be displayed and integrated into the overall application look and feel.

- The application can be integrated with a dock or system tray icon to provide easy access to common application functions.

- The application can display operating system-specific "chrome" (the graphics in the application window's border, title bar, and control icons).

- A status bar can be displayed at the bottom of the application window for string-based status messages.

Here's one example: The `WindowedApplication` component can display a status bar at the bottom of the application window. This display is controlled by two of the `WindowedApplication` component's properties:

- `showStatusBar:Boolean`: When `true` (the default), the application window displays a status bar.
- `status:String`: The string value displayed in the status bar.

The following modified custom `updateHTML()` function from the `NewTitlesReader` application updates the application's status bar with the title of the currently selected RSS item:

```
private function updateHTML():void
{
  myHTML.location = feedSelector.selectedItem.link;
  status = "Current Title: " + feedSelector.selectedItem.title;
}
```

Figure 30.16 shows the resulting display in the status bar at the bottom of the application window.

FIGURE 30.16

Displaying a message in the status bar

The application's status bar

Creating Remoting channels at runtime

When a Web-based Flex application communicates with an application server that supports Flash Remoting (known as the Remoting Service in LiveCycle Data Services and BlazeDS), it typically uses a channel definition with dynamic expressions that evaluate at runtime to the location of the server from which the application was downloaded. This is the default `my-amf` channel delivered with BlazeDS:

```
<channel-definition id="my-amf"
    class="mx.messaging.channels.AMFChannel">
  <endpoint
    url="http://{server.name}:{server.port}/{context.root}/
    messagebroker/amf"
    class="flex.messaging.endpoints.AMFEndpoint"/>
</channel-definition>
```

The <endpoint> element's url attribute uses dynamic expressions to evaluate the server name and port and the context root of the hosting instance of BlazeDS.

This approach doesn't work with desktop applications deployed with AIR, because the concept of "the current application server" doesn't have any meaning in a desktop application. Instead, you must provide the explicit location of the server-based application to which Remoting requests should be sent at runtime.

You can solve this in one of two ways:

- If the location of the server providing Remoting Services is always the same, you can define a custom channel in the application's services configuration file with a hard-coded url:

  ```
  <endpoint url="http://www.mycompany.com/messagebroker/amf"
      class="flex.messaging.endpoints.AMFEndpoint"/>
  ```

- For flexibility and the ability to set a url at runtime, declare a channel in either MXML or ActionScript code.

The RemoteObject component has a channelSet property, cast as a class named ChannelSet, that contains one or more instances of the AMFChannel component. To declare a runtime channel in MXML, nest the <mx:ChannelSet> tag inside a <mx:RemoteObject> tag pair's <mx:channelSet> property. Then nest one or more <mx:AMFChannel> tags, and assign each a uri property pointing to the selected server and its Remoting url.

> **TIP**   If you declare more than one AMFChannel tag inside the channelSet, they're treated as a list in order of preference. The client application always tries to use the first channel; if there's a communication failure, it goes to the next one, and so on.

The following RemoteObject instance declares a single AMFChannel at runtime:

```
<RemoteObject id="myRO" destination="myRemotingDestination">
  <mx:channelSet>
    <mx:ChannelSet>
      <mx:channels>
        <mx:AMFChannel uri="http://myserver/messagebroker/amf"/>
      </mx:channels>
    </mx:ChannelSet>
  </mx:channelSet>
</RemoteObject>
```

You can accomplish the same result with ActionScript. The following ActionScript code creates a
ChannelSet object, populates it with a single AMFChannel object, and adds it to the
RemoteObject component.

```
var endpointURL:String = "http://myserver/messagebroker/amf";
var cs:ChannelSet = new ChannelSet();
var customChannel:Channel =
  new AMFChannel("myCustomAMF", endpointURL);
cs.addChannel(customChannel);
myRemoteObject.channelSet = cs;
```

 You also can create channels at runtime for use with the Message Service, Proxy
Service, and Data Management Service when using LiveCycle Data Services or BlazeDS.

 When communicating with remote servers using the **HTTPService** or **WebService**
components in a desktop application, you don't have to deal with the cross-domain
security constraint as you do with Web-based Flex applications. Because the application loads locally,
it isn't subject to the restrictions of the Web browser's security sandbox and can make connections
freely over the Web just like any other local application.

A Conclusion about AIR

In addition to the features described in this chapter, AIR applications can accomplish the following
tasks that aren't possible with Flex Web applications:

- Full screen and spanned monitor display
- Integration with native visual components such the operating system's window and menu
  systems
- Creation of applications with transparency that serve as widgets
- Reading and writing files and folders on the local file system
- Persisting data in SQLite, a local database embedded in the runtime
- Synchronization of data managed on the server by LiveCycle Data Services
- Access to all network services supported by the Flex framework

The subject of building and deploying AIR-based desktop applications is worthy of an entire book,
and in fact there are many such books available. In particular, check out the *Adobe AIR Bible* (from
Wiley, of course!).

Summary

In this chapter, I described how to build and deploy desktop Flex applications with the Adobe Integrated Runtime. You learned the following:

- The Adobe Integrated Runtime (AIR) allows you to build and deploy cross-operating system desktop applications with Flex, Flash, or HTML.

- Users can download and install AIR freely from Adobe Systems.

- Flex Builder 3 includes everything you need to build and deploy AIR applications.

- Each AIR application requires an application descriptor file that determines how an application is packaged and delivered.

- You must provide a security certificate to create an AIR application installer file.

- Flex Builder 3 allows you to create a self-signed security certificate suitable for testing or deployment within an organization.

- For public deployment of AIR applications, a security certificate issued by a recognized certificate authority is strongly recommended.

- Flex applications built for AIR commonly use <mx:WindowedApplication> as the application's root element.

- The Flex framework's HTML control displays both HTML and PDF content.

- You can declare channels at runtime for use with Remoting destinations called from a Flex-based desktop application.

Glossary

ActionScript The scripting language used in Flex and Flash development.

ADL AIR Debug Launcher, an interim runtime for debugging AIR applications without having to install them.

ADT AIR Development Tool, a toolset for building and deploying AIR applications.

AIR Adobe Integrated Runtime, a desktop environment for installing and executing Flex applications and HTML/AJAX sites on the desktop, outside of the browser environment.

AJAX Asynchronous JavaScript and XML, a software development pattern that allows Web pages to make asynchronous calls to server resources without reloading the entire page.

AMF Action Message Format, the binary message format used in Flash Remoting with ColdFusion, the Remoting Service in LiveCycle Data Services and BlazeDS, and other server-based applications that can communicate with the Flex framework's RemoteObject component.

AMFPHP A free implementation of Flash Remoting and the AMF protocol designed to work with PHP.

application server A class of software applications that serve as middleware in multi-tier applications. The term can refer to both the server software itself (such as Tomcat, Jboss, WebSphere, WebLogic, PHP, or ASP.NET), or Java Enterprise Edition (JEE) applications that are hosted by a server, such as LiveCycle Data Services, BlazeDS, or ColdFusion.

ASP.NET Microsoft's application server that's used to build and deploy dynamic Web sites and services. Its XML Web Services feature can provide runtime services for Flex applications.

behavior A combination of an effect and a trigger that causes animation to occur in a Flex application at runtime.

binding expression An ActionScript expression used in MXML object declarations that sets up a broadcaster/listener relationship between a source value and a destination, both of which are identified as an object's property. Only explicitly bindable properties can serve as the source of a binding expression.

BlazeDS Adobe's free open-source implementation of the Remoting, Message, and Proxy Services for Java developers.

Cairngorm A microarchitecture for building and maintaining complex Flex applications using a strongly defined implementation of MVC.

CFC ColdFusion Component, a software module hosted by ColdFusion that provides runtime services that can be consumed by Flex applications.

ColdFusion Adobe's rapid application development application server.

component A software class definition. Components in the Flex framework are written in ActionScript, but can typically be instantiated with either MXML or ActionScript code.

component library An archive file with an extension of .swc that contains multiple software classes and supporting files.

925

constraint-based layout A style of controlling application layout that anchors objects to corners, borders, or arbitrary rows and columns of an application or component.

container A visual component that is designed to contain other objects. Flex containers are grouped as either layout containers that determine positioning of nested objects on the screen or navigator containers that determine which view of an application region is currently active.

control A visual component that incorporates display and, sometimes, interactivity.

CSS Cascading Style Sheets, the industry standard that's implemented in the Flex framework to manage application appearance.

Eclipse A free integrated development environment workbench that hosts the Flex Builder plug-in.

Eclipse perspective A particular arrangement of views and editors in Eclipse.

Eclipse view A window within the Eclipse interface that serves a particular software development purpose.

Eclipse workspace A system folder that manages and serves as a table of contents for Eclipse projects.

ECMAScript The language recommendation on which ActionScript and JavaScript are based.

effect An animation or sound that's defined and managed in ActionScript code.

event bubbling The process of passing an event object upward through a Flex application's containership hierarchy.

event listener A declaration that causes ActionScript code to be executed when a software event is handled. Event listeners can be declared as MXML attributes or with the ActionScript `addEventListener()` method.

event object An instance of an Event class that is generated and dispatched by a software object.

Flash The Flash authoring environment, currently in version Flash CS3.

Flash Player The browser plug-in/ActiveX control from Adobe that hosts Flash documents and Flex applications on a client system.

Flex Builder The Eclipse-based integrated development environment (IDE) from Adobe that supports rapid application development with the Flex framework.

Flex project A collection of one or more Flex applications managed in Flex Builder.

FlourineFX enA free implementation of Flash Remoting and the AMF protocol designed to work with ASP.NET.

instantiation The action of creating an instance of a software class. The resulting instance is then referred to as an *object*.

item renderers editors MXML and ActionScript classes that render and/or allow editing of data in the context of list controls.

JEE or J2EE Java Enterprise Edition, a software standard managed by Sun Microsystems. The older acronym, J2EE, has been replaced by Sun, but is referred to often in the Flex documentation and Flex Builder user interface.

LiveCycle Data Services Adobe's enterprise application server product that offers a complete suite of data and messaging services for Java developers. Formerly known as Flex Data Services.

MAMP An integrated server bundle for Mac OS X that includes Apache, PHP, and MySQL.

method A function that is a member of a class definition.

MVC Model-View-Controller, a software architecture used in large-scale application development to separate code that presents data (the view), manages data (the model), and handles application events (the controller).

MXML The XML markup-based language used in Flex development to express the layout of an application. MXML also can be used to declare instances of non-visual Flex components, to declare class metadata, and to wrap scripting sections in an MXML document.

MXMLC The Flex command line compiler, included with the Flex SDK. Used by developers who don't use Flex Builder or as part of an automated build process.

object An instance of a software class. When spelled with an uppercase initial character, it refers to the ActionScript Object class, which is a dynamic class that allows the developer to add arbitrary properties and methods at runtime.

OOP Object-Oriented Programming, a term that refers both to a style of programming and a particular type of language that uses software *objects* to encapsulate properties and behaviors of data entities.

Open Source A class of software that is offered in source code format and is typically licensed freely. Both the Flex SDK and the AIR SDK are open-source software.

package A collection of ActionScript classes and/or MXML components that are grouped together. Unless using external code libraries, the source files for all members of a package are stored in a single folder within a Flex project.

PHP A free application server product that can provide runtime services to Flex applications with a variety of messaging protocols.

property A data element that is a member of a class definition.

REST Representational State Transfer, a software pattern for providing runtime services that use generic XML as their message format.

RPC Remote Procedure Call, a software architecture implemented in Flex applications with asynchronous request/response communications. RPC components in Flex include HTTPService, WebService, and RemoteObject.

SDK Software Developers Kit. The Flex SDK and AIR SDK are free software kits that allow developers to create and deploy royalty-free applications on the Web and desktop.

skinning The process of replacing the graphical interface of a visual component.

SOAP The industry standard Web service architecture that supports RPC communications with a standardized XML-based messaging format.

static A type of class property or method for which there is only one instance, regardless of how many instances of the class are created. Static class members can be referenced from the class definition without having to instantiate the class.

transition An animation (effect) that's triggered by a change to the current view state.

trigger A component member that triggers an effect, typically related to a component event.

Value Object A design pattern that's used to implement software classes representing data for a single instance of a data entity. Also sometimes referred to as a Transfer Object, Data Transfer Object, or Bean.

view state An MXML-based declaration of an alternate presentation of an application or component. The current view state is determined by the component instance's currentView property.

WAMP An integrated server bundle for Windows that includes Apache, PHP, and MySQL.

WSDL Web Service Description Language, an XML-based language that describes a SOAP-based Web service's operations and other essential metadata.

XML Extensible Markup Language, the syntax standard that is the model for MXML, one of the core programming languages used in Flex application development. XML files also are commonly used for data storage and exchange and to store software configuration settings.

XML namespace A label that uniquely identifies a particular set of XML element and attribute names.

Index

SYMBOLS

: (colon)
   style selector separator, 286
   in XML namespace prefixes, 97
. (dot), descendant accessor operator, 655
. . (double dot), descendant accessor operator, 655
. (period), in style name selectors, 288
{ } (braces)
   denoting code blocks, 103
   in MXML binding expressions, 124
   in MXML property values, 404
& (ampersand)
   XML entity for, 99
   XML reserved character, 99
&& (ampersands), ActionScript operator, 105
' (apostrophe)
   XML entity for, 100
   XML reserved character, 99
* (asterisk)
   ActionScript operator, 105
   wildcard character, 103
   in XML namespace prefixes, 132
$ (dollar sign)
   in class names, 48
   in file names, 48
" (double quote)
   literals in ActionScript statements, 182
   XML entity for, 100
   XML reserved character, 99
= (equal sign). in flashVars variables, 119
== (equal signs), ActionScript operator, 105
!= (exclamation point equal sign), ActionScript operator, 105
> (greater than)
   ActionScript operator, 105
   XML entity for, 100
   XML reserved character, 99
< (less than)
   ActionScript operator, 105
   XML entity for, 99
   XML reserved character, 99

– (minus sign), ActionScript operator, 105
% (percent sign), ActionScript operator, 105
+ (plus sign)
   ActionScript operator, 105
   expanding a tree structure, 170
(pound sign), in hexadecimal color values, 296
' (single quote)
   literals in ActionScript statements, 182
   XML entity for, 100
   XML reserved character, 99
/ (slash), ActionScript operator, 105
_ (underscore)
   in class names, 48
   in file names, 48
   Linkage class name, 309, 311
| | (vertical bars), ActionScript operator, 105

A

absolute layout, 121–122
absolute positions, 259–261, 269
acceptDragDrop() method, 432–434
access modifiers
   methods, MXML components, 140–141
   omitting, 137
   variables, ActionScript, 103–104
<access> property, 768
Accordion container
   creationPolicy property, 354–355
   instantiating at runtime, 354–355
   keyboard shortcuts, 369–370
   nesting containers, 344
   sliding headers, 369–370
AC_FL_RunContent() function, 80
AC_OETags.js file, 75, 80
acompc component compiler, 24
Action Message Format (AMF). See AMF (Action Message Format)

C

G